# abc NEWS

## 75 YEARS IN THE MAKING

Text by JOHN BAXTER
Foreword by DAVID MUIR · Afterword by LINSEY DAVIS

 KINGSWELL

Los Angeles · New York

# ACKNOWLEDGEMENTS

First and foremost, the author would like to thank Wendy Lefkon for giving me the chance to work on this one-of-a-kind project, and for providing her usual expert and critically important guidance. Thanks also to Erin Zimring for her collaborative editorial vision in putting the book together, as well as Brett Oronzio, Michele Mustacchio, and Van Scott for their tireless assistance and valuable input. And thanks to Julie Rose for her masterful book design and to the entire Kingswell team including Monica Vasquez, Warren Meislin, Rachel Rivera, Jennifer Black, and Kate Milford. And finally, thank you to all of the ABC News personnel, past and present, that graciously consented to be interviewed for the book, especially Diane Sawyer, Byron Pitts, Sam Donaldson, David Muir, Rick Kaplan, Wendy Fisher, James Goldston, and the late Cokie Roberts. Thank you to Marc Gunther, whose excellent book, *The House That Roone Built*, served as an indispensable guide for some of the sequences of events described in this work.

John Baxter

The photography department wishes to thank Ken Niblock and Julie Townsend who embraced this project and gave us the resources and support we needed to do the work.

An extra special thanks goes to the editors on our team who dove into the ABC Photo Archives with commitment and zeal especially Brett Oronzio. Thanks also to our wonderful researchers Wendy Wallace, Patti O'Leary, Lorenzo Bevilaqua, and Hana Keiningham.

Thanks to Wendy Lefkon of Disney Publishing Worldwide, whose tremendous creative collaboration has energized our team.

Thank you to author John Baxter, Disney Publishing's Erin Zimring, and ABC News' Van Scott, who at the start of this project sat with our team in the photo studio, surrounded by contact sheets and black-and-white negatives, and acknowledged the intrinsic value of our images to tell this story.

To all the ABC News correspondents, publicists, producers, and crew members who have welcomed us to the sets over the years and enabled us to get the shot, we are grateful for the support.

Finally, to all of the photographers and editors whose imaginative efforts have produced the images in this book, we extend our heartfelt thanks. The history of ABC News runs parallel to the history of the world and through photography, the medium which captures an instant in time, we are able to revisit those historic moments, hold them still, and understand ourselves better.

Happy Anniversary ABC News!

Michele Mustacchio, Director, Walt Disney Television Photography

For information address Kingswell, 1200 Grand Central Avenue, Glendale, California 91201.

ISBN 978-1-368-05486-7      FAC-039745-21064      Printed in South Korea

First Hardcover Edition, June 2021      10 9 8 7 6 5 4 3 2 1

# CONTENTS

# FOREWORD

As I write this in early August 2020, we are still in the middle of a national emergency. This once-in-a-century pandemic has killed more than 160,000 Americans and nearly seven hundred thousand globally . . . and there are still no answers to the most crucial of questions: Will there be a second wave? How many more lives will be lost? Will the United States and the world produce a vaccine? (Note: At the time this book went to print, the death toll in the U.S. had surpassed three hundred thousand and globally it was more than 1.6 million.)

It is rare as Americans we would witness this intersection of a deadly public health crisis, an economy in historic contraction, and a test of leadership all at once. But this is our reality. And for how long, we simply do not know.

For many years as a journalist for ABC, I have preferred riding the New York City subway to work along with millions of others who, I'm sure, feed off of that same, invisible energy. This was one of the first changes to my daily rhythm as the anchor of *World News Tonight*. And I would soon learn there would be many, many more.

Early on, we were faced with the very real possibility we would have to broadcast from home given the ease with which COVID-19 spreads. We built a makeshift studio in my basement with a small camera that sits locked on a tripod, a couple of lights, and a TV screen propped up on a stand displaying an image of the globe that mirrors the one millions of viewers see behind me every night on the news broadcasts from the studio. In front of that small screen sits a lone chair where, if needed, I can sit and report the news. As of this moment, we consider ourselves lucky we have not had to use it. I still make the daily trip to ABC, but it is not the same.

As the pandemic was first taking hold in the United States, I will never forget those early rides to the ABC studios on the Upper West Side of Manhattan. ABC had hired the same driver to pick me up every day from my home in New York City's West Village. Each day we—I, wearing my mask, and the driver, Ralph, wearing his—would make our way uptown. In the first months of the crisis, I was greeted daily when leaving home by the sound of sirens. Soon, I began spotting the ambulances scattered throughout the city, parked in front of apartment buildings. I never lost sight that inside each one of those buildings someone was struggling, and first responders were putting their lives on the line to help save a patient they knew could have COVID-19.

Ambulances would race past us, their sirens drowning out the news bulletins coming from the radio. If ever there was a reminder of the role, the responsibilities we carry as journalists, this was it. We were—and still are—duty bound to carefully provide the facts, to acknowledge what we still do not know about this virus, and to help Americans make informed decisions about their own health . . . and the health of their loved ones.

Each day, when I arrive at ABC, there are immediate reminders that these are not normal times. All of the doors to the building are locked, but for one. We are all wearing masks and a guard sits behind a plastic shield at the front desk. Hand sanitizer stations are in place beside the escalators. There are markings on the floors to remind colleagues to keep a proper distance. The moment you walk down the second floor, where for decades producers have gathered in the newsroom for the *World News Tonight* broadcast, you instead find a series of closed doors.

Behind some of them, there is the hum of cable news and the voices of producers on speakerphone with their teams in the field, but now the vast majority of the offices are locked and dark. Much of our team is working from home, not unlike the rest of the country. When I walk down those hallways to get to the set, it's eerily quiet. I miss the electricity, the camaraderie, my work family. You're immediately reminded this is a different time, an unsettling time, and one whose story is still being written.

I make that walk to the studio alone, where I find the floor director and a writer waiting, both wearing masks, a safe distance from one another. I am grateful to have them with me every night. You'll notice as you watch from home, I have my laptop next to me on the set, often crafting what I'm going to say leading into each of our reports, right up until the moment we go on the air, which is a true reflection of the evolving nature of this pandemic.

We often remind ourselves as a team we cannot contribute to the noise that's out there. We have to find a way to cut through it all, and to stay calm and steady. There is a real anxiety in this country, and I think that part of our role as journalists is to find a way to ease some of that uncertainty. By sticking to the facts, no matter how dire they might be, it is my hope we have contributed in some small way to reducing that fear.

One night not long ago, I wrote in the "Good evening page," what we call "Page 2," "It is easy to get lost in all of these numbers night to night, but we stay focused on the stories of the families affected, and the doctors and nurses affected." We know these numbers are American lives. These are families forever changed by the cruelty of this virus. That stark reality makes our mission very clear.

David Muir, anchor and managing editor, *World News Tonight with David Muir,*
reporting from a near-empty studio during the pandemic

3

FROM MONDAY 3/16
UNTIL FURTHER NOTICE
we will be
CLOSED

online orders &
in-store pick-up
between 12-4
only! EMAIL US
FOR HELP AND FOR
RECOMMEDATIONS:

and FOLLOW US ON
INSTAGRAM
@cwpencilenterprise
FOR UPDATES AND FUN
AT-HOME CONTENT!

most importantly:
STAY SAFE, FRIENDS!

xo
CAROLINE,
ALYX, ESTHER, &
JULIANNE &
MAX

2020

# 2020
# THE PANDEMIC

**B**ook publishing is a deadline-driven business. And with nonfiction titles, it is an all too commonly experienced frustration that significant events of relevance to the subject covered occur after the cutoff date for a manuscript is set. Such changes can tamper with the focus or even perspective initially being made. Take this book: it was still being finalized when the coronavirus outbreak turned into a pandemic. And because this book celebrates the ascendancy of ABC News through its many decades of journalistic excellence, it was essential to include the network's coverage of the most significant global news event of the modern era.

ABC News has reported on wars, assassinations, terrorist attacks, and a host of other events of national and international importance since its founding. But there had never been anything like COVID-19 before (particularly when it came to modern news media and coverage), with its worldwide reach and the sudden, urgent, and universal need for accurate information it's created. The virus exposed the hidden vulnerability of *all humans* to infectious disease, as well as

the limits of science and medicine in responding rapidly to such large-scale outbreaks.

Simultaneously, it also underscored (on a daily basis) the critical importance of having a *trusted* news source to turn to during the information vacuum that can set in during a rapidly unfolding crisis. For the millions of regular viewers of *ABC World News Tonight with David Muir*, Muir and the news organization behind him had earned that trust over the years, so when the full

scope of the coronavirus threat became apparent, the network's reputation and Muir's ability to connect with viewers drew such a vast audience that the news program and operation did what no news program had ever done before in the history of television: it became the number one program across all of broadcast and cable in America! Not even the legendary "ratings king," CBS anchor/ newsman Walter Cronkite, had ever managed that.

That so many people were stuck at home watching the news so religiously every night was, of course, a unique circumstance created by the pandemic. But viewers did have the usual array of news sources to choose from—and a majority of them tuned in to *World News Tonight with David Muir* and stayed with the show as the pandemic raged on.

Throughout March 2020, Muir also anchored three *20/20* prime-time specials devoted to the then-still-developing COVID-19 story. The first was a live, two-hour program titled *Outbreak: What You Need to Know*, which aired on March 6. The special featured ABC News chief medical correspondent Dr. Jennifer Ashton, who would provide expert guidance throughout the crisis across all of ABC News' platforms.

That first special centered on the impact of the outbreak in China and on the plight of passengers (some of whom had either been diagnosed with

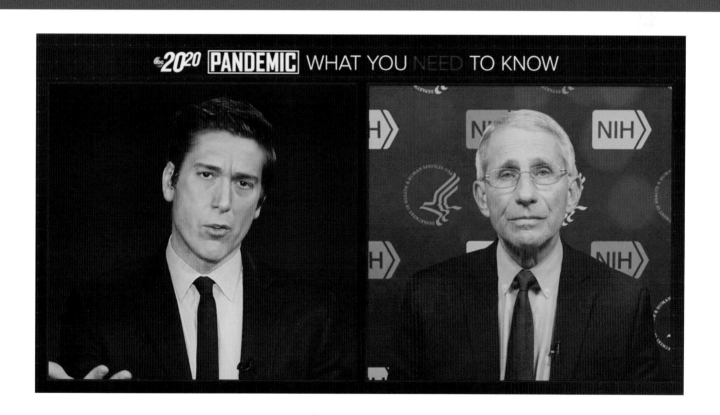

FACING PAGE, CLOCKWISE FROM TOP: Empty audience seats and minimal production staff during a taping of *The View*.

*Nightline* co-anchor Byron Pitts and the team pivoted quickly to provide viewers a look behind the headlines at what the COVID-19 news of the day might mean for them.

Eva Pilgrim was among the correspondents covering COVID-19 on *World News Tonight*.

ABOVE: As part of the ABC News *20/20* special *Pandemic: What You Need to Know*, David Muir interviews Dr. Anthony Fauci, director of the National Institute of Allergy and Infectious Diseases, who became the public face of America's medical research community during the pandemic.

or were showing COVID-19 symptoms) trapped aboard a cruise ship barred from docking as the world began closing its ports to international traffic. When the second special, titled *Pandemic: What You Need to Know*, aired a mere ten days later, the health crisis had turned global. The focus of each special also shifted in accordance with evolving audience priorities and concerns, so that the second show detailed the push to develop a faster coronavirus test, plus addressed the increasing anxiety being felt across America by allowing Dr. Ashton to answer viewer questions live from social media.

By the third installment, *America Rising: Fighting the Pandemic*, the emphasis was on the inspiring courage and superhuman daily efforts of frontline healthcare workers who continue battling a virus that at times has threatened to overwhelm the nation's hospital infrastructure—and puts them at lethal risk.

On May 5, David Muir also secured the first exclusive one-on-one interview with President Donald Trump during the pandemic that focused

on the state of the nationwide battle to contain the virus, the timing of the president's proposed reopening of the economy, how many deaths the country should be willing to accept in the pursuit of restarting the economy, and the likelihood a vaccine would be ready by the end of the year. (The interview was done "in person"—without masks—and therefore required careful social distancing between Muir and the president, providing viewers with the startling image of the two sitting and facing each other at more than ten feet apart from one another.)

Every component of the ABC News apparatus was pressed into service to cover the crisis. Early on, the decision was made to dedicate *Nightline* coverage solely to COVID-19 news five nights a week beginning on March 17, and to switch time slots with *Jimmy Kimmel Live* to provide late-night audiences with substantive updates on the pandemic at a slightly earlier time.

*Nightline* had come into being as a weeknight late-evening news program in March of 1980 as a result of the ongoing Iranian Hostage Crisis . . . and forty years later, the production staff was

ABOVE LEFT: Kenneth Moton, an anchor of the *ABC News Now* overnight broadcast.

ABOVE RIGHT: Dr. Jennifer Ashton, chief medical correspondent, provides much-needed information across all the ABC News shows and co-anchors *GMA3* along with Amy Robach and T. J. Holmes.

FACING PAGE, CLOCKWISE FROM TOP: David Muir conducts an exclusive interview with President Donald Trump in person more than ten feet apart.

Mona Kosar Abdi, an anchor of the *ABC News Now* overnight broadcast.

New York City residents don face masks early in the spring virus surge.

preparing to celebrate that remarkable milestone (but it was just as the COVID-19 outbreak reached pandemic status). The show had evolved into a multistory newsmagazine program over the years, but in an ironic twist, the all-consuming nature of the coronavirus crisis necessitated a return to its original, single-subject roots.

"The modern formula for *Nightline* is a magazine show with highly produced, edited pieces," observes co-anchor Byron Pitts. "The lead story on any given night might have been in the works for a day, a month, or a year. Then COVID hit, and suddenly all that mattered was what had happened in the last twenty-four hours—and sometimes the last three hours."

*Nightline* thus temporarily reinvented itself as the ideal news vehicle for viewers seeking a meaningful distillation of substantive developments in the COVID crisis after having been bombarded throughout the day by media noise. "By eleven thirty at night," says Pitts, "people knew what the headlines were, but they wanted to know what it all meant for them." Moreover, in those early days of the pandemic the news was unrelentingly grim, and Americans were already having enough trouble sleeping without the voice of doom being the last thing they heard at night.

"The *Nightline* team understood that," according to Pitts, "always seeking to end even the most sobering stories in such a way that they left viewers thinking, 'As bad as this is, we're going to be okay.'"

By late May, the pandemic had been raging long enough to begin assessing the staggering toll the virus was taking on multiple aspects of American life. To that end, on May 26, ABC News aired a one-hour, prime-time *20/20* special titled *Our New Reality: A Diane Sawyer Special*, in which the industry's preeminent journalist and her team explored the individual, human elements comprising America's response to the crisis. Sawyer traced the spread of the virus by examining some of the previously unrecognized outbreaks that occurred during the critical period in early March, when many Americans were under the impression it was a manageable cluster affecting other countries.

In addition, she examined the way a frightened public's need for answers was met initially with a flood of contradictory information from government officials on the political and medical fronts. The response underscored just how unprepared we were for a health crisis of such magnitude—during a period in which so little was known about the virus and its transmission that, as the special points out, the nation's surgeon general stated early on that "You can increase your chance of getting [the virus] by wearing a mask."

Sawyer went beyond the facts in the special, giving names and faces to some of the more heartrending fatalities, reminding us of the human beings behind all the charts and graphs and numbers and statistics swirling around the crisis. In addition to telling the harrowing and inspiring stories of the nation's many nonwhite, female healthcare workers on the exposed frontlines of the fight to save lives, the special touches on the role of "essential" workers in keeping the country going during quarantine lockdown at dire risk to their own health (and that of their families and loved ones), discusses the hope and faith that sustains Americans during these darkest of hours, and asked the all-important question of what happens next.

In the hands of Diane Sawyer, whose masterful long-form television journalism is always as moving as it is informative, the story of America's tragically slow reaction to the pandemic becomes an inspiring one of perseverance, of stepping up to serve friends and community, and of learning from adversity to hopefully better counter a crisis the next time. Sawyer says in the introduction to the special, "I hope tonight that all of us can stop together for a moment and just look back at what we've done. What we learned about who we are, and how we head into the future helping each other, renewing, reinventing, and I believe, once again, reaching for the sky."

In addition, *Good Morning America* never missed a beat. Despite the majority of the staff producing segments from their homes, the show still broadcast from its Times Square Studio live each morning, bringing viewers the latest on COVID-19 and how to stay safe. On March 3, *GMA* aired its first of many interviews with leading infectious disease expert Dr. Anthony Fauci. Other interviews included those with Centers for Disease Control and Prevention (CDC) director Dr. Robert Redfield, Clorox company president Linda Rendle, New York governor Andrew Cuomo, New York City mayor Bill de Blasio, and U.S. surgeon general Dr. Jerome Adams. As the number of COVID-19 cases in America skyrocketed (and slightly ebbed in some parts), the public's nearly round-the-clock interest in getting the latest pandemic-related facts was viewed as a mandate by ABC News to committing its full resources to maintaining the flow of information and analysis throughout the day and evening. In some cases, this could be accomplished by devoting an existing news program to the story, as with *Nightline*.

PREVIOUS PAGE: An impossibly empty Avenue of the Americas at midday in New York City during the height of the spring outbreak.

ABOVE: Flags flew at half-staff for months to honor victims of COVID-19.

FACING PAGE, LEFT TO RIGHT: Ian Pannell provided ongoing reports on the pandemic from Europe.

Linsey Davis, ABC News Live service's anchor, provides additional coverage about the pandemic with daily streaming programming.

However, in other cases, it meant refocusing a program to provide COVID-19 information updates. For example, beginning Wednesday, March 18, 2020, *GMA3*—anchored by Amy Robach, featuring Dr. Ashton, and produced by ABC News Live, the network's streaming news network—gave viewers the most up-to-date guidance on health and safety, as well as tips on adjusting to the challenges of America's new socially distant lockdown existence. Topics such as homeschooling and how to talk to kids about the virus were addressed daily in a forthright manner.

Because the pandemic also sparked widespread online misinformation and conspiracy theory claims, the show included segments debunking the many myths and fallacies that were adding to the public's confusion and anxiety. Balancing out the harsh subject matter were encouraging human-interest stories emphasizing the sense of unity and sacrifice that the crisis was also instigating, giving viewers some relief from the seemingly endless flow of disheartening news early on about the virus.

Similar special programming was aired across all of ABC News' varied platforms, such as ABC News Live, which began live-streaming *COVID-19: What You Need to Know* with a rotating group of anchors and a Q and A with Dr. Ashton every weekday at noon (EST) starting Wednesday, March 4. Additionally, ABC News Radio simulcast the ABC News Live shows, as well as the *20/20* COVID-related specials; ABC News' daily podcast *Start Here*, anchored by Brad Mielke, also provided coverage, posting special editions devoted to the pandemic (that included discussions with Dr. Ashton on up-to-the-minute medical developments).

In July, a special edition of *20/20*, *American Catastrophe: How Did We Get Here?*, examined what officials did and did not do in those early days and weeks when the nation first started to understand there was a new virus sweeping through China.

From a production standpoint at ABC News, covering the crisis was daunting, especially in the earliest days of the lockdown, but it also opened up new possibilities. ABC

CLOCKWISE FROM TOP LEFT: Stephanie Ramos has covered a variety of stories for several of the network's news programs, including *Good Morning America*.

Closed hiking trails and empty freeways became a common sight in Southern California.

James Longman, based in London, also offered the international overview on COVID-19.

FACING PAGE, LEFT TO RIGHT: Closed beach in Los Angeles County.

Matt Gutman did some of the earliest reporting on the first U.S. major COVID-19 outbreak in Washington State.

News' vice president, newsgathering, Wendy Fisher, describes the challenge this way upon reflection: "It gave us the opportunity to realize that we were more flexible than we thought—that we can work differently, that we can cover things differently, and that if we can't travel to cover something in person, we can do it remotely without sacrificing our standards." Still, even using the minimum personnel required in the studio and out in the field for broadcast production purposes meant employees leaving their homes and potentially being exposed to the virus.

According to Fisher, the process of deciding who could work and how it could be done safely was thorough and informed. "Our workplace decisions have been made with internal guidance from our own Dr. Ashton and the entire medical unit at ABC News, who report but also advise. In addition," she notes, "our decisions are informed by external guidance such as CDC [Centers for Disease Control and Prevention] recommen-

dations, and most importantly, by people's own comfort levels and their state of health."

ABC News' employees had kept its many platforms up and running at full strength while also offering frequent bulletins and expanded programming devoted to COVID-19 developments during a crisis that had most of the country sheltering in place and desperate for answers.

The decades spent by ABC News personnel (behind and in front of the camera) building the most consistently innovative, adaptable, and watchable television news network all seemed to have been leading up to the moment in early March 2020 when ABC News became America's go-to source of information about the most mysterious, frightening, and widespread threat to public health in modern history. It was a demonstration of the network's abilities that nobody saw coming, but one that millions of anxious Americans were grateful to witness and turn to over the uncertain weeks and months that have followed.

# BLACK
# LIVES
# MATTER

The early 2020 COVID-19 pandemic and the nearly planetwide lockdown that ensued in the desperate struggle to contain the virus forced billions of human beings to shelter in place, creating the eerie spectacle of empty streets in the world's most populous cities. Those empty streets also meant people were crowded together in their homes, anxiously watching the news all day and evening for weeks on end.

In the United States, the anxiety was compounded by a political divide that developed over how to respond to the crisis; and as the weeks turned into months, the nation's worst ever case of cabin fever added fuel to an already combustible mix of fear, resentment, and uncertainty.

Then, on May 25, during what began as a routine arrest in Minneapolis, a white police officer was captured on cell phone kneeling heavily on the neck of an African American man named George Floyd for nearly nine minutes while he was handcuffed and facedown on the pavement. Despite Floyd's pleading that he couldn't breathe—and demands from the growing and concerned crowd of witnesses that had gathered—the officer kept pressing his knee against Floyd's neck, even long after he'd become silent and unresponsive (and even for another full minute and a half after paramedics had arrived on the scene to treat the victim).

Several recorded the entire, stomach-churning sequence of events. Before long, the video was

circulating—globally. Millions of pandemic-weary Americans who had gone to sleep that night convinced things couldn't get any worse awoke to the news reports of Floyd's death with real-time footage of the incident.

Between the disturbing reality that police brutality continues to take place (even during a national crisis and pandemic that puts us all at risk)—and here accentuated by a lead white officer's brazen, indifferent stare while knowing he was being filmed harshly pinning down a helpless Black man—and the endless replay of the chilling footage to a captive audience of anxious viewers, it was all too much.

Things exploded. Years of widely publicized incidents involving unarmed people of color dying at the hands of white police officers had culminated with the death of George Floyd. That moment was the catalyst for an at-times chaotic release of pent-up rage that had been brewing for generations.

Americans watched what they sensed was the same gut-wrenching scenario playing out over and over with no hope of reform. Suddenly, huge numbers of "quarantined" citizens of all backgrounds, ages, and ethnicities filled the empty streets with some of the most vociferous and determined large-scale protests the country had ever seen, even going back to the 1960s and early 1970s.

As the television news leader, ABC News was positioned to quickly recognize that this was not just another postmortem protest against racist police brutality, but possibly a watershed moment in the history of race in America—a story that was big and important enough to temporarily push COVID-19 into the background of our national discourse.

*Nightline* co-anchor Byron Pitts, along with his millennial colleagues, sensed right away that George Floyd's death had the potential to be a game changer in the fight for racial equality. "Our

staff is so young and diverse and so thoroughly acquainted with progressive causes like BLM and DACA that they knew immediately how significant the death of George Floyd was," said Pitts, who's reported on a vast array of stories, including the end of apartheid in South Africa, the 1992 Los Angeles riots, and many high-profile cases of fatal police encounters with people of color in the interim.

"It felt like a purposeful moment," Pitts adds upon reflection. As an African American journalist, Pitts was undeniably well prepared to provide meaningful coverage and insight of and on the event. "I've been a professional journalist for thirty-eight years," he says, "but I've been

Black for fifty-nine years. So I knew that in that moment, I could apply all my journalistic skills and my experience covering civil unrest. But on top of that I could also lay my personal context, my shorthand about the Black experience."

Within days of George Floyd's death, ABC News began producing in-depth specials on the Black Lives Matter (BLM) protests and their roots, broadcasting a special report in prime time on May 30, and then streaming *A Nation Divided* on ABC News Live the next evening. On the eighth night following Floyd's death, with police and protesters still clashing in cities across the nation, ABC News aired a one-hour live special titled *America in Pain: What Comes Next?*

FACING PAGE: Protesters compelled by an overwhelming sense of injustice to march, even as a deadly pandemic rages, capture the existential seriousness of the Black Lives Matter movement.

ABOVE, CLOCKWISE FROM TOP LEFT: Alex Perez spent many days in Minneapolis providing in-depth reports on George Floyd's death and the social unrest in its aftermath.

Atlanta-based Steve Osunsami reported on local unrest and renewed attention to the death of Ahmaud Arbery.

Marcus Moore reported from Texas, including coverage of George Floyd's Houston funeral.

Anchored by Robin Roberts, David Muir, and Byron Pitts, the special examined the genesis of the Black Lives Matter movement and featured ABC News personnel discussing their own relevant experiences and observations as African Americans.

It was an emotionally charged segment and a vitally important one in that it allowed many white viewers to comprehend for the first time the difficulties—and dangers—that American citizens of color face every day of their lives. ABC News correspondent and *ABC News Live Prime* anchor Linsey Davis, while discussing what is known among African American families as "The Talk"—the grim life-or-death conversation that Black parents have with their children about how

to behave during police encounters—was unable to fight back tears in a profoundly moving, unscripted television moment that seemed to transcend the ordinary bounds of the medium. Raw emotion collided with serious journalism, and in the process conveyed a potent, visceral message that no parent watching will ever forget.

The next day Davis anchored an equally memorable episode of *ABC News Live Prime* titled "America in Pain: What Do We Tell Kids?" that followed up on the issue of how to discuss with children a deadly serious subject they are far too young and innocent to fully grasp.

Through its various platforms, ABC News kept a spotlight on the Black Lives

ABOVE LEFT: Rachel Scott reports from Washington, D.C.

ABOVE RIGHT: *Nightline* anchor Byron Pitts during one of the broadcasts focused on the Black Lives Matter movement.

FACING PAGE, TOP TO BOTTOM: Emmy Award-winning journalist Deborah Roberts appeared regularly on *GMA*, *World News Tonight*, and was a co-anchor of the Juneteenth special.

David Muir interviews George Floyd's brother Terrence during a memorial ceremony in Brooklyn, New York.

Matter movement as the protests continued and the nation struggled to find unity on a heavily politicized issue. On June 4, 2020, ABC News aired a special report on George Floyd's memorial service, which took place in Minneapolis, and then another covering Mr. Floyd's funeral in Houston on June 9. Then on June 19 came *Juneteenth: A Celebration of Overcoming*, a prime-time special devoted to explaining and exploring the origins, meaning, and current significance of the holiday that commemorates the emancipation of America's slave population in 1865, a few months after the Civil War ended. The special, which represented the first time Juneteenth was the subject of a network news program, was anchored by African Americans Byron Pitts, Linsey Davis, T. J. Holmes, Deborah Roberts, and Janai Norman, and also featured Whoopi Goldberg narrating an animation that explained the history and meaning of Juneteenth.

As sobering as the backstory of the holiday is, the special managed to strike a hopeful, inspirational tone and the anchors conveyed their own deeply felt sense of pride in being participants in the history of the moment, a sentiment perfectly encapsulated by Holmes in the opening segment: "So, here we are, in this studio, all of us, the six of us, descendants of the enslaved. They're the original authors of the story of Black life, of Black culture, of Black overcoming. They could probably never imagine that the six of us would be standing here, serving proudly, as their storytellers."

In September, *Turning Point* took over *Nightline* for one month of programming devoted to the racial reckoning sweeping

the nation and whether it could lead to lasting reconciliation.

Even as ABC News expanded their coverage of the Black Lives Matter protests, the network still continued to deliver the latest news on the pandemic and to air specials on developments in the quest to rein in, treat, and vaccinate against the COVID-19 virus.

This meant a longer and more grueling workload than ever before for the ABC News enterprise, especially given the continuing social distancing restrictions and in-person staff reductions everyone and the organization was grappling with. "I've covered three wars, five presidential campaigns, and every major natural disaster around the world over the past twenty years," points out Byron Pitts, "and nothing was more demanding of my time, my energy, my heart, my soul than balancing COVID with the eruption along racial lines in our country." However, Pitts managed to pull it off because of the support and resources available to him that permitted him to do justice to both stories.

"I feel so fortunate to be at ABC News," he says, "because the company was uniquely armed to respond to this time in history. Culturally, the company leans in to what's just over the next hill. That cultural infrastructure made it easy to embrace the challenge of covering the COVID-19 pandemic and the Black Lives Matter protests simultaneously.

"We embrace inclusion as a business model. So George Floyd wasn't a foreign story to our news organization because we have people reflective of every community in our country," Pitts adds. "COVID didn't seem overwhelming because the company spends a lot of time thinking about what's next. So that combination of cultural dynamics allowed us to be well positioned to cover both stories at the same time. We do big things well. So despite the travel and staffing limitations, this is a big thing and we're going to do it well."

# 2020 ELECTION

As this book went to press, the 2020 United States general election was being settled and President-elect Joseph R. Biden, Jr. and Vice President-elect Kamala D. Harris were declared the winners.

The ABC News team worked tirelessly as Election Day stretched into election week including five prime-time specials covering the historic election anchored by George Stephanopoulos, David Muir, and Linsey Davis.

ABOVE: Linsey Davis, and George Stephanopoulos provided insights during the extended coverage of the 2020 election.

LEFT: David Muir with then-nominees Kamala Harris and Joe Biden.

FACING PAGE, CLOCKWISE FROM TOP LEFT: White House correspondents Mary Bruce and Jonathan Karl contributed unique perspectives during the coverage.

Chief Justice Correspondent Pierre Thomas covered the ongoing legal challenges to the election results.

Martha Raddatz, Chief Global Affairs Correspondent reporting for ABC's *World News Tonight with David Muir*.

Cecilia Vega provided ongoing reports from Washington, D.C.

Robin Roberts talks to then nominees Joseph Biden and Kamala Harris.

Tom Llamas worked the electoral map, offering myriad scenarios as the results flowed in.

David Muir, George Stephanopoulos, and Linsey Davis anchored the Decision Desk.

**ABC ELECTION RETURNS**

| LOCAL RETURNS | | NATIONAL VOTING | | | |
|---|---|---|---|---|---|
| **MAYOR RECALL** | **SUPERVISOR 1st** | **ARIZONA** | **IDAHO** | **NEW MEXICO** | **UTAH** |
| YES  98228 | SMITH  2257 | 1st CONG. DIST. | 1st CONG. D. | 1st CONG. DIST. | 1st CONG. DIST. |
| NO  149324 | LEGG  3916 | MURDOCK  6667 | PFOST | FERNANDEZ  10.12 | GRANGER  22762 |
| ALDRICH  1271 | **PROP 'A'** | DIVELBLISS  4056 | WOOD | DEMPSEY  11757 | JONES  9115 |
| COLE  302 | YES | 2nd CONG. DIST. | 2nd C | MASON | 2nd CONG. DIST. |
| HUBBARD  260 | NO | PATTEN | BUD | ARMIJO | BOSONE |
| KENNY  4711 | **PROP 'C'** | CURNUTTE | HAW | **NEW YORK** | PRIEST |
| MATTHEWS  251 | YES  13621 | **COLORADO** | 1L | **SENATOR** | **WASHINGTON** |
| McHENRY  154 | NO  9368 | **SENATOR** | | | **SENATOR** |
| PARSONS  311 | | MILLIKIN  217537 | LU | | |
| **CALIFORNIA** | | CAR | | **GOVERNOR** | WILLIAMS |
| **GOVERNOR** | **12th CONG. DIST.** | **GOVERNOR** | X1 | LYN | **OHIO** |
| WARREN  765270 | HILLINGS  1505 | JOHNSON  222175 | SA | **SENATOR** | 2nd CONG. DIST. |
| ROOSEVELT  212163 | ZETTERBERG  1089 | THORNTON  127905 | CAPEH | JACK | CAMP |
| **ATTORNEY GEN'L.** | **14th CONG. DIST.** | 1st CONG. DIST. | | | **OREGON** |
| BROWN  37722 | HARDY  1363 | LUXFORD  6962 | | FERGUSON | **SENATOR** |
| SHATTUCK  29718 | YORTY  1274 | ROGERS  587 | SE | **OREGON** | LOVE |
| **SENATOR** | **16th DISTRICT** | 2nd CONG. DIST. | | **SENATOR** | |
| DOUGLAS  168767 | JACKSON  2302 | HILL  7621 | | | |
| NIXON  379561 | MURRAY  2331 | 3rd | | **GOVERNOR** | |
| **CONGRESS** | **18th DISTRICT** | MARSH  1263 | TYI | | **PENNSYLVANIA** |
| **1st DISTRICT** | DOYLE  545 | CRENSHAW  5966 | BU | | |
| SCUDDER  2329 | HOSMER  376 | 4th CONG. DIST. | | **WYOMING** | |
| KENT  2032 | **21st DISTRICT** | ASPIN | HENN | TO | |
| **4th DISTRICT** | SHEPPARD  13 | **CONNECTICUT** | | CO | |
| HAVENNER  11298 | REYNOLDS  12 | **SENATOR** | | BAR | |
| SMITH  6085 | **23rd DISTRICT** | 1st CONG. DIS. | | | |
| **7th DISTRICT** | McKINNON  576 | McMA | | | |
| ALLEN  123 | GEHRES  480 | TALB  240133 | MANSFIELD | AN | |
| COOK  53 | **PROP 'I'** | BENTO  315409 | McGINNIS  3317 | 1  1103 | |
| **9th DISTRICT** | YES  4971 | BUSBY  307235 | 2nd CONG. DIST. | BARN | |
| WHITE  29 | NO  3762 | HOLMES  4716 | D'EWART  4141 | ELL | |
| | **PROP 'G'** | **GOVERNOR** | | | |
| 3rd DISTRICT | YES  10684 | BOWLES  | **NEVADA** | | |
| 416 | NO  24302 | LO  | **SENATOR** | | |
| 229 | **PROP 10** | | McCARRAN  2607 | **PENNSYLVANIA** | |
| **ARIZONA** | YES  18340 | **IDAHO** | MARSHALL  1447 | **SENATOR** | |
| **SENATOR** | NO  17608 | **SENATOR** | **GOVERNOR** | MARSHALL  1467 | |
| **GOVERNOR** | | CLAR  5904 | PITTMAN  1601 | | |
| OWMILLER | | WELK  10966 | RUSSELL  7326 | | |
| JORE  5351 | | DWORSHAK  9635 | | | |
| WRJ  5054 | | BURTENSHAW  7326 | COA | | |
| | | BARING | | | |

**Italian Balm**

**KECA**

**LOCAL**

# 1945-1959

# 1945–1959

# THE THIRD NETWORK

In 1945, Americans were getting their information about the world outside their communities from newspapers, newsreels shown at the local cinema (usually before a feature attraction), and from the family radio. The still futuristic-sounding "television" had been created in the 1930s, but the technological exigencies of World War II had put its full development and integration on hold for the duration.

Radio, meanwhile, was more popular than ever, both for its entertainment content and for the daily news broadcasts to which millions had become addicted during the war. Moreover, World War II had taught the radio networks a lot about the business of serious news coverage, and had helped launch the careers of a legendary generation of correspondents, including future television news icons like Walter Cronkite, Eric Sevareid, and Howard K. Smith.

Before the war, there were three major radio networks: the Columbia Broadcasting System (CBS), the National Broadcasting Company (NBC), and the Mutual Broadcasting System. The biggest, oldest, and most powerful of the three was NBC, which

PREVIOUS SPREAD: Personnel in action at ABC News' affiliate in Los Angeles, KECA-TV (now KABC-TV), on election night, 1950.

BELOW: ABC News correspondent Merle Worster, covering the Dwight D. Eisenhower presidential inauguration on January 20, 1953, talks with Frank Marx of ABC engineering in front of the news division's custom designed Willys-Overland station wagons, collectively known as "the White Fleet." Each vehicle was a mobile and completely independent "electronic reporter."

was owned by RCA, which in turn was controlled by the industrial colossus General Electric. ABC came into being as a result of an antitrust suit against RCA, which was forced to divest itself of one of its two NBC radio networks. The NBC Blue Network, as it was called, was sold to Life Savers candy cofounder Edward John Noble in 1943; in June of 1945, the name of the network was officially changed to the American Broadcasting Company (ABC).

ABC remained a radio-only network until 1948, when its first affiliate television station, New York City-based WJZ-TV (which changed its call letters to WABC-TV in 1953), went on the air. CBS began TV operations around the same time as ABC, while NBC and the short-lived DuMont Television Network had entered television broadcasting only the year before. However, CBS and NBC had been in existence as radio networks since the 1920s, and their experience with

broadcast operations, along with their established base of affiliates across the country, gave them a major head start over a still fledgling ABC. In the early going, ABC's newcomer status led some to call it "the third network."

The first watershed moment in ABC's history was made possible by another antitrust suit that had forced the Paramount Pictures movie studio to sell off most of its theater chain participants. The newly created spin-off, United Paramount

FACING PAGE, CLOCKWISE FROM TOP LEFT: From November 2, 1948, WJZ-TV—the original designation of WABC-TV in New York City—personnel are shown using state-of-the-art analog graphics to help its audience visualize the U.S. presidential election results between Democratic incumbent Harry S. Truman and his Republican challenger, Thomas E. Dewey.

Edward J. Noble, cofounder of the Life Savers candy company in 1913, who purchased NBC's Blue Network in 1943. On June 15, 1945, the network's name was formally changed to the American Broadcasting Company (ABC).

Actor John Agar, who at the time was recently divorced from Shirley Temple, with ABC News commentator Quincy Howe, covering the 1952 general election. The informal set, complete with a well-used wooden in-box, exemplifies the ad hoc nature of early live television.

ABOVE: John Daly reporting on Eisenhower's second presidential inauguration ceremony, January 22, 1957.

LEFT: Although Leonard Goldenson paid scant attention to his news division in the 1950s, the development of hit entertainment shows like *The Adventures of Rin-Tin-Tin* brought in the advertising revenue necessary to grow the network, including the news organization's operational infrastructure.

JOHN DALY

Theatres (UPT), was barred from making movies, so the company sought other investment opportunities, eventually purchasing ABC from Edward Noble in 1953. The merger proved to be critical to the evolution of ABC, in part because it meant not only a huge and desperately needed infusion of cash for the network, but also because the merger was orchestrated by UPT's head, Leonard Goldenson—the decision maker who would preside over ABC's slow but steady ascent to the position of industry innovator and leader it still holds.

ABC-TV featured news programming from the very beginning, starting with *News and Views* in 1948. *News and Views* featured "cohosts" H. R. Baukhage and Jim Gibbons (the term "anchor" in this industry had yet to be coined). The show ran for fifteen minutes each weekday evening—and it was a much more basic presentation than what we have come to know as news programming (but was one of the first TV news broadcasts ever). It was cancelled in 1951 and replaced by *After the Deadlines*, which lasted a year and a half. A new show, *All Star News*, succeeded *After the Deadlines*, but was cancelled just months later.

The concept of television news was brand-new . . . and was being honed during a period of trial and error experimentation, which was reflected in this high turnover rate for news programming. Then, in 1953, came *John Daly and the News*, which would last seven years. Daly was a former radio correspondent for CBS who had been the first to break the news of the attack on Pearl Harbor in 1941; on television he was best known as the host of the CBS hit show *What's My Line?* Incredibly, Daly was such a popular figure that he also filled in

LEFT: ABC's first network newscasts were fifteen minutes long and read by radio veteran John Daly, who was so popular with television audiences that he worked for ABC, CBS, and NBC simultaneously in the 1950s.

as host of NBC's *Today* show on occasion. His additional role as the anchor of the brief evening news broadcasts on ABC would never allow the network to stand out.

Leonard Goldenson later admitted to paying little attention to the news department at ABC before 1960. In fairness to Goldenson, he was focused on expanding and improving the network's entertainment content, including material for younger viewers, which allowed ABC to compete on its own terms with the rival networks. To

this end, he began courting Hollywood—though his efforts were met at first with stiff resistance. The film industry had experienced a downturn in business in the postwar years, and television, which was growing in popularity at the same time, was labeled as an existential threat. It was so bad that Goldenson, a former Hollywood executive, was viewed by many of his ex-colleagues as a traitor to the medium.

However, Goldenson persevered and worked his contacts in the film industry until he got what

ABOVE: Producer and moderator Ruth Hagy, with guest and former first lady Eleanor Roosevelt, fielding questions from a panel of politically engaged students on *College News Conference*, the network's first iteration of a weekend policy talk show that would lead to *Issues and Answers* and eventually *This Week*.

FACING PAGE: A mobile ABC News crew outside the Capitol Building during the 1957 Eisenhower inauguration after his reelection a few months earlier in November 1956.

he wanted: Hollywood-quality entertainment content that would give ABC something the other networks lacked. Goldenson made a deal with Warner Brothers to produce the first television Westerns with ABC; and he, along with ABC executives Robert Kinter and Sidney Markley, agreed to invest half a million dollars in Walt Disney's new theme park—while it was still under construction—in return for a stake in the park and rights to air several seasons of a one-hour weekly anthology series then titled *Disneyland*. When the first episode aired in October 1954, over thirty million Americans tuned in—by far the largest audience for an ABC show yet. It went on to become the network's first top-rated program and firmly established the children's/family entertainment genre in television.

While ABC's focus was on building its entertainment programming core, the network hadn't given up on its news coverage efforts. One early ABC News program of note was *College News Conference*, produced and moderated by Ruth Hagy, with Peggy

Whedon also filling in for Hagy periodically. Whedon would go on to produce *Issues and Answers*, a kind of successor to *College News Conference* and the first homegrown ABC News show to achieve longevity (SEE THE 1960–1969 SECTION).

*College News Conference* featured a weekly "headliner," typically a politician in the news at the time, who would be interviewed by four politically astute college students from schools across the country. The show's minimal staff meant Whedon had to report, write, produce, and book both the headliners and the student interviewers, the latter being especially important to the success of the show. "They had to be sharp, occasionally pugnacious, with a strong personality and good news judgment," recalled Whedon. One such interviewer was a young law student from the University of Virginia named Ted Kennedy. *College News Conference* was cancelled in 1960, but it proved to be the beginning of a continuum of Sunday panel discussion shows on ABC that led ultimately to *This Week*.

While it was true that ABC still lagged

behind NBC and CBS in the ratings, the news division had quickly evolved from a few cameras into a serious news-gathering organization on a national level. Its live coverage of the Army-McCarthy Hearings in 1954 (from April 22 to June 17) was of considerable historical significance, given that the public got to witness the hearings on TV and see Senator Joe McCarthy's tactics firsthand, which aroused anger and was a factor in ending McCarthyism, or at least helping curtail it (and lead to the senator's downfall). Through the lenses of ABC News' cameras, television had officially arrived as a means of shaping public opinion . . . and its full potential was about to be realized as an eventful new decade loomed.

FACING PAGE: Quincy Howe and the ubiquitous John Daly report from ABC-TV headquarters during the 1958 midterm elections. Note the support staff off camera to the right, including two people wearing sunglasses, presumably to cope with the intense glare of the studio lighting.

BELOW: An ABC News unit, perched on a rooftop, strikes a pose for a publicity shot the network used while promoting coverage of the 1956 Democratic and Republican parties' national conventions.

# LEONARD GOLDENSON

Leonard Harry Goldenson (1905–1999) was raised in the small town of Scottdale in western Pennsylvania, before heading to Harvard and becoming a lawyer for Paramount Pictures in the early 1930s. Goldenson spent four years reorganizing Paramount's once unprofitable New England theater chain unit and turning it into a moneymaker, after which he was given control of all the company's 1,700 theaters. He was made vice president in 1942 and then a director at Paramount in 1944. But when antitrust stipulations were enacted that required the movie studios to divest themselves of their theater chains, Goldenson became president of the newly formed United Paramount Theatres (UPT). Believing that television was the future, Goldenson engineered the merger between his company and the then fledgling American Broadcasting Company (ABC), which led to the coining of his press moniker, "The man who wed television to the movies."

Goldenson spent the next quarter century forging a brand-new identity for the network that would allow it to compete on its own terms with its older more established rivals, NBC and CBS. He began by courting Hollywood for content, though at the time television was seen as ushering in the demise of film, and it was an uphill battle to say the least. However, Goldenson and his team eventually won over Walt Disney, after which *Disneyland* became ABC's first hit show, and then secured a contract with Warner Brothers to produce entertainment programming for ABC. Goldenson really had wed television to the movies, establishing a TV Western craze that lasted for twenty years.

As profits from ABC Sports grew and the network's entertainment programming began to win time slots in the late 1960s and 1970s, Goldenson was finally able to put money and time into the long-neglected ABC News division. Within a few years (and with the promotion of Roone Arledge to ABC News president), the decades long dominance of the news by CBS and NBC was finally broken by the upstart network Goldenson had founded.

A decade later, Goldenson would engineer another merger—with the much smaller Capital Cities, which he selected because he liked the company's philosophy and felt confident the newly combined entity would be able to resist any future hostile takeover bids. Defending the move shortly before retiring in 1986, after thirty-three years at the helm of ABC, Goldenson said, "Having built this empire worldwide, I didn't want it to be dismembered." With his wife, Isabelle Charlotte Weinstein, Goldenson cofounded the United Cerebral Palsy charity organization and successfully lobbied Congress to pass the Americans with Disabilities Act of 1990.

FACING PAGE: Leonard H. Goldenson of United Paramount Theatres orchestrated a merger with a cash-strapped ABC in 1953, becoming the first president of the new media entity and the lead figure who would preside over the network's steady climb from obscurity to relevance.

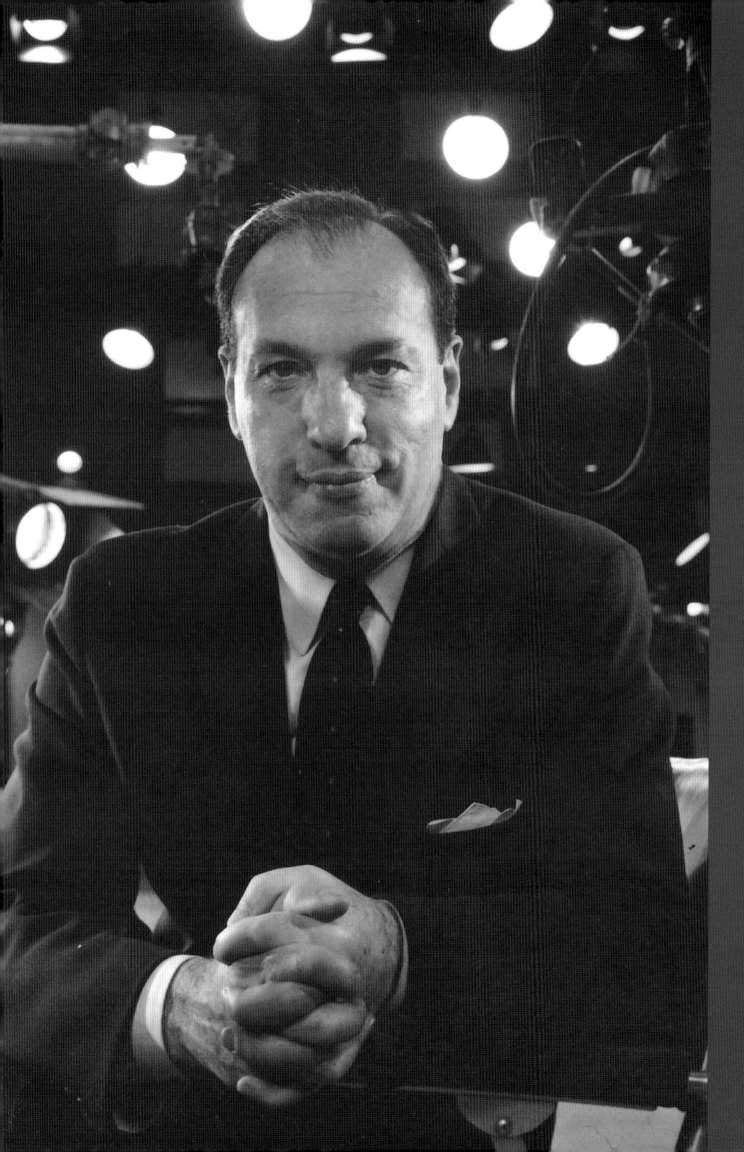

# 1960-1969

# 1960–1969

## ON THE MAP

One of the most turbulent and consequential decades in American history commenced in 1960. It was an election year, and for the first time, television would play a role in the outcome. The two presidential candidates, both in their forties, were considerably younger than their predecessors. Yet while John Kennedy, the Democratic Party's nominee, extolled the promise of America's future, his opponent, Republican vice president Richard Nixon, looked and sounded like a member of the old guard. However, when the first-ever televised presidential debate took place in September, the critical difference between them wasn't their ideology; Nixon treated the event as just another campaign appearance, while Kennedy fully appreciated the impact that TV would have on voter perceptions of the two candidates. He prepared relentlessly for the debate and sunned himself on his hotel rooftop to look his best on camera; Nixon, conversely, refused the makeup that would have improved his complexion, believing his debate experience would win out.

All three major television networks carried the debate live, and the audience consensus was that it had been a clear victory for Kennedy. However, the debate was also broadcast on radio, and that *listening* audience generally felt Nixon had prevailed . . . thus proving that television was going to change the nature of politics forever.

At about the same time that ABC was televising the landmark Kennedy-Nixon presidential debate, Leonard Goldenson was approached by John Pastore, the first Italian American ever elected a U.S. senator, who was then chairman of the U.S. Senate's Subcommittee on Communications. As a regulator of the still new and somewhat experimental medium of television, Senator Pastore wanted the networks to realize their full informational and educational potential! He urged Goldenson to develop more news and documentary programming. Goldenson was amenable to this: among his first steps toward accomplish-

ing this worthy approach was the hiring of Jim Hagerty, as a network vice president, in 1961 to oversee what would become a dedicated news division at ABC. Hagerty had been then President Dwight D. Eisenhower's press secretary—to date, the only person to have served two complete presidential terms in that position. He began his career outside reporting as Governor Thomas E. Dewey's press secretary and campaign manager in the forties, and later was also credited with

FACING PAGE, CLOCKWISE FROM TOP LEFT: Leonard Goldenson welcomes Senator and Mrs. Kennedy to the studio.

Emmy Award–winning correspondent and anchor Tom Jarriel joined ABC News in 1965, gaining national attention for his coverage of the Dr. Martin Luther King Jr. assassination and becoming the network's White House correspondent during the Nixon and Ford administrations; Jarriel later co-anchored *ABC Evening News* on Saturdays and became an investigative correspondent for *20/20* in 1979.

Howard K. Smith and Bill Lawrence sitting perpendicular to one another at their split-level news desk as they prepare for election night coverage, November 5, 1968.

ABOVE AND LEFT: Like Howard K. Smith, Bill Shadel had been a war correspondent protégé of Edward R. Murrow's during World War II, covering the D-Day landings for CBS Radio. Shadel, who served as an *ABC Evening News* anchor following the departure of John Daly, arrived at ABC News in 1960 and was chosen to moderate the third presidential debate between John Kennedy and Richard Nixon.

introducing TV cameras to White House press conferences in 1955.

Hagerty hired reporters and producers away from the other networks, which significantly raised the standard of news broadcasting at ABC. At the time, television—and especially ABC—was still feeling its way toward its own style of news presentation, so the networks primarily defaulted to former radio reporters like John Daly and Walter Cronkite to anchor their newscasts—and their occasional news specials/documentaries. But Hagerty, who was most familiar with the world of print media (and had started as a *New York Times* reporter), first turned to ex-newspaper heavyweights for his on-air talent, compiling a seven-man rotation of intelligent and experienced journalists to serve as anchors.

Then, in 1963, the personnel decisions at ABC News were taken over by its first president, former CBS and NBC news executive Elmer Lower. Lower had far more relevant experience than Hagerty in the medium, and he understood the dynamics of television production well. He immediately began laying the groundwork for a global news organization, setting up foreign bureaus and assigning ABC News film crews to other countries for the first time.

ABC's modest news division tripled in size during Lower's tenure, and he also invested in the network's future by hiring a stable of young journalists that included a number of future stars like Peter Jennings, Ted Koppel, and Sam Donaldson. ABC might have been third in the ratings, but to the fledgling correspondents Lower entrusted with legitimizing the network as a television news source, it was the place to be. As Koppel later put it, "We took a perverse

LEFT: After several years of using a multiple-anchor format, the *ABC Evening News with Ron Cochran* premiered in 1963. A former FBI man, Cochran was Canadian-born, like Peter Jennings, who would succeed him as the network news anchor a little under two years later.

kind of pride in being the youngest, the poorest, and in many instances the hardest working of the news divisions."

Nineteen sixty was also the year that ABC began broadcasting *Issues and Answers*, a serious discussion-style news program that ran on Sunday afternoons and typically featured newsworthy government officials responding to questions relevant to current events usually unfolding in the charged political world. It was hosted by a series of ABC News luminaries, including Howard K. Smith. *Issues and Answers* was created by ABC's first female correspondent, Margaret "Peggy" Whedon, who was also the show's producer for its entire twenty-one-year run.

Guests were usually national and world figures who agreed to field penetrating questions, which

ABOVE: First president of ABC News Elmer Lower, who laid the foundation for eventual greatness by expanding the division and hiring many of its future stars.

LEFT: Prior to a 1964 episode of *Issues and Answers*, Producer Peggy Whedon explains the technology behind the show to guest Under Secretary of State for Political Affairs W. Averell Harriman.

FACING PAGE. TOP TO BOTTOM: ABC News correspondent Malvin "Mal" Goode conducted an interview with then New York senator Robert Kennedy in a New York hotel in September 1965. Goode, who covered the United Nations, became the first African American network news correspondent at ABC News in 1962 after retired baseball great and activist Jackie Robinson complained to ABC executives about the lack of diversity among reporters.

ABC News units packing up their equipment to cover the 1960 national party conventions in Chicago and Los Angeles.

FOLLOWING SPREAD: A publicity still from 1960 titled "Newswomen of ABC" shows, from left to right, producers Peggy Whedon and Helen Jean Rogers, anchor Lisa Howard, and journalist/producer/host Ruth Hagy. Whedon worked at ABC News as a producer for nearly three decades, helming *Issues and Answers* for its entire twenty-one-year run. Rogers, who was married to ABC's founding Washington Bureau chief and White House correspondent John Secondari, won five Emmys and two Peabody Awards, and was also one of the first female teaching fellows at Harvard. Howard was a former soap opera actress who was the first American reporter to interview Khrushchev and later became ABC News' first woman reporter, as well as the anchor of the first demographic-specific news broadcast called *Lisa Howard and News with the Woman's Touch*.

often led to substantive conversations between panelists and some of the brightest and most controversial leaders, news makers, and personalities. Among the many important figures to appear on the show were Ronald Reagan, Bobby Kennedy, Yasser Arafat, Menachem Begin, Anwar Sadat, Madame Chiang Kai-Shek, Dwight Eisenhower, George H. W. Bush, Indira Gandhi, Che Guevara, Golda Meir, Richard Nixon, Gloria Steinem, Arnold Toynbee, and Eleanor Roosevelt. The anchors pursued their questions with a journalistic intensity that kept the discussion honest and focused, which resulted in an engaging and informative television experience.

After nearly a generation's worth of providing viewers with clarity on the complex political topics of the day, *Issues and Answers* went off the air in 1981. However, it was revamped as the landmark *This Week with David Brinkley*, which Whedon also helped produce in the early going and which retained the essential structure and focus of its predecessor show.

One other notable occurrence at ABC in 1960 was the hiring of a young Roone Arledge—as a sports producer. Although Arledge was many years away from taking over and transforming ABC News, he immediately put his stamp on the network's sports coverage and within a year had launched the groundbreaking *ABC's Wide World of Sports*. By the end of the decade, ABC was the undisputed leader of televised sporting events, and Arledge was being hailed as a TV production wunderkind.

Meanwhile, after the departure of John Daly in 1960, the ABC News division under Elmer Lower had used a series of combinations of news readers before settling on a single-anchor format with the launch of *ABC Evening News with Ron Cochran* in 1963. A

RIGHT: Roone Arledge, during his *Wide World of Sports* glory days, posing with his underwater cameraman during the Gold Cup Tarpon Championship in February of 1964.

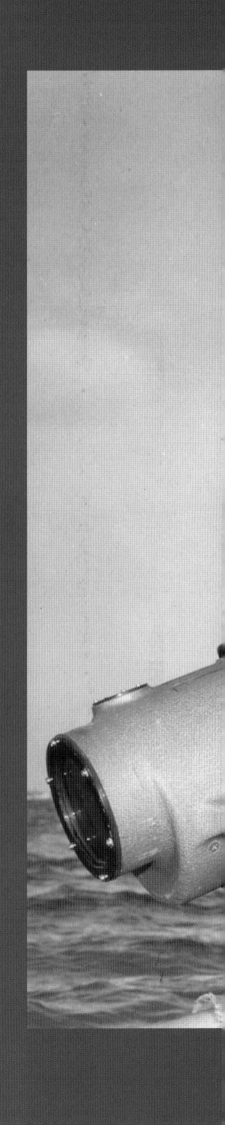

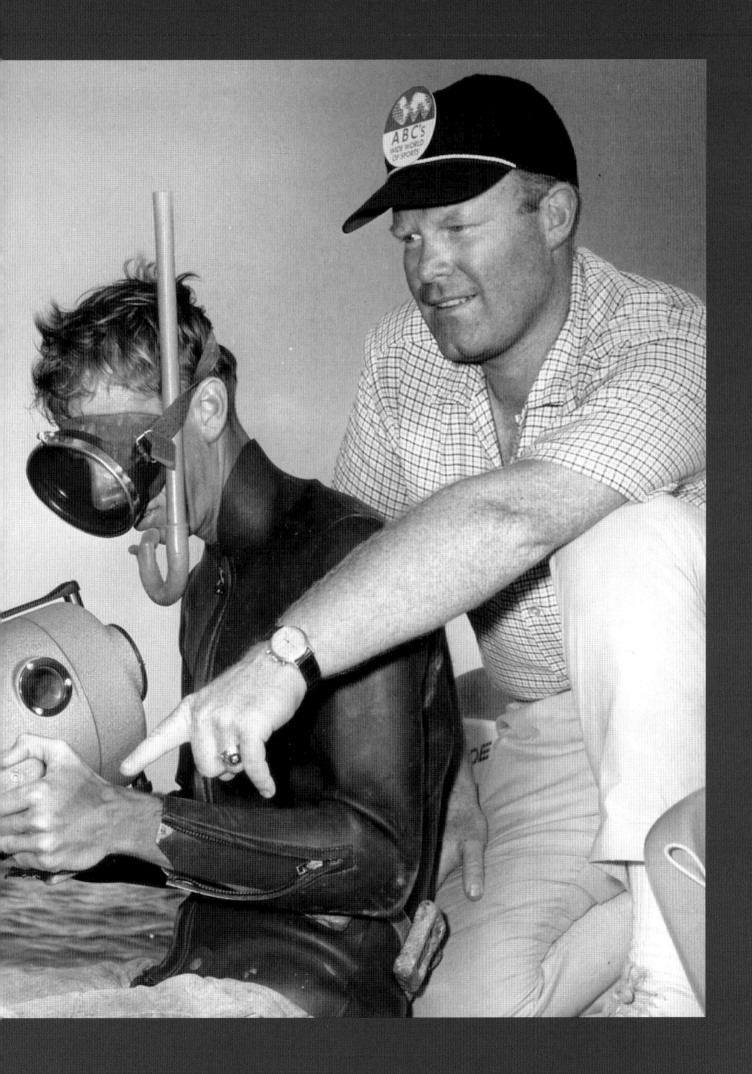

nearly twenty-year veteran of radio and television news, Cochran was the ABC anchor during its coverage of the assassination of President John Kennedy, in November 1963, and actually confirmed the president's death on the air several minutes before the official announcement was made by the White House. During Cochran's tenure, the evening news segment on ABC continued to lag behind the other main networks in the ratings and was still only fifteen minutes long,

despite NBC and CBS having switched to a half-hour news format.

In 1965, Lower replaced the fifty-three-year-old Cochran with a then twenty-seven-year-old fellow Canadian named Peter Jennings. *Peter Jennings with the News*, as the renamed broadcast was titled, also ran for only two years because the future ratings king was then deemed too green for the role of network news anchor.

In 1967, Lower decided to expand the news

FACING PAGE, CLOCKWISE FROM TOP LEFT: ABC News mobile crews covered the Civil Rights march in Selma, Alabama, in 1965.

*ABC Evening News* anchor and frequent *Issues and Answers* anchor Bill Lawrence was a longtime print journalist, working for two decades as a reporter and columnist at the *New York Times* before being hired by the network in 1961.

Former "Murrow Boy" Howard K. Smith was a twenty-year veteran newsman and a legend at CBS when he left to join ABC News in 1962.

Head of ABC News Jim Hagerty (seated on the left) and his department executives huddled together for a publicity shot during a daily morning conference on February 8, 1961. Standing, from left to right, are ABC News vice president Thomas Velotta, ABC director of news and public affairs John Madigan, ABC manager of public affairs Wiley Hance, ABC producer of special projects John Secondari, and ABC national news editor for radio Frank LaTourette; seated at right is ABC director of special events and operations Donald Coe.

BELOW: Peter Jennings, looking uncharacteristically overwhelmed, in his first incarnation as the face of ABC News in 1965. The critics roundly dismissed this early version of Jennings, who gave up the anchor chair after two unhappy years and became a highly respected international correspondent for the network.

broadcast to thirty minutes, retitled the show *ABC Evening News*, and brought on the middle-aged Bob Young as anchor. But Lower was astute enough to recognize the potential of a more seasoned Peter Jennings, so he reassigned him as an international correspondent for the time being. However, Young anchored the broadcast for less than a year, though he memorably covered the assassination of Martin Luther King Jr. in April 1968 for the network (just a month before leaving in May). Young's replacement was Frank Reynolds, a no-nonsense correspondent who would become a fixture at the network in various roles until his untimely passing in 1983.

In 1969, the redoubtable Howard K. Smith joined Frank Reynolds as co-anchor of *ABC Evening News*. Smith, a former Rhodes scholar, was a highly respected radio and television journalist and an original "Murrow Boy"—part of a team of CBS radio war correspondents working

continued on page 63

FACING PAGE: Jennings, who was among the first reporters to travel to Vietnam, with fellow correspondents and his film crew at the rooftop bar of the famed Caravelle Hotel in Saigon (now known as Ho Chi Minh City) in 1967.

ABOVE: Jennings on assignment in Moscow and Eastern Europe.

BELOW: Jennings tending to ABC News cameraman Larry Johnson, who was wounded by grenade shrapnel—a stark reminder of the hazards faced by news crews covering the Vietnam War.

FOLLOWING SPREAD: Sam Donaldson reporting from St. Patrick's Cathedral in New York City during a high requiem funeral mass for Senator Robert Kennedy two days after his assassination in Los Angeles, June 1968.

TOP: ABC News correspondents interview Vice President Lyndon B. Johnson for a special filmed at the White House on March 26, 1962; later as president, Johnson sought to eliminate the twin scourges of poverty and racial inequality through his ambitious Great Society programs that implemented reforms in American education, healthcare, housing, and transportation.

ABOVE LEFT: An ABC camera crew captures the action at the Las Vegas Invitational Skydiving Championships in January 1963.

ABOVE RIGHT: Jim McKay, host of *ABC's Wide World of Sports*, explains the finer points of logrolling during the 1962 Lumberjack World Championship. With *ABC's Wide World of Sports*, Roone Arledge demonstrated his ability to find entertainment value in virtually any form of athletic competition by connecting it with viewers on an emotional level.

continued from page 57

under the groundbreaking correspondent Edward R. Murrow during the Second World War. Smith had conducted interviews with Hitler, Himmler, and Goebbels before being expelled from Germany the day before the attack on Pearl Harbor by Japan, Germany's ally. After more than twenty years at CBS, Smith left the network and joined ABC in 1962, where he produced a documentary series called *Howard K. Smith: News and Comment* that ran for a year against the wildly popular *What's My Line?* on CBS.

ABC's willingness to experiment with anchor combinations also meant that audiences did not have time to develop loyalties, as CBS and NBC audiences had been able to do with Cronkite and Chet Huntley and David Brinkley (who co-anchored a daily weekday evening broadcast on NBC). However, if anything was holding ABC News down (and back) it was budget; the news was still serving as a prestige function for all three networks, never generating anything close to the advertising revenues of their entertainment programming. The steadily growing ABC network still lacked the financial clout CBS and NBC had, where the news division budgets were five to six times bigger than ABC's. To Leonard Goldenson, throwing any more money into the news division in order to improve ratings for what was essentially a loss leader product made no practical sense, especially now that ABC was beginning to dominate in other areas, like sports.

During the 1960s, television news had finally come into its own, surpassing print media for the first time as the American consumer's preferred source of information about current events. Part of the reason for this was the arrival of color television, which had a cultural impact that is difficult to appreciate today. Another was the fact that the big news stories of the decade—the civil rights movement; the war in Vietnam; assassinations; civil disturbances and uprisings in Watts, Detroit, Newark, and Chicago; the rise of the counterculture movement; the space race— were the kind of events whose physicality

continued on page 68

In 1968, the radio division of ABC News, which had been broadcasting from a single source since the network's founding in the mid-1940s, split up into four separate news programming services: the American Contemporary Network aired news five minutes before the hour on contemporary music stations in major markets like New York; the American Information Network ran the news at the top of the hour on big-market talk and information stations; the American FM Network broadcast news aimed at young adult listeners fifteen minutes past the hour on FM stations; and the American Entertainment Network aired the news at half past the hour on AM country music stations. Two additional news networks, ABC Rock and ABC Direction, were added in 1982 once the network shifted from ground lines to satellite.

ABOVE, CLOCKWISE FROM TOP LEFT: Talk radio pioneer Les Crane in 1964 on the set of his eponymous television show, which was originally called *Night Line*, and would later be renamed *Night Life*. Crane, whose show straddled the fence between entertainment and news, was a controversial anchor with a confrontational style, but his guests included many important figures of the day, such as Bob Dylan, Malcolm X, Norman Mailer, Jackie Robinson, and William F. Buckley.

The ABC buildings on West Sixty-Seventh Street in New York City in 1958.

An ABC News cameraman amid protesters during one of the pivotal marches on Selma, Alabama, in 1965.

FACING PAGE: Dr. Martin Luther King Jr. at his home in Atlanta, during an interview with Roger Sharp for the ABC News documentary *Crucial Summer: The 1963 Civil Rights Crisis*.

FOLLOWING SPREAD: The Rolling Stones make their first American television appearance on ABC's *The Les Crane Show*, June 13, 1964.

continued from page 63

was best conveyed through the visual medium of television. This trend would not just continue but come to dominate, and by the 1970s, television news would become popular enough to start attracting advertisers with deep pockets. It was the decade in which the news divisions at NBC and CBS would finally begin turning a profit . . . though the seventies would also mark the end of their hegemony over the evening news and the beginning of the golden age of ABC News.

ABOVE: On location for *The Agony of Vietnam*, a 1965 ABC documentary that focused on the impact of the war on the Vietnamese people.

FACING PAGE: The Washington, D.C. headquarters of ABC News during Dr. Martin Luther King, Jr.'s historic March on Washington for Jobs and Freedom in August of 1963, which helped pave the way for the passage of both the Civil Rights Act of 1964 and the Voting Right Act of 1965.

FOLLOWING SPREAD: Marchers gathered in Washington, D.C. to hear Dr. Martin Luther King Jr. deliver his famous "I have a dream" speech on August 28, 1963.

AKLAND COMMITTEE
FOR
OCIAL JUSTICE
ADOWS
CHICAGO CONF
ON RELIG
AND RA

CATHOLIC
INTER-RACIAL
COUNCIL of Chicago
CHICAGO, ILL.
CONFERENCE FOR
INTER-RACIAL JUSTICE

# SAM DONALDSON

Texas-born Sam Donaldson grew up on a farm in New Mexico and had his first job in journalism as manager of his college radio station. He joined the army in 1956 and served on active duty as an artillery officer, eventually reaching the rank of captain, at one point observing a nuclear test detonation from a slit trench a mere three thousand yards away. After leaving the army, Donaldson worked for a Dallas television affiliate before moving to New York City in search of broadcast work and eventually finding it in Washington, D.C., with WTOP-TV, where he reported from Capitol Hill and experienced handling his first presidential campaign while covering Republican nominee Barry Goldwater's in 1964.

When ABC News hired him as their Washington, D.C., correspondent in 1967, he began a forty-five-year career as one of the network's most popular and indispensable talents, co-anchoring a decade of unforgettable *Primetime Live* episodes, enlivening panel discussions and analyses on *This Week* for twenty-one years, covering American military action around the world, and completely redefining the role of White House correspondent, to the delight of the public and his fellow correspondents . . . but to the terror of presidents looking for slack or softball questions at press conferences.

Donaldson has won every TV journalism award of note, including four Emmys and three Peabodys, and though retired, his expert opinion continues to be sought through interviews. Donaldson's name will forever be invoked as the great example of the press speaking truth to power.

FACING PAGE: A youthful Sam Donaldson at the microphone for ABC-affiliate KEPO in El Paso, Texas. Donaldson joined ABC News in 1967 and was a fixture for nearly half a century, distinguishing himself as a formidable investigative reporter, a popular political convention coverage specialist, and the preeminent White House correspondent of his time.

FOLLOWING SPREAD: Vice President Spiro Agnew (left) being interviewed by Bill Lawrence, with the Apollo 11 rocket in the background, prior to launch, July 1969.

# 1970-1979

# 1970–1979

## GAINING GROUND

As the seventies dawned, world events kept the television news industry busy, and ABC News continued to experiment with its evening news-anchor formula. Howard K. Smith and Frank Reynolds were a great team, but the network was always willing to try new approaches. Thus far, most of the gains made by ABC News were the result of poaching talent from the other networks.

Elmer Lower continued the practice—for the most part. Most notably, the well-established and highly respected Harry Reasoner, who was good enough to sub for the mighty Walter Cronkite, was lured away from CBS. Reasoner commanded a hefty salary, but he was also one of the best in the business and worth every penny to a news organization in the ascendant. Reasoner became co-anchor with Smith, while Reynolds took over as ABC's chief Washington, D.C., correspondent. Av Westin, also a CBS ex-pat, was hired as executive producer, and the new configuration was renamed *ABC Evening News*. For the first time, critics raved, and a number of affiliates that had previously declined to air network news

PREVIOUS SPREAD: Barbara Walters conducts the first American television interview in twenty years with Cuba's Fidel Castro in 1977; Walters had doggedly pursued the interview for two years, and the results were well worth the effort.

BELOW: ABC News' Harry Reasoner surveying the chaotic scene below him during the 1976 Democratic National Convention at Madison Square Garden, in New York City, where the eventual winner, Jimmy Carter, was nominated for president.

started broadcasting *ABC Evening News*. The ratings push this provided was not a threat to the dynastic dominance of CBS, but *ABC Evening News* was unquestionably now a force to be reckoned with in the industry . . . and continued to attract its own loyal audience.

In 1972, ABC Sports was broadcasting the Summer Olympics from Munich, Germany, when eleven Israeli athletes were taken hostage and later killed by Black September terrorists.

Under Roone Arledge, television coverage of the Olympics, which had previously been a statically filmed record of athletic competition accompanied by monotone commentary, evolved into the emotionally charged entertainment spectacle that we take for granted today. The 1972 Olympics provided its share of sports drama, but when terrorism struck, Arledge switched gears instantly and turned the ABC Sports apparatus at his disposal into a de facto news organization for the duration

of the crisis. He had chosen the right people for the job, pressing into service Peter Jennings and Jim McKay to report on developments. And when the crisis ended disastrously, ABC's sensitive and restrained coverage provided audiences with a cathartic postscript to the tragedy. That this was accomplished by a sports coverage team made it all the more remarkable and further cemented the reputation Arledge already had as a production magician.

Nineteen seventy-four was a pivotal year at ABC Television. The sports division continued to grow under Arledge, but the all-important prime-time ratings were down, along with revenues; the news division would feel the pinch. Lower departed after twelve years and was replaced by Bill Sheehan, who had the unenviable task of trying to win the confidence of his new subordinates while announcing cutbacks and layoffs. But help was on the way in the form of longtime

FACING PAGE, CLOCKWISE FROM TOP LEFT: Correspondent Marlene Sanders, shown sitting on Havana, Cuba's Malecon esplanade and seawall during the ABC News special *Closeup: Cuba—The Castro Generation*, from 1977.

Roone Arledge during a press conference at the 1976 Summer Olympics in Montreal.

ABC News' resident space program expert, Jules Bergman, using one of his trademark scale models to demonstrate the heavily symbolic docking of the U.S. and Soviet spacecrafts that would take place in orbit in 1975, representing the thawing of Cold War tensions and a bright future for international scientific cooperation.

ABC correspondent and political party convention specialist Sam Donaldson, reporting from the 1976 Republican National Convention in Kansas City, Missouri, which featured the drama of a strong challenge to the incumbent, President Gerald Ford, by future nominee (in 1980) Ronald Reagan.

LEFT: Peter Jennings with Egyptian president Anwar Sadat in a scene from the Peabody Award-winning documentary *Sadat: Action Biography*, coproduced by Jennings in 1974.

ABC executive Fred Pierce, who was named president of ABC Television. Pierce, who started at ABC in 1956 as a research analyst, immediately hired CBS programming whiz Fred Silverman, and together the two Freds would fill ABC's prime-time lineup with ratings monsters like *Happy Days*, *Charlie's Angels*, *Laverne & Shirley*, and *Starsky & Hutch*.

ABC was soon the highest rated network in prime time, and profits began to soar. That very same year was also the year that documentary producer Pamela Hill directed, produced, and cowrote her first installment of the series *ABC Close-Up*, winning an Emmy, a Peabody, a duPont-Columbia University Award, and a National Press Club Award. Hill, who had joined the network the previous year, would be appointed head of the fifty-person *Close-Up* unit in 1978, replacing fellow television news pioneer Marlene Sanders.

In 1975, Pierce also launched *AM America*, which was ABC's long overdue answer to the NBC's *Today* show. It was co-anchored by Bill Beutel, a former London bureau chief who would anchor New York City affiliate WABC-TV's *Eyewitness News* for decades, and Stephanie Edwards, an actress and Los Angeles-based morning news and talk show host. It also featured Peter Jennings reading the news. *AM America* couldn't make it a full year, but it was not a dead end. The show was typical of ABC's experimental programming in that the network was willing to work through multiple iterations of a concept to get it just right.

And on November 3, 1975, the network unveiled *Good Morning America*. It was inspired by a local

RIGHT: Peter Jennings in 1971, as ABC News' bureau chief in Beirut, Lebanon, where Jennings had established the first American television news bureau in the Arab world in 1968.

FOLLOWING SPREAD: ABC News correspondent Malvin "Mal" Goode (left) interviewing Jackie Robinson in 1972, shortly before Robinson passed away.

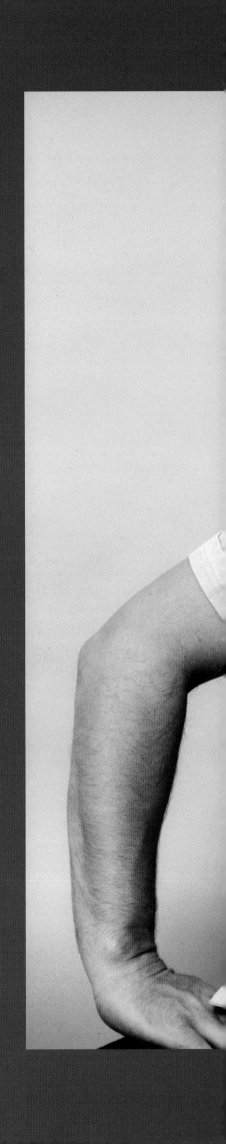

show in Cleveland called *The Morning Exchange* that aired on that ABC affiliate's WEWS-TV. The idea was to soften the overall tone, while adding regular segments on subjects ranging from health to entertainment. In keeping with the show's deliberate informality, the set was designed to look less like a newsroom and more like a room in someone's home. Another twist was that the hosts, David Hartman and Nancy Dussault, were not your usual journalists but audience-friendly

actors. *Good Morning America* would compete on its own terms by offering viewers a new kind of programming as an alternative to *Today*.

ABC News was making other major moves in 1975 as well—particularly with its evening network news broadcast. Howard K. Smith was shifted from co-anchor to correspondent, leaving Reasoner as the sole evening news anchor for the first time. Then the following year, Pierce made a decision that would alter the television journalism

FACING PAGE: Jules Bergman, during launch coverage for the ill-fated Apollo 13 lunar mission on April 11, 1970. Bergman joined ABC News as a writer in 1953 and became the network news' science editor in 1961, a post he held until his passing in 1987. His most memorable work was unquestionably his thoughtful and authoritative coverage of NASA's golden age accomplishments in the 1960s and 1970s.

ABOVE: Peter Jennings, shown here with sports artist LeRoy Neiman, at the opening ceremonies of the 1972 Summer Olympic Games in Munich, Germany. When terrorists took eleven Israelis hostage a week later, Roone Arledge had the advantage of assigning Jennings, an experienced foreign correspondent, to cover developments as the tragedy unfolded.

landscape forever. Back in the 1960s, ABC's Marlene Sanders, who had been the first female correspondent to report from Vietnam, was actually the first woman to anchor an evening news broadcast for a major network when she substituted for a male colleague who was out sick. It had made waves at the time . . . and now Pierce had his sights set on *Today* show star Barbara Walters becoming the first woman to be hired specifically for the role of network news anchor.

Pierce began trying to tempt Walters away from NBC—she was a hot commodity and the move was bound to generate attention and publicity . . . possibly more negative than positive, but either way it would push ABC News into the spotlight. According to Walters, the initial offer was made during a game of tennis between Pierce and his neighbor, who just happened to be head of television at the William Morris Agency, Lou Weiss. Walters would get a five-year deal, with half of her

ABOVE: The Reverend Jesse Jackson responds to a question from Sam Donaldson on a 1971 broadcast of *Issues and Answers*; Jackson appeared on the program to discuss his nonprofit organization Operation PUSH (People United to Save Humanity), which was formed with the goal of inspiring corporate and government action in the fight for social justice and racial equality. Also shown, to Reverend Jackson's right, is the long-serving U.S. representative John Conyers of Michigan.

FACING PAGE: A December 10, 1974, publicity photo for *AM America*, ABC News' first attempt at a morning program that could compete with NBC's *Today*. The show featured Stephanie Edwards and local New York City TV news figure Bill Beutel as co-anchors, and Peter Jennings as the news anchor. Jennings had recently returned to the United States after nearly a decade abroad to become ABC News' Washington correspondent. *AM America* lasted less than a year, but it served as the basic template for what would become *Good Morning America*.

89

salary paid by ABC News for her anchoring services and half by ABC Entertainment for a series of interview specials she would produce annually; the news slot would be expanded to an hour to accommodate her interviews. It was not the money—she was already well paid at *Today*—but the promise of making history as the first woman network news anchor that finally convinced Walters to take the offer and leave her NBC home after so many years.

Reasoner had always been the picture of on-air professionalism, but he was manifestly uncomfortable sharing airtime with Walters from the beginning. Whatever Reasoner's feelings about gender equality in the workplace, he was, as Walters put it, "in a lose-lose position" because an uptick in ratings would make it seem like Reasoner had needed her help to boost the show's popularity, and if the ratings tanked, they would both look bad. Still, Reasoner's hostility on

FACING PAGE: Peter Jennings, seen here with the Ayatollah Khomeini on November 18, 1978, was the first North American reporter to interview the Iranian religious leader, who was living in exile in Paris at the time.

ABOVE: The original cast, not including Barbara Walters, of the second iteration of *20/20*, from June of 1978. Left to right are Dave Marash, Sylvia Chase, Hugh Downs, Geraldo Rivera, and Thomas Hoving.

LEFT: The three-anchor format of *ABC World News Tonight* featured the all-star grouping of Peter Jennings, Frank Reynolds, and Max Robinson.

the set was palpable, and eventually critics began to comment on his coldness toward Walters, even during the broadcasts.

Sadly, between Reasoner's animosity and the chauvinist hue and cry in the press over her salary—they dubbed Walters "the million dollar baby"—the historic occasion of women being accepted into the hitherto all-male ranks of network news anchors was starting to look more like a case study in the obstacles faced by gender-

equality pioneers like Walters. Somehow, she managed to weather the frost for two years before Roone Arledge, who knew and liked Walters from his early days at NBC, eased Reasoner out the door and took Walters off the news to focus exclusively on her interview specials, for which she was already famous for on *Today* (but would soon become legendary at ABC). In fact, since arriving at the ABC Network, she had already conducted the first ever U.S. television interview

with Fidel Castro as Cuban prime minister, as well as a history-making joint interview in 1977 with Egypt's Anwar Sadat and Israel's Menachem Begin, plus a sit-down with the shah of Iran.

Once again, a bold ABC News experiment that didn't go quite as planned had nevertheless yielded something of lasting value to the network. Barbara Walters's first stint as a network news anchor has largely been forgotten now. Yet her two years of co-anchoring the news was historic because it was the first time a woman had ever been hired to sit in that chair—and it was also a

nationally televised reminder of how far we still had to go.

It is impossible to overstate the importance of Roone Arledge to the changes that occurred at ABC News after he became president of the unit in 1977. But it would also be unfair to discount the years of hard work put in by his predecessors in building up a respectable news division on a relatively meager budget. Arledge inherited a solid foundation on which to build, including what would become five of the brightest stars in the ABC News firmament in Barbara Walters,

Peter Jennings, Sam Donaldson, Ted Koppel, and Charles Gibson. Nevertheless, Arledge was a maverick with a vision; when he took over Sports at ABC, he transformed it into something that had never existed before in television, and while the core of ABC News would remain strong reporting, Arledge would look for ways to enhance the news experience for viewers.

One of his first actions was hiring David Burke as a vice president. Burke had had a remarkably varied background, working for years as a devoted "fixer" for the Kennedys, helping to engineer a merger for the Dreyfus Fund, and having a significant hand in ending the mid-1970s New York City fiscal crisis. Burke was a tenacious and versatile executive who would play a major role in creating some of ABC News' most storied programming. Arledge also lured charismatic Washington reporter Cassie Mackin from NBC with the offer of a big paycheck.

In addition, Arledge would retain the services of talented producer and fellow maverick Av

FACING PAGE: Harry Reasoner, Barbara Walters, and Howard K. Smith posing for a publicity shot as the upcoming ABC News election night coverage team, late October 1976.

ABOVE: Barbara Walters making television history as the first full-time female anchor of an evening network newscast, October 4, 1976. For the next two years, Walters would bravely endure co-anchor Harry Reasoner's palpable dissatisfaction with the arrangement.

FOLLOWING SPREAD: A historic joint interview with Egyptian president Anwar Sadat and Israeli prime minister Menachem Begin, 1977, courtesy of Barbara Walters and ABC.

Westin, which allowed for a sense of continuity without compromising the spirit of innovation that would characterize ABC News going forward. Arledge brought along some key staffers from the sports division as well, including director Roger Goodman, who would completely retool the on-screen personality of ABC News with new graphics, set designs, and musical themes.

The network's style of strong reporting would not change, but Arledge also wanted to make ABC the go-to source for breaking news, drawing on his years of experience as a producer of live sporting events, which gave him the ability to

ABOVE TOP: Barbara Walters at home with President Gerald Ford and First Lady Betty Ford for an ABC News special.

ABOVE BOTTOM: Walters interviews President Ford in his backyard.

FACING PAGE: Tom Jarriel, Sam Donaldson, and Frank Reynolds covering the 1976 presidential debates between Jimmy Carter and Gerald Ford.

adapt to changing circumstances instantly, as the Munich Olympics tragedy had proved. Arledge described his mission this way: "On the big, breaking stories that made a network's reputation, I wanted us always first and best. If we couldn't match Walter Cronkite [at CBS] . . . we would find our own way of competing."

Arledge wasted no time in changing the way ABC News conducted business. During his first week, Indonesian terrorists took over a commuter train in the Netherlands! Arledge flew multiple producers and their crews in to cover the siege. The crisis ended three weeks later when Dutch police stormed the train, and for the first time, ABC had

ruled the coverage of a major news story. While the drama in the Netherlands was still unfolding, Martin Luther King Jr.'s convicted assassin, James Earl Ray, escaped from a Tennessee prison, and Arledge flew multiple crews to that scene as well. If there was breaking news anywhere in the world, ABC News would spare no expense to obtain immediate and maximum coverage.

The rest of the television news industry—and more than a few ABC News staffers— reacted to the arrival of Roone Arledge with skepticism. It was conceded that Arledge had single-handedly made televised sports more popular and far more emotionally engaging—but sports was

ABOVE AND FACING PAGE: Barbara Walters interviewed First Ladies Mamie Eisenhower and Lady Bird Johnson in their homes for a 1979 ABC News special.

merely entertainment; the news was serious business. Network news in the late 1970s was still dominated by old-school print and radio veterans who worried that Arledge might bring unwanted change to their time-honored profession. It didn't help that he had a couple of missteps early on that seemed to validate everyone's notions about him, like his coverage of the arrest of New York City's Son of Sam killer, or the death of Elvis Presley (both in the summer of 1977). However, what the naysayers didn't realize was just how serious Arledge was about the news—and how he wanted to elevate the medium itself by connecting with viewers on a deeper level than ever before.

His critics assumed he was a one-trick pony,

that he had been good at making televised sports better simply because he was good at sensationalizing things. But it was the nature of sports that dictated his approach, not a *penchant* for sensationalism . . . and Arledge genuinely aspired to TV news greatness. Mastery would come in time, and he could be forgiven for a few awkward misfires along the way. Producer Rick Kaplan, who collaborated with Arledge on some of ABC News' most successful programming, puts it bluntly: "Look, I've worked for some heavy hitters, like Walter Cronkite, and I will tell you no one was more substantive, better read, or had a greater sense of responsibility to get the news right than Roone Arledge."

In 1978, as soon as Reasoner returned to CBS, Arledge and Westin implemented a new, three-anchor format at *ABC Evening News*. ABC stalwart Frank Reynolds would serve as the main anchor in Washington, while a more seasoned Peter Jennings would report on international news from London and Max Robinson, the first African American network news anchor, would broadcast the national news from Chicago, which was also a first. Robinson, who was a founder of the National Association of Black Journalists, had graduated from a segregated high school in Virginia and worked in radio before landing a local television news job, where he gained national attention for his Emmy Award–winning documentary on Black life, *The Other Washington*.

Complementing the new three-man configuration was Howard K. Smith, who would contribute commentary from Washington, and Barbara Walters, who ran a "special coverage desk" in New York. The cosmopolitan broadcast was appropriately re-titled *World News Tonight*, which reflected Arledge's determination to make ABC News a global force in news coverage. And while the novel format was a vast improvement over the tension-filled Reasoner and Walters experiment, Arledge and Westin continued to introduce innovations to the broadcast. Over the next few years, as Arledge further developed his news production sensibilities, viewership would increase, and by the end of the decade, ABC News could accurately boast that it was "fast becoming the most watchable news on television."

ABOVE: Former president Richard M. Nixon spoke with Barbara Walters at the ABC News desk on *20/20* in 1982.

FACING PAGE: President Ronald Reagan was interviewed by Barbara Walters for *20/20* at his Santa Barbara ranch during the first year of his presidency.

ABC News' programing presence started showing up outside the morning and early evening hours at this time as well. Ever since the CBS ratings juggernaut *60 Minutes* went on the air in the late 1960s, ABC had considered creating its own newsmagazine show; but nothing came of it until Arledge arrived in 1977 and promised to deliver one. And in June of 1978, he did. ABC premiered the first episode of *20/20*, the brainchild of Arledge and ABC Entertainment vice president Bob Shanks. It was not exactly an overnight sensation. But ABC had a history of patience with new concepts, as did Arledge, and he immediately began brainstorming ways of turning the new show into a winner. The show's writing and editorial choices would have to be addressed, but the first order of business was replacing the on-air talent.

The success of *60 Minutes* was tied to the gravitas and investigative reporting skills of co-anchors at various stages Mike Wallace, Harry Reasoner, Dan Rather, and Morley Safer, whereas *20/20* was anchored initially by Australian art critic Robert Hughes and former *Esquire* editor Harold Hayes. As Arledge was looking for replacements, he happened to turn on *Good Morning America* and saw former *Today* show anchor Hugh Downs filling in for David Hartman. Arledge immediately arranged a meeting, and to Downs's credit—even though he had seen the lackluster first episode of *20/20*—he still recognized the show's tremendous potential and agreed to anchor.

Arledge also took Westin off *World News Tonight* to replace Shanks as the show's producer,

and hired his favorite reporter, Geraldo Rivera, whose unorthodox style and strong personality were not an ideal match for straight reporting but turned out to be perfectly suited to the *20/20* ethos Arledge was looking to establish. The new version of *20/20* aired once a month for the remainder of the 1978 season, before settling into its regular prime-time slot on Thursdays at 10:00 p.m. in 1979, where it quickly gained an appreciative audience.

There was one other significant development at ABC News in 1979. It began when militant Iranian students seized the American embassy in Tehran on November 4. Stan Opotowsky, ABC's director of news coverage, immediately dispatched London radio reporter Bob Dyk—who was the only ABC News reporter available—and photographer David Greene to Iran to cover the story. Both CBS and NBC had vacillated on sending crews to the Iranian capital just long enough to miss the window of opportunity that existed for American network news crews before Iran closed its borders to Americans. As a result, ABC News had one of the biggest scoops of the decade—practically all to itself (in the American media market). It is likely that without Arledge's directive to make ABC the number one source of breaking news anywhere in the world, Opotowsky might also have hesitated before sending a crew into potentially hostile territory.

As a result, the ratings for *World News Tonight* went up by two points, and Arledge could claim,

fairly or not, that "We just sensed that it was a bigger story than the other two [CBS and NBC] did." Then four days later, Frank Reynolds anchored a late-night special about the siege, titled *The Iran Crisis: America Held Hostage*. When Arledge realized that the average American citizen was deeply concerned about the hostages, he decided the one-off special should be a nightly affair for the duration of the crisis. Such a move was unheard of, and Fred Pierce, whose approval was needed, fretted that the network would lose too much money on a nightly special; but ultimately, he gave his blessing. At the time, nobody thought the siege would last more than a few weeks or a month at most, and neither Pierce nor Arledge had any idea what they were committing to.

But *America Held Hostage* stayed on the air into the new decade, filling up the evening slot with detailed explanations for the crisis: Who were the militants? What is the difference between a Sunni and a Shiite Muslim? It was the first time that most Americans had ever given much thought to the problems of the Islamic world. This was exactly the sort of news coverage that fired up Arledge—an audience connection with current events that engaged their attention and kept them tuning in, night after night. Roone Arledge was going to give viewers the in-depth coverage of a complex news issue they wanted, and in the process, he would show the world just how good ABC News could be.

FACING PAGE: Hugh Downs, an early Roone Arledge hire and one of ABC's galaxy of stars anchors in the 1990s.

# BARBARA WALTERS

A pioneer among pioneers, Barbara Walters has broken clean through every professional gender barrier that ever stood in her way . . . often, it has seemed, by sheer force of her indomitable will, but always through hard work, abundant talent, and superhuman patience. Born in Boston to a well-known nightclub owner, Walters worked for a small New York City ad agency for one year after college before getting a job writing press releases for the local NBC affiliate.

After a period of making herself useful at the television station, she produced a fifteen-minute children's show in 1953 called *Ask the Camera* that was directed by a young Roone Arledge. She then had a brief stint at CBS as a writer for *The Morning Show*, before returning to NBC and working her way up the production ladder, eventually landing at the *Today* show as a writer and segment producer. It was there that Walters first demonstrated her unique ability to not only get the interview but to make it count by getting even the most tight-lipped of her subjects comfortable enough to open up.

After her groundbreaking move to ABC News and the co-anchoring role with its national network evening news broadcast from 1976 to 1978, a newly arrived to the news division Roone Arledge stepped in and allowed her to continue building on her legacy by adapting *20/20* to accommodate Walters's journalistic strengths. For the next twenty-five years, Walters would co-anchor and produce the show, along the way conducting some of the most absorbing and important interviews of the famous and the infamous, and winning every award for which she and the show were eligible.

Not content to rest on her countless achievements, in 1997 Walters cocreated and produced *The View*, a new breed of talk show primarily for women viewers that has since become one of the most politically important programs on television. It is difficult for us now, in an age of relative gender equality, to appreciate the level of hostility Walters endured, to say nothing of the endless unwanted advances she had to fend off earlier in her remarkable career. That she *did endure* is not only a testament to her strength, but also an inspiration to new generations of women journalists who might never have realized their professional dreams without her leading the way for so long.

FOLLOWING SPREAD: In her first special for ABC, Barbara Walters interviewed newly elected president Jimmy Carter and First Lady Rosalynn Carter in December 1976. It was during this interview that President Carter famously raised eyebrows by mentioning that he and Rosalynn would be sharing a double bed in the White House.

1980-
1989

## ARRIVAL

When Roone Arledge became president of ABC News, the brilliant and vastly experienced Ted Koppel was anchoring the network's *Saturday Evening News*, doing a daily radio commentary, and producing occasional specials. ABC news president Bill Sheehan had previously offered Koppel the evening news producer and vice president positions, which he had turned down in order to spend more time with his children while his wife completed her first year of law school (though he continued to work weekends as the *World News* anchor). Koppel also declined the offer because he was not interested in behind-the-scenes roles. A former State Department correspondent, Koppel was used to being in the thick of it, having also covered Vietnam, run two foreign news bureaus, and traveled extensively with Henry Kissinger even before he was secretary of state. Moreover, he had developed formidable interviewing skills along the way that would be utterly wasted anywhere but in front of the camera.

When Arledge took over, he sent Koppel back to his old State Department job, shattering the latter's dream of becoming an ABC News anchor. But then in the spring of 1979, he and producer Mike Von Fremd created an eleven-part series for *World News Tonight*

PREVIOUS SPREAD: Princess Diana and Prince Charles shortly after the royal couple exchanged vows in what was billed as the wedding of the century.

BELOW: Massachusetts senator Edward Kennedy in Boston shortly before announcing his ill-fated candidacy to be the Democratic Party nominee over incumbent president Jimmy Carter during the 1980 presidential election.

titled "Second to None," which examined the relative military preparedness of U.S. and Soviet Union forces. The entire series was eye-opening, but there was a particular nine-minute segment that employed graphics to depict what a nuclear exchange would look like. In a lesser reporter's hands, the segment might have easily slipped into lurid sensationalism, but Koppel's superlative journalistic skills made it both riveting and informative.

Arledge was impressed enough to vigorously promote the series, and the week it aired on *World News Tonight*, the show came in second in the ratings for the very first time; in the history of this business—and the competition it brings, no second-place finish was ever so welcomed. Later that year, Koppel filled in for Frank Reynolds one night as anchor of *America Held Hostage*, and when Reynolds opted to focus his already divided energies on covering

the 1980 presidential campaign, Koppel took over the show.

Once Koppel's anchoring and interviewing skills were properly showcased, it was clear to Arledge that he had a very special talent on his hands. And when he decided to make *America Held Hostage* a permanent nightly show even after the hostage crisis ended in January 1981, Koppel would continue as anchor. In its 11:30 p.m. time slot, the show was giving *The Tonight Show*

*Starring Johnny Carson* stiffer competition than the NBC fixture had ever experienced before, and Arledge wanted to keep it going.

In addition, Arledge had been trying to come up with another new concept for a news program . . . and here it was, already audience-tested and with the production infrastructure in place. *Nightline*, as the new iteration was called, debuted March of 1980, a few months after the Lake Placid, New York, Winter Olympics concluded. And while it

FACING PAGE, CLOCKWISE FROM TOP LEFT: The inimitable Barbara Walters in her milieu, in front of a camera preparing for one of her many exclusive and highly anticipated interviews.

Barbara Walters during an interview with Fawn Hall, secretary to Lt. Col. Oliver North of Iran-Contra fame; Hall helped North destroy key evidence relating to the political scandal.

Barbara Walters conducts a prison interview with Mark David Chapman, the assassin of a beloved music icon, former Beatle and activist John Lennon.

Joan Lunden covering the impending royal wedding.

LEFT: Peter Jennings and Barbara Walters in London during the network's coverage of the royal wedding between Prince Charles and Lady Diana Spencer in 1981.

FOLLOWING SPREAD: Max Robinson, with Executive Producer Jeff Gralnick, in the ABC News newsroom in the early 1980s. Gralnick was the talented and tireless production whiz behind *ABC World News Tonight*.

was not an instant hit with the critics, the show soon found its footing. Koppel was too good not to learn and grow from any early missteps, plus Arledge had brought in Bill Lord as executive producer. Lord was a longtime ABC News veteran who had worked his way up from reporter to vice president; he turned out to be the perfect choice to produce *Nightline*, because he had a technical grasp that Koppel lacked, and his mainstream editorial instincts balanced out Koppel's, which tended to heavily favor foreign-policy stories.

The combination of Koppel and Lord, along with a staff replete with bright go-getters and a virtually unlimited budget, turned *Nightline* into a unique and consistently compelling force in television news. The ratings climbed steadily, and by early 1981, when the show was expanded from twenty to thirty minutes and to five nights a week, the critics were won over. Tom Shales of the *Washington Post* called it "the most successful programming initiative in ABC News history" . . . and he was right.

When the Iran hostage crisis ended, ABC News bookended its coverage with a three-hour special titled *America Held Hostage: The Secret Negotiations*, which focused on how Jimmy Carter's administration had attempted to secure the release of the American hostages through back channels. The investigation had been spearheaded by ABC News Paris bureau chief and former President Kennedy press secretary Pierre Salinger, whom Arledge had hired back in 1977—and the result was a fascinating and absorbing glimpse into the world of off-the-books international diplomacy and a fitting coda to ABC's proactive coverage of the crisis from day one.

Meanwhile, *World News Tonight* was also gaining viewers, in large part because of all the positive attention that *Nightline* was getting. Another factor was Arledge's choice of executive producer, Jeff Gralnick, to take over when Av Westin left to produce *20/20*; Gralnick was a driven TV news veteran, and his exacting production standards raised the journalistic

bar at ABC significantly. Arledge also redesigned the look and feel of *World News Tonight* in a successful bid to attract younger viewers. In retrospect, Arledge seemed to be the only network news executive at the time who understood how best to use the medium of television to engage viewers so that important news stories always found a receptive audience.

The three-anchor format of *World News Tonight*, meantime, had made sense as a means of establishing a strong news presence around the country and the world. But Arledge still yearned for a single anchor with the star power to unseat Walter Cronkite. His first choice had always been Dan Rather, whom he courted for months. He offered Rather everything a network anchor could

possibly want—money, control, flexibility—but Rather was reluctant to leave CBS and turned the offer down. However, Arledge's full-court press recruiting ultimately forced CBS to offer Rather more money and to promise him the anchor position when Cronkite retired (which, to placate Rather, he was persuaded to do six months early), instead of Roger Mudd, whom everyone at CBS assumed was next in line. Apparently, Arledge and Burke even went so far as to contact Mudd about the anchor position simply to convince CBS that he was being courted, with the hope that they would make him an offer and lose Rather in the process. In any event, when the CBS spot went to Rather, Mudd was furious and defected immediately to NBC.

FACING PAGE: In addition to covering political conventions, summit meetings, and being the first woman to serve as in-studio anchor for ABC's coverage of the Winter Olympics in 1984, the versatile Kathleen Sullivan debuted *ABC World News This Morning* with co-anchor Steve Bell in 1982. She would also anchor *ABC World News Saturday*, as well as sub for Joan Lunden on *Good Morning America*.

ABOVE: Steve Bell covered the Vietnam War for ABC News beginning in 1967, at one point being held in detention in neighboring Cambodia while investigating the massacre of a hundred Vietnamese civilians by Cambodian soldiers. After the war reporting assignment, Bell served in a number of on-air roles at ABC News and was the news anchor for *GMA* from 1975 to 1986.

This was not the first time Arledge's maneuverings had impacted the other networks. His offers of six-figure salaries to people he wanted on his team put the other networks in the position of having to match his enticements and incentives in order to keep their staffs intact. Linda Ellerbee, who was at NBC at the time, said, "All of us who worked as correspondents owe Roone a great deal because he single-handedly upped salary levels at all three networks simply by bidding across the board." Arledge then went after Tom Brokaw, and the net result was exactly the same: Brokaw ultimately declined, but NBC was forced to give him the anchor position, which had been offered to Roger Mudd, and to convince John Chancellor to retire six months ahead of schedule to accommodate the Brokaw offer. Owing perhaps partly to the chaos that Arledge had sown at the rival networks, *World News Tonight* took the top spot in the Nielsens for the first time in July of 1981.

Over at *20/20*, Hugh Downs had settled comfortably into his role as anchor, and reporter Geraldo Rivera's fame and influence continued to grow. (Rivera was popular enough to have been wooed by Ted Turner to leave ABC for CNN.) And with Arledge's patronage and protection, he operated almost as an independent unit. He used his own handpicked producers and staffers and followed his own agenda, and was answerable only to Av Westin and above. Rivera did some terrific reporting on some very important subjects, such as a series of pieces on the AIDS epidemic in the gay community, which at the time no other network would go near, and investigating defense contractors and the Pentagon for wasteful spending.

Arledge also moved forward with a program he had been considering that would help maintain journalistic credibility at ABC News. The new show was called *Viewpoint*, with ABC News vice president George Watson as its executive producer and Koppel as the anchor; it would air periodically in the *Nightline* time slot. The ninety-minute program, broadcast live, invited TV news professionals and critics on to debate various subjects relating to media accountability, and was followed by a Q and A session with a studio audience. The show may have seemed like an unusual reach for Arledge, but so much of what he had done with sports—and was now doing with news—was tied to explaining the details and the backstory of a subject in order to more deeply involve the viewer. *Viewpoint* explained to viewers how ABC News stories were vetted and reported, with the goal of reassuring them that there was no ratings-based bias involved in the process. It was a sincere bid for transparency from Arledge the showman, who was nevertheless serious about preserving the integrity of the medium he sought to revolutionize.

Despite the growing popularity of *20/20*, the show faced a challenge in the fall of 1981 when NBC premiered the police drama *Hill Street Blues* at 10:00 p.m. on Thursdays. Arledge countered with a fresh infusion of star power, convincing a reluctant Barbara Walters to team up with *20/20* anchor Hugh Downs. Walters, who had worked with Downs on *Today* for nine years, had been offered the anchor job back in 1978, but had declined because her unhappy stint as news co-anchor with Harry Reasoner had just ended and she was not ready to take on another risky career experiment. Walters had done dozens of interviews on the show since then, but she was concerned that a co-anchor position would interfere with her carefully cultivated image as television's premier interviewer. But in the end, the two sides negotiated a deal whereby Walters would gain even more control over her choice of assignments and take a job as not quite a co-anchor, but more than a correspondent. Downs was permitted to retain the *appearance* of sole anchor, sitting alone at his desk facing the camera, with Walters off to the side and at an angle to the viewer. This arrangement continued until the fall of 1984, when Walters was officially introduced as Downs's co-anchor.

There were still a few lingering clashes of ego, as when deciding who literally got the last word at the end of the broadcast (it was Downs), but the two went on to become one of the most successful pairings in television history, remaining co-anchors of *20/20* for the next fifteen years.

By 1981, ABC's *Issues and Answers* had been around for over twenty years and a thousand episodes—Hall of Fame numbers, to be sure. But next to Arledge's state-of-the-art news programs *Nightline* and *20/20*, it felt structurally antiquated and in need of an overhaul. That same year, the venerable David Brinkley was planning his departure from NBC when senior vice president Dick Wald reached out to him about doing a

new ABC Sunday morning news show, as well as some spot political coverage. Arledge considered Brinkley one of a handful of true giants in the business, and welcomed the "instant credibility" that he would bring to ABC News.

To Arledge, all of the Sunday morning shows were "dinosaurs," and he envisioned something new and exciting in their place. He wasn't sure exactly what the new show would be, and he tasked weekend news producer Dorrance Smith

ABOVE: Maxie Cleveland "Max" Robinson was a trailblazing African American journalist who battled systemic racism and rose to the top of his profession, eventually serving as co-anchor of *ABC World News Tonight* for five years alongside Peter Jennings and Frank Reynolds. Tragically, Robinson was an early AIDS casualty, succumbing to the disease in 1988 at the age of forty-nine.

ABOVE: Henry Kissinger (top) and Gerald Ford discuss Ronald Reagan's landslide victory with Barbara Walters on election night, 1980. The presence of Walters on shows like election night specials gave ABC News an edge when it came to booking big-name guests.

FACING PAGE: President Ronald Reagan calls to order the 1984 Republican National Convention in Dallas.

with developing the format. Smith played around with ideas, but once ABC signed Brinkley, with his legendary status, his strong personality, and his distinctive voice and speech patterns, "Then it fell into place," said Smith. Also, once ABC could sell the concept with Brinkley as anchor, its affiliates agreed to carve out a full hour of airtime for the show. Brinkley, for his part, was pleased to be going to a network where he was considered broadcasting royalty, and a deal was reached very quickly. As a bonus, Brinkley recruited his friend, columnist George Will, to appear as a weekly guest.

*This Week with David Brinkley* premiered on November 15, 1981, and like almost all of Arledge's innovations, it got off to a slow start but then settled into success, brilliance, and longevity. In the beginning, Arledge felt the show too closely resembled the familiar Sunday morning shows it was designed to supplant, so he decided to shake things up. Inspired by a *Nightline* piece on Muammar al-Qaddafi, Arledge called Smith and told him to book the Libyan dictator for the

FACING PAGE: Peter Jennings and Barbara Walters during the 1986 ABC News special *Liberty Weekend*, which celebrated the hundredth anniversary of the Statue of Liberty.

ABOVE TOP: Longtime ABC News science correspondent and space enthusiast Jules Bergman in 1985 with a model of the space shuttle *Columbia*, which would tragically break up during reentry in 2003, effectively ending NASA's space shuttle program.

ABOVE BOTTOM: Before there was breaking news, there was the ABC News Bulletin.

following Sunday. Smith protested, assuming it would be impossible to line up this guest. But he made the arrangements, and come Sunday, there was Qaddafi on a satellite link. The ploy worked, and on Monday morning, *This Week with David Brinkley* was the talk of the television news industry. But Arledge also knew that they couldn't book a Qaddafi every week, so he threw the brash, tenacious, and highly respected Sam Donaldson into the mix. Donaldson, who had been at ABC News since 1967, recalls with some amusement that the network originally hired him because he was "a twofer"—a reporter who could also produce his own pieces.

Apart from covering Vietnam, Donaldson became a convention-coverage specialist and eventually a White House correspondent, earning the admiration of his peers as a pit bull who always got the sound bite and someone who wasn't afraid to shout questions at the president of the United States when necessary. As Arledge anticipated, the volatile chemistry between Will and Donaldson led to many a spirited debate, with the genteel Brinkley always providing the show's on-screen center of gravity. After three months on-air, the show pushed NBC's *Meet the Press* into third place for the first time in the program's long history. *This Week* became the show that every influence peddler and every influence seeker in Washington wanted to be on. Roone Arledge had done it again.

By 1983, *World News Tonight* was cruising along when co-anchor—and the revered leader of ABC's remaining old guard—Frank Reynolds died suddenly and unexpectedly after what appeared to be a brief illness. Arledge and Burke later learned that Reynolds had been diagnosed with terminal bone cancer in 1979, and had been told he had another three or four

RIGHT: Frank Reynolds (left) and Ted Koppel covering the 1980 Democratic National Convention from Madison Square Garden in New York City.

Among the talent that joined ABC News in the new decade was the trailblazing Carole Simpson, who had become the first African American woman to anchor a major network newscast in 1975. Simpson was hired in 1982 and would go on to enjoy a twenty-four-year career at ABC News, during which time she anchored the weekend edition of *World News Tonight* for fifteen years, as well as serving as the first woman of color to moderate a presidential debate in 1992.

years to live. Reynolds, an intensely private man for a public figure, had chosen to continue working until the end, and he knew that revealing his diagnosis to ABC News would have meant stepping down; so he kept it secret. After Reynolds's sudden passing, Arledge decided that rather than attempt to replace him the broadcast would return to the single-anchor format. In his mind, the choice was between Koppel and Jennings; but when Arledge called to sound out Koppel on the subject, Koppel immediately said, "Roone, let me make this easy for you. I think Peter will be a terrific anchor for *World News Tonight*, and I think you ought to go sign him up."

Koppel wasn't being noble in stepping aside—he had the perfect job already as anchor of *Nightline*, and genuinely wasn't interested in switching. Jennings also felt very comfortable in his London correspondent role,

and he was still a little gun-shy after his experience on *Peter Jennings with the News* back in the 1960s. He was also in his element when reporting in the field, and didn't relish being "chained" to a news desk after so many years having the freedom to chase stories around the globe. However, becoming the sole anchor of the network's flagship news broadcast was too tempting to pass up. Jennings took the job.

Another problem was that shortly before Frank Reynolds died, *World News Tonight* executive producer Jeff Gralnick had quit; after four years of running the show, Gralnick was burned out. As he put it, "*World News Tonight* was a seven-day-a-week, twenty-four-hour-a-day job for anyone who cared about where the news division was going." With the dependable Gralnick gone, Arledge tapped longtime ABC producer Robert Frye for the position, hoping his broad experience and managerial

FACING PAGE: Ted Koppel and Frank Reynolds anchored coverage of the 1980 Democratic National Convention at Madison Square Garden in New York City.

tact would serve him well in the post. Frye tried to remake *World News Tonight* in his own image, which was not a perfect match for the successful production style Arledge and Gralnick had worked so hard to put in place. Frye also had to cope with an industry shift when Ted Turner's brand-new CNN started to eat into the evening news market share of all three of the major networks, while at the same time ABC's prime-time dominance flagged as the entertainment division struggled to replace their megahit lineup from the 1970s. Frye lasted only a year and was replaced by *Nightline* executive producer Bill Lord. Jennings and Lord managed to produce an outstanding newscast for the next three years until Lord was succeeded by Paul Friedman, who would develop a strong rapport with his anchor and oversee the emergence of *World News Tonight with Peter Jennings* as the number one evening news program beginning in 1989.

Nineteen eighty-five was a consequential year for ABC News—and the entire network. First, in March, the company was bought by Capital Cities for $3.5 billion, which was the first sale of a broadcast network since United Paramount Theatres merged with ABC in 1953. (Coincidentally, both deals had been overseen by Leonard Goldenson.) Fred Pierce and Arledge would now report to Cap Cities chairman Tom Murphy and president and COO Dan Burke, signaling a new era of frugality at ABC. Before long, Pierce, who had made a number of costly sports and entertainment programming commitments for the coming years, was replaced by Cap Cities executive John Sias. And while Arledge was still wondering how he would manage without Pierce as his corporate ally, he was informed that he would no longer be president of ABC Sports.

In fairness to Cap Cities, the formerly profitable sports division was hemorrhaging

money at the time, and Murphy could not be expected to share Arledge's sentimental attachment to the sports-coverage apparatus he had built from scratch. Moreover, the new management wanted him to focus solely on news now that it was poised to become the industry leader.

In March of 1985 as well—back on the news coverage front—*Nightline* broadcast a history-making program from South Africa, where Ted Koppel moderated a split-screen debate between South Africa's foreign minister, R. F. Botha, and Nobel laureate Bishop Desmond Tutu. For the first time, South Africans got to see both sides of the apartheid issue facing off against one another on television; the show had been the brainchild of Koppel and African American producer Lionel Chapman. The historic broadcast proved to be the opening of a dialogue that would help bring about the end of the country's apartheid policy within a few years.

A few years later, in 1988, Cokie Roberts joined the staff of *World News Tonight with Peter Jennings* as a political correspondent after ten years in the same role for National Public Radio, which Roberts had helped bring to prominence. As the daughter of the late Democratic Louisiana congressman Hale Boggs, Roberts had been immersed in the politics of the nation's capital since childhood and understood its machinations perhaps better than any other journalist of her time. Roberts became a regular fill-in anchor for Ted Koppel on *Nightline*, and would later co-anchor *This Week* next to Sam Donaldson.

As ABC News became competitive under

FACING PAGE: ABC News stalwart and convention coverage specialist Sam Donaldson, doing what he does best at the 1980 Democratic National Convention.

ABOVE: The "Magnificent Seven," plus one: ABC News' star-studded pool of homegrown and poached talent poses for this group shot in 1989 alongside the man who brought them all together, Roone Arledge.

loyal second-in-command, walked out the door to become president of CBS News.

It was a pivotal moment for Arledge; he was eager to prove he could keep ABC in the ascendant without Burke, who would now be his direct competition. Fortunately for Arledge, Tom Murphy was not happy with the move because he and CBS head Larry Tisch were friends . . . and they had so far refrained from hiring talent away from one another. Now it was Murphy's turn. Arledge had been in hot pursuit of Diane Sawyer for years, and Murphy gave him his blessing to go after her, to create a news vehicle for her, and to promise her a minimum two-year commitment to the new show to give it time to find an audience.

The new show was created by *This Week* executive producer Dorrance Smith and Phyllis McGrady, Barbara Walters's prime-time specials producer. McGrady, who at thirty-four had been one of the youngest women ever to executive produce a morning show, was a critical factor in making *Good Morning America* the number one breakfast show in the early 1980s. In general, her peerless production instincts had proven essential to the rise of the news division to its status now of industry leader, and they enabled her to translate Arledge's rough vision into groundbreaking programming.

McGrady was herself being wooed by NBC at the time; she mentioned the offer to Walters, who said she should hold off on deciding until she arranged a meeting with Arledge. "Roone asked me to help develop a new magazine show that Diane Sawyer would anchor once he pried her away from CBS," says McGrady. "His excite-

Arledge, it also became his turn to worry about the other networks raiding his carefully assembled galaxy of star anchors and correspondents. Jennings, Koppel, Donaldson, Walters, and Brinkley had all been courted by either CBS or NBC, but to Arledge's relief, they all turned down the offers or were convinced to stay by ABC's counteroffers. However, all Arledge could do was watch helplessly when David Burke, his

ABOVE: The late Cokie Roberts, former National Public Radio pioneer and ABC News' most experienced Beltway insider.

ment and creative ideas, along with the bold move of stealing Diane, convinced me to stay at ABC News." Arledge told McGrady he wanted a program with more immediacy than *20/20*, one that could react to current news events and, where possible, cover them live in prime time. "He wanted to team Diane with Sam Donaldson, who had become a huge news personality as the White House correspondent for ABC News," McGrady adds. "Roone knew that Sam could respond to breaking news and brought a tremendous energy and grit to the job, and would not hold back in interviews." McGrady was named executive producer and she began hiring the best available producers and correspondents, including Chris Wallace. But when a family illness forced McGrady to step down less than two months before the show's premiere, she was replaced by Rick Kaplan.

Such a setback might easily have thrown the whole production off, but Kaplan, who had been executive producing *Nightline* since 1984—and had been responsible for many of the show's most important and memorable segments (including the historic South African broadcasts)—was able to slide right into the role and keep things on track and on schedule. The show, initially called *Primetime Live*, launched in August of 1989, and—as was par for the course with Roone Arledge's experiments—did not find an audience right away. One problem was the live element of the show was not working because newsworthy events were not typically occurring on Thursday nights at 10:00 p.m., traditionally a fairly quiet time of the week. But then came the show's cov-

erage of the unexpected opening of the Berlin Wall a few months later in November, which was an ideal story to test out all the moving parts of *Primetime*. The story gave everyone on the show a glimpse of what was possible.

Yet even before that momentous historic event, *Primetime* had gotten to put on full display the

benefits it would bring to its audience, when a destructive earthquake hit San Francisco October 17. It was right before Game 3 of the World Series between the hometown Giants and Oakland A's was set to begin. ABC Sports, ironically, was broadcasting the game. But soon after, ABC News took charge through *Primetime Live*. News was back in its element—and would cover the bulk of an unfolding crisis.

Still, the show struggled to find its identity for the entire first season. But fortunately, ABC was committed to two years, and Arledge, as he always did, would find a way to turn things around.

Despite the challenges facing the new show, ABC News ended 1989 on a celebratory note: *World News Tonight* won the Nielsen ratings for the entire year. ABC News had been producing superior coverage for decades, but Roone Arledge had found new ways of presenting strong reporting that resonated with a larger audience. After twelve years of chipping away at the CBS News empire, the numbers finally vindicated Arledge, whose only goal had been to make ABC the best television news organization in the business. He savored the victory and heaped praise on the whole ensemble that had helped him realize his dream.

RIGHT: Peter Jennings and Leonard Goldenson in the busy ABC News room in New York City.

# PETER JENNINGS

Canadian-born Peter Charles Archibald Ewart Jennings (1938–2005) was the son of a famous radio broadcaster with the Canadian Broadcasting Corporation (CBC), and yet he followed an unlikely path to the top of the broadcast journalism world. He was hired by the news department of a local radio station in the province of Ontario in 1959, then found his way to a fledgling television station in Ottawa, Canada's capital, doing interviews . . . until his superiors decided he had Dick Clark–like appeal and made him the host of a dance show that was a Canadian clone of *American Bandstand.*

A year later, he joined CTV, a brand-new, privately owned rival of the CBC, as co-anchor of a late-night news program. Then, while covering the 1964 Democratic National Convention for CTV, Jennings had a chance encounter with ABC News' president, Elmer Lower, which led to a job offer in New York as a correspondent—and within a year, twenty-six-year-old Peter Jennings was anchoring ABC's evening news broadcast. It proved to be a learning experience for Jennings, who had the unenviable task of going up against the great Walter Cronkite at CBS and the one-two punch of Chet Huntley and David Brinkley at NBC every night.

Jennings managed to hang in there for two years before leaving the anchor desk to work as a foreign correspondent. When the change came, he threw himself into his new role, seeing it as an opportunity to do important journalism while rebuilding his industry credibility from scratch. He was among the first American correspondents to cover Vietnam, and reported from Moscow, Paris, Rome, the Balkans, and Beirut, where, in 1968, he established the first American television news bureau in the region. Ironically, it was while co-anchoring ABC Sports' coverage of the 1972 Summer Olympics in Munich that Jennings covered his first significant breaking news story when Black September terrorists took Israeli athletes and coaches hostage in the Olympic village. Jennings managed to hide with his camera crew close enough to where the Palestinian terrorists and their victims were being held to provide ABC News with footage of the masked perpetrators, and was able to deliver insightful commentary on the group pulling off the attack based on his years of experience in the Middle East.

In the aftermath of the Munich Olympics tragedy, Jennings continued to focus on the region, and work on various documentaries. One of his projects from this period was the Peabody Award–winning profile documentary *Sadat: Action Biography.*

Jennings returned to the United States in 1974 to become ABC News' Washington correspondent, as well as the news anchor for ABC's short-lived *Good Morning America* predecessor, *AM America.* Through no fault of Jennings's, the show was cancelled, and he moved abroad again in 1975, this time with the title of chief foreign correspondent. After a few more years of handling primarily Middle East coverage, Jennings, after Roone Arledge became ABC News president, soon was broadcasting from London as one of three anchors of the new-look network evening news, along with Frank Reynolds in Washington and Max Robinson in Chicago. The broadcast slowly gained viewers over the next five years, and when Reynolds became ill, Jennings relocated to Washington to fill in for him temporarily.

Reynolds's sudden and unexpected death forced Arledge's hand, and he decided that Jennings was ready to carry the evening news by himself. On September 5, 1983, *World News Tonight with Peter Jennings* was born . . . and the era of ABC News' dominance began. For the next twenty-two years, until his own sudden passing from cancer, Peter Jennings would compete for ratings supremacy with Tom Brokaw (NBC) and Dan Rather (CBS), often winning that battle, amassing shelves full of awards, and always delivering serious news coverage that engaged viewers on both an intellectual and an emotional level—a perfect balance straight from the playbook of Roone Arledge himself.

# 1990-1999

# 1990–1999

## GOLDEN

The 1990s promised to be golden years for ABC News: *World News Tonight, 20/20, This Week with David Brinkley,* and *Nightline* were all drawing critical praise and were consistently at or near the top of the ratings, thus making money for the network. The friction generated by Roone Arledge's spare-no-expense philosophy running up against Cap Cities' determination to rein in spending had settled into a period of productive détente, with Arledge accepting the new fiscal reality at ABC while his superiors acknowledged his successful track record by allowing him some budgetary leeway on occasion. After all, he had been swelling the network's coffers ever since he was first hired in 1960, and even with a few notable misfires to his credit, Arledge was as bankable as any television programmer in the business.

A case in point was his determination to aim for younger viewers as a way of building a new viewership independent of the older adult audiences that tended to watch CBS and NBC. The strategy was working! Moreover, Arledge's youth movement was paying even bigger dividends now that advertisers were also going after younger demographics, and this translated into significantly higher rates paid for ABC

PREVIOUS SPREAD: Barbara Walters with Bill Clinton.

BELOW: Roone Arledge on the set of *World News Tonight with Peter Jennings*.

airtime than that of its rivals, regardless of who won the ratings battle for a particular week.

Arledge's priorities for the decade ahead were to continue to develop innovative news programming while finding ways of keeping existing successes from going stale. For example, now that Peter Jennings and executive producer Paul Friedman were in sync, *World News Tonight* was the top network newscast. Yet there was always room for improvement, and in 1990, they intro-

duced a new regular segment to the broadcast called "American Agenda." Just as *Viewpoint* had been created to help assuage public skepticism about journalistic bias, "American Agenda" was intended to counter the growing perception among viewers of all networks that the news was just an unrelenting flow of negativity. It departed from typical "bad news" segments by offering solutions or at least exploring possible answers to life's challenges. It was an attempt at what

in later years would be referred to as "service journalism," or as Friedman put it, "a grown-up way of doing 'news you can use.'" The segments required extra time and money to produce, which Arledge provided, and while the new segment did not significantly impact the medium or last forever, it demonstrated that *World News Tonight* was still evolving, willing to experiment, and not taking its audience's allegiance for granted.

In May 1990, the fortunes of *Primetime Live*

FACING PAGE, CLOCKWISE FROM TOP LEFT: ABC News correspondent Ann Compton reporting from the Bush-Gorbachev summit at the White House in June 1990.

ABC News' Diane Sawyer conducts a rare U.S. television interview with British prime minister Tony Blair in 1998.

Peter Jennings meeting with Cambodian troops on February 15, 1990, as part of the ABC News special *Reporting: The Return of the Khmer Rouge.*

Leonard Goldenson with Peter Jennings on the set of *World News Tonight* in December of 1990.

ABOVE AND LEFT: Peter Jennings produced a number of ABC News specials designed to explain to children intimidating adult concepts like war and foreign policy, using terms and diagrams they could easily process. Here, Jennings anchors *War in the Gulf: Answering Children's Questions*, a live, ninety-minute broadcast that answered questions from young people, both in the studio and from those who called in on the phone.

were still at a low ebb when Arledge arranged a dinner meeting with Diane Sawyer, Sam Donaldson, and Rick Kaplan to discuss ways of fixing whatever was wrong. The show's often inorganic combination of live coverage and taped pieces was one issue; by trying to give equal time and effort to both, neither approach was well served, and the live pieces especially tended to be unwieldy. Arledge had made what, to some, was the surprising decision to pair Sawyer and Donaldson, despite their different on-air approaches. In terms of making changes, his options were limited—Sawyer was Arledge's most important hire to date, and Donaldson was a well-established and popular figure at ABC.

At the dinner, Sawyer recalls that Arledge simply asked them, "What is it you believe in? Let's do that." Donaldson, who had kept his home in Washington, offered to return to the capital and generate taped pieces from there, leaving Diane to anchor in New York. On paper it looked potentially awkward, like a trial marital separation, but the plan worked. Both anchors were given their own stage, enabling them to focus on their respective stories without having to manufacture on-camera bonhomie with a co-anchor. In addition, both worked with their own segment producers who specialized in investigative reporting. Ultimately, *Primetime* became a big success, making a name for itself as a consistent ratings leader and often landing first in Nielsen's ratings.

By de-emphasizing the live element, the show became less of an innovation and more of a traditional newsmagazine show, but the results were often game-changing. Sawyer's hidden camera revelations about poorly run New Orleans day care centers and Donaldson's confrontation with fugitive Nazi war

LEFT: The "Big Three"—Russian presidents Gorbachev and Yeltsin and ABC News president Roone Arledge, inside the Kremlin during the filming of a National Town Meeting for an ABC News special in 1991.

ABOVE, CLOCKWISE FROM TOP LEFT: Diane Sawyer

Ted Koppel

The once-called "Magnificent Seven" with Roone Arledge (center), the visionary responsible for providing them with news vehicles that maximized their individual talents.

Hugh Downs

criminal Erich Priebke in Argentina were examples of investigative journalism at its best, because they elicited viewer sympathy and outrage that prompted action. As Sawyer puts it, "There's nothing more energizing than a story that can make a difference."

From the beginning, *Primetime Live* featured important stories in absorbing and informative detail that were not covered elsewhere, such as "Return to the Killing Fields," which retraced the harrowing wartime odyssey of Cambodian journalist Dith Pran. Other stories ranged from exposing a culture of rape and sexual assault in the military and examining racial inequality, gender bias, and age discrimination in the workplace, to consumer-protection segments on the tobacco, automobile, and fast-food industries. Every episode covered multiple subjects and often featured Sawyer doing exclusive interviews with world leaders and those in the news such as Boris Yeltsin, Mark Fuhrman, and the family of slain Israeli prime minister Yitzhak Rabin, as well as field pieces like the 1996 episode in which Sawyer filmed life inside a maximum security prison for women.

Sawyer also conducted many hidden-camera investigations of fraudulent businesses, substandard healthcare institutions, and other entities threatening the welfare of the American consumer. Once the show found its footing, it became must-watch television for millions every Thursday night and reaped a steady flow of awards and industry accolades.

Early the next year, at 6:35 p.m. on January 17, 1991, Peter Jennings was delivering the day's headlines on *World News Tonight* when bombs began falling on Baghdad, Iraq, and he went live to a telephone call from ABC's Gary Shepard. Shepard was on the scene, describing the pyrotechnics lighting up the sky over the Iraqi capital from his hotel window, thus beginning an ABC News special report that would last a record forty-two hours. They had scooped everybody on the commencement of Operation Desert Storm, including the White House, which issued an official announcement twenty minutes later.

Roone Arledge had been preparing for this moment since the invasion of Kuwait by Iraqi forces back in August 1990, dispatching Ted Koppel to Baghdad where he and his *Nightline* team were the first Western journalists to arrive and interview the Iraqis. Unfortunately for Arledge, the ABC News triumph of having Gary Shepard on the air first was short-lived, because once the Iraqis cut the phone lines, only CNN, which had earlier paid the Iraqis to hook up their own independent phone line, was broadcasting live from the scene. Also, because CNN was a dedicated news channel, they focused extensively on the war twenty-four hours a day and continued covering it long after the networks resumed airing their entertainment and sports programming, which established the cable network as a news contender despite having a fraction of the experience and resources that drove ABC News. This disparity would eventually begin to show as the visually compelling bombardment phase of the war gave way to White House, Pentagon, and State Department briefings, the kind of coverage at which ABC News was second to none.

ABC viewers of regularly scheduled shows were kept apprised of developments with hourly "Gulf War Updates," and the network aired prime-time specials that explained the historical and geopolitical context of the conflict. In the end, the first Gulf War proved the superior capacity of the ABC News machine to deliver sustained and substantive coverage. It also gave a relatively unknown ABC News reporter named Forrest Sawyer the opportunity to advance his career with aggressive field reporting that produced some of the network's most indelible images of Operation Desert Storm, including the first ground war video footage. To no one's surprise, Ted Koppel and *Nightline* performed flawlessly in the role thrust upon them by the conflict, and *Primetime Live* attracted a sizable audience with its Gulf War coverage—the kind of unfolding drama for which the show's format was originally designed.

Arledge was especially fond of trying to create

new kinds of star-driven prime-time newsmagazine shows. His third such venture (after *20/20* and *Primetime Live*) was *Day One*, anchored by Forrest Sawyer and later Diane Sawyer (no relation!), which generally featured investigative pieces. *Day One* debuted in March of 1993 and won awards, including a Peabody, but ran only two seasons and was cancelled in 1995; given the accolades, the program was not a complete failure, but still a rare instance of Arledge losing his magic touch.

The other magazine show in development was *Turning Point*. Arledge and *Primetime Live* cocreator Phyllis McGrady brainstormed about a program that would devote its entire hour to a single subject, rather than the usual three or four topics such programs usually covered. "We were hoping to reach a younger audience by reinventing the documentary form," says McGrady. Documentaries were widely perceived as slow-moving and dry, and McGrady and Arledge wanted to upend that perception by creating a new form that combined solid reporting with dramatic storytelling techniques. McGrady explains, "I cited as an example a *20/20* piece about the Hyatt Regency walkway collapse [at their hotel in Kansas City in 1981] titled 'Moment of Crisis,' which had broken down the disaster into a minute-by-minute analysis of what had occurred. Our working [show] title became *Moment of Crisis*, which we soon replaced with *Turning Point* because it created a built-in question underlying each story—in any given crisis or triumph or otherwise notable event, what was the turning point?"

ABOVE: Charles Gibson on location in Lower Manhattan in the early 1990s.

Another twist was that the show would have one overarching story line that lasted an hour, but that hour would comprise separate component chapters with their own story arcs that ultimately contributed to the show's conclusion. And it would not be anchored by a single ABC News personality but by many of them.

When the format was set, McGrady assembled a handpicked staff of producers with a wide range of experience and expertise, and got to work. The premiere episode aired in March of 1994, and was the top-rated show of the week. Bob Iger, who was then head of ABC Television, sent McGrady a congratulatory bouquet of flowers, and when the second episode also scored a number one rating, more flowers arrived from Iger—though this time with a note that said, "I

ABOVE, TOP TO BOTTOM: Diane Sawyer with President Bill Clinton.

Peter Jennings, above, and Sam Donaldson, below, interviewing troops during Operation Desert Storm in 1991.

CLOCKWISE FROM RIGHT: Although a posed shot, the smiles seem a genuine testament to how comfortable Diane Sawyer, Peter Jennings, and Barbara Walters felt with the direction of things at ABC News under Roone Arledge.

The well-traveled Peter Jennings en route to Cuba for a *World News Tonight* segment in 1990.

George Will, Cokie Roberts, David Brinkley, and Sam Donaldson of *This Week with David Brinkley*, serving as the ABC News coverage team for the 1992 Democratic National Convention at Madison Square Garden in New York City.

FACING PAGE: Diane Sawyer interviews Egyptian president Hosni Mubarak in Cairo during the Gulf War in 1991.

can't keep doing this!" By the end of the show's five-year run in 1999, it had earned multiple awards, including five Emmys, and it had been anchored by an impressive group of ABC News A-listers, including Diane Sawyer, Peter Jennings, Barbara Walters, Charles Gibson, Forrest Sawyer, and Meredith Vieira.

With *Turning Point*, Roone Arledge—whose vision and innovative genius had transformed both televised sports and network news (and whose most significant creations continued to dominate the ratings)—had launched his last new program. As much as Cap Cities wanted to keep him, the more stringent fiscal regime imposed by the new power structure at the network was no longer compatible with Arledge's style of program development and resource management. He was still deeply respected around ABC—and still sorely missed by the sports division—plus he had the full support of Bob Iger, who felt Arledge was

himself a star with the same importance to the ABC News brand as Jennings, Koppel, or Sawyer. His programming legacy would continue to exist for years to come, but by the end of 1996 he was out as president of ABC News, though he retained the title of chairman until his passing in 2002.

If ever there was a clearly defined era in the history of ABC News, it was the Arledge years, from 1977 to 1998. It was also a golden age for the organization . . . not in the sense that its future

looked any less bright without Arledge at the helm, but because he made ABC News an industry leader for the first time in its history.

At a 1995 media conference in Sun Valley, Idaho, Warren Buffett was on his way to play golf with Tom Murphy when he bumped into Disney CEO Michael Eisner. Buffett, who had helped engineer the Cap Cities purchase of ABC ten years earlier, was the majority shareholder in ABC/Cap Cities at the time, and the two men

had an informal chat about a possible merger. A few weeks later, on July 31, Disney announced it would be acquiring ABC/Cap Cities for $19 billion—then the third largest merger in history. The deal, which was finalized February 9, 1996, was a winner for both sides, as it enhanced the content and financial clout of ABC while providing Disney with a top-rated television platform; unlike the 1985 merger, the Disney purchase had no disruptive impact on ABC News, which continued to dominate the industry.

A few years later, David Westin took over

ABOVE: *GMA*'s Denise Richardson on assignment in Somalia in December 1992.

LEFT: Cokie Roberts covering the 1996 elections.

FACING PAGE, TOP TO BOTTOM: Diane Sawyer interviews actor Robert Downey Jr. after a series of arrests that led to a court order for him to enter a drug rehabilitation program.

Moderator Peter Jennings (center) and the president during a special from February 1993 titled *President Clinton: Answering Children's Questions.*

as president of ABC News in 1997. One of his top priorities was to breathe new life into *Good Morning America*. Despite its increased focus on hard-news segments over the years—breaking news overseas often occurred overnight and was covered on *GMA*'s morning watch—the show was only made part of ABC News in 1995. At the time of Westin's arrival, NBC's *Today* had just begun to enjoy a resurgence of popularity when Matt Lauer joined anchors Katie Couric and Bryant Gumbel; meanwhile, at *GMA*, Joan Lunden was departing after seventeen years, and co-anchor Charles Gibson would leave the following year (after more than a decade). Their successors, Lisa McRee and Kevin Newman, were replacing two

continued on page 154

ABOVE TOP: Barbara Walters never shied away from sit-downs with controversial figures, as she demonstrates here by interviewing Louis Farrakhan in April of 1994.

ABOVE BOTTOM: Diane Sawyer and Saddam Hussein during her exclusive interview with the Iraqi leader in 1990.

ABOVE TOP: Peter Jennings reporting from Haiti in July of 1994 as part of the ABC News special *Reporting: House on Fire: America's Haitian Crisis.*

ABOVE BOTTOM: Peter Jennings in front of the Smithsonian while filming the ninety-minute ABC News special *Peter Jennings Reporting: Hiroshima: Why the Bomb Was Dropped.*

continued from page 151

beloved television icons of long standing, and it would take audiences time to adjust.

However, Westin decided the show needed a complete overhaul, including a new executive producer to see the show with fresh eyes and to bring a new energy to the production. For anchor, Westin wanted Diane Sawyer because her prestige would immediately be felt in the ratings. At first glance, morning television did not seem to be a natural fit for Sawyer, whose greatest successes had all happened in prime time; but she was the consummate risk-taker, and she agreed to fill in temporarily as anchor. Then Westin went to work on convincing Charles Gibson to return to co-anchor with Sawyer, appealing to his sentimental attachment to a show that had largely defined his career. Gibson relented. Next, Westin hired Shelley Ross, who had worked with Sawyer on many of her best *Primetime Live* segments, as executive producer . . . and the exciting new iteration of *Good Morning America* debuted in January 1999.

As Westin had hoped, ratings went up dramatically the very first week. However, it was still a rebuild in progress, and that September, the show was moved to a studio in New York City's Times Square. By then, both Gibson and Sawyer had agreed to make the arrangement permanent, and *GMA* entered into a new era of market dominance. Over the next seven years, Diane and Charlie used their industry clout to help elevate the status of the show to that of a bona fide news program, securing many exclusives and firsts. The combination of these returning veteran co-anchors was not only a revenue generator for the network, but a reminder that after coveting the Cronkites and Rathers of the industry for decades, ABC News had now been at the top for long enough

RIGHT: The brilliant director, producer, and all-around television pioneer Roger Goodman (left), who was with the network for forty-three years, is shown in action in the control room. ABC News president David Westin said of Goodman, "Roger's profound affect on television news and sports cannot be overstated."

155

to have its own legendary talent on the wish lists of its rivals and competitors.

Ultimately, the 1990s were golden years for ABC News, but also a reminder that adaptability had become the key survival trait in tech-driven industries like TV news. There was barely time to savor the triumphs of the decade because it was also a period of significant change: in addition to the departure of Roone Arledge and his replacement by Westin and the Disney merger announcement in 1995, the inimitable David Brinkley retired in 1996 and was replaced on *This Week* by the ABC News institution Sam Donaldson and trailblazing correspondent Cokie Roberts as co-anchors. In addition, *Primetime*

*Live* was cancelled in 1998 (and its elements temporarily subsumed by *20/20*). *Turning Point* was cancelled in 1999, and Hugh Downs, one of Roone Arledge's first hires, stepped down from *20/20* the same year, leaving Barbara Walters as the sole anchor for the next three years.

For ABC News, it was a decade of continued experimentation, of fiscal downsizing, and of successfully adapting to a market altered forever by the advent of cable television. But the news division had proved that it could survive strong market shifts and extreme corporate thrift, though nothing in the 1990s could have prepared ABC News for the technological sea change that was coming in the new millennium.

ABOVE LEFT: Barbara Walters interviews Kato Kaelin.

ABOVE RIGHT: Diane Sawyer with the family of Nicole Brown Simpson.

FACING PAGE: From a tent city created in ABC's New York studios in January of 1996, Peter Jennings anchors the family special *Bosnia 101: Who Lives There, Who Died There, Why Are We There?* Throughout his career at ABC News, Jennings was always looking for viewer-friendly ways of explaining the geopolitical complexities behind the news headlines of the day.

ABOVE TOP: Diane Sawyer did an exclusive interview with Fidel Castro in 1993.

ABOVE BOTTOM: Peter Jennings in the thick of it at the 1992 Democratic National Convention.

FACING PAGE, CLOCKWISE FROM TOP LEFT: Barbara Walters with Henry Kissinger in front of Brandenburg Gate in Berlin.

Barbara Walters had Monica Lewinsky on her *The 10 Most Fascinating People of 1999* TV news special. Lewinsky first met with Walters in February of that year to discuss the relationship that shocked the world and changed her life forever.

The ABC News family celebrating with Hugh Downs as he steps down from co-anchoring *20/20* in 1999.

Peter Jennings during coverage of the war in Bosnia.

# ROONE ARLEDGE

Roone Arledge (1931–2002) was born in Forest Hills, a section of the New York City borough of Queens, and grew up just east of there in suburban Long Island. His first experience with news media was gathering around the family radio each night during World War II and following the progress of American and Allied military forces. After attending Columbia University, he landed an entry-level position at the DuMont Television Network, and later became a stage manager for NBC in New York, where he won his first Emmy for a show featuring puppeteer Shari Lewis.

Then in 1960, Arledge was hired by ABC, where he proceeded to revolutionize televised sports. Before Arledge, TV coverage of football and baseball was a minimalist documenting of games, designed to deliver just enough visibility to follow the sport without discouraging fans from attending the games in person. Arledge changed all that. He created *ABC's Wide World of Sports* and *Monday Night Football*, along the way raising viewer expectations forever by introducing dynamic camera setups that elevated sporting events to high drama and captured the previously hidden sights and sounds of the action.

Arledge's holistic approach to televising a game meant giving the home audience a view of the event curated for maximum entertainment value, zooming in on individuals and on details that would be invisible to a ticket holder sitting in the stands. Arledge loved to orchestrate the coverage from the truck himself, but even when he wasn't at the game, he would often phone in changes in coverage via a special hotline he had set up.

Arledge was becoming well known in the industry as the man who put show business into sports, but he became a household name after the riveting 1972 Munich Olympics broadcasts—which attracted a vast global audience once it unexpectedly veered into news (after Israeli athletes were attacked and murdered by Palestinian terrorists). His deft repurposing of his sports coverage team into hard-news field correspondents would be remembered later in the decade, when ABC News needed a leadership change.

As with all innovators, Arledge had to overcome initial resistance to doing things differently. But he proved the doubters wrong with a vengeance, turning *World News Tonight* into the industry gold standard and creating new and exciting news shows like *20/20*, *Primetime Live*, and *Nightline*. Arledge changed the face of broadcast news forever—and for the better—by creating programming that realized the medium's full potential for connecting with audiences through strong reporting that resonates with viewers. And his influence can still be felt today in every news program, both on network and on cable.

FOLLOWING SPREAD: Barbara Walters interviewing Yasser Arafat as part of an ABC News special in October 1995.

# 2000-
# 2009

# 2000–2009
# THE NEW REALITY

The experience of the previous two decades had made it clear that change at ABC News would be a constant in the new millennium. The reach of cable news continued to expand rapidly and the fledgling Internet was laying the groundwork for another twenty-four-hour-a-day source of information, leaving the network news organizations scrambling to find new ways of hanging on to their market share. One consequence of this was fierce competition among the many prime-time newsmagazine shows that the networks were airing as less expensive alternatives to sitcoms and other more traditional prime-time fare. In 2000, for example, the previously cancelled *Primetime Live* was relaunched as *Primetime Thursday*, with Charles Gibson replacing Sam Donaldson, who, apart from continuing at *This Week*, would soon anchor several experimental ABC News digital platforms.

The true beginning of the new millennium, 2001, was a relatively slow news year . . . until al-Qaeda struck, destroying New York's famed World Trade Center towers. The terrorist attacks of September 11,

PREVIOUS SPREAD: The view of Lower Manhattan and the World Trade Center from a Circle Line Sightseeing Cruises segment on *Good Morning America*, four months before the September 11, 2001, attacks.

BELOW: Ted Koppel with a group of children in the Congo. In 2001 he anchored a weeklong *Nightline* special, "Heart of Darkness."

2001, represented the worst national trauma in America since the surprise bombing of Pearl Harbor nearly sixty years earlier that put us into World War II. But unlike the 1941 attack, much of 9/11 unfolded on live television, and like every cable and network news entity around the world, ABC News threw the full weight of its resources into covering the event.

The in-depth investigative reporting tracing the origins and planning of the attacks would take time; and in any case a dazed nation was struggling to comprehend what it was seeing on the screen, so the immediate task for ABC News was simply providing its audience with a reliable source of the basic information that everyone was desperately craving in the fog of the immediate aftermath. *Good Morning America* (*GMA*) was on the air when news broke of an explosion and fire at the World Trade Center; veteran anchors Charles Gibson and Diane Sawyer shifted imme-

diately into hard-news mode, and were talking live with ABC reporter Don Dahler, who was on the scene, when the second plane hit the South Tower and erased all doubts as to the nature of the attacks. As soon as Peter Jennings arrived at the newsroom, he took over lead coverage and proceeded to deliver a seventeen-hour newscast that calmly guided millions of viewers through their raw grief and outrage and assuaged their anxiety by imparting a sense that he was there with them

FACING PAGE, CLOCKWISE FROM TOP LEFT: Bob Woodruff was teaching law in Beijing when he was hired as an interpreter by CBS during the Tiananmen Square protests in 1989; Woodruff switched careers on the spot and began working as a correspondent for ABC News in 1996, later succeeding Peter Jennings as a co-anchor of *World News Tonight* in 2005, before being critically wounded on assignment in Iraq the next year.

Chief Justice Correspondent Pierre Thomas at the Capitol in 2003.

Diane Sawyer interviews President George W. Bush at the White House in December 2003.

Diane Sawyer interviews Whitney Houston in her suburban Atlanta home for a special edition of *Primetime* in 2002.

ABOVE: Cynthia McFadden, who worked as a correspondent for ABC News from 1994 to 2014, also served as a co-anchor of both *Nightline* and *Primetime*.

LEFT: A former radio news editor and local affiliate reporter, John Quiñones has co-anchored *Primetime* and reported for *20/20*, *Good Morning America*, *ABC World News Tonight*, and *Nightline*, winning a Peabody, seven Emmys, and a host of other prestigious awards along the way.

in their living rooms and that clear answers to their questions were forthcoming. The personal connection Jennings had worked so hard to establish with his evening news audience over the years proved to be especially critical during an unprecedented televised moment like this, and as a result, countless Americans trusted ABC News and Peter Jennings to give them the straight story when it was needed most.

At the seventeen-hour mark, Charles Gibson relieved Jennings, and then later, other ABC anchors were rotated in, with everyone eventually contributing and either staying at their posts for days on end or traveling to Washington, D.C.; Shanksville, Pennsylvania; and anywhere else in the world with an important nexus to the story. Diane Sawyer is as proud of the network's coverage of the event as any story she has ever worked on. "It was a powerful news division operating with all the excellence it could bring to bear on the most important of stories—a luminous example of professionals, with full heads and full hearts, doing their work when it was needed most." In the gloomy weeks and months following the catastrophe, ABC News remained a reassuring presence and a steady and determined voice of inquiry.

In 2002, the pall of 9/11 gradually lessened to the point where Americans were curious once again about what was happening in the world—in addition to the latest about the war on terror; ABC News provided that balance of coverage, from the shocking bankruptcy of retail giant Kmart, to a massive volcanic eruption in Congo, to the Golden Jubilee celebrations for Queen Elizabeth II. In the fall, former New York City deputy police commissioner and then ABC News correspondent John Miller joined Barbara Walters as co-anchor of *20/20*, which Walters had been helming solo for several years. The following year, Miller was succeeded by longtime *20/20* investigative correspondent John

RIGHT: George Stephanopoulos interviews Illinois senator Barack Obama.

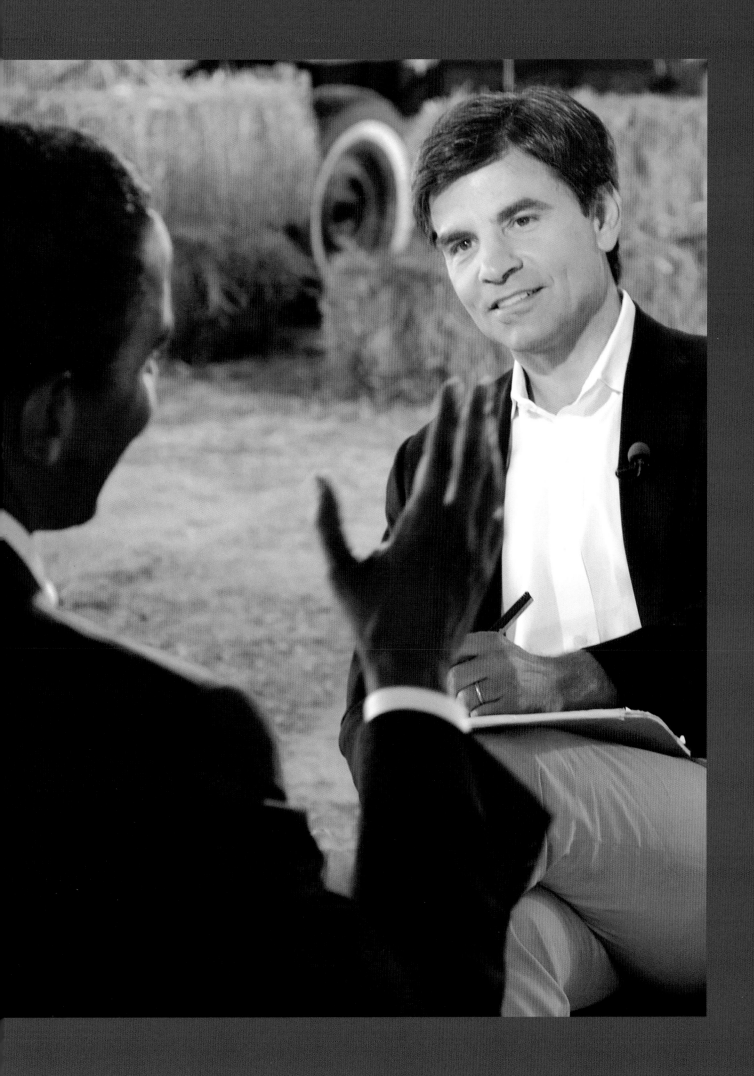

Stossel. Stossel proved to be a good fit for the anchor chair, and when Walters stepped down from her regular duties on the show in 2004—though she would continue as a special contributor—Stossel remained and was paired with *GMA* alum and weekend *World News Tonight* anchor Elizabeth Vargas. Stossel would depart the network at the end of the decade, but the popular Vargas had found a home at *20/20* and would continue to anchor the show until 2018.

In addition to her *GMA* and *World News Tonight* stints, the versatile Vargas also anchored a *20/20* spin-off and innumerable news specials during her years with ABC, prompting Executive Producer Phyllis McGrady to call her "one of the most flexible talents I've ever worked with."

Staff changes proceeded as ABC News kept pace with world events in 2002 as former White House communications director George Stephanopoulos took over as anchor of *This Week*.

In the continuing effort to keep the *Primetime* concept viable, the show was rebooted again in

FACING PAGE, CLOCKWISE FROM TOP LEFT: *Primetime Live* and *Good Morning America* producer Shelley Ross, whose live television production skills are the stuff of legend.

*Nightline* co-anchor Juju Chang and special guest Dominique Jackson, star of the Fox series *Pose*, present a special edition, "Am I Next?: Trans and Targeted."

A week after the terrorist attacks on the World Trade Center and Pentagon, Diane Sawyer interviews firefighters gathered at the Fireman's Memorial, which was donated by the state of Missouri to New York City.

ABOVE: Martin Bashir (left) and Terry Moran (right) joined Cynthia McFadden as the new co-anchors of *Nightline* when Ted Koppel stepped down in 2005. Bashir, an interview specialist, left the network after five years, while Moran, who had previously served as ABC News' chief White House correspondent, went on to become the unit's chief foreign correspondent in 2013 and since 2018 has served as the network's senior national correspondent.

2004 as *Primetime Live*, with the emphasis once again on investigative reporting, featuring a rotating team consisting of future ABC News star David Muir and fellow correspondents Chris Cuomo, Cynthia McFadden, and John Quiñones. In terms of extending the life of shows that had been around for long enough to be considered television institutions, experimenting with formula, even in the form of reverting to previously discarded approaches, was clearly working for the network: between *World News Tonight*, *20/20*, and *Primetime Live*, the programming legacy set by Roone Arledge continued to be critical to ABC News' market dominance well into the twenty-first century.

ABC turned its attention in 2004 as well to the burgeoning Internet news industry by launching *ABC News Now*, a digital television, broadband, and streaming video program on ABCNews.com. Although it was ABC's second attempt at establishing an Internet presence (Sam Donaldson had previously anchored a twenty-minute online news program in 1999), it was the first effort by ABC to become a twenty-four-hour news network; and beginning in 2008, it also extended ABC's reach to Germany, Spain, and Belgium. *ABC News Now* lasted only until 2009, but it provided valuable experience that ABC would apply to its future Internet ventures.

The sudden passing of Frank Reynolds in 1983 had signaled the end of an era at ABC News, and he was mourned by the industry for which he had helped to carve out a permanent place in the cultural landscape. His death had also led to the prominent emergence of Peter Jennings as

continued on page 178

FACING PAGE, TOP TO BOTTOM: ABC News correspondent Bob Woodruff and cameraman Doug Vogt, who were both seriously injured by an IED in Iraq in 2006, are seen here during a reunion special.

George Stephanopoulos became a fixture of Sunday morning news programming beginning in 2002.

ABOVE: In an hour-long special that aired in August of 2002, Diane Sawyer spoke with widows of the World Trade Center attacks about life without their husbands and the mixed emotions they experienced giving birth to babies after 9/11. Here, the chaos involved in trying to photograph all sixty-three babies at once at this photo shoot is evident.

RIGHT: In December 2009, Juju Chang became the first Korean American to anchor a U.S. morning news television show when she joined *Good Morning America*.

ABOVE: The faces of Charles Gibson and Diane Sawyer, shown here a few days after the World Trade Center attacks in 2001, are etched with the same concern and deep sense of loss that all Americans were experiencing at the time. Outside the windows of their Times Square studio, behind them, are a display of American flags created by construction workers in the area.

FACING PAGE, CLOCKWISE FROM TOP LEFT: In the aftermath of the 9/11 attacks, Cynthia McFadden reports from a barricade near Ground Zero.

Diane Sawyer prepares to fly in an F-15 jet, at Otis Air National Guard in Cape Cod, Massachusetts, at the end of September 2001. The segment focused on how the military was patrolling the skies after the terrorist attacks.

ABC News correspondent Don Dahler was one of the first journalists on the scene September 11, 2001, and was reporting live when the second plane hit the South Tower. This photo was taken September 17, 2001.

In December 2001, Barbara Walters tours Ground Zero with Mayor Rudy Giuliani; in the background, the remains of the fallen towers are visible and the extensive damage to the surrounding buildings is evident. Also in the photo is a fire truck from Squad 288, which, despite being based miles away across the river in the borough of Queens, responded to the attack and lost eight firefighters on 9/11.

continued from page 174

the voice and face of the ABC News brand for the next twenty-two years, so there was a sad irony in Jennings's passing with little warning, also from cancer, in August of 2005. For the network, it was a devastating loss, because Jennings seemed irreplaceable, both as a journalist and as the human nexus between ABC News and its audience. Apart from his unique combination of natural gifts and hard-won expertise, Jennings's long years of developing a strong rapport with viewers was not something that could be easily replicated. When Jennings stepped down from anchoring in April, Charles Gibson, Elizabeth Vargas, and Bob Woodruff were pressed into service as interim co-anchors while the network ago-

nized over how to proceed on a permanent basis. Finally, after nearly eight months of consideration, Vargas and Woodruff were announced as the new *World News Tonight* team.

The loss of Peter Jennings alone would have made 2005 an extraordinarily tough year for ABC, but when Ted Koppel also retired from *Nightline* after a quarter century as the essence of the franchise, it must have seemed to everyone in the news division that the world was ending. As with filling Jennings's spot at *World News Tonight*, the idea of replacing a legendary heavyweight like Koppel with any other single candidate was out of the question, leading the network to go with a three-anchor format of Cynthia McFadden, British journalist Martin Bashir, and ABC's chief White House correspondent, Terry Moran. The new configuration proved to be successful for years to come. In addition to the personnel change, the show transitioned to a format that addressed multiple topics each night and broadened the scope of subject matter. As impossible as such a move would have been during the Koppel years, audience preferences for the time slot were changing and late-night programming needed to reflect that shift in order to compete with the 11:30 entertainment vehicles on CBS and NBC. (Sure enough, by the fall of 2006, the "new" *Nightline* was popular enough to beat out CBS' *Late Night with David Letterman* for three straight weeks at one point.)

One of the biggest news stories of 2005 was the historic devastation wrought by Hurricane Katrina along the Gulf Coast. As part of ABC News' intensive coverage of the event and its lingering aftermath, newly promoted *GMA* co-anchor Robin Roberts broadcast a series of deeply moving reports from some of the hardest hit communities, including her hometown of Pass Christian, Mississippi. It was the kind of relevant and substantive reporting that eventually earned Roberts a Walter Cronkite Award for Excellence in Journalism—an accolade that Roone Arledge would no doubt have relished.

David Muir reported on the ground from New Orleans from inside the Superdome with

FACING PAGE: Robin Roberts and Diane Sawyer at the *GMA* news desk.

RIGHT: David Muir outside the New Orleans convention center in the devastating aftermath of Hurricane Katrina.

thousands before Katrina even hit and stayed in the city for weeks uncovering the unfolding crisis, from the patients trapped at the flooded Charity Hospital to the families desperate for help at the convention center.

In January of the following year, Bob Woodruff and cameraman Doug Vogt were both seriously injured by an exploding IED while riding in an Iraqi military convoy. The incident was a sobering reminder of the hazards war correspondent work entails, though ABC News personnel have never shied away from assignments in war zones, beginning during the Vietnam War. To date, thirteen correspondents and producers have been killed in the line of duty. Both Woodruff and Vogt sustained head wounds. Woodruff suffered a traumatic brain injury and was not expected to survive. Miraculously, Woodruff did pull through and was eventually able to resume

BELOW: Charles Gibson

RIGHT: Elizabeth Vargas

FACING PAGE: Robin Roberts interviews President Barack Obama at Wakefield High School in Arlington, Virginia, in September 2008.

his career at ABC News, but in the meantime, his spot at *World News Tonight* was conspicuously vacant. With occasional help from Charles Gibson and Diane Sawyer, new mother Elizabeth Vargas anchored the broadcast alone until May. She returned to *20/20* later that year and continued to anchor *20/20* and ABC News specials. Fortunately for ABC News, Gibson, who had returned to *GMA* in 1999, once again stepped in and *World News with Charles Gibson* was born.

In 2007, after more than a half century of stable expansion, ABC Radio, along with its twenty-two radio stations and the ABC Radio Networks, merged with Citadel Broadcasting, though it still broadcast ABC News content. This arrangement would last for eight years, at which point ABC Radio returned to syndicating its radio content in-house while using Skyview Networks as its distributor.

The next few years were quiet ones at ABC

News television—at least on the business side of things, with no new programming and no major personnel changes. From a news perspective, however, the decade itself was unrelentingly turbulent. The 2000s had heralded in a steep rise in both international and domestic terrorism, the launching of two U.S.-led wars in the Middle East and central Asia, the advent of social media, the demise of the *Concorde* and NASA's space shuttle program, a devastating worldwide eco-

nomic crisis, and the election of Barack Obama, the first African American president. With all of this and more going on in the world, ABC News welcomed the internal structural stability of 2007 and 2008; but it was not to last.

In 2009, the great Charles Gibson, a veteran of ABC News for thirty-four years, as well as the longtime face of ABC's morning and evening news programming—and one of the last survivors of ABC's golden age pantheon—retired from the television broadcasting field. This time, however, there was no hand-wringing over who would replace Gibson as the evening news anchor; Diane Sawyer was the clear choice, and for the next five years she performed brilliantly in a role that she seemed born to assume. Her co-anchoring position on *Good Morning America* (next to Robin Roberts) was taken over by George Stephanopoulos, who was still anchoring *This Week*. Stephanopoulos, who was rapidly becoming a valuable utility player at ABC News, would also periodically substitute for Sawyer on *World News*.

The other 2009 departure was that of John Stossel, who had been with *20/20* in one capacity or another for twenty-eight years. A cantankerous, controversial yet consistently popular figure, Stossel was irreplaceable in his own way, but the hallmark of *20/20* had always been its ability to survive change . . . and the show ultimately thrived with its new combination of ABC News' jack-of-all-trades Elizabeth Vargas and *Primetime* veteran (and *GMA* news anchor) Chris Cuomo.

For ABC News, the decade had been one of adapting not just to the departures of legendary on-air talent, but also to the new reality that shifting cultural values and emerging technologies were altering the fundamental nature of television news. Just as *Nightline*, in changing its format and broadening its focus, had found a new journalistic identity, so had ABC News, which had embraced the digital age.

However, all that really mattered was that it would retain the Roone Arledge philosophy of a commitment to vigorous reporting that fostered an emotional and intellectual connection with its viewers! And in the next decade, ABC News would follow that precept as closely as it had ever done under Arledge himself.

ABOVE: In addition to his co-anchor duties for *20/20*, Chris Cuomo anchored the *Good Morning America* news summaries for six years, both behind the desk and on assignment around the globe, frequently covering the war on terrorism with military forces in the Middle East.

FACING PAGE: Robin Roberts spent time in her hometown of Pass Christian, Mississippi, in the aftermath of Hurricane Katrina.

# CHARLES GIBSON

Charles deWolf Gibson grew up in Washington, D.C., and attended Princeton University, where he caught the broadcast journalism bug working as a news director for the college radio station. After gaining some production and reporting experience at RKO General and later WLVA-TV in Lynchburg, Virginia, Gibson was hired by an ABC network affiliate back in his hometown before being assigned to cover the Watergate scandal for the syndicated news service TVN.

In 1975, Gibson joined ABC News directly and worked as a general assignment reporter and as a White House correspondent, followed by a memorable six-year stint covering the U.S. House of Representatives (where he gained a reputation for holding politicians' feet to the fire). When he replaced the beloved David Hartman as co-anchor of *Good Morning America* (*GMA*), alongside Joan Lunden, in 1987, the show's ratings continued to soar.

Gibson left in 1998 to co-anchor the Monday edition of *20/20* with Connie Chung, but returned to *GMA* in 1999—to the great relief of millions of the program's fans—to team up with Diane Sawyer for the next seven years.

In addition to his anchor duties on various hallmark ABC news programs, Gibson is known for his political party convention coverage skills, his work moderating presidential debates and conducting interviews with seven sitting presidents, and his on-location reporting on critically important stories from around the world. Gibson also co-anchored *Primetime Thursday* from 1998 to 2004—while still co-anchoring *GMA*—where he produced a number of memorable one-hour investigative pieces, including his Emmy Award–winning special on the tragic loss of the space shuttle *Columbia*.

When Peter Jennings passed away suddenly in 2005, everyone knew he would be a very tough act to follow. Yet the network was confident that the venerable Gibson could do it, and the following year he reached the pinnacle of professional success at ABC News when he became the anchor or *World News Tonight*, where he remained until his retirement in 2009.

# GEORGE STEPHANOPOULOS

George Stephanopoulos was born in Fall River, Massachusetts, to parents deeply involved with the Greek Orthodox Church. He contemplated entering the priesthood himself for a time, eventually earning a master's degree in theology at Oxford as a Rhodes scholar.

Although he had worked as a sports broadcaster while studying political science at Columbia University, Stephanopoulos came to television journalism after a meteoric rise and brilliant career as an adviser and strategist at the highest levels of American politics. Beginning as a congressional aide, Stephanopoulos then worked on Michael Dukakis's 1988 bid for the U.S. presidency as the Democratic Party's nominee.

After that campaign, Stephanopoulos became floor man for U.S. House of Representatives majority leader Dick Gephardt before being hired as a key member of Bill Clinton's successful 1992 campaign for the U.S. presidency (as the next Democratic Party's next nominee).

After four years as an influential White House insider, Stephanopoulos left politics, wrote a *New York Times* bestseller about his experiences, and then began his long association with ABC News, first as a political analyst and correspondent for news formats as varied as *This Week*, *World News Tonight*, and *Good Morning America* (*GMA*).

Stephanopoulos's rise to prominence at the network was just as dramatic as his ascent in politics, and by 2002 George was hosting *This Week*. In 2005, he was named chief Washington correspondent. Then, in 2009, he took over Diane Sawyer's co-anchoring chair at *GMA* (upon her becoming the newly appointed *World News Tonight* anchor).

Stephanopoulos became chief anchor at ABC News in 2014, and he continues to lead the network's coverage on all major live events and breaking news.

Valued for his range and his unique background in and mastery of political science and analytic journalism, George Stephanopoulos has won every prestigious industry award, including three Emmys. He is among the most vital and irreplaceable assets at ABC News.

2010-
2019

# 2010–2019

## UPWARD

**M**ore change was in store for ABC News in the new decade, not just among the on-air talent but also at the highest corporate level. David Westin had been president of ABC News since the spring of 1997, and during his tenure the division had prospered, reaping dozens of prestigious industry awards across all categories. He also oversaw the maintenance and makeovers of *Nightline*, *Primetime Live*, *20/20*, and the rest of the news-programming legacies he had inherited from the Roone Arledge era, all of which continued to thrive under his leadership.

But early in 2010, Westin announced he was stepping down later that year; he was succeeded by Ben Sherwood. Sherwood, who had served as executive producer of *Good Morning America* (*GMA*) from 2004 to 2006, was also a published writer and a long-time journalist with ABC News.

British-born James Goldston, the senior executive producer of *Good Morning America* (who had previously overseen the transition of the post-Koppel *Nightline* into a three-anchor format, with wildly successful results), now hunkered down with Sherwood and Goldston's second-in-command, Tom Cibrowski, and set to work reconfiguring the *GMA* template.

PREVIOUS SPREAD: Newtown, Connecticut, scene of one of America's most horrific mass shootings.

BELOW: When the 113th Congress was sworn in January 2013, it was the high-water mark for female representation in the U.S. Senate. Diane Sawyer gathered nearly all the women for an exclusive conversation in the historic Kennedy Caucus Room. Left to right: Barbara Boxer, Susan Collins, Patty Murray, Barbara Mikulski, Elizabeth Warren, Deb Fischer, Claire McCaskill, Kay Hagan, Jeanne Shaheen, Amy Klobuchar, Diane Sawyer, Mazie Hirono, Kirsten Gillibrand, Lisa Murkowski, Debbie Stabenow, Maria Cantell, Dianne Feinstein, Mary Landrieu, Tammy Baldwin, Kelly Ayotte.

The stellar co-anchor team of Robin Roberts and George Stephanopoulos would remain in place, but they would now be joined by a supporting cast consisting of Josh Elliot (reading the news), Sam Champion (with the weather), and Lara Spencer (handling entertainment). The infusion of these vibrant new personalities into the *GMA* mix resonated with the audience. The positive word of mouth began to attract new viewers, and in the spring of 2012, *Good Morning America* beat NBC's *Today* for the first time in sixteen years. In the world of television ratings, the victory was almost on a par with Arledge's *World News Tonight* finally triumphing after decades of incremental improvement. And indeed, upon reflection, *Today*'s dominance had long seemed as unassailable as *CBS Evening News*' broadcasts had been till the early 1980s under Walter Cronkite.

The same year that Ben Sherwood arrived also

FACING PAGE, CLOCKWISE FROM TOP LEFT: In January 2010, David Muir reported from Haiti after the devastating earthquake. He has returned to Haiti multiple times since the earthquake hit, uncovering attacks on women and the unfolding mental health crisis in Port-au-Prince.

Robin Roberts in Haiti playing with an orphan on the six-month anniversary of the earthquake that devastated the country. The broadcast was part of *Good Morning America*'s "Road to Recovery" reports that aired the week of August 23–27, 2010.

George Stephanopoulos and a somber Chris Cuomo and Diane Sawyer in Newtown, Connecticut, covering the unspeakable tragedy of the shooting at the Sandy Hook Elementary School.

ABOVE: David Muir and Diane Sawyer reporting from Ground Zero the day Osama bin Laden was killed in 2011.

LEFT: Ginger Zee, chief meteorologist, during a New York City snowstorm. Zee covers weather and climate for *Good Morning America* and *World News Tonight*.

saw the departure of Martin Bashir from *Nightline*—and his replacement by Bill Weir. Weir, a former sports anchor in Chicago and Los Angeles, had been co-anchoring the weekend edition of *Good Morning America* since 2004. In addition, that same year, George Stephanopoulos left *This Week* and was succeeded by Christiane Amanpour, a twenty-seven-year veteran at CNN. However, Amanpour left less than two years later, at which time Stephanopoulos was prevailed upon to return to the show.

Meanwhile, *America This Morning*, which Arledge had created in 1982 as *ABC World News This Morning*—and which airs as a lead-in to local ABC morning newscasts—was moved to the 4:00 a.m. slot to accommodate the many network affiliates that now begin their news day coverage at 4:30.

The next round of personnel changes came in 2013, when Weir left *Nightline* after three years, giving way to Dan Harris, who had also succeeded Weir as the weekend *GMA* anchor in 2010. Harris spent time in various Middle Eastern war zones and had covered a broad variety of stories, from major disasters, to the 2013 papal conclave, to the mass shootings in Newtown, Connecticut; Aurora, Colorado; and Tucson, Arizona. As a field reporter of the first rank, Harris brought all the best qualities of an experienced correspondent to the *Nightline* desk. Chris Cuomo also had left the network that year, and was replaced on *20/20* by rising star David Muir.

Then, in 2014, a truly seismic shift occurred at ABC News when Diane Sawyer stepped down as anchor of the *World News Tonight* broadcast.

RIGHT: Michael Strahan and Robin Roberts in London covering the wedding of Prince Harry and Meghan Markle for *Good Morning America*. NFL Hall of Famer and New York Giants legend Michael Strahan parlayed his trademark gap-toothed grin and charismatic on-air presence into a career in television, first with *Live! With Kelly and Michael* for four years, before joining Roberts as a co-anchor of *Good Morning America* in 2016.

Although she would remain with the network as an anchor of long-form prime-time specials and continue to interview top news makers, Sawyer's departure from the *World News Tonight* anchor chair was a turning point in that she was the last of the group he called the "Magnificent Seven" that Roone Arledge had assembled back in the 1980s—and an entire generation of ABC News watchers could hardly imagine a week of programming that didn't somehow include Diane Sawyer! Many wondered how *World News Tonight* could possibly compete without her . . . and with no venerable news icon seemingly waiting in the wings to succeed her.

But they needn't have worried. Since the beginning of network evening news broadcasts at ABC, the one constant has been the importance of the personality of the anchor; as much as brilliant reporting and producing have always been essential to the success of *World News Tonight*, the main reason the show eventually beat its CBS and NBC counterparts was that audiences preferred Peter Jennings over his rivals.

Don't forget . . . in this, the digitized information age, we are bombarded with news stories from the moment we first look at our phones in the morning to the point that by the time the evening news rolls around, we have become thoroughly familiar with the day's headlines. Therefore, in addition to being likable and charismatic, the contemporary evening news anchor must also bring a value-added dimension to the newscast. It is not enough to just curate the mass of information that has piled up since the last broadcast and separate the news from the noise; the anchor must also find the angle that resonates with viewers. And perhaps above all else, in this the era of the global village, the audience needs to be assured that the anchor has been out in the world, chasing down stories long enough to know what is newsworthy.

By all of these metrics, nobody at ABC News was better qualified to slide into the *World News Tonight* anchor chair than David Muir, who officially succeeded Diane Sawyer on September 1,

FACING PAGE: George Stephanopoulos interviewing President Barack Obama.

ABOVE: Robin Roberts interviewing First Lady Michelle Obama.

2014. In addition to having substituted many times for Sawyer when she was away on assignment or vacation, Muir had been a workhorse for ABC News since 2003, anchoring early-morning and weekend news programming, and co-anchoring *Primetime* and *20/20*. But he was also a tireless correspondent in the field, filing stories from such far-flung locations and hot spots as the Israeli-Lebanese border during the war between Israel and Hezbollah, Gaza during the Hamas coup that overthrew the Palestinian Authority, Cairo's

Tahrir Square during the Egyptian revolution, and Peru after a devastating earthquake. Muir was also in the New Orleans Superdome when Hurricane Katrina devastated the city and peeled the roof off the behemoth structure in 2005. Muir risked his own safety during the assignment, wading through chest-deep water to find survivors trapped in a flooded hospital. Therefore, when Muir took over as anchor of *World News Tonight*, he had the background to assure viewers that he understood the news from the ground up,

ABOVE LEFT: Former *Good Morning America* desk mates Diane Sawyer and Robin Roberts reunite for an *Adweek* cover shot in 2019. Sawyer considers her time with Roberts as history-making female co-anchors of a morning news program to be among her most enjoyable years in broadcast journalism.

ABOVE RIGHT: Like her late ABC News colleague Cokie Roberts, Martha Raddatz got her start in the business at National Public Radio, where she covered the Pentagon. In addition to being a best-selling author, Raddatz has moderated a number of important presidential and vice presidential debates, including the 2015 Democratic presidential debate at St. Anselm College in Manchester, New Hampshire, in December 2015. Raddatz worked her way up at ABC News, starting as the State Department correspondent, before being named its senior national security correspondent. Raddatz has been the network's senior foreign affairs correspondent since 2008.

CLOCKWISE FROM TOP LEFT: David Muir and Diane Sawyer

Amy Robach

George Stephanopoulos

Robin Roberts

and he also possessed the qualities of instant likability and of being able to establish a deep connection with his audience. Not surprisingly, Muir is an admirer of Peter Jennings, so it is perhaps no coincidence that he has cultivated in himself so many of the late anchor's best journalistic attributes.

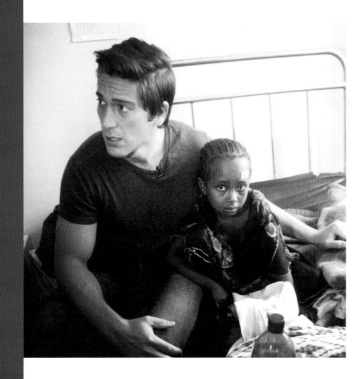

David Muir is a devoted student of the careers of past and retired ABC News giants like Peter Jennings, Diane Sawyer, and Charlie Gibson, but he is also very much an anchor for the new millennium. Perhaps the single most important difference between television news in the current decade and in years past is that social media has created an around-the-clock town hall atmosphere in which the public can provide nearly instantaneous feedback on what they are seeing on television. As Muir puts it, "I always used to marvel at the conversation that Peter Jennings was having with viewers, and now it's a two-way conversation." Muir is clearly a good listener, because his newscasts have resonated with viewers sufficiently to make *World News Tonight* the top-rated evening newscast during 2019–2020 across all key demographics for the first time in twenty-four years—a feat not accomplished since 1996 when Peter Jennings was anchor.

The future of ABC News is brighter than

ever because the core values of strong reporting and a determination to always get the story right are still in place. There are still the periodic departures of ABC News fixtures like Elizabeth Vargas and Cynthia McFadden; yet at the same time, the network manages to find new audience favorites like Martha Raddatz, Juju Chang, Amy Robach, and ex-New York Giant Michael Strahan.

Similarly, periodic corporate leadership changes are seamless because the organization is replete with experienced replacements, as when Ben Sherwood was promoted to president of the Disney-ABC Television Group in 2015 and was able to hand over the reins to his longtime associate James Goldston.

Moreover, the spirit of innovation that Roone Arledge imparted to the ABC News DNA is still a driving force at the network. This applies to the development of new programming, of course, though its application to existing shows is perhaps even more important, as with the reworked formats of *Nightline*, *Primetime*, and *20/20* over the years. A less obvious but no less important example of this is *The View*. When Barbara Walters first created the all-women panel talk show in 1997, it was an entertainment division vehicle at ABC and an immediate hit with audiences. Over the subsequent twenty-four seasons, *The View* has been able to maintain its relevance and popularity

FACING PAGE, TOP: George Stephanopoulos interviews former Federal Bureau of Investigation director James Comey.

FACING PAGE. BOTTOM: In 2013 David reported from Ethiopia on "Gift of Sight," featuring an American doctor and his team that's helping hundreds.

ABOVE: In his first week of anchoring *World News Tonight* in 2014, David Muir stayed true to his reporting roots and did a story from the Lebanon/Syria border on child refugees working to support their families.

ABC News has done more than just keep pace with the evolution of broadcast technology—it has become an award-winning industry leader across the many digital platforms through which it now provides news content. To accommodate the demand for around-the-clock streaming news coverage, ABC News Live was launched in 2018 and is available on more than twenty platforms and devices. Two years later Linsey Davis and Tom Llamas were named anchors for the streaming channel's prime-time programming and breaking news coverage. Diane Macedo and Terry Moran officially joined the lineup later that year. The news division also premiered a daily news program for Facebook Watch called *On Location*. In addition, ABC News reimagined *GMA Digital*, featuring a new website, morning newsletter, and original videos. The digital portfolio also includes FiveThirtyEight, the famed data visualization and journalism site for politics, sports, and science founded by the renowned statistician Nate Silver. FiveThirtyEight has seen its number of unique visitors and page views skyrocket since joining ABC in 2018.

through periodic personnel changes, by focusing on topics of importance to viewers, and by never shying away from controversy. Eventually, *The View* became so talked about that politicians began lining up to make appearances on the show, just as they had for *Nightline*, and when it was taken over by ABC News in 2014 after a short-lived dip in the ratings, it confirmed the fact that *The View* was no mere talk show but a hybrid entertainment-news program in a class by itself—and a vital platform for the discussion of serious topics . . . usually those at the heart of

ABOVE: In 2019 David Muir traveled deep into the Anbar desert in Iraq, not far from the Syrian border, with U.S. forces during an operation to take out ISIS fighters. David Muir also traveled to Afghanistan in 2019, where he interviewed the top U.S. commander and gained rare access to the fight against the Taliban.

FACING PAGE: David Muir in a helicopter near the Syrian border.

Jonathan Karl and Cecilia Vega at a White House news briefing.

America's ideological polarization.

*The View* not only demonstrates Barbara Walters's peerless television instincts that originated the Emmy Award-winning talk show, but also the fact that our shifting cultural sensibilities are creating a market for different forms of news presentation that ABC has positioned itself to pioneer.

In the three quarters of a century of ABC's existence, the news division has evolved from an

underfunded afterthought into an industry leader that in many ways has transformed the medium. The long, slow march toward relevance at ABC News in the 1940s, 1950s, and 1960s was more than compensated for by the brilliant successes and the flurry of game-changing innovation that marked the following decades at the network. And after a brief period of uncertainty in the new millennium, as the generational talent of the Arledge era began retiring and the media landscape sud-

FACING PAGE: Barbara Walters celebrates her final co-hosting appearance on *The View* in May 2014.

CLOCKWISE FROM TOP LEFT: Former *60 Minutes* reporter and the once and future CNN anchor Christiane Amanpour anchored *This Week* at the beginning of the decade.

Bill Weir joined ABC News in 2004 as a breaking news and global trends correspondent, later co-anchoring the weekend edition of *Good Morning America*, as well as *Nightline*, along with Martin Bashir and Cynthia McFadden.

New York senator Chuck Schumer with New York's WABC-TV's Bill Ritter and Lori Stokes at Ground Zero in New York City during coverage of the tenth anniversary of the 9/11 attacks.

denly expanded to accommodate digital forms of communications, ABC News reasserted itself as the premier source of information about the world.

"The story of the last five years is one of rapid transformation in the news and media landscape, from a linear news environment to a multidimensional streaming future," says ABC News president James Goldston. Part of the continuing appeal of ABC News is its signature strengths: solid reporting and the ability to always find the story angle that engages and resonates with the audience without resorting to embellishment. "It's more important than ever to take a straightforward, down-the-line approach to news," observes Goldston. "As others embrace a more political agenda, ABC News believes our future lies in doing what we've always done—giving people the news and the facts in as straightforward a fashion as we can."

Another factor in the ongoing success of ABC

News is its inherent adaptability—a vestige of its days as the scrappy newcomer that relied on ingenuity in place of the lavish budgets enjoyed by its competitors. Thus, as technology continues to shape the destiny of the industry, ABC News will continue to stay ahead of the curve for the next seventy-five years and beyond, turning the challenges of rapid progress into a competitive advantage. "This is the most exciting moment for ABC News since the era of Roone Arledge," adds Goldston. "You're suddenly seeing growth and opportunities for us to do creative storytelling in ways that weren't possible a generation ago. We're branching out into documentaries, podcasts . . . new mobile forms of storytelling and series ideas. There's so much more to come."

FACING PAGE: David Muir moderated an Emmy Award-winning town hall with President Barack Obama, *The President and the People: A National Conversation*, about race, policing, and efforts to bridge the divide.

ABOVE: David Muir with Pope Francis in 2016 during Muir's historic and exclusive town hall special, *Pope Francis and the People*, which won a Gabriel Award for News and Information.

LEFT: George Stephanopoulos anchoring ABC News' coverage of the Democratic Party debate in Houston in 2019.

# DIANE SAWYER

Diane Sawyer is an ABC News anchor, tackling some of the biggest issues of our time in new ways with original reporting, prime-time specials, long-form interviews, and in-depth investigations. One of the most respected journalists in the world, she has traveled the globe delivering breaking news reports, and has conducted interviews with almost every major newsmaker of our time. Her prime-time documentaries have won critical acclaim for shedding light on difficult and previously underreported topics.

A Kentucky native, she attended Wellesley College, and returned to her home state to work as a weather forecaster for WLKY-TV in Louisville, later being promoted to a general assignment position. Restless for a new challenge, Sawyer eventually moved to Washington, D.C., where she found work as an assistant to White House Deputy Press Secretary Jerry Warren. Soon she was drafting public statements for President Richard Nixon, and shortly afterward became his staff assistant, forming a long working relationship with the president that continued into the late 1970s, even after his presidency ended.

In 1978, Sawyer returned to broadcast journalism, working her way up the ladder at CBS and joining *60 Minutes* as the show's first female correspondent. Five resoundingly successful years later, Roone Arledge convinced the star journalist to join ABC News, where she proceeded to draw critical praise and huge audiences for her work as the co-anchor of *Primetime Live*, *20/20*, and *Good Morning America*, and as sole anchor of *ABC World News*. During her time at ABC News, Sawyer has interviewed world leaders, including both President Bushes, President Obama, Prime Minister Tony Blair, Saddam Hussein, and Fidel Castro. She also interviewd some of the world's most notable figures, including Whitney Houston and Caitlyn Jenner.

She's created many highly acclaimed prime-time documentaries that have called attention to neglected but vitally important issues, such as her in-depth reporting on the troubled U.S. foster care system and her groundbreaking study of poverty in America. Her series of award-winning investigative pieces titled "Hidden America," her award-winning reports aimed at shining a light on stories of American struggle and hope in the face of great adversity. The series also spotlights people who make a difference. Previous programs include award-winning documentaries on children in Camden, New Jersey, one of America's poorest cities; the crisis of the foster care system; children raised on Native American reservations; an in-depth look inside Rikers Island, one of America's most infamous and dangerous jails; and a documentary on a remarkable principal trying to turn around one of America's most dangerous schools.

# ROBIN ROBERTS

Born in Tuskegee, Alabama, and raised in a small Gulf Coast town in Mississippi, Robin Roberts was a star basketball player in college before embarking on a career in television journalism as a sports anchor and reporter. After a series of local television posts in Mississippi, Tennessee, and Georgia, Roberts was hired as a sportscaster by ESPN in 1990 and quickly established herself as a fan favorite. Her dynamic, entertaining presence also helped grow the ESPN brand for the next fifteen years.

Concurrently, she worked for *Good Morning America* (*GMA*) beginning in 1995, first as a featured reporter and later as a news anchor. In 2005, she left ESPN to co-anchor *GMA* with Diane Sawyer. Then, after Sawyer's departure in 2009, she teamed up with George Stephanopoulos—and the pair have kept the show in the ratings stratosphere ever since.

In addition to breaking through multiple glass ceilings and conquering the broadcast television world, Roberts has also courageously and very publicly battled breast cancer and MDS, bringing much-needed national attention to these conditions as well as successfully promoting the donation of bone marrow for lifesaving transplants. Her wide-ranging professional triumphs and personal bravery have earned Roberts an impressive array of accolades, including the Walter Cronkite Award for Excellence in Journalism, the George Foster Peabody Award, a Gracie Award, and the Arthur Ashe Courage Award.

Roberts has also been inducted into the Broadcasting and Cable Hall of Fame, the Sports Broadcasting Hall of Fame, and the Women's Basketball Hall of Fame, and was named a Disney Legend in 2019. She has authored two books and founded Rock'n Robin Productions, which creates original broadcast and digital content for ABC and other networks.

Robin Roberts is more than just a revered and invaluable member of the ABC News community. She is a universally beloved cultural icon and one of the most trusted faces on television.

# DAVID MUIR

A native of Syracuse, New York, Emmy award-winning journalist David Muir is known for his global dispatches from Afghanistan, Iraq, Iran, Tahrir Square, Mogadishu, Gaza, Guantanamo, Fukushima, Beirut, Amman, and the Syrian border. Muir is the anchor and managing editor of *ABC World News Tonight with David Muir*, which during his tenure, has become the most-watched newscast in America. Muir is also the co-anchor of *20/20*. He has been honored with multiple Edward R. Murrow and Emmy awards. His exclusive interviews make global headlines, landing the historic one-on-one with President Obama in Cuba in 2014 and the first interviews with President Trump in the White House in 2017 and later during the COVID-19 pandemic in 2020. Muir also conducted the historic sit-down with Pope Francis inside the Vatican, moderating the first-ever town hall, *Pope Francis and the People*, conducting the town hall in Spanish. Muir moderated a town hall with President Obama as well, *The President and the People*, on race, policing, and efforts to bridge the country's racial divide, earning an Emmy for his work.

Muir knew he wanted to be a reporter from an early age, first visiting his local television station when he was just thirteen. He grew up watching Peter Jennings and would begin a journey that would eventually lead him to the same chair. Graduating magna cum laude from Ithaca College, Muir also attended the Institute on Political Journalism at Georgetown, and studied at the University of Salamanca in Spain, before returning to Syracuse to begin his career at WTVH-TV. At twenty-three, Muir's first international reporting trip took him to the Middle East after the assassination of Israeli prime minister Yitzhak Rabin, earning him top honors for his work. He moved on to WCVB-TV in Boston, where he reported on the 9/11 terrorist attacks, earning him an Edward R. Murrow Award.

In 2003, Muir was hired by ABC News as anchor of their overnight news program, *World News Now*, and quickly became a lead correspondent. His early reports from flashpoints, including Tahrir Square during the revolution in Egypt, Fukushima after the deadly tsunami and nuclear disaster, and from New Orleans during Hurricane Katrina, led to his role as weekend anchor, and principal substitute for Diane Sawyer before being named to the post in 2014.

Muir's reporting roots are key to the broadcast, taking viewers to Afghanistan to interview the top U.S. commander amid talks with the Taliban, and to Iraq to interview top American military leaders in the fight against ISIS. Muir reported *The Children of Auschwitz*, documenting Holocaust survivors returning to Poland seventy-five years later and *Return to Normandy*, profiling World War II veterans returning to France seventy-five years later, after changing the course of history. And in 2020, with the world suffering through a once-in-a-century pandemic, Muir's newscast spent several months as the most-watched program on all of television, a reflection of the times, and of Muir's enduring connection with the viewers.

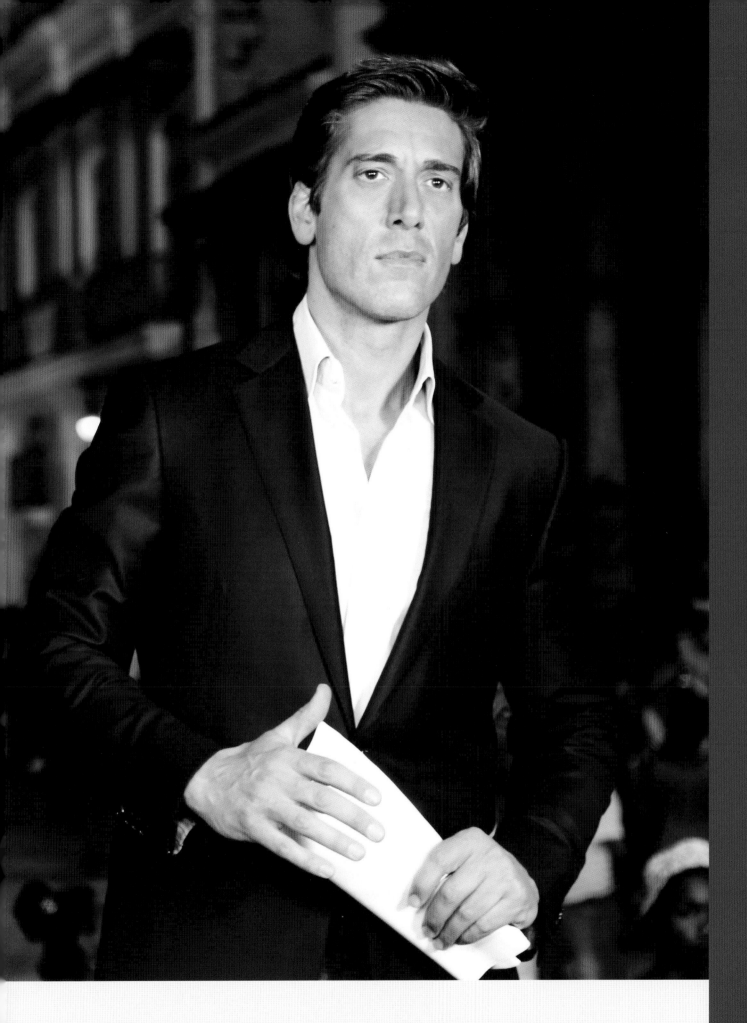

FOLLOWING SPREAD: David Muir interviews surviving D-Day veterans in 2019 on the seventy-fifth anniversary of the pivotal battle and campaign to reclaim Western Europe from the Nazis.

# AFTERWORD

While caskets are not ordinarily catalysts for change, a handful of deaths in American history have been so explosive, such marked moments of depravity, that the singular act of death serves the dual purpose of both traumatizing and galvanizing a nation. Until Memorial Day 2020, those select, transformative funerals existed merely as archival footage—grainy or black-and-white images from yesteryear, buried in the distant past of at least more than half a century ago.

But because of an uncanny parallel between one courageous act in 1955 and another in 2020, we find ourselves back in the same unrest sixty-five years later, as a nation grappling with racism, injustice, and inequality. While the decision of Emmett Till's mother to have an open casket at the funeral for all to see the mutilated face of her brutally murdered fourteen-year-old son is credited with helping inspire the civil rights movement, seventeen-year-old Darnella Frazier's act of pulling out her cell phone and hitting the record button during what would have otherwise been a routine walk to the corner store has triggered a similar outcry.

As a result of that teen's actions, the world watched that officer grind his knee into George Floyd's neck, all the while with his hand in his pocket. We all bore witness to the brutal act and subsequent grief that has given way to inconsolable outrage marching down our streets.

But there is at least one remarkable difference: when pictures of Emmett Till's corpse were printed in 1955, it's reported that "Black Americans across the country shuddered." The collective anguish this time is a unifying outrage, not limited to Black America. In fact, it is not even limited to the shores of this country.

It was Benjamin Franklin who once said, "Justice will not be served until those who are unaffected are as outraged as those who are." And while the jury is still out on whether justice will be served going forward, what our cameras captured (and what the words in my shorthand scrawled across my notebook reflected) on June 4, 2020, is that glaring difference from movements in the past.

For on that day of George Floyd's Minneapolis memorial service—as I stood, perched on a crate in front of a camera, just outside Cups Foods convenience store (where the forty-six-year-old Floyd exhaled his final breath)—this moment did not just look different, it felt different. I spent more time than usual with my back to the camera, really observing the scene and the moment (or movement) at large. I found myself marveling at the white fists punching the air; there were hundreds of them. It was a mark of solidarity typically reserved for African Americans as a symbol of Black power seemingly culturally appropriated on this day in a way that people at the location seemed to appreciate and even revel in.

The scene was in sharp contrast to the images so many of us have seared in our mind's eye from the March on Washington in 1963, when the predominantly Black crowd seemingly only had a sprinkling of white advocates. The crowd at Floyd's Minneapolis memorial, however, was overwhelmingly white. Sure, there were Black people present, but they were overwhelmingly the minority.

The message: the group of stakeholders looked different . . . a sea of non-Black people using their own power, dare I say privilege, to put some skin in the game and say, "Enough!" There were bowed heads, interlocked fingers from hands of varying hues, and high fives among strangers sharing food and fellowship despite a global pandemic that implores social distancing.

The notion that Floyd's memorial service (and a few days later his funeral in Houston) played out with the backdrop of the pandemic only added to the cocktail of emotions that made this moment so remarkable. Anyone who had passed away in the three months leading up to it (at least since early March)—regardless of how large they loomed in life—had to contend with their funeral or memorial service being a restrained gathering, one limited to ten people . . . maximum. But on this occasion, hundreds of mourners turned out, ending up packed inside the chapel. Hundreds more filled the surrounding streets. Paying respect superseded calls for limiting social interaction.

Concerns about the spread of coronavirus were seemingly secondary to the need for solidarity, at least to those who deemed their presence here essential. It felt like history in the making. Ink smudged on the knuckles of those present as it was being written.

For on this unseasonably hot, sunny day in June 2020, the cross section of America crowded together at the intersection of Thirty-Eighth Street and Chicago Avenue, calling for equality, demanding change, and taking a stand for justice . . . many, for the very first time.

Linsey Davis, *ABC News Live Prime* anchor

# PHOTOGRAPHY CREDITS

# INDEX

J. Michael Padgett

*with contributions by*
William A. P. Childs *and*
Despoina Tsiafakis

Nathan T. Arrington

Beryl Barr-Sharrar

Michael Bennett

Jennifer Y. Chi

Jasper Gaunt

Stephen Gavel

Janet B. Grossman

Joan T. Haldenstein

Mary Louise Hart

Seán Hemingway

John J. Herrmann Jr.

John F. Kenfield

Peter Lacovara

Kenneth D. S. Lapatin

Karen Manchester

Susan B. Matheson

David Gordon Mitten

Jenifer Neils

Aaron J. Paul

Jeffrey Spier

Conrad M. Stibbe

Alessandra Balco Sulzer

Carrie E. Tovar

Rex Wallace

# The Centaur's Smile

## The Human Animal in Early Greek Art

Princeton University Art Museum

This book has been published on the occasion of the exhibition
*The Centaur's Smile: The Human Animal in Early Greek Art.*

Princeton University Art Museum
October 11, 2003 – January 18, 2004

Museum of Fine Arts, Houston
February 22 – May 16, 2004

Paper and cloth editions have been published by
the Princeton University Art Museum,
Princeton, New Jersey 08544-1018

Cloth edition distributed by Yale University Press,
New Haven and London

Managing Editor: Jill Guthrie
Editor: J. Michael Padgett
Copy Editor: Sharon R. Herson
Editorial Assistants: Nathan T. Arrington, Mary Cason, Nicola Knipe
Design: Anthony McCall Associates
Indexer: Kathleen M. Friello
Printer: Snoeck-Ducaju & Zoon, Ghent, Belgium

The book was typeset in Centaur and Shaker and
printed on 115 lb. Parilux Silk Text and 93 lb. Parilux Silk Cover.

Cover illustrations: Front: Statuette of a Centaur, detail (cat. no. 24)
Back: Statuette of a Satyr (cat. no. 56)

Frontispiece: Red-Figure Bell-Krater with the Wedding
of Cheiron, detail (cat. no. 38).

Library of Congress Control Number: 2003104045
ISBN: 0-300-10163-5 (cloth); 0-943012-40-6 (paper)

Printed and bound in Belgium

Support for this publication has been provided by the
Publications Committee of the Department of Art and Archaeology,
Princeton University, and The Andrew W. Mellon Foundation.
Additional support for the exhibition and programming has been
provided by the River Foundation, the Judy and Michael Steinhardt
Foundation, William R. Suddaby, Donna W. and Hans Sternberg,
Walter Banko, Friends of the Princeton University Art Museum,
Partners of the Princeton University Art Museum, and
anonymous donors.

# Contents

# Foreword

IN 1997, ONE OF THE FINEST surviving Greek bronzes in the world, a late-sixth-century B.C. statuette of a centaur (illustrated on the cover of this catalogue), entered the permanent collection of the Princeton University Art Museum. This extraordinary work was the inspiration for a seminar in 1999 on *Mischwesen*, or composite creatures comprised of both human and animal elements, taught by J. Michael Padgett, curator of ancient art at the museum, and William A. P. Childs, professor of art and archaeology at Princeton University. This exhibition and publication are a direct outgrowth of this exemplary collaboration and a reaffirmation of the museum's commitment to presenting the permanent collection in the context of new research and scholarship. As a university museum, our mission to highlight objects in the collection that may serve to illuminate aspects of the curriculum allows us to serve as a catalyst that brings together the coordinated, cooperative study of important works of art by scholars within the Princeton community and beyond. No fewer than twenty objects from the permanent collection are included in this exhibition.

Bringing the entire project to fruition stems from Michael Padgett's scholarly rigor and intellectual originality. He has demonstrated considerable skill, working in concert with the two other authors of the essays as well as the many noted scholars responsible for the catalogue entries, and diplomatic tenacity in securing loans from numerous lenders, both public and private. The resulting exhibition both challenges the mind and satisfies the imagination.

An exhibition of this complexity would not have been possible without the extraordinary efforts of each and every member of the museum staff. From the initial conception of the project to the final installation of the objects, the staff, in particular Becky Sender, associate director, Maureen McCormick, chief registrar, Mike Jacobs, senior preparator, Caroline Cassells, curator of education and academic programs, Michael Brew, business manager, Craig Hoppock, building superintendent, Karen Richter, assistant registrar, and Ruta Smithson, public information officer, have been invaluable in attending to all aspects of this presentation. Special thanks to Jill Guthrie, managing editor, and her colleagues, Nicola Knipe, assistant editor, and Mary Cason, editorial assistant, for

their masterful job of producing a catalogue with the editorial acuity, precision, and good humor that, by necessity, must accompany a project of this scope. I would also like to extend special thanks to Katherine Rohrer, vice-provost, and Amy Gutmann, provost, for their important support of the museum's initiatives. Through their encouragement and that of President Shirley Tilghman, the museum is flourishing, committed to advancing the teaching and appreciation of art through its exhibitions and programs.

We are delighted to share this exhibition with the Museum of Fine Arts, Houston, which also served as the venue for another important Princeton exhibition, *The Olmec World: Ritual and Rulership*, in 1996. It was during another presentation of ancient art at Princeton, the installation of the Roman collection on the occasion of the publication of *Roman Sculpture in The Art Museum, Princeton University* (2001), that Frances Marzio, curator of the Glassell Collection in Houston, and I first discussed the *Centaur's Smile*. Her enthusiasm inspired us to consider Houston as a second site for the exhibition. Our thanks extend to Peter C. Marzio, director of the Museum of Fine Arts, and to Frances Marzio, for their support of this project.

Important financial support for the catalogue has been provided by the Publications Fund generously allocated by the Publications Committee of the Department of Art and Archaeology, chaired by Patricia Fortini Brown, and The Andrew W. Mellon Foundation. Additional funding for the exhibition and programming has been given by the River Foundation, the Judy and Michael Steinhardt Foundation, William R. Suddaby, Donna W. and Hans Sternberg, Walter Banko, and several donors who wish to remain anonymous. The Friends of the Princeton University Art Museum have always funded significant exhibition undertakings, and this project is no exception. Their generous contribution to the exhibition and catalogue has ensured that the greatest possible audience can learn from and enjoy this exhibition. Thanks also to the Partners of the Princeton University Art Museum, our newest affiliate group, which generously supports museum programs and exhibitions.

Susan M. Taylor
*Director*

# Preface

THE TITLE OF THIS EXHIBITION is taken from an article written in 1983 by the late Barbara Hughes Fowler. In Pindar's ninth *Pythian*, Apollo, who has fallen in love with the nymph Cyrene, asks the wise old centaur Cheiron, "Might it be becoming if I were to lay my famed hand on her body, even shear her honey-sweet meadow grass in bed?" The centaur "smiles greenly" (*chloarón*) and replies, "Hidden are the keys of wise Persuasion" (*Pyth.* 9.36–39). Apollo took that for yes—Cyrene eventually bore him two sons—but scholars have argued about the meaning of Cheiron's "green" smile, just as they have about the "Archaic smile" of sixth-century Greek sculptures, an enigma no less intriguing than the nature of centaurs themselves. Half horse and half man, centaurs stand—like humanity itself—with legs in two worlds. Wild and libidinous, like Nessos, who assaulted the wife of Herakles, centaurs also could be noble and wise, like Cheiron, the teacher of Achilles, Jason, and Asklepios. Their bifurcated form perfectly symbolizes the fundamentally ambivalent nature of the human being: part beast, part angel. This is a heavy load to bear, and in Western culture the centaur has been pressed into the service of both high art and low comedy, appearing in everything from comic books to illuminated manuscripts; from prints by Picasso to Disney's *Fantasia*. In studies of Greek art, the many battle scenes between Greeks and centaurs are commonly explained as symbolizing the struggle between civilization and brutality, or even, as in the metopes of the Parthenon, the historical conflict between the Greeks and the Persians. These interpretations are certainly correct, but hardly the whole story, for such simple symbolism—man good, brute bad—ignores the human half of the centaur as well as the bestial side of Man, an element of humanity well understood by the Greeks.

If centaurs had the heads of horses and the bodies of men, they would be brutish indeed, but instead we perceive them as the Greeks did, as men who are part horse. It is not their human half, however, that puzzles and intrigues us. Rather, we ask what part of them, besides their legs, is horse, and why? Their character is so different from that of the satyrs, another baffling creature in which horse and man are even more mysteriously intermixed. Closely related but occupying different conceptual realms, centaurs and satyrs are seldom considered together, and yet it may be that the one cannot be understood without the other. Similar connections may be found among other composite creatures: sphinxes, sirens, Gorgons, and the other "human animals" of Greek mythology, including individual gods and demons such as Pan, Acheloos, Triton, Typhon, and the bull-headed Minotaur. They, too, have persisted in our collective memory, in some cases adapted to serve distinct metaphorical ends.

*The Centaur's Smile: The Human Animal in Early Greek Art* is an exhibition for both general and scholarly audiences that investigates the phenomenon of such mixed beings (*Mischwesen*) in early Greek art. Organized by the Princeton University Art Museum, the exhibition is on view at Princeton from October 11, 2003, to January 18, 2004, and thereafter at the Museum of Fine Arts, Houston, from February 22 to May 16, 2004.

Neither the exhibition nor the catalogue attempts to survey the history of composite beings throughout the ages—an enormous subject. For encyclopedic lists of Greek *Mischwesen* by type and activity, the reader is directed to the relevant sections of the *Lexicon Iconographicum Mythologiae Classicae*, which itself is necessarily selective. Instead, the focus here is exclusively on "human animals"—griffins and other creatures lacking a human element are excluded—from their early, formative years to their maturity in the art of the Archaic period. The subject is the Greek imagination itself, in its purest form, before the advent, in the late fifth century, of that combination of self-awareness and fatalistic skepticism that—no less than the ideals of Reason and Liberty—is among the more durable legacies of ancient Greece.

Human animals played a central role in Greek myth and are ubiquitous in Greek literature and art. Diverse in form, origin, and character, some of these fantastic creatures first appeared in Greece during the Bronze Age—in Minoan and Mycenaean art—only to vanish during the subsequent cultural hiatus of the Greek Dark Ages (ca. 1100–950 B.C.). Their reappearance in the sculpture and ceramics of the Protogeometric and Geometric periods (ca. 950–700 B.C.) heralded a new era of contacts between Greece and the cultures of Egypt and the Near

East that was to prove decisive in the formation of a distinctive Greek culture. As such, the evolving forms and roles of human animals in early Greek art are important indicators of the nature and degree of contact between Greece and older Near Eastern cultures.

There is no question that the distinctive forms of many Greek composite creatures were derived from Egyptian and Near Eastern sources, as demonstrated by their appearance in everything from Mesopotamian cylinder seals to Phoenician ivories. One focus of the exhibition and catalogue is to examine the possible oriental origins of centaurs, sphinxes, and other human animals through the juxtaposition of selected objects—Greek, Egyptian, Near Eastern. A Sumerian stone carving of a human-headed bull (cat. no. 1), dating to the third quarter of the third millennium B.C., testifies to the antiquity of the idea of visualizing the divine as a combination of human and animal elements.

Beyond the question of origins, an issue of greater importance is the meaning these creatures had for the Greeks themselves. Sirens, for example, have a limited role in myth, confined essentially to their encounter with Odysseus. In art, however, sirens are exceedingly common, often in contexts that suggest they had multiple or layered meanings, primarily as symbols of death and as enforcers of divine will or retribution. The Sphinx is best known for its deadly riddle and the famous solution by Oedipus, but it, too, is a very common figure in Greek art, normally in ostensibly decorative rather than overtly narrative contexts. There is only one Sphinx in the Oedipus myth, but in art they are multiplied freely as the occasion warrants, unencumbered by narrative but, as some scholars believe, still redolent with meaning. Whether such images can be deconstructed to arrive at their core significance or whether instead such analyses are forced and illusory are among the questions pondered.

In order to focus more closely on the initial significance and development of human animals in Greek art, the Greek works in the exhibition are limited to examples dating from the Late Geometric to the Early Classical period (ca. 750–450 B.C.). Joining these is a selection of contemporary Etruscan objects produced under the influence of Greek models and demonstrating the ways in which composite creatures adopted by the Greeks from Near Eastern sources were further transformed by Italian artisans. The narrative scenes on the painted ceramics portray the full range of relevant Greek myths, including—to take only the example of centaurs—Herakles' rescue of Deianeira from Nessos, the battle of the Lapiths and the centaurs at the wedding of Peirithoos, the death of Kaineus, Herakles as the guest of the good centaur Pholos, Herakles driving off the thirsty centaurs of Mount Pholoë, Cheiron encouraging Peleus to seize Thetis, and Cheiron accepting the tutelage of their son Achilles.

Different aspects of the exhibition's theme are treated in three essays. In the first, "Horse Men: Centaurs and Satyrs in Early Greek Art," I discuss the possible origins of centaurs and satyrs, describe their similarities and differences and the manner in which they are represented in early Greek art, followed by a survey of their iconography. I consider the possibility of a conceptual relationship between horse-demons and human horsemen founded on the propagation and reinforcement of aristocratic social values. In the second essay, "The Human Animal: The Near East and Greece," William A. P. Childs, professor of art and archaeology at Princeton University, examines the demons and *Mischwesen* of the ancient Near East and their impact on early Greek iconography. Ranging over a variety of types and media from different areas and periods, he investigates some of the proposed antecedents of sirens, sphinxes, and other composite creatures and evaluates the validity of their alleged relationships in the light of literary, archaeological, and art historical evidence. The third essay, "'ΠΕΛΩΡΑ': Fabulous Creatures and/or Demons of Death?" by Despoina Tsiafakis, assistant professor and classical archaeologist at the Cultural and Educational Technology Institute, Xanthi, Greece, surveys the broad range of non-equine human animals in Greek art. Discussing their evolving forms and changing roles, she gives particular attention to sirens, sphinxes, and Gorgons, with additional remarks on the iconography of Pan, Acheloos, Triton, Typhon, and the Minotaur.

The exhibition focuses primarily on questions of iconography, but the objects selected are also of the highest artistic quality: painted ceramic vases, sculptural reliefs in stone and clay, bronze and terracotta statuettes, jewelry and metalwork in gold, silver, and electrum, engraved gems in rock crystal, jasper, and carnelian. Of the 101 pieces from thirty-seven lenders, more than a third are centaurs. Twenty-one works are drawn from the collection of the Princeton University Art Museum, including an exceptional bronze statuette of a centaur (cat. no. 24). The remaining objects are borrowed from fifteen public and twenty-one private collections. The international loans are limited to three key works from museums in Paris and Madrid, a testament to the rich diversity of material in American collections. Many pieces are published here for the first time.

The most important debt of gratitude is owed to the lenders, both public and private, who made this exhibition possible. I am especially grateful to colleagues at museums here and abroad whose assistance was essential in arranging these loans; they are here mentioned with their museums: Allen Memorial Art Museum, Oberlin College (Lucille Stiger); Arthur M. Sackler Museum, Harvard University Art Museums (David Mitten, Amy Brauer, Karen Manning); Art Institute of Chicago (Karen Manchester, Mary Gruel); Bibliothèque Nationale de France, Paris (Sylviane Dailleau); Cleveland Museum of Art (Michael Bennett, Rachel Rosenzweig, David Smart); J. Paul Getty Museum, Malibu (Marion True, Karol Wight); The Metropolitan Museum of Art, New York (Carlos Picón, Seán Hemingway); Michael C. Carlos Museum, Emory University (Jasper Gaunt, Stacey Gannon); Museo Arqueológico Nacional, Madrid (Dra. Alicia Rodero Riaza, Jefe del Departamento de Protohistoria y Colonizaciones); Museum of Art and Archaeology, University of Missouri-Columbia (Jeff Wilcox); Museum of Fine Arts, Boston (John Herrmann, Mary Comstock, Christine Kondoleon, Brenda Breed); Tampa Museum of Art (Aaron Paul); Virginia Museum of Fine Arts, Richmond (Margaret Mayo); Walters Art Museum, Baltimore (Barbara Fegley); Yale University Art Gallery (Susan Matheson, Kathleen Coulombe).

Many people contributed to the success of the exhibition at Princeton. Credit for the initial idea goes to former director Allen Rosenbaum. In 2000, the exhibition proposal was presented to acting director Peter C. Bunnell and subsequently was approved by Susan M. Taylor, director of the Princeton University Art Museum, who has given the project her full support.

Many budgeting, and scheduling tasks have been shouldered by the associate director of the museum, Rebecca Sender. I am particularly grateful to Nancy Stout, executive assistant to the director, for her many good deeds. The tasteful design of the exhibition at Princeton was the work of Daniel Kershaw. The exhibition was installed with unflustered efficiency by senior preparator Michael Jacobs and preparators Calvin Brown, Mark Harris, and Gerritt Meaker, the latter also supervising the lighting. Museum superintendent Craig Hoppock and assistant superintendent Kenneth Harris provided much practical assistance. The silk-screening was done by Gene Clarici; the mount-making by David La Touche, of Benchmark. The museum's curator of education, Caroline Cassells, assisted in the preparation of labels, wall texts, and other didactic material, and also coordinated a range of educational programming. Ruta Smithson managed the publicity for the Princeton venue, and Albert Wise and Gayle Everett supervised exhibition security. A special debt is owed to Princeton registrar Maureen McCormick, and to assistant registrars Alexia Hughes and Virginia Pifko, who managed the movement of objects from the many lenders with dispatch and aplomb.

Among our friends at the Museum of Fine Arts, Houston, we are particularly grateful for the support given by the director, Peter Marzio; by Isabel B. Wilson, chairman of the Board of Trustees and chairman of the Antiquities Committee; and by the members of the Antiquities Committee for their help in bringing *The Centaur's Smile* to Houston. I especially wish to thank Frances Marzio, curator of the Glassell Collection, who was the project coordinator for the Houston venue. Her support and encouragement were of tremendous importance to me.

William Childs penned not only an essay but also ten entries, including some for which he generously assumed responsibility at a very late date. Many of the exhibition's themes were first explored in a class taught by Professor Childs and me in a seminar at Princeton in the spring of 1999. His influence has extended into nearly every area of the project, and it is a particular pleasure to acknowledge his contributions. We are grateful also to our third essayist, Despoina Tsiafakis, whose participation has been vital to the success of the project.

Among the authors of the catalogue entries are curators of ancient art from museums all over America: Karen Manchester (Art Institute of Chicago); Jasper Gaunt and Peter Lacovara (Carlos Museum of Art and Archaeology, Emory University); Michael Bennett (Cleveland Museum of Art); Janet Grossman, Mary Hart, Ken Lapatin, and Carrie Tovar (J. Paul Getty Museum); Seán Hemingway (Metropolitan Museum of Art); John Herrmann (Museum of Fine Arts, Boston); David Mitten (Arthur M. Sackler Museum, Harvard University), Aaron Paul (Tampa Museum of Art), and Susan Matheson (Yale University Art Gallery). The loans from the Shelby White and Leon Levy Collection were catalogued by curator Jennifer Chi, who also wrote an exhibition handout. Eminent specialists were enlisted to catalogue engraved gems (Jeffrey Spier), architectural terracottas (John Kenfield), Greek bronze statuettes (Conrad Stibbe), Etruscan inscriptions (Rex Wallace), Near Eastern antiquities (Stephen Gavel), Attic and Etruscan pottery (Jenifer Neils and Joan Haldenstein), and classical metalwork (Beryl Barr-Sharrar). The involvement of students in museum publications is a tradition at Princeton. Graduate student Kyriaki Karoglou wrote gallery handouts for the exhibition, and the catalogue features entries by Alessandra Sulzer, a Harvard undergraduate, and Nathan Arrington, Princeton Class of 2002.

The research, writing, and production of the catalogue were aided by many friends and colleagues who offered information, advice, attributions, photographs, translations, and other forms of assistance. In particular, I wish to thank Sidney Babcock, Judith Barringer, Robin Benningson, Max Bernheimer, Larissa Bonfante, Jacklyn Burns, Tom Carpenter, Andy Clark, Joseph Coplin, Dimitri Gondicas, Robert Guy, Florent Heintz, Mario Iozzo, Caroline James, Shari Kenfield, Richard Keresey, Kenneth Kitchen, Vasilis Lambrinoudakis, Adrienne Mayor, C. W. Neeft, John Oakley, Nadia Perucic, Beate Pongratz-Leisten, Cornelius Vermeule,

Stark and Michael Ward, and Bonna Wescoat. In behalf of other contributors, Karen Manchester examined and measured several objects in distant collections, and did more besides. All the authors benefited from the helpful comments of the anonymous outside reader.

Bruce M. White photographed the Princeton loans and many others as well: he is the best at what he does. Assistant registrar Karen Richter oversaw the photography process. The catalogue's handsome design is owed to David Zaza, Doug Clouse, and Mark Nelson of Anthony McCall Associates. The printing was professionally executed by Michael Sakkalli, Stijn Blontrock, and Gudrun Huvelier of Snoeck-Ducaju & Zoon, Ghent, Belgium. Publication assistant Mary Cason and assistant editor Nicola Knipe scanned, copied, formatted, unjammed, and generally greased the wheels of the whole project. Kathleen M. Friello created the index with her usual painstaking attention to detail. The map of the eastern Mediterranean and the Near East and the drawing of the Etruscan temple were produced by Jill Moraca, on whom we have come to rely.

Nathan Arrington, curatorial research assistant, was my right arm throughout the last year of the project. Very special thanks are owed to Jill Guthrie, managing editor at the Princeton University Art Museum, for her oversight of the entire process of catalogue production and her thorough understanding of curatorial psychology; and to Sharon Herson, whose responsibilities extended well beyond expert copyediting to the roles of mediator, diplomat, and counselor. Above all, I wish to thank my wife, Judith Boothe Padgett, for her loving support in this and all my endeavors.

J. Michael Padgett

## Lenders to the Exhibition

Allen Memorial Art Museum, Oberlin College, Ohio

Arthur M. Sackler Museum, Harvard University Art Museums

Art Institute of Chicago

Bibliothèque Nationale de France, Paris

Cleveland Museum of Art

J. Paul Getty Museum, Malibu, California

The Metropolitan Museum of Art, New York

Michael C. Carlos Museum, Emory University, Atlanta

Mr. and Mrs. Nicholas M. Evans

James E. and Elizabeth J. Ferrell

Sheri and Stuart Jamieson

Museo Arqueólogico Nacional, Madrid

Museum of Art and Archaeology, University of Missouri-Columbia

Museum of Fine Arts, Boston

Richard F. Plechner and Mary Lou Strahlendorff Plechner

Princeton University Art Museum

Sol and Colleen Rabin

Arthur S. Richter

Michael and Judy Steinhardt

William Suddaby

Tampa Museum of Art

Virginia Museum of Fine Arts, Richmond

Walters Art Museum, Baltimore

Shelby White

Yale University Art Gallery, New Haven

Private Collections

# Abbreviations

## MUSEUM NAMES

| | |
|---|---|
| Aigina | Aigina Archaeological Museum |
| Aleppo | Aleppo Museum |
| Amsterdam | Allard Pierson Museum, Archaeological Museum of the University of Amsterdam |
| Ancona | Museo Archeologico Nazionale delle Marche, Ancona |
| Athens, Acrop. Mus. | Acropolis Museum, Athens |
| Athens, Agora | Athenian Agora Museum, Athens |
| Athens, Goulandris | Goulandris Museum of Cycladic Art and Ancient Greek Art, Athens |
| Athens, Kerameikos | Kerameikos Archaeological Museum, Athens |
| Athens, Nat. Mus. | National Archaeological Museum, Athens |
| Atlanta, Emory | Michael C. Carlos Museum, Emory University, Atlanta |
| Baghdad | Iraq Museum, Baghdad |
| Baltimore | Walters Art Museum, Baltimore |
| Basel | Antikenmuseum und Sammlung Ludwig, Basel |
| Belgrade | National Museum, Belgrade |
| Berlin | Antikensammlung, Staatliche Museen zu Berlin—Preussischer Kulturbesitz |
| Bonn | Akademisches Kunstmuseum der Universität Bonn |
| Bologna | Museo Civico Archeologico, Bologna |
| Boston | Museum of Fine Arts, Boston |
| Brussels | Musées Royaux d'Art et d'Histoire, Brussels |
| Budapest | Szépmüvészeti Múzeum, Budapest (Museum of Fine Arts) |
| Buffalo | Albright-Knox Art Gallery, Buffalo |
| Cambridge, Fitz. | Fitzwilliam Museum, University of Cambridge |
| Capua | Museo Provinciale Campano, Capua |
| Catania | Museo Civico Castello Ursino, Catania |
| Cerveteri | Museo Nazionale Cerite, Cerveteri |
| Chicago | Art Institute of Chicago |
| Cleveland | Cleveland Museum of Art |
| Copenhagen, Nat. Mus. | National Museum, Copenhagen |
| Copenhagen, Ny Carlsberg | Ny Carlsberg Glyptotek, Copenhagen |
| Delphi | Delphi Archaeological Museum |
| Dresden | Staatliche Kunstsammlungen Dresden |
| Eleusis | Eleusis Archaeological Museum |
| Eretria | Eretria Archaeological Museum |
| Ferrara | Musei Civici di Arte Antica, Ferrara |
| Florence | Museo Archeologico Nazionale, Florence |
| Geneva | Musée d'Art et d'Histoire, Geneva |
| The Hague | Gemeente Museum, The Hague |
| Hamburg | Museum für Kunst und Gewerbe, Hamburg |
| Harvard | Arthur M. Sackler Museum, Harvard University Art Museums, Cambridge, Massachusetts |
| Heidelberg | Antikenmuseum und Abgußsammlung des Archäologischen Instituts der Universität Heidelberg |

| | |
|---|---|
| Herakleion | Herakleion Archaeological Museum |
| Istanbul | Archaeological Museum, Istanbul |
| Kassel | Hessisches Landesmuseum, Kassel |
| Kos | Kos Archaeological Museum |
| Lecce | Museo Provinciale "Sigismondo Castromediano," Lecce |
| Leiden | Rijksmuseum van Oudheden, Leiden |
| London, Brit. Mus. | British Museum, London |
| London, V&A | Victoria and Albert Museum, London |
| Los Angeles | Los Angeles County Museum of Art |
| Madrid | Museo Arqueológico Nacional, Madrid |
| Mainz | Römisch-Germanisches Zentralmuseum Mainz |
| Malibu | J. Paul Getty Museum, Malibu |
| Melos | Melos Archaeological Museum |
| Munich | Staatliche Antikensammlungen und Glyptothek, Munich |
| Naples | Museo Archeologico Nazionale, Naples |
| Newcastle upon Tyne | Museum of Antiquities of the University and the Society of Antiquaries of Newcastle upon Tyne |
| New York, Met. | The Metropolitan Museum of Art, New York |
| New York, Morgan Lib. | J. Pierpont Morgan Library, New York |
| Nicosia | Cyprus Museum, Nicosia |
| Olympia | Olympia Archaeological Museum |
| Orvieto | Museo Civico "Claudio Faina," Orvieto |
| Oxford | Ashmolean Museum of Art and Archaeology, University of Oxford |
| Paestum | Museo Archeologico, Paestum |
| Palermo | Museo Archeologico Regionale "Antonio Salinas," Palermo |
| Paris, Cab. Méd. | Bibliothèque Nationale de France, Cabinet des Médailles, Paris |
| Paris, Louvre | Musée du Louvre, Paris |
| Philadelphia | University of Pennsylvania Museum of Art and Archaeology, Philadelphia |
| Prague | National Museum, Prague |
| Princeton | Princeton University Art Museum |
| Reggio Calabria | Museo Nazionale di Reggio Calabria |
| Rhodes | Rhodes Archaeological Museum |
| Richmond | Virginia Museum of Fine Arts, Richmond |
| Rome, Mus. Cap. | Museo Capitolino, Rome |
| Rome, Mus. Naz. | Museo Nazionale Romano delle Terme, Rome |
| Rome, Pal. Cons. | Palazzo dei Conservatori, Rome |
| Rome, Vatican | Vatican, Museo Gregoriano Etrusco, Rome |
| Rome, Villa Giulia | Museo Nazionale di Villa Giulia, Rome |
| St. Louis | Saint Louis Art Museum |
| St. Petersburg | State Hermitage Museum, St. Petersburg |
| San Antonio | San Antonio Museum of Art |
| San Simeon | Hearst State National Monument, San Simeon, California |
| Sofia | National Museum of History, Sofia |

| | |
|---|---|
| Stockholm | Medelhavsmuseet, Stockholm |
| Stuttgart | Württembergisches Landesmuseum Stuttgart |
| Syracuse | Museo Archeologico Regionale "Paolo Orsi," Syracuse |
| Tampa | Tampa Museum of Art |
| Taranto | Museo Archeologico Nazionale, Taranto |
| Toledo | Toledo Museum of Art |
| Toronto | Royal Ontario Museum, Toronto |
| Toulouse | Musée-Saint-Raymond, Musée des Antiques de Toulouse |
| Vienna | Kunsthistorisches Museum, Vienna |
| Volos | Athanassakeion Archaeological Museum, Volos |
| Würzburg | Martin von Wagner Museum der Universität Würzburg |
| Yale | Yale University Art Gallery, New Haven |

## PUBLICATIONS

| | |
|---|---|
| *AA* | *Archäologischer Anzeiger* |
| *AAA* | Αρχαιολογικά ανάλεκτα εξ Αθηνών *(Athens Annals of Archaeology)* |
| *AAS* | *Annales Archéologiques de Syrie (Annales Archéologiques Arabes Syriennes)* |
| *ABL* | C. H. E. Haspels, *Attic Black-Figured Lekythoi* (Paris 1936) |
| *ABV* | J. D. Beazley, *Attic Black-Figure Vase-Painters* (Oxford 1956) |
| *ActaArch* | *Acta Archaeologica* [Copenhagen] |
| *AfO* | *Archiv für Orientforschung* |
| *AJA* | *American Journal of Archaeology* |
| *AM* | *Mitteilungen des Deutschen Archäologischen Instituts, Athenische Abteilung* |
| *AnatStud* | *Anatolian Studies* |
| *ANET* | *Ancient Near Eastern Texts Relating to the Old Testament*, edited by J. B. Pritchard, 2d ed. (Princeton 1955) |
| *AnnLiv* | *Annals of Archaeology and Anthropology* [Liverpool] |
| *AntJ* | *Antiquaries Journal. The Journal of the Society of Antiquaries of London* |
| *AntK* | *Antike Kunst* |
| *AR* | *Archaeological Reports* [supplement to *JHS*] |
| *ArchCl* | *Archeologia Classica* |
| *ArchDelt* | Αρχαιολογικόν Δελτίον |
| *ArchEph* | Αρχαιολογική Εφημερίς |
| *ARV²* | J. D. Beazley, *Attic Red-Figure Vase-Painters*, 2d ed. (Oxford 1963) |
| *AsAtene* | *Annuario della Scuola archeologica di Atene e delle Missioni italiane in Oriente* |
| *AuA* | *Antike und Abendland* |
| *BABesch* | *Bulletin antieke beschaving. Annual Papers on Classical Archaeology* |
| *BAdd²* | *Beazley Addenda: Additional References to ABV, ARV² and Paralipomena*, edited by T. H. Carpenter, 2d ed. (Oxford 1989) |
| *BaM* | *Baghdader Mitteilungen* |
| *BCH* | *Bulletin de correspondance hellénique* |

| | |
|---|---|
| *BClevMus* | *Bulletin of the Cleveland Museum of Art* |
| *BdA* | *Bollettino d'arte* |
| *BICS* | *Bulletin of the Institute of Classical Studies of the University of London* |
| *BMC* | *Catalogues of the Greek Coins in the British Museum* (London 1873– ) |
| *BMFA* | *Bulletin of the Museum of Fine Arts, Boston* |
| *BMMA* | *The Metropolitan Museum of Art Bulletin* |
| *Boreas* | *Boreas. Münstersche Beiträge zur Archäologie* |
| *BSA* | *Annual of the British School at Athens* |
| *CECy* | *Centre d'Études Chypriotes, cahiers* |
| *ClAnt* | *Classical Antiquity* |
| *CP* | *Classical Philology* |
| *CQ* | *Classical Quarterly* |
| *CSCA* | *University of California Studies in Classical Antiquity* |
| *CVA* | *Corpus Vasorum Antiquorum* |
| *Dacia* | *Dacia. Revue d'archéologie et d'histoire ancienne* |
| *FGrH* | F. Jacoby, *Fragmente der griechischen Historiker* (Berlin 1923–58) |
| *FuB* | *Forschungen und Berichte. Staatliche Museen zu Berlin* |
| *GettyMusJ* | *J. Paul Getty Museum Journal* |
| *Gnomon* | *Gnomon. Kritische Zeitschrift für die gesamte klassische Altertumswissenschaft* |
| *Graef and Langlotz* | B. Graef et al., *Die antiken Vasen von der Akropolis zu Athen*, I i–iii (Berlin 1901–14); B. Graef and E. Langlotz, *Die antiken Vasen von der Akropolis zu Athen*, I iv and II i–iii (Berlin 1925–33) |
| *Gymnasium* | *Gymnasium. Zeitschrift für Kultur der Antike und humanistische Bildung* |
| *HBA* | *Hamburger Beiträge zur Archäologie* |
| *Hephaistos* | *Hephaistos. Kritische Zeitschrift zur Theorie und Praxis der Archäologie und angrenzendes Wissenschaften* |
| *Hesperia* | *Hesperia. Journal of the American School of Classical Studies at Athens* |
| *IrAnt* | *Iranica antiqua* |
| *Iraq* | *Iraq* [published by the British School of Archaeology in Iraq] |
| *IstMitt* | *Istanbuler Mitteilungen* |
| *JbMusMainz* | *Jahrbuch des Römisch-Germanischen Zentralmuseums, Mainz* |
| *JCS* | *Journal of Cuneiform Studies* |
| *JdI* | *Jahrbuch des Deutschen Archäologischen Instituts* |
| *JEOL* | *Jaarbericht van het Vooraziatisch-egyptisch Genootschap "Ex Oriente Lux"* |
| *JHS* | *Journal of Hellenic Studies* |
| *JNES* | *Journal of Near Eastern Studies* |
| *JRAS* | *Journal of the Royal Asiatic Society* |
| *JWalt* | *Journal of the Walters Art Museum* |
| *Klio* | *Klio. Beiträge zur alten Geschichte* |
| *LIMC* | *Lexicon Iconographicum Mythologiae Classicae*, 8 vols. (Zürich and Munich 1981–97) |
| *Maia* | *Maia. Rivista di letterature classiche* |
| *MarbWPr* | *Marburger Winckelmann-Programm* |
| *MASCA* | *Museum Applied Science Center for Archaeology, University Museum, University of Pennsylvania* |
| *MASCAP* | *MASCA Research Papers in Science and Technology* |
| *Meded* | *Mededeelingen van het Nederlands Historisch Instituut te Rome* |

| | |
|---|---|
| *MeddelGlypt* | *Meddelelser fra Ny Carlsberg Glyptotek* |
| *Minerva* | *Minerva. The International Review of Ancient Art and Archaeology* [London] |
| *MIO* | *Mitteilungen des Instituts für Orientforschung* |
| *MM* | *Madrider Mitteilungen* |
| *MMAJ* | *Metropolitan Museum of Art Journal* |
| *MonAnt* | *Monumenti antichi* |
| *MonPiot* | *Monuments et mémoires. Fondation E. Piot* |
| *MüJb* | *Münchener Jahrbuch der bildenden Kunst* |
| *MuM* | *Münzen und Medaillen, A.G.* [Basel] |
| *Muse* | *Muse. Annual of the Museum of Art and Archaeology, University of Missouri — Columbia* |
| *NumAntCl* | *Numismatica e antichità classiche. Quaderni ticinesi* |
| *OJA* | *Oxford Journal of Archaeology* |
| *ÖJh* | *Jahreshefte des Österreichischen archäologischen Instituts in Wien* |
| *OlBer* | *Bericht über die Ausgrabungen in Olympia* |
| *OlForsch* | *Olympische Forschungen* |
| *OpRom* | *Opuscula romana* |
| *Paralipomena* | J. D. Beazley, *Paralipomena: Additions to Attic Black-Figure Vase-Painters and Attic Red-Figure Vase-Painters* (Oxford 1971) |
| *Prospettiva* | *Prospettiva. Rivista d'arte antica e moderna* |
| *RA* | *Revue archéologique* |
| *RAssyr* | *Revue d'assyriologie et d'archéologie orientale* |
| *RdA* | *Rivista di archeologia* |
| *RDAC* | *Report of the Department of Antiquities, Cyprus* |
| *RE* | Pauly-Wissowa, *Real-Encyclopädie der klassischen Altertumswissenschaft* (1893 –) |
| *REA* | *Revue des études anciennes* |
| *Record* | *Record of the Princeton University Art Museum* |
| *RivIstArch* | *Rivista dell'Istituto nazionale d'archeologia e storia dell'arte* |
| *RLA* | *Reallexikon der Assyriologie und vorderasiatischen Archäologie.* Vols. 3 (1957 – 71) and 4 (1972 – 75), ed. E. F. Weidner and W. von Soden. Vols. 5, (1976 – 80), 6 (1980 – 83), 7 (1987 – 90), and 8 (1993 – 97), ed. D. O. Edzard. Berlin |
| *RM* | *Mitteilungen des Deutschen Archäologischen Instituts, Römische Abteilung* |
| *Roscher* | W. H. Roscher, *Ausführliches Lexikon der griechischen und römischen Mythologie* (Leipzig 1897 – 1902; 2d ed. 1965) |
| *RSGR* | S. Reinach, *Répertoire de la statuaire grecque et romaine*, 6 vols. (Paris 1897 – 1924) |
| *SBWien* | *Sitzungsberichte, Österreichische Akademie der Wissenschaften* [Wien], *Philosophisch-historische Klasse* |
| *SEG* | *Supplementum epigraphicum Graecum* (1923 –) |
| *SIMA-PB* | *Studies in Mediteranean Archaeology and Literature. Pocketbook* |
| *StEtr* | *Studi etruschi* |
| *Sumer* | *Sumer. A Journal of Archaeology and History in Iraq* |
| *Syria* | *Syria. Revue d'art oriental et d'archéologie* |
| *TAPA* | *Transactions of the American Philological Association* |
| *TAPS* | *Transactions of the American Philosophical Society* |
| *ZA* | *Zeischrift für Assyriologie und vorderasiatische Archäologie* |

Faesulae •
ETRURIA
• Pesaro
I T A L Y
Chiusi •
Orvieto •
Narce • • Satricum
Vulci • Falerii Veteres • • Chieti
Tarquinia • Capena
Caere • • Capua • Rome
LATIUM
Capua • CAMPANIA
Nola •
Ischia • MAGNA GRAECIA
Foce del Sele • • Paestum
• Taras
CALABRIA
• Sybaris
Medma •
• Locri Epizephirii
Naxos • • Rhegion
Selinus • SICILY • Katane
Gela • • Grammichele
• Camarina

• Trebenishte          THRACE
                       • Abdera          Byzantium •
MACEDONIA
Pydna •         THASOS
                SAMOTHRACE  Kamir-Blur •
GREECE                      • Troy
CORFU   • Dodona            • Assos            LYDIA
Mons Repos •  AKARNANIA  Mount Pelion ▲  Rhitsona
              THESSALY  EUBOIA  Tanagra
              Mount Oita ▲ Thebes  Lefkandi
              Thermon  Ptoion  Chalkis   IONIA
AITOLIA  Delphi  LOKRIS  Eretria  CHIOS  • Çesme  Sardis •
              Perachora Menidhi  BOIOTIA
              Mantineia • Marathon
              Sicyon  Corinth • Athens  TENOS  SAMOS •
Olympia ▲ Mount Pholoë  ARCADIA Argos  Mycenae  AIGINA  DELOS  Miletos •
              PELOPONNESE          CYCLADES  NAXOS
              Sparta • • Amyklai            KOS
              LACONIA  Phylakopi •          Kameiros •
              MALEA    MELOS  Thera •  RHODES •
                                         Siana •
CRETE  Prinias •                         Xanthos
Phaistos • Arkades •
         Kato Syme •

A E G E A N   S E A
MAEANDER

M E D I T E R R A N E A N   S E A

• Cyrene

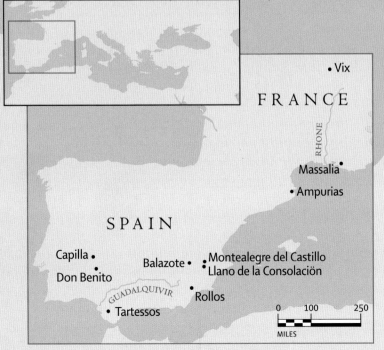

• Vix

FRANCE

RHONE

• Massalia
• Ampurias

S P A I N

Capilla •
                Balazote • • Montealegre del Castillo
Don Benito •            • Llano de la Consolaciön
GUADALQUIVIR  • Rollos
• Tartessos

0        100        250
MILES

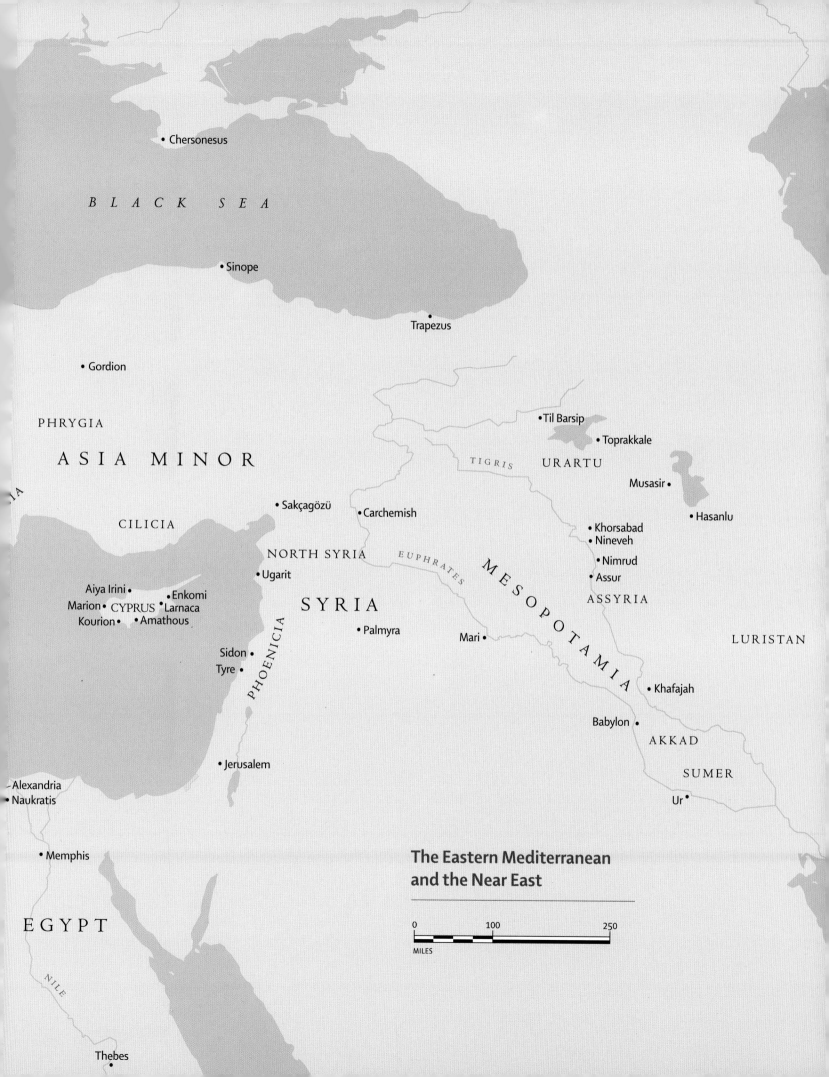

The Eastern Mediterranean
and the Near East

BLACK SEA

• Chersonesus

• Sinope

• Trapezus

• Gordion

PHRYGIA

ASIA MINOR

CILICIA

• Sakçagözü

NORTH SYRIA

• Ugarit

Aiya Irini •
Marion •      • Enkomi
    CYPRUS  • Larnaca
Kourion •    • Amathous

SYRIA

PHOENICIA

Sidon •
Tyre •

• Palmyra

• Jerusalem

• Alexandria
• Naukratis

• Memphis

EGYPT

NILE

• Til Barsip

• Toprakkale

TIGRIS      URARTU

Musasir •

• Hasanlu

• Carchemish

EUPHRATES

MESOPOTAMIA

• Khorsabad
• Nineveh
• Nimrud
• Assur

ASSYRIA

Mari •

LURISTAN

• Khafajah

Babylon •

AKKAD

SUMER

Ur •

Thebes

0        100        250
MILES

## Notes to the Reader

The subdivisions of the book are set forth in the Contents and discussed briefly in the Preface. The three essays deal successively with centaurs and satyrs in early Greek art ("Horse Men"), the Near Eastern antecedents of Greek composite creatures ("The Human Animal"), and the broad range of non-equine Greek *Mischwesen* such as sphinxes, sirens, and Gorgons ("ΠΕΛΩΡΑ"). These are followed by the catalogue of the exhibition, comprising 101 objects in 100 entries. Each entry contains basic information in a "tombstone" heading, followed by a brief summary of the object's condition and a full description and analysis, with endnotes and a selected bibliography that gives the publication history of the object in chronological order. The author's initials appear at the end of the main text section of each entry (see the list below). With few exceptions, the references in the notes of the essays and entries are in abbreviated form: author and year of publication. The full reference of every work abbreviated in this fashion can be found in the Bibliography of Works Cited.

Although authors are listed alphabetically in the Bibliography, individuals with the same last name appear chronologically; for instance, "Morris 1984," by Sarah P. Morris, precedes "Morris 1988," by Ian Morris. Greek titles are in Greek and not transliterated.

There are two lists of abbreviations: one for journals and standard reference works, which is based on that of the *American Journal of Archaeology*, and another for museums, which are abbreviated by city, e.g., "Cleveland," for the Cleveland Museum of Art. Objects in museums are identified by inventory number, when known, e.g., Cleveland 1986.88. If a given city has more than one museum with a significant collection of ancient art, these are distinguished: e.g., Athens, Nat. Mus.; Athens, Acrop. Mus.

All dimensions are given in centimeters; it has not been thought necessary to state that the measurements of fragments are their "preserved" dimensions, as they could hardly be otherwise. All dates are B.C.

Cross-referencing within the essays and entries is either by catalogue number or with reference to a particular essay. The spelling of Greek names generally favors the Greek—e.g., Boiotia, Aigina, Aischylos—but there are notable exceptions: e.g., Homer, Athens, Pindar. Most place names are located on the Map of the Eastern Mediterranean and the Near East. Architectural terms such as antefix, columen, and geison revetment are explained on a section drawing of a typical Etruscan temple in the Glossary.

### AUTHORS OF CATALOGUE ENTRIES

| | |
|---|---|
| NTA | Nathan T. Arrington |
| BB-S | Beryl Barr-Sharrar |
| MB | Michael Bennett |
| JYC | Jennifer Y. Chi |
| WAPC | William A. P. Childs |
| JG | Jasper Gaunt |
| SG | Stephen Gavel |
| JBG | Janet B. Grossman |
| JTH | Joan T. Haldenstein |
| MLH | Mary Louise Hart |
| SAH | Seán A. Hemingway |
| JJH | John J. Herrmann Jr. |
| JFK | John F. Kenfield |
| PL | Peter Lacovara |
| KDSL | Kenneth D. S. Lapatin |
| KM | Karen Manchester |
| SBM | Susan B. Matheson |
| DGM | David Gordon Mitten |
| JN | Jenifer Neils |
| JMP | J. Michael Padgett |
| AJP | Aaron J. Paul |
| JS | Jeffrey Spier |
| CMS | Conrad M. Stibbe |
| ABS | Alessandra Balco Sulzer |
| CET | Carrie E. Tovar |
| RW | Rex Wallace |

# Horse Men:
# Centaurs and Satyrs
# in Early Greek Art

J. Michael Padgett

**CENTAURS AND SATYRS** are familiar creatures. Like sirens and sphinxes, they are denizens of the mythical fantasy world of the ancient Greeks, and because of the role of the Greeks in the formation of Western civilization, they are part of our fantasies as well. With only occasional exceptions, sirens and sphinxes are female, as are the three Gorgons, daughters of Phorkys and Keto. Centaurs and satyrs, on the other hand, are aggressively masculine, like Acheloos and the Minotaur, who are part bull, and Triton and Typhon, whose serpentine lower bodies are suggestively phallic in form. They are not more violent than the females, nor more bestial, and may even show sparks of humanity that are lacking in the feminine monsters. From the beginning, both satyrs and centaurs were thought of as wild, woodland creatures that dwell on the mountainsides and in gorges, caves, and forest glades. Like the nymphs, they "rank neither with mortals nor with immortals" (*Hym. Hom. Aph.* 259). They are not evil but rude, their unbridled sensuality frequently giving way to unthinking violence. They do not deal in riddles or woo with lilting songs; they are not subtle. Their principal concern is the satisfaction of their own mundane appetites for sex, food, and alcohol. They may travel in packs, but the satyrs in particular have scant regard for one another; there is little of the family feeling that is the one saving grace of the Gorgon sisters. The centaurs are "rude, lawless, savage, unapproachable, unmatched in might" (Soph. *Trach.* 1096–97). They are worthy of a hero's attentions because they are brave themselves and willing to fight for what they want. In contrast, satyrs are cowardly and inclined to whine. There are even some "good" centaurs, Cheiron and Pholos, who are friends to humankind and renowned for their wisdom and hospitality. With the exception of Silenos, who was said to have fathered Pholos (Apollod. *Bibl.* 2.5.4), the satyrs lack such paragons, and although they are more human in form than the centaurs, only in later times do some of them take on individual personalities.

Figure 1. Black-figure Horse-head amphora: profile head of a horse. Greek, Attic, early sixth century B.C., workshop of the Gorgon Painter. Princeton University Art Museum, museum purchase, Carl Otto von Kienbusch Jr. Memorial Collection Fund (1997-54).

The link between centaurs and satyrs is not human but equine: each is part horse. In Hellenistic and Romans times, satyrs became partially conflated with the goat god Pan, sprouting horns and a short caprine tail, but in the first centuries of their existence they were horse-demons. The difference in character between satyrs and centaurs to some extent reflects differing Greek attitudes about horses on the one hand and donkeys and mules on the other. Although the two are closely associated in art, satyrs were not thought of as part donkey, for even when they

are represented with equine legs, they never have the characteristic dark stripes (*myklai*) that mark the legs of donkeys, and their bushy tails are like those of horses and mules. A mule is a half-breed, the offspring of a mare and a male donkey. The physique of satyrs reflects a similar, generalized melding of two natures, horse and man, while centaurs, on the other hand, are neatly divided in twain, the equine portion unmixed with the human, with only a narrow line of contact between them. Satyrs, then, are like mules in this sense, but just as they are not part donkey, neither are they part mule, since mules are sterile and unable to reproduce their own kind, let alone give rise to the race of satyrs. While centaurs retain many of the noble qualities of both horse and man, satyrs exhibit the worst traits of each. Just as satyrs were considered worthless and ignoble, so were mules and donkeys derided in comparison with horses.[1]

The horse was an important animal in Greece, and its ownership was a mark of significant class distinction.[2] As is true today, only the wealthy could afford to feed and care for a horse, and in early Greece the wealthy were those who owned land, the aristocracy, "the beautiful and the good" (*kaloi k'agathoi*). Every town, or polis, was dominated by a few landed families with slaves, flocks, vineyards, and olive groves, who rented plots to smaller farmers, married their daughters to one another, exchanged gifts and hospitality with others of their class in neighboring towns, and through their power and patronage controlled the sacred and civic institutions of the polis, including priesthoods and magistracies. From what little we know of military organization in the early first millennium B.C., when the polis went to war with the people over the hill, the aristocracy provided the cavalry and were backed by ranks, or in some cases a rabble, of armed tenants, bondsmen, and peasants, as well as tradesmen and artisans. By the end of the eighth century B.C., the role of the cavalry had begun to diminish because of accelerating improvements in military technology, the so-called Hoplite Reform.[3] The heavy infantryman, the hoplite, went to battle clad in bronze armor—helmet, greaves, breastplate—and carrying a heavy shield that, when massed together in overlapping ranks with those of his fellow citizen-soldiers, was proof against cavalry and anything else except a larger and more determined formation of hoplites. The hoplites were not the wealthiest aristocrats but men of more middling status, who through trade, toil, and thrift were able to save up the price of a suit of armor, which ate no grass and needed no groom.

The changes in Greek society caused by these developments, and the tensions and insecurities associated with them, have been much discussed by historians, with particular attention to their expression in art. The clash of hoplites became a favorite theme on Corinthian and Attic vases in the seventh and sixth centuries, but the horsemen are there as well, sometimes proceeding in a stately cavalcade, other times standing in the wings, watching the clash of armored ranks. As the cavalry became less essential in actual warfare, the horseman class, the *hippeis*, found new outlets to maintain its status, one of which was racing, whether of individual horses or of chariot teams, the most expensive game of all. A class of Attic black-figure amphora that began development in the last years of the seventh century features on either side the profile head of a horse set in majestic isolation within a reserved panel, as on this intact example in Princeton (fig. 1).[4] Horse-head amphorae, as they are called, disappeared before the mid-sixth century, at roughly the same time that the Panathenaic Games at Athens were reorganized by the tyrant Peisistratos. Scholars have linked this reorganization with the appearance of the first Panathenaic prize amphorae, vases filled with olive oil awarded to victors in the games and decorated with images of Athena and of athletic contests, including horse and chariot races.[5] The Horse-head amphorae may have been the predecessors of these later prizes, at least for the equine events, their restrained imagery glorifying the ethos of the *hippeis*.

Earlier, in the Geometric period (ca. 900–700 B.C.), when small bronze horses were among the most common dedications at the panhellenic sanctuary of Olympia, bronze centaurs also made their first appearance, alongside their counterparts in terracotta and painted pottery. They precede the earliest satyrs by a good century, which would not be surprising if we assume that centaurs, with their manly qualities of courage and comradeship and

their sense of aggressive self-entitlement, may, like the horse itself, have been associated with aristocratic values. Until the fifth century, centaurs and satyrs are almost never shown together, for each existed in a different conceptual sphere, the one heroic, the other Dionysiac.[6] Half horse and half man, they stand—like humanity itself—with legs in two worlds, between the rough freedom of nature and the reasoned ascent that is human culture. In their ambivalent characters lies a key to the Greek soul, and by examining their role in early Greek art, we may find clues both to their essential meaning and to their particular significance in Greek culture.

## THE CENTAURS

### Form and History

Of all the composite "human animals" of the Greek imagination, the centaur usually has been considered among those least reliant on direct inspiration from Near Eastern models.[7] From this point of view, the notion of combining the anatomies of a human and a horse need not have been based on any particular foreign models, being something that might occur to people in different times and places, wherever the horse had been domesticated and mounted horsemen were to be seen. For many observers, however, the general indebtedness to longstanding oriental antecedents such as sphinxes, lion-centaurs, and human-headed bulls has seemed too obvious to ignore, and they have sought the origin of centaurs in the imagery of the ancient Near East.[8] The identities of the eastern models and the legends and symbolism associated with them need not have traveled with their images, which could have been adapted by Greek artisans to give form to their own indigenous myths. It has even been suggested that some motifs and scenes copied by Greek artists may have inspired poets and others to have invented myths to explain the otherwise inscrutable images.[9] There is no reason, however, to believe that the Greek imagination was so impoverished as to need such prompting.

The claim of independent creation of the Greek centaur has been supported by the lack of exact correspondences in Near Eastern iconography. The creature

Figure 2. Impression of a cylinder seal: winged centaur hunting gazelles. Middle Assyrian, thirteenth century B.C., rose quartz. Private collection.

that hunts ibexes on a Middle Assyrian cylinder seal in the exhibition has the body of a horse and the torso of a bearded man, like a Greek centaur (fig. 2; cat. no. 11). Unlike them, however, he is winged—a general signifier of divine or demonic otherness in Near Eastern art— and his tail is not that of a horse but of a scorpion. This winged archer-centaur, who eventually became the astrological symbol Sagittarius, dates to the thirteenth century B.C. He appears on a number of Middle Assyrian, Kassite, and Neo-Babylonian seals,[10] as well as on Kassite boundary stones (*kudurrus*),[11] but he has no direct correspondent in early Greek art, where centaurs frequently are on the receiving end of arrows but do not shoot them themselves.[12] The motif of the archer-centaur apparently was rejected by Greek artists in the formative years of the late eighth and early seventh centuries as not meeting their pre-existing narrative needs. Instead, the tables were turned, and another oriental stock figure, the kneeling bowman, was adopted to represent the archer Herakles,[13] whose victims, as often as not, are centaurs.

Another Middle Assyrian seal (cat. no. 12), previously unpublished, portrays an altogether different sort of creature, apparently unique in Near Eastern art. It is a fully developed centaur, with the torso of a bearded man and the body of a horse: no wings, no scorpion tail. Unlike the "Sagittarius," he is bareheaded. He holds a bow, but whether the weapon belongs to him or to the naked man standing before him, who also grasps it, is unclear. The man has long hair, parted in the middle, and a beard tied with a cord. William Childs identifies him as a powerful hero, a *laḫmu*, and suggests that the centaur also may be a *laḫmu*, since his hair, beard, and frontal face are identical to the man's.[14] As a sign of their power, and perhaps of their kinship, both figures also take hold of the same small animal, possibly a goat. The tableau remains enigmatic, but the unambiguous depiction of the "centaur" represents the first proof that a demon of this type was fully conceived in Late Bronze Age Assyria and consequently was available for possible emulation by Greek artists.

This is not altogether surprising, since a handful of Mycenaean Greek "centaurs," roughly contemporary with these Mesopotamian parallels, have been identified. One, from Phylakopi, on Melos, is a rude terracotta statuette of a nude male, dated to the twelfth century B.C., with a break in the buttocks that can best be explained by the loss of a horizontal extension in the form of an animal's hindquarters.[15] Another example, recently identified by Ione Shear, is from Ugarit (Ras Shamra); even simpler in form, like a standard Mycenaean bull figurine of about 1300 B.C., it clearly combines a human torso with a quadruped body.[16] In neither case is the preservation or modeling sufficient to establish that the figure is a true centaur, for the animal part may just as well have been that of a bull.[17] Bull-bodied monsters of various sorts are common in the Near East, and bull-sphinxes appear on Mycenaean pottery and sarcophagi from the mainland and Cyprus.[18]

Like the Mycenaean sphinx, these centaurs, if that is what they are, had few immediate successors in the "Dark Ages" of the eleventh and tenth centuries. The figure identified as a centaur on a Sub-Mycenaean pyxis from the Athenian Kerameikos is too schematic to be at all convincing.[19] From Kos comes a tenth-century plastic vessel in the tradition of Late Mycenaean duck askoi, with a hollow, wheel-made body and the torso of a stubby-armed male rising at the front;[20] again, the animal part could be either horse or bull. A more schematic wheel-made Cypriote statuette from Enkomi has not one but two heads, which rise directly from the animal body, without torsoes.[21] Other statuettes of suggestive form, from Crete, have been plausibly interpreted as sphinxes rather than centaurs.[22] More convincing are some of the earliest of the wheel-made statuettes from the Cypriote sanctuary at Ayia Irini, which are probably tenth century in date. Although their animal anatomy is not certainly equine, and some of their later successors at the shrine have bull's horns, it has rightly been noted that there is otherwise nothing to distinguish most of these statuettes from centaurs.[23]

There is no uncertainty about the Cypriote centaur painted on the bottom of a Black Slip Painted II plate from Larnaca, dating to the late tenth century (Cypro-Geometric II).[24] The cartoonish figure has spiky hair, a human torso and arms, and a quadrupedal body of uncertain species, with what look like human feet in front. What clinches the identification is the branch that the creature holds in one hand in exactly the same manner

as generations of centaurs to come, a diagnostic attribute that obviates further speculation about whether the hindquarters are more equine than bovine. Whether this and the terracottas from Ayia Irini are enough to justify identifying Cyprus as the essential link in the transmission of the centaur concept from East to West is still debated. Phoenician and Assyrian influence in Cyprus was direct and, in the case of the Phoenicians, of long duration, and there is no question that the island was a major intersection of Near Eastern and Hellenic cultures. What is missing is a direct link to another island, where the first indisputable centaur makes its appearance in the Greek homeland.

The Lefkandi Centaur is named for the site of its discovery on the island of Euboia (fig. 3).[25] The head, torso, and legs of the large (h. 36 cm.) terracotta statuette are solid and handmade, while the body is wheel-made and hollow in the tradition of the composite figures and vessels described above. Unlike the votives from Ayia Irini, it was a funerary offering, but curiously the head was found in one tomb, the body in another. The associated grave goods and the painted designs on the statuette, which are related to those of Euboian Protogeometric pottery, date it with relative security to the end of the tenth century B.C. The centaur's forelegs lack human feet but have vaguely humanoid knees; nevertheless, the impression is one of a human torso rising above the chest and forelegs of a horse. Although it is simple in form— it lacks genitals but is clearly male—what is remarkable about the Lefkandi Centaur is that it is so successful as a work of art and, as a centaur, is so fully conceived a century and a half in advance of its nearest successors, the bronze and terracotta statuettes of the Late Geometric period. Traces of a missing object on the centaur's left shoulder suggest that he probably held in his left hand a branch or small tree, a motif not securely attested again until these rude weapons became the standard accoutrements of centaurs on Late Geometric vases, seals, and diadems (e.g., cat. nos. 15–17). Even more surprising is the gash on the centaur's left foreleg, which some have interpreted as representing the wound accidentally inflicted on the wise centaur Cheiron by one of Herakles' poison arrows.[26] The mark, which is clearly intentional

Figure 4. Krater: two centaurs. Greek, Early Protoattic, early seventh century B.C. Musée du Louvre, Paris (CA 3256).

and difficult to explain in any other way, removes the sculpture to a different conceptual realm, away from vague associations with askoi and cylinder seals to the world of Greek mythology.

Euboia lies across the straits from Mount Pelion, in Thessaly, the mythical home of the centaurs, including Cheiron. Although excavations at Lefkandi found evidence of extensive trade relations with other regions of the eastern Mediterranean, the centaur is surely Euboian-bred and stands at the head of the line of Greek centaurs. We can explain the gap between it and its successors in the Geometric period by positing an oral tradition that kept alive the tales of Cheiron and the centaurs of Mount Pelion until such time as changes in society and art called them back into visible form. This need not preclude the eventual discovery of more tangible evidence linking them over the centuries.

The famous bronze group from Olympia, in the Metropolitan Museum of Art (cat. no. 13), marks the re-emergence of the centaur in the Late Geometric aesthetic of the third quarter of the eighth century.[27] A helmeted hero grapples with a centaur who has a fully human body attached to the barrel and hindquarters of a horse. The equine portion closely resembles that of the many bronze horses found at Olympia and other Greek sanctuaries in this period, lean distillations of horseflesh that are not so much simple as smartly stylized.[28] The bronze horses and their painted counterparts represent in reduced form the chariot teams seen in procession on massive funerary

vases and fashioned in clay on pyxis lids, symbols of the wealth of the aristocracy and of its pride in a heroic past. In contrast, bronze horsemen are rare in this period,[29] and bronze centaurs even scarcer: aside from the extraordinary group in New York, only two have been published, isolated figures standing on the same type of pierced, rectangular bases as the horses.[30] They precede by a generation the first painted centaurs, which do not appear on Attic vases until Late Geometric IIb (ca. 720–700 B.C.),[31] at the same time as human horsemen.[32] The painted centaurs nearly always carry one or two branches and, like the riders, are represented both singly and in procession.[33] The centaurs continue on Early Protoattic vases of the early seventh century, their iconography little changed, although now their role as hunters may be emphasized by the substitution of a deer or goat for one of the branches they hold.[34] The two centaurs on a standed krater in the Louvre are essentially sub-Geometric in style (fig. 4), differing only in the outline drawing of the forelegs.[35]

The bronze centaur in New York (cat. no. 13) also may have carried a branch.[36] The action of the group has been debated, with some even seeing a friendly embrace rather than a struggle, perhaps representing the encounter between Herakles and the good centaur Pholos.[37] The object sticking from the side of the centaur, however, is the broken blade of his attacker, and there is no doubt that we are dealing with a classic confrontation between hero and monster. The intrusion of narrative adds a new degree of sophistication. Although fights between warriors and

Figure 3 (left). The Lefkandi Centaur. Greek, Euboian, late tenth century B.C., terracotta. Eretria Archaeological Museum (8620).

between men and beasts become relatively common on Late Geometric vases, no comparable encounter of man and centaur is yet known.[38] This may change with new discoveries, for such a fight does occur on the Late Geometric gold diadem in the exhibition (cat. no. 17), where a pair of centaurs has killed one man and possibly a second.

The inevitable question of whether such scenes ought to be identified with known myths applies to nearly all Late Geometric and Early Protoattic action scenes. Some scholars see attempts to identify action scenes with specific narratives as anachronistic and potentially misleading, since there was no real canon of myth in early Greece; many legends existed in numerous variants and fragmented oral narratives had not yet been knit into coherent epics, at least not to our knowledge.[39] Klaus Fittschen argued that early centaurs, like sphinxes and sirens, can be divided into anonymous demons and creatures of myth, depending on their interaction with human figures.[40] However, we cannot really know what meaning may have attached to individual or processional centaurs. In part, the question of their identity is linked to their formal typology, which in the early stages was anything but consistent.

On the krater in the Louvre (see fig. 4), the forelegs of the centaurs have been outlined in order to emphasize their human shape. This type of centaur, with a fully human man encumbered with half a horse *a tergo*, is by far the most common in Geometric and Early Archaic art. The Lefkandi Centaur, however, seems to have equine forelegs, as does the centaur attacked by an archer on a famous Late Geometric seal in Paris (cat. no. 14). Both types of centaur appear side by side on an early-seventh-century gold diadem from Corinth, along with human horsemen.[41] Although less common, the type with four horse legs was present from the beginning. This is not surprising, since we have seen that it is the type with close Near Eastern parallels. Most of the latter are winged, and this type, too, appears in a few early Greek examples (without the scorpion tail),[42] as do centaurs with clawed feet, recalling Assyrian lion-centaurs.[43] The Gorgon-horse is featured on some early-sixth-century intaglios (fig. 5), probably East Greek in origin,[44] and makes a surprising

Figure 5. Impression of a scarab seal: Gorgon-centaur. East Greek, early sixth century B.C., carnelian. Location unknown. After Boardman 1968, 27, pl. II, no. 31.

appearance on an earlier, seventh-century Cycladic relief-amphora from Boiotia (see Tsiafakis, "ΠΕΛΩΡΑ," fig. 13), where the horse-bodied Medusa is decapitated by Perseus.[45] The intaglio in figure 5 shows the centauresque Medusa grappling with an overmatched lion, her stony glare turned toward the viewer.[46] From her back springs a pair of wings, appendages that the majority of Archaic Greek artisans apparently deemed sufficient to set Medusa and her sisters apart as demonic figures, eschewing the horse's body as too easily confused with that of the centaurs.[47]

The example of these stillborn hybrids has encouraged scholars to ask whether the addition of equine hindquarters was used in the seventh century as "an indicator of the generally monstrous."[48] One image that has been the subject of considerable discussion is on a Middle Protocorinthian aryballos of about 680 B.C., in Boston (cat. no. 31), where a centaur with human legs battles a male figure grasping a scepter and brandishing a peculiar spiky object.[49] Ernst Buschor identified the object as a thunderbolt and the subject as the fight between Zeus and the monster Typhon.[50] The latter is never described as having an equine body, and indeed, he came to be represented most commonly with a serpentine lower body (see cat. no. 98). Buschor's interpretation has been accepted by many, but Fittschen has made a good argument for instead identifying the spiky object as one of the firebrands used by Herakles to drive off the thirsty centaurs of Mount Pholoë (Apollod. *Bibl.* 2.5.4), and this may well be correct.[51] In either case, we are compelled to resort both to much later literary accounts and to a vocabulary of attributes based on later images to attempt to make sense of a scene created in a period when the canons of myth and imagery were not yet set.

After experimenting with these and other permutations, most early Greek artists settled on the two basic types of centaur—with either human or equine forelegs—both of which continued until the Early Classical period of the mid-fifth century, by which time the type with human legs had long been reserved for the "civilized" Cheiron (see below). There are regional and geographic preferences, but in general, efforts to designate either of the two basic types as "Attic," "Laconian," or the like are futile.[52] A possible exception is East Greece, where sixth-century vase-painters and gem-engravers frequently represented centaurs with human forelegs ending in hooves,[53] a trait found also on some early coins of Thasos and Macedonia,[54] and on Caeretan hydriae painted by immigrant East Greek artists in Etruria.[55]

The few bronze centaurs of the Geometric period have even fewer successors in the seventh century, but there are several terracotta examples, mostly from Boiotia (cat. no. 21)[56] and Cyprus (cat. nos. 19, 20); a multitude of painted centaurs on Protoattic and Protocorinthian vases (cat. nos. 30, 31); seals in ivory, stone, and metal (cat. nos. 15, 16); a beautiful series of electrum plaques from Rhodes (cat. no. 18); and reliefs in bronze, clay, and precious metal (cat. no. 32). It is not until the third quarter of the seventh century that we again see another bronze centaur, found at a sanctuary of Hermes and Aphrodite at Kato Syme, Crete.[57] Like the centaurs on the Rhodian plaques, the Cretan centaur has human legs and is in the Daedalic style, with a triangular face and wiglike hair. He walks to the right, turning his torso toward the viewer, his hands resting on his hips. This basic type was continued in the sixth century, when bronze centaurs were still extremely rare, much more so than sphinxes, sirens, and Gorgons, all of which became popular as cast handles and ornaments on bronze vessels and implements.

A bronze centaur in Athens, found on the Acropolis, is in much the same pose as his Daedalic forebear, but he

Figure 6. Statuette of a centaur. Greek, Laconian, found on the Athenian Acropolis, second quarter of the sixth century B.C., bronze. National Archaeological Museum, Athens (6680).

Figure 7. Tomb guardian from Vulci: a centaur. Etruscan, ca. 550 B.C., nenfro. Museo Nazionale di Villa Giulia, Rome. After Settis 1985, 72, fig. 127.

Figure 8. Statuette of a centaur. Greek, ca. 510–500 B.C., bronze. Private collection.

now gallops instead of walks and carries a branch over his left shoulder (fig. 6).[58] His right arm is swung back, the hand attached to the flank of his equine body. The style is Laconian, as is that of a slightly later bronze centaur, also from the Acropolis and now in Paris (cat. no. 23).[59] The Paris centaur is in the same posture, the left hand holding a rude club, the right one attached to the flank, but the torso is more muscular and in better proportion to the legs, which are spread wide, while the horse legs in the rear are set close together.[60] These little bronzes once may

have had slender base plates, like that of a later, fifth-century centaur from South Italy (cat. no. 26). This is by no means certain, as a third bronze centaur from the Acropolis had none;[61] it is poorly cast but follows generally the same formula as the other two, differing only in details (he wears a cap of some sort, and the long club in his left hand rests on his back). The statuettes with base plates originally may have been decorative attachments on the rims of hammered bronze vessels, or they might have been dedicated as votives, like the earlier one from Crete and like a pair of bronze centaurs from a sanctuary at Çesme, in Ionia (cat. no. 22).[62]

Although we have only a handful of Archaic bronze centaurs, the same basic model—human forelegs, head and torso turned partly toward the viewer, one hand swung back and attached to the body—apparently was widespread, for it appears even in a bronze found in distant Spain (cat. no. 25),[63] probably from a native Iberian workshop under strong Greek influence. The torso and head are turned perpendicular to the legs and equine body, making the piece even more one-sided in orientation. The sickle-shaped beard and corkscrew tresses are quite unlike those of the Greek centaurs, but the modeling of the horse and human musculature is bold and convincing. Similar tresses occur on a statue of a centaur carved from volcanic stone (nenfro) that once stood at the entrance of a tomb near the Etruscan city of Vulci (fig. 7).[64] Like the Greek models from which it ultimately derives, the equine body of the Etruscan centaur, which dates about 550 B.C., is nearly cylindrical; it attaches with almost casual abruptness to the rump of a bearded male figure, whose nakedness alone would set him apart from most depictions of Etruscan males. Unlike the Greek centaurs, he faces forward with rigid frontality, a characteristic also of smaller bronze centaurs from Etruria (e.g., cat. no. 43).[65]

It is instructive to compare the Iberian centaur (cat. no. 25) with a Greek example in a private collection (fig. 8).[66] The basic pose is reversed, with the right leg forward, the left hand attached to the flank, and the right hand raised to carry a now missing branch or club. The feet and hooves are attached to a base plate, the curve of which again suggests a vessel rim, although it would have been a massive vase indeed to support a figure of this size.

Figure 9. Statuette of a centaur. Greek, possibly Attic, ca. 530 B.C., bronze. Princeton University Art Museum, gift of Damon Mezzacappa (1997-36).

There is a swing in the centaur's gait, but though the torso turns out, the head looks forward, raised and alert. The tubular barrel and stunted legs of the horse half would not be out of place in a centaur of an earlier century, but the man's figure is well modeled, with taut muscles, a washboard belly, barbered pubic hair, and a trim beard and moustache that contrast with the long, herringboned hair in the back. These elements together suggest a date of about 510–500 B.C.

At this point in the sculptural evolution of the centaur, a figure like this bronze is already an anachronism. In following the formula established by Dorian Peloponnesian and Cretan bronze workers more than a century before, it clings to the schema of a horse's hindquarters attached to the otherwise complete body of a man. In this case, the intrusion of the horse's barrel at an unnaturally low spot on the buttocks only highlights the apparent absurdity of the combination. In contrast, an earlier centaur in Princeton (fig. 9; cat. no. 24), not later than 530 B.C., is more in keeping with the popular iconography of Attic black-figure vase-painting, in which the centaur with four equine legs had long been dominant.[67] The union of horse and man was never effected with greater "naturalism" than in this small sculpture. The horse's anatomy is accurately rendered and has the appropriate mass in proportion to the human element. Although fully modeled in the round, the body has a slight curvature, and the hair in the back is not incised. These characteristics suggest that the figure was not meant to be seen from behind. A deep indentation in the back of the head is possibly an accommodation for a structural element of a large vessel or tripod. Unlike its Laconian counterparts from the Acropolis, this centaur may have been made in Athens itself. He has a broad, hairy chest[68] and muscular arms that are flexed in a manner imparting added vigor to the traditional twist of the torso. The right hand may have held a branch. He differs from most black-figure centaurs in retaining human ears, a holdover from the tradition of the more fully human type. The beard, a pendant mass of parallel locks scored with herringbone incision, seems to hang from the ears, framing a face with high cheeks, bulging eyes, and a classic "Archaic smile" of the type that Barbara Fowler so

elegantly connected with the "green" smile of Pindar's Cheiron.[69] The expression is open and alert, though perhaps not in response to things we would readily imagine. The smile and, in particular, the eyes resemble those of "Bluebeard," the triple-bodied monster with a snaky lower body from an Archaic pediment on the Acropolis,[70] reminding us that the centaur's human half is an illusion: like the monster on the pediment, he is not one of us. A masterpiece of the mature Archaic style, the Princeton bronze epitomizes the Greek conception of the centaurs of legend. If it does not represent a specific personality, like Cheiron or Pholos, it eloquently evokes the mythical landscape they shared.

## Centaurs in Myth and Legend

Greek scholars offered no etymology for "centaur" (κένταυρος) beyond the eponymous Kentauros, whose conception was described by Pindar (*Pyth.* 2.21–48) and Apollodoros (*Epit.* 1.20). Ixion, king of the Thessalian Lapithae, was purified by Zeus after murdering his own father-in-law. Invited to sup with the gods, he tried to seduce Hera, who reported the outrage to Zeus. The king of the gods fashioned a cloud, Nephele, in the form of the sleeping Hera, and when Ixion slept with her, the resulting offspring was Kentauros. Ixion's punishment was to be tied to a perpetually spinning wheel, but Kentauros was nurtured by Nephele and coupled with the Magnesian mares on the spurs of Mount Pelion, engendering the race of centaurs, "the mare's likeness in the parts below, and the manlike father above" (Pind. *Pyth.* 2.48).[71]

Ixion was succeeded as king by his son Peirithoos, whose paternity some ascribed instead to Zeus.[72] To his wedding with Hippodameia (or Deidameia),[73] Peirithoos invited the centaurs as well as his friend Theseus. The centaurs got drunk and fell upon the Lapith women, setting off a bloody battle that became the model for all future "centauromachies," from the west pediment at Olympia to Ovid's lengthy account in *Metamorphoses* (12.210–535), in which he lingers lovingly over every gory detail.[74] Homer singled out the centaur Eurytion as the principal offender of the Lapiths (*Od.* 21.295–304), but he never mentions a wedding, alluding elsewhere only to the vengeance that

Figure 10. The François Vase, black-figure volute-krater: the Death of Kaineus.
Greek, ca. 570 B.C., signed by Ergotimos and Kleitias. Museo Archeologico Nazionale, Florence (4209).

Peirithoos wreaked on the "hairy beasts" (*phéres*), which he drove from Pelion (*Il.* 2.741–44).[75] Theseus distinguished himself in the fight, and others present were Nestor, Dryas, and the centaur Nessos. Among the Lapith casualties, the most celebrated was Kaineus, who had been born a woman, Kainis. Raped by Poseidon, he granted her a compensatory wish, which was to change her sex and thus never again suffer the same indignity. Poseidon made Kaineus invulnerable, but the centaurs at the wedding battle overcame this by pounding him into the earth.[76]

The death of Kaineus became a favorite subject in art, first appearing in the third quarter of the seventh century on a hammered bronze relief at Olympia, where the Lapith is represented as an armored hoplite between a pair of centaurs who batter him with trees.[77] Already he is sunk in the earth to mid-calf, a motif that makes Kaineus instantly recognizable in any depiction of the Thessalian centauromachy. The subject does not reappear with certainty for another sixty years,[78] when it forms the centerpiece of the centauromachy on the neck of the François Vase (fig. 10), the great Attic black-figure volute-krater in Florence, which dates about 570 B.C. and is signed by the potter Ergotimos and the painter Kleitias.[79] Kaineus has sunk to the bottom of his cuirass but fights

Figure 11. Tondo of a red-figure kylix: Lapith Killing a Centaur. Greek, Attic, ca. 480 B.C., attributed to the Foundry Painter. Staatliche Antikensammlungen und Glyptothek, Munich (2640). After Ohly-Dumm and Hamdorf 1981, 119, pl. 53.

on against three centaurs, one wielding a tree, the other two boulders. In the many subsequent versions of this scene in Greek vase-painting—mostly Attic, but also East Greek, South Italian, and Etruscan—the basic composition remains the same, with Kaineus partially sunk into the ground and attacked by at least one and as many as four centaurs (cat. nos. 27, 28). Kaineus is always represented as a Greek warrior, usually fully armored and always wearing at least a helmet; he frequently carries a shield and defends himself with a spear or, more often, a sword. Sometimes he stabs both attackers simultaneously with a pair of swords, as he does on the Olympia relief.[80] Depictions of a warrior who is not sunk into the ground but is besieged on either side by centaurs might be discounted as representing Kaineus were it not for the fact that an early example, a Tyrrhenian amphora in Rome, is inscribed with the Lapith's name.[81]

In addition to Kaineus, the other Lapiths and centaurs on the François Vase also are named. The Lapiths include Antimachos, Therandros, Dryas, and Hoplon, as well as Peirithoos's Athenian friend, Theseus. The centaurs who pummel Kaineus are Hylaios, Akrios,

and Asbolos, while others named are Petraios, Pyros, Orosbios, and Melanchaites. Theseus and Dryas are mentioned in the description of the fight in the Hesiodic *Shield of Herakles*, as are the centaurs Petraios and Asbolos. The combatants on the shield "were in silver, but the fir trees they had in their hands were golden, and they were streaming together, as if they were alive, and battering each other in close combat with spears and fir trunks."[82]

The flood of black-figure centauromachies that followed the François Vase gave artists scope to experiment with new and more complicated figural compositions, with hirsute centaurs brandishing boulders and tree trunks while galloping, rearing, and wheeling about in frenzied combat, now and then falling to earth with gushing wounds and flailing hooves.[83] The inscriptions on the François Vase are the exception, for most often the antagonists are anonymous. The iconography remains consistent, however, with Lapiths normally represented in hoplite armor, as on a splendid red-figure cup in Munich of about 480 B.C. (fig. 11), attributed to the Foundry Painter.[84] Since Herakles was not present at the wedding of Peirithoos, fights between hoplites and centaurs are generally regarded as representing the Thessalian centauromachy, while those in which Herakles appears ought to refer instead to one of his adventures; compare, for example, the two sides of a black-figure neck-amphora

Figure 12. South metope 31 from the Parthenon: Lapith and centaur. Greek, Attic, ca. 438 B.C., marble. British Museum, London.

Figure 13. Drawing of a painted alabastron: possibly Cheiron and Chariklo. Greek, Early Corinthian, last quarter of the seventh century B.C. Rhodes Archaeological Museum (11.550). After Jacopi 1929, 78, fig. 69.

in the exhibition (cat. no. 34), with centaurs battling Herakles on one side and a Lapith on the other.[85]

In the fifth century, the Thessalian centauromachy became an important theme for sculptors and painters, forming the subject of the sculptural decoration of the west pediment of the temple of Zeus at Olympia (ca. 456 B.C.).[86] The theme was especially popular in Athens, where the exploits of Theseus against the centaurs and the Amazons came to symbolize the defeat of barbarism, in particular, the Persians.[87] It appears on the west frieze of the Hephaisteion (430s)[88] and the south metopes of the Parthenon (ca. 438 B.C.), in which the fight is represented as a series of duels (fig. 12).[89] It was carved in relief on the edges of the sandals of Pheidias's statue of Athena Parthenos (Pliny, *HN* 36.18) and was engraved by Mys, after a design by Parrhasios, on the bronze shield of the Athena Promachos, another work by Pheidias (Paus. 1.28.2).

The fight with the Thessalian centaurs traditionally had been represented as taking place on the slopes of Mount Pelion, but in the second quarter of the fifth century, Early Classical vase-painters began depicting it in

an indoor setting, at the actual wedding feast, with the men not wearing armor and the combatants using stools, jars, table legs, and lampstands as weapons.[90] Theseus plays the leading role in these scenes, in some of which the Lapith women also appear, as they do on the west pediment at Olympia, where they struggle against the importunate centaurs. The inspiration for both the vase-paintings and the Olympia pediment has been attributed to a mural of the late 470s that Pausanias saw in the Theseion in Athens, possibly by the painter Mikon, though some give it to Polygnotos.[91] All we know about this painting, however, is that Theseus was shown already having killed a centaur. There is too much variety in the vase-paintings for them to have been based on a single work,[92] nor is there any reason to believe that the Olympia pediment, a major work designed for the eyes of the entire Greek world, was likely to have been based on a painted prototype that Pausanias happened to see centuries later and whose brief description happens to have survived.

Among the centaurs of Pelion, the most renowned was Cheiron, "justest of the centaurs" (Hom. *Il.* 11.832), a friend to men and the teacher of heroes. Unlike the

Figure 14. Black-figure amphora: two horsemen.
Greek, Attic, ca. 540 B.C. Formerly in the Hunt Collection.

Figure 15. Black-figure dinos: Cheiron at the wedding of Peleus. Greek, Attic, ca. 580 B.C., signed by Sophilos. British Museum, London (1971.11-1.1).

other centaurs, he was not descended from Ixion but was an immortal, the son of Kronos and the ocean nymph Philyra.[93] Surprised in flagrante delicto by his wife Rhea, Kronos turned into a horse, accounting for Cheiron's shape, "half like a horse, half like a god."[94] In art, the latter description remained truer for Cheiron than for other centaurs, for long after they had begun to be depicted with equine forelegs, he continued to be represented as a man with the hindquarters of a horse. This tribute to Cheiron's humanity was reinforced by Attic vase-painters, who usually draped his human half in a chiton, himation, or both (see cat. nos. 39, 40). Cheiron lived on Pelion with his mother Philyra[95] and his wife, the nymph Chariklo, by whom he had three daughters: Okyrrhoë, a prophetess whom the gods turned into a mare because she could reveal the future (Ov. *Met.* 633–75); Theia, also changed into a mare; and Endeis, who, in one tradition, married Aiakos and gave birth to Peleus.[96]

Cheiron's marriage to Chariklo is depicted on a red-figure bell-krater of about 440 B.C., attributed to the Eupolis Painter (cat. no. 38). This charming image of a centaur wedding is so far unique; an Early Corinthian alabastron in Rhodes, however, may show Cheiron with his bride nearly two centuries earlier (fig. 13).[97] That the Corinthian centaur is fully human in front is not significant, since most centaurs are represented this way in Corinthian vase-painting. The branch in his raised right

hand is standard centaur equipment. Although his genitals are depicted, so are the sleeves and collar of a tunic, human attire normally reserved for the "civilized" centaurs Cheiron and Pholos. Standing beside him, a woman wearing a belted peplos embraces him with both arms. If she is Herakles' wife, Deianeira, and the centaur is her molester, Nessos, this tender gesture is hard to explain, as is the fact that the centaur does not a lay a hand upon her.[98] Herakles is normally present in scenes of Deianeira's abduction, and when he is not, as on the bronze shield band in the exhibition (cat. no. 36), the subject is made explicit by placing Deianeira sidesaddle on the centaur's back.[99] This woman is not molested, she is in love. To her right, floating amid the rosettes of the background, is a large horse head with a bridle and a flowing mane, not unlike those of Attic Horse-head amphorae (see fig. 1). Its presence here is curious, for it looks almost as though it has fallen off the equine body attached to Cheiron. One wonders if the painter felt a need to put additional emphasis on the horsey character of the old centaur, whose divine bloodlines and successful wooing of the lovely nymph otherwise threaten to move him into a different class altogether, leaving his bestial part literally behind him.

Such fractional horse bodies may have had more significance than we can fathom at this distance. On a black-figure amphora of about 540 B.C., with a pair of

Figure 16. Black-figure band-cup: Cheiron watching Peleus wrestle Thetis. Greek, Attic, ca. 540 – 530 B.C., attributed to the Oakeshott Painter. Michael C. Carlos Museum, Emory University, Atlanta (2000.1.2).

mounted warriors on either side, the shield device on the obverse consists of the head and forelegs of a white horse, while the shield on the reverse has a horse's disembodied hindquarters (fig. 14).[100] A horse's arse is not a particularly martial emblem, but a joke seems out of the question: the warriors and their mounts are drawn with singular elegance and decorum. Instead, we may think of the sandwiched warriors as bridging the gap between the shields with their own centaur-like strength and prowess. Centaurs are a relatively common shield device,[101] and by giving us only the hindquarters as a device, the complete subject—horse or centaur—is left to the viewer's imagination. By the same token, the horse protome on the obverse could just as easily be completed by the serpentine body of a hippocamp. This kind of playful rearrangement of centaur and horse anatomy is far from unique.[102]

Cheiron's fame as a hunter was emphasized in his iconography, for he is commonly represented holding a tree hung with game, as he does on a black-figure dinos in London, signed by the painter Sophilos (fig. 15).[103] The subject is the procession of gods at the wedding of Peleus and Thetis, in which Cheiron is said to have led the other centaurs (Eur. *IA* 1058–64), though only he is represented. Like the other guests, Cheiron's name is inscribed, but by this date, about 580 B.C., the old centaur is readily recognizable by his human legs and attire—a belted

chitoniskos suitable for hunting—and, above all, by the tree laden with game, in this case a stag, two does, a fawn, and a hare.[104] The gnarled stick in his right hand is a lago bolon, a throwing stick for stunning small game. Sophilos was the first to depict the Wedding of Peleus and Thetis, painting it a second time on a fragmentary dinos from the Acropolis.[105] Chariklo is present on both occasions, and Cheiron, too, was surely among the guests on the second dinos. After Sophilos, the subject was repeated by Kleitias on the François Vase, where it again occupies the principal frieze. Now Cheiron has the honor of leading the procession alongside Iris, while Chariklo walks behind with Demeter and Hestia.[106] The prominence afforded this subject on these large mixing bowls, which probably functioned as centerpieces at symposia, highlights the ideals of the aristocracy: of noble birth supported by divine favor; of hunting and horses—the principal gods do not walk, but ride; and of ostentatious rites of passage, including not only the wedding on the François Vase but also the funeral games of Patroklos on the neck above.

The centrality of Peleus and Achilles to the iconography of the François Vase is well recognized, and anyone seeing Cheiron at the wedding would instantly recall the centaur's role in both their lives. The old centaur taught Peleus as a boy and was his constant friend thereafter. He cured the blindness of Peleus's friend Phoinix (Apollod. *Bibl.* 3.13.8), and when the jealous Akastos hid Peleus's sword and left him to the beasts of Mount Pelion, it was Cheiron who rescued him, a subject depicted on a few Attic vases.[107] At his wedding, Cheiron gave Peleus an ashen spear, which became legendary.[108] It was Cheiron who advised Peleus to seize the volatile Thetis and hold her tight no matter how many fierce creatures or elements she transformed herself into (Apollod. *Bibl.* 3.13.5). This was a favorite subject of vase-painters, who frequently showed the centaur standing nearby, watching the turbulent wooing and encouraging his protegé, as he does on a band-cup in the exhibition, attributed to the Oakeshott Painter (fig. 16; cat. no. 96).[109]

Cheiron was well known for his tutelage of young gods and heroes, including Asklepios, Jason, Achilles, and a host of others whom ancient authors eventually enrolled in his "school."[110] His moral and practical wisdom was embodied in the *Precepts of Cheiron*, a didactic poem in the form of advice directed at the young Achilles, the few fragments of which are preserved in the Hesiodic corpus.[111] His healing arts he passed on to Asklepios and his son Machaon (Hom. *Il.* 4.219), and to Achilles, who in turn taught them to Patroklos (*Il.* 11.831). Like the sons of the aristocracy, his pupils learned to play the lyre, and indeed, it has been noted that his "curriculum," designed especially for mythic heroes, is more in harmony with the schools of the music teacher and the gymnasium instructor than with the teacher of letters.[112] For Euripides, Cheiron's tutoring of Achilles was principally focused on morality and proper behavior, "that he might not learn vile men's ways" and "tread no tortuous paths" (Eur. *IA* 709, 927). Venery was another important focus of instruction, and it was from Cheiron that the hunters Meleager and Aktaion learned their craft.[113] Even Apollo looked to Cheiron for advice, asking him if he might not lie with the nymph Cyrene and receiving a wry but smiling reply (Pind. *Pyth.* 9.26–66).

Cheiron's most famous charge was Achilles, the offspring of Peleus and Thetis. Many Attic vase-paintings of the sixth and early fifth centuries show Peleus bringing the young Achilles to Cheiron, either handing him over as an infant or leading him forward as a young boy (cat. no. 40).[114] The subject begins much earlier, however, on Protoattic kraters of the mid-seventh century by the

Polyphemos and Ram Jug Painters.[115] On one of these, by the Ram Jug Painter,[116] Cheiron is recognizable not only by the context but also by the tree he shoulders, which is hung with game—a lion, a boar, and a wolf—foretelling the same creatures that Achilles would soon drag "gasping" to the house of Philyra.[117] The wise centaur knew his young pupil was special: "Prophetic Chiron, / the son of Philyra, / laying hands / on the blond curls / of Achilles, / often declared Fate: / 'Scamander chokes / on the Trojan marauders.'"[118]

Cheiron's death also was the stuff of legend. Ovid (*Fast.* 5.397–414) says that he was visited by Herakles, and while the old centaur was examining the hero's arrows, the tips of which were poisoned with the blood of the Hydra, one fell from the quiver and stuck in his left foot. The poison soaked into Cheiron's bones, and all of his medical skills were helpless to assuage the pain. Being immortal, he could find no relief in death, but Zeus agreed to let him die in place of Prometheus, who assumed the centaur's immortality.[119] Cheiron then became a constellation,[120] like so many other lamented mythological figures. In Ovid's telling, Cheiron's unlucky meeting with Herakles took place in his cave on Mount Pelion, but Apollodoros (*Bibl.* 2.5.4) says it happened in Malea, in the southern Peloponnesos. In this version, the arrow of Herakles is shot clean through the arm of a centaur named Elatus, striking Cheiron in the knee with the same dire results. Elatus was among the centaurs battled by Herakles in the aftermath of his encounter with Pholos, a *parergon,* or side adventure, in the course of Herakles' search for the Erymanthian boar, the fourth of his canonical Labors.

The story of Herakles' meeting with Pholos is told most fully by Apollodoros, Diodorus Siculus, and, much later, Tzetzes.[121] Passing through the mountain range of Pholoë, between Elis and Arcadia, Herakles stopped at the cave of Pholos, a hospitable centaur of mild disposition, who invited him to dine, setting roast meat before the hero while he ate raw. Spying a large jar of wine, Herakles asked for a drink. Pholos warned him not to lift the lid because the scent would attract the wild centaurs dwelling on the mountain round about. Ignoring his host's advice, Herakles opened the jar anyway, with

Figure 17. Black-figure amphora: Pholos and Herakles. Greek, Attic, ca. 530 B.C., attributed to the Group of Würzburg 199. Museo Archeologico Nazionale, Florence (3812).

predictable consequences: the centaurs smelled the sweet wine and laid siege to the cave, arming themselves with boulders and trees. A savage fight ensued, but Herakles drove the centaurs off, first with brands from the cook fire and then with his bow, killing several of them and driving the rest as far as Malea.

This Peloponnesian centauromachy has obvious parallels with the Thessalian, with the same race of savage, cloud-born centaurs transplanted whole from the slopes of Pelion to those of Pholoë, driven thence by the Lapiths. Cheiron joined this exodus, but his presence here is superfluous, for the Peloponnesian myth has its own "good" centaur, Pholos, and its own Dorian hero and hammer of centaurs, Herakles, who takes the place of the Ionian Theseus and his friend Peirithoos. Once again the centaurs savagely violate the rules of hospitality and are justly punished. Although most of the later mythographers said that the episode on Pelion preceded

that on Pholoë, not all agreed (Schol. *Il.* 1.266), nor is it certain that one myth is significantly older than the other. Diodorus (4.12.8) has Pholos, like Cheiron, die from an accidental prick from one of Herakles' arrows. This need not indicate that the story of his demise is simply adapted from that of Cheiron; indeed, it is Cheiron's death that seems an afterthought to this particular Peloponnesian story.

Herakles and Pholos were painted together on many Attic vases, both black-figure and red-figure, beginning in the last quarter of the sixth century and continuing to the mid-fifth.[122] Among the earliest are some by the Antimenes Painter and his associates that depict the initial meeting between hero and centaur, who converse or shake hands in the presence of Hermes.[123] More common are scenes of Herakles and Pholos on either side of a large jar, a pithos, full of wine and partially buried in the earth. Herakles usually is shown either removing the lid

Figure 18. Relief from the temple of Athena at Assos: Pholos, Herakles, and fleeing centaurs. Greek, ca. 550–530 B.C., andesite. Museum of Fine Arts, Boston, gift of the Archaeological Institute of America (84.67).

or filling his cup (cat. no. 29). The scene on a black-figure amphora in Florence is one of a few that instead shows Herakles reclining like a symposiast and being served by his host, who in this case fills his guest's kantharos from an oinochoe (fig. 17).[124] The opened pithos is at the left, its lid propped against it. As is customary, Pholos is distinguished from Cheiron by having the forelegs of a horse and a bare human torso.[125] The one element borrowed from Cheiron's iconography is the tree hung with small game that rests on his shoulder. On the other side of this vase, it is Dionysos who is shown reclining, served by a satyr; the pairing with Herakles is not unintentional, recalling vase-paintings of these two sons of Zeus drinking together.[126] Pholos was said to be the son of Silenos by a Melian nymph (Apollod. *Bibl.* 2.5.4), and in his role as cupbearer on this vase he is purposefully contrasted with his horsey cousin, the satyr on the obverse.[127]

Representations of Herakles and Pholos long predate their appearance in Attic pottery. The episode of the jar is preserved in a fragmentary clay relief from Praisos, in Crete, of about 600 B.C.,[128] but more common are depictions of the subsequent fight between Herakles and the centaurs (cat. nos. 30–34). The combat was among the sixth-century reliefs on the Chest of Kypselos at Olympia[129] and on the Amyklai Throne in Laconia,[130] but there are much earlier renditions in vase-painting. One of

the earliest is a Protocorinthian aryballos of about 660–650 B.C., with Herakles kneeling to shoot at four fleeing centaurs, their hairy bodies peppered with arrows.[131] This became a standard composition, first on Corinthian vases and then on Attic, the number of centaurs varying.[132] Pholos is normally absent, but on a Corinthian skyphos of the early sixth century, in the Louvre, he stands behind Herakles as the hero hurls firebrands at eleven fleeing centaurs.[133] He appears as well in two sixth-century sculptural representations: in the metopes from the east front of the first Archaic temple of Hera at Foce del Sele,[134] near Paestum, and in the frieze from the temple of Athena at Assos,[135] in the Troad (fig. 18), the first dating about 550 B.C., the second about 550–530. In each case, Pholos has human legs but his equine hindquarters are largely lost.

The Assos frieze is the more traditional, with some sixteen centaurs in flight before Herakles, two of them discovered as recently as 1987.[136] Separate sections are preserved in Assos, Boston, Paris, and Istanbul. Carved in local andesite, the reliefs are unusual in occupying the architrave of a Doric temple that also had sculpted metopes, at least two of which feature galloping centaurs.[137] Other sections of the frieze include heraldic bulls and sphinxes, lions attacking prey, Herakles wrestling Triton, and a symposium with four reclining banqueters drinking wine from a krater. This seemingly incongruous combination of themes has been elegantly deconstructed by Bonna Wescoat. Noting the prominence of the communal wine vessel in both the Pholos scene and the symposion, she interprets the myth of Pholos as a "failed symposion," with the inhospitable centaurs—metaphors for the negative potential in human behavior—thwarting Pholos's efforts to honor Herakles as a guest and thus violating the sacred rules of guest friendship (*xenia*).[138] "The centauromachy is juxtaposed with its purely natural and fully civilized counterparts, represented on the one hand by lions savaging prey and on the other by the congenial symposion."[139] This interpretation does not account for the relief of Herakles and Triton, but in this period we should not expect a consistent intellectual program but rather a paratactic tapestry in which established myths, ancient animal symbolism, and expressions of particular societal values are interwoven.

In the sculptures from Foce del Sele, the missing section of the metope with Pholos may have included the sunken pithos; its appearance doubtless resembled that of the pithos in another metope from the same temple, in which the cowardly Eurystheus hides when Herakles threatens him with the Erymanthean boar. Herakles had been looking for the boar when he encountered Pholos, a fact probably well known to the sculptor. In the fight sequence, three or four centaurs, one to a metope, charge toward Herakles rather than flee. Those closest to the hero's deadly arrows stumble and fall, their flailing limbs presenting a challenge to the sculptor, as they did to the vase-painters.[140] On Attic vases, Herakles uses his club or sword to dispatch the centaurs as often as he does his bow, laying about him on all sides. In the art of Italy and Magna Graecia, however, the bow was the favored weapon, with Herakles standing to one side and shooting at his prey as though they were a herd of buffalo: we find it not only on the metopes from Foce del Sele but also on black-figure vases produced in South Italy, Sicily, and Etruria.[141]

Although literary accounts describe Herakles as killing the centaur Nessos with an arrow, in art he normally attacks Nessos with a club or sword (fig. 19). Consequently, when no woman is represented, depictions of Herakles shooting at a single centaur are more than

likely intended to evoke the fight on Mount Pholoë; the silver gilt lamina in the Metropolitan Museum of Art is an elegant example (cat. no. 32).[142] This is only a rule of thumb, and it would be reckless to stretch it to include such early examples as the fight between archer and centaur on the Geometric seal in Paris (cat. no. 14), just as we cannot assume that the close combat of the Geometric bronze group in the Metropolitan represents Herakles and Nessos (cat. no. 13).

Another metope from Foce del Sele shows Herakles again kneeling to draw his bow, this time accompanied by a gesticulating woman. The most convincing arrangement of the reliefs connects this metope with one of a single centaur charging to the left with a raised branch. If this is correct, the woman must be Herakles' wife, Deianeira, and the centaur is Nessos.[143] The story of Nessos's death and his ultimate revenge on Herakles is the subject of Sophokles' *Trachiniae* and is also told by several other authors.[144] When Herakles and his bride, whom he had won in contest with Acheloos, approached the river Evenus, in Aitolia, the centaur Nessos, a refugee from the rout in Thessaly, offered to carry Deianeira across. The amorous centaur assaulted Deianeira in midstream, but Herakles cut him down with a well-placed arrow. As he lay dying on the bank, Nessos told Deianeira to

Figure 19. Amphora: Herakles killing Nessos. Greek, Protoattic, mid-seventh century B.C. The Metropolitan Museum of Art, Rogers Fund, New York (11.210.1).

Figure 20. Black-figure amphora: Herakles killing Nessos. Greek, Attic, ca. 620–610 B.C., the name-vase of the Nettos Painter. National Archaeological Museum, Athens (1002).

take a vial of his blood, now mixed with the venom of the Hydra, assuring her that it was a powerful love potion that would restore Herakles' affections should he ever forsake her for another woman. Many years later, when Herakles planned to leave her for Iole, Deianeira sent him a robe smeared with the potion, which tortured him with burning agony. Deianeira killed herself in remorse and Herakles built his own funeral pyre on Mount Oita, from which he was snatched by the gods to live alongside them in Olympos.[145]

As the quintessential story of man versus centaur, the Nessos myth has been perceived, rightly or wrongly, in even the earliest centauromachies, including the bronze group in New York and the Geometric seal stone in Paris (cat. nos. 13, 14).[146] Uncertainty is eliminated when the three principal protagonists are present, as they are on fragments of a Protoattic stand from the Argive Heraion, dating to the second quarter of the seventh century:[147] the human-legged Nessos maintains his hold on Deianeira though he is already dying from the arrow in his side; Herakles moves in for the kill, but only his raised sword is

preserved. This may be the earliest certain depiction of the myth, but it is followed very soon after by a grander (h. 108.6 cm.), and better preserved work, an amphora in the Metropolitan Museum of Art that probably served as a grave marker, since the figure decoration is confined to one side (fig. 19).[148] The decoration is in the "black-and-white" style, with the stocky, rubber-limbed figures executed in a technique combining black-figure and outline drawing. The wounded Nessos, painted in black-figure with human legs, has dropped his branch and is falling to his knees. In a gesture of supplication, he reaches out to touch the knee of Herakles, who dismounts from his chariot to seize Nessos by the hair, his sword drawn and ready for the deathblow. The hero's legs are outlined, perhaps to emphasize his humanity in contrast to the bestial centaur. An owl hovers above the scene, a bird of omen. Seated in the chariot, facing backward toward the action, is Deianeira, wrapped in a checkered gown. The arm of the charioteer, perhaps Iolaos, is preserved behind her, holding the reins of the four horses, whose heads rise from their single, conflated body like the blades of a pocketknife. More horses graze on the shoulder of the vase, and on the neck a lion is killing a deer, recalling the combination of heroic and bestial violence on the frieze from Assos.

The somewhat baroque composition of the New York amphora has no real successors. Instead, another mid-seventh-century Protoattic vase, an ovoid krater in Berlin, features a tighter grouping of man and centaur, without Deianeira.[149] Herakles—as he must be—again holds Nessos by the hair as he stabs him with his sword. The same pairing, with variations in postures, appears on contemporary Protocorinthian vases,[150] as well as on ivory reliefs and seals.[151] This swift dispatching of a single centaur by the son of Zeus could be rendered by artists with brutal simplicity and was surely identified with ease by ancient viewers. The inscriptions naming Herakles and "Nettos" (the Attic spelling of Nessos) on the name-vase of the Nettos Painter were already superfluous by the time the amphora was placed on top of a grave in Athens about 620/10 B.C. (fig. 20).[152] The antagonists are confined to a compact space on the neck of the vase while the body is given over to the three Gorgons. The action is more dynamic than in any previous depiction, with Herakles planting his foot on Nessos's back and jerking his head back by the hair. The centaur, whose shaggy beard and bristling moustache are intentionally contrasted with his killer's neatly groomed appearance, touches Herakles on the chin, a pitiable gesture of supplication recalling that on the earlier Protoattic amphora in New York. The figures are drawn in the pure black-figure technique, with no outlining, which seems somehow to impart a new somberness to the action. The yanking of the hair recurs in even more brutal form on an ivory relief from Sparta, in which the composition is quite similar to that of the Nettos amphora, but with Deianeira present.[153]

Similar portrayals of the death of Nessos continued throughout the sixth century, but the iconography never became completely standardized, and we have many versions that include all three of the principal protagonists (cat. no. 37) or that lack either Deianeira (cat. no. 35) or Herakles (cat. no. 36). Nessos is normally the only centaur present, but sometimes others are shown coming to his aid, resulting in a melée confusingly similar to the fight with the centaurs on Mount Pholoë.[154] Although the literary accounts make the poison arrow a central motif in the Nessos myth, in Archaic art Herakles instead normally attacks Nessos with a club or sword. This has led some to suggest that Sophokles may have invented the arrow motif, but there is evidence that it predates the playwright's version.[155] When Deianeira is present she may grapple with Nessos, ride on his back, or stand nearby, sometimes accompanied by her father Oineus (see cat. no. 37), or even by a crowd of onlookers, as on several Tyrrhenian amphorae of the second quarter of the sixth century.[156] In one of the most common compositions, Nessos gallops to the right with Deianeira either on his back or held in his arms, while at the left Herakles charges up from behind, weapon in hand.[157] Sometimes Herakles grabs his wife, but more often he seizes Nessos as he attacks him with club or sword. So common is this arrangement that we recognize the subject even when Deianeira is absent, as was already possible in the earlier vase-paintings of the seventh century.

A red-figure stamnos in Naples, signed by Polygnotos, and another in London, from the same artist's workshop,

are painted with scenes that accord in nearly every way with traditional depictions of Herakles, Nessos, and Deianeira.[158] On the Naples vase, Deianeira is labeled and so is her father Oineus, but the name written near the centaur that assaults her is not Nessos but Dexamenos. Apollodoros (*Bibl.* 2.5.5) says that after cleansing the stables of Augeus, Herakles was entertained by King Dexamenos of Olenos. The centaur Eurytion, who had escaped the massacre on Mount Pholoë,[159] had forced Dexamenos to give him as a bride his daughter Mnesimache, whom some other writers call Hippolyte (Diod. Sic. 4.33) or Deianeira (Hyg. *Fab.* 31.33), as she is on the Naples stamnos. Despite the confused inscriptions, this little-known *parergon* of Herakles must be the subject of the Naples vase and by extension of the London stamnos as well.[160]

By the time these vases were painted in the mid-fifth century, when, as we have seen, the imagery of the Thessalian centauromachy began to be modified, a general sea change is discernable in the iconography of centaurs. Some have detected a new feeling in Sophokles' treatment of Nessos in the *Trachiniae*, as well as in the metopes of the Parthenon, where the centaurs occasionally get the upper hand.[161] Herakles' brutal treatment of Nessos on the Nettos Amphora and in other Archaic representations would have won the centaur no sympathy,[162] but Athenians of the Classical period were conscious of their own hubris in building a powerful empire at the expense of smaller Greek states, and this may be reflected in the more evenhanded treatment of the centauromachy on the Parthenon. The bell-krater by the Eupolis Painter, with the marriage of Cheiron and Chariklo (cat. no. 38), dates to the period when the metopes were being carved. It dwells on a tender moment between husband and bride that emphasizes the centaur's humanity, but at the same time his anatomy finally has been changed to conform to the longstanding Attic practice of representing all other centaurs with four equine legs.[163] The result is paradoxically more "naturalistic," and the romantic scene elicits our empathy and establishes an emotional connection with the race of centaurs that would have been impossible a generation or two before, as late as the temple of Zeus at Olympia.

From depicting the wedding of a centaur, it was but a small step to the first representation of a female centaur. This occurred at the end of the fifth century when Zeuxis painted a celebrated panel of a centauress nursing her children, one suckling from one of her human breasts, the other from her mare's teat. In Lucian's lengthy description,[164] he says that the top half of the centauress was that of a very beautiful woman, excepting only her equine ears, and he makes a point of noting that Zeuxis's audience, while appreciative of the painting's aesthetic qualities, was even more struck by the strangeness of the idea and the freshness of the sentiment, which were quite unprecedented.

When the horse-demons of legend could become mere mutable motifs in the repertory of a sophisticated artist like Zeuxis, and the gods themselves serve as pliable metaphors for Euripides and the sophists, there is no question that we are entering a new and more skeptical era. Centaurs continued uninterrupted in Hellenistic and Roman art, either reduced to ornament or imbued with new symbolism remote from their Archaic origins. The dispassionate Galen looked on them as a curious problem in anatomy,[165] while Aelian wonders aloud if the old legends about creatures who are half horse and half human were not simply born of "rumour, more ductile than any wax, and more credulous."[166] Philostratus salaciously contemplates the idea of female centaurs, noting that "the delicacy of their female form gains in strength when the horse is seen in union with it."[167] As useful vehicles of metaphor—they served Freud as a symbol of the wedding of Id and Ego—centaurs continue to occupy a place in our imagination. As for their original significance for the Greeks, we can do no more than review the fragmentary evidence and speculate. In the plains of Thessaly and Euboia, where a man's horses defined his worth, centaurs may have been bearers of aristocratic values. The heroes of legend needed worthy foes, otherworldly creatures endowed with preternatural power. Their initial form suggested by foreign models, the centaurs rapidly took their place in the renewed figural imagery of Iron Age Greece, slipping into established narratives and inspiring new tales of courage, hubris, and violent desire.

Figure 21. Black-figure neck-amphora: satyr with Dionysos and Ariadne. Greek, Attic, ca. 530 B.C., in the manner of the Lysippides Painter. Princeton University Art Museum, museum purchase, Classical Purchase Fund (y1987-55).

## THE SATYRS

The imagery of satyrs, perhaps born in a lighter corner of the Greek imagination than that which produced the centaurs, also underwent a change in the fifth century.[168] Satyr children had appeared early in the century, and in the Classical period there was an increasing number of teenage satyrs, beardless and bald, whose amorous interest in the maenads seems somehow natural and appropriate. In the century after the Peloponnesian War, a considerable change in Dionysiac imagery took place that included a shift to a more youthful, beardless Dionysos and a concomitant favoring of youthful satyrs. Pans and "paniskoi," beardless young Pans with the horns and legs of goats, began to intrude in Dionysiac scenes, even joining the bearded satyrs in pursuit of the maenads.[169] This set the stage for the eventual conflation of Pan and the satyrs, who by Roman times had come to be thought of as part goat. These are deep waters, requiring a separate study; here we are concerned with the role of satyrs in early Greek art, when their horsey nature was not in question.

The form and character of satyrs are well known. Satyrs are so plentiful in Attic vase-painting of the Archaic period that no accurate count of them can be made, as new examples are constantly coming to light. The satyr on a black-figure neck-amphora in Princeton, of about 530 B.C., is typical (fig. 21).[170] The skin over his shoulder contains wine, and indeed the wine god Dionysos is himself present, standing with his bride Ariadne. The satyr has the body of a nude man but the long ears and tail of a horse. His expressive features emphasize his bestiality: mouth open, nose large and rounded, forehead bulging slightly. In red-figure, satyrs often are depicted as bald (e.g., cat. no. 62), but the hair and beard of this satyr are long and full, more so than is customary in depictions of human males. These deviations from the ideal are intentional, for from their earliest appearance, satyrs were conceived as representing the opposite of the Greek ideal of youthful, straight-nosed, masculine beauty, just as their behavior was considered the antithesis of *sophrosyne*, the ideal standard of restraint, moderation, and sober self-control.[171] It is a mistake to think of satyrs merely as expressions of the male libido

Figure 22. Red-figure amphora: charging satyr. Greek, Attic, ca. 490 B.C., attributed to the Flying-Angel Painter. Museo Nazionale di Villa Giulia, Rome.

Figure 23. Statuette of a satyr. Greek, Laconian, found in Spain, third quarter of the sixth century B.C., bronze. Musée du Louvre, Paris (MNC 2375).

or as representing man's natural and healthy desire to live freely in a state of nature without the encumbrance of societal constraints. Instead, satyrs functioned as cautionary models of antisocial irresponsibility. Cowardly, thieving, mischievous, and sexually frustrated, their antics were amusing but not to be emulated. As François Lissarrague has put it, the "race of satyrs . . . is not an exaggerated reflection of the world of men but rather a countermodel to humanity."[172]

Like most Attic satyrs, the one in Princeton has human legs and feet, but on rare occasions the vase-painters represent them with the legs and hooves of horses.[173] The two types are sometimes shown together,[174] suggesting that the difference was one of artistic whim and does not reflect any meaningful distinction. A third type occurs in East Greece, where satyrs, like centaurs, often are represented with human legs ending in hooves.[175]

On a red-figure amphora in Rome, of about 490 B.C., attributed to the Flying-Angel Painter, the swordsman on

one side of the vase prepares to fight the satyr on the other side, who is charging toward him (fig. 22).[176] With both hands, the satyr raises a small tree, the favored weapon of the centaurs. Neither the tree nor the bravery with which it is wielded is a typical attribute of satyrs. They may be sufficiently overcome by lust to attack a woman, or even a goddess, as they do on the metopes at Foce del Sele, where their assault on Hera is foiled by Herakles,[177] but they normally shy away from combat with armed warriors. The exception is when they assist Dionysos in the battle with the giants.[178] The swordsman on the Rome vase, however, wears a chlamys and petasos, unusual garb for a giant. On another vase, a column-krater formerly in the art market, the Flying-Angel Painter depicted a satyr attacking with a phallos-staff, but the reverse is occupied by a harmless reveler, a komast. The wild hair and equine ear of the satyr in Rome are characteristic of the breed, but the usual tail is conspicuously absent. We might be tempted to wonder if this is a satyr at all: perhaps the artist meant to paint a centaur and simply forgot to add the equine body in the back. But except for Cheiron, Attic centaurs nearly always have four equine legs, and this fellow has the legs and feet of a man. It is highly unlikely that an Attic centaur would loose his equine hindquarters and gain human legs at the same time.[179]

The lack of a tail on the satyr in Rome is unusual but not unprecedented.[180] Satyrs without tails are the rule in some regions, especially in Laconia, where a number of fine bronze statuettes of satyrs were produced in the sixth century.[181] A satyr now in the Louvre was found in Spain (fig. 23),[182] but unlike the bronze centaur in Madrid (cat. no. 25), which is probably a local product, this is a Spartan import. Like the bronze volute-kraters found in France and Macedonia, and the statuettes of centaurs from the Athenian Acropolis (fig. 6; cat. no. 23), the satyr testifies to the reputation and widespread popularity of Laconian bronzes in this period. The bronze satyr in the exhibition (cat. no. 56), while not certainly Laconian, is broadly Peloponnesian in style but could have been made in a South Italian center such as Taras

or Sybaris.[183] The figure's flattened physique suggests that it was a decorative adjunct to a vessel or utensil, a function more often met by more apotropaic *Mischwesen*, like Gorgons and sphinxes.

On the François Vase, Kleitias represented the Return of Hephaistos to Olympos, with the god riding on a mule preceded by Dionysos and followed by horse-legged satyrs, who in this instance are labeled as *silenoi* (fig. 24).[184] Among writers of the Archaic and Classical periods, satyrs (*satyroi*) and silenoi were interchangeable terms, referring to the same half-human, half-horse creatures. Satyrs, "creatures worthless and unfit for work," are first mentioned in a fragment of the post-Hesiodic *Catalogue of Women*, which states that they, along with the Kouretes and the mountain nymphs, were the offspring of Hekateros and the daughter of Phoroneus.[185] Surprisingly, the word *satyros* does not recur in surviving literature until Euripides,[186] unless one counts a fragmentary inscription of about 500 B.C. on a red-figure cup by the Ambrosios Painter.[187] Silenoi are first mentioned in the seventh-century Homeric *Hymn to Aphrodite*, where

Figure 24. The François Vase, black-figure volute-krater: the Return of Hephaistos.
Greek, Attic, ca. 570 B.C., signed by Ergotimos and Kleitias. Museo Archeologico Nazionale, Florence (4209).

Figure 25. Krater: bearded figure wielding stones. Greek, Protoattic, mid-seventh century B.C. Antikensammlung, Staatliche Museen zu Berlin–Preussischer Kulturbesitz (A 33). After CVA Berlin 1, Germany 2, pl. 20.

they are said to mate with the mountain nymphs in the depths of pleasant caves.[188] More than a century passes before Herodotos refers both to the contest between Apollo and the silenos Marsyas (Hdt. 7.26.), and to the capture of the wise satyr Silenos by the Phrygian king Midas (see below).[189] Both of these myths are set in Asia Minor, suggesting a possible Ionian origin for the name *silenos*.[190] There is no question, however, that by the fifth century, silenoi and satyroi were interchangable terms in Athens. In Plato's *Symposium*, Alkibiades compares Sokrates' appearance both to the silenoi made by the sculptors and to the satyr Marsyas,[191] whom Pausanias, as we have already have seen, refers to as a silenos. Pausanias agrees with Herodotos in calling Marsyas a silenos,[192] but Herodotos is contradicted by Xenophon when he mentions the spring where "Midas caught the satyr" (Xen. *An.* 1.2.13). Silenoi eventually came to be the designation reserved for satyrs of advanced age (Paus. 1.23.6), a distinction possibly owing to the example of satyr plays,[193] where it is frequently implied that the old, white-haired Pappasilenos, is the father of the satyrs in the chorus (e.g., Eur. *Cyc.* 82).

The silenoi on the François Vase, which for the sake of consistency I shall hereafter call satyrs, are grotesquely ithyphallic, and the artist was at pains to carefully distinguish the clearly human form of their phalloi from that of Hephaistos's mule. The propinquity of the satyr's phallos to the rump of the mule is suggestive, and in fact there are numerous depictions of satyrs mating with donkeys and

mules, even when they are being ridden by Dionysos or Hephaistos.[194] They also copulate with deer, goats, and other animals, and when these are not available, may even fall upon one another, as on the fragment of a black-figure dinos in the exhibition, attributed to Sophilos (cat. no. 53). The unabashed lustiness of the satyrs is a function of their role as negative role models, for in Greek art, ideal nude males are commonly represented with noticeably short, thin penises.[195]

The randiness of the satyrs is in one sense a more fundamental character trait than their thirst for wine, for it is their tumescence that distinguishes the earliest satyrs from their human counterparts and from the "padded dancers"[196] and "wild men" with whom they often are confused. The wild men in question are so called because they are covered with hair, like the curious figure tucked beneath the handle of a mid-seventh-century Protoattic krater in Berlin (fig. 25).[197] Painted black, in contrast to the figures in the principal scene where Orestes murders Agamemnon, he nonetheless is bearded like them and is garbed in the same short breeches. In either hand he wields what are probably stones, weapons associated more often with centaurs. Two similar figures, also thowing stones, are under the handle on the opposite side, but their bodies are not hairy. The figure's genitals are not represented, and there seems no compelling reason to believe, as often has been suggested, that he is some kind of "proto-satyr."[198] In fact, we have no idea who he is, but as a satyr he is no more convincing than the majority of hairy wild men who turn up here and there in the late seventh and early sixth centuries, some of whom, at least, are impressively ithyphallic.[199]

The fragment by Sophilos (cat. no. 53) dates to about 580 B.C., at least a decade before the François Vase. The latter is not only the earliest depiction of the Return of Hephaistos but also the earliest known association of the satyrs with Dionysos. Earlier satyrs seem to have had no connection with the god.[200] They are more interested in sex, a subject that seldom touches Dionysos directly. On another fragment by Sophilos, in Istanbul,[201] one of these early, pre-Dionysiac satyrs, again covered with hair and sexually aroused, roughly grabs a woman by the arm. A contemporary vase from the Athenian Agora shows an

Figure 26. Black-figure amphora: satyrs at the vintage. Greek, Attic, probably from Vulci,
ca. 540 B.C., attributed to the Amasis Painter.  Martin von Wagner Museum der Universität Würzburg (265).

Figure 27. Red-figure kylix: two satyrs approaching a sleeping maenad. Greek, Attic, ca. 490 B.C., attributed to Makron. Museum of Fine Arts, Boston, Henry Lillie Pierce Fund (01.8072).

even hairier satyr in full pursuit of another woman, who, like her sister in Istanbul, is surely a nymph.[202] The nymphs are identified by an inscription on the François Vase, where one of them is again the object of a satyr's violent passion. The nymph on an earlier lekythos in Buffalo flees from a satyr who pursues her on muleback,[203] which makes one wonder if the terracotta statuette in the exhibition of a satyr riding a mule is giving us the whole story (cat. no. 55).

After Kleitias's masterful portrayal of the Return of Hephaistos, the satyrs and nymphs did, indeed, become closely associated with Dionysos and remained with him for centuries thereafter. On innumerable vases they form his riotous entourage, the *thiasos*—dancing, playing the pipes, pouring wine, reeling to and fro in drunken ecstasy. The subject was one of inexhaustible popularity, not least among the Etruscans, who imported Attic vases to Italy by the thousands, making them an integral component of their funerary offerings.[204] On an amphora by the Amasis Painter, probably found in an Etruscan tomb in Vulci but now in Würzburg (fig. 26),[205] the satyrs are busy bringing in their master's vintage, picking the grapes from the vine and trampling them in a basket, the sweet juice flowing into a sunken pithos like the one in the cave of Pholos (cf. cat. no. 29).

When they are not looking for wine, the satyrs continue their quest for sex. By the middle of the sixth century, the nymphs largely give way to the maenads, idealized representations of mortal female worshipers of Dionysos who convene to drink themselves into a fit of madness and then roam the hills, tearing small animals to pieces.[206] They, too, dance attendance on Dionysos, and the decoration of many an Attic vase consists of the god standing amid a small crowd of satyrs, maenads, or both (e.g., cat. no. 29). The satyrs pursue the maenads as relentlessly as they did the nymphs and with equal lack of success, for it is notorious that satyrs, for all their excessive sexuality, are almost never shown consummating their lust.[207] On a cup in Boston, attributed to Makron (fig. 27), two ithyphallic satyrs approach a sleeping maenad, identified by her thyrsos, a fennel wand tipped with ivy.[208] She leans against a rock fast asleep, oblivious to the satyr who has raised her skirt and is spreading her legs. On the other side of the cup, the maenad awakes just in time to fight off her attackers, whose desires are once again frustrated. This subject was repeated several times on other cups, and we are left to wonder what satisfaction it gave the painter or his customers. Was it perhaps a charm against poor sexual performance by the drinker,

Figure 28. Tondo of a red-figure kylix: maenad scourging a satyr. Greek, Attic, ca. 500–490 B.C., signed by Douris. Private collection.

après symposium, transferring onto the satyrs yet another bad character trait, as an Athenian male would have regarded it, and thus reinforcing the line between the drinker and his negative alter ego? It is impossible to say, but part of the charm of Attic vases—and of satyrs—is the opportunity they afford for such speculation.

When Makron painted the cup in Boston, in the first decade of the fifth century, the maenads were beginning to show even more determination to resist the importunity of the satyrs; their defense becomes doughty, even violent.[209] In the tondo of a cup signed by Douris, in a privatecollection, the tables have turned completely (fig. 28).[210] A maenad grabs a satyr by his beard as she scourges him with a whip. The hapless satyr has fallen to one knee, howling in terror and raising his hands in supplication. On the exterior of the cup, other satyrs also get their comeuppance as maenads whip them, pull their tails, and pound them with thyrsoi. It is a Greek woman's fantasy, painted by a man, and again one wonders if the idea was not to exalt liberated women but rather to lump them together with satyrs, the anti-paragons of male behavior.

Beginning in the late sixth century and throughout the fifth, Attic vase-painters moved beyond repetitive scenes of the Dionysiac thiasos to portray satyrs in more unusual situations. Sometimes they mimic human behavior, as when the satyrs on a black-figure lekythos in the exhibition dance to the pipes while holding peltae, light infantry shields (cat. no. 60). They are dancing a pyrrhic, a ritual war dance, like those performed by ranks of young warriors at civic festivals. Since satyrs were not models of exemplary citizenship but rather functioned as cautionary archetypes of antisocial irresponsibility, this behavior can only be a parody. It is not clear, however, whether it was dreamed up by the vase-painter or inspired by the satyr mummery—men dressed in masks and hairy costumes with tails and pendulous phalloi—that traditionally accompanied the worship of Dionysos in Attica.

In addition to taking on human roles—chef, sailor, warrior, athlete—satyrs of the Late Archaic and Early Classical periods are sometimes shown interacting with gods and heroes in mythological situations where they otherwise are out of place. White-haired satyrs carrying scepters listen to the riddle of the Sphinx;[211] an old satyr leaning on a cane is conducted toward the boiling cauldron by a daughter of Pelias;[212] a group of satyrs carrying hammers pound the ground to release Persephone from the earth.[213] These scenes and others like them have been explained as reflecting or actually illustrating contemporary satyr plays, comic parodies of myth written by the great playwrights of the age and produced in association with dramatic trilogies.[214] Nearly all such plays have been lost except for a few fragments, but dozens of titles survive, offering a constant temptation to scholars wishing to draw connections between surviving artistic representations and equally fragmentary literary remains. The influence of satyr drama is manifest in scenes where satyrs are represented wearing the tail, mock phallus, and short breeches (*perizoma*) of satyr actors, as they do on a red-figure hydria in Boston, attributed to the Leningrad Painter (fig. 29).[215] A chorus of five satyrs in masks and breeches dances about with the components of a couch or throne, which they apparently are in the process of erecting. An aulos player in formal attire sets them a tune, while a man in a himation, possibly the producer, the *choregos*, stands at the far right. It has been suggested that the scene derives from the *Thalamopoioi*, a lost play, possibly satyric, by Aischylos, but this is much debated.[216]

The vast majority of painted satyrs are not depicted in costume, but Guy Hedreen has argued that these, too, represent satyr actors, and that even black-figure satyrs on vases predating the introduction of formal satyr plays at the end of the sixth century are based on satyric performances connected with the worship of Dionysos. I have argued elsewhere against this point of view,[217] which gives too little credit to the imagination of the vase-painters and their clientele. Satyr performances there undoubtedly were, and in clear cases of mythic parody involving satyrs the costumes of the actors need not be represented overtly. But the same folk belief in wild, woodland spirits that provided the initial impetus for satyr mummery in cult surely also must have sufficed to bring these same creatures to life in vase-painting. The majority of painted satyrs are not pictures of performances: they are pictures of satyrs.

Beyond their role in cult and theater, there also were myths associated with satyrs, but these usually are local

Figure 29. Red-figure hydria: satyr actors. Greek, Attic, ca. 470 – 460 B.C., attributed to the Leningrad Painter. Museum of Fine Arts, Boston, Francis Bartlett Donation (03.788).

tales concerning the sprite of a particular valley, spring, or wood. The Danaid Amymone was accosted by a satyr as she went to the spring at Lerna and was rescued by Poseidon (Apollod. *Bibl.* 2.1.4). A storm-tossed mariner told of sailing to the Island of Satyrs, whose lusty inhabitants seized and tortured women (Paus.1.23.7). Before he himself was killed by Hermes, the multi-eyed Argos was said to have killed a satyr who stole the cattle of the Arcadians (Apollod. *Bibl.* 2.1.2). Some of these local tales achieved a wider circulation, like that of the satyr Marsyas, who found the pipes discarded by Athena and bragged that his music surpassed even that of Apollo.[218] The god defeated Marysas in a musical contest and then skinned him alive to punish his hubris, both episodes becoming popular subjects in Hellenistic and Roman art.[219] The presumed setting of the story was the banks of the River Marsyas, a tributary of the Maeander, in Asia Minor; the Ionians of Kelainai, nearby, revered Marsyas as a protector of their city (Paus. 10.30.2).

The name *Silenos* attached to a particular satyr who had a separate identity as a local god or daimon in Asia Minor, long before his later association with Dionysos. Like Marsyas, the first mention of him is in Herodotos,[220] but there are a number of sixth-century vase-paintings depicting his capture by the Phrygian king Midas; the earliest, of about 565 B.C., is signed by Ergotimos, the potter of the François Vase.[221] Silenos was renowned for his wisdom, a curious trait in a satyr, and Midas wanted his secrets. Luring him to a spring or fountain by mixing wine with the water, Midas's henchmen captured Silenos and took him before the king. Each episode of the story was depicted by the vase-painters, not only in Athens, but also in Sparta and Chios.[222] In Roman times, the fat old Silenos was thought of as the personal attendant and caretaker of Dionysos (Diod. 4.4.3 – 4), but this figure is not connected with the original Silenos, and instead is likely descended from the Pappasilenos of the satyr plays.

Figure 30. Red-figure chous: maenad offering wine to a satyr toddler.
Greek, Attic, ca. 440 B.C., attributed to the Phiale Painter.
Michael C. Carlos Museum, Emory University, Atlanta (2001.1.1).

The gradual change in satyr iconography mentioned earlier began in the fifth century B.C. as part of the broader movement from an Archaic to a Classical sensibility, with the growth of rational philosophy and the retreading and retirement of old motifs in art. Along with the female centaur of Zeuxis, we now have satyr "families," like the charming scene on a jug (*chous*) in Atlanta, of about 440 B.C., attributed to the Phiale Painter (fig. 30).[223] A motherly maenad, a fawn skin draped over her peplos, offers a small chous of wine to a toddler whose tail, pointed ears, and bald pate identify him as a satyr. Similar scenes with mortal children appear on other jugs of this shape, which are associated with the Anthesteria, a festival of Dionysos at which children were given miniature jugs appropriate to their age.[224] The Phiale Painter, who painted several satyr children,[225] may have had a special interest in Dionysiac cult. The scene on a krater in Paris, with a maenad following a satyr boy carrying a chair, has been interpreted as the Basilinna, the wife of a priestly magistrate, on her way to be the ritual bride of Dionysos.[226] A stamnos in Warsaw, also by the Phiale

Painter, shows a group of women, presumably maenads, who have been ladling wine from a stamnos, a scene perhaps connected with the Lenaia festival.[227] One of them cradles an infant satyr, who could be the brother of the child in Atlanta.

In time and temperament, these harmless satyr tots seem a world away from their horse-demon predecessors. The early satyrs, mulishly independent of Dionysos, seem to have come into being not in response to the demands of narrative but rather to represent a type of antisocial male misbehavior. Some of the earliest satyrs appear on dinoi, the centerpieces at upperclass drinking parties where a degree of drunkenness was expected but its less pleasant consequences not necessarily tolerated. As with the centaurs, the partly human nature of the satyrs exempted them from duty alongside the sphinxes and sirens relegated to the animal friezes on early Attic vases. After the satyrs were summoned by Kleitias to join for the first time the train of Dionysos, their subsequent association with the wine god was so natural and appropriate as to never again be in doubt. In parallel with these developments in art, satyr mummery became an integral part of rustic Dionysiac cult. It is possible that the shenanigans of village "satyrs" at rural festivals were in part lampoons on the pretensions of the horse-owning aristocracy. These horse-demons were everything the brave and haughty centaurs were not, and it was thus as anti-paragons that satyrs were co-opted and given form by Attic vase-painters who, at least in the early sixth century, worked largely in the service of the elite. It was then, before the huge expansion of Attic exports and the mass production of Dionysiac images for the Italian market, that the identity of the satyrs was established. As creatures combining the good and bad elements of horses and humans, centaurs and satyrs were opposite sides of the same coin. Whatever their origins and initial significance, their place in the imagination of the Greeks and in the fantasies of their cultural descendants eventually evolved and faded but never completely passed away.

## Notes

1  On satyrs, mules, and donkeys, see Padgett 2000.

2  See Eaverly 1995, 47–56 and bibliography.

3  What follows condenses a very complex subject; see Ducrey 1985; Bugh 1988; Lissarrague 1990B, 191–231; Hanson 1991; Snodgrass 1993. It is interesting that what may be the earliest shield device on an Attic vase (LGIIB) is a horse: see Tölle 1963, 648, fig. 5.

4  Princeton 1997–54: *Record* 57.1 (1998), 195. For Horse-head amphorae, see *ABV* 15–17, 679; *Paralipomena* 9–10; *BAdd²* 4–6; Picozzi 1971; Birchall 1972.

5  For Panathenaic prize amphorae, see Beazley 1986, 81–92; Neils 1992, 29–51; Bentz 1998.

6  Cf. a red-figure ram's-head rhyton in the manner of the Sotades Painter: Athens, Nat. Mus. 10461 (*ARV²* 768.27; Wolters and Bruns 1940, pl. 23.1).

7  The literature on centaurs is immense, but general studies are few. The lists and classifications of Baur (1912) were superceded and augmented by Schiffler (1976), who built on the work of Fittschen (1969, 88–128). More recent bibliography and copious illustrations are to be found in *LIMC* 8 (1987), 671–721, pls. 416–81, s.v. "Kentauroi et Kentaurides" (Leventopoulou et al.). See also *Neue Paulys* 6 (1999), 413–15, s.v. "Kentauren" (Walde and Ley).

8  This is an old debate, and one cannot cite every opinion pro and con. Baur (1912, 135), without real evidence, posited a Hittite origin for centaurs, while Demargne (1929, 125–28) believed they were introduced from the Near East via Cyprus or Rhodes. Karageorghis (1966, 169) and Demetriou (1989, 52) emphasized the role of Cyprus. Nilsson (1932, 158), whose opinion was influential, rejected an eastern origin because there were no close oriental prototypes, and this point of view has persisted in many quarters (e.g., Kirk 1970, 157), even as others have continued to try to construct a chain of influence from East to West (e.g., Arnold 1972).

9  See Powell 1997; Petropoulos 2001, 18. It has been suggested that the discovery of the fossil remains of large prehistoric animals provided an impetus for tales and images of monsters, such as griffins (Mayor 2000). Perhaps, but every literary or visual motif does not require a corporeal source of inspiration. The human fears that give form to monsters, in particular, have no need of such tangible catalysts: a bump in the night is sufficient.

10  E.g., Frankfort 1939, 198, pls. XXXIf, XXXIVd; Porada 1948, pl. CXIII, no. 749E; Smith 1965, 25, 147, figs. 4b, 4d. See also Fittschen 1969, 89 n. 458; *RLA* 5, 569–70, s.v. "Kentaur" (Calmeyer).

11  King 1912, pl. XXIX; Baur 1912, 2–3, no. 2; Arnold 1972, 120–21; Seidl 1989, 176–78 (listing all previously known oriental centaurs). The archer on a *kudurru* of Nebuchadnezzar I has a human torso on the body of a scorpion: Collon 1995, 121, fig. 98.

12  I. M. Shear (2002, 151), in arguing for the oral transmission of the concept of the centaur from Mycenaean times, specifically points to the absence of wings and scorpion tails on early Greek centaurs as a reason for doubting a Near Eastern origin. Demetriou (1989, 52), in contrast, believes "the scorpion's tails and the wings . . . were discarded by the Cypriots," before passing on the centaur concept to mainland Greece. Morris (1984, 66 n. 108) argues that Greek artists transformed the wings into the branches commonly carried by centaurs, but it is not clear why they would have had more trouble recognizing them as wings than we do, or, if recognizing them, why they would have felt compelled to transform them into anything at all, instead of simply discarding them, which is what they did from the very beginning. (For the few exceptions, see n. 42 below.)

13  This seems obvious if one compares such examples as the Herakles on the Assos relief (fig. 18) or a bronze statuette of Herakles in Boston (98.657: Comstock and Vermeule 1971, 23, no. 21) with figures like the bowman on the Syro-Phoenician bowl in Princeton (cat. no. 9) or the archer on an engraved Luristan situla in Los Angeles (M.76.97.357: Moorey et al. 1981, 87, no. 431).

14  See the comments by Childs under cat. no. 12.

15  Melos 592: E. French, in Renfrew et al. 1985, 223, 229, fig. 6.12, pls. 36b, 37a–b, d; Lebessi 1996, 148–49, pl. 54. French noted the similarity of the figure's painted decoration to that of the Lefkandi Centaur but reconstructed it with a clay prop instead of an animal's body. Lebessi makes the case for restoring it as a centaur, a suggestion first proposed by P. Warren (*Antiquity* 60 [1986], 156) in a review of Renfrew et al. 1985.

16  Aleppo 8315: Shear 2002, pl. 3a–c. Shear (148, pl. 3e–f) identifies part of a second such figure among the published Mycenaean figurines from Ugarit (Courtois 1978, fig. 55, no. 5).

17  The same could be said of the "centaur" on a Middle Minoan prism-seal of about 2000 B.C., which certainly had no successors, whatever its identity: see Baur 1912, no. 1, fig. 1; Evans 1909, 77, fig. 5b; see also the analysis by V. E. G. Kenna in an addendum to Karageorghis 1966, 170–72. Boardman (1963, 54–55) and Kenna (ibid. 172–73) believe the "centaurs" identified on an LHIII stone from Prosymna (Blegen 1937, 277–78, fig. 589) are actually goats, though Shear (2002, 148 n. 15) is not fully convinced.

18  Kourou 1991, 113–14, pls. XXVI.2, XXVIII.1.

19  Kourou 1991, 112, fig. 1. The figure stands before a tree, the weapon of choice for centaurs, which may have influenced some to read more into this stick figure than it deserves.

20  Kos 1104: Guggisberg 1996, 121–22, no. 418, pl. 30.2.

21  Karageorghis 1966, pl. XXIa.

22  Desborough, Nicholls, and Popham 1970, 28.

23  Desborough, Nicholls, and Popham 1970, 29. For the centaurs from Ayia Irini, see Karageorghis 1966, 164–66, pls. XXIII–XXIV; Karageorghis 1993a, 69; Karageorghis 1996, 1, 3–6, figs. 2–3, pls. II–IV. See also the discussion by Demetriou (1989, 51–52).

24  Paris, Louvre AM 961: Schiffler 1976, 284, cat. Z 1; Karageorghis 1991b; Karageorghis 1998, 41, fig. 14.

25  Eretria 8620: the fullest description is Desborough, Nicholls, and

Popham 1970. See also Arnold 1972, 93, no. 29; Schiffler 1976, 77–80, 279, cat. EU-S 1; *Human Figure* 1987, 58–60, no. 1; Popham, Sackett, and Themelis 1980, 169–70, 344–45; *LIMC* 8, 675, no. 20, pl. 417, s.v. "Kentauroi et Kentaurides"; Lebessi 1996, pls. 50, 53; Shear 2002, 149, pl. 4a–b. Lebessi's arguments (1996) for a strong Cretan influence on the style of the Lefkandi Centaur are based on very slender evidence.

26 V. Desborough, in Popham, Sackett, and Themelis 1980, 345. For a detail, see Lebessi 1996, pl. 53D. For the story, see Apollod. *Bibl.* 2.5.4. Lebessi (1996, 149–50) embraces the identification as Cheiron, which she believes explains why the figure was so prized that its broken pieces were placed in the graves of two separate individuals, for it "could have been prized only if it was charged with an ideological message referring to an association developed during the lifetime of the [buried] individuals." The association she has in mind is that of *erastes* and *eromenos* on the Cretan model, with Cheiron, the teacher of heroes, the ultimate example of the "mature teacher–young student" paradigm. This is an elegant argument, but the evidence she marshals of ostensible Cretan stylistic influence on the centaur is not compelling.

27 New York 17.190.2072: see the description and bibliography in cat. no. 13.

28 For Geometric bronze horses, see Herrmann 1964, 20–32; Zimmermann 1989.

29 I know of only six Geometric bronze horsemen. Two, in the same private collection, are Peloponnesian in style: a small horse and rider (Mitten and Doeringer 1967, 35, no. 14) and a larger, helmeted rider who has lost his mount (unpublished). The other four examples, of which only one is published, are Northern Greek: two in the private collection mentioned above; another, in the art market, who carries a pelta and spear; and Copenhagen, Ny Carlsberg I.N. 3359 (Christiansen 1992, 50–51, no. 17). There are a few bronze statuettes of women riding sidesaddle, presumably on mules or donkeys (Schweitzer 1971, pls. 194–96).

30 Athens, Nat. Mus. 6188, from Olympia (Br. 5073: Baur 1912, 78–79, no. 202, fig. 14; Casson 1922, 210, fig. 3a; Herrmann 1964, 43, figs. 26–27; Schiffler 1976, 320, cat. V 12) and Athens, Nat. Mus. 14495 (Schiffler 1976, 173 [drawing], 320, cat. V 13). An otherwise unremarkable Geometric bronze horse, now in a private collection, has a deeply cut intaglio of a centaur on the underside of the base plate: Basel, Jean-David Cahn, A.G., illustrated brochure for the TEFAF Fair, Maastricht, March 14–23, 2003.

31 An unpublished tankard in Florence that Rombos (1988, 420, no. 63) attributes to the Hirschfeld Painter (LGIb, ca. 760–730 B.C.) is not Attic but rather the product of a workshop of immigrant Greek vase-painters in Vulci, active at the end of the eighth century (see F. Canciani, in Martelli 1987, 9–15, 66–76). For centaurs on Attic LGII vases, see Schiffler 1976, 243–44, pl. 1; Coldstream 1977, 118, fig. 36b, 354; *LIMC* 8, 674, nos. 3, 4, 6, pl. 416, s.v. "Kentauroi et Kentaurides."

32 See Schweitzer 1971, 307 n. 42, no. 26, pls. 50, 64.

33 E.g., Karlsruhe 60/12 (Thimme 1960, 58, fig. 12) and a hydria neck in Athens (Goulandris Museum, Polites 92: Papadopoulou-Kanellopoulou 1989, 50–52, no. 25).

34 E.g., Berlin 31006 (*CVA* Berlin 1, Germany 2, pl. 41.1; Boardman 1998, fig. 197); Geneva, G. Ortiz Collection (Beazley 1986, pl. 4.1; Van Gelder 1994). Processions of centaurs continue on Middle Protoattic vases: e.g., a fragmentary krater by the Oresteia Painter (Athens, Kerameikos Mus. 98: Morris 1984, 63, pl. 14).

35 Paris, Louvre CA 3256: Kourou 1991, pl. XXVII.4 ("Early Proto-attic"); Boardman 1998, fig. 70 ("LGIIb").

36 See the reconstruction in Fittschen 1969, fig. 16.

37 Richter 1930a, 337; Schweitzer 1971, 150–51, fig. 185.

38 On an amphora in Copenhagen (Nat. Mus. 7029), with a file of branch-carrying centaurs on the belly, a panel on the neck features a centaur carrying a pair of branches confronted by a man holding two branches of his own: the effect is more fan dance than fight: see Webster 1955, 49, fig. 53; *CVA* Copenhagen 2, Denmark 2, pl. 73.3; *LIMC* 8, 682, no. 127, pl. 422, s.v. "Kentauroi et Kentaurides." Schweitzer (1971, 47) and Cook (1934–35, 169) called the tableau in Copenhagen a fight, but men do not fight with branches. Webster (1955, 49) called it "a peaceful meeting, such as Peleus with Cheiron." On the opposite side of the neck, two centaurs face one another, each holding a branch in one hand and sharing a third branch in the other, as though participating in a dance (cf. the dancers with branches on Tübingen B4: Akurgal 1966, 197, pl. 62).

39 See Snodgrass 1998; Petropoulos 2001.

40 Fittschen 1969, 88–128. Schiffler (1976, 161) rightly takes issue with this division.

41 Berlin GI 310: Baur 1912, 5–6, no. 5, fig. 3; Ohly 1953, 35, cat. A 21, fig. 20; Schiffler 1976, 265, cat. A-S 2; *LIMC* 8, 680, no. 109, pl. 421, s.v. "Kentauroi et Kentaurides." Another early example of a centaur with equine forelegs occurs on an eighth-century White Painted III (CG III) jug from Cyprus (Nicosia 1985/X-19/1: Karageorghis 1986, 51–52, pl. X.5). The centaur incised on an early-seventh-century tripod ornament from Dodona has human forelegs, but they are carefully stippled with hair like the horse body behind (Athens, Nat. Mus. Karapanos 95; Carapanos 1878, 195, pl. XIX.5).

42 E.g., Athens, Nat. Mus. 894: Schweitzer 1971, pl. 65; Arnold 1972, 82–90, no. 28; Boardman 1998, fig. 72. Boardman (p. 27) calls the creatures on this LGIIb bowl "sphinxes which seem to have horse-legs like centaurs," but sphinxes normally do not have arms. There is no question of the winged centaur on the Early Protoattic hydria Athens BS 179 being a sphinx, for it has both human arms and forelegs: see Brokaw 1963, 71, Beil. 34.5; *LIMC* 8, 700, no. 345, pl. 455, s.v. "Kentauroi et Kentaurides." See also the discussion in Kourou 1991, 120.

43 Geneva, G. Ortiz Collection: Beazley 1986, pl. 2; Van Gelder 1994. Unlike the Ortiz centaur, the lion-centaur on an Early Protoattic stemmed dish in the British Museum has a lion's feline body (London, Brit. Mus. 1910.6-16.1: Kourou 1991, 120, pl. XXVII.6).

44 For Boardman's Gorgon-horse Group, see Boardman 1968, 27–30, pl. II, nos. 31–37. Most are carnelian scarabs.

45 Paris, Louvre CA 795: Boardman 1967, 93, fig. 53; *LIMC* 4 (1988), 312,

no. 290, pl. 183, s.v. "Gorgo, Gorgones" (Krauskopf and Dahlinger); Snodgrass 1998, fig. 31. See also the comments of D. Tsiafakis, "ΠΕΛΩΡΑ," in this volume. One wonders if there is some remembrance of these early Gorgon-horses in the myth of the birth of Pegasos from the neck of the decapitated Medusa.

46  Location unknown: see Boardman 1968, 27, pl. II, no. 31; Napier 1986, 62, pl. 23; Boardman 2001a, 180, pl. 282.

47  Within the same Gorgon-horse Group are seals with similar depictions of the winged Egyptian god Bes seizing a goat or boar, with Bes having the hindquarters either of a horse or a lion: see Boardman 1968, 27–28, pl. II, nos. 34–35; Boardman 2001, pls. 283–84.

48  Snodgrass 1998, 85.

49  Boston 1895.12: see the discussion by K. Manchester under cat. no. 31, with bibliography. Cf. the confrontation of man/god with centaur/monster on the fragment of a relief-amphora from Rhodes (Maiuri 1923–24, 337, fig. 222B).

50  Buschor 1934, 128–29.

51  Fittschen 1969, 113, no. SB 5, 119–24.

52  E.g., Pipili 1987, 9–10.

53  Baur 1912, 130–34, nos. 318–25; Richter 1968, no. 157; Cook 1981, no. 29; LIMC 8, 683, no. 143, pl. 423, s.v. "Kentauroi et Kentaurides"; Zwierlein-Diehl 2000, 399, fig. 4; Boardman 2001a, pl. 306. A Cypriote limestone statuette of a centaur in Geneva (P 620) has legs and hooves in the East Greek style: Baur 1912, 134, no. 326, fig. 38; Karageorghis 1998, 90, fig. 48.

54  BMC Thrace, 217, no. 15; BMC Macedon, 147, no. 9, 148, no. 1, 149, no. 1; Price and Waggoner 1975, 32–35, pls. V–VI, nos. 62–99.

55  E.g., Paris, Louvre E 700 (Baur 1912, 132–33, no. 322, fig. 37) and a hydria formerly in the Hirschmann Collection (Bloesch 1982, 28–31, no. 11; Cook and Dupont 1998, 112, fig. 13.3).

56  For bibliography on these and on centaurs in the other media here listed, see the relevant catalogue entries.

57  Herakleion 3141: Lebessi 1973, 109, fig. 7; Schiffler 1976, 283, cat. KR–S 3; LIMC 8, 676, no. 38, pl. 418, s.v. "Kentauroi et Kentaurides."

58  Athens, Nat. Mus. 6680: Baur 1912, 98, no. 236; Schiffler 1976, 320, cat. V 15; Niemeyer 1964, 29–30, pl. 27. See the comments by C. Stibbe under cat. no. 23.

59  Paris, Cab. Méd. 514: see cat. no. 23.

60  This formula dates back at least a century: cf. the centaur on the Protocorinthian kotyle in Richmond (cat. no. 30).

61  Athens, Nat. Mus. 6684: de Ridder 1896, 145–46, no. 429; Baur 1912, 98, no. 238; Schiffler 1976, 320, cat. V 14.

62  See Haynes 1952. Another possible votive centaur is a charming group of Nessos carrying Deianeira that was found at the sanctuary of Aphaia on Aigina: see Maass and Kilian-Dirlmeier 1998, 60–61, fig. 1.

63  Madrid 18536: see cat. no. 25.

64  Rome, Villa Giulia: Hus 1961, 144–61, no. 17, pl. XXIII; Spivey 1997, 123, figs. 106–7.

65  For Etruscan centaurs, see Schiffler 1976, 125–50, 303–18, pls. 11–14;

66  Previously unpublished. This is the largest of the Archaic bronze centaurs (h. 16.3 cm.). See the comments by C. Stibbe under cat. no. 23, n. 11, and cat. no. 25, n. 3.

67  Princeton 1997.36: see cat. no. 24.

68  "δασυστέρνου" (Soph. Trach. 557).

69  Pind. Pyth. 9.38; Fowler 1983. For other opinions on this passage, see Woodbury 1972; Francis 1972.

70  Boardman 1978, fig. 193; Fowler 1983, 168, fig. 11.9.

71  For all translations from Pindar quoted here, see Lattimore 1976. Diodorus Siculus (4.69.5) says instead that the centaurs resulted directly from the union of Ixion and Nephele, and that Ixion was thus father both to them and to Peirithoos. His subsequent account of the conflict between the Lapiths and centaurs is notably confused, and he elsewhere unhelpfully states that Apollo begat both Lapithes and Kentauros (4.69.1). The centaurs Cheiron and Pholos were of different parentage, the former a son of Kronos, the latter of Silenos (Apollod. Bibl. 1.2.4; 2.5.4).

72  Peirithoos is usually called the son of Ixion (Apollod. Bibl. 1.8.2; Ov. Met. 12.210), but Homer says he was sired on the wife of Ixion by Zeus (Il. 2.741; 14.317–18).

73  Hippodameia: Homer Il. 2.742; Diod. Sic. 4.70.3. Deidameia: Plut. Thes. 30.3. Ovid (Met. 12.210) calls her Hippodame.

74  Aelian (VH 11.2) says that the battle was the subject of an early epic poem by Melisandros of Miletos, but this work is lost.

75  Nestor, another guest who sided with the Lapiths in the fight, makes no mention of a wedding, recalling only that the Lapiths defeated the "the beast men living within the mountains" (Il. 1.267–68). The battle is described as depicted on the Shield of Herakles (Hes. Scut. 178–90), but again no wedding is mentioned. In Ovid (Met. 12.219), Eurytion has become "Eurytus, wildest of the wild centaurs."

76  For Kaineus, see Ap. Rhod. Argon. 1.57–64; Ov. Met. 12.459–532; Apollod. Epit. 1.22.

77  Olympia BE IIa: Boardman 1967, 87, fig. 48; Human Figure 1987, 102, no. 25; LIMC 5 (1990), 888, no. 61, pl. 573, s.v. "Kaineus."

78  The man between a pair of centaurs on an Early Corinthian aryballos from the Samian Heraion, ca. 630–600 B.C., could be Kaineus, but he is not sunk into the ground (Walter 1959, 67, Beil. III.1–5, 114.3). The Thessalian centauromachy is otherwise rare in Corinthian vase-painting; Payne (1931, 325, no. 1374) lists only one example, a late aryballos (Munich 346) "strongly influenced by Attic work."

79  Florence 4209: ABV 76.1; Paralipomena 29; BAdd² 21; Minto 1955. For the centauromachy on the neck, including the death of Kaineus, see Cristofani, Marzi, and Perissinotto 1981, 128–29, pls. 66–69, and 161, pls. 126–27; LIMC 5, 889, no. 67, pl. 574, s.v. "Kaineus." For Kaineus in Greek art, see Schauenburg 1962a; Brommer 1973, 499–501; Schmidt-Dounas 1985; Laufer 1985; LIMC 5 (1990), 884–91, s.v "Kaineus" (Laufer).

80  Cf. the relief on a late-sixth-century South Italian terracotta altar in the art market (Hecht 1995, 10).

LIMC 8 (1997), 721–27, pls. 482–93, s.v. "Kentauroi (in Etruria)" (Weber-Lehmann).

81 Rome, Mus. Cap. 39: *ABV* 98.44; *Paralipomena* 37; *BAdd*² 26; *LIMC* 5, 885, no. 2, pl. 563, s.v. "Kaineus." The likelihood is increased when the warior is fallen and both centaurs rear in unison to administer the coup de grace, as, for example, on a red-figure cup by Oltos: Copenhagen, Nat. Mus. 13407 (*ARV*² 59.57; *Paralipomena* 326; *BAdd*² 164; Schefold 1992, 169, fig. 207).

82 Hes. *Scut.* 188–90, trans. R. Lattimore. For a summary of the names on the François Vase, see the appendix in Minto 1960, Zona II.B.

83 The similarity between such sixth-century centauromachies and the one described so vividly in the *Shield of Herakles* is among the reasons that this work probably postdates Hesiod. Individual combats between a man and a centaur on seventh-century Corinthian and Attic vases seem to have more in common with Herakles' fights with Nessos and the centaurs of Mount Pholoë than with the Thessalian centauromachy. A jar painted in Sicily about 650–625 B.C. in a style resembling Protoattic, with two centaurs seizing a pair of women, most likely illustrates their behavior at the wedding of Peirithoos (Paris, Louvre CA 3837: Ahlberg-Cornell 1992, 128, 384, fig. 230; *LIMC* 8, 683, no. 137, pl. 423, s.v. "Kentauroi et Kentaurides"). The identification of the same subject on fragments of a skyphos from Perachora is not convincing (Athens, Nat. Mus.: Ahlberg-Cornell 1992, 128, 385, fig. 231). Other seventh-century candidates are wanting, since the charging centaurs on the neck of an amphora by the Piraeus Painter, ca. 610 B.C., lack pre-served adversaries (Athens, Kerameikos Mus. 658: *ABV* 3; *Paralipomena* 1; *BAdd*² 1). One of the earliest and finest black-figure centauromachies is on a dinos by the Kyllenios Painter, from the second quarter of the sixth century (Hannover L9.1989: *CVA* 2, Germany 72, pls. 21–24). Near this in date is an unusual amphora with decoration on one side only, from the Athenian Agora (P 13126), with a fine melée of Lapiths and centaurs: see Moore 1997, 115–16, pl. 14, no. 118. Another example of this date, a column-krater formerly in the art market, features a pair of Lapiths surrounded by two pairs of centaurs, a doubling of the usual Kaineus composition: see London, Sotheby's, July 11, 1988, lot 139.

84 Munich 2640: *ARV*² 402.22; *Paralipomena* 370; *BAdd*² 231; Ohly-Dumm and Hamdorf 1981, 119, pl. 53; *LIMC* 8, 686, no. 175, pl. 426, and 687, no. 191, pl. 428, s.v. "Kentauroi et Kentaurides."

85 Only rarely are Herakles and a warrior represented together in the same centauromachy: see cat. no. 34, n. 7.

86 Ashmole and Yalouris 1967, 17–22, pls. 62–142; Boardman 1985, figs. 21.1–8; Herrmann 1987, 31–54, pls. 1a, 2–21; *LIMC* 8, 689, no. 211, pls. 430–31, s.v. "Kentauroi et Kentaurides."

87 For Theseus in the centauromachy, see Shefton 1962; *LIMC* 7 (1994), 943–45, pls. 662–64, s.v. "Theseus" (Neils).

88 See Dörig 1985; Boardman 1985, figs. 113, 114.6–7. In the fourth century the subject also appears on friezes from the temple of Apollo at Bassae (see Kenner 1946; Madigan 1996) and the heroon at Trysa (see Eichler 1950; Oberleitner 1994).

89 The relief in figure 12 is Parthenon south metope 31: Boardman 1985, fig. 91.10; *LIMC* 8, pl. 434. For the centauromachy metopes from the Parthenon, see Brommer 1979; Boardman 1985, figs. 90, 91.1–11; *LIMC* 8, 689, no. 212, pls. 432–34, s.v. "Kentauroi et Kentaurides."

90 See Shefton 1962, 338–44, 353–65; for a list of vase-paintings with the indoor centauromachy, see pp. 365–67. Two of the finer examples occur on the neck of a volute-krater by the Painter of the Woolly Satyrs (New York, Met. 07.286.84: *ARV*² 613.1; *Paralipomena* 397; *BAdd*² 268–69; Shefton 1962, pl. 110); and on the column-krater that is the name-vase of the Florence Painter (Florence 3997: *ARV*² 541.1; *Paralipomena* 385; *BAdd*² 256; Esposito and de Tommaso 1993, 63, pl. 96).

91 Paus. 1.17.2. See Shefton 1962, 362–65; Barron 1972; Woodford 1974. Barron believed that the Theseion mural, which he dated 478–470 B.C., was the source of the new type of wedding-feast centauromachy, including that of the Olympia pediment. For the question of the artist, see Shefton 1962, 362 n. 124; Barron 1972, 23.

92 Mannack (2001, 85) notes that the fallen centaur mentioned by Pausanias usually does not appear in centauromachies with Theseus, but he does appear on vases that predate the painting by Polygnotos (see the examples in his note 320).

93 *Oidipodeia* 6; Pind. *Pyth.* 3.3; Ap. Rhod. *Argon.* 1231–41. Nearly every author from Hesiod on (*Theog.* 1001–2) agrees that Philyra was his mother, but Xenophon (*Cyn.* 1.4) says he was born of the nymph Nais.

94 Ap. Rhod. *Argon.* 1240–41. See also Schol. ad Ap. Rhod. 1.554.

95 Pindar (*Nem.* 3.43) says Achilles "lived in the house of Philyra."

96 Schol. Pind. *Nem.* 5.7 (12); Hyg. *Fab.* 14. Another tradition made Endeis the daughter of Skiron (Apollod. *Bibl.* 3.12.6; Paus. 2.29.7). A historical clan of healers who called themselves the Cheironidai claimed to be descended from Cheiron (Colvin 1880, 135).

97 Rhodes 11.550, from tomb 277 at Ialysos: *CVA* Rhodes, Italy 9, pl. 2.9; Jacopi 1929, 78, fig. 69.

98 Cf. Deianeira's description of the assault in Soph. *Trach.* 565: "he touched me with wanton hands" (trans. F. Storr).

99 Cf. also the tondo of a red-figure cup by the Ambrosios Painter (London, Brit. Mus. E 42: *ARV*² 174.20; *BAdd*² 184; Boardman 1975a, fig. 121): Deianeira touches the arm of Nessos in a similar way, but her identity is made explicit by her riding on his back. The Cypriote lime-stone statuette in Geneva (see n. 53 above) is an exception: Deianeira stands before Nessos, but she keeps her own hands at her side while he grasps her shoulders.

100 Formerly in the Hunt Collection: Bothmer et al. 1983, 48–49, no. 2; New York, Sotheby's, June 19, 1990, lot. 2.

101 For centaurs as shield devices, see Chase 1902, 44–45; Vaerst 1980, 275–76; Bothmer 1985, 123–24; Neils 1996, 27 n. 26. To these, add a cup by the Ambrosios Painter: London, Sotheby's, December 14, 1995, lot 84.

102 In some depictions of Peleus bringing Achilles to Cheiron, black-figure artists of the Leagros Group back Cheiron against the right frame of the scene, concealing his equine extension off stage, while at the far left only the rump and hind legs of Peleus's chariot horses intrude into the scene, as though the centaur had come full circle: cf. Berlin

1901 (*ABV* 361.22; *BAdd*² 96; *LIMC* 1 [1981], 45, no. 22, pl. 59, s.v. "Achilleus" [Kossatz-Deissmann]) and Berlin 1900 (*ABV* 385.27; *BAdd*² 102; *LIMC* 7 [1994], 265, no. 196, pl. 203, s.v. "Peleus" [Vollkommer]).

103 London, Brit. Mus. 1971.11–1.1: *Paralipomena* 19.16 bis; *BAdd*² 10–11; Schiffler 1976, 32 (drawing), 257, cat. A/Ch 2; Bakir 1981, 64, pls. 1–2, no. A.1; Williams 1983; *LIMC* 3 (1986), 240, no. 41, pl. 190, s.v. "Cheiron" (Gisler-Huwiler); *LIMC* 7, 267, no. 211, pls. 206–7, s.v. "Peleus." For Cheiron in Greek art, principally Attic vase-painting, see Schiffler 1976, 30–37, 257–61; *LIMC* 3, s.v. "Cheiron."

104 The tree laden with game is later adopted by the other civilized centaur, Pholos, who normally is represented with equine forelegs. Consequently, the motif by itself becomes unreliable as a distinguishing attribute of Cheiron, but in combination with human forelegs it allows us to tentatively identify as Cheiron the solitary centaur on a late-sixth-century silver gilt rhyton from Kelermes, now in St. Petersburg (Schiffler 1976, 97 [fig.], 289, cat. O-S 8; Boardman 1980, 261, fig. 304). For the tree hung with game in the iconography of Cheiron and Pholos, see Schnapp 1997, 435–52.

105 Athens, Nat. Mus. Acrop. 587: *ABV* 39.15; *BAdd*² 10; Bakir 1981, pls. 3–5, 89–90, no. A.2; *LIMC* 3 (1986), 190, pl. 150, no. 1, s.v. "Chariklo I" (Finster-Hotz).

106 For a detail, see Cristofani, Marzi, and Perissinotto 1981, fig. 133.

107 Pind. *Nem.* 4.57–65; Apollod. *Bibl.* 3.13.3. In depicting Peleus's ordeal on Pelion, vase-painters showed him in a tree surrounded by wild beasts: e.g., New York 46.11.7 (*ABV* 434.3; *Paralipomena* 187; *BAdd*² 111; Milne 1947; Schefold 1992, 187, fig. 224; Schnapp 1997, 442, fig. 526) and Haverford College EA-1989-8 (Ashmead 1999, 24–27, figs. 29–32). On an amphora in Rome, Peleus is rescued by Cheiron (Villa Giulia 24247: *CVA* 1, Italy 1, pl. 9.3–4; *LIMC* 3, 239, pl. 187, no. 15, s.v. "Cheiron"). In the Hesiodic *Catalogue of Women* (frag. 56; Evelyn-White 1982, 185), it is the centaurs that endanger Peleus on Pelion.

108 Hom. *Il.* 16.139–44; *Cypria* 5 (Evelyn-White 1982, 497); Apollod. *Bibl.* 3.13.5.

109 Atlanta, Emory Univ. 2000.1.2: see cat. no. 96. For the Rape of Thetis, see Krieger 1973; Barringer 1995, 69–94, pls. 71–108. For depictions that include Cheiron, see *LIMC* 3, 239–40, pls. 187–90, s.v. "Cheiron"; and *LIMC* 7, 261–62, pls. 197–98, 200, s.v. "Peleus." See also the references cited in cat. nos. 39 and 96. On the Harvard lekythos (cat. no. 39), Cheiron carries not a tree but a pair of torches, an allusion to the nocturnal Athenian wedding procession; cf. the centaur's own wedding on the bell-krater by the Eupolis Painter (cat. no. 38), where his mother Philyra carries the torches. The Rape was represented on the ivory Chest of Kypselos at Olympia, but Cheiron was absent (Paus. 5.18.5).

110 Xenophon (*Cyn.* 1.2) lists twenty-one heroic or divine students of Cheiron. Hesiod (*Theog.* 1000–1001) adds another, Medeios, the son of Jason. Apollodoros (*Bibl.* 3.4.4) adds Aktaion.

111 Evelyn-White 1982, xx, 72–75.

112 Beck 1975, 10.

113 When Aktaion turned into a stag and was devoured by his dogs,

the hounds missed their master and sought him in the cave of Cheiron, who fashioned an image of Aktaion to soothe their grief (Apollod. *Bibl.* 3.4.4).

114 For this subject in vase-painting, see cat. no. 40 with bibliography. It was represented as well on the Amyklai Throne (Paus. 3.18.12), a sculpted monument in Laconia surrounding a statue of Apollo and the tomb of Hyakinthos.

115 See cat. no. 40, n. 3.

116 Berlin 31573 (A 9): Morris 1984, 55–56, pl. 12; Beazley 1986, 9–10, pl. 9.3–4; Ahlberg-Cornell 1992, 302, fig. 72.

117 Pind. *Nem.* 3.43–52. Apollodoros (*Bibl.* 3.13.6) says Cheiron fed the infant on the innards of lions and wild swine and the marrows of bears. On this, see Beazley 1986, 10.

118 Bacchylides, frag. 27 (Fagles 1998, 67).

119 Apollod. *Bibl.* 2.5.4; 2.5.11. Her father's predicament had been predicted by Cheiron's prophetic daughter, Okyrrhoë (Ov. *Met.* 2.649–54). The role of Herakles' arrow in Cheiron's death is mentioned by Sophokles (*Trach.* 714–15).

120 Ov. *Fast.* 5.413–14. Pausanias (1.19.9) says that a centaur with human legs on the Chest of Kypselos was explained as representing Cheiron, who "when he was free from humanity and permitted to live with the gods, came to give Achilles some relief in his grief" (trans. P. Levi). It is curious that the formerly immortal horse man was thought of as having been "freed from his humanity." For a speculative restoration, see Splitter 2000, 48, fig. 37.

121 Apollod. *Bibl.* 2.5.4; Diod. Sic. 4.12.3–8; Tzetz. *Chil.* 5.111–37. There is no mention of the story in Homer, Hesiod, or Pindar, but a fragment of Stesichoros, *Geryoneis* (Davies 1991, 19 = frag. 181; Ath. 11.499), describes the huge cup handed to Herakles by Pholos. There is reason to believe that the story was recounted by two authors of epic poems about Herakles, Peisandros of Kameiros and Panyasis of Halikarnassos, the former in the seventh century, the latter in the fifth, when it also was the subject of a comedy by Epicharmos (see Colvin 1880, 113). Frequent allusions are made to the subsequent fight between Herakles and the centaurs, with and without reference to Pholos: e.g., Soph. *Trach.* 1096–97; Eur. *HF* 181, 364, 1271.

122 For vase-paintings of Herakles and Pholos, see Luce 1924, 301–9; Schauenburg 1971; Schiffler 1976, 37–41, 261–65; Brommer 1973, 178–82; Ahlberg-Cornell 1992, 102–5, figs. 178–83; *LIMC* 8, 691–95, 706–9, pls. 442–50, 456–57, s.v. "Kentauroi et Kentaurides." To these, add two examples of the opening of the jar, both formerly in the art market: a black-figure hydria (London, Sotheby's, July 11, 1988, lot 131) and a red-figure column-krater by the Eucharides Painter (London, Sotheby's, July 1, 1969, lot 105; Langridge 1993, 349, cat. E19).

123 See Verbanck-Piérard 1982; Burow 1989, pls. 53–56, 69; Schefold 1992, 135, fig. 158. An earlier (ca. 550 B.C.) depiction of the meeting of Herakles and Pholos may occur on a Laconan dinos in Paris, where Herakles grabs the wrist of a centaur with human forelegs while around them other centaurs fall or run away (Louvre E 662: Baur 1912, 53–54, no. 161, fig. 8;

Pipili 1987, 7–9, fig. 10; Schefold 1992, 135, fig. 157; *LIMC* 8, 693, no. 254, pl. 446, s.v. "Kentauroi et Kentaurides"). On this vase, most of the other centaurs have four horse legs, but one, who threatens to intrude on a scene of Achilles ambushing Troilos, also has human legs, so it is not clear whether the centaur with Herakles is his host or his next victim.

124 Florence 3812: *ABV* 289.23; *BAdd²* 75; Schauenburg 1971, pl. 33; Esposito and de Tommaso 1993, 47, fig. 60; Schnapp 1997, 450, fig. 553. For variations on this composition, including Pholos reclining alongside Herakles, see Baur 1912, 52, no. 157, fig. 7; Schauenburg 1971, pls. 29–31, 33–35; Wolf 1993, 41–42, 171–72, figs. 123–30; *LIMC* 8, 708, nos. 360–63, s.v. "Kentauroi et Kentaurides." Lucian (*Symp.* 13.14) refers to the habit of later artists representing the two reclining together. On a black-figure lekythos by the Athena Painter, once in the art market (*Paralipomena* 256; *BAdd²* 129; Wolf 1993, fig. 58), Herakles reclines with Hermes, while Pholos stands nearby holding a pair of torches, like Cheiron at the Rape of Thetis (cf. cat. no. 39).

125 As usual, there are exceptions to the rule, and Pholos, too, is sometimes given human legs and attire: e.g., Zürich Univ. L 551; Baur 1912, 109, pl. 4, no. 268 (for other examples, see under Baur no. 267).

126 For Herakles and Dionysos reclining together, see Wolf 1993, 22–29, figs. 38–45, 47–55, 69, 72–73; *LIMC* 4 (1988), 818–19, pls. 544–45; and *LIMC* 5 (1990), 154–55, pl. 144, s.v. "Herakles" (Boardman et al.); Padgett 2002, 265–66.

127 Some vase-painters seem to have intentionally placed satyrs in contexts recalling the Pholos episode. The Gela Painter shows a trio of satyrs dipping wine from one buried pithos and water from another (once art market: *Paralipomena* 215; Basel, *MuM*, Auktion 26, *Kunstwerke der Antike*, October 5, 1963, lot 118, pl. 40). A closer connection with Pholos is suggested on a column-krater formerly in the Borowski Collection (New York, Christie's, June 12, 2000, lot 87), attributed to the Harrow Painter [Padgett], with two centaurs dipping wine from a buried pithos—the communal jar of the Arcadian centaurs(?)—while on the reverse a single satyr dips from the same or a similar pithos.

128 Paris, Louvre AM 840–842: Demargne 1902, 576, fig. 3; *LIMC* 8, 708, no. 358, pl. 456, s.v. "Kentauroi et Kentaurides."

129 Paus. 5.19.9. See Splitter 2000, 49–50. For the date of the chest, see Payne 1941, 351 n. 4; Carter 1989.

130 Paus. 3.18.10. The throne also had a carving of Herakles' fight with a centaur named Oreios (Paus. 3.18.16).

131 Berlin 2686: Baur 1912, 91–92, no. 226, fig. 19; Payne 1933, pl. 21; Amyx 1988, 37, no. 1; Ahlberg-Cornell 1992, 104, 355, fig. 178; *LIMC* 8, 691, no. 235, pl. 441, s.v. "Kentauroi et Kentaurides."

132 For Herakles driving off the centaurs of Mount Pholoë, see the sources and examples cited in cat. no. 30. In addition to Corinthian and Attic vases, the subject appears on a variety of other painted fabrics, including Boiotian (e.g., Munich 7740: Kilinski 1990, pl. 16.3; *LIMC* 8, 693, no. 253, pl. 446, s.v. "Kentauroi et Kentaurides"); Eretrian (e.g., Eretria ME 16618: Boardman 1998a, fig. 465.2); and Laconian (e.g., Louvre E 662: see n. 123).

133 Paris, Louvre MNC 677: Baur 1912, 93–94, no. 228, fig. 12, no. 228; Payne 1931, pl. 31.9–10; Ahlberg-Cornell 1992, 104, 357, fig. 183; *LIMC* 8, 693, no. 252, pl. 445. This painting is the basis for Fittschen's identification of the figures on the Protocorinthian aryballos in Boston (cat. no. 31) as Herakles and an Arcadian centaur (see nn. 49–51 above).

134 Paestum, Mus. Naz: Zancani and Zanotti 1954, pls. 52–60; *LIMC* 4, 6, no. 1698, pl. 7, s.v. "Herakles"; Schefold 1992, 137, fig. 162; *LIMC* 8, 695, no. 281, pl. 449, s.v. "Kentauroi et Kentaurides"; Greco 2001, 61–63, figs. 67–72.

135 Boston 84.67; Istanbul 257; Paris, Louvre MA 2830-31; Assos depot A48; Comstock and Vermeule 1976, 13, no. 19; Boardman 1978, fig. 216.5–8; Finster-Hotz 1984, 24–33, 104, 127–30, pls. 1–3; Wescoat 1995, 296, 313–16, figs. 11.9–12, 11.20; *LIMC* 8, 695, no. 282, pls. 450, 457, s.v. "Kentauroi et Kentaurides."

136 In 1987, Bonna Wescoat discovered a fragment on the eastern slope of the Assos acropolis with parts of two running centaurs that joins Louvre 2830 (see Wescoat 1995, 316, fig. 11.12).

137 Finster-Hotz 1984, 145–46, metopes 5–6, pl. 20. It is not certain from what narrative sequence these may derive.

138 Wescoat 1995, 296.

139 Wescoat 1995, 296.

140 There are fallen centaurs on the kotyle in the Louvre (see n. 133 above) and the aryballos in Berlin (see n. 131 above), both Corinthian. In one of the earliest Attic centauromachies with Herakles, a louterion signed by Sophilos, a dying centaur has fallen hard, his equine legs scrambling for purchase on the bloody ground: Athens, Nat. Mus. 15918 and 15942 (*ABV* 40.21 and 42.36; *Paralipomena* 18; *BAdd²* 11; Baur 1912, 11–12, fig. 4; Callipolitis-Feytmans 1965, pl. XVII; Bakir 1981, 68, no. A20, pl. 9, fig. 17).

141 E.g., a South Italian black-figure column-krater in the art market (Basel, Jean-David Cahn, A.G., Auktion 3, *Kunstwerke der Antike*, October 18, 2002, lot 25); a pseudo-Chalcidian neck-amphora in Berlin (F 1670; *LIMC* 8, 693, no. 255, pl. 447, s.v. "Kentauroi et Kentaurides"); and a Caeretan hydria formerly in the Hirschmann Collection (Bloesch 1982, 28–31, no. 11; Cook and Dupont 1998, 112, fig. 13.3). On a "Pontic" oinochoe in Cleveland (1986.88: Neils 1998, 13–19, figs. 7a–d.), Pholos stands behind Herakles, as he does on the Assos relief and in the sequence of metopes at Foce del Sele. "Pontic" vases may have been produced by immigrant Ionian artisans, but before identifying this arrangement as deriving from East Greek models, it is well to remember the similar composition on the Corinthian kotyle in Paris (Louvre MNC 677: see n. 133 above). The subject's appearance in Etruscan art would seem to argue against Van Keuren's suggestion (1989, 157) that the centauromachy at Foce del Sele refers to conflicts with the native population or the Etruscans.

142 For other examples, see cat. no. 30, n. 16.

143 *LIMC* 4, 6, pl. 6, no. 1698, s.v. "Herakles"; Greco 2001, 66, fig. 79 and 70–71, figs. 84–85. The centaur metope could instead belong to the sequence with Herakles and Pholos. The Nessos story is otherwise rare in Archaic sculpture, though it was said to be among the reliefs on the

Amyklai Throne (Paus. 3.18.12). Cf. also the bronze statuette from Aigina (see n. 62 above).

144 Soph. *Trach.*, esp. 555–81; Apollod. *Bibl.* 2.7.6–7; Diod. Sic. 4.36; Sen. *Herc. Oet.* 500–544.

145 Some say the potion was the centaur's poisoned blood mixed with his spent semen (Apollod. *Bibl.* 2.7.6; Diod. Sic. 4.36). For the presence of Nessos at the Thessalian centauromachy, see Apollod. *Bibl.* 2.5.4; Ov. *Met.* 12.308–9. Hesiod (*Theog.* 341) refers to Nessos as a river, along with Acheloos. Pausanias (10.38.1) repeats a local legend that Ozolian Lokris got its name when the mortally wounded Nessos escaped there and his rotting corpse began to smell (*ozein*).

146 For Nessos in art, particularly vase-painting, see Dugas 1943; Fittschen 1970; Brommer 1973, 153–58; Schauenburg 1973; *LIMC* 6 (1992), 838–47, pls. 534–55, s.v. "Nessos" (Díez de Velasco).

147 Athens, Nat. Mus. 27697g: Baur 1912, 92, no. 227, fig. 20; Cook 1934–35, 191, pl. 52f; Morris 1984, 70–71, pl. 17; *LIMC* 6, 843, no. 89, pl. 549, s.v. "Nessos"; Ahlberg-Cornell 1992, 107, no. 108, and 360, fig. 188.

148 New York, Met. 11.210.1: Richter 1912; Morris 1984, 65–70, pl. 15; Beazley 1986, 6–7, pl. 5; *LIMC* 6, 840, no. 36, pl. 541, s.v. "Nessos"; Ahlberg-Cornell 1992, 107–8, 361, fig. 109.

149 Berlin A 21: *CVA* Berlin 1, Germany 2, pl. 10; Morris 1984, 74, pl. 19; *LIMC* 6, 844, no. 114, pl. 553, s.v. "Nessos"; Ahlberg-Cornell 1992, 108, 364, fig. 194 (she hesitates over the identification).

150 E.g., Syracuse 42648: Payne 1931, pl. 7.

151 See Ahlberg-Cornell 1992, 362–63, figs. 190, 192.

152 Athens, Nat. Mus. 1002: *ABV* 4.1; *Paralipomena* 1; *BAdd*[2] 1–2; Boardman 1974, fig. 5; Beazley 1986, pl. 10.2–4; Carpenter 1991, fig. 224; Ahlberg-Cornell 1992, 107, 362, fig. 191; *LIMC* 6, 844, no. 113, pl. 553, s.v. "Nessos." In Attic inscriptions, one "t" does the work of two, hence the label "Netos."

153 Athens, Nat. Mus. 1002: Ahlberg-Cornell 1992, 107, 362, fig. 190. Deianeira's hand is preserved on Herakles' shoulder.

154 See cat. no. 33, n. 6.

155 See Gabbard 1979, 65, who apparently was unaware that there are a few vase-paintings predating the *Trachiniae* (ca. 447–442 B.C.) in which Herakles does use his bow against Nessos: see cat. no. 30, n. 12. A fragment (frag. 147) of Archilochos suggests that the motif of the poisoned arrow was known much earlier than Sophokles (see Bérard 1981). If the "wound" on the leg of the Lefkandi Centaur identifies him as Cheiron, the motif may be as old as the tenth century.

156 Tyrrhenian: see Baur 1912, 16–20, nos. 32–40, pl. 1; Schauenburg 1962b, 63–66, figs. 5–6; Fittschen 1970, pl. IV, fig. 4; Schiffler 1976, 246–47, cat. A 35–40; *LIMC* 6, 839, nos. 1–12, pls. 534–37, s.v. "Nessos." See also cat. no. 33.

157 This composition occurs on the earliest (ca. 600–580 B.C.) Attic depiction after the Nettos painter, the name-vase of both the Deianeira Class of lekythoi and of the Deianeira Painter (London, Brit. Mus. B 30: *ABV* 11.20; *BAdd*[2] 3; Baur 1912, 57, no. 163, fig. 9; Williams 1986; *LIMC* 6, 840, no. 38, pl. 541, s.v. "Nessos"). So standard is this basic composition

that we can recognize it even when only the upper bodies of the figures are preserved, as on a black-figure lekythos fragment in a Florida private collection, here attributed to the Painter of the Boston Polyphemos. The subject is rare in fifth-century red-figure, when it is adapted to serve in depictions of Theseus, but the same composition recurs as late as a pair of cups signed by the painter Aristophanes (ca. 410 B.C.): Boston 00.344 and 00.345 (*ARV*[2] 1319.2–3; *Paralipomena* 478; *BAdd*[2] 363; Fittschen 1970, pl. V, fig. 7; *LIMC* 6, 841, no. 63a–b, pl. 545, s.v. "Nessos").

158 Naples H 3089: *ARV*[2] 1050.4; Fittschen 1970, pl. IV, fig. 5; *LIMC* 3 (1986), 359, no. 2 (drawing), s.v. "Deianeira II" (Vollkommer); Matheson 1995, 217–19, pl. 164, no. PGU 5. London, Brit. Mus. 98.7-16.5: *ARV*[2] 1027.2; *LIMC* 3, 359, no. 3, pl. 267, s.v. "Deianeira II"; Matheson 1995, 217–19, pl. 38, no. P 2.

159 Apollod. *Bibl.* 2.5.4. (He adds that the other survivors were received at Eleusis by Poseidon, who hid them in a mountain). For the subject in art, see *LIMC* 3, 359–61, pls. 266–68, s.v. "Deianeira II."

160 R. Vollkommer also identifies the subject on some fourth-century Attic and South Italian vases: see *LIMC* 3, 359–60, nos. 4–8, pls. 267–68, s.v. "Deianeira II."

161 Gabbard (1979, 6–69) thinks Herakles is like Nessos in his savagery and considers the Nessos of Sophokles to be lustful and vindictive but not cruel like his killer. This more sympathetic approach she discerns as well in the metopes of the Parthenon (pp. 74–88), which she agrees still symbolize the defeat of the Persians: "Unlike the *Odes* of Pindar and the Temple of Zeus at Olympia, which show centaurs as grotesque, hubristic intruders in a world of virtuous heroes and their Olympian sponsors, Sophocles and the Parthenon sculptors give us centaurs with many more human qualities" (p. 88). Like Herakles and Nessos, Pheidias achieved balance between men and centaurs. The *sophrosyne* extolled by Pindar and others is put into effect.

162 Hurwit (1985, 177) seems to disagree.

163 One of the last depictions of Cheiron with human legs is on a pointed amphora in the collection of Shelby White and Leon Levy, attributed to the Copenhagen Painter (real name Syriskos), dating to 470–460 B.C., where the centaur participates in the wedding of Peleus and Thetis: see Bothmer 1990, 168–71, no. 121; Oakley and Sinos 1993, 36–37, 112–14, figs. 108–11; *LIMC* 7 (1994), 233, no. 5, pl. 172, s.v. "Peirithoos" (Manakidou); Reeder 1995, 347–49, no. 109. In the tradition of some earlier black-figure scenes of Cheiron receiving the infant Achilles (see n. 102 above), the equine portion of the centaur's anatomy is largely concealed.

164 Lucian, *Zeuxis or Antiochus* 3–7.

165 Gal. *De usu part.* 3.1.

166 Ael. *NA* 17.9, trans. A. F. Scholfield.

167 Philostr. *Imag.* 2.3, trans. A. Fairbanks. We can imagine what Philostratus would have thought of the many websites today devoted to centaurs, half of them openly pornographic. For "sightings" of satyrs and centaurs in Roman times, see Mayor 2000, 236–41.

168 For an overview of satyrs/silenoi in art, with extensive bibliography, see *LIMC* 8 (1997), 1108–33, pls. 746–83, s.v. "Silenoi" (Simon).

See also Brommer 1937; Carpenter 1986, 76–97; Lissarrague 1988; Lissarrague 1990c; Lissarrague 1990d; Hedreen 1992; Lissarrague 1993; Padgett 2000. Despite the general similarity of bipedal bull-men in Near Eastern Seals and sculpture (e.g., King 1912, pl. XXIX, face B), satyrs seem to be distinctly Greek in origin.

169 E.g., on a lekanis lid in St. Petersburg: *Compte-rendu de la Commission Impériale Archéologique* (St. Petersburg 1862), pl. II. On the beginnings of the confusion between Pan and the satyrs, see Simon 1982b, 144–45.

170 Princeton y1987-55, attributed by Robert Guy to the manner of the Lysippides Painter: *Record* 47.1 (1988): 46–47 (illus.); Padgett 1995–96, 80, fig. 11.

171 Nowhere is this more evident than in the satyrs' penchant for masturbation: see *LIMC* 8, 1113, nos. 111–19, pls. 764–66, s.v. "Silenoi." To the vases listed in *LIMC*, add a lively bronze statuette formerly in the art market: Basel, *MuM*, Auktion 60, *Kunstwerke der Antike*, September 21, 1982, lot 96, pl. 32.

172 Lissarrague 1990c, 66.

173 For some Attic satyrs with hooves, see Carpenter, 1986, 77, n. 4. Cf. also a black-figure pelike formerly in the art market: London, Sotheby's, December 11, 1989, no. 374.

174 Some examples: Würzburg 252 (*ABV* 315.1; *BAdd*²85; Koch-Harnack 196, fig. 98); Paris, Louvre E 876 (*ABV* 90.1; *BAdd*²24; Peirce 1993, fig. 10); Berlin 1966.1 (*ABV* 285.1; Lissarrague 1993, 209, fig. 13); Madrid, Mus. Arq. [no number] (London, Sotheby's, December 10, 1996, lot 162).

175 For some examples, see Carpenter, 1986, 77 n. 4; Boardman 1998a, fig. 347 (Clazomenian). Satyrs with human legs and hooves also appear on "Chalcidian" vases, probably made at Rhegion (e.g., Boardman 1998a, figs. 472, 479); and on Caeretan hydriai and vases of the Northampton Group, both probably made in Etruria by immigrant East Greek artisans (Boardman 1998a, figs. 485.2, 495). For a bronze satyr of this type in the Louvre, see Charbonneaux 1962, pl. XVI.2. For East Greek centaurs with hooved human legs, see n. 53 above.

176 Rome, Villa Giulia: *ARV*² 279.4.

177 Schefold 1992, 75–76, figs. 88–89; Greco 2001, 64–65, figs. 74–77. The same subject occurs on a cup by the Brygos Painter (London, Brit. Mus. E 65), where both Hera and Iris are assaulted by satyrs (*ARV*² 370.13; *Paralipomena* 365; *BAdd*² 224; Boardman 1975a, fig. 252; Simon 1982b, pl. 30). On two other cups, it is Iris alone who is attacked: Boston 08.30a (*ARV*² 135; *LIMC* 8, 1125, no. 158, pl. 771, s.v. "Silenoi") and Berlin 2591 (*ARV*² 888.150). Simon (1982b, 125–29) suggests that the attack on Iris was the subject of an early satyr play. This is unlikley in the case of the Foce del Sele metopes, and Schefold (1992, 76) instead suggested a link with a lost "Silenomachy" by Stesichoros. On a fragmentary skyphos by the Kleophrades Painter (Florence 4218: *ARV*² 191.102; *BAdd*² 189; Esposito and de Tommaso 1993, 54, fig. 75; Williams 1997, 195–96, fig. 1), Iris is attacked not by satyrs but by centaurs, a seeming variant of the story but one that can hardly be based on a satyr play. Williams (1997, 196) suggests that Iris may have been sent by Zeus to intercede at the Thessalian centauromachy.

178 *LIMC* 8, 1122–23, nos. 129–40, pls. 768–69. Cf. the satyr raising a boulder in the gigantomachy on Ferrara 2892, a calyx-krater in the manner of the Peleus Painter (*ARV*² 1041.6; *Paralipomena* 443; *BAdd*²319; Matheson 1995, 196, pl. 153).

179 Cf. the composition on the neck-amphora Munich 2316, by the Kleophrades Painter, with Herakles on one side and a charging centaur on the other (*ARV*² 183.12; *BAdd*²187; *CVA* Munich 5, Germany 20, pl. 209.3–4). The centaur wields a boulder and has four equine legs.

180 Pipili's contention (1987, 104 n. 656) that Attic red-figure satyrs always have tails is not correct; for some examples, see Padgett 2000, 57 n. 49.

181 See Pipili 1987, 65–68. To Pipili's list of tailless Laconian bronze satyrs, add two reclining examples: in Karlsruhe (Schumacher 1890, 87–88, no. 474) and in a Swiss private collection (Lullies 1964, no. 17); add also a walking satyr, less clearly Laconian, formerly in the Hunt Collection (Bothmer et al. 1983, 97, no. 23).

182 Paris, Louvre Br 133, from Llano de la Consolación (near Montealegre del Castillo, province Albacete); height 9.0 cm.: Herfort-Koch 1986, 121, no. K 153. See the comments under cat. no. 23.

183 The frontal faces of satyrs eventually took on an apotropaic role, to judge by the regularity with which they appear on late-sixth-century black-figure vases (e.g., cat. nos. 57, 58); on Greek and Italic antefixes (e.g., cat. no. 59); and on coins and bronze handles from the early fifth century onward. See *LIMC* 8, 1126–29, pls. 772–75, s.v. "Silenoi."

184 For the François Vase, see n. 79 above. For details of the Return of the Hephaistos, see Cristofani, Marzi, and Perissinotto 1981, 140–41, figs. 90–93; *LIMC* 8, 1113, no. 22, pl. 747, s.v. "Silenoi."

185 Strabo 10.3.19; Evelyn-White 1982, 277. The *Catalogue of Women* probably dates to the sixth century. Papyrological studies have shed new light on this fragment, suggesting that the satyrs and nymphs were derived from the family of Dorus; see Carpenter 1986, 76.

186 Eur. *Bacch.* 13 and *Cyc.* 100.

187 Würzburg 474: *ARV*² 173.10; *BAdd*² 184; Simon 1982b, pl. 32a.

188 *Hym. Hom. Aph.* 262; Evelyn-White 1982, 424–25. For the date, see Evelyn-White 1982, xxxviii; Carpenter 1986, 77 n. 6.

189 Hdt. 8.138. Herodotos says the garden where Silenos was caught is in Macedonia, which seems rather far from Phrygia.

190 Because the satyr play was said to have came to Athens from the Peloponnesos, introduced by Pratinas of Phleious at the end of the sixth century, it has been suggested that *satyros* was the Peloponnesian name and *silenos* the Ionian name used in Athens during the sixth century. For this question, and for the debated role of Pratinas, see Brommer 1937, 2–5; Stoessl 1975; Hedreen 1992, 162–63. Hedreen rightly points out the lack of evidence to support a neat geographical division of terminology. Already in the fifth century, both names were used as personal names in Athens (Stoessl 1975, 193).

191 Pl. *Symp.* 215a,b; 216c,d; 221d,e.

192 Paus. 1.24.1; 2.7.8; 2.22.9.

193 As suggested by Brommer (1959, 3).

194 For examples, see Padgett 2000, 49 n. 20.

195 On this subject, see McNiven 1995; Padgett 2000, 46–47. For the varied sex life of satyrs, see Lissarrague 1990c.

196 Padded dancer is the name given a type of reveler on some early-sixth-century Corinthian and Attic vases who wears a short, belted tunic and has a fat, rounded belly: see Payne 1931, 118–24; Seeberg 1971; Hedreen 1992, 130–36. Hedreen believes that an ithyphallic pair witnessing the Return of Hephaistos on Athens 664, a Middle Corinthian amphoriskos, are padded dancers wearing the costumes of satyrs (Payne 1931, 119, fig. 44G, 314, no. 1073; Metzger 1972, 32–33, figs. 3–4; Isler-Kerenyi 2001, 70, fig. 13). They do wear the usual tunic, but so do many monsters and *Mischwesen* in this period, such as Typhon (cat. no. 98) and Nereus (cat. no. 96). The tunics are conventions, not costume illustrations. Satyrs are exceedingly rare in Corinthian vase-painting, and while I can believe that these figures represent a hesitant attempt at depicting satyrs by an artist more used to painting padded dancers, that is no reason to interpret them as human mummers dressed as satyrs. Simon (1982c, 16, 28–29, 43 n. 56) is probably right in seeing the padded dancers as the forerunners of the comic, rather than the satyric, chorus.

197 Berlin A 33: Metzger 1972, 32, figs. 1–2; Morris 1984, 62–63, pl. 13; Beazley 1986, 8, pl. 8; Boardman 1998a, fig. 29; Isler-Kerenyi 2001, 30, 35–36, figs. 4–5.

198 E.g., Beazley 1986, 8. Isler-Kerenyi (2001, 35–36) finds the figures in Berlin the only convincing candidates for satyrs dating before 600 B.C. Morris (1984, 61–62), while agreeing that they may be early comic figures or proto-satyrs, calls them "monsters" and, not surprisingly, finds their inspiration in the Near Eastern minor arts.

199 I have come to disagree with Payne's (1931, 320, no. 1258) conclusion that the running, hairy, ithyphallic man on the Late Corinthian aryballos Brussels A 83 is not a satyr, for all its lacking a tail. Hedreen (1992, 128–30) speaks of "non-equine silens," by which he means hairy and occasionally ithyphallic figures without tails, i.e., wild men. I do not believe, however, that a satyr can *be* "non-equine"; if he is, then he is not a satyr. There are many ways to represent a horse-demon, and a tail is not necessarily de rigueur. For the debate about the identity of such figures, see Metzger 1972; Carpenter 1986, 80–81 n. 19; Hedreen 1992, 128–29; Isler-Kerenyi 2001, 29–80.

200 See cat. no. 53, n. 12.

201 Istanbul 4514: *ABV* 42.37; Bakir 1981, 71, no. A.35, pl. 35, fig. 66; Carpenter 1986, pl. 18A.

202 Athens, Agora P 334: *ABV* 23; *BAdd²* 7; Moore and Philippides 1986, 178–79, no. 610, pl. 58; *LIMC* 8, 1113, no. 29, pl. 751, s.v. "Silenoi"; Isler-Kerenyi 2001, 107, figs. 33–34.

203 Buffalo G 600: *ABV* 12.22; *Paralipomena* 8; *BAdd²* 3; Boardman, 1974, fig. 15.

204 Because so many vases with Dionysiac imagery are found in tombs, they occasionally have been interpreted as symbolizing the happy afterlife of the deceased in the thiasos of Dionysos, where men are transformed into satyrs (Langlotz, 1967, 476). Symbolism of this type would seem more at home in the Hellenistic and Roman periods.

205 Würzburg 265: *ABV* 151.22; *Paralipomena* 63; *BAdd²* 43; Carpenter 1986, pl. 20A; Hedreen 1992, pl. 29; *LIMC* 8, 1114–15, no. 38, pl. 752, s.v. "Silenoi."

206 For the conversion from nymphs to maenads, which some scholars question, see Henrichs, 1987, 100–103; Hedreen, 1994; Carpenter, 1997, 52–55. For maenads in Attic vase-painting, see Moraw 1998.

207 This phenomenon, now widely acknowledged, was apparently first discussed in detail by Sheila McNally (1978). There are rare exceptions where the satyr gets the girl: e.g., Boston 08.30a (*ARV²* 135; Lissarrague 1990c, 79, fig. 2.24). The satyrs on "Chalcidian" and Caeretan vases are modestly more successful with the ladies: see Boardman 1998a, figs. 479.2, 495.2.

208 Boston 01.8072: *ARV²* 461.36; *Paralipomena* 377; *BAdd²* 244.

209 For this change, see McNally 1978.

210 Previously unpublished. The cup is of Type B, burned and fragmentary, with an offset inner rim; height 10.6–10.9 cm.; diameter 28.8 cm.; width with handles 36.7 cm.; diameter of foot 12.5 cm.; diameter of tondo 15.8–16.2 cm. The inscription *"Panaitios kalos"* is written on both sides and in the tondo. The name of Douris ([Δ]ORIΣ), without a verb, is painted in the reserved exergue of the tondo. This is unusual, and one remembers that not every vase inscribed with the name of Douris is his work (e.g., the lekythoi of the Cartellino Painter [*ARV²* 452]). In this case, however, there is no question that the cup is an early work by Douris, one that demonstrates a strong kinship with Onesimos in his early, Panaitian phase. The frame of the tondo, a labyrinthine maeander with dotted squares, resembles that of Malibu 83.AE.217, a large cup painted by Douris and signed on the foot by the potter Kleophrades (Buitron-Oliver 1995, no. 38, pl. 24). Another cup by Douris, Berlin 2283 (*ARV²* 429.21; *BAdd²* 236; Buitron-Oliver 1995, pls. 22–23, no. 34), not only has a similar tondo frame and *kalos* inscriptions praising Panaitios, but also has an offset inner rim. The foot attached to the Berlin cup, which might belong to it or to another cup, Berlin 2284 (*ARV²* 429.22), also is signed by the potter Kleophrades. The foot of the cup in figure 28 is not signed, but a comparison of its profile with the one attached to Berlin 2284 suggests that it, too, may have been potted by Kleophrades. It must be added that another foot signed by Kleophrades, Malibu 80.AE.54, might belong to either of the Berlin cups (see Bothmer 1981c).

211 Würzburg (loan): Simon 1982b, pl. 37a–b.

212 Ancona 105: Simon 1982b, pl. 35b.

213 Ferrara 3031: *ARV²* 612.1; *Paralipomena* 397; *BAdd²* 268; Simon 1982b, pl. 38b.

214 For satyr plays, see Guggisberg 1947; Pohlenz 1965; Chormouziades 1974; Seaford 1976; Sutton 1980. For their reflection in art, both real and imagined, see Buschor 1943; Brommer 1943; Brommer 1959; Brommer 1978–79; Brommer 1983c; Webster 1971, 29–39; Simon 1982b; Lissarrague 1990d; Hedreen 1992, 105–80; Green and Handley 1995, 22–29; Padgett 2000, 45–46.

215 Boston 03.788: *ARV²* 571.75; *Paralipomena* 390; *BAdd²* 261; Caskey and Beazley 1963, 51–52, pl. 86, no. 151; Simon 1982b, 135, pl. 36b; Lissarrague 1990d, 231, pl. 10; Hedreen 1992, pl. 33; *LIMC* 8, 1124, no. 153, pl. 770, s.v.

"Silenoi." For the costume of the satyr play, see Brommer 1959, 10–18;
Kossatz-Deissmann 1982; Green 1985, 111, 117–18; Caruso 1987;
Hedreen 1992, 107–12.

216 Caskey and Beazley 1963, 52; Simon 1982b, 135; Lissarrague 1990d, 231.

217 Padgett 2000, 45–6.

218 The earliest mention of Marsyas is in Herodotos (7.26). The story is
told by Apollodoros (*Bibl.* 1.4.2).

219 The earliest depiction of Marsyas may be on the red-figure oinochoe
Berlin 2418 (*CVA* Berlin 2, Germany 21, pl. 147; Richter 1929, 207, fig.
587), where he finds the pipes of Athena. For Marsyas in art, see *LIMC* 6
(1992), 366–78, pls. 183–93, s.v. "Marsyas" (Weis).

220 Hdt. 8.138. See also Xen. *An.* 1.2.13; Ov. *Met.* 11.85–193.

221 Berlin 3151: *ABV* 79–80; *Paralipomena* 30; *BAdd*² 22; Brommer 1941, 38,
fig. 1; Lissarrague 1990b, 119, fig. 66; Schefold 1992, 77, fig. 90;
Carpenter 1991, fig. 6.

222 For Attic examples, see Brommer 1941; *LIMC* 8 (1997), 846–51,
pls. 569–72, s.v. "Midas" (Miller). To these, add a black-figure
lekythos formerly in the art market (Galerie Günter Puhze, Katalog 11,
*Kunst der Antike* [Freiburg am Breisgau 1995], no. 186), with the henchmen
of Midas leading the bound Silenos. For Spartan and Chiot versions,
see Pipili 1987, 38–39. The subject of the bound Silenos affected the
composition of black-figure lekythos Athens 516 (*ABV* 508; Brommer
1959, figs. 30–32), where Herakles leads a coffle of bound satyrs whom
he probably has caught trying to rob him.

223 Atlanta, Emory 2001.1.1; height 16.5 cm.; previously unpublished; attribution by Padgett. Cf. another chous recently in the art market
(London, Christie's, October 5, 2000, lot 221), attributed to the manner
of the Phiale Painter (Oakley and Padgett); the satyr crouches humbly
like a child, but now he is a grizzled adult, and the maenad wisely
runs off.

224 See Hamilton 1991.

225 On Princeton 1997-68 (Buitron 1972, 132–33, no. 73), a damaged
calyx-krater that John Oakley believes is near the Phiale Painter and
possibly from his hand, one of the satyrs pulling a war chariot is a
teenager. Standing nearby, a much smaller child satyr holds a torch
next to an adult satyr.

226 Paris, Louvre G 422: *ARV*² 1019.77; *Paralipomena* 440; *BAdd*² 315; Simon
1963, pl. 7.5; Oakley 1990, 79, pl. 59. The identification with the Basilinna
was suggested by Simon (1963, 21–22).

229 Warsaw 142465: *ARV*² 1019.82; *Paralipomena* 441; *BAdd*² 315; Oakley 1990,
80, pl. 62. For the connection with the Lenaia, see Oakley 1990, 35–36.

# The Human Animal:
# The Near East and Greece

William A. P. Childs

**HERODOTOS,** the historian and guide to the peculiar traits of the barbarian world surrounding Greece in the fifth century B.C., hesitates only occasionally in accepting as truth accounts of strange beasts that lived on the periphery of the then-known world: flying snakes that invade Egypt from Arabia (2.75), giant ants that dig gold in India (3.102), and griffins that guard gold on the hither side of the land of the Hyperboreans (4.13).[1] The extraordinary composite beasts that had so inspired Greek artists of the seventh century are mentioned just in passing. By the mid-fifth century, such creatures had lost much of their hold on the Greek imagination or had become tamed. Take, for example, the fearsome Gorgons (Hdt. 2.91); Perseus had his hands full when he set out to bring back the head of Medusa and needed all sorts of divine aid.[2] By the middle of the fifth century, Medusa was gradually being transformed into a rather human, even attractive, girlish figure, though she continued on occasion to have wings.[3] But the terrible face—with fangs, projecting tongue, and snaky locks—was most of the time forgotten. The nature of the terrifying had radically changed.

A quick perusal of Greek art of the later eighth and the seventh century reveals a signal fascination with composite creatures of all sorts. Pride of place belongs to the Gorgons, centaurs, sphinxes, and sirens. All but the first, whatever name one attaches to them, are at home in the art of the ancient Near East or Egypt, and the Gorgon could derive from various Near Eastern models. These borrowings, along with the introduction of a wealth of curvilinear and vegetal motifs also at home in the eastern Mediterranean, long ago gave the name of Orientalizing period to Greek art of the seventh century.[4] There is, however, ample room for debate about the nature and consequences of the borrowing. Did the Greeks understand the images they borrowed, or were they motivated primarily or exclusively by aesthetic considerations? The pervasive Orientalizing character of Greek art of the seventh century certainly

Figure 1. Relief from the palace of Assurbanipal, Nineveh: lion-centaur and lion-demons. Assyrian, middle of the seventh century B.C. British Museum, London (WA 118912).

areas, this was usually subsidiary to their purpose as apotropaic genies. The designation "apotropaic" must not be taken narrowly. The *Oxford English Dictionary* defines the word as "having or reputed to have the power of averting evil influence or ill luck." As we shall see, many of the composite creatures in the Near East had the dual function of averting evil and procuring good. The use made by the Greeks of a select variety of these creatures in the later eighth century, and particularly in the seventh century, to "decorate" clay vases, shield straps, and just about any utensil or weapon suggests strongly, as I shall argue, that the Near Eastern values and functions were imitated in Greece to surround the activities of daily life, ritual, and war with protective and beneficent beings.

Let us begin with a brief look at composite creatures in Mesopotamia and dependent cultures. The study of composite creatures in the ancient Near East is complex for a variety of reasons. First, the ancient Near East consisted of a medley of related cultures, each of which had its own religious and artistic traditions. Second, Near Eastern art began more than two thousand years before the historical Greeks started to produce figural representations. Third, even in a given region and period, there was apparently no rigorous iconographic system comparable to that developed in Greece during the Archaic and Classical periods. In the period with which we are here primarily concerned, the Iron Age from about 1100 to 600 B.C., Assyria gradually conquered and administered the "ancient Near East" and progressively homogenized the artistic traditions. Yet scholars are convinced that Neo-Hittite, Aramaean, Phoenician, Assyrian, and Mesopotamian iconographic traditions, among others, persisted and frequently can be identified. Even within any of these local traditions, variations occur that cannot all be explained satisfactorily. For example, a recent iconographic dictionary lists five different composite creatures based on the lion: lion-centaur, lion-demon, lion-dragon, lion-fish, and lion-humanoid, and all occur in the Iron Age in Assyrian art.[7] The lion-centaur is straightforward: a lion body walking on all fours has a human male torso with head and arms and sometimes wings (fig. 1, lower register).[8] The lion-demon has a human male body with

suggests a profound fascination with everything Oriental, whether iconographic models or broad decorative elements such as the guilloche, palmette, or lotus bud. The complexity of the issues involved here is revealed by the more or less close reflection of Near Eastern and Anatolian, perhaps also Egyptian, models in early Greek cosmology and divine and heroic mythology.[5] One recent commentator has even proposed that some Greek myths were invented to suit borrowed Oriental images.[6]

As will be argued below, the function of the composite creatures that are the subject of this essay was largely similar in both the Near East and Greece. Although some of the creatures had roles in the myths of their respective

Figure 2. Relief from the temple of Ninurta, Nimrud: Anzû. Neo-Assyrian, ninth century B.C.
British Museum, London (WA 124571). After Layard, from Frankfort 1970, 163, fig. 188.

the head of a lion, long donkey-like ears, and the feet of a bird of prey (fig. 1, upper register). The lion-dragon has the body of a bird with wings, the forepaws of a lion, the hind legs of a lion but with the talons of a bird of prey, and the head of a lion. This creature may become Anzû in later representations, such as that on a Neo-Assyrian relief in London (fig 2).[9] The generic lion-demon has at least two identities: at first it was a companion of Nergal, the god of the underworld, but later it became the *ugallu* (big weather-beast), a beneficent being protective against evil demons and illnesses.[10] The lion-fish and the lion-humanoid are rather rare and simply combine the two beings at about mid-section.[11] Other part-lion creatures are probably Lula (Latarak), Lamaštu, and Pazuzu.

Some basic principles are useful to our discussion if not taken too strictly.[12] First, all the composite lion figures do not belong to a single category of being, since the lion-humanoid wears a horned cap and is, therefore, a god. This is true also of some winged male sphinxes, such as that on a Middle Assyrian seal (cat. no. 10) and the lion-centaur on the Assyrian relief in the lower register of figure 1. Without the horned cap, the species of being is either a demon or a genie. (I use the latter term in generic contexts because many of the composite creatures are not malignant, and the word "demon" has such a connotation.[13]) Second, the images alone are not adequate to define the beings in question, and thus inscriptions and texts are necessary to elucidate their functions and characters. Unfortunately, these do not always exist. Third, there are very few connections that can be made between the representations of composite beings and narrative mythological texts. Indeed, ancient Near Eastern iconography is far

Figure 3. Impression of a cylinder seal: possibly Gilgamesh and Enkidu
killing Humbaba. Neo-Assyrian, late ninth–early seventh centuries B.C.
Antikensammlung, Staatliche Museen zu Berlin–Preussischer Kulturbesitz
(VA 4215).

Figure 4. Impression of a cylinder seal: bull-man and hero.
Akkadian, Early Dynastic II, third quarter of the third millennium B.C.
British Museum, London (WA 89308).

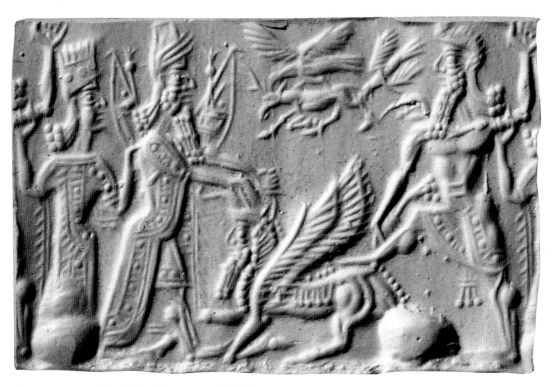

Figure 5. Impression of a cylinder seal: two men attacking the
Bull of Heaven. Neo-Babylonian, late seventh–early sixth centuries B.C.
British Museum, London (WA 89435).

more concerned with the representation of basic religious
statements than with narratives.[14] Although modern
commentaries are littered with references to the deeds
of Gilgamesh known from various Sumerian and later
poems, the evidence is at best circumstantial for corre-
lating pictures with the hero. A good example is the
depiction of Gilgamesh and Enkidu killing Humbaba
(fig. 3).[15] The recurrent motif of two men attacking
a third between them, who is always represented with
frontal face, may be an image of the killing of Humbaba,
but the iconographic pointers are few and subtle.[16]

Although some of the composite creatures of the
ancient Near East had some form of divine status, the
majority from the very beginning appear to be of lowly
rank, and, as the iconography developed in the third and
second millennia, they became first adjuncts of the great
gods and then sometimes rebellious entities.[17] The bull-
man is one such—a bull with human torso and head but
with horns, standing upright—who first appeared in the
Early Dynastic II period on cylinder seals and remained

popular thereafter (fig. 4).[18] At first, he was a protector
of flocks, then he probably represented the mountains
that border Mesopotamia on the east whence the sun rises,
and was therefore an associate or servant of the sun-god
Utu/Shamash,[19] an attendant whom the god must on
occasion also conquer.[20] As with the lion, images of a
composite bull and man are numerous and varied in their
appearance. For example, the relationship of the human-
headed quadruped bull (e.g., cat. no. 1) to the bull-man
is unclear.[21] He wears on occasion the horned cap of
divinity and was adopted by the Assyrians as a monumental guardian of palace gates.[22] The relationship of this
figure to the Bull of Heaven, which Ishtar sends against
Gilgamesh, is also unclear.[23] On Neo-Assyrian seals in the
British Museum, an archer aims at the human-headed
winged bull,[24] while on a Neo-Babylonian seal, two men,
possibly Gilgamesh and Enkidu, try to kill it (fig. 5).[25]
Of interest in the present context is the obvious relationship between these human-headed bulls and Acheloos in
the Greek repertory, the earliest example of which may be

Figure 6. Orthostat blocks at Carchemish, North Syria: composite genie. Neo-Hittite, early ninth century B.C. After Hogarth 1914, pl. B 9a.

on a Middle Protocorinthian oinochoe of just before the middle of the seventh century, the date of which at least suggests the possibility of a Near Eastern origin for the image of Acheloos.[26] Yet the Bull of Heaven belongs to Anu, the sky god, and has no obvious connection with streams and water, the realm of Acheloos in Greece (Hes. *Theog.* 340), so the manner of acquisition of the figure by the Greeks remains obscure. Since it is *a priori* unlikely that all Greek composite creatures were borrowed directly from the Near East, the image of Acheloos may simply have been created on the analogy of Near Eastern creatures. A tenuous connection could have been the parallel concept of the bull as an image of fertility in both the Aegean and the Near East. If the Greeks knew of the Near Eastern creature, they may have encountered it as a sign of the zodiac, since the Bull of Heaven was the constellation Taurus, and astronomical figures may have played some role in the transmission of iconographic types, a hypothesis discussed briefly below.

In the Iron Age the composite genie appears to play a very specific role: to ward off evil and to foster good.[27] This is amply illustrated by the carved orthostat blocks of the North Syrian/Neo-Hittite area, such as those of Carchemish (fig. 6),[28] and the discovery of small figurines, mostly of unfired clay, in brick boxes and other containers at significant locations in temples, palaces, and houses. First identified by Robert Koldewey at Babylon,[29] the clay figurines have been found also at Assur (fig. 7),[30] Ur,[31] and Nimrud.[32] The figurines and related incantation texts have been widely studied.[33] One large and easily recognized group of these is the antediluvian "Seven Sages," or *apkallē*. Two major forms of the *apkallu* are the bird- or griffin-man and the fish-garbed genie (fig. 7; and Princeton plaques, cat. nos. 4, 5). These are clearly described in incantation texts, which prescribe in detail the procedures for protecting a house or person from malignant demons:

Seven statues of the Wise Ones which are . . . their own
and furnished with faces of birds (and) carrying in their right hands the "purifier"
(and) in their left hands the ritual cup,
clad in gypsum and cloaked with birds' wings upon their [shoulders]
thou shalt make. Seven statues of the Wise Ones of [clay]
clad in gypsum for their garments, fishes' skins [in black wash]
thou shalt trace upon them, carrying in [their right] hands
the purifier, (and) in their left hands the r[itual cup].[34]

These descriptions perfectly characterize not only the two Princeton plaques, but also the rather large number of similar figurines discovered in excavations.[35]

The function of the above-cited text was for the protection and purification of a private house. Figurines and plaques of the *apkallē* in the form of bird- or griffin-men and fish-garbed genies from excavated contexts show that they were actually deposited in groups of seven at points of entry into rooms to guard these critical areas, a function they appear to have shared with the monumental representations on the stone orthostats of Neo-Assyrian palaces. The correlation between the texts and composite genies of the Assyrian palace reliefs is, in fact, quite close, as Julian Reade has demonstrated.[36] Although there is no consistent pattern through the various Assyrian palaces from the ninth to the seventh century, the number of griffin-men and fish-garbed genies associated with doors is remarkable.[37]

As guardians, the griffin-men and the fish-garbed genies were benign. Other figures served the same apotropaic function. In the text KAR no. 298[38] appear the raging serpent (*mušḫuššu*),[39] the goat-fish (*suḫurmašû*),[40] the scorpion-man (*girtablullû*),[41] the god Latarak,[42] and the lion-centaur (urmaḫlullu).[43] Of these, the scorpion-man, the lion-centaur, and possibly the raging serpent also are depicted, though rarely, on Assyrian palace reliefs.[44] But many such figures occur in the reliefs on *kudurrus*—stelae that mark royal gifts, frequently of land[45]—which emphasizes their role as protectors and defenders.

There were also malignant figures that apparently were used to ward off the evil they bore. Such in part were the *utukkē* (*udug*), demons of disease.[46] An inscribed lion-headed figure in the British Museum (fig. 8) states: "Destroyer of the evil throat, the hurrying, smeared with

Figure 7. Figurine of a fish-man (an apkallu).
Assyrian, ninth–seventh centuries B.C., found at Assur, terracotta.
Antikensammlung, Staatliche Museen zu Berlin–Preussischer
Kulturbesitz (VA 3727).

Figure 8. Inscribed lion-headed figurine. Neo-Babylonian,
late seventh–early sixth centuries B.C., bronze.
British Museum, London (WA 93078).

Figure 9. Statuette of Pazuzu. Assyrian/Neo-Babylonian,
seventh–early sixth centuries B.C., bronze.
Musée du Louvre, Paris (MNB 467).

sucked blood, tireless runner, may he cut off the feet of his
comrades."[47] This has been interpreted by some, beginning
with Carl Frank in 1908, to mean that the figure represents
an *utukku*, but the present consensus is against this.[48]
However, a figure similar to the statuette is described in
the dream of an Assyrian prince and is called *utukku lemnu*,
evil spirit.[49] The description and the figure in London
also resemble the *ugallu*, lion-demon (fig. 1, upper register).[50]
As has been remarked above, iconography is not always
consistent, and the ambiguity here demonstrates rather
clearly that apotropaic figures are dual in nature: they
are terrifying and horrible themselves, yet they protect
humans from their own kind.

The figure of Pazuzu illustrates the point well.[51]
Generally considered a malignant demon of the underworld,

Pazuzu certainly was a guardian against the goddess/demon
Lamaštu. In form, Pazuzu has a leonine or doglike head
(see cat. no. 7) with prominent crest, scaly humanoid
body, human arms with leonine paws, four wings, and
talons for feet (fig. 9).[52] The details vary from figure to
figure, but the above description covers the most frequent
traits of the demon. In the same fashion as the *apkallē*,
figurines and amulets of Pazuzu guarded the passages in
houses.[53] One of the clearest statements in images of the
nature and function of composite creatures in the Near
East is a small Neo-Babylonian bronze plaque now in the
Louvre.[54] A figure of Pazuzu presides over the scene: his
body is modeled on the back of the plaque so that his
head projects over the top (figs. 10, 11). The front of the
plaque is divided into four horizontal registers. The top

Figure 10. Plaque, obverse: Lamaštu on a boat on the river of the
underworld. Neo-Babylonian, late seventh–early sixth centuries B.C.,
bronze. Musée du Louvre, Paris (AO 22205).

Figure 11. Plaque, reverse: Pazuzu. Neo-Babylonian, late seventh–early sixth centuries B.C., bronze. Musée du Louvre, Paris (AO 22205).

conventional running-knee position on the back of a donkey that stands on a boat that floats on a stream with five fish; two trees grow on the bank to the viewer's right. Lamaštu's head projects up into the frieze band above; she holds out two snakes in her hands; two animals (dog and pig) hang on her breasts. Her head is leonine with large ears, an object like a large nail sticks into the cranium, her body is covered with fur indicated by short incisions, and her legs end in bird talons. To the viewer's left is a winged figure with human torso, arms, and legs but bird talons for feet, paws for hands, and a ghastly head, possibly another figure of Pazuzu. To the viewer's right are nine objects, not all easily recognizable. There appear to be two vases, a bowl, a box, and possibly the leg of an animal. A reasonable interpretation is that these are the gifts that are prescribed in the incantation texts to bribe Lamaštu to leave a sick person alone.[57]

The interpretation of the Louvre plaque appears quite straightforward: Lamaštu is shown on her pet animal, the donkey, on a boat on the river of the underworld. She is being driven off by the genie on the viewer's left, probably Pazuzu, and enticed to depart by the gifts on the right. Above, the sick man is tended by the two *apkallē* fish-garbed genies and is surrounded by an army of demons, probably, as noted above, benign. The whole scene takes place under the symbols of the great gods in the topmost register, and Pazuzu embraces the whole plaque behind (and above).

The plaque in the Louvre has at least two more or less full parallels,[58] but more important is the existence of a large number of smaller and simpler plaques and amulets that represent only Lamaštu, often inscribed with her name.[59] These simpler representations reveal a number of variants in the figure of the demon, such as wings for arms, the addition of wings, and several long, slightly sinuous protrusions (horns?) on the head.[60] The use of these plaques and amulets must have been to ward off the very figure depicted on them.[61] A common prayer written on the various figurines and amulets of all types is "Bring in the good, keep out the evil."[62] The dual character of any of the figures treated above is clear in the inscriptions on the two lions that guard the northeast entrance to the city at Til Barsip on the upper Euphrates in the eighth

band is filled with symbols of the great gods.[55] Next below is a row of seven demons with human bodies and various animal heads, all facing to the right with the right hand raised and the left extended diagonally in front.[56] The identification of these demons is unknown; their placement in the space below the symbols of the gods and in close proximity to the fish-garbed genies below suggests that they are benign. Below this is a complex scene: on the left is a stand, possibly an incense burner, then a fish-garbed genie facing to the right, a bed with a bearded man supine on it, another fish-garbed genie now facing to the left, then two lion-demons (*ugallē*) facing each other, and finally an indistinct, bearded figure with right arm raised facing to the right. The last frieze band at the bottom is the tallest. In the center is a large figure of Lamaštu in the century: "The impetuous storm, irresistible in attack, / crushing rebels, / procuring that which satisfies the heart" and "He who pounces on rebellion, / scours the enemy, drives out the evil / and lets enter the good."[63]

From the modern point of view, the representations of composite genies in the Near East retain a high degree of ambiguity. For example, the birdlike depictions of Lamaštu are not very different from, and easily confused with, griffin-men, which are *apkallē* (the "Seven Sages"). The lion-demon is difficult to distinguish from an *utukku* and resembles the lion-dragon and Lamaštu.[64] A more puzzling relationship is that between the biped bird-man or griffin-man (e.g., fig. 6, extreme right orthostat block; cat. no. 4), which is also known as a griffin-genie or griffin-demon, and the quadruped griffin, which has a more or less leonine body (e.g., on the Urartian quiver, cat. no. 3). Although the two basic types of griffin share a number of characteristics, they are also quite distinct creatures.[65] Both types have the head of a bird of prey, and they frequently share one or more long locks that descend from the top of the head along the neck. This lock is not shared by the Assyrian griffin-genies, who have a prominent crest on the top of the head that descends down the back of the neck,[66] but the lock is common to all the griffin types of the Syro-Palestinian area.[67] A mark of similarity is that both beings are depicted symmetrically flanking a "sacred tree."[68] But on Phoenician ivory plaques, quadruped griffins are frequently shown hunted and killed by a male god or hero.[69] The brief review given earlier of the various manifestations of lion-genies demonstrates that it is not necessary to assume more than a general relationship between the griffin types. The distinction becomes most interesting when the Greeks borrowed the griffin.

Griffins first appeared in Greece near the end of the eighth century as protomes riveted onto the rims of large bronze cauldrons imported from the Near East. These have been found principally at the sanctuary of Zeus at Olympia (fig. 12), but they have also been discovered in other sanctuaries, such as the Acropolis of Athens, Delphi, and in East Greece, in Samos and Miletos.[70] It is difficult to tell whether the griffin protome is a griffin-genie (biped) or

a plain griffin (quadruped). The long neck covered in a scale pattern emphasizes the birdlike qualities of the biped beast, contrasting with the leonine emphasis of the quadruped creature.[71] Perhaps the best comparison in the Near East is with the lion-dragon (fig. 2)[72] with some traits of the *mušḫuššu*,[73] which explains the leonine lower jaw, a signal trait of some of the Syrian/Neo-Hittite griffin-genies.[74] The Greeks adopted the griffin protome as their own. From rather small figures made in hammered

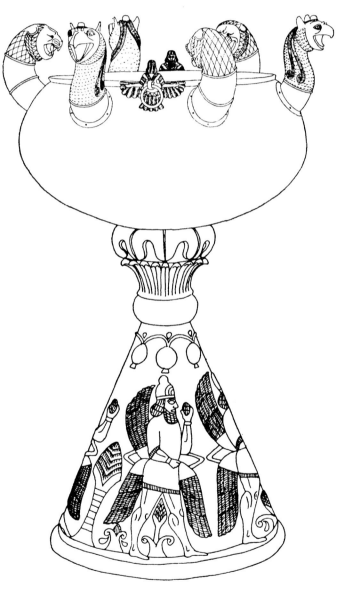

Figure 12. Cauldron with griffin and lion protomes. Syrian, early seventh century B.C., found at the sanctuary of Zeus at Olympia, Greece. After Herrmann 1972, 82, fig. 49.

Figure 13. Skyphos: man between two lions. Greek, Attic, Late Geometric, late eighth century B.C. National Archaeological Museum, Athens (14.475).

bronze, the griffin protome grew into an elegant cast figure, the development of which can be traced in some detail from the late eighth century to the end of the seventh, and can be used to characterize the essence of the birth of Greek representational art and aesthetic principles.[75]

The interesting problem is that scholars cannot decide whether the earliest griffin protomes were imported from the Near East or made in Greece. This is a serious matter. If the griffin is an Oriental iconographic type and Greek imitations cannot be distinguished from the model, early Greek art can be construed as a mere mechanical reflection of Eastern forms, for which there is no other evidence. The difficulty lies in the lack of essential information. Almost all commentators agree that the earliest cauldrons found in Greece were probably made in the area of North Syria. Cauldrons of similar type have, indeed, been found in the Near East, but with the single exception of a large cauldron found in tomb 79 at Salamis on the island of Cyprus,[76] they do not have griffin protomes attached to them. On this cauldron, the griffin protomes are attached over the wings of the "siren" handle

attachments, suggesting a secondary elaboration of the decoration of the cauldron. The idiosyncratic nature of both the hammered "siren" handle attachments and the cast griffin protomes strongly suggests a local Cypriote work. It has been suggested that the griffin protomes were from the beginning Greek additions to the imported bronze cauldrons. A significant argument against this is that the griffin protomes do not reflect the prevailing rectilinear style of the Late Geometric period in the way that the clearly copied "siren" handle attachments do (see, e.g., cat. no. 74).[77] Another, equally weighty argument against the Greek invention of the griffin protome is that the metallurgical analysis of a number of the cauldrons, "siren" handle attachments, and protomes reveals a distinct difference between the earliest hammered griffin protomes and indigenous Greek metallurgy.[78] Only two propositions appear to explain the scanty archaeological evidence: (1) bronze griffin protomes existed in the Near East but by chance have not been found; (2) griffin protomes were produced in Greece but made by Near Eastern migrant smiths.[79]

The griffin protomes are the most popular figures on cauldrons, but lion protomes and snakes are also known.[80] What is interesting in the present context is that the Greeks certainly understood the dual meaning of the lion in the Near East right from the beginning. On a Late Geometric skyphos, a small male figure stands between two beasts with huge mouths (fig. 13),[81] but he merely reaches out and touches the beasts in the manner of the Near Eastern Master of Animals (fig. 14).[82] On a kantharos in Copenhagen, a far less lucky man is being devoured by the pair of lions on either side of him (fig. 15).[83] Similar images are found in Crete on one of the bronze votive shields from the cave sanctuary of Zeus on Mount Ida.[84] Here a lion devours a man and a nude Mistress of Animals stands between two felines that raise a paw to her, a gesture of reverence. This gesture, though without the divine figure, is frequently found on Greek vases of the Late Geometric and Early Orientalizing periods.[85]

The parallel appearance of lions in the Near East and Greece suggests a broad understanding by the Greeks of the motifs they were borrowing from their eastern neighbors. The appearance of the griffins on the bronze cauldrons together with lions, both in the form of protomes, suggests that there is a parallelism in meaning. In this case, the griffin protomes were derived from the bird-man/griffin-genie (combined, as noted above, with the lion-dragon) and are benign beings that guard the cauldron. The Greek iconographic tradition is ambiguous because the rest of Greek art does not adopt the bird-man/griffin-genie but instead uses the quadruped griffin. How this came about is obscure. Some evidence suggests that there was a continuity of iconography between the Aegean Bronze Age, when the Aegean knew the quadruped griffin, and the beginnings of Greek art in the eighth and seventh centuries.[86] The griffin protomes on the bronze cauldrons must derive from the contemporary Near East, but they remain isolated from the representations of quadruped griffins on vases and plaques from Greece and Etruria (compare, e.g., cat. nos. 42, 67). An additional characteristic of Greek quadruped griffins is that they normally do not interact with humans, whereas in the Near East

Figure 14. Statue base: Master of Animals. Neo-Hittite, eighth century B.C., from Zincirli (Sam'al). Archaeological Museum, Istanbul (7768).

Figure 15. Kantharos: man devoured by lions. Greek, Attic, Late Geometric, second half of the eighth century B.C. National Museum, Copenhagen (727).

a popular appearance of the quadruped griffin is as the victim of a "hero," who spears the beast on innumerable Phoenician ivory plaques.[87]

The origin and nature of the other composite beasts in this exhibition are hardly less ambiguous than the figure of the griffin. The "siren" provides a typical case. By definition, a "siren" is a bird with human head or face.

Sirens appear on the Oriental bronze cauldrons as the supports for the large ring handles. Here there is no debate possible about their origin in the Near East because they are found on examples of such cauldrons from Urartu (fig. 16),[88] Phrygia, Cyprus, and, no longer attached to a cauldron, from Assyria.[89] The Greeks were copying these "siren" handles by the beginning of the seventh century (cat. no. 74); such copies are easily distinguished from the Oriental originals but only in style. Otherwise, the Greek and Oriental types are extremely close in form. Curiously, "sirens" are not frequently encountered in the art of the Near East other than in the form of handle attachments for the large cauldrons.[90] In Egypt, however, the human-headed bird is well known as the *ba*-bird, a representation of the "spirit" of the deceased (e.g., cat. no. 8). Given the close resemblance between the *ba*-bird and the appearance of the Greek siren, it appears possible that there is once again a distinct difference between the origin of the cauldron "sirens" and that of the siren of Greek vases and plaques.[91]

The distinction between the iconographic origin of the composite creatures attached to the bronze cauldrons and the rest of Greek art may derive from the very specific function of the cauldrons. At first imported from the Near East, cauldrons have been found exclusively in sanctuaries. As such, cauldrons were among the first monumental votives and must have been imbued with religious awe. Their reception is attested by several representations on Greek painted pottery of the late eighth century and the first half of the seventh.[92] Representative of these is a fragmentary Protocorinthian krateriskos from the Heraion of Samos, dating from the early seventh century.[93] A recognizable cauldron with three griffin protomes is flanked on one side by a partially preserved centaur and on the other by a grazing deer; further to the right is a feline possibly attacking a crouching man, who is followed by a striding quadruped that could be any number of different animals. On the extreme left of the frieze as published is Athena with spear and shield facing right and a sphinx that touches her robe with one paw in a gesture of reverence. The meaning of all these figures is unclear, but the divine and powerful world in which they exist is unmistakable. A related scene appears on a small Protocorinthian aryballos in Boston (cat. no. 31):[94] a male

Figure 16. "Siren" handle attachment. Urartian, seventh century B.C., from Toprakkale, bronze. Archaeological Museum, Istanbul (1271). After Akurgal 1961, fig. 19.

figure strides to the left toward a centaur; with his arm raised, he brandishes at the centaur an object that looks a bit like an inflated rubber glove. The object probably is a thunderbolt and the figure Zeus.[95] To the right of Zeus, a man holding a sword moves rapidly to the right where a dinos or cauldron on a conical stand is flanked by two birds in the field with two more birds perched on its rim. How the set of figures is to be interpreted remains completely open to speculation, but the presence of the cauldron suggests an importance rarely given mere objects in early Greek art.

Another instance of the importance of the cauldrons with griffin protomes is very different in nature but equally informative: the Protoattic amphora in Eleusis by the Polyphemos Painter (see this volume, Tsiafakis, "ΠΕΛΩΡΑ," fig. 14).[96] On the belly is a scene of Perseus chased by the two sisters of Medusa; Perseus flees on the extreme right. Athena faces toward the two Gorgons who pursue Perseus;

on the extreme left is the horizontal, headless body of Medusa. Only a perfunctory look is necessary to see that the heads of the two Gorgon sisters resemble the form of a cauldron with snake protomes, very like the Phoenician silver vessel from Praeneste in the Villa Giulia.[97]

The complexity of the relationship between composite creatures in Greek art and those in the Near East and Egypt varies with each figure. Consider for a moment another beast, the Chimaera, which Bellerophon must subdue. Bellerophon is a Corinthian hero sent to Lycia at the southwest corner of Asia Minor where he must perform a series of impossible feats. The earliest descriptions of the Chimaera are in the *Iliad* (6.179–82; 16.328–29) and the *Theogony* (304–25), and the beast appears on a Protocorinthian skyphos (ca. 660 B.C.) just as described: a lion with the head of a goat growing from its back.[98] Although the rear of the beast is missing from the skyphos, other Protocorinthian representations make clear that it also had a snake's head at the end of a long tail.[99] A figure of very similar appearance occurs on the orthostat reliefs of Carchemish[100] (see fig. 6, extreme left orthostat block) and Zincirli,[101] though in both cases the head growing from the back of the lion is human, a variant that occurs on one Protocorinthian aryballos.[102] The location of Bellerophon's feat in western Asia Minor, though not the Near East proper, suggests an understanding on the part of the Greeks that the Chimaera belonged to that area, very nearly where the artistic prototype existed.

The use made of the Chimaera in Greek art is interesting particularly because it indicates a selective adaptation and use of composite Near Eastern creatures. On the orthostats of the Neo-Hittite sites, the Chimaera had no narrative context and served only an apotropaic function, but in Greece the beast was to be conquered by a hero. The best parallel in the Near East is the quadruped griffin speared by a "hero," already mentioned above. When the various composite beasts of the Near East, such as the scorpion-man,[103] are shown in action, they appear for the most part to be attacking the forces of disorder. An exception is the lion-dragon, who is frequently presented as the enemy of a god or hero,[104] though it is also an animal sacred to various gods, who often stand on its back.[105] The most impressive representation of the battle between a genie or god and the lion-dragon is on a relief from Nimrud discovered by Layard (fig. 2).[106]

There are connections between Near Eastern representations of composite creatures and the Greek narrative use of similar creatures in heroic and divine mythology. The most important group of certified enemies of civilization in the Near East was a motley crowd of monsters first associated with the warrior god Ningirsu/Ninurta. They first appeared in Gudea's account of his rebuilding of the temple of Ningirsu at Girsu in the late third millennium.[107] Here representations of the enemies of the god were hung in various locations in the new temple, and organized cults devoted to these "slain enemies" transformed them into minor divinities.[108] They reappeared in the later *Lugal-e* and the *Angim* with some variations[109] and were eventually transformed into members of the army of Tiamat in her battle with Marduk in the Babylonian *Enuma Eliš*, where they became a spottily recognizable series of figures:

> Mother Hubur, who fashions all things,
> Contributed an unfaceable weapon: she bore giant snakes,
> Sharp of tooth and unsparing of fang (?).
> She filled their bodies with venom instead of blood.
> She cloaked ferocious dragons with fearsome rays
> And made them bear mantles of radiance, made them godlike,
> "Whoever looks upon them shall collapse in utter terror!
> Their bodies shall rear up continually and never turn away!"
> She stationed a horned serpent, a *mušḫuššu*-dragon, and a *laḫmu*-hero,
> An *ugallu*-demon, a rabid dog, and a scorpion-man,
> Aggressive *ūmu*-demons, a fish-man (*kulullû*), and a bull-man
> Bearing merciless weapons, fearless in battle.[110]

Of all these "slain enemies," one figure has drawn particular attention, the *mušmaḫḫu* or *muš-sag-imin*, a seven-headed snake.[111] Although not represented in art after the Akkadian period, it continues in literature into the Iron Age.[112] Scholars have sought to connect it with the Greek Hydra, the enemy of Herakles, and, by the way, to posit a relationship between Herakles and Ningirsu/Ninurta.[113] Of all the "slain enemies" and the creatures of the army of Tiamat, only the *mušmaḫḫu* might have inspired a Greek monster, which does not exclude the borrowing, but it does stress the selective adaptation of the Near Eastern composite creatures by the Greeks of the eighth and seventh centuries.

Another possible link between Greek and Near Eastern composite creatures may exist in the case of the Hittite storm god's battle with Illuyanka[114] and Zeus's battle with Typhon. On the orthostat reliefs from Malatya,[115] which are of uncertain date but perhaps belong in the early Iron Age, the storm god faces a snaky beast that vaguely resembles the figure of Typhon on a Chalcidian hydria (see this volume, Tsiafakis, "ΠΕΛΩΡΑ," fig. 20)[116] and on a Laconian cup of the sixth century B.C. (cf. also cat. no. 98).[117] Here the connection may be through literary descriptions rather than imagery,[118] since the Greek examples are so much later.

For other Greek composite creatures, such as the Minotaur, the relationship with Near Eastern models is difficult to establish. The bull is very much at home in the Aegean as a divine power, and little or no external influence appears necessary: the bull form of the Minotaur is explicit in the narrative, and the human element turns the creature into an awful monster. The possible contemporary Near Eastern models combine different parts of the two beings: man above the waist and bull below. This is the reverse of the Greek type. Early Mesopotamian bull-men do have horns and are shown fighting with the nude hero (fig. 4),[119] but the type was unknown in the Iron Age, when the horns disappeared and the bull-man did not fight.[120] Perhaps the relationship of the Greek Minotaur to the Near Eastern bull-man lies mainly in the combination of animal and human forms to depict a powerful creature, and was not based on actual borrowing of an image, since the closest Near Eastern models were so very much earlier than the alleged Greek reflections.

Several Near Eastern composite creatures borrowed by the Greeks—sirens, sphinxes, and griffins—are distinctive because they played almost no role in Greek myths. When they appear in the seventh century, they parade around on vases and other utensils. The sphinx can be taken as relatively typical: it had a role in the myth of Oedipus (e.g., cat. no. 63 and this volume, Tsiafakis, "ΠΕΛΩΡΑ," fig. 9) but was a favorite of seventh- and early-sixth-century vase-painters simply for itself, either together with various real animals in friezes or emphasized in heraldic pairs (e.g., cat. nos. 33, 66).[121] Even though the sphinx had its origin in Egypt, it is clear that the Greeks learned of it from the Levant, where it was particularly popular with the Phoenicians (cf. the sphinx on the Syro-Phoenician bowl in Princeton, cat. no. 9). This avenue of transmission is important because it emphasizes the minor role Egypt played in the Greek "Orientalizing revolution." Greek sphinxes became explicitly apotropaic when they began to occupy the crests of Attic grave stelae,[122] a role they ceded to sirens in the fourth century.[123] As already noted, the griffin closely followed the pattern of the sphinx (e.g., cat. no. 42), except that the combat of "hero" and griffin popular in Phoenician ivories was not copied. Sirens have a minor role in the adventures of Odysseus, but otherwise they are rare outside of seventh- and sixth-century vases (e.g., cat. nos. 75, 76).[124]

Other composite creatures, notably centaurs and the Gorgons, participate in myth and also function as independent creatures. In Greek art, centaurs appear individually and in groups from the late eighth century on, and are portrayed as beings that inhabit the wild (e.g., cat. nos. 14, 15)[125]—images similar to Middle Assyrian (cat. nos. 11, 12) and other Near Eastern seals.[126] Admittedly, the depiction of Medusa as a female centaur on a Cycladic relief-pithos in Paris of the early seventh century does indicate that centaurs can be terrifying creatures (see this volume, Tsiafakis, "ΠΕΛΩΡΑ," fig. 13), but their composite nature already assures the viewer of that.[127] The earliest example of a centaur in Greece after the Bronze Age is the magnificent terracotta figurine from Lefkandi (see this volume, Padgett, "Horse Men," fig. 3),[128] found divided between two tombs and therefore serving in some fashion as guardian of the tombs, a function which hardly suggests the malignant figure of the later Cycladic pithos. Totally apart from the question as to whether the Lefkandi centaur is a Bronze Age memory[129] or the product of influence from the Near East[130]—the existence of which at Lefkandi is proved by the presence at the site of imported bronze bowls of roughly contemporary date[131]—the Greeks appear to have had a clear idea of the different realms of the composite beast. As a genie of the wild, the centaur in the Near

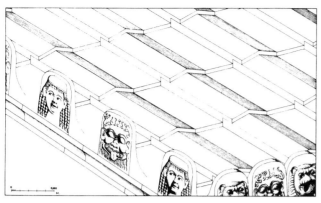

Figure 17. Drawing of reconstructed antefixes on the early temple of Hera, Corfu. Greek, sixth century B.C. After Winter 1993, 116, fig. 13.

East and Greece had an apotropaic function, since its presence on Late Geometric and Orientalizing vases in non-narrative contexts can only be explained as such.

The same is true of the Gorgons. As a gorgoneion, simply the head of one of the Gorgons, the motif is wildly popular on Greek vases of the sixth century (e.g., cat. no. 82). The use of gorgoneia on antefixes surrounds the eaves of a building with emblems of a powerful figure that bears no reference to the mythical adventure of Perseus (fig. 17; cat. nos. 88, 89).[132] Even when the Gorgons are part of a scene with Perseus, the prominent depiction of the two sisters chasing the hero frequently emphasizes them more than the story (e.g., cat. no. 81).[133] When the Mistress of Animals on a Rhodian plate appears with the head of a Gorgon,[134] a connection is made with the pediment of the temple of Artemis at Corfu, since Artemis is the normal form of the Mistress of Animals and one of the pediments of her temple on Corfu displays a monumental Gorgon in its center (see this volume, Tsiafakis, "ΠΕΛΩΡΑ," fig. 15).[135] The choice of the Gorgon as an alter-ego of Artemis is not arbitrary. The Gorgon appears to have been created as a composite of Lamaštu, Bes, and perhaps the mask of Humbaba,[136] and Lamaštu was specifically an enemy of pregnant women, women in childbirth, and babies—the very same arenas in which Artemis also was active, though as protectress. A running Gorgon also appears as a strongly benign force on the predella of an Archaic Attic grave stela,[137] which recalls the centaur from Lefkandi, found (as noted above) in two parts in adjoining graves.

The terrifying composite genies of the Near East that were nonetheless benign, such as the lion-demon and the fish-garbed genie, did not inspire Greek enthusiasm, even though they knew the creatures, as is proved by the reuse of a Near Eastern bronze relief for a statue about the middle of the seventh century at Olympia.[138] Conversely, the man-fish could be the origin of Triton (e.g., cat. nos. 95, 96),[139] but once again the generalized Near Eastern creature, like the Chimaera, was inserted into narrative myths and given a more distinct personality than is attested for the alleged Near Eastern model. A related Greek sea monster, the Ketos, experienced a process of development, which suggests that it was a native Greek invention.[140] Other than blatant content, how did the Greeks even know what the various composite creatures meant? In the *Theogony*, Hesiod (306 ff.) groups a large number of terrible beasts as children of Echidna and Typhon: Orthos, the dog of Geryon; Kerberos; the Hydra; the Chimaera; the Sphinx (though the father was Orthos); and the Nemean lion. Still very much in the family was the snake that guarded the apple tree of the Hesperides (333 ff.); the serpent was the youngest child of Keto and Phorkys, and thus he was related to Echidna (295 ff.), as were the Gorgons (274 ff.).[141] Although M. L. West believes that the transmission of the Near Eastern cosmogony on which the *Theogony* depends must have occurred in the Bronze Age, there is no cogent reason why this must be so, or perhaps better, must alone be so.[142] All will agree, I suspect, that the Minoan-Mycenaean world belonged within the eastern Mediterranean cultural sphere, and that parts of this *koine* survived the Dark Ages. The pictorial tradition makes it eminently clear, however, that historical Greek culture was powerfully refertilized by contact with the Near East in the eighth and seventh centuries. Even though Near Eastern imports are known from Lefkandi on Euboia at the very end of the tenth century,[143] these have no resonance in Greek art until after 800. Although the concentration of composite monsters in the *Theogony* resembles the similar group in the army of Tiamat cited above, there is no further relationship.

Though West wishes to draw a close relationship between Hesiod's *Theogony* and the Hurrian/Hittite myth of Kumarbi, Hesiod's construction does not closely resemble either the Kumarbi myth or the *Enuma Eliš*, nor really the theogony of Dunnu, to which it is closely related in the violence of the succession of the gods.[144] Hesiod has recast the Near Eastern theogonies much as the Greeks recast Lamaštu and Bes into the Gorgon. No long time span is required for these transformations because they do not constitute mere borrowing; rather, they represent conscious adaptations right from the beginning. This can be seen in another area of the relationship. The earliest stone statues of women in Greece, such as that dedicated by Nikandra, dated about the middle of the seventh century,[145] seem to follow the pattern of Assyrian male statues such as that of Ashurnasirpal II[146] and his followers. The earliest Greek statues of men in the second half of the seventh century[147] follow the pattern of the *laḫmu*, or naked hero, with long hair, such as the figure on the left of a Middle Assyrian cylinder seal (cat. no. 12) and on the right of an Akkadian seal (fig. 4).[148] In each case, the motivation for the borrowing is different and can be understood only as responding to a Greek concept of what was to be represented.

The means of transmission of the motifs must have been varied. As has been suggested, textual descriptions probably played a role in the creation of an image of Typhon, and immigrant craftsmen may well have had a hand in the making of the bronze griffin protomes for the seventh-century cauldrons. Astronomy/astrology as another avenue of transmission of the composite creature from the Near East to Greece deserves at least brief mention. Various creatures of the Near East existed as constellations,[149] and any sailor plotting a path across the Mediterranean would have had to be familiar with the pattern of stars and to have been able to discuss these in the language(s) of the numerous ports of call. In one case, that of the Hydra, the Near Eastern name and its image are preserved in a text of Seleucid/Hellenistic date: $^{mul}muš$, a version of the *mušḫuššu*.[150] The $^{mul}maš_2$ is the goat-fish, which is the constellation Capricorn.[151] Another figure, the $^{mul}ud$-$ka$-$duḫ$-$a$, is the "storm that tears open the mouth," possibly the lion-dragon.[152] As a constellation, it is variously recognized as Sagittarius, Pegasos, and Cygnus, but Sagittarius is usually recognized as the centaur ($^{mul}pa$-$bil$-$sag$).[153] Anzû is also known from astrological texts.[154] Finally, the Bull of Heaven is the constellation Taurus.[155] This is not a long list, comprising as it does only two or three figures adopted by seventh-century decorators of vases or by Greek mythology; nevertheless, it emphasizes the variety of paths for the acquisition of knowledge and understanding of Near Eastern motifs by the Greeks. The omission of so many figures which the Greeks clearly knew, such as the fish-garbed genie on the bronze sheet reused at Olympia for a piece of a statue, stresses how selectively the Greeks adopted and adapted the composite creatures of the Near East for their own purposes. An obvious corollary is that the process of selection was guided by the appropriateness of the content to the new function (griffins, sphinxes, Gorgons, centaurs) or a conception that suited the borrowed form (Acheloos).

The relationship of the Near Eastern composite creatures to those adopted by the Greeks in the late eighth and in the seventh century may shed some new light on the Greek propensity to cover their objects with mythological representations, not just the powerful composite creatures of principal concern in this essay.[156] As suggested at the beginning of this paper, the Greek use of composite creatures is very similar to that in the ancient Near East: the creatures both guard the object, building, or space from malignant forces/beings *and* attract positive ones, as is specifically engraved on the guardian lions of Til Barsip and many of the clay figurines buried in Near Eastern buildings. The representation of composite creatures in early Greek art is not, therefore, merely a decorative imitation of things Oriental, but a conscious statement of cultural values. It comes as no surprise that sympotic vessels are our main source for such representations, with military gear—shields, breast-plates, helmets—in close competition.

An understanding of the meaning of the Oriental-izing representations on early Greek vases and military armor suggests an approach to the adoption of mytho-logical narratives for the same purposes. A basic function of myth in Greece was to serve as a model for right action. Since right action is closely linked to the approbation and even support of the gods, myth served as a promoter of divine order. As such, myth—or the representation of myth—differs imperceptibly from the burying of apotropaic creatures in Near Eastern dwellings, palaces, and temples and the parallel depictions of figures and creatures on the Assyrian palace orthostat reliefs or the Syrian versions of the same. This is amply underscored by the representation of mythological scenes gradually replacing the sphinxes and other apotropaic composite creatures on Greek sympotic vessels. Although this Greek practice of covering their pottery, furniture, armor, and buildings with myths and composite creatures may at first seem strange, it is worth noting that the Christians fol-lowed the same practice in representing the stories of the Old and New Testaments on their buildings and on all and sundry objects. Even in contemporary society, the very function of art does not, on close inspection, appear very different from the ancient Near Eastern use of apotropaic creatures: statues, reliefs, and paintings expound values and ideals that surround or articulate both public and private spaces. Princeton University's program of adorning the campus with lions and tigers, the new statue of John Witherspoon, and modern works by a wide variety of artists attempts to define the community and connect it with the inspirational and protective power that is thought to reside in art objects.

## NOTES

I am grateful to Dr. Beate Pongratz-Leisten for discussing aspects of the present paper with me and for reading a draft, saving me from numerous pitfalls. As always, I alone am responsible for any remaining errors of fact or thought.

1 Mayor 1994. In general, see Pritchett 1993, 27–29, 90–94, 281–85.

2 Gantz 1993, 304.

3 *LIMC* 4 (1988), 312–13, nos. 299, 301, pl. 183, s.v. "Gorgo, Gorgones" (Krauskopf).

4 For the source of the name, see Cook 1960, 298, 305–6.

5 Burkert 1992; Burkert 1987, 10–40; Penglase 1994; West 1997.

6 Powell 1997, 154–93.

7 Black and Green 1992, 119–22. See also Ellis 1977, 67–78.

8 London WA 118912: Barnett 1976, pl. LV. Wiggermann (1992, 181–82) notes that the wingless lion-centaur is the *urmaḫlullû*, first correctly identified by Ellis (1977, 74), which seems to mean that it was considered a different beast from the winged lion-centaur.

9 London, Brit. Mus. WA 124571: Layard 1853, vol. 2, pl. 5; Barnett and Forman n.d., pl. 4 (partial photograph); Gray 1969, 36, fig. (photograph of complete block). See Wiggermann 1992, 185 and Kolbe 1981, 71–77; Engel 1987, 81–84. Black and Green (1992, 35–36) have proposed that this figure may be one of the manifestations of the mythological figure Asag (Asakku), who is defeated by the god Ninurta in the Sumerian poem *Lugal-e*; but see the commentary of Dijk (1983, 22–23), where it is clear that the physical appearance of Asag varies considerably according to the texts.

10 Black and Green 1992, 121; Wiggermann 1992, 169–72.

11 Wiggermann 1992, 182–83, 172–74; *RLA* 8, 242 (§ 7.5), s.v. "Mischwesen A" (Wiggermann) and 250–51 (§ 3.5), s.v. "Mischwesen B" (Green); Kolbe 1981, 132–33, pl. XIV, figs. 1–2. The distinction between the-lion-humanoid (human body above the waist and lion below) and the lion-man (lion's head and otherwise totally human body) is unknown: *RLA* 7, 100 (§ 2), s.v. "Löwenmensch" (Braun-Holzinger).

12 Van Buren 1946, 1–45.

13 Black and Green (1992, 63) make a distinction between demon (upright) and monster (quadruped); Reade (1979, 35–46) uses for all the term "genie," which I follow, because the word has a mildly Oriental flavor and suggests neither a malignant nor a beneficial character. Those writers who prefer the word "demon" do so on the basis of its derivation from the Greek δαίμων, but, since "genie" is well established in the literature, there is no need to multiply terms.

14 Green 1997, 135–58.

15 Berlin VA 4215: Moortgat 1940, no. 608; Lambert 1987, pl. VIII.7.

16 Lambert 1987, 37–48, pls. VII–XI; Green 1997, 137–39. Another reasonably likely mythical scene is the story of Etana, king of Kish, carried off to heaven on the back of a bird.

17 Van Buren 1946, 2; *RLA* 8, 226–27 (§ 2.1–2.2), 231 (§ 2.5), s.v. "Mischwesen A." Black and Green (1992, 63) give a simplified sketch of the evolution of composite creatures in the ancient Near East.

18 London, Brit. Mus. 89308: Frankfort 1939, 46–47, 60–61, 86, pl. XVIIh; Moortgat 1967, 37–38; Amiet 1980, 147–52.

19 Frankfort 1939, 72–73, 99–100, 161, pl. XVIIIg; Amiet 1976b, 18; Amiet 1980, 147–52; Wiggermann 1992, 174–79; *RLA* 8, 226 (§ 21),

230 (§ 2.4), s.v. "Mischwesen A"; Amiet 1956, 116–18. Bull-men on the orthostats of Tell Halaf support the sun disk (Frankfort 1970, 295, fig. 345).

20 Frankfort 1939, 86, pl. XVIIIj; Wiggermann 1992, 153; *RLA* 8, 227–28 (§ 2.2), s.v. "Mischwesen A."

21 Frankfort 1939, 61–62; Amiet 1980, 147, 137–40; *RLA* 8, 223, s.v. "Mischwesen A."

22 Engel 1987, 13, 29; Frankfort 1939, 200–201; Kolbe 1981, 1–14; *RLA* 6, 446–53, s.v. "Lamma/Lamassu A" (Foxvog, Heimpel, and Kilmer).

23 Frankfort 1939, 72–73, pl. XIIIh; on pl. XXIIe and g, the figure identified as the Bull of Heaven does not have a human head. See most recently Lambert 1987, 48–51; Green 1997, 139; Black and Green 1992, 49; *RLA* 4, 413–14, s.v. "Himmelstier" (Borger).

24 Collon 2001, 42, nos. 14, 17, 18.

25 London, Brit. Mus. WA 89435 (1853–822,6): Collon 2001, no. 340, pl. XLII.

26 Syracuse 42684: Amyx 1988, 21, no. A2, pl. 4.1 (Toulouse Painter); *LIMC* 1 (1981), 13, no. 1, s.v. "Acheloos" (Isler); Isler 1970, 48–49, 94, 95, 133–34, no. 60; Payne 1931, 13, fig. 6. The identification of the figure on the vase in Syracuse is difficult: the monster appears to have human arms for forelegs and a feline rump and tail. Payne (1931, 91) puts Acheloos in quotation marks; Amyx (1988, 630 n. 32) denies the identification. Isler leaves the identification open but accepts a Near Eastern origin for the figure. The first certain representations of Acheloos appear in the first half of the sixth century. The Syracuse oinochoe has recently been published in Bennett, Paul, and Iozzo 2002, 224–25, no. 47, with color plate.

27 Amiet 1956, 123, 126.

28 Hogarth 1914, pl. B 9a. For a general discussion, see Orthmann 1971.

29 Koldewey 1925, 57, 59, 203 with fig. 128 on p. 206; 218, 220–21 with figs. 140–41 on p. 223; 226 with figs. 145–46; 288 with fig. 243 on p. 289 (the pagination of the 5th edition [Munich 1990] is slightly different, but the figure numbers are the same).

30 Berlin VA Ass 3727: Klengel-Brandt 1968, 28, pl. 6; in general, see 19–37, pls. 1–10.

31 Woolley 1926, 698–713, pls. IX–XIII.

32 Mallowan 1954, 85–94; Mallowan 1966, vol. 1, 102, 226, fig. 191.

33 Gurney 1935, 31–96; Van Buren (1930, 189–244) lists with full bibliography a large number of such figurines and related deposits (section entitled "Religion and Magic"); Rittig 1977; Green 1983, 87–96.

34 Gurney 1935, 50–53 (text I, obverse 3, lines 35–42).

35 See particularly Rittig 1977, 70–77, 80–96; Green 1983, 88–90.

36 Reade 1979, 35–43; Green 1983, 93.

37 Kolbe 1981, 14–30 (Types B and C). The use of *ugallê* flanking doors in Assurbanipal's palace at Nineveh is no less remarkable; see Barnett 1976, pls. IV, XXI, XXXVII, XLV; Wiggermann 1981–82; Wiggermann 1992, 169–72. Kolbe (1981, 108–115) confuses *ugallu* and *utukku*, not a difficult thing to do.

38 Gurney 1935, 71–72.

39 Gurney 1935, 71, no. 3; Seidl 1968, 168–69; Black and Green 1992, 166 (snake-dragon).

40 Gurney 1935, 71, no. 4; Seidl 1968, 178–81; Wiggermann 1992, 184–85; Black and Green 1992, 93.

41 Gurney 1935, 71, no. 8; Seidl 1968, 169–71 (nos. XLIV–XLV), fig. 10, pl. 23a; Wiggermann 1992, 180–81; Black and Green 1992, 161.

42 Gurney 1935, 71, no. 14; Black and Green 1992, 116.

43 Gurney 1935, 72, no. 15; *RLA* 7, 100, s.v. "Löwenmensch" (Braun-Holzinger).

44 Kolbe 1981, 79–83, 123–31, 132–36.

45 Slanski 2000, 95–114. For the appearance of the figures on the *kudurrus*, see nn. 39–41 above, with references. I am indebted to Dr. Beate Pongratz-Leisten for the reference to Dr. Slanski's article.

46 Black and Green 1992, 179, s.v. "*udug (utukku)*." Gurney 1935, 77–95 (text III, from the series *Utukkē Limnūti*: ritual for healing a sick man).

47 London, Brit. Mus. WA 93 078: Kolbe 1981, 111–12. For earlier translations, see Thompson 1904, frontispiece and Frank 1908, 27. Cf. Seidl 1968, 173–74. Rittig (1977, 108–10) translates the passage very differently and on that basis rejects the identification of the figurine as an *utukku*. In addition, see Green 1983, 90.

48 See previous note.

49 Foster 1996, 719: "Pituh, gatekeeper of the netherworld (had) a lion's head, human hands, and bird's feet." See *RLA* 8, 224 (§ I), s.v. "Mischwesen A."

50 Wiggermann 1992, 169–72.

51 Thureau-Dangin 1921, 189–94; Black and Green 1992, 147–48; Saggs 1959–60, 123–27. The book by N. P. Heeßel, *Pazuzu: Archäologische und philologische Studien zu einem alt-orientalischen Dämon* (Leiden 2002), was not available in Princeton at the time of the completion of this essay. References have been added in the following notes, but the text has not been altered.

52 Paris, Louvre MNB 467: Frankfort 1970, 195, fig. 221; Heeßel 2002, 119–20, no. 12, fig. on p. 192.

53 For amulets, see Thureau-Dangin 1921, 189–94; Saggs 1959–60, 123–27; Heeßel 2002, 41–53.

54 Paris, Louvre AO 22205; Frank 1908; Thureau-Dangin 1921, 171–74, 183–89; Black and Green 1992, 181, fig. 151; Heeßel 2002, 128–29, no. 30, figs. on pp. 209–10.

55 Frank 1908, 85; Thureau-Dangin 1921, 172–73.

56 At least one of these has a lion head: Frank 1908, 11–12. The distinction between the lion-headed figure with an otherwise totally human body and the lion-headed human with bird talons for feet is unclear: *RLA* 7, 100 (§ 2), s.v. "Löwenmensch"; Seidl 1968, 173–74.

57 Frank 1908, 85–87.

58 Frank 1908, pls. III–IV; Thureau-Dangin 1921, 174–77; Heeßel 2002, nos. 15–29, 31, figs. on pp. 195–208, 211.

59 *RLA* 6, 439–46, s.v. "Lamaštu" (Farber), with earlier literature.

60 Klengel 1960, 341, fig. 3; 350, fig. 10a; 353, fig. 12a; pl. IV.

61 *RLA* 6, 445, s.v. "Lamaštu"

62 In various versions: Rittig 1977, 54, 61, 67, 99, 100, 112–13, 117, 122.

63 Thureau-Dangin and Dunand 1931, 150, cited by Frankfort 1970, 300;

cf. the inscriptions on the Ishtar Gate of Babylon in Lambert 1985, 87.

64 Wiggermann (1992, 185) reviews briefly various associations and split personalities.

65 *RLA* 3, 633, s.v. "Greif" (Börker-Klähn); Herrmann 1979, 10.

66 Stearns 1961, pls. 60–64, 70, 75–81.

67 Akurgal 1992, 35–37. An ivory griffin-man from Nimrud presents a rare example of both Assyrian crest and side curls: Mallowan 1966, vol. 2, 594, no. ND10228, fig. 575. The lock with curl at the end occurs at least as early as Gudea in the second millennium on figures of the *mušmuššu*, the snake-dragon or roaring dragon: Heuzey 1906, 96 with drawing; Frankfort 1970, 98, fig. 101; Strommenger 1962, pl. 144. Curled locks in one form or another are found also on *mušmuššē* on the *kudurrus*; see, e.g., Seidl 1968, 48 (no. 80, fig. 14), 50 (no. 84, fig. 16), 61 (no. 108, fig. 23).

68 Barnett 1975, pl. IX, nos. D8, D9, p. 184, fig. 79, no. G2. For Assyrian griffin-men on either side of a tree, see Stearns 1961, pls. 70, 75.

69 Mallowan 1966, vol. 2, figs. 455, 456, 485, 558, 559; Mallowan 1978, figs. 39, 42, 67; Orthmann 1975, pl. 261b. On a seal in New York (Morgan Lib.), a griffin-man fights a quadruped griffin (Porada 1948, pl. 86, no. 607).

70 Herrmann 1966; Herrmann 1979; Picard 1991, 156 (no. 18, figure on p. 155).

71 Herrmann 1979, 10.

72 Frankfort 1970, 163, fig. 188; *RLA* 8, 258 (§ 3.25), s.v. "Mischwesen B."

73 Green 1993–97, 258 (§ 3.25). The relationship is recognized by the confusing alternate name for the lion-dragon—"lion-griffin." A beautiful bronze protome from the Schimmel Collection, now in New York (Met. 1989.281.27) is, based on the long ears, either a lion-dragon or a lion-demon (*ugallu*): Muscarella 1974, no. 139. A similar piece was in the Pomerance Collection: Terrace et al. 1966, 41, no. 47. Since the neck of the latter is incised with a scale or feather pattern, it should be a lion-dragon. Given the close resemblance of the two protomes (apart from the pattern on the neck), they are probably both lion-dragons.

74 Akurgal 1949, 84; Akurgal 1992, 35. Herrmann (1979, 11) notes the peculiar idiosyncrasy of the Greek griffins: they have teeth from the very beginning, even though their lower jaw resembles a beak and is unlike the heavy animal jaw common in the Syrian area.

75 Jantzen 1955.

76 Karageorghis 1973, 97–108, no. 202, figs. 18–24, pls. frontispiece, CXXIX, CXXX, CXLIII, CCXLV; Rolley 1986, 80, 82, fig. 51.

77 Amandry 1958, 81, 95; Rolley 1986, 82; Akurgal 1992, 39. Cf. the "siren" handle attachment in the exhibition to any of the Oriental examples, such as the Urartian example illustrated in figure 16 of this essay.

78 Filippakis et al. 1983, 111–32. That the early hammered protomes were filled with a substance 27.60 percent bitumen adds some weight (but is not conclusive) to the argument for Oriental origins; see Jantzen 1955, 30–31; Amandry 1958, 85–87.

79 Akurgal 1992, 40.

80 Herrmann 1966, pls. 1–4; Markoe 1985, figs. on pp. 284–85.

81 Athens, Nat. Mus. 14.475: Schweitzer 1969, fig. 70.

82 Istanbul 7768, from Zincirli: Orthmann 1971, pl. 62 (E/1); Schweitzer 1969, fig. 71; Frankfort 1970, 300, fig. 351; cf. Orthmann 1971, pl. 32 (F/17 and H/11); Akurgal and Hirmer 1961, pl. 109; Akurgal 1968, pl. 21a, from Carchemish.

83 Copenhagen, Nat. Mus. 727: Schweitzer 1969, fig. 69.

84 Kunze 1931, pls. 3, 5, 10, 12, 15 and fig. 30 on p. 205.

85 Boardman 1998a, figs. 102.1 (Boiotian), 188.2 (Early Protoattic).

86 Benson 1970; Kourou 1991, 110–23.

87 See n. 69 above.

88 Istanbul 1271: Herrmann 1966, 56, no. 3, pl. 24.

89 Herrmann 1966, pls. 22, 24–26.

90 ED III seal: Frankfort 1939, pl. XIIIh, lower frieze, center left. Akkadian seal: Frankfort 1939, 133–34, pl. XXIIIe. Assyrian seal of the ninth to seventh century: Moortgat 1940, no. 710 (VA 4996); Amiet 1980, 144–46. The bird-man or bird-lions discussed by Collon (2001, 9) appear to be yet another creature.

91 A curious Late Antique phenomenon is the use of a pair of human-headed birds for the zodiac sign of Gemini; see Hartner 1973–74, 103, 115, 124.

92 Herrmann 1966, 1–3, figs. 1–4.

93 Walter 1959, 57–60, pls. 99–101, 114.1; Hermann 1966, 149–50, fig. 25; Ahlberg-Cornell 1992, 102, 104, no. 102, fig. 180; Benson 1995, 165, pl. 37a; *LIMC* 8 (1997), 682, no. 123, s.v. "Kentauroi et Kentaurides" (Leventopoulou et al.) (= 609 with drawing, no. 1, s.v. "Gryps" ([Leventopoulou]).

94 Boston 95.12: Schefold 1966, 29, fig. 4; Ahlberg-Cornell 1992, 102–4, no. 99, fig. 6 on p. 111; *LIMC* 8, 682, no. 129, s.v. "Kentauroi et Kentaurides" (= 317, no. 16, pl. 219, s.v. "Zeus" [Tiverios]).

95 See cat. no. 31, where different interpretations are presented.

96 Eleusis 2630: *LIMC* 4, 313, no. 312, pl. 184, s.v. "Gorgo, Gorgones" (= *LIMC* 7 [1994], 341 with drawing, no. 151, s.v. "Perseus" [Roccos]).

97 Markoe 1985, figs. on pp. 284–85; Bossert 1951, no. 816.

98 Aigina 235: *LIMC* 7 (1994), 227, no. 212, pl. 167, s.v. "Pegasos" (Lochin).

99 Boston 95.10: Boardman 1998a, fig. 173.

100 Orthmann 1971, pls. 27 (E/8), 33 (H/4?).

101 Orthmann 1971, pl. 61 (B31b).

102 Boston 6507: Boardman 1980, 79, fig. 79; Ahlberg-Cornell 1992, fig. 223.

103 A Neo-Assyrian seal shows a "hero" shooting an arrow at a scorpion-man; see Moortgat 1940, no. 696.

104 Frankfort 1939, pls. XXXIVa and XXXVb; Moortgat 1940, nos. 468–70 (Old Babylonian); Porada 1947, nos. 73–74 (Middle Assyrian) and 80, 82 (Neo-Assyrian) = Porada 1948, nos. 607, 608, 689, 690.

105 Frankfort 1939, pl. XXIIa, d, e (Akkadian); Porada 1947, no. 34 (Akkadian) = Porada 1948, no. 220; Moortgat (1940, nos. 595 and 615) depicts a god (Ninurta?) on a lion-dragon attacking a lion-dragon; Moortgat-Correns 1988, 124–26; *RLA* 8, 223 (§ 1), s.v. "Mischwesen A." For a variety of types, see Collon 2001, pl. V.

106 Layard 1849–53, vol. 2, pl. 5; Moortgat-Correns 1988, 120, fig. 3 on 121

(Ninurta and Anzû); Kolbe 1981, 63–79, pl. VIII.1; Frankfort 1970, 163, fig. 188.

107  Edzard 1997, 85 sections xxv 24–xxvi 16; Black 1988, 21–25.

108  Black 1988, 21.

109  Cooper 1978, 63 (line 39a), 65 (line 62), 81 (line 138 = a descriptor of Ninurta's seven-headed mace), 141–54; Dijk 1983, 10–18.

110  Dalley 1989, 237 (= *ANET*, p. 62, tablet I, lines 132–43); see also Engel 1987, 85–91.

111  *RLA* 8, 244 (§ 28a–b), s.v. "Mischwesen A" and 259 (§ 3.28), s.v. "Mischwesen B."

112  Frankfort 1939, 71, 121–22, text fig. 27 on p. 72, pl. XXIIIj; Van Buren 1946, 18–20, pl. IV, figs. 16–17; Black and Green 1992, 164–65; Hansen 1987, 60–61, pl. XVI, fig. 29; similar to a cylinder seal from Tell Asmar (As. 32/738): Frankfort 1939, pl. XXIIIj; Powell 1997, 169, fig. 9. See Dijk 1983, 15, 17, 68–69, lines 128–35. See also *RLA* 8, 227 (§ 2.2), 244 (§ 7.28a), s.v. "Mischwesen A" and 259 (§ 3.28), s.v. "Mischwesen B"; Engel 1987, 91. The constellation Hydra was in later times equated with the snake-dragon; see Weidner 1967, pls. 5–6; *RLA* 8, 461–62, s.v. "*mušh-muššu*" (Wiggermann).

113  Dijk 1983, 11, 12, 15, 17–18, 19; Powell 1997, 167–69, 176–83. Cf. Boardman 1998c, 32–33. Wiggermann (*RLA* 8, 227 [§2.2b], s.v. "Mischwesen A") distinguishes between the *muš-sag-imin* and the *muš-mah*, the first an enemy, the second a weapon of Ninurta.

114  Haussig 1965, s.v. "Illujanka"; Lebrun 1985, 101–2; Hoffner 1998, 10–14, no. 1; *ANET*, 125–26.

115  Orthmann 1971, pl. 40 (A/8); Akurgal 1961, pl. 104, bottom; Akurgal 1968, 101, fig. 60.

116  Schefold 1966, pl. 66.

117  Boardman 1998a, fig. 435.

118  West 1997, 300–304.

119  Collon 1986, nos. 104a, 114, etc. (see list on p. 41, s.v. "bull-man").

120  Collon 2001, 10, s.v. "bull-man."

121  Scheibler 1960, 20–29, 34–42, pl. 1, fig. c.

122  Richter 1961, 6, pls. 1 ff.; Boardman 1978, figs. 224–28.

123  Boardman 1995, figs. 115–16, 126.

124  *LIMC* 6 (1992), 962, nos. 150–56, pls. 632–33, s.v. "Odysseus" (Touchefeu-Meynier); *LIMC* 8 (1997), 1102, nos. 117, 118, pl. 743, s.v. "Seirenes" (Hofstetter). For depictions of sirens in the Odysseus story, see also this volume, Tsiafakis, "ΠΕΛΩΡΑ," figs. 3, 4.

125  For example, *LIMC* 8, 674, 680–82, nos. 2, 3, 6, 99, 109, 114, 125, pls. 416, 420–22, s.v. "Kentauroi et Kentaurides"; Schiffler 1976, 15.

126  Frankfort 1939, pl. XXXIf (late Kassite; winged, scorpion tail); for a general discussion of Near Eastern centaurs, see Seidl 1968, 176–78. Since the horse is a late introduction to the Near East, it and its derivatives do not appear in the index of Amiet 1980. See Brentjes 1971, 95.

127  Paris, Louvre CA 795: Schefold 1966, 32, pl. 15b; Fittschen 1969, 152; Ahlberg-Cornell 1992, 113, no. 115, fig. 198.

128  Eretria 8620: *LIMC* 8, 675, no. 20, pl. 417, s.v. "Kentauroi et Kentaurides"; Desborough, Nicholls, and Popham 1970, 21–30;

Popham, Sackett, and Themelis 1980, 168–70 (Toumba, tombs 1 and 3), pls. 251–52; Lebessi 1996.

129  Schiffler 1976, 77–80.

130  See the observations of Calmeyer in *RLA* 5, 570, s.v. "Kentaur."

131  Popham and Lemos 1996, pls. 63 top, 144 (Toumba, tomb 55); pls. 70, 145 (tomb 70); Popham 1995, 103–107.

132  Winter 1993, 116, fig. 13.

133  Athens, Nat. Mus. 1002 (Nessos Painter): Boardman 1974, fig. 5.2. Paris, Louvre E 874 (Gorgon Painter): Boardman 1974, fig. 11.1–2.

134  London 1860.4–4.2: Boardman 1998a, fig. 297.

135  Boardman 1978, fig. 187.

136  *LIMC* 4, 317, s.v. "Gorgo, Gorgones"; Burkert 1992, 82–87.

137  Richter 1961, fig. 83; Boardman 1978, fig. 231.

138  Borell and Rittig 1998, fish-garbed genies, 27–29, pls. 6 top row, 67; there is possibly also a lion-demon (30).

139  *LIMC* 8 (1997), 68–73, s.v. "Triton" (Icard-Gianolio).

140  Boardman 1987.

141  See Gantz 1993, 19–25.

142  West 1988, 28.

143  See n. 131 above.

144  Hallo 1997, 402–4; Dalley 1989, 278–81. The reference was kindly provided by Dr. Beate Pongratz-Leisten.

145  Boardman 1978, fig. 71.

146  Frankfort 1970, 152, fig. 175.

147  Boardman 1978, figs. 57–59.

148  Amiet 1980, 147, 149–52; Wiggermann 1981–82; Wiggermann 1992, 164–66; Kolbe 1981, 89–108; Engel 1987, 87–89. I have suggested elsewhere that the very idea of the dedication of statues as votives in Greek sanctuaries may have been inspired by the example of Cyprus, where the practice was early and broad, yet Cypriote style played no role in early Greek sculpture; see Childs 2001b, 115–28.

149  *RLA* 8, 230 (§ 2.4), s.v. "Mischwesen A"; *RLA* 3, 75–78 (§ 6–7), s.v. "Fixsterne" (Weidner). See also Rochberg 1998, 28–30; I am indebted to Dr. Beate Pongratz-Leisten for the latter reference.

150  Weidner 1967, 9, pls. 5–6; *RLA* 8, 461–62, s.v. "Mischwesen A"; Wiggermann 1989; Deimel 1950, no. 284. It is worth noting that this is not the *muš-mahu*, or seven-headed snake, often equated by scholars with the Hydra on the basis of the physical resemblance of the two beasts.

151  Deimel 1950, nos. 263, 344; Weidner 1957–71, 78 (§ 7).

152  Deimel 1950, no. 144. See the kudurru relief Berlin VA Bab. 4375. On this relief, see Seidl 1968, 40–41, no. 63 and RLA 8, 223 (§ I), s.v. "Mischwesen A"; in the latter, Wiggermann identifies the figure as the lion-dragon ("Roaring Day").

153  *RLA* 3, 77–78 (§ 7), s.v. "Fixsterne."

154  Deimel 1950, no. 196.

155  Deimel 1950, nos. 73, 75–77, 96, 200, 279; Weidner 1957–71, 76, 77.

156  Schnapp 1988.

# "ΠΕΛΩΡΑ"
# Fabulous Creatures and/or Demons of Death?

Despoina Tsiafakis

SPHINX, SIREN, GORGON, satyr, centaur, Minotaur, Acheloos, Triton, Typhon, Pan: these names of πέλωρα conjure images of some of the most characteristic and widely represented composite creatures in ancient Greek art.[1] The Greeks were attracted to fantasy elements that conveyed various aspects of their lives, and their mythology, based on heroes who fight monsters, envisages the beasts in the form of hybrids.[2] Many other peoples have also conceived of supernatural creatures that incorporate aspects of diverse natural beings—half-human, half-animal. These creatures, not necessarily divine, represent the world beyond fantasy, combining understandable traits such as human intelligence, physical strength (lion), and the power of flight (bird). The mixture of animal and human features in Greek fantasy appears to be similar for any kind of hybrid without implying shared qualities simply on account of common physical characteristics. Thus, the combination of a bull with a man creates two quite different figures: Acheloos, who is a god, and the Minotaur, who is mortal.

Fabulous beasts pictured in Minoan and Mycenaean art disappeared during the so-called Greek Dark Ages (ca. 1100–950 B.C.) and, as far as we currently know, "reappeared" in relatively early historic times, in the Geometric period.[3] They are represented in every kind of medium, adorning architecture, sculpture, painting, pottery, and the minor arts throughout the course of antiquity. Occasionally, they participate as principal figures in popular episodes of Greek mythology, and it is not unusual for them to be genealogically related to each other. The characteristic forms taken by the most distinctive Greek composite creatures have been related to beings found in Egyptian and other Near Eastern cultures; the original forms gradually were altered and integrated into Greek myth and imagination.[4] This paper explores the class of human-animal hybrids in Greek art and thought, following them from their appearance in the Geometric period into late Archaic times.[5]

## FEMALE HYBRIDS

The sirens, sphinx, and Gorgon depicted together on the Attic black-figure plate by the Gorgon Painter (cat. no. 82) are generally considered female composite creatures, even if their gender was not fixed from the very beginning. All three may appear bearded in various regions and media of Greek art as late as the sixth century B.C. Medusa maintained a beard as a principal attribute,[6] but unlike the bearded sirens and sphinxes, her female character was never questioned. The earliest surviving representations of the female hybrids in Greek art date a little before the end of the Late Geometric period, and they became very popular during Archaic times. Employed by all major workshops, they were particularly prevalent in Corinthian, Attic, Laconian, Cycladic, and East Greek art.

### Sirens

The human-headed birds known as sirens (see figs. 1–4, 6) were famous for their irresistibly beautiful voices; their songs, which enticed sailors to death, contributed to their strong association with the afterlife.[7] They are usually mentioned as daughters of a Muse and the river Acheloos or the sea demon Phorkys.[8] In either case, they are closely associated with the water and connected by family ties to other hybrids such as the Gorgons (daughters of Phorkys), the Sphinx (as a descendant of Phorkys), and, of course, Acheloos. Their number varies from two to three,[9] and the written sources speak of two different groups: Thelxiepeia, Aglaope, and Peisinoe, the sirens of the Greek mainland; and Parthenope, Ligeia, and Leukosia, the sirens of South Italy.[10] Anthemoessa, a mythical island close to Italy, was believed to be their place of residence; and it was also in South Italy, on the Sorrentine peninsula, that they were worshiped as early as the fifth century B.C. in a temple dedicated to them.[11]

In Greek mythology, the sirens first appear in Homer's description of the adventures of Odysseus, and they played a key role in the story of the Argonauts.[12] Pausanias adds that they competed with the Muses in singing but that they lost the contest and the Muses punished them by plucking out their feathers to make crowns for themselves.[13] Through their musical skills, the sirens charmed men and kept them away from home forever. With the exception of Orpheus and Odysseus, no mortal heard the sirens' song and lived to tell the tale. The music of Orpheus proved more powerful and overcame the sirens' voice, while Odysseus defeated them by having himself strapped to the mast of his ship. Lykophron (*Alex.* 712–13) describes their final fate: unable to bear the failure of not beguiling every human, they committed suicide.

Homer, our earliest extant source for the sirens, does not provide any description of their physical appearance. His are two in number and female, but there is no indication that his audience had any idea about how they looked. The bird-bodied female is not found in Minoan or Mycenaean art, and it seems that Greek artists employed Near Eastern models for the visualization of the creatures. Although the musical sirens, such as the ones in Homer, do not occur in Egypt, the human-headed *ba*-birds (e.g., cat. no. 8) might have looked appropriate for the representation of the Greek sirens, and the Greek artists adapted the type for their own needs.[14]

The earliest representations of sirens in Greek art are dated in the late eighth to the early seventh century B.C. and occur mostly as attachments on bronze vessels or in vase-painting along with the sphinxes and the griffins (cat. no. 74).[15] A rare exception is the Geometric bronze figurine of a human-headed bird (cat. no. 73), perhaps an early attempt to form a siren.[16] By the sixth century, sirens were among the most popular figures on Archaic monuments. They found their place in the animal friezes or heraldic compositions decorating the vases of various Greek workshops and as individual creations such as the plastic vases in clay or metal. They were used as supports of handles on vessels or mirrors and as a decorative element on carved gems, as well as on stone and metal reliefs. Corinth, as a chief center of the ceramic industry and of foreign trade during the Archaic period, played a leading role in the diffusion of the canonical siren type by using it extensively on its products (e.g., cat. nos. 75, 76). Sirens from this early period were also popular with other Greek workshops, particularly in East Greece (cat. no. 78) and the Cyclades.

With the exception of the Clazomenian, South Italian, and Sicilian workshops, which appear to depict exclusively unbearded sirens, the rest of the Greek workshops were not very decisive about the gender of the creature. Judging by the presence or absence of a beard, the earliest Greek sirens could be either female or male (e.g., cat. nos. 75, 76),[17] and the same is true for representations of sphinxes (see below). The artistic evidence is supported by an inscription from the Heraion on Samos that mentions a male siren but does not give any other details.[18] The dual representation of the *ba*-birds, with or without a beard, might have had an influence on the early Greek sirens. When one adds to this the general belief that every species needs both genders to survive, we may begin to approach the reasons behind this double representation. By the fifth century B.C., however, only female sirens were being represented, and the bearded males have disappeared.

During the earlier period, however, when both sexes were depicted, some vase-painters emphasized the female character of the siren. A good example is the siren under the horizontal handle of a Late Corinthian hydria by the Tydeus Painter (fig. 1).[19] The sense of color is striking, with the white body in sharp contrast to the dark plumage and hair. Since the flesh of women in Attic black-figure and Corinthian vases is normally tinted with added white slip, the femininity of the figure is highlighted through the white that totally covers the face, neck, body, tail, and feet. In addition, the vase-painter has added a necklace and a diadem, also to stress that this is a female creature.

Another interesting detail in the iconography of these human-headed birds is the occasional presence of human arms (fig. 2; cat. no. 79). This attribute is also found on some Egyptian *ba*-birds and on the sirens decorating the bronze cauldrons (cat. no. 74). In Greek representations, however, there is a practical reason for arms, related to sirens' association with music. Musical instruments look appropriate in the hands of the sirens, to accompany their song, and they become common features, appearing as early as the seventh century B.C.[20] The lyre, kithara, and aulos are the most frequently depicted musical instruments held by the sirens.[21] The representation of arms strengthens the human part of the siren, and more specifically, when they hold mirrors, beads, or wreathes, the feminine part.[22] It is clear that the later addition of human breasts was an attempt to emphasize the female character of the beings.[23]

Figure 1. Hydria: siren. Greek, Late Corinthian, mid-sixth century B.C., attributed to the Tydeus Painter. Staatliche Kunstammlungen Dresden (135).

The domination of the human part of the siren increased gradually from the fifth century B.C. onward, with sirens eventually resembling humans more than birds.[24]

The identification of those human-headed birds with the name of sirens, as provided by Homer, is confirmed by the inscription ΣΙΡΕΝ (siren) next to a human-headed bird on two Attic vases dated to the mid-sixth century B.C.[25] It is because of the inscriptions that all the similarly formed hybrids are named sirens, whether or not they refer to the Homeric creatures who beguiled humans. In reality, depictions of Homer's sirens are very rare in Greek art compared to the innumerable examples of individual

Figure 3. Aryballos: Odysseus and the sirens. Greek, Late Corinthian, second quarter
of the sixth century B.C. Museum of Fine Arts, Boston, Henry Lillie Pierce Fund (01.8100).

bird-bodied humans. There is no visual representation
of Odysseus with the sirens before the sixth century B.C.,
and even then, only a very few are known.[26] Corinthian
workshops appear to have been the first to introduce the
Homeric story into art, with Athenian artisans following.
The earliest indisputable depiction of Odysseus's adventure
is found on a Corinthian aryballos from the second quarter
of the sixth century B.C.; it shows Odysseus's ship and crew,
and the hero bound to the mast while two sirens are sitting
on a rock and singing (fig. 3).[27] The next examples are Attic
and date from the late sixth century B.C. They all follow the
same basic pattern as on the Corinthian aryballos, with the
sirens standing on rocky cliffs that tower over the sea and
looking at the hero in his boat. Among the more interesting
examples is an Attic white-ground/black-figure lekythos by
the Edinburgh Painter, showing Odysseus bound to a pillar
and two sirens on either side of him playing musical instruments.[28] Unlike other examples, the ship is missing, and
only the leaping dolphins denote the sea. Red-figure artists
seem even less interested in the subject: there is only one
known example, an Attic stamnos in the British Museum, of
about 490 B.C., the name-vase of the Siren Painter (fig. 4).[29]
Here, the hero is again bound to the mast as his ship passes
two rocks, each with a siren on top. More remarkable is that
the vase-painter has included a third siren plunging into the
sea—this is the earliest known reference to their demise.

Despite the rarity of the Homeric story in Greek art
and an apparent dearth of depictions of the episode with
Orpheus,[30] sirens remained very popular throughout

antiquity. The variety in their representations alludes to
some difficulty in defining a single significance and symbolic meaning, particularly because this meaning might
have changed over time. Though their decorative role
obviously cannot be denied—especially when they parade
in the animal zones of the Archaic vases—they were also
more than that. Their connection to death was clearly
suggested by Homer as well as by later sources. Sirens

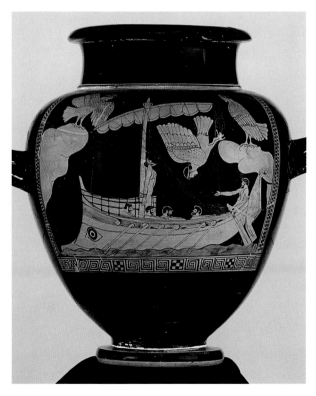

Figure 2. Siren-shaped askos.
Greek, South Italian, 470–460 B.C., bronze.
J. Paul Getty Museum, Malibu (92.AC.5).

Figure 4. Red-figure stamnos: Odysseus and the sirens.
Greek, Attic, ca. 490 B.C., the name-vase of the Siren Painter.
British Museum, London (1943.11-3.31 [E 440]).

were well known as the musical birds of Hades, and Plato (*Cra.* 403 d) related that their home was the underworld. According to Euripides (*Hel.* 168–78), sirens were the companions of Persephone, and Apollonios of Rhodes (*Argon.* 4.896–97) verifies Persephone's relationship with sirens by stating that they tended Demeter's daughter and sang for her. Their association with the underworld also can be confirmed in art, as they often appear on graves or in funerary scenes as mourners for the dead. Their connection with the funerary lament occurred as early as 600 B.C., as shown by an Attic black-figure pinax in Boston with a *prothesis* scene in which a siren stands under the bier of the deceased.[31] Numerous ceramic vases in the form of a siren have been found in Archaic and Classical graves, and by the fourth century B.C., sirens commonly appeared on stone grave markers.[32]

A similar interpretation can be given to a series of representations of sirens carrying a person in their human arms, recalling depictions of sphinxes carrying off youths (see below) or scenes depicting erotic pursuits, such as Eos with Kephalos or Tithonos.[33] Though the theme is relatively uncommon, it is found in sixth-century vases and gems and continues sporadically into the fifth century.[34] The subject appears on a Late Corinthian alabastron and a Laconian cup, both sixth century in date,[35] but the best-known examples of this subject are the siren reliefs (misinterpreted in the past as Harpies) on the early-fifth-century so-called Harpy Monument from Xanthos in Lycia.[36] In this case, the type of monument itself, a tomb, is indicative of the role of these "kourotrophos-type" sirens.

Sirens were frequently interpreted as omens of death.[37] Their popularity, however, and particularly their presence in sanctuaries as dedications,[38] cannot be adequately explained if they were considered only as unpleasant beings associated with death. Furthermore, nothing in their appearance makes them as fearful as other death demons. Their connection with the underworld may allow them to have been seen as a positive aspect of death, since through their charming music, sirens could accompany the dead into their graves. Their melodic song may have conveyed a hopeful message of life after death, one promising to tell people how they would be remembered.

## Sphinxes

Related to, but different from, the siren is the sphinx, another popular human-animal hybrid in Greek art and one of earliest-known composite creatures in Greece.[39] In the most widespread type, the sphinx possesses the body of a winged lion and a human female head (figs. 5–8). Variations include the wingless sphinx and the sphinx with a bearded male head, as well as some combining other human, canine, or bovine elements.[40] Representations of this composite being occur often in Near Eastern art, but its origins lie in Egypt.[41] A male human head placed on a lion's body comprises the common form of an Egyptian sphinx. The Assyrians gave the sphinx wings; the Hittites altered its hairstyle, preferring curly hair to the traditional corrugated wig lappets. It seems that the Greeks, adopting it in the Bronze Age, were attracted to the type only after most of these alterations and transformations had occurred. As a rule, Greek sphinxes, either female or male, are winged. A further distancing from the original Egyptian model is evident in the apparent lack of interest on the part of the Greeks in the traditional recumbent type of Egyptian sphinx. Instead, the watchful sphinx, seated on its haunches with front legs upright and erect, is the most widespread type in the Greek world. Unlike the immobile Egyptian sphinxes, Greek sphinxes also get up and walk, as they do in Phoenician art.

Despite the early appearance of the Sphinx in art, Homer does not mention her, although he refers to Oedipus (*Il.* 23.679–80; *Od.* 11.271–80). Hesiod (*Theog.* 326) provides the earliest extant reference, calling her a murderous monster without, however, giving any physical description. In Hesiod, the Sphinx is the daughter of Echidna and Orthos (brother of Kerberos) and sister of the Nemean lion. According to other versions of the genealogy, her father was Typhon and her mother, the Chimaera.[42] Although the term used for the creature in Near Eastern languages and the origin of the name *Sphinx* remain obscure, in popular etymology the word *sphigx* or *sphix* seems to derive from the Greek verb *sphiggo* (to tighten or strangle), perhaps influenced by the Theban story related to her.[43] Hesiod, however, names her *Phik*, a word suggestive of the mountain Phikion, the monster's supposed place of residence.

# The Centaur's Smile
## The Human Animal in Early Greek Art

# Fantastic Creatures

Oil bottle in the form of a siren. East Greek, sixth century B.C., Aphrodite Group; ceramic. Princeton University Art Museum, museum purchase, gift of John B. Elliott, Class of 1951. (y1989-31)

The mythical hybrid creatures referred to in this exhibition as "human animals" are prominent characters in the stories and legends that the ancient Greeks developed not only to entertain, but also to examine and explain themselves, their history, and their surroundings. Because the Greeks had no fixed mythological canon and no standard religious text, the roles of human-animals changed over time and varied from place to place. They could be feared foes, guardians of a grave, transporters of the dead, devices for warding off evil, or decorative ornaments. Fantastic figures such as sphinxes, sirens, and satyrs adorn a wide range of artifacts in a variety of materials, from stone to gold, including pottery, jewelry, armor, and architecture. This exhibition presents the wide variety of Greek mythological composite creatures in the Geometric, Archaic, and Early Classical periods, from the eighth to the mid-fifth century B.C., demonstrating the richness of the Greek imagination and Greek civilization's debts to Near Eastern traditions.

### Centaurs
Creatures combining the body and legs of a horse with the head and torso of a man (although early centaurs were often represented with a horse's hindquarters attached to a fully human body). With the exception of Cheiron, a civilized centaur who was the tutor to many Greek heroes, and Pholos, a creature of mild and hospitable nature, centaurs were known for their excessive fondness for wine and their subsequent unruly behavior.

### Satyrs
Also known as **silens**. Part man and part horse but differing from centaurs in walking upright on two legs, either human or hooved. Satyrs represent an antithesis to the Greek ideals of youthful beauty and self-controlled behavior. Frequent companions of Dionysos, the god of wine, the satyrs' unbridled yet unsatisfied lust leads them into humorous situations. Some of the depictions of satyrs on Attic vases were inspired by satyr plays, comic parodies of myth with satyr choruses.

### Sphinxes
Creatures with the body of a winged lioness and the head of a woman. According to a famous myth, the Sphinx came to Thebes and posed the following riddle, "What has one voice and becomes first four-footed, then two-footed, and finally three-footed?" Each day that the riddle remained unanswered, the Sphinx killed a youth. Oedipus finally provided the correct response—Man, who crawls, then walks, then uses a cane—and eliminated the menace. Although episodes from the myth are occasionally represented, sphinxes in art more often have essentially decorative roles or, when placed on funerary monuments, act as guardians of the dead.

## Sirens

Human-headed birds whose irresistible songs lured sailors to their death. In form, they resemble the *ba*-birds of Egyptian art, but in contrast are generally female. Sirens were associated with the underworld, sometimes appearing on vessels used in funeral rites. Often, however, they are depicted as benign creatures and, like sphinxes, were a favorite decorative motif of Corinthian vase-painters.

## Acheloos

An immortal, man-headed bull who is a personification of the longest river in Greece. Herakles fought him to acquire the hand of Deianeira and tore off his horn during the struggle.

## Minotaur

A monster with the body of a man and the head of a bull. He lived in the Labyrinth, on Crete, where King Minos exacted a tribute of fourteen Athenian youths and maidens to feed him. The Minotaur died at the hands of Theseus, the mythical unifier of Attica.

## Nereus

A wise old fish-man who could mutate into different forms. He was forced by Herakles to reveal the way to the Garden of the Hesperides, located at the ends of the earth. The Garden contained the golden apples that Gaia (Earth) gave to Zeus' wife Hera as a wedding gift and that Herakles was required to steal as one of his Labors. In the course of the sixth century B.C., the fight with Nereus seems to have been supplanted by Herakles' struggle with another fish-man, **Triton**, about whom little is known outside his appearance in art.

## Typhon

Often represented with wings and a serpentine lower body. A huge monster who embodied the destructive forces of wind and fire, he was defeated by Zeus and buried under the volcanic Mount Etna.

## Pan

The Arcadian god of the flocks. He is depicted either as a goat or as a human with the head of a goat (and often the legs as well). Pan assured the Athenians of his special favor at the Battle of Marathon (490 B.C.), when they soundly defeated a larger force of invading Persians. It seems that only after this event did Pan begin to appear in Greek art.

## Gorgons

Three monstrous sisters whom artists depicted with wings, grimacing frontal faces with tongues lolling between curved fangs, and often with serpents for hair. Medusa, the only mortal Gorgon, had a face so horrible that it turned to stone anyone who gazed at her. King Polydektes of Seriphos ordered Perseus to bring back Medusa's head, hoping he would die in the attempt. The young hero succeeded, however, with help from Athena and Hermes, and returned with the head, which he used to petrify Polydektes. Medusa's disembodied head, the *gorgoneion*, became a common device for warding off evil, a tradition begun by the goddess Athena when she placed Medusa's head on her shield.

Nathan T. Arrington
Curatorial Research Assistant
Princeton University Art Museum

# The Centaur's Smile
## The Human Animal in Early Greek Art

# Centaurs in Greek Mythology

Tyrrhenian Amphora with Herakles battling the centaurs, detail. Greek, Attic, ca. 560–550 B.C., attributed to the Fallow Deer Painter. Private collection.

The personalities of centaurs reflect their physical duality: savage and brutal on the one hand, brave and benevolent on the other. Wild creatures, they were believed to live in the forests of Mount Pelion in Thessaly, feeding on raw flesh. In art, they are usually represented with the body and legs of a horse and the torso, head, and arms of a man. The myths of the centaurs became vehicles for the Greeks to explore the institutions of war, marriage, and guest friendship (*xenia*). Invariably, the centaurs' violation of culture reaffirms the superiority of male humans over their bestial enemies.

Kentauros—the offspring of Ixion, king of the Thessalian Lapithae, and Nephele, a cloud in the form of Hera—was said to have engendered the race of centaurs by mating with the wild mares of Magnesia. The centaurs make their first dramatic appearance in Greek mythology at the wedding of Ixion's heir, Peirithoos, to Hippodameia. Intoxicated by the wine at the feast, they assaulted the Lapith women; one of the centaurs, Eurytion, even tried to carry off the bride. The Lapiths, assisted by Theseus, king of Athens, drove the centaurs away but suffered some casualties, most notably Kaineus. Although Kaineus believed he had been made invulnerable by Poseidon, the centaurs killed him by hammering him into the ground with the trunks of pine trees. This archetypal battle between men and centaurs, known as the Thessalian Centauromachy, was a favorite subject in ancient art and came to symbolize the triumph of Greek civilization over brutality and barbarism.

Like humans, centaurs have their own heroic figures, who are far more "civilized" than other members of the species. Cheiron, renowned for his wisdom and justice, was the only centaur who was immortal, descended not from Ixion but rather from the union of Kronos and the Ocean nymph Philyra. He served as tutor for heroes such as Peleus and his famous son Achilles, as well as Jason, Meleager, and Aktaion. In Cheiron's "school," practical wisdom, morality, and proper behavior were taught alongside music, hunting, and the healing arts. Cheiron suffered an accidental death while inspecting the arrows of Herakles, which were tipped with the poisonous blood of the monstrous, nine-headed Hydra. Cheiron dropped one of the arrows on his foot, and to relieve him from his pain, Zeus let him surrender his immortality and die. He was commemorated among the stars as the constellation Sagittarius.

The centaur Pholos resided in Pholoë, a mountain range between Elis and Arcadia, together with the centaurs driven from Pelion by Theseus and the Lapiths. When Herakles visited the cave of Pholos, the hospitable centaur offered him roasted meat, but the hero called for wine with his meal. Pholos stored a big wine jar in his cave but hesitated to open it because it belonged to all the centaurs in common. Herakles insisted, however, and soon the smell of the fragrant wine attracted the other centaurs, who stormed the cave. Pholos hid, but Herakles stood against the centaurs, who attacked him with trees, boulders, and axes. Using firebrands at first and then his bow and arrows, Herakles managed to kill most of the centaurs and routed the others down to Cape Maleas at the southernmost tip of the Peloponnese. While burying the dead, Pholos was wounded by an arrow that he extracted from one of his comrades, and died. He was immortalized in the sky as the constellation Centaurus.

The encounter between Herakles and the centaur Nessos, narrated in Sophokles' *Trachiniae*, is a necessary forerunner to the hero's eventual demise. Nessos attempted to rape Herakles' wife Deianeira while ferrying her across the river Evenos. Herakles promptly shot Nessos, but before dying the centaur offered Deianeira his blood mixed with the poison from the hero's arrows, calling it a love charm that would keep Herakles ever faithful to her. Many years later, when she discovered that Herakles was about to take a new bride, Iole, Deianeira anointed a robe with Nessos's drug and sent it as a gift to Herakles. The hero, unable to bear the terrible pain caused by the poison eating into his flesh, immolated himself on a funeral pyre, while Deianeira committed suicide upon learning the outcome of her deed.

Kyriaki Karoglou
Department of Art and Archaeology
Princeton University

FURTHER READING
Carpenter, T. H. *Art and Myth in Ancient Greece.* London 1991.
Gantz, T. *Early Greek Myth: A Guide to Literary and Artistic Sources.* Baltimore 1993.
Padgett, J. M. "Horse Men: Centaurs and Satyrs in Early Greek Art." In *The Centaur's Smile: The Human Animal in Early Greek Art.* Exhib. cat. Princeton University Art Museum, Princeton 2003.

# The Centaur's Smile
The Human Animal in Early Greek Art

# Gorgons

Running Gorgon, Greek, ca. 540 B.C.; bronze.
Yale University Art Gallery, gift of Cornelius
C. Vermeule III, in memory of Emily Townsend
Vermeule (2002.95.2).

The Gorgons, whose name derives from the
Greek word *gorgos*, meaning terrifying or fearful, were
monstrous female hybrids defined by an inherent
duality: deadly, yet also serving as powerful protective figures. Born to the sea monster Keto and the
sea god Phorkys, the Gorgons were three sisters—
Stheno, Euryale, and Medusa—whom Athena
turned into monsters after Medusa lay with
Poseidon in a grove sacred to the goddess. Medusa
was the only one of the three who was mortal, but she also possessed the power to petrify anyone
who gazed upon her. Apollodorus tells us that King Polydektes commanded Perseus to kill
Medusa and bring back her head. With the help of Athena and Hermes, who provided him with
winged boots and a special sack (*kibisis*) to carry off the head, the young hero was able to complete
this seemingly impossible task. In the *Iliad*, Athena wears Medusa's head on her goatskin aegis,
while Agamemnon carries it on his shield, both, therefore, transforming the head of a dreaded
demon into an apotropaic device capable of averting evil.

Of all the composite "human-animals" in Archaic Greek art, Gorgons are among the most prevalent,
appearing everywhere from precious gems to the pediments of monumental temples, their popularity probably due to their protective powers. In contrast to the common Archaic convention of
representing figures in profile, Gorgons are typically depicted with their heads turned frontally,
facing the viewer. By the beginning of the Archaic period, around 600 B.C., Greek artists had
attached these hideous, mask-like faces to the winged body of a female, thus creating a powerful
demonic image that was to remain popular for centuries to come. While the iconography of
Gorgons is decidedly Greek, the formulation of their imagery owes much to Egyptian and Near
Eastern precedents, most notably Bes, an Egyptian apotropaic divinity who was also rendered with
a distorted, frontally posed face, and Pazuzu, a Mesopotamian winged demon with an equally
deformed countenance.

On the massive bronze volute krater included in the exhibition, Gorgons adorn both the vessel's
handles and its three-legged stand (*hypokraterion*), clearly dominating its figural decoration. Standing
at a restored height of 122.5 cm., the exceptionally well-preserved krater includes a strainer with a
cast figure of a flute player standing at its center; two cast volute handles with running Gorgons;
a separately cast rim and foot, both elaborately articulated; cast appliqué horsemen circling the
neck; a body of hammered metal (now almost fully restored); and a cast stand with kneeling
Gorgons and diving eagles.

On the krater's handles, the Gorgons are shown running to the right on top of an Ionic capital. Their arms and legs are posed in the so-called *knielaufen* posture, a visual device employed during the Archaic period to suggest rapid motion. Both wear a short belted chiton with three central zigzag pleats. Four sickle-shaped wings emerge from behind the Gorgons' backs, the lower pair extending out past their knees, the top two wrapping around the lower end of the volute handle. Their hair is bound into thick bundles below their ears and then separates into four long tresses. Large, protruding eyes and gaping mouths, which expose their teeth and characteristic lolling tongues, define their full faces. Emerging from beneath each Gorgon are two bearded snakes, meant to emphasize their demonic character.

Like the volute handles, the three Gorgons forming part of the stand illustrated here are solid cast. Instead of running, however, they kneel on top of lion's paw feet, their arms held akimbo, their faces rendered frontally in the characteristic manner. Each wears a beaded-tongue necklace and a long belted chiton, which falls in vertical pleats on the outside of both legs. The faces of the Gorgons are similar to those on the volute handles, but their hair is rendered more simply, with notched tresses framing the forehead and the rest pulled loosely behind the head.

The krater was most likely produced on the Greek mainland, perhaps in Laconia, in the Peloponnese, a region renowned for its bronzeworking throughout the Mediterranean world in the seventh and sixth centuries B.C. Earlier examples, such as the magnificent krater from Vix, in France, depict only a bust of a Gorgon on the shoulder strap of the handle (the handle from another krater of this earlier type is also in the exhibition). The more developed representation of a Gorgon running on an Ionic capital dates this krater slightly later, in the third quarter of the sixth century B.C., placing it toward the end of a sequence of such Gorgon handles that lasted at least two generations.

In Archaic Greek society, the two most common contexts for such a krater were the symposium, where it would have been employed for mixing wine and water, or in a tomb, where it would have made a particularly magnificent grave gift. In the first instance, the Gorgon's presence may have warned the symposium's participants of the potency of the wine held within, while at the same time protecting them from its ill effects; in a tomb, the vessel would not only have enhanced the tomb's opulence, but the Gorgons may have been meant to protect the remains of the deceased laid within.

FURTHER READING:
Boardman, J. *Archaic Greek Gems: Schools and Artists in the Sixth and Early Fifth Centuries B.C.* London 1968.
Krauskopf, I. And Dahlinger, S. C. "Gorgo, Gorgones." In *Lexicon Iconographicum Mythologiae Classicae*, vol. 4 (1988).
Gaunt, J. *The Attic Volute Krater.* Ph.D. diss., New York University 2002.
Roccos, L. "Perseus." *Lexicon Iconographicum Mythologiae Classicae*, vol. 7 (1994).
Stibbe, C. M. *The Sons of Hephaistos: Aspects of the Archaic Greek Bronze Industry.* Rome 2000.
———. *Trebenishte: The Fortunes of an Unusual Excavation.* Rome 2003.
Tsiafakis, D. "Fabulous Creatures and/or Demons of Death?" In *The Centaur's Smile: The Human Animal in Early Greek Art.* Exhib. cat. Princeton University Art Museum, Princeton 2003.

In Greek mythology the Sphinx became a central figure in the great saga of the Labdacidae, in Hesiod's native Boiotia.[44] The story implied in Hesiod's reference is told in detail in the fifth century B.C. by Sophokles (*OT* and *OC*). In the most widespread version, Hera sent the Sphinx to Thebes to punish Laios for his love for Chrysippos.[45] The monster, which inhabited the mountain Kithairon or Phikion, terrorized Thebes by seizing any travelers, mostly young men, who could not solve her riddle. The riddle— "What goes on four legs in the morning, two in the afternoon, and three in the evening?"—was finally answered by Oedipus, who replied that man crawls as a child, walks upright as an adult, and supports himself with a stick as an old man (Apollod. *Bibl.* 3.5.7–8). The legend of the Sphinx as a devourer was widely disseminated throughout Greek culture from the Archaic period onward, and the exotic creature of Near Eastern origin was gradually transformed into an active beast.

The earliest representations in Greek lands of a winged lion with a female head are found in Minoan and Mycenaean art, where they are depicted in different media such as seals, vases, and bronzes.[46] There, they could have a decorative role or appear as guardians of sanctuaries without participating in any narrative. Until recently, it was generally accepted that the sphinx vanished during the Dark Ages only to reappear in the Geometric period. Theodora Rombos, however, attempts to narrow this chronological gap by presenting a few depictions of sphinxes as early as the ninth century B.C.[47] Moreover, the basically nonfigurative nature of early Greek Geometric vase-painting may have contributed to the absence of the sphinx in the early Iron Age.

The sphinx took her place in Greek art after the middle of the eighth century B.C. with representations peaking during the Archaic period (seventh and sixth centuries B.C.).[48] Crete appears to have played a significant role in the iconography of the early examples.[49] Of particular interest are the depictions of the helmeted or crowned sphinx, found mostly on Cretan vases and bronzes of the eighth and seventh centuries B.C., perhaps under the influence of Near Eastern art.[50] Crete retained her interest in this hybrid creature from the Bronze Age on, creating a distinctive type that influenced the other Greek

workshops. The *polos* headdress worn by Corinthian sphinxes is recognized as a Cretan influence,[51] as is the lock-like motif on top of the head that characterizes the early Greek examples.[52] The significance of this motif, if there was one, remains unknown, but the motif may have Near Eastern origins. Despite this, it is obvious that the unnatural topknot and spiral curls, combined with the natural elements of a lion, a female, and wings, contribute to the supernatural character of the beast.

The early sphinx types do not appear within a narrative context, and their symbolism, if any, remains obscure. They parade usually within the animal friezes on Late Geometric and Protoattic vase-paintings (e.g., fig. 5). Single or heraldic pairs of sphinxes are found on Archaic vases (e.g., cat. no. 66),[53] gold diadems, engraved seals, bronze helmets, and bronze and clay figurines and reliefs (e.g., cat. no. 67).[54] This creature, however, is not the predatory and ravenous beast that devoured the people of Thebes. That famous Theban monster, along with the tomb guardian and the chthonic demon, is clearly recognizable by the sixth century B.C.

Figure 5. Krater fragment: sphinxes. Greek, Protoattic, mid-seventh century B.C. After Cook 1934–35, 194, fig. 9.

Figure 6. Neck-amphora: siren and sphinxes.
Greek, Late Corinthian, 570 – 560 B.C., attributed to the
Tydeus Painter. Musée du Louvre, Paris (E 640).

Greek literature is clear about the gender of the sphinx: she is always female, and this character is often emphasized by Greek tragedians.[55] Only Herodotos (2.175.5) refers to male sphinxes, and this is in relation to the male statues he had seen in Egypt. Greek iconography, however, is not as decisive, and some early representations show the beast as *dimorphon* (double-natured).[56] On a Corinthian amphora in Paris (fig. 6), the vase painter emphasizes the female character of the sphinxes by painting them white.[57] This vase also is interesting for the combination of two hybrids: sphinx and siren.

Male sphinxes (cat. no. 69), like male sirens, occur in Archaic art, and both disappeared after the sixth century B.C. Their initial appearance can be explained as a translation of the Egyptian male sphinx into the bearded or helmeted examples seen in early Greek iconography. Bearded sphinxes, like bearded sirens, were most often chosen by the Attic, Corinthian, and Peloponnesian workshops. The earliest sphinxes in Corinth, in Protocorinthian vase-painting of the seventh century B.C., were female; male examples did not appear until the advent of the classic Corinthian style in the sixth century B.C.[58]

Human arms, a common feature on the sirens, are rare on the sphinxes. There are a few examples, the earliest dating to the last quarter of the eighth century B.C.[59] Since arms were not of any particular use for the sphinxes — these creatures could carry the dead youths in their front legs and did not play musical instruments — they were not adopted by Greek artists other than experimentally or for matching the sirens.

It was in the seventh century that Greek artists for the first time represented the sphinx in what might be a narrative context. The Corinthian potters' quarter seems to have first introduced the motif of sphinxes surrounding human figures.[60] A Laconian ivory comb of about 650 B.C.[61] and an architectural relief from Mycenae of about 630 B.C.,[62] each portraying two sphinxes standing over a male figure, are among the earliest depictions of the beast as a devourer of youths. Whether and to what extent these early representations can be related to the Oedipus myth remains problematic and, frankly, doubtful. Their demonic aspect, however, is evident, and they are perhaps more easily associated with *Ker*, the Homeric demon of death.[63]

The development of this subject can be followed into the sixth century in depictions of the sphinx chasing or carrying off youths (e.g., fig. 7; cat. no. 64). The model can be traced again to Near Eastern art, as is shown in numerous Egyptian and Phoenician examples.[64] In Greek art, the theme is found on gems, bronze shield bands, and a series of ceramic vases beginning about 560 B.C.; it was especially popular during the late Archaic period (ca. 500 – 480 B.C.) and declined thereafter.[65] Beginning somewhat later are vase-paintings of sphinxes flanking scenes of battle or hunting;[66] in contrast to those cases where the sirens might be considered omens of death, here the sphinxes may be present to effect the actual transfer to the underworld. Aischylos (*Sept.* 522, 541–54) confirms the use of the motif as a shield device. The theme of the sixth-century sphinx carrying a dead youth, however, probably relates to the Theban legend and depicts the fate of the traveler who could not solve the riddle (fig. 7).[67] But apparently it goes beyond that. The scene itself was adopted by and not invented for the Oedipus myth. In Attic vase-painting, the theme recently has been interpreted as symbolizing the Athenian ephebe awaiting initiation as a hoplite, the class of adult citizen who served in the militia as an armored infantryman.[68] Another interesting interpretation is that this sphinx can be both a dangerous and an erotic interlocutor of youths, posing them riddles on manhood while they are still inexperienced.[69] The erotic overtones in some of the scenes are undeniable, with the sphinx straddling the nude youth in a suggestive manner (fig. 7; cat. no. 64). The rape by a sphinx is characterized by the actions of chasing and lifting up, and both perfectly fit an erotic pursuit.

The iconography of the sphinx reached maturity in the sixth century B.C. To begin with, the inscription ΣΦΙΧΣ on an Attic black-figure cup of about 540 B.C. (fig. 8) confirms that this type is the Hesiodic creature.[70] There, instead of being an active participant, the sphinx, placed on either end of the main scene depicting Theseus and the Minotaur, plays the role of a framing ornament or boundary to another state (see below). Two more sphinxes flank the Kalydonian boar hunt on the reverse of the cup. Sphinxes were common motifs on Attic black-figure vases, especially eye-cups from the last decades of the sixth

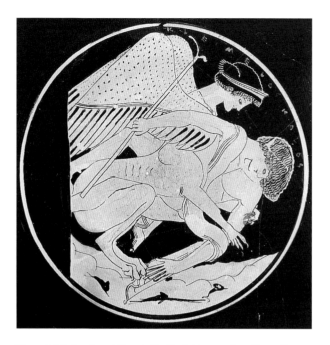

Figure 7. Interior of a red-figure kylix: the Sphinx carrying off a youth. Greek, Attic, ca. 500 B.C., attributed to the Kleomelos Painter. J. Paul Getty Museum, Malibu (85.AE.377).

century.[71] Plastic vases in the form of a crouching sphinx, although made by Corinthian potters from the late seventh to the early sixth century,[72] are very limited in number; the shape apparently was not as popular as the siren vases. Plastic ceramic sphinxes appeared again later, from the fifth century onward, in the form of *rhyta*, also in limited numbers.[73] In addition, sphinxes served as acroteria or antefixes on buildings, mainly after the middle of the sixth century B.C., with the Peloponnese playing a significant role in their development as terracotta architectural ornaments.[74]

Figure 8. Black-figure band-cup: sphinxes flanking Theseus and the Minotaur. Greek, Attic, ca. 540 B.C., signed by Archikles and Glaukytes. Staatliche Antikensammlungen und Glyptothek, Munich (2243).

Although the sphinx is not connected to any particular deity, it often served as a votive offering in sanctuaries.[75] The most representative example is the great marble sphinx dedicated about 580 B.C. by the Naxians at the sanctuary of Apollo at Delphi. Although it has been suggested that this was a symbolic grave marker for the Python's tomb,[76] its votive character cannot be ignored. Similar monuments are known from Cyrene, Delos, and possibly Aigina, Naxos, Paros, and Thasos.[77] Artistic evidence also suggests association of the sphinx with Athena. It is known that a sphinx decorated the helmet of her cult statue in Athens, the Athena Parthenos by Pheidias; and on a Protocorinthian krateriskos from Samos, the beast raises one forepaw toward the goddess.[78]

Greek art also employed the sphinx on stone funerary monuments. The composition of a sphinx occupying the crest of a marble grave stela is a purely Attic invention with a limited duration in the sixth century.[79] Written sources also attest to the use of sphinxes in a funerary context. On a fifth-century B.C. tombstone from Pagasai, the sphinx is addressed as "Dog of Hades, whom do you . . . watch over, sitting over the dead?"[80] and Diogenes Laertius (1.89), although much later (third century A.D.), refers to sphinxes placed on tombs. The abandonment of the sphinx as a grave marker in the fifth century might very well be connected to a general change in Greek—and, in particular, Athenian—thought, with the demonic aspect becoming less powerful.[81] Supporting such a view is the iconography of the fifth century B.C., which favors a gradually less violent repertoire that ends with scenes at the *gynaikonitis* (female scenes at home) and idyllic scenes with Aphrodite and Eros.[82]

From the sixth century onward, artists chose to illustrate two episodes related directly to the Theban Sphinx:[83] the meeting of Oedipus with the monster on his way to Thebes (e.g., cat. no. 63) and the Sphinx surrounded by the Thebans. In the earliest extant representation of Oedipus and the Sphinx, dated about 530 B.C., the scene already follows the standard form known from later depictions.[84] Oedipus is sitting before the Sphinx, who stands on a column. A number of seated Thebans watch the contest. The form of the Sphinx-on-a-column that becomes standardized for the Oedipus episode recalls the Archaic votive sphinxes, like the one at Delphi. The name-cup of the

Attic red-figure artist known as the Oedipus Painter, of about 480 B.C., is perhaps the best-known representation of Oedipus as solver of the riddle; from that time on, the subject became popular in Athenian vase painting.[85] During the last decades of the sixth century B.C., there appeared a related episode of the Theban story: the Theban citizens seated around the Sphinx and attempting to solve the riddle.[86] The scene can be seen as a rite of passage or transition ritual for crossing the boundaries from one state or status to another: they either begin a new life as distinguished citizens or they are led to death. And the Sphinx is the initiator of this transformation.

According to the most popular version of the myth, the Theban Sphinx brought about her own destruction by flinging herself from the acropolis of Thebes when foiled by Oedipus.[87] In contrast to the sirens' suicide, which is represented in Attic vase painting (fig. 4), there is no extant representation of the Sphinx falling to her death. A late-fifth-century Attic red-figure squat lekythos in the manner of the Meidias Painter, however, depicts a different end of the story, not preserved in the literary sources (fig. 9).[88] Here Oedipus clearly kills the Sphinx. This version of the subject has puzzled modern scholarship, and Jean-Marc Moret, in his study on the Theban Sphinx, believed that there was a tradition behind it.[89] In her monograph on the Meidias Painter, Lucilla Burn supported the existence of two alternative traditions: she suggested that the version depicted on the lekythos was the less common but was still present in the fifth century B.C.[90] On a series of black-figure vases, a man is shown attacking a sphinx. Since iconography often preserves otherwise unknown versions of myths, it is possible that these scenes are related to the myth of Oedipus.[91]

Although only a brief accounting of the occurrence of the sphinx in Greek art has been presented here, it is clear that the representations are many and diverse. The ornamental role played by the sphinx is undeniable, but the significance of the beast goes beyond the purely decorative. A funerary inscription probably written under the Saïte Dynasty (663–525 B.C.) echoes the words of an Egyptian sphinx: "I protect the chapel of the tomb. I guard thy sepulchral chamber. I ward off the intruding stranger. I hurl thy foes to the ground."[92] The role of the sphinx as guardian of the underworld is as clear in the epigram as it is in the inscription from Pagasai mentioned earlier. The creature's funerary significance is evidently tied to her demonic aspect, which means she functions in an apotropaic role. This is supported by the numerous representations of sphinxes in a heraldic, confronting position, which is particularly common among funerary sphinxes and gives the impression that the creatures act as guardians.[93] They keep away the "evil eye" by forcing the spectator to keep a distance. This prophylactic role might be hinted at alongside the ornamental, as in their use on warriors' helmets[94] or as attachments to bronze mirrors.[95] The creature's function as a demon of death is attested most explicitly in relation to funerary cult practices, when the sphinx is depicted on grave stelae and on vases placed in graves as votive offerings. Her presence in funerary scenes, the depictions of her carrying dead youths, and her role in the myth of the Theban riddle itself confirm this relationship with the underworld. Indeed, in the Theban episode, the sphinx is portrayed as the creature that completes the transformation of the living into the dead.

The rapacious, violent aspect was maintained until the end of the Archaic period, but in the Classical period, the appearance of sphinxes sweetened and became more feminine—they even are shown wearing the *sakkos* (hairnet) or *sphendone* (headband), as in figure 7. There is no doubt that much of the initial symbolic and religious significance was gradually lost, and the ornamental role, which existed from the beginning, became more important in later Greek iconography, alongside the involvement of the Sphinx in the Oedipus saga.

**Gorgons**

The third of the female hybrids presented here, the Gorgon, the fearful monster who turns men to stone with her glance, is, like the sphinx, commonly found either as an individual or in a group. In Greek mythology, the Gorgons were three sisters, Stheno, Euryale, and the best known, Medusa.[96] They were daughters of Phorkys and Keto, who also gave birth to Echidna, the mother of the Chimaera, and to the reptile Ladon, who guarded the Garden of the Hesperides. Hesiod (*Theog.* 277–78) states that of the three sisters, only Medusa was mortal, without offering any explanation of this odd situation. That detail, though, explains the

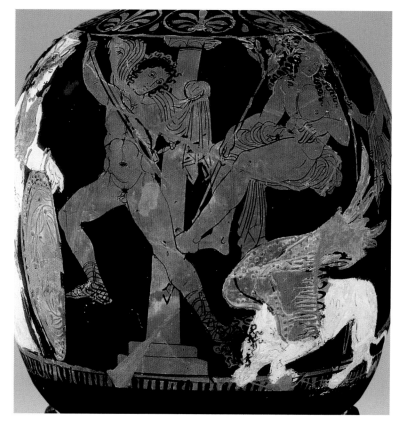

Figure 9. Red-figure squat lekythos: Oedipus killing the Sphinx Greek, Attic, end of the fifth century B.C., in the manner of the Meidias Painter. British Museum, London (E 696).

beheading of Medusa by Perseus (Hes. *Theog.* 280). A full account of this episode is provided by Apollodoros (*Bibl.* 2.4.1–5). The story starts with Akrisios, king of Argos, and his daughter Danaë. Because of an oracle that the king's grandson would be the cause of his death, Akrisios locked up Danaë to prevent her from having a child. But Zeus came to her in the form of a golden rain, and Danaë gave birth to Perseus. Akrisios did not believe that story and threw mother and baby into the sea. They were rescued by Diktys on the island of Seriphos. The brother of Diktys, Polydektes, king of the island, fell in love with Danaë and, in order to get Perseus out of the way, sent him off to bring back the head of the Gorgon. Through the Graiai, daughters of Phorkys, Perseus found the Nymphs, who gave him the means to protect himself: the famous *kibisis*, a bag in which to put the Gorgon's head; the cap of Hades with which to make himself invisible; and winged shoes.

The head of Medusa turned into stone anyone who gazed at it. Therefore, when Perseus came upon the Gorgons and cut off Medusa's head, he averted his eyes, and carried back the head in the sack. From the severed neck of Medusa sprang Chrysaor and Pegasos, offspring of Poseidon. Pegasos was the winged horse that helped Bellerophon to kill another hybrid, the Chimaera. Chrysaor, who fathered Geryon, had human form but enormous size. The immortal Gorgon sisters pursued Perseus, but he managed to escape using the cap of Hades. After Perseus returned to Seriphos, he showed Medusa's head to Polydektes and his friends, and turned them into stone. He gave the *kibisis* and the winged shoes to Hermes, and the Gorgon's head to Athena, who inserted the gorgoneion into the middle of her shield.

Bold frontality is the principal characteristic of the visualization of the Gorgon, whose name and related words derive from *gorgos*, meaning scary, fearful, terrifying.[97] Hesiod was the first to mention Medusa in the context of the myth, but he leaves out any description of her or her two sisters. Details of the physical appearance of the monsters were therefore left to the inventive imaginations of individual artists (as will be seen below). The Gorgon appears to be a Greek invention, composed, however, from features borrowed or inspired by Near Eastern and Egyptian prototypes: features from Humbaba, Bes, Hathor, Pazuzu, and Lamaštu, for example, can be recognized in the Greek creature.[98]

The Greek Gorgon is in every aspect a terrifying figure, with a mask-like face placed on a female body (fig. 15; cat. no. 84). She has a long tongue protruding from a great red grimacing mouth with bared teeth and long fangs. On either side of the broad nose, the eyes petrify the observer. Her hair falls in long, undulating locks down her back and forward across her shoulders. Some of the locks are particularly lively in the form of snakes, a feature adequately explained because of her family relations. Other snakes are often tightened around her waist like a belt. Although the head of the Gorgon Medusa preserves its major features, it loses its terrifying character gradually through the centuries. In the Classical period, the entire look is sweetened, as for the sphinx, and finally she becomes a lovely girl, distinguished only by the snakes knotted beneath her chin, and the wings in her wild hair.[99]

Greek art distinguishes between Gorgon and gorgoneion (γοργείη κεφαλή), the frontal face of a Gorgon (fig. 10). Homer knows of the apotropaic face,[100] but he does not mention the beast as a mythological figure. Both the running Gorgon and the gorgoneion are among the most popular demonic subjects of early Greek art, and they appear almost simultaneously in the early seventh century B.C.[101] Although there has been some controversy as to which came first, Gorgon or gorgoneion, most scholars agree that the image of the disembodied head is older and that the body is a later addition.[102] The dominant part of this creature is certainly the face, the menacing mask to which could be attached a body with normal arms and legs. The Corinthian potters' quarter in the seventh century B.C. appears to be among the earliest Greek workshops to employ the gorgoneion, on Protocorinthian vases. The early examples to a great extent resemble lions, with mane, ruff, mouth, and occasionally, the animal's nose.[103] Laconian gorgoneia also are found on clay and metal vessels,[104] like the bronze amphora handle in Princeton (cat. no. 85). The East Greek workshops made the gorgoneion (actually the bust of a Gorgon) in the form of plastic vases in the first half of the sixth century B.C.;[105] the aryballos in Boston is an exceptionally good example (cat. no. 83). From the same period date the earliest gorgoneia on Greek gems.[106] Gorgoneia also were employed in architecture as acroteria, simas, metopes, and antefixes from the seventh century B.C. on (e.g., cat. nos. 88, 89).[107]

Although gorgoneia were known as early as the Protocorinthian period (ca. 710–640 B.C.), it was not until the inception of the Attic eye-cup, about 535 B.C., that they became a standard decoration in the tondo of cup interiors.[108] These Attic tondo-gorgoneia are based on the earlier Corinthian type and represent a mix of human and animal (especially leonine) features. The foreheads of the gorgoneia are sporadically decorated with dots that recall tattoos (δερματοστιξία), known from art and literary sources, decorating the face and body of northern barbarians (fig. 11).[109]

Gorgoneia, as well as more complete Gorgons, are often featured in the decoration of Archaic bronze vessels, especially hydriae and volute-kraters. Among the finest is a series with the Gorgon herself found at the handles of

**Figure 10. Red-figure Panathenaic amphora: running Gorgon. Greek, Attic, ca. 500–490 B.C. Staatliche Antikensammlungen und Glyptothek, Munich (2312).**

Figure 11. Black-figure amphora: detail of gorgoneion at the base of a handle.
Greek, Attic, ca. 540–530 B.C., attributed to the BMN painter. Musée du Louvre, Paris (F 99).

volute-kraters dated to the sixth century B.C. (e.g., cat. no. 86).[110] The snake legs of the Gorgon emerging from her garment on some of these vessels, such as the great Vix krater,[111] allude to demonic figures like Typhon; through them, the demonic and apotropaic aspects of the monster are emphasized, creating a wild image on the cold metal. A similar role is recognizable in the synthesis of the two plastically rendered snakes that spring from a monstrous gorgoneion under the handle of a vase in Paris (fig. 11).[112]

Because of its mythical power to paralyze an opponent, the Greeks employed the head of Medusa on military armor and shields, a practice confirmed by Homer, who places it on the shield of Agamemnon and the aegis of Athena. Despite this early mention, the aegis and the gorgoneion were not visualized together in art before the sixth century B.C., when they were combined, especially in Athenian iconography.[113] The gorgoneion occurs often as the device (ἐπίσημα) emblazoned on warriors' shields, where its role is obviously protective and apotropaic through its natural aggressiveness. In addition, the gorgoneion is found both on real bronze shields and shield bands and

on numerous representations of shields on painted vases. On an Attic black-figure amphora attributed to Group E, for example, with the battle between Herakles and the three-bodied Geryon, the frontal face of Medusa is depicted on the shield of the monster (fig. 12).[114] Enormous, its height takes up the entire figural surface, its eyes fixed on the viewer; a loud cry seems to issue from its open mouth.

Figure 12. Black-figure amphora: Herakles battling Geryon.
Greek, Attic, ca. 550–540 B.C., signed by Exekias as potter and attributed to a painter of Group E. Musée du Louvre, Paris (F 53).

86

Figure 13. Relief-pithos: Perseus killing Medusa. Greek, Cycladic, found in Boiotia, second quarter of the seventh century B.C. Musée du Louvre, Paris (CA 795).

The placement of the shield in a frontal position at the center of the scene not only attracts spectators but also keeps them away. An analogous function can be seen in all similar representations, suggesting that the gorgoneion was being used as subliminal imagery.

It is difficult to pinpoint when Greek artists first began to depict the Gorgon of the Perseus myth, but it was probably by the first half of the seventh century.[115] From then on, throughout antiquity, Medusa was depicted in the same media as gorgoneia—vase-painting, sculpture, architecture, and the minor arts. The typical form of Medusa is that of the female body crowned by a gorgoneion. Other principal attributes include the wings, which appeared before the end of the seventh century but are not always found in the early examples. Of interest is the clearly experimental character of the early representations.

One of the earliest extant examples is a Cycladic relief-pithos from Boiotia dated in the second quarter of the seventh century B.C. (fig. 13).[116] The moment depicted is the decapitation of Medusa by Perseus. The hero, with the *kibisis* over his shoulder, is about to behead Medusa with his sword; he turns away his face so as not to be petrified by the Gorgon's gaze. The composition of the scene might be considered already standardized were it not for the unique appearance of Medusa herself. To a frontal view of a clothed female figure, the artist has awkwardly attached the hindquarters of a horse in profile. This centaur-gorgon wears a long garment that covers her legs; she has no wings, no snakes or tusks or protruding tongue; in fact, she possesses none of the facial peculiarities, except rotundity of outline, that are connected with the regular Archaic type. The relationship of Medusa to the horse—

Figure 14. Amphora: the Gorgons pursuing Perseus. Greek, Protoattic, ca. 670–650 B.C., attributed to the Polyphemos Painter. Eleusis Archaeological Museum (2630).

the connection with *hippios* Poseidon, who made her the mother of Pegasos—and the later use of the epithet *gorgos* with the meaning of *tachys* (rapid) to characterize the same animal might be responsible for the equine-human combination.[117]

The Protoattic amphora in Eleusis by the Polyphemos Painter, dated about 670–650 B.C.[118] (fig. 14), is the earliest vase that preserves the next episode of the myth, where Medusa, already beheaded, lies amid flowers, while her monstrous sisters pursue Perseus. Unusual features here

include the heads of the Gorgons—cauldron-shaped with snake protomes—possibly a deliberate reference to bronze cauldrons of the period that in fact do have animal attachments. The Gorgons are dressed in a long garment, probably a peplos, with the skirt split so that one leg issues from it, a way of indicating that the female is running. A horrific contrast is accomplished through the use of this running motif: the nude female leg is revealed, suggesting a sexual element, and this is simultaneously obliterated by the totally appalling face.

Figure 15. Pediment of the temple of Artemis at Corfu: detail of Medusa, Pegasos, and Chrysaor.
Greek, ca. 590–580 B.C., limestone. Corfu Archaeological Museum.

This convention of the leg issuing from the garment continues until the sixth century when it is replaced by the so-called *Knielaufschema*—legs and arms bent in pin-wheel fashion, denoting the rapid movement of the human body. The Gorgon at the very center of the pediment of the temple of Artemis at Corfu (fig. 15),[119] dated about 590 B.C., is an outstanding example of this motif. The ferocious character of the beast is emphasized through the snakes extending off her shoulders and the reptiles used as a belt around her waist. Her son Pegasos stands to her right, reminding the viewer of her decapitation. The story of the two children of Medusa, Pegasos and Chrysaor, was a favorite subject in the Archaic period and one that declined in popularity in the Classical era.[120]

In addition to depicting episodes related to the Perseus story, artists of the Archaic period were also interested in individual Gorgons, or in groups of two, along with scenes not found in later periods, such as the Gorgon as Mistress of Animals (*Potnia Theron*).[121] Perhaps the most characteristic example is an East Greek plate of about 630 B.C. on which the Gorgon/Potnia holds two geese by the neck.[122] As Mistress of Animals, the Gorgon adopts

a role similar to that of Artemis. The only difference from the standard type of Potnia is that she has been given the apotropaic head of Medusa. It seems that there are certain similarities between Artemis and the Gorgon as Potnia Theron.[123] That the Greek goddess was wild nature deified is confirmed by her titles Potnia Theron and *Agrotera* (of the fields). Homer (*Il.* 21.511) referred to her as *Keladeine* (noisy, echoing), a characteristic that recalls the noise coming out the Gorgon's open mouth. Artemis might also appear winged, as on the handles of the François Vase.[124] Both Potnia and the Gorgon were powerful and apparently frightening figures, and this integration might reflect an earlier aspect of Medusa as a deity. Further, the association between the two appears to be made visible in the presence of the Medusa on the pediment of the temple of Artemis (the official Greek Potnia Theron) at Corfu.[125]

The mixture of features belonging to diverse creatures is another characteristic of the iconography of the Gorgons in Archaic times.[126] The centaur-gorgon is not limited to the scene showing Perseus decapitating Medusa (described above; fig. 13); it is also found on some Greek gems of the sixth century B.C.[127] Another interesting mixture, which occurred particularly during Archaic times, is the placement of the gorgoneion on the body of a lion.[128] These gorgon-sphinxes recall the related type of Bes-sphinx found in Egypt and the Near East.[129] Archaic artists also experimented with other human-animal combinations, including birds and panthers,[130] before settling on the form that was to become the standard Gorgon.

The apotropaic role of the Gorgon and gorgoneion is made clear beyond any doubt by the horrible face of the monster.[131] Her gaze kept away any intruder, whom she otherwise would turn into stone. The monster's large, distended mouth conveys to the spectator the idea of a terrifying roar. In the *Iliad*, the head has Terror and Rout as its companions. The connection to death suggested by those features is made explicit in Euripides' *Ion* (1012–14): when Erichthonios was born, Athena gave him two drops of the Gorgon's blood, one drop to give death but the other to heal and prolong life.

All these associations provide the Gorgon with a dual role: she is a demon with an apotropaic aspect and, at the same time—like Artemis—she acts as a guardian. Whether her presence in sanctuaries is as votive offering or as architectural ornament, this dual aspect should always be kept in mind.[132] The protective function of the Gorgon is clearly noted by Pausanias (8.47.5) in his account of Tegea, in the Peloponnese, where Athena cut off some of Medusa's hair in token of her promise that the city should never fall. The hair was kept in a bronze urn and would turn back an enemy from the city walls. Elsewhere, Pausanias (1.21.3) describes a gilded gorgoneion surrounded by an aegis and placed on the south wall of the Athenian Acropolis.[133]

The "prophylactic" role of the eye in Greek tradition is well known and remains unchanged to the present day.[134] Surely a protection against the "evil eye" is the placement of a gorgoneion between two giant eyes on some Attic black-figured cups.[135] This may also have been intended to protect the banqueter from the ill effects of the drink or simply to magnetize him. Even more interesting is the actual incorporation of the gorgoneion into the eyes, as on a eye-cup in Cambridge.[136] There the monstrous face replaces the pupils of the eyes decorating the vase, and the spectator looks at eyes within eyes. The gorgoneion is an image purely for spectacle. Lacking the body, it is only a face, enigmatic and fascinating, a source of supernatural force. The total effect is of a terrifying mask, inhuman; it is not a face but rather a negation of the face, already belonging to the invisible beyond. This confrontation between the viewer and the Gorgon is the major difference between this female hybrid and other Greek *Mischwesen*. Sirens and sphinxes remain distant, whereas the Gorgon, with or without a body, creates an almost immediate connection, something like a mirror game in which she flashes a reflection of her powers toward the viewer.

Magnetism, allure, and fierceness are all characteristics common to these female monsters. The siren, the sphinx, and the Gorgon act as symbols of death with the face of a woman, man-killers with a frightening power that is conveyed clearly through visual signs.[137] They are females challenging males, and ultimately their death must be brought about by males. The fearsome aspects associating them with death and the underworld are clearly depicted on the features of the sphinx and the Gorgon but are carefully hidden under the charming looks of the siren. Because of their connection to a world of fear, the death of these beings was a welcome event for humans, and almost all the stories about them conclude with their defeat and death at the hand of mortals.

The fifth century B.C. was the boundary that separated the bestial aspect emphasized during the Archaic period in the representation of sirens, Gorgons, and sphinxes from the almost civilized form these creatures assumed in the following centuries. Thereafter, they followed the common path of Greek iconography, gradually becoming more humanized and eventually making their appearance— at least the sirens and Medusa—among the more beautiful women of Hellenistic art.

## MALE HYBRIDS

The Minotaur, Acheloos, Triton, Typhon, and Pan are among the best-known male *Mischwesen* of Greek mythology. Their gender was fixed from the beginning, and Greek artists never depicted them with female characteristics.

## The Minotaur

Of the male hybrids, only the Minotaur is mortal and a genuine hybrid born from the union of a human with an animal. According to the myth, told in detail by Apollodoros (*Bibl.* 3.1.3–4; 3.15.7–16.9), Pasiphaë, daughter of Helios and wife of Minos, king of Crete, was driven mad with desire for a bull. With the help of Daidalos, she was able to fulfill this unnatural passion. Daidalos constructed a hollow wooden cow and once Pasiphaë was concealed within it, she mated with the bull. The offspring of this union was the Minotaur, whose personal name was Asterios. He had the face of a bull, but the rest of him was human. The Minotaur was confined in the Labyrinth, and Minos exacted a tribute of seven youths and seven maidens from Athens to feed him. Theseus, son of Aegeus, came to Crete as one of the victims and killed the monster with help from Ariadne, daughter of Minos. To find the way out of the Labyrinth, he used a ball of yarn, which Ariadne gave him in return for a promise of marriage.

The early representations of the Minotaur, whose name means "bull of Minos," indicate that he was thought of as a man-bull hybrid of undetermined shape.[138] By the sixth century B.C., however, the artistic tradition had chosen the existing figure of the bull-headed man to represent the creature slain by Theseus (e.g., cat. no. 91). The two-figure composition of the hero fighting a monster is a common and well-known motif that finds models in the Near East.[139] The story of Minos and Theseus is the only myth in which the Minotaur is involved, and Greek artists had begun depicting his battle with Theseus by the middle of the seventh century B.C.[140] Gold reliefs, shield bands, and vases are the principal classes of objects representing the story. Surprisingly, it was not Attica but the Peloponnese, along with the Cyclades, that introduced this deed of the Athenian hero into art; the Athenian potter's quarter did not include the Theseus legend in its repertoire before the sixth century B.C. The theme reached its peak in the second half of the sixth century and became one of the most popular in Attic black-figure (fig. 16).[141] Red-figure artists continued to render it throughout the fifth century, albeit with decreasing frequency.[142]

Figure 16. Black-figure amphora: Theseus and the Minotaur. Greek, Attic, ca. 550–540 B.C., attributed to Lydos or a painter close to him. J. Paul Getty Museum, Malibu (86.AE.60).

Among the numerous preserved representations, of particular interest here are a few vases depicting not only the Minotaur, but also other hybrids. The band-cup by Archikles and Glaukytes with the central scene of Theseus and the Minotaur flanked by sphinxes has already been mentioned (see fig. 8). The same pattern is found on another Attic black-figure cup, dated about 530 B.C., again depicting Theseus and the Minotaur.[143] The presence of the sphinx as a secondary motif is not unusual, but here it makes us think of the devouring monster who is waiting to grasp the defeated and carry him away, as she does with the dead youths on many other vase paintings. The only difference is that instead of the expected youth, in this case the sphinx will carry away the dead Minotaur, a subject unfortunately not preserved in the art.

Two other vases depict the greatest Greek heroes killing hybrids composed of elements of the same beings: the man-bull and the bull-man. The first is a Corinthian black-figure cup of the Gorgoneion Group, dating about 570–560 B.C.[144] Here Theseus's battle with the Minotaur is combined with the fight of Herakles and Acheloos. The same subjects are rendered on another vase, an Attic hydria of about 510 B.C. (fig. 17).[145] Striking is the alignment

Figure 17. Black-figure hydria: Theseus fighting the Minotaur and Herakles struggling with Acheloos. Greek, Attic, ca. 510 B.C., attributed to the Leagros Group. British Museum, London (313).

of the scenes on the vertical axis, occupying the center of both figural panels: the battle with the Minotaur is placed on the shoulder of the hydria and consequently is smaller in scale than the Acheloos scene on the body. It is remarkable that the vase-painter uses the same poses to render the motif of the monster-fighting hero. Both monsters turn their head and upper body to face their opponent at the left, and both heroes grasp the horn of the hybrids.

## Acheloos

Acheloos, like the Minotaur, also is a bull-man, but in reverse order: he is a man-headed bull (cat. nos. 92, 93). According to Hesiod (*Theog.* 340), he was the son of Okeanos and Tethys, or, as is recounted elsewhere (Serv. *Georg.* 1.8), his mother was Gaia (Earth).[146] A river deity, Acheloos was considered the father of numerous nymphs and of the sirens. A cult place of Acheloos is mentioned

by Plato (*Phdr.* 230b), in the Ilissos area of Athens. Nymphs, Pan, and other deities were also worshiped at the same sanctuary. Archilochos (287w) and Pindar (Fr. 249a SM) tell of a battle between Acheloos and Herakles, but a full account of the story is not preserved before that of Sophokles (*Trach.* 1–27). The episode is related to Herakles' desire to marry Deianeira, the daughter of Oineus of Kalydon. In order to fulfill his wish, Herakles had to fight the river god Acheloos, who already was courting Deianeira. As they wrestled, the hero broke off the horn of Acheloos and finally defeated him.

Acheloos as an individual figure without a narrative context appeared in art as early as the seventh century B.C., with the East Greek workshops having a prominent role in his initial representations.[147] The episode with Herakles, however, was introduced in Attic black-figure, the first depictions of the myth thus dating to the second quarter of the sixth century B.C.[148] Corinthian and Caeretan pottery workshops followed suit. Although the theme was not completely abandoned later, the majority of the depictions date from the Archaic period. Acheloos is most commonly represented with the body of a bull and the head of a bearded man. On the hydria by the Leagros Group (fig. 17), however, Acheloos has the body of a horse and a human torso, like a centaur; were it not for the large horn on the river god's head, the scene could easily be mistaken for Herakles and Nessos (cf., e.g., cat. nos. 35, 37). The most remarkable representation of Acheloos, however, was painted by Oltos on a red-figure stamnos of about 520 B.C. (fig. 18).[149] Here Acheloos has the fishlike body normally reserved for monsters of the sea rather than freshwater deities. Only the inscription ΑΧΕΛΟΙΟ (running from right to left), which identifies the figure as the river god, and the way that Herakles grasps his prominent horn enable us to distinguish this combat from that with the sea monster Triton.

## Triton

Triton is not mentioned by Homer. The earliest reference to him is in Hesiod's *Theogony* (930 ff.), where he is described as a horrible god (*deinos theos*)[150] and the son of Poseidon and Amphitrite. The visualization of this monster was a merman named Triton, who, according to Herodotos (4.179),

Figure 18. Red-figure stamnos: Acheloos with a fishlike body. Greek, Attic, ca. 520 B.C., signed by the potter Pamphaios and attributed to Oltos. British Museum, London (E 437).

acted as a seer to the Argonauts. The account of Herodotos and that of Apollonios Rhodios (*Argon.* 4.1537–1619) relate Triton to Lake Tritonis in Libya. The term "triton" is used for rivers, springs, nymphs, and aquatic figures. It has therefore been suggested that in pre-Hellenic times the word meant "water" or something similar.[151]

Triton is a male *Mischwesen*, characterized in archaic Greek art as a man above the waist and a fish below. His just-noted connection to water provides a logical justification for this depiction and at the same time emphasizes his aquatic connection. The combination of an elderly, civilized figure with a fish body was not limited to Triton but also was used in representing sea demons such as Nereus and Proteus.[152] The three are so alike that often it is not clear which one is being portrayed. The origins of the type can be traced once again to the Near East. The Greeks borrowed the iconography during their Orientalizing period to personify their own mythical sea monsters. It is probable that the various dangers of marine voyages led to this personification of the constantly

Figure 19. Black-figure neck-amphora: Nereus watching Herakles wrestling Triton. Greek, Attic, ca. 520–510 B.C., near the Group of Toronto 305. British Museum, London (B 223).

changing aspects of the sea and that the combative wrestling pictured between the sea demon and the heroes paralleled the Greeks' real struggle to succeed in marine navigation.

Representations of Triton began with certainty in the sixth century B.C. and depicted him as a composite creature whose head and upper body were human and whose lower body was that of a fish with a long tail. The battle of Triton with Herakles, the principal subject depicted in art (fig. 19), is not preserved in the literary sources. Ancient authors, however, emphasize the dreadful character of the sea monster and his dangerous aspect for humans. A tradition regarding his conquest by the greatest of heroes, therefore, was undoubtedly welcome. The struggle of Herakles with Triton appears to be an Athenian invention, for it appears almost exclusively on Attic vases and reliefs limited primarily to the second half of the sixth century B.C., with a particular popularity in the years 530–510 B.C. Furthermore, the name Triton is never found outside Attic art;[153] a series of inscriptions on Athenian vases identifies the hybrid and the subject. It appears that the scene replaced the struggle between Herakles and another sea demon, Nereus, about 560 B.C. The fight with

Triton has been regarded as having political symbolism, referring perhaps to some Athenian maritime success at the time of the Peisistratids.[154] Even though the iconography of the fight between Herakles and Triton is very close to that with Nereus, there are some differences that allow them to be distinguished: Triton is neither old nor mutating and Herakles does turn around.[155] Of interest are some representations in which Nereus watches the struggle between Herakles and Triton,[156] such as on a neck-amphora of about 520–510 B.C.[157] (fig. 19). Here Nereus, depicted as an old man holding a stick, looks on as his successor fights their common opponent. By the fifth century, the episode with Herakles had been abandoned, and Triton thereafter would appear in scenes with his parents and Theseus, as on a cup by Onesimos of about 500–490 B.C.[158]

## Typhon

The dangers of the sea, embodied by Triton, are even more powerful in the personification of Typhon, by virtue of his additional and equally destructive natural powers of wind and fire.[159] Typhon, known to Homer (*Il.* 2.780–783), is a demonic figure and, according to Hesiod (*Theog.* 820–80), the youngest son of Gaia (Earth) and Tartaros, and father of the unpleasant winds. In Greek mythology, Typhon was born to prevent the gods from establishing themselves as rulers of the world after their victory over the Giants. Despite Gaia's desire, Zeus destroyed him with his thunderbolt and hurled him into Tartaros. The model of this combat with Zeus and the origin of the hybrid figure of Typhon in art are traceable to the Hittite myth about the dragon Illuyanka.[160]

Hesiod describes Typhon as having human legs and one hundred snakes' heads growing from his shoulders. Some centuries later, Apollodoros (*Bibl.* 1.6.3) reverses this, presenting him with a human upper body and serpents instead of legs; in addition, he is said to have wings, wild hair and beard, and one hundred dragons' heads projecting from each hand. The fierceness, hostility, and danger posed by snakes and dragons are emphasized through the great number of reptiles common to both descriptions of Typhon. The serpent form seems ideal for this mythical monster because it suggests his chthonic origin and nature.[161]

Figure 20. Black-figure hydria: Zeus and Typhon. Greek, Chalcidian, probably made at Rhegion in Sicily, ca. 540–530 B.C. Staatliche Antikensammlungen und Glyptothek, Munich (596).

Typhon entered the repertoire of Greek artists in the seventh century B.C., appearing first at Corinth. His appearance in art, however, does not quite correspond to the earliest—and nearly contemporary—descriptions provided by the literary sources. He is shown with wings and serpents, but the latter are placed differently. The isolated being depicted on Protocorinthian vases and recognized as Typhon is a winged hybrid with a human torso and head, and a serpent body instead of legs.[162] He usually has wild hair and beard and occasionally two serpents instead of one. The depiction of this same creature in a fight with Zeus on bronze shield bands from Olympia[163] allows us to identify him with the demon on the vases.

It is noteworthy that no certain depiction of Typhon is preserved in Attic art,[164] which suggests that the myth with Zeus could be a Peloponnesian invention. Except for a Chalcidian hydria, probably made at Rhegion in Sicily (fig. 20), all other known representations come from the Peloponnese, especially Laconia.[165] Nonetheless, the most impressive depiction of the battle between Zeus and Typhon may be on the strikingly colorful Chalcidian vase, which dates to about 540–530 B.C.[166] Zeus rushes at Typhon, brandishing his thunderbolt. The monster, except for his face, is rendered frontally so that there is no mistaking the identity and power of the enemy, who is roughly twice as large as the figure of Zeus.

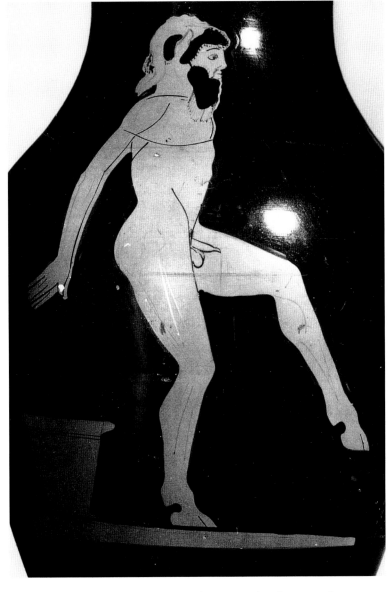

**Figure 21. Red-figure oinochoe: Pan. Greek, Attic, ca. 470–460 B.C., attributed to the Geras Painter. Museo Archeologico Nazionale, Naples (126056).**

## Pan

Nonnos (*Dion.* 1.409–534) provides an interesting version of the story of Zeus and Typhon, in which the goat-god Pan is involved. The music of Pan's instrument, the syrinx, bewitches the monster and makes him dream that he is already lord of Olympos; in reality, though, the song celebrates the coming victory of Zeus and is only a trap. This form of the story does not occur in Archaic art, and

Pan is not included in the iconography of Typhon. Pan, however, is also a hybrid figure, a mixture of goat and human. A rustic god closely related to shepherds, Pan was considered the son of Hermes and Dryope. His liking for music—the syrinx, or Pan's pipes, is his principal instrument—dancing, flirting, and drinking wine, in combination with a bestial animalism like that of the satyrs, connects him closely to Dionysos. The name Pan derives from the root *pa(s)*, meaning the "guardian of the flocks."[167] In the Homeric Hymn to Pan (19.45–47), however, his name is related to the Greek word *pan*, meaning all (*olos*), from the way he delighted *all* the gods.

Pan started as an Arcadian deity whose cult was introduced into Athens at the time of the Persian Wars, after his supposed intervention at the battle of Marathon.[168] His goatlike appearance corresponds to descriptions by the ancient authors. Artistic and literary evidence for him do not predate the fifth century B.C.[169] Greek art depicts him as a man-goat, at first with the animal's features predominating, but over time gradually evolving into a more humanized creature. In the beginning, in the early fifth century, he is almost entirely a goat; nevertheless, a representation showing a goat chorus cannot be identified with certainty as a depiction of multiple Pans.[170] Very soon, however, he is given a human torso and arms but with a goat's legs and tail, and a goat's head, bearded and horned (e.g., cat. no. 99).[171] This becomes one of his standard forms along with a partially human shape that might have either a human head or human legs (fig. 21).[172]

The scenes in which Pan is included are most frequently related to the world of Dionysos and the satyrs, rustic scenes, and erotic pursuits. These representations indicate that with Pan, the Greeks found a deity through whom they could express otherwise unacceptable behavior. From the fifth century through the Roman period, he is depicted in a variety of media, and occasionally multiple Pans and female *Paniske* are also found. Since the goat-god is not involved in any of the major Greek myths, he either functions as a side figure or appears in scenes without any particular narrative content.

With the exception of his physical appearance, Pan is not really closely associated with the other composite creatures presented in this essay. Although literary sources attest that his appearance caused *panic* (a word deriving from his name),[173] this trait is much less fearsome than the attributes of Medusa or Typhon. Furthermore, he is not connected to death, nor can he be identified as a demon or guardian. "Otherness," however, as well as an element of the exotic, is found in all these creatures. Of all the Olympian deities, Pan is the only animal hybrid, very different from the rest of the gods. In that sense, he shares the generally barbaric behavior that characterizes all the other, more terrifying hybrids.

## CONCLUSION

All those fabulous creatures, with the exception of Pan, made their appearance or reappearance in the Greek world sometime between the end of the eighth and the early seventh century B.C. The Peloponnese appears to have been the leader in introducing many of those beings into Greek art or to have played an important role in the development of their iconography.[174] At about the same time, literary sources began to provide information for the existence and genealogy of the hybrids. Homer knew only few (sirens, Typhon),[175] but Hesiod in his *Theogony* provided a full account, excluding—surprisingly—the sirens, the Minotaur (who is not preserved in the literary sources until Hellanikos,[176] in the fifth century), and the god Pan. Many of them belong to the *genos* of Pontos, as is stated in the *Theogony*, and they have Phorkys and Keto as their ancestors.

Although Hesiod does not provide a full description of those creatures, contemporary Greek art preserves their earliest indisputable images. Wild hair, beards, grimacing faces, and snakes are attributes used frequently to denote the fearsome character of some of the demonic beings. Wings appear also to be a common attribute for a wide range of these hybrid creatures, perhaps under the influence of Near Eastern art. Their use, however, in the Greek composite creatures might be an indication of rapid movement in an unconventional, supernatural way.[177] Until the sixth century B.C., it seems there was not a standard way of rendering the composite creatures; artists experimented with mixing different forms of existing creatures that served as prototypes for other unusual demons. In this way can be explained the appearance in early Greek art of hybrids composed of other hybrids, such as the gorgon-sphinx, the Chimaera-sphinx, or the sphinx with two bodies and one head.[178]

Equine elements are not unknown on some early hybrid creatures. Among the earliest representations of the Perseus myth is the relief-pithos already mentioned, with the Gorgon in the form of a centaur (fig. 13).[179] An equine element is also fairly common on some early sphinxes. On a late Geometric Attic skyphos, for example, two sphinxes with equine legs and hooves are depicted facing one another.[180] They are winged, with feline tails and human heads, and they retain the spiral-like motif on the head, an attribute of many early sphinxes. Typhon is the third hybrid recognized in the form of a centaur: an eighth-century bronze group shows a man fighting a centaurlike figure (cat. no. 13); and a Protocorinthian aryballos depicts a similar scene (cat. no. 31).[181] The Minotaur might also be depicted in an equine form on a Cycladic relief-amphora of the seventh century B.C.[182] Thus, the combination of human and horse seems in the early Archaic period to have been a device utilized to represent several different kinds of monsters (at the same time, we cannot be absolutely certain that the earliest centaurs were even conceived in this form). The association of the horse with deities and demons of the underworld might be related to this preference.[183]

The fluid forms of these creatures, as evidenced by the various artistic attempts at their visualization and the absence or insufficient description provided by the literary sources, point toward their origin in and connection to the Near East. Their amorphous shapes also suggest that these monsters existed in the Greek imagination prior to their visualization and that it was not necessarily the Near Eastern *Mischwesen* that led to the creation of the Greek myths. A direct Near Eastern origin would have required a fixed form of representation from the very beginning, with changes expected to come later. Thus, the Greeks may be said to have borrowed the forms from the Near East to visualize their own mythological creatures. Moreover, it should not be forgotten that all those hybrid creatures express beliefs, fears, superstitions, and perhaps myths held in common by different cultures.

The many artistic attempts to embody those creatures of fantasy before their standardization, plus the indecisiveness about gender, might be related to a different role previously played by the hybrids. Reading their hidden meaning and significance can be particularly complicated, especially because we might be missing the right password.[184] It is known that superstitions, fear, and demonic powers had much more influence on the Greeks of the Archaic period than in the Classical period and later. Iconography also shows that hybrid forms and monsters had less of an appeal for the Greeks of the fifth century than for their forebears of the Orientalizing period or even for the Greeks of the sixth century. And this cannot be unrelated to a general change in the repertoire that occurred in Greek art by the late Archaic period: violent, warlike scenes diminished and were replaced by scenes of daily life and other, less aggressive subjects. Considering those parameters, we may begin to think about some of the reasons that led to the gradual humanization of the earlier monstrous figures and their full absorption into mythology.

Death provides one link among the creatures. The exotic "foreignness" reflected in their composite nature was deemed the appropriate imagery of an unknown world, the underworld. The sphinx and the siren, for example, were widely employed on grave markers honoring and commemorating the dead. The Gorgon petrified those who turned their gaze upon her, depriving them of their senses. Triton embodied the threat in the sea, while Typhon destroyed humans through storm and fire. All the πέλωρα also have in common that they combine in one body three ontological characteristics: animal, human, and superhuman. This mixture of human and nonhuman features was suitable for a dual purpose: first, in their ferocious animal form, the hybrids protected against hostile supernatural forces in day-to-day living; and second, through their human element, they enabled mortals to conquer those symbols of death. Their complex, antithetical nature made of them "mediators between worlds."[185] But which worlds? The only undeniable answer is that the πέλωρα mediated between the actual world and that of fantasy. The greatest Greek heroes—Herakles, Theseus, Odysseus, Oedipus, Perseus—were all monster-slayers, as was Zeus, first among the Olympians. And thus it is not surprising that in the end, human heroes or gods triumphed over all the supernatural beasts.

## NOTES

I thank Michael Padgett for his invitation to contribute to the present volume, as well as for his constructive criticism and editorial advice, including corrections of my English. The interesting remarks and suggestions of the anonymous reader were helpful and appreciated. I am also grateful to Elena Walter-Karydi for access to her text on the sphinx prior to publication and for the useful discussions we had on *Mischwesen*. I would also like to thank Eleni Manakidou and Vana Machaira for providing copies of articles and references for titles I could not easily obtain, and Sharon Herson for her editorial comments and advice.

1 The name πέλωρα ( *pelora* ) characterizes oversized and giant creatures, usually malevolent beings like monsters, for example: Hom. *Il.* 18.410; *Od.* 9.428; 12.87; Homeric Hymn to Apollo 374, 401. For Gaia and her offspring: Hes. *Theog.* 159, 173, 295, 479, 505, 731, 821. For gorgoneion: Hom. *Il.* 5.741 and *Od.* 11.634; Karagiorga 1970, 69.

2 For hybrids, see Müller 1978, passim.

3 See below for the individual hybrids.

4 Akurgal 1968, 162−224.

5 Centaurs and satyrs in early Greek art are presented in Michael Padgett's essay, "Horse Men," in this volume; they are mentioned here only as part of the group of *Mischwesen* with human features.

6 Of interest is the explanation given by Pipili (1987, 89 n. 131): the moustache and the beard of the Gorgon probably represent a lion's rough hide and mane, and are not male characteristics added to a female figure to enhance its hideous character (cf. Floren 1977, 15−16, 34−35, 58 ff.). For all three female hybrids, see Stibbe 2001, 1−38.

7 The bibliography on sirens is immense. See *RE* III A 1 (1927), 290 ff., s.v. "Sirenen" (Philipp); Roscher IV (1965²), 602−17, s.v. "Seirenen" (Weicker); Weicker 1902; Kunze 1932; Buschor 1944; Gropengiesser 1977; Hofstetter 1990; *LIMC* 8 (1997), 1093−1104, pls. 734−44, s.v. "Seirenes" (Hofstetter); Tsiafakis 2001, 7−24. For Corinthian plastic vases in the form of a siren, see Biers 1999, 135−46. For Laconian, Corinthian, and South Italian bronze sirens, see Stibbe 2001, 6−8, 24−27.

8 The ancient authors provide several different names for their mother, including the Muses Terpsichore, Melpomene, and Kalliope; another is Sterope, the daughter of Helios. See Weicker 1902, 67−68; *RE* III A 1, 294−95, s.v. "Sirenen"; Roscher IV, 604, s.v. "Seirenen." See Soph. Fr. 852 for Phorkys as the father of the sirens.

9 Homer (*Od.* 12.39−46) knows only two sirens, in contrast to later authors like Apollodoros (*Epit.* 7.18), who, for example, gives three names.

10 Apollodoros, *Epit.* 7.18.

11 Ps.-Arist., *Mir. ausc.* 103; Strab. 6.252; Weicker 1902, 39−40.

12 Hom. *Od.* 12.39−46; 12.158−160; 12.197−200; 23.326. Ap. Rhod. *Argon.* 4.905−9.

13 Paus. 9.34.3. The story recalls the musical contest described by Homer (*Il.* 2.594−600) between the renowned Thracian musician Thamyras

and the Muses, a contest that Thamyras lost. As punishment for his hubris, the Muses blinded him and took away his musical skills. Pausanias also recounts this story (1.3.3).

14  Buschor 1944, 11–14; Cooney 1968, 265–67; Touchefeu-Meynier 1968, 179–88; Tsiafakis 2001, 7; see also Childs, "The Human Animal," in this volume.

15  Tsiafakis 2001, 7, no. 12 with earlier bibliography.

16  Cf. *LIMC* 8, 1095, nos. 8, 13, pl. 734, s.v. "Seirenes," possibly a next stage in the depiction of the hybrid.

17  Weicker 1902, 36, 42; Buschor 1944, 19–23; Schefold 1964, 91; Hofstetter 1990, passim; Tsiafakis 2001, 7, no. 15.

18  Buschor 1944, 22, 41; Tsiafakis 2001, 11, no. 16.

19  Late Corinthian hydria, mid-sixth century b.c., Dresden 135: Amyx 1988, 271, C2.19; Knoll 1998, 46–47, no. 15.

20  Kunze 1932, 133, pl. V.5; *LIMC* 8, 1096–97, nos. 35–39, pl. 736, s.v. "Seirenes." Kitharas and *krotala* (rattles) are the earliest musical instruments found in the hands of sirens.

21  Hofstetter 1990, passim; Vedder 1985, 276–83. Cf. the bronze askos in the form of a siren holding a syrinx, in Malibu (Getty 92.AC.5; fig. 2 above): Tsiafakis 2001, 7–24.

22  Cf. an Archaic engraved cornelian scarab in The Hague: Boardman 1968, 66, no. 140.

23  The attribute is found from the fifth century onward. A characteristic example shows the sirens on the Harpy Monument from Xanthos (now in London, Brit. Mus. B 287): Hofstetter 1990, 243–49, pls. 22–23. See also n. 36 below.

24  Cf. a red-figure Apulian loutrophoros in Malibu (Getty 86.AE.680), by the Painter of Louvre MNB 1148: Hofstetter 1990, 268, no. W45, pl. 29.1. See also the large terracotta sirens in Malibu (Getty 76.AD.11): Bottini and Guzzo 1993, 43–52. Attic statues of sirens from fourth-century b.c. graves also look more like women than birds: see Vedder 1985, 68–69, 103, 277, no. S 7a, figs. 43, 47, 51.

25  Black-figure hydria of the Archippe Group, Paris, Louvre E 869: *ABV* 106.2; *Paralipomena* 43; *BAdd²* 11; *CVA* Louvre 2, pls. 12.1 and 3, and 13; *LIMC* 8, 1097, no. 50, pl. 736, s.v. "Seirenes." Black-figure band-cup by the potter Neandros, Boston 61.1073: *Paralipomena* 69; MuM Auktion XXII (May 13, 1961), pl. 38, no. 125; Hofstetter 1990, 97, no. A115.

26  Brommer 1973, 441–43; Hofstetter 1990, 33–35, 116–20, 130–32; *LIMC* 6 (1992), 962–64, nos. 150–89, pls. 632–33, s.v. "Odysseus" (Touchefeu-Meynier); Schefold 1978, 267–68. The subject reappears in the Hellenistic period on a group of almost thirty Etruscan cinerary urns. See Candida 1971, 214–15, no. 7, pl. II, fig. 1; Touchefeu-Meynier 1968, 174, no. 332; *LIMC* 6 (1992), 975, no. 93, pl. 648, s.v. "Odysseus/Uthuze" (Camporeale).

27  Boston 01.8100: Schefold 1978, 267–68; Hofstetter 1990, 34, 58, no. K90; Buitron and Cohen 1995, 31, pl. 39. Cf. a Middle Corinthian aryballos of about 590 b.c. (Basel BS 425.1966) depicting both a man standing on a boat and a siren, but their placement on the vessel makes the identification of the theme problematic: Amyx 1988, 180–81, 344, pl. 67.2;

28  Hofstetter 1990, 33–34, 47, no. K47; Buitron and Cohen 1995, 31, pls. 44–45.

28  Athens, Nat. Mus. 1130: *ABV* 476; *Paralipomena* 217; *BAdd²* 120; Hofstetter 1990, 94–95, 117–18, no. A90; Buitron and Cohen 1995, 34, pls. 49–50.

29  London, Brit. Mus. 1943.11–3. 31 (E 440): *ARV²* 289.1; 1642; *Paralipomena* 355; *BAdd²* 210; Hofstetter 1990, 17, 122, 124–26, 130–31, no. A178, pl. 27.2; Buitron and Cohen 1995, 33, pl. 47.

30  On an Attic black-figure lekythos in Heidelberg (68/1), it is doubtful that the man standing between two sirens is Orpheus; see Tsiafakis 1998, 45 n. 161 with the earlier discussion. A possible depiction of the subject is on the terracotta group at the Getty Villa in Malibu (n. 24 above). Cf. also an Attic black-figure lekanis (Dresden ZV.1464) by the Painter of the Dresden Lekanis, first quarter of the sixth century b.c. (*ABV* 21.1; *BAdd²* 7; Knoll 1998, 50, no. 16); a male flanked by two sirens places his hands on their necks as if he is their master or is trying to beguile them. Is he Orpheus or some other male tempted by them?

31  Boston 27.146: Gropengiesser 1977, 593, fig. 15; Hofstetter 1990, 10, 81, 88, 192, no. A55. See also Huber 2001, passim.

32  Vedder 1985, 65–78. For animal symbolism in Greek vase-painting, see also Edlund 1980b, 31–34.

33  For Eos pursuing Kephalos or Tithonos, see Kaempf-Dimitriadou 1979, 16–21, 81–93, pls. 8–11.

34  Boardman 1968, 72; Rizza 1996, 139–43.

35  Late Corinthian alabastron in Berlin (V.I.4285): Amyx 1988, 653; Hofstetter 1990, 61, fig. 1, pl. 3.1. Laconian black-figure cup in Catania (KC 4712): Rizza 1996, 135–43.

36  London, Brit. Mus. B 287: Hofstetter 1990, 243–49, pls. 22–23, with the earlier discussion and bibliography; *LIMC* 8, 1099, no. 73, pl. 739, s.v. "Seirenes." Sphinxes also decorate this monument. Harpies are related to myth of the Thracian king Phineus, and they are depicted as winged female creatures very different from sirens. Hesiod (*Theog.* 266–69) presents them with beautiful hair and rapid wings. Homer (*Od.* 1.241; 14.371; 20.77) regards them as personified storm winds and clearly relates them to death. The Nettos Painter krater fragment (once in Berlin F 1682: *ABV* 5.4; *Paralipomena* 2, 8; *LIMC* 4 [1988], 446, no. 1, pl. 266, s.v. "Harpyiai" [Kahil and Jacquemin]) preserves an early, indisputable representation of Harpies as winged women through the inscription ΑΡΕΠΥΙΑ next to them. For Harpies, see Smith 1892–93, 103–14; *LIMC* 4, 445–50, pls. 267–71, s.v. "Harpyiai." For the confusion surrounding the Harpies and other winged creatures, including their interchangeability, see Cohen 1997, 143–55.

37  For sirens as omens of death, see Gropengiesser 1977, 593–96.

38  Bevan 1986, 300–302, 309–11.

39  On the sphinx, see Roscher IV (1965²), 1298–1408, s.v. "Sphinx" (Ilberg); Payne 1931, 89–90; Verdélis 1951, 1–37; Dessenne 1957; Demisch 1977; Bosana-Kourou 1979; Rhyne 1982; Dierichs 1993, 33–54; *LIMC* 8 (1997), 1149–74, pls. 794–817, s.v. "Sphinx" (Kourou,

Komvou, and Raftopoulou); for the Sphinx in Etruria, see *LIMC* 8 (1997), 1165–69, nos. 235–63, pls. 809–10, s.v. "Sphinx" (Krauskopf). For the Chian sphinx, see Zacharou-Loutrari 1998.

40 *LIMC* 8, 1158–60, nos. 123–64, pls. 801–4, s.v. "Sphinx."

41 See also Childs, "The Human Animal," in this volume; Akurgal 1968, 187 and passim for representations of sphinxes in Egyptian and Near Eastern Art.

42 Apollod. *Bibl.* 3.5.8; Schol. Hes. *Theog.* 326.

43 For the name, see Roscher IV, 1329, s.v. "Sphinx"; Demisch 1977, 13; *LIMC* 8, 1150, s.v. "Sphinx," with the early discussions on an Egyptian origin of the name.

44 For the myth, see Gantz 1993, 23–24, 495–98; Hausmann 1972, 7–36. For an analysis of the myth of Oedipus and the Sphinx, see Edmunds 1981, 147–73; Edmunds 1988, 213–27; Hoffmann 1994, 71–80.

45 Apollod. *Bibl.* 3.5.8, whose version follows closely that of Sophokles.

46 Poursat 1973, 111–14; Mylonas 1980, 352–62; Rhyne 1982, 3, 6, 264. See Demisch 1977, 65–69; Dessenne 1957, 122–53; esp. for Mycenaean pottery, see Vermeule and Karageorghis 1982, V27, V28, VI16–18, VIII30–32, X42, XI65, XI91. For connections between Crete and Egypt, see Warren 1995, 1–18.

47 Rombos 1988, 244–54, and they are all Cretan productions: a bell-krater from Tekke, Tomb E, near Knossos, dated about the middle of the ninth century B.C.; a bronze quiver from Fortetsa and a gold relief from Kavousi by the so-called Knossian Workshop, dated about the late ninth to the middle of the eighth century B.C. Note that Kourou (*LIMC* 8, 1156, no. 86, pl. 799) dates the krater even earlier, about 900 B.C.

48 Although not rare, representations of the sphinx become less popular from the fifth century B.C. onward: see Schefold 1964, 74; *LIMC* 8, 1149–65, pls. 794–817, s.v. "Sphinx." For the sphinx in Archaic relief-pithoi, see Anderson 1975, passim.

49 See Rombos 1988, 246–50; *LIMC* 8, 1158, nos. 123–25, 127, 139–41, pls. 801–2, s.v. "Sphinx."

50 Rombos 1988, 248–50; *LIMC* 8, 1158, nos. 123–28, pl. 801, s.v. "Sphinx." Helmeted sphinxes are known earlier from the Near East: cf. a bronze bowl of about 900 B.C., probably from North Syria and found in Lefkandi, depicting helmeted sphinxes flanking Trees of Life (Lemos 2000, 12–13).

51 Payne 1931, 90. According to Payne, the Ionian sphinxes are bareheaded. For Cretan influence on Laconian sphinxes, see Anderson 1975, 67.

52 Dierichs 1993, 33–54. Cf. also the sphinx on the Chigi Vase (see n. 178 below).

53 Cook 1933–34, 165–219; Verdélis 1951, 1–37; Whitley 1994b, 63; Kyrkou 1997, 428–30, figs. 10–13. For the sphinx in Cycladic vase painting, see Zapheiropoulou 1985, 56–58.

54 *LIMC* 8, 1152–57, s.v. "Sphinx." For Laconian, Corinthian, and South Italian Archaic bronze sphinxes, see Stibbe 2001, 2–4, 8–20.

55 Soph. *Oed. Tyr.* 508, 1199; Eur. *Phoen.* 806, 1042.

56 The term is borrowed from Diodoros (4.64.3), who addresses the Sphinx with this epithet but without further explanation.

57 Late Corinthian amphora by the Tydeus Painter (Paris, Louvre E 640): Payne 1931, pl. 40; Amyx 1988, 270, 330, 588.

58 Payne 1931, 89. For bearded sphinxes, see *LIMC* 8, 1158, nos. 129–34, pls. 801–2, s.v. "Sphinx."

59 Attic Late Geometric IIa cup from the Athens 894 Workshop (Athens, Nat. Mus. A 784): Rombos 1988, 244–45, cat. no. 202, pl. 46b; *LIMC* 8, 1158, nos. 135–38, pl. 802, s.v. "Sphinx."

60 The scene is found on Middle Protocorinthian vases. See Amyx 1988, 661; *LIMC* 8, 1161, nos. 189–90, s.v. "Sphinx."

61 *LIMC* 8, 1161, no. 188, s.v. "Sphinx."

62 Athens, Nat. Mus. 2870: Gantz 1993, 24.

63 Hom. *Il.* 2.302; 3.454; 11.332; 12.326–27; 13.665; 16.687; 21.548; 18.115–18, 535–40; 22.202; 23.78–79; *Od.* 3.410; 4.502; 5.387; 11.171, 398; 14.207; 17.500, 547; 19.558; 22.66; 23.332. Aischylos (*Sept.* 776) also uses the term *Ker* for the Sphinx. Cf. Walter 1960, 66–67, who recognizes the *Ker* in the sphinxes of the eighth–seventh centuries B.C. For *Ker* as demon of death, see *LIMC* 6 (1992), s.v. "Ker" 14–23, pls. 11–12 (Vollkommer).

64 Moret 1984, 15–17, figs. 1, 2, pls. 10.2–3, 11.

65 Moret 1984, 24–26; *LIMC* 8, 1160, nos. 172–81, pls. 804–5, s.v. "Sphinx." On gems, see esp. Boardman 1968, 65–76. For the sphinx as man-killer, see Cohen 2000a, 103–6.

66 Pairs of sphinxes flanking warrior or battle scenes are found on black-figure vases of the sixth century B.C. See *LIMC* 8, 1161, nos. 190–92, pl. 805, s.v. "Sphinx." Of interest is a Middle Protocorinthian aryballos painted in a style close to that of the Huntsmen Painter in Syracuse (Payne 1931, pl. 1.4; Amyx 1988, 25, no. 3), depicting a warrior between two male sphinxes. See also the sphinxes flanking the Kalydonian boar hunt on the François Vase, the famous Attic black-figure volute-krater by Kleitias and Ergotimos (Florence 4209): *ABV* 76.1; *Paralipomena* 29–30; *BAdd*[2] 21; Minto 1960; Cristofani, Marzi, and Perissinotto 1981.

67 Attic red-figure cup by the Kleomelos Painter of about 490–480 B.C. (Malibu, Getty 85.AE.377): *GettyMusJ* 14 (1986): 190; Cohen 2000a, 104–5. Pausanias (5.11.2) relates that Theban youths seized by the monster were carved on the front legs of the throne of Pheidias's colossal chryselephantine statue of Zeus in Olympia. For a recent discussion of this statue, see Lapatin 2001, 79–85, 136.

68 Oakley and Langridge 1994, 41–42, no. 28; Hoffmann 1997, 82–83.

69 Vermeule 1979, 171; Moret 1984, 9–29; Cohen 2000a, 105; Hurwit 2002, 18. See also discussion above for sirens carrying off youths.

70 Band-cup by Archikles and Glaukytes (Munich 2243): *ABV* 1633.2; *Paralipomena* 68; *BAdd*[2] 47; *LIMC* 8, 1155–56, no. 82, pl. 799, s.v. "Sphinx."

71 Jordan 1988, 194–97.

72 Higgins 1959, 37, 40, pls. 27–28.

73 Cf. the two sphinx vases in the British Museum, from the so-called Brygos tomb at Capua, dated to the second quarter of the fifth century

B.C.: the first is attributed to the Athenian potter Sotades (E 788: *ARV*² 764.8); the second to the Tarquinia Painter (E 787: *ARV*² 870.89). For the vases, see Williams 1992, 617–36; Hoffmann 1994, 71–76; Hoffmann 1997, 77–88. An interesting example is the sphinx vase dated to the fourth century B.C., from Phanagoria, now in St. Petersburg, Hermitage Φα 1869-7: Demisch 1977, 95, fig. 265.

74 Danner 1989; Winter 1993, 21, 26, 37, 50, 112, 126, 128–30, 141–43. The preserved examples indicate that Corinth and the areas under its influence employed sphinxes as acroteria. Their use as antefixes in the Arcadian system is especially distinctive. In contrast, sirens are not common in architecture as acroteria or antefixes. Cf. a terracotta antefix from Gela, dated in the sixth century B.C. (Winter 1993, 279).

75 Bevan 1986, 293–97, 302–3, 312–14.

76 Homolle 1909, 54.

77 *LIMC* 8, 1153, no. 31, s.v. "Sphinx."

78 The chryselephantine statue that stood in the cella of the Parthenon is dated 438 B.C.; it is known only from copies and literary sources: *LIMC* 8, 1155, no. 71, s.v. "Sphinx"; for this and other chryselephantine statues, see Lapatin 2001. For the Middle Protocorinthian krateriskos of about 670 B.C. in the Samos Museum, see Walter 1960, 65, pl. 5.15; Benson 1995, 165, pl. 37a.

79 They occurred between 600 and 530 B.C. and were then abandoned. It seems that they yielded this role to the sirens in the fourth century B.C. (Richter 1961, 15–36). On this subject, see Woysch-Méautis 1982, 83–87; Hoffmann 1997, 79–80; and Walter-Karydi 2002, 63–70.

80 Volos 690: Kurtz and Boardman 1971, 239; Müller 1978, 335.

81 Walter-Karydi 2002, 68–70. The explanation that connects the abandonment of the funerary sphinx with an Athenian law limiting luxury (see Richter 1961, 38–39; Kurtz and Boardman 1971, 89–90) is no longer accepted by many scholars: see Shapiro 1991, 631; Morris 1992, 38.

82 Vase-painting is our principal source for this change. For the repertoire during the sixth century B.C., see Boardman 1974 passim; for the fifth century, see Robertson 1992, passim and Boardman 1975a, passim.

83 The scene with the sphinx carrying a dead youth cannot, as was stated earlier, be exclusively related to this story. For Oedipus and the Sphinx, see Brommer 1973, 481–83, 551; Hausmann 1972, 7–36; Schefold 1978, 87–88. For suggested representations of the Theban Sphinx in the seventh century B.C., see Ahlberg-Cornell 1992, 45–46.

84 Chalcidian black-figure amphora in Stuttgart (65/15): Hausmann 1972, 22–23, figs. 21–23; Moret 1984, no. 101, pl. 58; *LIMC* 7 (1994), 6, no. 46, pl. 11, s.v. "Oidipous" (Krauskopf).

85 Attic red-figure cup in Rome (Vatican 16541: *ARV*² 451.1; *LIMC* 7, 4, no. 19, pl. 7, s.v. "Oidipous." The subject appeared only sporadically during the sixth century.

86 *LIMC* 8, 1160–61, nos. 183–84, pl. 805, s.v. "Sphinx"; Hoffmann (1997, 81–82) interprets the scene as "the city's future hoplites, awaiting initiation — submitting to the terror of death, from which they will emerge reborn."

87 Apollod. *Bibl.* 3.5.8. See also Soph. *Oed. Tyr.* 391–98 and Eurip. *Phoen.* 806–11.

88 London, Brit. Mus. E 696: *ARV*² 1325.49; *BAdd*² 364; Burn 1987, 46–48, pl. 32; Moret 1984, 80–82, no. 105, pl. 63; cf. also Gantz 1993, 497.

89 Moret 1984, 80–82, with bibliography.

90 Burn 1987, 46–48.

91 Moret 1984, 77–93; Hausmann 1972, 9–10; *LIMC* 7, 8–9, nos. 75–77, pl. 13, s.v. "Oidipous"; *LIMC* 8, 1161, no. 186, pl. 805, s.v. "Sphinx." Add also an Attic black-figure oinochoe, Rhodes 12368: *ABV* 428.2 (Collar-of-Esses Class); Lemos 1997, 458, fig. 2.

92 Hanfmann 1953, 230.

93 The major distinction between the votive and the funerary sphinx is the frontal head of the latter, which faces the viewer of the stela. In contrast, the head of the votive sphinx follows the direction of the body: see Walter-Karydi 2002, 63.

94 *LIMC* 8, 1152–53, nos. 8, 38, pl. 794, s.v. "Sphinx."

95 Ibid., 1153, no. 40.

96 Hes. *Theog.* 270–82. Gantz 1993, 19–22; Besig 1937; Schauenburg 1960; Vernant 1985.

97 For the name, see Riccioni 1960, 127–28; Howe 1954, 209. Gerojannis (1927/28, 144) claimed that Medusa and Eurymedusa were common female names without a particular significance, at least from Homeric times onward; cf. Hom. *Il.* 2.727; *Od.* 4.627, 696. Pausanias (10.26.9) calls Medusa one of Priam's daughters.

98 For the various suggestions on the origin and meaning of the Gorgon, see Roscher I, 2 (1965), 1695–1727, s.v. "Gorgones" (Furtwängler); Frothingham 1911, 349–77; Marinatos 1927/28, 13–41; Hopkins 1934, 341–58; Howe 1954, 209–22; Riccioni 1960, 127–206; Boardman 1968, 37–39; Karagiorga 1964, 116–22; Karagiorga 1970, 23–45. See also Childs, "The Human Animal," in this volume.

99 Floren 1977; *LIMC* 4 (1988), 298–99, nos. 127–44, pls. 172–73, s.v. "Gorgo, Gorgones" (Krauskopf).

100 *Il.* 5.741–42; 8.349; 11.36–37; *Od.* 11.633–35.

101 For their representation in Greek art, see Besig 1937; Schefold 1964, 38, 49, 52; Karagiorga 1970; Brommer 1973, 274–283; Floren 1977; *LIMC* 4, 285–330, s.v. "Gorgo, Gorgones" (literary sources: Dahlinger); cf. also Payne 1931, 79–89; Riccioni 1960, 127–206; Boardman 1968, 28 ff.; Rizzo 1992–93, 233–57.

102 Besig 1937, 5–7; Riccioni 1960, 129–57; but cf. Touloupa 1969, 877: Gorgons may have existed earlier than the seventh century B.C. 103 Payne (1931, 79–89) provides a full discussion of the type and its development, from the Protocorinthian to the Late Corinthian period; see also Amyx 1988, vol. 2, 626.

104 For the gorgoneion in Laconian art, see particularly Pipili 1987, 14–18.

105 Higgins 1967a, 31. The Gorgoneion Group of plastic vases is named after this type.

106 Boardman 1968, 27–44, 89–102.

107 Belson 1981, passim; Winter 1993, 110, 114, 123, 125–26, 129, 137, 141–44, 199–200, 223–24, 227–28, 258, 261–62, 266–69, 279, 303. Use of the gorgoneion on a pediment is not common in mainland Greece, but it is known from Sicily (Belson 1981, 38–39; Riccioni 1960, 161, fig. 44).

108 Connor 1983, 23–31; Jordan 1988, 59–65.

109 For tattooing as a barbarian attribute, see Hdt. 5.6, 2.113; Tsiafakis 2000, 372–73; Tsiafakis 1998, 38, with earlier bibliography. For gorgoneia decorated with dots, cf. Jordan 1988, 68–69. Cf. also the dots decorating the entire face of a gorgoneion on a Corinthian alabastron by the Scale Painter of about 550 B.C. (Philadelphia, MS 553): Payne 1931, no. 457, fig. 24b; Amyx 150, 290; Karagiorga 1970, 106, fig. 13; LIMC 8, 1163, no. 223, pl. 808, s.v. "Sphinx." The dots on the forehead occur mostly on Attic gorgoneia; they have been interpreted as hints at the creature's animal-like nature. See Jordan 1988, 68–69 n. 86, with a summary of the earlier discussion.

110 Hitzl 1982, 57–58, 247–54, 256–70, pls. 14–16, 18, 22; Vokotopoulou 1997, nos. 98, 100–102, 105. Cf., for example, a bronze volute-krater handle in London (Brit. Mus. Br 585 [73.8-20.99]): Pipili 1987, 18, fig. 27. For Laconian, Corinthian, and South Italian Archaic bronze Gorgons, see also Stibbe 2001, 4–6, 20–24.

111 Joffroy 1954; Joffroy 1962; Rolley 1982, 57–71; Vokotopoulou 1975, 106, 108–19, 182, pl. 42b; Thouverin 1990, 301–4.

112 Attic black-figure amphora, Paris, Louvre F 99: Connor 1983, 24, fig. 5.

113 The aegis was initially a plain skin that was fringed with snakes; eventually it was frequently covered with scales. The Gorgon's head was attached to it after about 530 B.C. (Besig 1937, 5; Carpenter 1991, 46).

114 Paris, Louvre F 53, about 550–540 B.C.: ABV 136.49.

115 For representation of the myth in Greek art, see Schauenburg 1960; Schefold 1978, 81–85; Schefold 1988, 100–107; LIMC 4, 311–15, nos. 289–342, pls. 182–88, s.v. "Gorgo, Gorgones"; Amyx 1988, 625–26; Carpenter 1991, 104–6 (with a brief summary of the development of the myth in Greek art); LIMC 7 (1994), 332–48, pls. 272–308, s.v. "Perseus" (Roccos).

116 Paris, Louvre CA 795: Frothingham 1911, 373–74; Howe 1954, 214; Riccioni 1960, 146–49, fig. 28; Karagiorga 1970, 2, 14, 151, no. I 9, pl. 5a.

117 Earlier scholarship has suggested three different interpretations for the equine shape of Medusa: (1) desire to emphasize her monstrous character; (2) association with an equine-type earth goddess, who had mated with the horse-like Poseidon; (3) birth of Pegasos. See Ahlberg-Cornell (1992, 144, with earlier discussion), who believes that the artist portrays the birth of Pegasos in his own way. Fittschen (1969, 128) suggests that the equine form of Medusa is connected to her having given birth to one human (Chrysaor) and one horse (Pegasos), and therefore that she must be part of each. Accordingly, he does not accept that the scene on the pithos in Louvre CA 795 depicts the very act of giving birth. For the relation of Medusa with Poseidon and the horse, see also Papachatzis 1987, 109–15; Burkert 1985, 138, 222; Simon 1985, 71; Vernant 1992, 46–47.

118 Eleusis 2630: Mylonas 1957; Riccioni 1960, 151–55, figs. 36–38; Karagiorga 1970, 13, 151, no. II 9, fig. 2; Whitley 1994b, 63–64; Carpenter 1991, 233–34, figs. 340–41.

119 Rodenwaldt 1939; Hampe 1935/36, 269–99; Kunze 1963, 74–89; Benson 1967, 48–60; Stucchi 1981, 7–86; Marinatos 2001, 83–88.

120 LIMC 4, 313–15, nos. 307–42, pls. 184–88, s.v. "Gorgo, Gorgones."

121 For the extant examples, see Boardman 1968, 27–29; LIMC 4, 310–11, nos. 279–88, pls. 181–82, s.v. "Gorgo, Gorgones." See also Karagiorga 1970, 73–78.

122 London, Brit. Mus. 748: Riccioni 1960, 137, fig. 13; Karagiorga 1970, 33, 153, no. IV 10, pl. 6a; Carpenter 1991, 106, fig. 157.

123 Howe 1954, 214–15; Vernant 1992, 34–36, 44–47.

124 See n. 66 above. Worthy of note is that on the inner face of the handles are two Gorgons with outstretched tongues and hair comprised of serpents.

125 For the Corfu pediment, see Hampe 1935/36, 269–99; Kunze 1963, 74–89; Benson 1967, 48–60; Simon 1985, 170–71; Bevan 1986, 277. In his discussion of the Corfu pediment, Marinatos (2001, 83–88) also refers to the relationship between the Gorgon and Artemis. For similarities between the two, see also Vernant 1992, 34–36.

126 LIMC 4, 315–16, nos. 344–51, pl. 188, s.v. "Gorgo, Gorgones."

127 Boardman 1968, 27–28, pl. 2.

128 Riccioni 1960, figs. 14–15; Boardman 1968, 29; LIMC 4, 315–16, no. 348, s.v. "Gorgo, Gorgones."

129 LIMC 4, 315–16, nos. 345–46, pl. 188, s.v. "Gorgo, Gorgones."

130 Ibid.

131 For the meaning of the Gorgon and the gorgoneion, cf. also Frontisi-Ducroux 1989, 151–65; Vernant 1985.

132 Bevan (1986, 277–85) also accepts the earlier interpretation of the Gorgon image as a symbol of the sun.

133 Although the gilded gorgoneion, a gift from Antiochus IV, king of Syria in the second century B.C., is much later than the period under study, its placement on the battlements is still indicative of its protective role. As an apotropaic demon, it kept enemies away from the city.

134 Even today, every newborn baby gets as a gift at least one *mataki* [little eye] that is placed over the clothes in order to protect the baby and to keep away the "evil eye."

135 Attic black-figure eye-cup of about 520 B.C., Munich 2027: ABV 205; LIMC 4, 291–92, no. 41, s.v. "Gorgo, Gorgones."

136 Attic black-figure eye-cup, Cambridge, Fitz. 61: ABV 202.2; Frontisi-Ducroux 1989, 163, fig. 230.

137 On the sphinx and other female killers, see Cohen 2000a, 98–131.

138 Cf. the human-headed equine Minotaur depicted on a Cycladic relief-amphora of the mid-seventh century B.C. in Basel (Kä 601): Fittschen 1969, 166, no. SB 63.

139 Young 1972, 102–3, 122; Neils 1987, 22. See also Childs, "The Human Animal," in this volume.

140 For the Minotaur in Greek art, see Roscher II, 2 (1965), 3004–11, s.v. "Minotauros" (Helbig); Schefold 1964, 12, 24, 37, 58, 66, 70; Fittschen

1969, 166–68; Young 1972; Schefold 1978, 150–53; Neils 1987, 22–27; Schefold 1988, 253–58; *LIMC* 6 (1992), 575, 577, nos. 6, 7, 33, pls. 316, 321, s.v. "Minotauros" (Woodford); Ahlberg-Cornell 1992, 123–24; *LIMC* 7 (1994), 940–43, nos. 228–63, pls. 661–62, s.v. "Theseus" (Woodford). Among the earliest representations are five identical gold reliefs from Corinth, dated about 675–650 B.C., in Berlin (G I 332–336): Ahlberg-Cornell 1992, 123, 225, no. 138, fig. 225.

141 Attic black-figure amphora by Lydos or a painter close to him, of about 550–540 B.C., in Malibu (Getty 86.AE.60): *Getty Antiquities* 2002, 60.

142 For the representations of the theme, see Brommer 1973, 226–43.

143 For the Archikles and Glaukytes cup, see n. 70 above. The other cup is in London, V&A 373-1883: *LIMC* 8, 1162, no. 219, s.v. "Sphinx."

144 Brussels, A 1374: Payne 1931, pl. 34.6; Amyx 203–4, 627, 630; *LIMC* 7, 940, no. 228, s.v. "Theseus"; photograph in *LIMC* 1 (1981), 27, no. 246, pl. 50, s.v. "Acheloos" (Isler).

145 Black-figure hydria attributed to the Leagros Group (London, Brit. Mus. 313): *ABV* 360.1; Carpenter 1991, fig. 225.

146 For Acheloos, see Roscher I, 1 (1965), 6–9, s.v. "Acheloos" (Stoll); Schefold 1964, 21, 22, 66, 70; Isler 1970; Schefold 1978, 146–47; *LIMC* 1 (1981), 12–36, pls. 19–54, s.v. "Acheloos" (Isler); Schefold 1988, 185–90; Gantz 1993, 28–29.

147 For early East Greek, *LIMC* 1, 13, nos. 2, 3, pl. 19, s.v. "Acheloos." The subject is extremely rare in Corinthian vase painting; see Amyx 1988, 630, and cf. a Middle Protocorinthian oinochoe, Syracuse 42684: Payne 1931, 13, fig. 6; *LIMC* 1, 13, no. 1, s.v. "Acheloos." In the discussion in *LIMC* 1, 30–32, Isler provides an overview of the representations of Acheloos as an individual figure. The Syracuse oinochoe has recently been published in Bennett, Paul, and Iozzo 2002, 224–25, no. 47, with color plate.

148 Brommer 1973, 3–4.

149 Attic red-figure stamnos signed by the potter Pamphaios (London, Brit. Mus. E 437): *ARV*$^2$ 54.5; *LIMC* 1, 27, no. 245, pl. 50, s.v. "Acheloos."

150 For Triton, see Roscher V (1965), 1150–1207, s.v. "Triton" (Dressler); Payne 1931, 77–78; Shepard 1940, passim; Brommer 1973, 143–51; Schefold 1978, 128–30; Glynn 1981, 121–32; Brommer 1983a, 103–9; Ahlberg-Cornell 1984; Ahlberg-Cornell 1992, 105–7; Barringer 1995, 155–62; *LIMC* 8 (1997), 68–73, pls. 42–46, s.v. "Triton" (Icard-Gianolio).

151 Roussos 1986, 246.

152 For Nereus and Proteus, see Shepard 1940, passim; Glynn 1981, 121–32; Brommer 1983a, 103–9; *LIMC* 6 (1992), 825–27, nos. 1–6, 16–25, pls. 516, 519–20, s.v. "Nereus" (Pipili); *LIMC* 7 (1994), 560–61, s.v. "Proteus" (Icard-Gianolio).

153 Brommer 1983a, 103; Glynn 1981, 126.

154 Boardman 1972, 59–60, 70; Glynn 1981, 121–32; Ahlberg-Cornell 1992, 106–7.

155 Apart from the iconography, it is also the literary tradition (Pherekydes, *FGrH* 3 F 16a; Hellanikos, *FGrH* 4 F 164; Apollod. *Bibl.* 2.5.11) that refers to Nereus's changes during his fight with Herakles.

156 *LIMC* 6, 833–34, nos. 107–24, pls. 529–33, s.v. "Nereus."

157 Attic black-figure neck-amphora, near the Group of Toronto 305 (London, Brit. Mus. B 223): *ABV* 284.7; *Paralipomena* 125; *BAdd*$^2$ 74; *LIMC* 6, 833, no. 107, pl. 529, s.v. "Nereus."

158 Attic red-figure cup in Paris, Louvre G 104: *ARV*$^2$ 318.1, 1645; *Paralipomena* 358; *BAdd*$^2$ 214; Denoyelle and Pasquier 1994, 110–11, 192, no. 50. For other representations of the subject, see *LIMC* 8, 71, no. 23, s.v. "Triton."

159 The name Typhon is related to the verb *typhein* (to consume in smoke). See Roscher V (1965), 1441–42, s.v. "Typhon" (Schmidt). Typhon is called Seth and Sutech in Egypt (Seippel 1939, 5).

160 Akurgal 1968, 165–66; Burkert 1982, 7–9. See also Childs, "The Human Animal," in this volume.

161 Cf. another hybrid, Kekrops, the legendary first king of Athens, who was the incarnation of autochthony. Sources say he was born from the earth rather than from a female (Apollod. *Bibl.* 3.14.1) and was characterized as a man who had the lower part of his body in the form of a snake.

162 Roscher V, 1426–54, s.v. "Typhon"; Payne 1931, 76–77; Seippel 1939; Schefold 1964, 15, 19, 20, 26, 27, 29, 32, 36, 49–51, 60, 61; *LIMC* 8 (1997), 147–52, pls. 112–13, s.v. "Typhon" (Touchefeu-Meynier). Pausanias's information (5.19.1) that Boreas was represented with snakelike legs on the Chest of Kypselos calls into question the identification of the figure with Typhon. In either case, however, we have a wind-demon.

163 *LIMC* 8, 149, nos. 16–19, pl. 113 s.v. "Typhon."

164 For two uncertain depictions, see ibid., 150, nos. 25–26.

165 For Typhon in Laconian iconography, see Pipili 1987, 68–69. For his presence in Etruscan art, see *LIMC* 8 (1997), 151–52, s.v. "Typhon" (Krauskopf).

166 Munich 596: *LIMC* 8, 149, no. 14, pl. 113, s.v. "Typhon."

167 Borgeaud 1988, 181; Roscher III (1965), 1404–6, s.v. "Pan" (Roscher).

168 Htd. 6.105; Borgeaud 1988, 133–35.

169 *LIMC* 8 (1997), 923–41, pls. 612–34, s.v. "Pan" (Boardman).

170 Ibid., 924, nos. 1, 2, pl. 612, s.v. "Pan."

171 Cf. the name-vase of the Pan Painter (Boston 10.185): *ARV*$^2$ 550.1; *BAdd*$^2$ 256–57; Cohen 2000a, 116–17, fig. 4.5.

172 Attic red-figure oinochoe by the Geras Painter, about 470–460 B.C. (Naples 126056): *ARV*$^2$ 287.32; Boardman 1997, 925.22.

173 According to Ailianos Taktikos (27), he instilled panic on the Persians at Marathon; for Pan's effect on the Trojan guards, see Eur. *Rhes.* 36–37.

174 According to Whitley (1994b, 61), the adoption of Oriental and Orientalizing imagery in Greece began when the conventions of the Attic Geometric were slowly breaking down, and "[c]ommunities such as Corinth, whose Geometric tradition was less established, . . . were in the forefront of these developments."

175 The Gorgon is not included since Homer refers only to the gorgoneion.

176 *FGrH* 4 F 164.

177 For winged figures, see Kenner 1939, 83–95; Cohen 1997, 141–51.

178 *LIMC* 8, 1159, nos. 154−61, pls. 803−4, s.v. "Sphinx." It is remarkable that the majority of those examples are Peloponnesian creations. The static, bicorporate sphinx, in particular, appears to be a Corinthian invention. Cf. the sphinx on the Chigi Vase, a Protocorinthian olpe by the Chigi Painter, about 650−640 B.C. (Rome, Villa Giulia 22679): Amyx 1988, 369; Hurwit 2002, 1−22, with all the earlier bibliography on the vase and esp. p. 10 for the double sphinx.

179 Relief-pithos, Paris, Louvre CA 795. See n. 116 above.

180 Athens, Nat. Mus. 784: Rombos 1988, 244−45, cat. no. 202, pl. 46b; see also 248−49 for Cretan sphinxes with equine body.

181 Bronze group, New York, Met. 17.190.2072 (this volume, cat. no. 13): see Akurgal 1968, 170−72; Fittschen 1969, 111, 119, no. SB1, fig. 16; *LIMC* 8, 150, no. 27, s.v. "Typhon." Protocorinthian aryballos attributed to the Ajax Painter, Boston 95.12 (this volume, cat. no. 31): see Fittschen 1969, 113, 119, no. SB5; *LIMC* 8, 150, no. 22, s.v. "Typhon" (picture in *LIMC* 8, 317, no. 16, pl. 219, s.v. "Zeus" [Tiverios]). The identification with Typhon was proposed by Buschor (1934, 128−32) and accepted by Kunze and Schefold. For a different opinion and the earlier discussion, see Fittschen 1969, 119−28; Ahlberg-Cornell 1992, 25−26, 103−4.

182 Relief-amphora from Boiotia (Basel, Ciba Collection): Fittschen 1969, 166−68, no. SB63.

183 Papachatzis 1987, 111; Burkert 1985, 138.

184 For a new reading of the Chigi Vase, see Hurwit 2002, 1−22. Cf. also Edlund 1980b, 31−35; Hoffman 1994, 71−80; Whitley 1994b, 51−70.

185 Hoffman 1994, 74.

Catalogue of the Exhibition

# 1

# Human-Headed Bull

Mesopotamia, Early Dynastic III or possibly Akkadian,
ca. 2500 – 2200 B.C.
Fine-grained white limestone
Height 7.3 cm., width 4.7 cm., length 13.4 cm.
Private collection

CONDITION
The surface is well preserved, with gray incrustations
concentrated on the proper right side and scattered
incrustation throughout. The tenon, broken on the
proper left side at the rear, splits off from a vertically
drilled attachment hole, one side of which is preserved.

The forepart of a human-headed bull with its two front
hooves tucked up under its ample beard/mane is carved
from a fine-grained white stone. The protome tapers to a
smooth section in front of a flange with a tenon (now
broken) that once had a hole drilled through it to aid in
its attachment to another element. Similar objects with
animal protomes in front of a pierced flange have been
interpreted either as antefixes or as pegs by which carved
plaques were mounted to temple walls, but the protome
pegs usually feature lions rather than human-headed
bulls.[1] This piece is most similar in form to one showing
a human-headed bull found in an altar in Nintu Temple
VI at Khafajah. The Khafajah piece (now in Philadelphia),

which has a mortise and a horizontal drill-hole rather
than a vertical one, has been identified as an armrest
attachment for a throne; this seems the most likely use
for nearly all such objects.[2] The beard on the bull in the
exhibition, with its undulating rows of plaits ending in
outward spirals, is much longer and more plastic in handling
than that of the Khafajah specimen; similarly, its human
face is more fully three-dimensional, with fleshier cheeks
and lips and thickly outlined eyes. This suggests that it is
slightly later than the Khafajah bull, perhaps Akkadian,
when such plasticity was more common.

The association of the human-headed bull with
kingship has a long history in Sumer and Akkad. At the
"royal" cemetery of Ur, seals showing such animals (with
long beards like the one on this piece) protecting the
sacred tree from bird monsters (sometimes aided by a
human hero/leader) appear often among the grave goods.[3]
An even more common scene is a contest in which a
human-headed bull and a hero either fight each other or
help protect herds of domesticated animals.[4] Human-
headed bulls appear on the famous harp plaque from Ur,
flanking a hero in the top panel.[5] The human-headed bulls
that are most similar to the stone protome in the exhibition are found on two alabaster vessels discovered in the fill
of two important graves at Ur, which Sir Charles Leonard
Woolley dated late in the Early Dynastic period or early
in the Akkadian period (2500 – 2250 B.C.); he related the
carved human-headed bulls on these vessels to an inscribed
Akkadian mace head carved with a similar creature.[6]

Early in their rule of Mesopotamia, the Akkadians
adopted many of the attributes of Sumerian kingship,
even if they eventually changed them drastically by the
time of Naram Sin, who on his famous stele in the Louvre
declares himself divine and wears the bull-horned crown
of divinity. The iconography of the human-headed bull as
the protector of flocks and of the Tree of Life continues,
especially in seal carving, all the way through the Sumerian
and Akkadian periods.

Without clear evidence, some scholars have sought
to relate the prevalence of human-headed bulls in these
early works to Enkidu, the wild-man companion of
Gilgamesh, the semimythical first king of the Sumerians.
Although such associations are possible, based on literary

descriptions of Enkidu's nature and attributes, it seems preferable to view such imaginary beings as supernatural protective figures who aided the king in asserting human control over the wild forces feared by the early Mesopotamians.[7] Many early rulers sought to associate themselves with the control of such divine forces. The presence of the human-headed bull in the "royal" tombs at Ur, and on possible throne arms like this object and the one from Khafajah, thus reinforces a linkage between royalty and the supernatural embodiment of divine protection. Such creatures are the distant ancestors of the *lamassu* figures who protect the kings of Assyria in their palaces nearly two thousand years later. Stories about these creatures thus remained a constant element of Near Eastern culture until they were introduced into the Western tradition via the Persians.

—SG

**BIBLIOGRAPHY**
Unpublished.

**NOTES**

1 An onyx lion protome with a horizontal drill hole through its flange, inscribed to Ur-Nanshe, king of Lagash, ca. 2500 B.C., was found at Tello: see Spycket 1981, 140, fig. 46. A lion peg of pink stone, in the New York art market, has been interpreted as a plaque support used to lock a grain-room door by means of ropes sealed by clay bearing an official's seal mark. Hansen (1963, 148 n. 18) suggested this interpretation, but he doubted the use of these animal protome pegs as functional plaque supports. They may, however, have been attached to such functional pegs as decorations, since functional pegs that have been found do have decorative knobs attached to them by flanges and dowel holes (ibid. 148).

2 See Frankfort 1943, 10, pls. 49–50 and Frankfort 1970, fig. 61.

3 See Woolley 1934, pl. 192.12.

4 See Zettler et al. 1998, fig. 40.

5 Zettler et al. 1998, 55, cat. no. 3.

6 Woolley 1934, 378. One of the alabaster vessels, now in Philadelphia, was associated with an early Akkadian grave; the one in London, with a late Early Dynastic III grave. This bull-man is closer in style to that on the London vessel: the long beard and wide eyes are particularly comparable (see Woolley 1934, pl. 182b). Zettler et al. (1998, 69) suggest, based on its style, that the London vessel may be late and perhaps from Lagash, which points to a late date for this bull as well.

7 See the discussion in Zettler et al. 1998, 50.

## 2

# Cheekpiece in the Form of a Winged Human-Headed Bull

**Western Iran, Luristan, ca. 800–600 B.C.**
**Bronze**
**Height 14.7 cm., width 11.6 cm.**
**Princeton University Art Museum, gift of**
**J. Lionberger Davis, Class of 1900 (y1952–6)**

**CONDITION**
The cheekpiece is complete but for the missing part of the left hair curl, which appears not to have been cast, rather than having been lost. The piece has a fine, green patina throughout.

A common type of horse trapping from Luristan, this piece originally would have been joined by means of a horizontal bit to a mate facing left to form the cheekpieces of the elaborate horse garniture favored by the relatively unknown but presumably nomadic elite of northwestern Iran during the early Iron Age.[1] Such objects often contain elements like the rings and prongs (probably goads) on the back, which could be used for actual attachment to the controlling reigns of a horse. Whether such objects were so used, however, or were instead only tomb offerings is debated; many complete pairs were said to have been found in tombs under the head of the deceased, but excavation reports still remain too spotty to ascribe specific meaning or function to the pieces.[2]

The Princeton cheekpiece shows a winged human-headed bull with a frontal face, passant to the right.[3] The eyes are indented dots, and two horizontal incision lines indicate his mouth and beard. The wing is segmented by somewhat carelessly incised lines, the last three of which extend onto the body. The horns appear to be part of a headdress through which the ears extend, although this detail is unclear. The composition of the piece is well designed, with the curves of the tail, the wing, the horns, and the hair curls gracefully balancing and echoing one another.

The general type of animal cheekpiece is fairly common, but the clearly articulated bull's hooves and the suggestion of male anatomy preclude the common appellation of "sphinx" for this example. Both the wings and the horned headdress of this otherworldly animal would have signified a divine force in Mesopotamia proper, where such human-headed bulls were common in almost all periods. Stone reliefs show that elite Assyrian horsemen adopted similar horse cheekpieces from their eastern neighbors in Luristan.[4] The Lurs had a longer tradition of horsemanship than the Assyrians, but the Assyrians had a longer history of depicting human-headed bulls, in particular to show a *lamassu*, an apotropaic guardian figure. In this cheekpiece we thus see evidence of a symbiotic diffusion in which the Lurs adopted an iconographic type and the Assyrians adopted the type of functional object. Such powerful syncretic symbols of elite strength, especially as these relate to the possession of equine material culture, appear in almost all the cultures of the Near East in the early Iron Age. The horse-loving early Greek traders who came east at the beginning of the eighth century appear to have emulated this aristocratic image tradition, even acquiring eastern-style horse cheekpieces.[5] How much of the original symbolism and cultural context they would have adopted with the imagery remains controversial.

—SG

## BIBLIOGRAPHY

Waldbaum 1973, 10–11, fig. 8.

## NOTES

1 For debates about how nomadic the inhabitants were, and the suggestion that the cheekpieces were cast in closed molds for an aristocratic cavalry and/or chariot warrior elite, see Muscarella 1988, 155–57. On Luristan social structure, see also Moorey 1971, 289.

2 See Muscarella 1988, 156; Moorey 1971, 107.

3 The general type is common: see Potratz 1966 (his group V) and Pope 1938, pls. 32–33. The Princeton piece is clearly not a "sphinx," as the type is usually called, although in style it is close to this type. The sphinx group has segmented leonine feet and often a downward tail. The closest parallel to the Princeton piece is another human-headed bull formerly in the Heeramaneck Collection (Los Angeles M.76.97.99: Moorey et al. 1981, 42, no. 151; Potratz 1966, fig. 63c; Pope 1938, vol. 4, pl. 32B), although this has more incised details than the Princeton piece. It is also similar to a pair of cheekpieces in New York (Met. 32.161.24: Muscarella 1988, 164, no. 256), although the feet on these are less clearly those of a bull. Somewhat similar in form are cheekpieces in St. Louis (inv. 234:1955: *Saint Louis Art Museum* 1975, 27)

and a pair once in the Davis-Weill Collection (Amiet 1976a, pl. iii). Moorey (1971, 119 and 304) speculates on why fantastic composite creatures in this period appear only in this specific horse cheekpieces group, and sees their ancestry in Elam and Babylon. Assyria, however, also had such creatures, especially in its seal-carving traditions: see Harper et al. 1995, cat. no. 64.

4 For the Assyrian adoption of Iranian traditions and a clear drawing of an Assyrian relief showing such bits in use, see Peltenburg 1991, 100.

5 No horse cheekpiece that is definitively from Luristan has been found in Greece, but Assyrian versions of such objects have been discovered (Muscarella 1988, 156), suggesting an international, cosmopolitan taste for such images and associations. The shared elite horse culture of Greece and the Near East played an important role in encouraging trade during the Orientalizing period; on this, see Crielaard 1992, 235–40.

# 3

# Quiver with Eight Relief Registers

Anatolia, Urartian, ca. 800 – 600 B.C.
Bronze
Height 61.4 cm., width 10.85 cm. (without rings),
maximum depth at top 5.8 cm.
Collection of Michael and Judy Steinhardt, New York

CONDITION
The quiver is complete except for the back section,
which probably was made of leather; in quivers of
this type it often is lost. The leather would have
been attached by pins, the holes of which punctuate
the sides of the quiver. The base, a separate piece
of bronze attached by rivets, is preserved. There is a
uniform green patina throughout, with more traces
of corrosion on the reverse.

This quiver is decorated in repoussé and chasing with
files of creatures derived from Assyrian art but presented
with the imaginative flair typical of Urartian work. The art
of Urartu, in eastern Turkey and Armenia, was strongly
influenced by that of its southern neighbor, Assyria, with
which it traded early in the ninth century, but from which,
in the eighth century, it sought to gain independence by
forming a resistance with the semi-independent city-states
of North Syria and Phrygia.[1] Assyrian reliefs illustrate
how such quivers were worn by soldiers and hunters, slung
over their shoulder and supported by straps attached to
two rings, like those still preserved on this example.[2]
Similar quivers have been found in votive deposits at
important Urartian temple complexes along with helmets
also decorated with processions in relief.[3] The Assyrian
annals, recounting their sack of the Urartian cult center
of Musasir in 714 B.C., record that among the metal votives
taken from the temple were decorated quivers.[4] A quiver
in the Ebnöther Collection is of almost exactly the same
size and style as this one, and its processional friezes have
been related to such votive contexts.[5]

The Steinhardt quiver is divided into eight registers
by an elaborate decorative scheme, in which all the figures
are shown passant to the left, in profile, with frontal eyes.

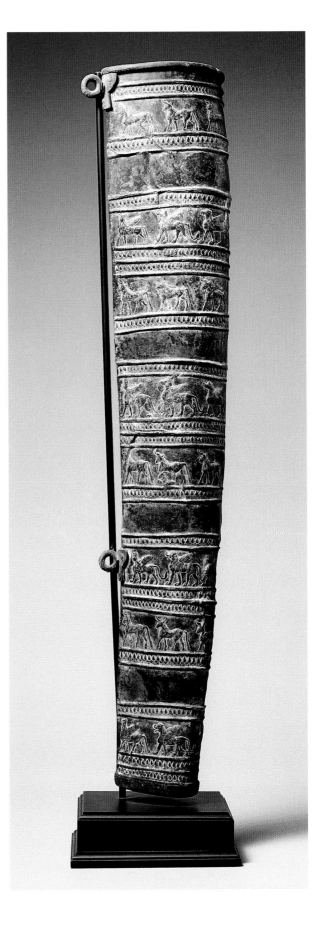

A frieze of three bulls occupies the top register and is repeated three times below, alternating with a different frieze showing various combinations of three fantastic animals (*Mischwesen*) composed of composite animal parts. Below each bull frieze is a single bud garland, and below each *Mischwesen* frieze is a double band of bud garlands. Further, each bull frieze has a blank register below it, and each *Mischwesen* frieze has a blank register above it. The first frieze at the top, below the out-turned lip of the quiver, is composed of three bulls passant to the left. The second frieze consists of a winged human-headed bull, followed by a winged quadruped with an elephant-like head, a long upturned nose, and a leonine body. This creature is followed by a griffin with an eagle-like head and leonine body. A sphinx with a horned headdress with a round symbol on top leads the fourth frieze, followed by

another griffin and another elephant creature. The sixth frieze also begins with a sphinx, followed by the elephant creature and another sphinx. The eighth frieze begins with a winged human-headed bull, followed by the elephant creature and a griffin.

These same composite animals appear on other Urartian objects dispersed in various collections, and each may be associated with specific local deities.[6] Perhaps the tripartite friezes of *Mischwesen* on the quiver were meant to allude to a typically Near Eastern triad of divine forces, which in Urartu were represented by Haldi, Teisheba, and Shiuini.[7] All the fantastic creatures on the quiver suggest a protective divine force that, in the Near East, is often associated with royal power. The quiver itself reinforces this connection, since arrows also are related to the power of the king in Assyrian palace reliefs, where the ruler hunts or wages war under the protection of similar specific deities. In Assyrian palaces, the winged human-headed bulls (*lamassu*) and lions are emblems of divine protection over the king.

The *Mischwesen* for which Urartian artists are famous have a long life both in local myths and in the Western stories of fantastic beasts like centaurs and sirens that may in part derive from them. In both the West and the East, the earliest examples of *Mischwesen* objects appear in tombs and sanctuaries, suggesting that many of the images were imported to the West within a shared elite context that had some understanding of the objects' original meanings and functions.[8]

—SG

### BIBLIOGRAPHY
Unpublished.

### NOTES

1 For good discussions of the indebtedness of Urartian art to Assyria, as well as of its unique elements, see Van Loon 1966 and Muscarella 1988, 421. For the anti-Assyrian alliances in the early eighth century, which depended on Assyrian weakness and Urartian ascendancy at the time, see Winter 1973, 126–30.

2 See Madhloom 1970, pls. xxiv–xxv. A similar quiver is worn by the archer on the bronze bowl in this exhibition (cat. no. 9).

3 Especially from Kamir-Blur (see Merhav et al. 1991, 125); these are often inscribed to a king. The processional imagery and the find spot suggest that such helmet/quiver groups were first dedicated to the king and then rededicated as votives to Haldi, the main god of the Urartians.

4 See Kendall 1977, 27–28.

5 Merhav et al. 1991, 132, pl. 17a, b.

6 Based on the similarity in iconography and style, a pair of three-part horse side ornaments may have been made by the same hand (see Merhav et al. 1991, pl. 62.1–3; Haerinck and Overlaet 1984, 55–70). On them, one can see the sphinx wearing the headdress with horn and round ornament (at bottom), winged human-headed bulls, regular bulls, and griffins in a strikingly similar style. For the elephant-like creature (perhaps an exaggerated goat?), see Eichler 1984, 15, pls. 2–3 (though these lack the leonine body). The bud garland border appears on many Urartian objects: cf. Merhav et al. 1991, pl. 44, a frontlet.

7 See Kendall 1977, 40–45. Haldi, the warrior god, is often associated with lions; Teisheba, the storm god, with bulls; and the sphinx with solar/lunar headdress could easily be seen as a female divinity in an Anatolian trinity.

8 For contrasting views, see Carter 1972 and Gombrich 1960, 116–45, who regard such images as being imported without any pre-existent meaning or understanding.

## 4

# Molded Plaque with a Griffin-Genie (*Apkallu*)

Neo-Assyrian, late ninth–seventh centuries B.C.
Said to be from Nineveh [1]
Terracotta
Height 13.12 cm., width 9.32 cm., thickness 1.37–1.53 cm.
Princeton University Art Museum, gift of Mrs. Évi Bossányi Loeb (y1982–94)

CONDITION
The plaque is in good condition, with minor damage along the upper left side and left corner and at the upper right corner and along the right side. At the lower right corner is a protrusion left over from the removal of the plaque from the mold. On the right and left sides are marks of a string used to cut the plaque from a longer band of clay. The top and bottom edges are plain. On the back are fingerprints and striations from a tool used to press the clay into a mold.

The griffin-genie stands facing to the viewer's right and wears a short, belted kilt that reaches his knees. A double tassel hangs from his belt between his legs. His wings are attached to the shoulder, one raised and the other lowered. He extends his arms out in front and holds a vertical staff that is only partially preserved along the right edge of the plaque. The whole figure is offset slightly to the right of the plaque: the wings are 1.0–1.5 centimeters from the left edge. The rear foot was never present; the right foot is chipped away.

The griffin-genie's head conforms to the standard Assyrian type with a high crest along the top of the head and down the neck.[2] The beak is only partially visible: the tip of the beak and the lower jaw are largely missing, suggesting a worn mold. The faint vertical striations on the side of the head, which are meant to indicate long locks of hair, are also signs of a worn mold, as is the lack of detail on the upper part of the lower wing.

The griffin-genie is one of the *apkallē*, the antediluvian sages of Mesopotamian myth. Another prominent *apkallu* is the fish-garbed genie (cf. cat. no. 5).[3] These are benign creatures that ward off evil demons and disease. The griffin-genie is a frequent subject of Assyrian palace reliefs of Assurnasirpal II and Sargon in the ninth and eighth centuries B.C.[4] Plaques similar to the one in Princeton are known from the excavations at Assur.[5] There are also small figurines of the creature found in the excavations of several Mesopotamian and Assyrian sites.[6] These have been discovered in various types of containers, frequently brick boxes, buried beneath the floors of rooms. From incantation texts we learn that these figures were intended to protect the spaces, particularly passageways, from evil spirits in the same fashion as the monumental figures of the palace reliefs.[7]

The date of the Princeton plaque is difficult to establish. It compares in all details with a plaque from Assur in Berlin.[8] Evelyn Klengel-Brandt has dated the Berlin example to the Middle Assyrian period (13th– 10th centuries B.C.) on the basis of the short kilt and long tassels, which she correctly points out are found in precisely the same form on two Middle Assyrian seals in the J. Pierpont Morgan Library.[9] However, a similarly dressed griffin-genie appears on a now-lost relief from the late-eighth-century palace of Sargon at Khorsabad, though the tassels are different;[10] and a Neo-Assyrian seal also in the Morgan Library shows a griffin-man in a short kilt, though without tassels.[11] On the other hand, the early seals depict the genie with wings spread out behind the figures, while the Berlin, Princeton, and Khorsabad figures all have the wings set more vertically and close to the body, as does the Neo-Assyrian seal in the Morgan Library. The similarities between the Berlin and the Princeton plaques are so close that they could be from the same mold, only the Princeton plaque shows a more worn state of the mold, as mentioned above.[12] The balance of the evidence, although not conclusive, indicates a Neo-Assyrian date of the late ninth to seventh centuries B.C. for both the Princeton and Berlin plaques.

—WAPC

**BIBLIOGRAPHY**

*Record* 42.1 (1983): 69 (illus.).

**NOTES**

1 The gift by Mrs. (Joel T.) Loeb was made in the name of her stepfather, Howard Spencer Levy, in honor of Joel Traitel Loeb, Class of 1937, and Nicholas Howard Loeb, Class of 1981. Howard Spencer Levy took part in the excavations of Nineveh led by Ephraim Speiser of the University Museum, University of Pennsylvania, and the provenance from Nineveh marked in pencil on the back of the plaque is supported by this connection. Two plaques very similar to the Princeton plaques y1982-94 and y1982-95 are in Amsterdam (Rittig 1977, figs. 23, 31), but these also have no secure provenance. The only excavated plaques of this type come from the site of Assur: Klengel-Brandt 1968.

2 Cf. Reade 1979, pl. 10; Stearns 1961, pls. 60–64, 70, 75–81.

3 Green 1983, 88–89; Wiggermann 1992, 75–76; *RLA* 8, 242–43 (§ 7.9), s.v. "Mischwesen A" (Wiggermann); *RLA* 8, 252–53 (§ 3.9), s.v. "Mischwesen B."

4 Kolbe 1981, type B, 15, 20–30; Reade 1979, 39.

5 Berlin VA 4884–4887: Klengel-Brandt 1968, 20–22, 29–30, pls. 1.2, 2.3–4, 8.6–7. Amsterdam: Rittig 1977, 75, no. 5.1.9, fig. 23.

6 Woolley 1926, 693–94, pl. IX.2; Mallowan 1954, 86, pls. XVII–XVIII; Green 1983, pl. 9b.

7 See Childs, "The Human Animal," fig. 7 and related text, in this volume.

8 Berlin VA 4885: Klengel-Brandt 1968, pl. 1.2.

9 Klengel-Brandt 1968, 24–25; Porada 1948, nos. 608, 609.

10 Kolbe 1981, pl. IV.1.

11 Porada 1948, no. 702.

12 The Berlin plaque is slightly larger than the one in Princeton: height 15.1 cm., width 9.0 cm. (Klengel-Brandt 1968, 21). The very similar plaque in Amsterdam cited in n. 7 above measures 12 x 8.5 cm.

## 5

# Molded Plaque with a Fish-Clad Genie (*Apkallu*)

**Neo-Assyrian, late ninth–seventh centuries B.C.**
**Said to be from Nineveh[1]**
**Terracotta**
**Height 11.97 cm., width 5.11 cm., thickness 1.5–1.7 cm.**
**Princeton University Art Museum, gift of**
**Mrs. Évi Bossányi Loeb (y1982.95)**

CONDITION

**Damage to the plaque is minimal, at the bottom left corner and in the center of the top edge. The top and bottom sides are rough, while the left and right sides are smooth, as is the somewhat domed back. A fingerprint is visible near the top right corner.**

The fish-clad genie stands facing to the viewer's left; he holds in his proper right raised hand something that is indecipherable but that may be stalks of a plant, next to which is a shallow cutting in the clay. In his left hand, held obliquely downward, he holds a situla (a type of bucket). The gesture of the raised right hand is common for figures that are tending a sacred object; the situla presumably contains the purifying substance for which the stalks would serve as the applicator.

The figure consists of a man with long beard who wears a fish skin that reaches to his ankles; its open-mouthed head serves as a kind of hood over his own head. The creature is a common companion of the griffin-genie (see cat. no. 4), and like it, is an *apkallu*, an antediluvian sage, who appears in the same incantation texts.[2] The fish-garbed genie is commonly confused with the *kulullû*, which has the body of a fish with a human head and arm(s);[3] it is the *kulullû* that is named in the *Enuma Eliš* in the army of Tiamat in her battle with the god Marduk.[4]

That the fish-clad genie does not seem to be a truly composite creature but is rather a bearded man wearing a fish cloak has led several scholars to surmise that he may be a priest dressed in a ritual garment.[5] This supposition is extremely unlikely because the fish-clad genie appears only in the same roles as the griffin-genie, and these are all apotropaic in nature. Not only does the fish-clad genie occur on plaques such as the one in Princeton, but he is also found in multiple examples in the form of clay figurines in containers buried under the floor to protect rooms and passageways.[6] He is not, however, a popular presence on the Assyrian palace reliefs, where his appearance is limited to the reign of Assurnasirpal II (ninth century), one example at Til Barsip (eighth century), and ten at Khorsabad under Sennacherib (early seventh century).[7] Fish-clad genies flank a sick man on the bronze Neo-Babylonian plaque in the Louvre,[8] and they appear quite regularly on Neo-Assyrian cylinder seals.[9]

The date of the Princeton plaque must fall in the Neo-Assyrian period of the late ninth to the seventh century B.C. The fish cloak of the fish-clad genies of Assurnasirpal's palace is short, reaching only to the hip,[10] while the representation of the same garment on a series of terracotta plaques scattered in various museums is so close to that of the Princeton plaque as to suggest contemporaneity.[11] The prominent appearance on the tank of Sennacherib from Assur, in Berlin, of a fish-clad genie that generally resembles the Princeton figure supports this suggestion.[12]

—WAPC

**BIBLIOGRAPHY**

*Record* 42.1 (1983): 69 (illus.).

**NOTES**

1 For the provenance, see cat. no. 4 n. 1.

2 Wiggermann 1992, 76–77; *RLA* 8, 252 (§ 3.8), s.v. "Mischwesen B" (Green); Reade 1979, 38–39.

3 Rittig 1977, 94–96, 215–16; Wiggermann 1992, 182–83; *RLA* 8, 257 (§ 3.22), s.v. "Mischwesen B"; Reade 1979, 40. The *kulullû* appears in the "List of the Types of Gods" (*Göttertypentext*) associated with the god Ea, god of the fresh waters; the description there suggests confusion over the types of composite fish-men: Köcher 1953, 81, 95: commentary to § 6.12. For a likely representation of a *kulullû* on a seal, see Porada 1948, no. 433; Black and Green 1992, 131–32, s.v. "Merman and Mermaid."

4 Langdon 1923, 88–89 with n. 6; Klengel-Brandt 1968, 35.

5 Gurney 1935, 39; Kawami 1974, 9. Opposed to this interpretation are Wiggermann 1992, 76; *RLA* 8, 242 (§ 7.8), s.v. "Mischwesen A" (Wiggermann); and Rittig 1977, 86.

6 Woolley 1926, 693, pl. IX.1; Klengel-Brandt 1968, 22–23, 27–28, 37, pls. 3, 6.1, 10.3; Green 1983, 89–90, pl. X.b–d; Kawami 1974. See also Childs, "The Human Animal," fig. 7 in this volume.

7 Kolbe 1981, 16, table 1 (type C); Kawami 1972, 146–48, pl. IIIa–b.

8 See Childs, "The Human Animal," fig. 10 in this volume.

9 Porada 1948, nos. 772, 773.

10 Layard 1849–53, vol. 2, pl. 6; Kolbe 1981, pl. IV.4; Black and Green 1992, 83, fig. 65.

11 Amsterdam B 1702: Rittig 1977, 86, no. 8.5.2, fig. 31. New York, Met. 51.72.4: Kawami 1974, 12, pl. 3.3.

12 Kawami 1974, 12, pl. 3.4.

## 6

## Cosmetic Vessel
## in the Form of Bes

Egyptian, Saïte period, Dynasty 26, ca. 664–525 B.C.
Glass frit ("Egyptian Blue")
Height 14.3 cm., width 9.6 cm., depth 8.6 cm.
Virginia Museum of Fine Arts, Richmond, the Adolph
D. and Wilkins C. Williams Fund in memory of
Bernard V. Bothmer (93.110)

CONDITION
The piece is in good condition. There is a break at the
top right corner of the modius, and the right hand
is missing. The right kneecap and left thumb, once
broken, have been restored. There is some cracking
in the surface, particularly in the area of the belly.

The Egyptian household god Bes was portrayed as a
dwarf, with a large head, broad nose, furrowed brow, and
leonine features, including a long mane, feline ears, and a
panting tongue.[1] The fearsome aspects of his depiction
served in his role as protector of the home and of women
(especially in childbirth), yet his bandy-legged comical
aspects, such as the rotund belly emphasized on this
example, made him quite appealing. Because of his association with women, the image of Bes was frequently
used to decorate cosmetic equipment.[2]

Stylistically, this piece can be dated to the Saïte
period (Dynasty 26) and is of particularly fine workmanship. Bes is depicted squatting on a plinth; his huge, round
stomach droops to the ground. Around his neck and down
his back he wears a leopard skin to underscore his animal
power. At the top of his head, he sports a rectangular
modius, bordered by a cavetto cornice. The hole in the
center allows access to the interior and was probably
plugged with the feathered headdress usually worn by Bes.
It has been suggested that he would have held a stick in
each fist with which to apply the cosmetic *kohl* contained
within the vessel.[3] Kohl was a black eye-paint, sometimes
galena but more often simple carbon-black, which would
be traced around the eyes and eyebrows of women and
men, not only to enhance their features, but presumably
to protect them from the glare of the sun, like modern
football players. Traces of kohl were found in a similar
vessel that is now in Cleveland.[4] The kohl-applicators would
have been long sticks swelling to blunt, rounded ends,
probably in wood or metal. Held in Bes's hands, this would
have been a play on the knives, serpents, or other apotropaic devices often depicted as being brandished by the god.

Occasionally, just the face of Bes is used as a decorative motif. In this, it is not unlike depictions of the Greek
gorgoneion, with its broad, curly beard, wide, staring eyes,
broad nose, and grimace. Indeed, Greek artists originally
may have based their conception of the Gorgons on Bes
and other Egyptian and Near Eastern gods and demons.
—PL

BIBLIOGRAPHY
J. F. Romano, in Capel and Markoe 1996, 68–70; Mayo 1998, 22–23;
Goldstein 2001, 23 and 192.

NOTES
1 See *LIMC* 3 (1986), 98–112, pls. 74–86, s.v. "Bes" (Hermary).
2 J. F. Romano, in Brovarski, Doll, and Freed 1982, 226–27.
3 Goldstein 2001, 192. For some other examples of kohl vessels in the
  form of Bes, see Friedman 1998, 108, 209–10, nos. 73, 74.
4 Personal communication (2002) from Dr. Lawrence Berman, curator
  of Ancient Egyptian, Nubian, and Near Eastern Art, Museum of
  Fine Arts, Boston.

# 7

# Head of Pazuzu

**Neo-Assyrian, reign of Assurbanipal (668 – 631/627 B.C.)**
**Hematite**
**Height 10.75 cm., width ear-to-ear 6.65 cm.,**
**depth 8.16 cm.**
**Private collection**

CONDITION
**The head is in excellent condition, with only minor breakage at the bottom right of the neck.**

The head is a composite of dog (mouth), lion (muzzle),[1] and human elements (ears and eyes). The prominent mouth appears to grin with gritted teeth on the side, but the tongue is still able to protrude slightly in front between the canines. The lower jaw

has a short beard-fringe; the whiskers are deeply cut on the muzzle below the two nostrils that are bored out. Below the large, domed eyes are two sets of wrinkles that radiate from the bridge of the nose, much like some Assyrian lions.[2] The eyes are framed by deeply cut concentric curves topped by hatched ridges that look like eyebrows but extend to the back and curve around the ear down the neck.

Seen from behind, the eyebrow ridges almost meet toward the base of the skull, which is deeply furrowed in the middle and separated from the neck by a pair of bulges that resemble human buttocks. The vertical line that bisects the back of the head continues down the back of the neck, causing the two neck segments to look like legs below the "buttocks" protrusions immediately above them.[3] Between the side ridges is a cuneiform inscription in fifteen lines:[4]

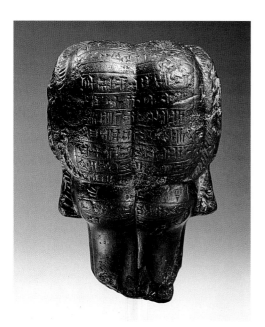

(1) Ù SAG.DU ᵈPa-zu-zu
(2) šá ʿᵈ30-MAN.KÚR LÚ.SAG
(3) šá ʾAš+šur-DÙ-[A M]AN ŠÚ
(4) MAN KUR ʾAš+šurᴷᴵ a-na DIN-šú
(5) [BA?]
(6) ÉN gá-e ᵈPa-zu-zu
(7) dumu ᵈHa-an-pà
(8) LUGAL-líl-lá-e-ne hul-a
(9) hur!-sag kala-ga mu-un-huš

(10) ba-an-e₁₁-dè gá-e-me-en
(11) im-ne-ne lú šà gin-na
(12) im-mar-tu igi-ne-ne
(13) ba-an-gar
(14) dili-e-ne pa!-e-ne
(15) ba-an-haš!

This is the head of Pazuzu
which Sin-shar-usur the Eunuch
of Assurbanipal king of the world
king of the land of Assur for his life
[presented?]
Incantation: I, Pazuzu
son of Hanpu
king of the evil demons
the mighty mountain (against which)
I have been seized with wrath
I myself will go up (against)
The winds which go against its heart
to the west-(wind) their face
is placed.
One by one their wings
I have broken.

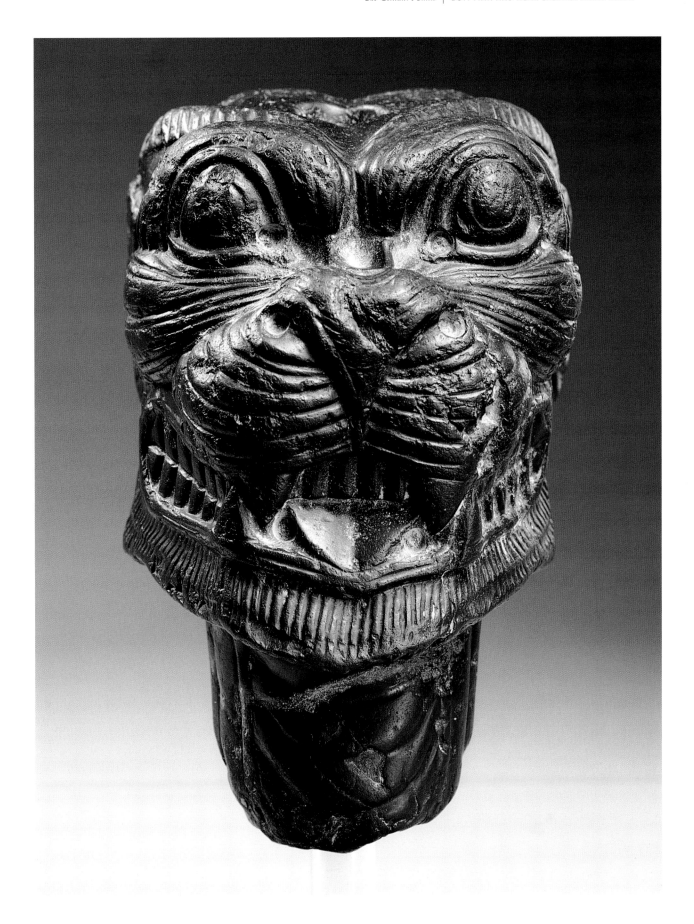

Pazuzu was a malignant demon of disease, but images of him also served to ward off the very ills he could bring.[5] A large number of amulets and small figurines depicting just the head and neck of the demon are known. Their usual height ranges from four to seven centimeters. The present head is among the largest known. Three others approach it in size, two in the British Museum and one in the Louvre, and one in Baghdad exceeds it (12.6 cm.).[6] Like many examples in its class, the head is pierced vertically by a hole 1.05 centimeters at the opening both above and below, and, like them, was probably set on some kind of support for display, since most of these stone examples are far too heavy to have been worn as amulets.[7]

Pazuzu's head is among the most easily identifiable of all Near Eastern composite creatures: the square muzzle and vertical plane of the eyes hardly vary in the preserved examples. Although the vast majority of representations of Pazuzu are, as here, confined to the head and long neck, there are a number of representations of the whole demon (see Childs, "The Human Animal," this volume, figs. 9–11).[8] On occasion, he has the tail of a scorpion; sometimes he is ithyphallic; frequently he is winged.[9]

From the evidence of excavated examples of Pazuzu amulets and figurines, the demon first appeared in the

second half of the eighth century B.C. The majority of the datable examples fall between this earliest date and the end of the Neo-Babylonian period in the first half of the sixth century B.C.[10] The inscription (lines 1–4) on the head dates the piece precisely to the reign of Assurbanipal (668–631/627 B.C.)

All the known heads vary quite considerably in the emphasis on one or another aspect of the demon. The present head displays the fullest range of the variant characteristics and is among the finest in the quality of its workmanship.

— WAPC

**BIBLIOGRAPHY**
Unpublished.

**NOTES**

1   Heeßel (2002, 10 with n. 6) argues that the muzzle also is canine, but a comparison with the lion held by a genie from Khorsabad in the Louvre suggests that the wrinkles between the snout and the eyes are at least derived from Assyrian lion types: Parrot 1961, fig. 38; Strommenger 1962, pl. 223.

2   See n. 1 above.

3   Compare the back of the head in Baghdad IM 73111: Ismail 1974, 128, fig. 1.

4   Transliterated and translated by W. W. Hallo. The incantation part of the inscription (lines 6–15) is well known on many Pazuzu heads and is called "Standard inscription A." See Heeßel 2002, 55–69, 95 ff.

5   Heeßel 2002, 51–53, 82–85; see also Childs, "The Human Animal," fig. 9 and accompanying text, in this volume.

6   London, Brit. Mus. WA 22459 (48-10-31,1) from Nineveh: height 10.2 cm. London, Brit. Mus. WA 91876: height 9.8 cm. Paris, Louvre AO 26591: height 9.5 cm. Baghdad IM 73111 (also from Nineveh): Ismail 1974, 121–28. On all the preceding heads, see Heeßel 2002, nos. 91, 94, 99, 108.

7   Heeßel 2002, 47–48, 51. At a recent auction in Paris, a hematite head of Pazuzu was described as an amulet; it is 5.1 centimeters tall and has a hole bored vertically through the head: Drouot-Montaigne, *Archéologie*, March 17–18, 2003, no. 451. A carnelian head of Pazuzu was offered for sale by Sotheby's New York, June 13, 2002, no. 8. This head, only three centimeters tall, was also pierced vertically and is described as having "fragments of a bronze suspension loop" preserved. These references were kindly supplied by Michael Padgett.

8   Heeßel 2002, nos. 2–30.

9   Heeßel 2002, nos. 2 and 17.

10  Heeßel 2002, 23–33.

8

## *Ba*-Bird

Egyptian, Late Dynastic – Early Ptolemaic period,
ca. 525 – 305 B.C.
Wood, painted gesso
Height 9.9 cm., width 2.8 cm., length 7.7 cm.
Museum of Fine Arts, Boston, Hay Collection, gift of
C. Granville Way (72.4182)

CONDITION

The figurine is in very good condition. There is some
minor abrasion to the painted surface, particularly
at the tip of the nose. At the center of the base, a drill
hole has been made to accept a peg to attach this
piece to a larger composition; a plugged hole on
the proper right side of the base and a section of
a transverse drill hole across the bottom suggest
that this may have been a reused piece of wood.
Such reuse of wood in Egypt was commonplace,
particularly for funerary equipment.

Carved of a soft local wood, this figurine would have
decorated an item of funerary furniture, as, for example,
a wooden stela.[1] Few of these sculptures come from excavated contexts. Like the figures of mummified hawks and
Anubis jackals found on coffins, canopic chests, and other
items of tomb equipment in Dynasties 25 and 26 (ca. 653
−525 B.C.), statuettes such as this were probably used as
decorations for various kinds of funerary furniture.[2] The
image, commonly referred to as a *ba*-bird, is of a human-
headed bird wearing a divine wig.[3] The wig is of ancient
tradition: long and with lappets descending down either
side of the neck. It is painted blue to represent lapis
lazuli—the hair of the gods in Egyptian myth. On its
chest three drooping lines represent a broad collar; the
black ticks below and on the legs represent feathers.

The *ba* represented the mobile aspect of the soul to
the ancient Egyptians, who believed it could fly between
the tomb, where the portion of the soul known as the
*ka* remained with the body, and the heavens, where the
third part of the soul, the *akh*, abided. The *ba* was the most
familiar aspect of the soul and figures in a famous literary
text, wherein a man debates with his soul the value of

life over suicide.[4] Aside from its appearance as a human-
headed bird, the usually benign Egyptian concept of
the *ba* would seem to have little relation to the sinister
sirens of Greek art and legend.

—PL

BIBLIOGRAPHY
Unpublished.

NOTES

1  Munro 1973.
2  D'Auria, Lacovara, and Roehrig 1988, 173−76.
3  For similar examples, see D'Auria, Lacovara, and Roehrig 1988,
    199−200.
4  Simpson 1972, 201−9.

## 9

# Bowl with Figural Relief

**North Syria and/or Yemen, ca. 700 B.C.**
**Bronze**
**Height 9.0 cm., diameter 22.5 cm., diameter of base 8.0 cm.**
**Princeton University Art Museum, museum purchase, Carl Otto von Kienbusch Jr. Memorial Collection Fund (2001 – 169)**

CONDITION
**There is minor restoration to the base of the bowl, especially in the rosette and the ground line on which the figures walk. Smaller restorations are scattered throughout. The interior of the bowl has been cleaned; the exterior retains incrustations and bright green corrosion.**

This bronze bowl is decorated on the interior with a frieze in chased repoussé relief. The subject, a lion hunt from a chariot in association with a bull and a sphinx, relates closely to bowls found at Nimrud, Delphi, and Olympia.[1] The Princeton bowl's robust figural style, with its deep outlining, is very close to that of the Nimrud bowl, yet the iconography, in which the horse-drawn chariot of the Nimrud bowl is replaced by a sphinx-drawn chariot in both the Princeton bowl and the two

Greek bowls, suggests that the three sphinx bowls are later adaptations and compressions of the Nimrud model. The guilloche border around the inner rim of the bowl and the rosette design of the medallion also are paralleled in the Nimrud bowl and the two bowls from Greece.[2] The Nimrud bowl is usually thought to be of North Syrian workmanship, and many of the peculiarities of the Princeton bowl also are found in the art of North Syria, suggesting that it is an early version close to the North Syrian workshops.[3]

The pictorial frieze of the bowl begins and ends at the lizard, whose vertical form divides the lion facing left from the kneeling archer facing right and highlights the adjacent inscription. The kneeling archer wears a belted, long-sleeved tunic and a quiver topped with a drooping palmette; he comes to the aid of a companion, who stabs a rearing lioness(?) with a sword.[4] Five arrows hit the lioness (one seems to have hit the man's head but may be meant to be seen as behind him). Another arrow flies toward a fleeing hare, already hit in the shoulder; the hare seems to float above the lioness, but perhaps it, too, is intended to be seen as behind the other figures. To the right of the lioness, a bull walks to the left in a papyrus grove inhabited by birds.[5] Farther right is a sphinx with outspread wings; she walks to the left, her oddly masculine face turned back to the viewer's right. She wears a tall Egyptian-style crown with a spiral tassel on top and an apron, shown frontally, that covers almost her whole torso but allows us to see her lion's feet shown in profile beneath the apron's border.[6] The sphinx is attached by an unusually stout and curvaceous pole to a square chariot with eight-spoked wheels that are mounted in mid-carriage.[7] The reins are held by a charioteer wearing a short-sleeved tunic and holding an odd, fluttering whip. Behind him in the car, facing right, an armored archer fires an eighth arrow at a large snarling lion, whose right paw is raised above a cowering pygmy.[8] A buzzard flies above the lion, whose upturned tail curves down to touch the kneeling archer's shoulder directly above the vertical lizard.[9]

The shape[10] and iconography of the Princeton bowl are at home in North Syria and Phoenicia at the end of the eighth century B.C., yet it has an inscription (just above the kneeling archer) in Old South Arabian that should

not date earlier than the fifth century B.C.[11] The North Syrian artistic sphere peters out with the Assyrian conquest of the area about 700 B.C., and thus this bowl suggests two possible scenarios as to its place and time of manufacture. Perhaps the Assyrians, as was their custom after a territorial expansion, resettled some North Syrian craftsmen in northern Yemen,[12] which had contacts with the Assyrian court. Or possibly an Assyrian king gave North Syrian objects from his storeroom to a trading partner from Yemen, and these were kept as heirlooms and inscribed later, as some bowls were in the West.[13] The Nimrud bowl dates to the end of the eighth century, and the two Greek bowls with similar iconography are dated by context to the late eighth or early seventh century, strongly suggesting that the Princeton bowl was made about the same time, perhaps in a somewhat provincial

context in which spatial concerns and true profiles were less important than in Greece and North Syria proper. The two Greek bowls, although clearly deriving from the same North Syrian tradition, show a more organically formed and more feminine sphinx type than the Princeton bowl, suggesting perhaps that the artisans already were tailoring their output to their respective new markets after the Assyrian destruction of the North Syrian luxury goods workshops at the end of the eighth century.

—SG

### BIBLIOGRAPHY

*Record* 61.1 (2002).

### NOTES

1 See Markoe 1985, 36, comparative photo 5 (Nimrud), cat. no. G4 (Delphi), cat. no. G7 (Olympia), all with earlier bibliography. The Nimrud bowl shows the sphinx but has horses drawing the chariot.

2 See Imai 1977, 88–91, 122–23. The Princeton bowl's guilloche is closest to bowls from Nimrud.

3 These North Syrian parallels for distinctive iconographic details in the Princeton bowl will be found in the notes below, keyed to the description.

4 The two figures appear on another Nimrud bowl: Markoe 1985, comparative photo 3; Curtis and Reade 1995, cat. no. 104, where the same Egyptian-style skirt is worn by the figures; and also on a North Syrian ivory pyxis: Barnett 1975, pl. XVIII. The hairstyle of the figures is unusual, but such curls appear on some ivories and Aramaean reliefs in North Syria. The kneeling archer also appears in Assyrian and North Syrian reliefs: see Orthmann 1971, B/6, from Zincirli.

5 See Falsone 1985 for very similar bulls and a discussion of "bull bowls"—usually thought to be North Syrian and early—some of which also were found at Olympia (see Markoe 1985, cat. no. G5). For a parallel in ivory, see Barnett 1975, cat. no. S129. The Princeton bull is much more decorated, perhaps wearing some kind of covering attached by straps(?) at the base of the tail, the rump, and the base of the shoulder. Unlike these other examples, the artist here shows the tip of the rear horn (and perhaps a second ear), as if uncomfortable with true profile, suggesting a more provincial imitation of North Syrian style. The papyrus grove, evoking a so-called marsh scene, also appears on other Nimrud bowls and ivories.

6 Similar winged sphinxes appear on other Nimrud bowls (Layard 1849–53, vol. 2, pl. 68) and on ivories from Nimrud, although the extreme frontality of the apron is unusual: (Barnett 1975, 83–85, pls. XLVI, LVI; similar sphinx crowns on pls. XX and XIX, and spirals on sphinx crowns, pl. XXXIV). The Princeton sphinx's face and general form are quite close to a stone relief at Carchemish (Orthmannn 1971, E/8, pl. 71), and its somewhat masculine countenance finds parallels

in the distinctly male sphinxes in North Syria, such as those at Sakçagözü (see Orthmann 1971, pl. 51A/12). The exaggerated flame pattern on the haunch of the sphinx is also seen in many North Syrian animals (e.g., on the pyxis in Barnett 1975, pl. XVIII).

7 Wheels with eight spokes and mid-carriage mounting are an old type that appears in North Syria at Tell Tainat (Winter 1973, 237; Orthmann 1971, Tainat 2, pl. 52f); on a lost gold-foil sheet from Cyprus (Barnett 1975, fig. 43); and on a gilded silver bowl from Praeneste (Markoe 1985, cat. no. E2). The odd double quivers(?) on the Princeton chariot box seem to be misunderstood versions of the North Syrian type. The curved chariot pole appears on the Delphi and Olympia bowls, which also show mid-carriage wheel mounting.

8 The lion is quite close to the Nimrud bowl discussed above in n. 1 (Markoe 1985, comparative photo 5), which goes back ultimately to the reliefs at Sakçagözü (ibid., comparative photo 6; Orthmann 1971, pl. 51c).

9 Buzzards appear on another Nimrud bowl: Layard 1849–53, vol. 2, pl. 62; Curtis 1995, cat. no. 103.

10 See Howes Smith 1986, bowl shape type 1B-1, which is not attested after the seventh century.

11 K. A. Kitchen, in a letter of July 2001, interprets the inscription to read: *y d/ sh r y k m* ("hand [of] Shariyakum"), with a late (or at least unattested earlier) *sh* sign, which ought not to predate the fifth century. The exact meaning remains unclear, but ownership seems to me to be the likely interpretation, unless the inscription is earlier than the letter forms suggest, in which case it could be an artist's signature.

12 For a discussion of how Assyrian conquests may have dispersed North Syrian artistic workshops, see Winter 1973, 477–82.

13 Many bowls show signs of having been inscribed long after manufacture, and some seem to have been inscribed, abraded down, and reinscribed as heirlooms; for two such bowls from Cyprus, see Markoe 1985, 72–74, cat. nos. Cy 20 and Cy 8.

## 10

# Cylinder Seal with Prancing Winged Male Sphinx

**Middle Assyrian, middle of the thirteenth century B.C.**
**Rock crystal**
**Height 4.02 cm., diameter 1.37 cm.**
**Private collection**

### CONDITION

**The seal is in excellent condition, with only slight chipping along the upper and lower edges and minor pitting in the field.**

The seal is a long, narrow cylinder pierced through its length for suspension on a cord.[1] There is but one figure, a prancing, winged and bearded sphinx within a wreath or garland composed of tripartite buds joined by curved double lines. At the base of each bud is a small hemisphere from which the buds spring. The same pattern is used along the upper and lower borders of the seal. At the top and bottom edges of the garland enclosing the

sphinx are cuneiform signs that read "seal of Ubru" *kunuk Ubru*), who was *limu*, or eponymous magistrate, under Shalmaneser I (1273–1244 B.C.).[2] The placement allows the signs to appear symmetrically arranged around the sphinx when the seal is rolled out to make an impression.

The sphinx is represented in a peculiar stance that was extremely popular for all sorts of animals in Middle Assyrian representations beginning in the thirteenth century: one rear and one front leg are raised in a prancing gait.[3] The pattern may have arisen as a means of representing an animal fallen in combat, but it became generalized, as here. The sphinx wears a low, rounded cap with horns on its lower rim, a sign of divinity.[4] The face is frontal and bearded. The feathers of the wings are plastically rendered and differentiated into primary and secondary groups. Along the belly of the creature is a ruff of hair. The musculature of the legs is emphatic; the wings are spread out with the nearer one to the back and the further one to the front. This pattern was common before the twelfth century, at which time it became more frequent to represent only one wing—the nearer—

IMPRESSION

set to the back, sometimes with the edge of the rear wing shown in outline above the front wing.[5]

The rather complex pattern of the bud garlands and the elegant stance of the sphinx create a busy decorative surface that is unusual in Middle Assyrian seals, though not without some parallels. A seal impression from the excavations of Sheikh Hamad, Syria, shows a winged bull in a similar stance and similarly surrounded by a bud garland;[6] the border is not preserved. A bearded and winged sphinx with horned cap on a seal impression in Berlin also closely resembles the sphinx on the seal under discussion: his profile head faces to the viewer's left, and he prances in a largely lost vegetal wreath.[7] Its somewhat fussy appearance recalls Kassite seals, and the garland appears to be derived from the same source, though Assyrian garlands have more attenuated buds or flowers.[8] Since the bud or palmette garland is frequently associated with sacred trees, its function on the present seal is clearly to emphasize the divine character of the sphinx.

The modeling can be compared to a thirteenth-century seal in the British Museum of a lion fighting a winged horse,[9] but the decorative surface recalls patterns of the end of the fourteenth century such as occur on a seal in the Boston Museum of Fine Arts.[10] The known dates of the owner of the seal, Ubru, place the seal in the second quarter of the thirteenth century; and the date of the impression from Sheikh Hamad (mentioned above), from the early years of the reign of Tukulti-Ninurta I (1243–1207 B.C.), confirms a date for our seal about the middle of the thirteenth century.

— WAPC

**BIBLIOGRAPHY**
Unpublished.

**NOTES**

1 Collon (1987, 108–11) discusses and illustrates various means of stringing cylinder seals, some of which had elaborate settings. It should be noted that Dr. Barbara Feller of the Vorderasiatisches Museum, Berlin, has suggested on the basis of photocopies of photographs that this and the other two Middle Assyrian seals (cat. nos. 11 and 12) in the exhibition may be forgeries. Although there are several unusual iconographic or formal elements in each of the three seals, these elements do not disqualify them as genuine because there are so few Middle Assyrian seals or seal-impressions known and published, and autopsy of the seals argues strongly for the authenticity of all three.

2 Transliterated and translated by Dr. Beate Pongratz-Leisten. For Ubru see Freydank 1991, 41, 53 with n. 138.

3 Mortgat-Correns 1964, 171–73, figs. 5–7; Moortgat 1967, 122, fig. 90. Mayer-Opificius (1986, 163) claims a late date under Tukulti-Ninurta I (1243–1207 B.C.) for the beginning of the pattern.

4 Moortgat (1944, 31, 32, figs. 19–20, 23–25) illustrates several twelfth-century male sphinxes, although none with frontal face.

5 Matthews 1990, 105. Cf. Moortgat 1944, figs. 15–27.

6 Der Az-Zor Museum inv. 2532: Kühne 1980, 102–3, no. 51; Kühne 1984, 166, fig. 17; Matthews 1990, no. 411. Kühne dates this seal in the second half of the thirteenth century based on the name of its owner, the *limu* (eponymous yearly official) Mušallim-Adad; a man of this name was *limu* in the early years of the reign of Tukulti-Ninurta I (1243–1207 B.C.); see Freydank 1991, 41, 48–49, 153.

7 Berlin VA 18007 and 18109: Fischer 1999, 134, no. 5; Freydank 1991, 171.

8 Matthews 1990, 64 with n. 97, 92. The Assyrian garland can at times become a palmette chain: Collon 1987, no. 916; Matthews 1990, no. 335 (BM 102535).

9 London, Brit. Mus. WA 129572: Moortgat 1941–42, 63–65, fig. 25; Orthmann 1975, 351–52, pl. 271g; Collon 1987, no. 282.

10 Boston 25-67: Frankfort 1939, pl. XXXIIb; Beran 1957, 157–58, fig. 26; Orthmann 1975, 351, pl. 271c; Matthews 1990, 91 with n. 31, no. 290.

## 11

# Cylinder Seal with Winged Centaur Hunting Gazelles

**Middle Assyrian, first half of the thirteenth century B.C.**
**Red jasper with inclusions**
**Height 4.44 cm., diameter 1.61 cm.**
**Private collection**

CONDITION
**The seal is in nearly perfect condition.**

This is a long and narrow cylinder, pierced along its axis to be suspended from a cord, exactly like the seal shown as catalogue number 10.[1] The main figure is a winged centaur with scorpion tail. He gallops to the right with the two hind legs together and the two forelegs stretched out in front of him, an age-old pattern in the Near East to depict swift movement of quadrupeds. He wears a rounded cap or helmet and a quiver on his back. The treatment of the feathers of his single visible wing is linear, and there is a distinction between the primary and secondary groups of feathers. The body of the horse element, the upper human torso, and the lower abdomen of the human torso are articulated by short cuttings; in the first two

cases they may represent ribs. The marks on the abdomen and three shallower cuttings on the rump suggest folds of skin and hide (see cat. no. 12).

The winged centaur is hunting three gazelles or antelopes together with a dog that occupies the space in front of him in the middle ground. A fourth gazelle lies on its back under the belly of the centaur, transfixed by an arrow. Above, seven birds are in flight to the right. Four of these are partially covered by a horizontal band on which is a cuneiform inscription: "seal of Ištar-ēriš son of Šulmānu-qarrād" (*kunuk Ištar-ēriš mār Šulmānu-qarrād*).[2] Ištar-ēriš was *limu* under Shalmaneser I (1273–1244 B.C.).[3] The band was clearly cut into the seal in a second use and obliterated much of the four upper birds.

The hunting winged centaur is broadly represented on Near Eastern seals.[4] The present example is close to a late-fourteenth-century Mitannian seal impression of a hunting centaur, now in Philadelphia.[5] The flock of birds along the top border also resembles another Mitannian seal reconstructed from multiple impressions preserved in Istanbul.[6] Even closer is still one more Mitannian seal closely resembling the previous one and known from many impressions: a flock of ten birds flies in two rows at the top of a scene of an anthropomorphic mountain holding two griffins.[7] These two seals date to the early

IMPRESSION

IMPRESSION

**BIBLIOGRAPHY**
Unpublished.

**NOTES**

1 For the authenticity of this seal, see cat. no. 10, n. 1.

2 Transliterated and translated by Dr. Beate Pongratz-Leisten.

3 Freydank 1991, 39–41.

4 Some examples follow. (1) Paris, de Clercq 363: Frankfort 1939, pl. XXXIf; Matthews 1990, 98, no. 355, dated twelfth century and considered Assyrian; Seidl 1968, 176, no. 2b (Kassite). (2) Berlin, VAT 16 397, 16 394, 16 396 (three impressions): Moortgat 1944, 41–42, figs. 42–44; Seidl 1968, 177, nos. 2c–e, twelfth century, Assyrian. (3) Leiden, Rijksmuseum van Oudheden: Orthmann 1975, pl. 272g, Neo-Assyrian. (4) Paris, Louvre MNB 1179: Frankfort 1939, pl. XXXIVd; Collon 1987, no. 881, Neo-Assyrian. (5) New York, Morgan Lib.: Porada 1948, no. 749; Collon 1987, no. 364, Neo-Babylonian. For a general discussion, see Fittschen 1969, 89–90 n. 458; *RLA* 8, 256 (§ 3.19), s.v. "Mischwesen B" (Green).

5 Philadelphia CBM 3176, Kassite, King Kurigalzu III, 1331 B.C.: Porada 1952, fig. 2; Seidl 1968, 176, no. 2a; Orthmann 1975, 346–48, fig. 103e; Matthews 1990, no. 161; Matthews 1992, 39, no. 158.

6 Porada 1952, fig. 5; Collon 1987, no. 842; Matthews 1990, no. 131; Matthews 1992, no. 148.

7 Matthews 1992, no. 149.

8 Matthews 1992, 34–36.

9 Porada 1948, 67; see also Moortgat 1967, 118–19, 124, pl. 242.

10 Seidl 1968, 177: nos. 12, 14, 27, 63, and possibly 64.

11 *RLA* 3, 77 78 (§ 7), s.v. "Fixsterne" (Weidner).

12 Borger 1964, 321–22; Koch-Westenholz 1995, 163–64.

13 Mayer-Opificius 1986, 161.

and mid-thirteenth century, respectively.[8] The present Assyrian seal is distinguished from the Mitannian ones by a sense of open space where a naturalistic scene is portrayed with a real ground line and palpable bird-filled air above.[9]

The arrow-shooting centaur is also known on *kudurrus*, or stelae,[10] and was a constellation known as $^{mul}$*pa-bil-sag*,[11] which was taken over into the Graeco-Roman zodiac as Sagittarius.[12]

The relationship to the Mitannian seals cited above suggests a date early in the thirteenth century, which is underscored by the extreme slimness of the centaur's torso.[13] Since the inscription with the name of *Ištar-ēriš*, *limu* under Shalmaneser I (1273–1244 B.C.), was cut into the seal obliterating part of the flock of birds above, it can only be assumed that the seal antedates the *limu*. Accordingly a date in the first half of the thirteenth century is indicated. The tangible sense of open space and the extremely elegant forms qualify this seal, along with its two companions in the exhibition (cat. nos. 10 and 12), as a masterpiece of Middle Assyrian glyptic.

—WAPC

## 12

# Cylinder Seal with *Laḫmu* and Centaur

**Middle Assyrian, middle to late thirteenth century B.C.**
**Rose quartz**
**Height 3.84 cm., diameter 1.53 cm.**
**Private collection**

CONDITION
**The seal is in nearly perfect condition, with only slight chipping along the top and bottom edges.**

This seal depicts the only known pure equine centaur from the ancient Near East, although Ione Mylonas Shear has recently discovered two Mycenaean terracotta centaurs from Ugarit.[1] (The deviations of several of the earlier known Near Eastern centaurs from the "pure" equine type are minimal.) Our centaur paces to the viewer's left though the torso and head are frontal. He grasps a small upside-down quadruped by the forelegs, while to the viewer's right a *laḫmu*, or nude hero, with six elegant locks of hair, holds the animal by the rear legs.[2] The small diameter of the seal allows the centaur and the *laḫmu* to hold a bow between them with their other hands. An inscription in two lines is written above the back of the

centaur; one sign appears to the left of his head. The inscription reads: "seal of Da''āni-Šamaš son of Sîn-ašarēd" (*kunuk Da''āni-Šamaš mār Sîn-ašarēd*).[3] The owner was a high official in the reign of Tukulti-Ninurta I (1243 –1207 B.C.).[4] A distinct line marks the surface on which the figures stand, and a similar line runs just below the top of the cylinder.

The plastic muscularity of both figures is emphatic. Particularly noteworthy are the horizontal cuttings on the torso and abdomen of the hero, as well as on the centaur, to indicate the ribs and folds of flesh, similar to the treatment of the winged centaur of catalogue number 11. This kind of articulation is not infrequently used to depict the ribs of animals,[5] but its use for human anatomy is unknown to me other than on the seal just mentioned.[6] Also noteworthy on the centaur are the small hooks or curls on the legs, lower chest, back, and rump. These elegant flourishes seem in strong contrast to the plasticity of the anatomy but are found on a number of Middle Assyrian seals of the thirteenth and twelfth centuries.[7] This seal is distinctive in its rendering of the hair and beards of the two figures. The hair is clearly parted in the center and combed to the side in two slightly convex sections that end in the top curl on either side of the face, somewhat like handlebar moustaches. A similar pattern

IMPRESSION

IMPRESSION

evidence to support the hypothesis, the composite creature bringing down a bull on a twelfth-century B.C. seal impression in Berlin may be precisely one of the new varieties of *laḫmu*.[12] As Wiggermann suggests, the identification is established through the frontal head with six elegant locks of hair framing the face,[13] which characterizes the composite creatures of the seal impressions in Berlin and our centaur. It is therefore extremely likely that *both* figures on our seal are *laḫmus*.

The date of the seal is broadly determined by the name of its owner, who was a high official under Tukulti-Ninurta I (1243–1207 B.C.), a date that confirms the stylistic analysis. The stylized hooks appear over a relatively long period in the thirteenth and twelfth centuries.[14] The strong modeling and clear ground also point to this same time span. That the human *laḫmu* is nude — in contrast to the introduction by the Assyrians of a similar figure with a kilt — might suggest the earlier part of this period,[15] but nude *laḫmus* continued to appear on seals well into the thirteenth century.[16] The relationship of the seal to the newly identified terracotta centaurs from Ugarit, which are dated to the Late Helladic IIIA/IIIB period (ca. 1300 B.C.), must remain open.
— WAPC

**BIBLIOGRAPHY**
Unpublished.

**NOTES**

1 Shear 2002, 147–53. Shear also resurrects the identification of centaurs on two Mycenaean seals. For a list of Near Eastern centaurs, see Seidl 1968, 176–78. Although two of the fourteen examples do not have wings, both creatures that lack wings have scorpion's tails and one has two heads (lion and human). For the authenticity of this seal, see cat. no. 10, n. 1. As remarked there, Dr. Barbara Feller has tentatively questioned this seal. One of her observations deserves comment here and should have been included in the original discussion: the stance and detailing of the legs of the centaur. Both are closely paralleled in a seal impression in Berlin with a winged centaur depicted as Sagittarius: VAT 16 396 (Moortgat 1944, 42, figs. 44a–b).

2 Wiggermann 1981–82.

3 Transliterated and translated by Dr. Beate Pongratz-Leisten.

4 Freydank 2001, 105.

5 Collon 1987, no. 280 (BM 102507); Moortgat 1940, no. 593; Matthews 1990, 332, 341, 346.

6 Sidney Babcock observed to me that the indication of ribs and folds

is found on other Middle Assyrian seals.[8] The beard of each figure is very clearly divided into three strands that descend from the corners of the mouth and the chin to a double horizontal element that represents some sort of binding. Below this, the beard spreads out in a fanlike shape that has several parallels.[9] It is the detail of the horizontal binding that is singular.

This unique depiction of a real, Greek-like centaur deserves some comment. Clearly he is related to his winged brethren, since he is characterized here as a hunter. The clear resemblance of the head of the centaur to his companion *laḫmu* is noteworthy. F. A. M. Wiggermann has suggested that a similar pairing of a *laḫmu* and a winged figure on two seal impressions in Berlin actually represents two *laḫmus*.[10] Such a variation in the appearance of a *laḫmu* is supported by the late *Göttertypentext* that describes several composite creatures as "*laḫmu*."[11] Although there is no of flesh does appear in a similar manner in Akkadian art, both on seals (Boehmer 1965, 34 and pl. XXI, figs. 236–37) and on reliefs (Strommenger 1962, pls. 117–18); this is an archaism not untypical of Middle Assyrian art.

7 Moortgat 1941–42, fig. 38; Mayer-Opificius 1986, 162, fig. 10, pl. 30, illus. 1; Matthews 1990, 100–101, nos. 337–39, 394.

8 There are three different seals or impressions: (1) Moortgat 1941–42, 57, fig. 10 (Newell 685 [Matthews 1990, no. 403]); (2) Moortgat 1941–42, 61, figs. 21a–c (Berlin VAT 12 993); (3) Moortgat 1944, 38–39, figs. 40a–b (Berlin VAT 15490).

9 Moortgat 1941–42, 61, figs. 21a–c; Matthews 1990, nos. 357–58.

10 Wiggermann 1981–82, 104–5; Moortgat 1941–42, 60–62, figs. 21a–c; Freydank 1974, 8, pl. I.6–8; Matthews 1990, 101, nos. 357–58.

11 Freydank 1974, 8; Wiggermann 1981–82, 97–99. Cf. Haussig 1965, 93–94, s.v. "Laḫama, Laḫamu" (Edzard).

12 Moortgat 1944, 38–41, fig. 40a–b; Orthmann 1975, 353, fig. 105g; Matthews 1990, no. 394.

13 Wiggermann 1981–82, 98–99. Orthmann (1975, 353 to figure 105g) identifies the figure on the impression in Berlin as "ein sechslockiger Dämon."

14 Matthews 1990, 100–101.

15 Moortgat 1941–42, figs. 9–10; Matthews 1990, nos. 290–91, 345.

16 Perhaps the latest is Paris, Louvre AO 4770 (A 900): Delaporte 1920–23, 27, pl. 95; Frankfort 1939, pl. XXXVIh; Moortgat 1944, 40, fig. 41; Collon 1987, no. 381; Matthews 1990, 103 (list). Moortgat dates the seal in or close to the reign of Tukulti-Ninurta I or slightly before; Frankfort and Collon date it to the Neo-Babylonian period (sixth century B.C.); Matthews is uncertain.

## 13

# Man Fighting a Centaur

**Greek, Peloponnesian, Late Geometric period, ca. 750 B.C.**
**Bronze**
**Height of man 11.1 cm., height of centaur 9.9 cm., length 14.3 cm.**
**The Metropolitan Museum of Art, New York, gift of J. Pierpont Morgan, 1917 (17.190.2072)**

### CONDITION
The figures appear to be intact except for the following losses: the tip of the man's helmet, his right forearm and hand, the right forearm and hand of the centaur, and whatever objects were held by both figures. There is a crack in the man's right forearm just below where the centaur lays hold of him. The worn surface exhibits a reddish brown patina with greenish tinge in places.

This magnificent bronze statuette represents a man and a centaur locked in combat. The man stands upright, naked except for a broad belt and a tall conical helmet.[1] With both legs firmly planted on the ground, he towers over the centaur, reaching out with his extremely elongated left arm and holding back the raised right arm of the centaur. It is likely that the centaur held the branch of a tree or another weapon in this hand. With his left hand the centaur grasps the man's right arm, which held a weapon, a spear or sword, the remains of which protrude from the centaur's side.[2] The centaur also stands upright with all four legs firmly planted on the ground. Depicted with the body of a man attached to the hindquarters of a horse, the centaur wears a tall conical helmet similar to that of his antagonist. A line of hair, represented as a herringbone pattern, delineates the centaur's equine spine all the way to the tail. The general characteristics of man and centaur—the proportions of the bodies, the large rounded heads with small pointed beards and pronounced ears—are similar, but the man is distinguished by his taller stature and deep-set eyes, which originally may have held inlay. The simplified geometric style belies the tense action of the scene and imbues it with a static, almost monumental quality.

On the underside of the base, concentric rectangles frame two symmetrical zigzag patterns, whose hollow areas pierce the base as a series of triangles between the legs of the centaur. The tail of the centaur is grounded on a small extension of the base at the back, and the man stands on a slightly larger extension at the front. Careful ornamentation of both the top and bottom of the base is characteristic of many fine small bronze statuettes

of this period, but the precise interpretation of this ornament is not clear.[3] Nonetheless, the interest in the geometry of form so evident in this work and the tendency to finish all parts of the object, even those not readily visible, such as the underside of the base, become fundamental underlying tendencies of the best Greek art in the ensuing centuries.

Figural groups are rare in Geometric Greek art, and this is among the finest.[4] The statuette is said to come from Olympia[5] and may be associated with a Laconian[6] or other Peloponnesian[7] workshop. The lack of attributes and of close parallels for the scene at this early date make it impossible to identify the figures with any certainty, although a mythological scene is almost certainly represented.[8] A careful reading of the action clearly indicates that it is a violent scene of combat, particularly evident from the blade in the centaur's side, rather than a scene of greeting, as one might surmise from the static poses of the figures.[9] Scholars have suggested a variety of plausible possibilities. The figures could represent Zeus and an early conception of the monster Typhon.[10] Alternatively, the scene has been identified as Zeus and one of the Titans,[11] or even Zeus and Kronos.[12] Another scholar has suggested a Lapith battling a centaur.[13] More likely, the scene depicts the hero Herakles and one of the centaurs, such as Nessos.[14] The superior height of the man and the mortal wound of the centaur indicate the outcome of the combat. On a generic universal level, the scene represents the battle between civilized man and wild beast, the conflict between order and chaos that is a central tenet of ancient Greek philosophical thought. As such, it foreshadows the centauromachies that become so popular in Archaic and Classical Greek art.

—SAH

### SELECTED BIBLIOGRAPHY

Sambon 1906b, 429, fig. 3; Baur 1912, 79, fig. 15; Richter 1917, 43–44, fig. 17; Casson 1922, 209, fig. 2, 210–11; Richter 1927, 51–52, fig. 29; Lawrence 1929, 89–90, fig. 5; Kunze 1930, 143–47, pl. 38.1; Richter 1930a, 51, 337, fig. 13; Buschor 1934, 129–31, fig. 2; Dörig and Gigon 1961, 39–41, pl. 18; Herrmann 1964, 40, fig. 21; Himmelmann-Wildschütz 1964, 9, 12, figs. 37–38; Akurgal 1968, 170–71, pl. 18; Fittschen 1969, 111–12, no. SB1, fig. 16; Schweitzer 1971, 150–51, fig. 185; Arnold 1972, 27–30,

no. 3; Boardman 1978, 10, fig. 13; Hurwit 1985, 108–9, fig. 47; Zimmermann 1989, 143–44; Thomas 1992, 56, fig. 41; Rolley 1994, 102, 109.

**NOTES**

1 This backward-tilted helmet of conical type is represented on a number of figurines from Greece (Snodgrass 1964, 9, 215 n. 24). Actual examples are less common but, interestingly, two such helmets have been found in Olympia, the alleged provenance of the Metropolitan group (Arnold 1972, 29). On the importance of the belt in representations of early Greek warriors, see Bennett 1997.

2 The statuette is a solid lost-wax casting. One could conjecture that the fragment identified here as the man's weapon is instead a channel or vent left from the casting process, but the piece is otherwise clearly finished in all details: note, for example, the finely incised hair on the equine spine of the centaur. It is most unlikely that the jutting element would have been left unfinished by the craftsman. For a discussion of how these statuettes were made and an illustration of the process, see Hemingway 1996, 3, figs. 3–4.

3 For a discussion and illustrations of horse statuettes with such decorative bases, see Zimmermann 1989, 314–15, pls. 73–79.

4 Two Greek Geometric bronze statuettes of centaurs also are known: one is from Olympia (Athens, Nat. Mus. 6188: Schiffler 1976, 320, cat. V 12), and the other is from Phigalia (Athens, Nat. Mus. 14495: Schiffler 1976, 320, cat. V 13). Cf. also a related terracotta group of man and centaur from Athens (Nat. Mus. 12508: Kunze 1930, 44–45, pls. 38.2, 39).

5 Mertens 1985, 19.

6 Herrmann 1964, 42; Mertens 1985, 18; Zimmermann 1989, 143–44.

7 Schweitzer (1971, 150) argues for Elis, near Olympia.

8 For further discussion on this topic and the difficulties of interpretation, see Hurwit 1985, 108–9.

9 The evident violence of the scene, therefore, makes the identification of the centaur as Pholos (Richter 1930a, 337; Schweitzer 1971, 150–51, fig. 185) or Cheiron (Sambon 1906b, 429) less likely.

10 Buschor 1934, 130; Akurgal 1968, 170.

11 Mertens 1985, 19.

12 Dörig and Gigon 1961, 39–41.

13 Kübler 1970, 95 n. 344.

14 Fittschen 1969, 124; Boardman 1978, fig. 13; Thomas 1992, 56.

# 14

## Seal with Centaur and Archer

**Greek, Peloponnesian (Argive?), late eighth century B.C.**
**Said to be from Crete**
**Black serpentine**
**Height 2.0 cm., width 2.2 cm., thickness 1.0 cm.**
**Paris, Bibliothèque Nationale de France, Cabinet des**
**Médailles (M 5837); from the collection of E. Babelon**

CONDITION
**The seal is intact and in good condition, with only minor chips and surface scratches.**

The large face of the seal bears the image of a standing man aiming a bow and arrow at the back of a centaur, who holds two branches in his raised hands. In front of the centaur is a lizard (or frog?), and below him is a filling ornament. Engraved on one short side of the tabloid is another standing figure, similar in appearance to the archer, who leans on a crooked stick. The back is ornamented with a geometric pattern of four quadrants of engraved chevrons, and the other short side is engraved with a similar zigzag pattern.

Although finely engraved seal stones were made in quantity in Minoan and Mycenaean Greece throughout the Bronze Age, the skills to produce them were lost during the Dark Ages (ca. 1100–950 B.C.). By the mid-ninth century, however, a revival of interest in seal cutting began in Greece, spurred by the influx of imported seals from Syria and the Near East, and perhaps even by immigrant artisans. The earliest seals, found in tombs in Athens dating to the ninth and eighth centuries B.C., were carved in ivory with simple designs.[1] By the late eighth century, seals cut in soft stones, such as serpentine and steatite, were being made in the Peloponnese, as well as in the islands and Crete. Seals of various shapes (square, hemispherical, tabloid, and in the form of animals) are especially well attested among the finds of the Argive Heraion and are most likely of local origin. A number of tabloid seals from the Argive Heraion provide close parallels to the Paris seal in shape, although no other is so finely engraved.[2] The chevron and zigzag decoration on the back of the gem is also seen on some Argive seals.[3] The stylizations

BACK 1:1

TOP 1:1

FRONT 2:1

IMPRESSION OF FRONT 2:1

IMPRESSION
OF BASE 2:1

of the figures—their triangular torsos, angular limbs, and profile legs with accentuated musculature—are very much within the conventions of the Peloponnesian Geometric style.[4] John Boardman suggests that the quality of the seal indicates a relatively early date in the series.[5]

The scene itself is remarkable, for an archer shooting a fleeing centaur must surely recall the story of Herakles and Nessos. Similar compositions are found in the sixth century B.C. in a variety of media, including East Greek engraved gems and Attic and Caeretan vases, and thereafter as part of the Classical iconographic repertoire,[6] but the prototype for the imagery was evidently created in the Peloponnese in the eighth century B.C., with this gem being the earliest surviving depiction. Another tabloid of similar though perhaps slightly later style may portray another part of the same story, the centaur Nessos grasping the arm of Herakles' wife Deianeira.[7] Other narrative mythological scenes on seals of this date are known, including two warriors (Herakles and Apollo?) fighting over a tripod.[8] A slightly later (mid-seventh century B.C.) ivory seal from Perachora depicts a man (Herakles?) fighting a centaur.[9] Centaurs, usually brandishing branches, continued to be popular on Peloponnesian stone and ivory seals throughout the seventh century.[10]

—JS

**BIBLIOGRAPHY**

Perrot and Chipiez 1911, 4, pls. 1.1, 2.8, 20; Casson 1927, 41, pl. 5; Babelon 1930, 12, pl. 6; Casson 1933, 45, fig. 17b; Boardman 1963, 120, C13, pl. 14; Richter 1968, 29, no. 3; Zazoff 1969, 183–85, pl. 30.1–5; Coldstream 1977, 151, 354, fig. 50b; Boardman 2001a, 112 and 134, pl. 208.

**NOTES**

1 Boardman 2001a, 108.

2 Boardman 1963, 119–21, C1–19; Boardman 2001a, 112, 133, figs. 162–64.

3 Boardman 1963, 119, B5 and B9 (hemispherical seals); and 119, C9 and C10 (tabloids).

4 Zazoff (1969, 185) notes similarities to figures in contemporary Argive vase-painting.

5 Boardman 1963, 120.

6 *LIMC* 6 (1992), 838–47, nos. 80–92, s.v. "Nessos" (Díez de Velasco).

7 Boardman 1963, 120, C14; Brandt 1968, no. 101; Zazoff (1969, 184–87) suggests an Attic origin for the seal, a proposal rejected by Boardman in favor of Argos; see Boardman 2001a, 134.

8 Boardman 1963, 120, C15; Boardman 2001a, 112 and 133, fig. 162, from Brauron, Attica.

9 Stubbings 1962, 414, no. A29, pl. 175.

10 See the following: Boardman 2001a, 133, fig. 164 (a tabloid at Yale); Boardman 1963, 131, G24 and G25 (steatite disks from Perachora); 132, G33 (steatite disk); 133, G40 (serpentine disk); 146, pl. 17b (ivory disk from Siphnos); Boardman 2001a, 134, pl. 212 (shell seal from Melos); and Stubbings 1962, 424, no. A65, pl. 180 (ivory stepped seal from Perachora).

# Seal with Centaur

Greek, Peloponnesian(?), ca. 700 B.C.
Formerly in the collection of Major General
Cornelius Mann of Shooters Hill
Olive green steatite lentoid, pierced
Height 2.20 cm., width 2.22 cm., thickness 0.68 cm.
Sol and Colleen Rabin Collection, Los Angeles

CONDITION
The gem is intact and in excellent condition.

The centaur holds a short branch in his raised hand
and grasps a longer branch, held downward before his
body. There is crude filling ornament in front of and
below him. A tooth border encircles the image.

The style is Late Geometric and finer than most
stone seals of this period. The frontal, triangular torso,
the profile legs, and the angular face and beard are
similarly depicted on contemporary vase-painting.
Other lentoid seals engraved in a related but slightly later
(sub-) Geometric style have been found on Crete
and in the Peloponnese at the Argive Heraion and in
Perachora.[1] The material, an olive green steatite, is
typical for Peloponnesian seals of the late eighth and
seventh centuries B.C.

There is little evidence to suggest how seals were used
in the Late Geometric period.[2] Nearly all the stones were
pierced and were probably worn by individuals, but there
is no evidence to show that seals were actually used to
make impressions, with the exception of two instances of
the same large rectangular stamp, decorated with the
image of Ajax carrying the body of Achilles, impressed
on a clay plaque found at Samos and on the neck of a jar
discovered on Ischia.[3] Most seals from known contexts are
votive dedications found in sanctuaries, and originally
they may have been worn merely as personal decoration.
—JS

BIBLIOGRAPHY
New York, Christie's, December 18, 1998, lot 200.

NOTES
1 Boardman 1963, 127–32, G1–9 (Cretan group), G16–20 (Argive
Heraion), and G23–30 (Perachora). For other centaurs on
Peloponnesian seals of seventh-century date, see this volume,
cat. no. 14, n. 10.
2 See the comments by Boardman 2001a, 112.
3 Boardman 2001a, 112, fig. 166.

## 16

## Double-Sided Seal with Centaur and Two Men

Greek, Peloponnesian(?), early seventh century B.C.
Lead, circular seal of "stepped" shape, pierced
Maximum diameter 2.79 cm., diameter of smaller
side 1.59 cm., thickness 0.6 cm.
Princeton University Art Museum, museum
purchase, Fowler McCormick, Class of 1921, Fund
(2002–284)

### CONDITION

The seal is in good condition, with only minor nicks
in the edges and some damage to the heads on the
reverse. Both surfaces are covered with a smooth,
tan incrustation or weathering layer.

The obverse shows an image in relief of a centaur standing facing right, holding a branch in his outstretched right arm. His left arm is down at his side. Before him is another branch, perhaps to be understood as held in his left hand. Below him a bird faces upward. The smaller reverse surface preserves only the center of the image, which depicts two men standing facing frontally with a zigzag (staff? serpent?) between them.

The seal appears to be unique both for its material and for the devices rendered in relief rather than in intaglio. The shape—two joined circular discs, one smaller than the other ("stepped" in profile)—was, however, often used in the Peloponnese for steatite seals, datable to the late eighth and early seventh centuries B.C.,[1] and for an extensive series of fine ivory seals of seventh-century B.C. date found at the Argive Heraion, at Perachora, at the sanctuary of Artemis Orthia at Sparta, and elsewhere, again primarily in the Peloponnese.[2] In view of the shape, and despite the devices being in relief, it seems that the lead piece was intended to serve as a seal. It may have been created by pressing an actual stone seal with devices in intaglio into a (wax?) mold and then making a cast of the impression in the appropriate shape.

The style of the centaur is similar to, but somewhat finer than, that seen on stone seals from the Argive Heraion.[3] It retains many of the purely Geometric stylizations found on some earlier seals cut in limestone, notably a square seal from Melos now in Oxford, which depicts two standing men.[4] Pairs of standing figures also appear on a number of other Late (or sub-) Geometric stone seals from Argos, although the meaning is uncertain.[5] A contemporary tabloid seal depicting Nessos and Deianeira(?) similarly adds a bird below the centaur.[6]
—JS

### BIBLIOGRAPHY

Unpublished.

### NOTES

1 Seals of this shape are best attested at Argos and Megara; see Boardman 1963, 129–30, G12–14; and Boardman 2001a, 111–12.
2 Boardman 1963, 145–48, and fig. 15 for the shape; Boardman 2001a, 114–18 and 418, fig. 167, for the shape. For the seals from Perachora, see also Dunbabin 1962, pl. 191, B13 (for the shape), B14 and B17 (centaurs).
3 Cf. Boardman 1963, 129–30, G11–12.
4 Boardman 1963, 115, A4; Boardman 2001a, 115, color pl. 1, and 133; and Coldstream 1977, 210, fig. 68.
5 See, e.g., Boardman 1963, 129–30, G11, 12, G14.
6 Boardman 1963, 120, C14; Brandt 1968, no. 101; Zazoff 1969, 184–87. See this volume, cat. no. 14, n. 7.

# Fragmentary Diadem with Centaurs, Dancers, and Boxers

Greek, possibly Euboian, Late Geometric, ca. 725 – 700 B.C.
Gold
Band A: height 2.8 cm., width 9.6 cm.
Band B: height 4.0 cm., width 10.1 cm.
Band C: height 2.8 cm., width 9.6 cm.
Sol and Colleen Rabin Collection

CONDITION
The diadem is in three pieces, each with torn edges and consequent loss of some design elements. Many fold lines remain after modest attempts to return the fragments to flat, legible condition.

The three bands (A–C) have numerous wrinkles and pleats that make the embossed design difficult to read in places. The thin, hammered gold is embossed with sixteen figures, most in a single frieze framed by horizontal lines. The central position of B is established by the remains of a second figured zone above the first, its sloping sides once having formed a rounded tongue. Despite their ragged ends, the two lateral bands are identical in size. Band A has a single string hole at either end; similar holes are preserved at the right end of C and the left end of B. The placement of these holes and the parity of dimen-

sions suggest that the three bands may have been made separately and were only united by attachment to a cloth backing. The original placement of A and C is uncertain; the arrangement here is conjectural.

Gold bands of this type, while rare, are well known from eighth-century cremation burials, mostly in Attica but also in Euboia, Crete, and Rhodes.[1] Although rich in appearance, they actually are thrifty offerings, being very thin and light. Dieter Ohly suggested that some may have served as chin-bands for the deceased,[2] but most probably they were worn as diadems. The figures were worked over a matrix, most likely of bronze.[3] This allowed for repetition of ornament and of individual figures and scenes, although that is not the case with this example. Some diadems show traces of a second frieze, proving that the band was cut from a larger sheet made for another purpose, most likely the sheathing of a box.[4]

Associated grave goods, particularly painted pottery, help date the majority of figured gold diadems from Attica to the Late Geometric period (ca. 750 – 700 B.C.). Earlier examples from the end of the Middle Geometric, about 760, feature animal imagery strongly suggestive of Near Eastern influence.[5] These continued well into the Late Geometric, but by the 730s new themes emerged: human scenes full of spirited movement — horsemen, athletes, dancers, warriors, women carrying jugs — as well as centaurs.[6] These subjects are familiar from Late Geometric pottery. Diadems from graves at Eretria, in Euboia, have similar figural scenes but differ from their Attic counter-

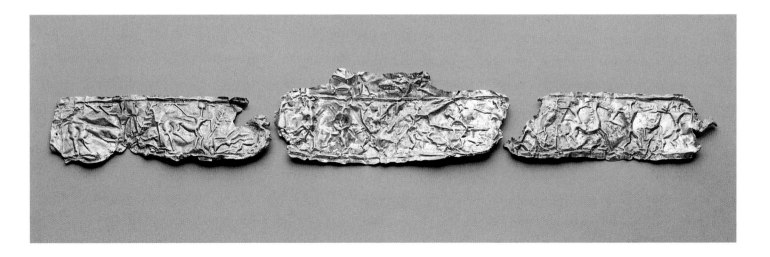

parts in having a central tongue that rested against the forehead.[7] This diadem has such a tongue, but the figure style seems closer to that of Attica. The dearth of any form of subsidiary ornament is unusual in diadems of either region. The origin of the diadem therefore remains uncertain.

All the figures on this diadem appear to be male. They are rendered in accordance with Late Geometric conventions: triangular torsos; round, featureless heads with slight projections indicating chins or beards; thin, angular arms but legs having a degree of volume. On band *A*, two centaurs with human forelegs advance to the right, each holding a pair of branches, one swung back in the right hand and the other held forward in the left.[8] They battle with their human enemies, two of whom lie fallen at the right. The first victim is stretched full length while the second is apparently falling, his right leg extended and his left leg bent beneath him; the string hole in his torso shows that his upper body was cut off at this point by the goldsmith.

The two distinct scenes in the lower frieze of band *B* are separated by a vertical line. At the left are three warriors carrying curvaceous "Dipylon" shields that conceal their torsos. Each warrior holds a pair of spears and wears a crested helmet. The first and third warriors walk to the right, but the central one moves to the left, his right leg kicked so high that one feels he must be dancing. A similar animation characterizes the three unarmed figures in the

scene at the right. Here again, the first and third figures advance to the right while the central one goes left; his pose is even more agitated, bending far forward, with one arm flung above his head. The warriors may be performing a "pyrrhic" war dance, beside which the goldsmith chose to place less warlike dancers from a different matrix.[9] On diadems in Copenhagen and Athens, unarmed dancers, one of whom holds a branch, are shown next to a branch-wielding centaur, but the latter faces away from the dancers and seems unconnected to them.[10]

The remains of the second, upper frieze on *B* preserve only the legs of two figures and a pair of plump fish, common intruders in Geometric figural scenes. At the left end of band *C*, another fish seems to swim through the air behind a mounted spearman, who rides to the right, holding his spear high in his right hand and clutching the horse's spiky mane with his left. Like the centaurs on *A*, the horse's anatomy is rendered schematically but with a certain volumetric naturalism. The spearman gallops toward a pair of boxers who square off over a bronze tripod, the prize for the victor. The combination of fish and horseman is a common one in pottery and incised metalwork of this period,[11] and it seems unlikely that they are connected with the boxers in any narrative sense. Mounted spearmen appear on other gold funerary bands, as do warriors, dancers, centaurs, and fish. There are a few examples in Geometric art of a pair of helmeted warriors fighting over a tripod, inevitably identified as Herakles and Apollo dueling for the Delphic tripod.[12] The bareheaded combatants on the diadem, however, ignore the tripod, which is relegated to the background, and their postures leave little doubt that they are pugilists.[13]

The centauromachy on band *A* is unique in Geometric art, with the centaurs victorious over their human antagonists. In most later centauromachies, centaurs are only shown as winners when they overcome the Lapith warrior Kaineus (see cat. nos. 27, 28). The fallen figures on this diadem, however, are not driven into the ground, and the two branch-wielding centaurs are essentially stock types. We cannot know if the artist had some narrative in mind or if he simply wanted to emphasize the dangerous violence of the centaurs by repeating a formula. Ohly argued that the deadly combats among warriors and horsemen on the diadems, sometimes interspersed with centaurs, lions, or sphinxes, reflected their exclusively funerary usage,[14] and a similar reading could be imposed on the imagery of this diadem. On one end, overmatched humans are defeated by the preternaturally powerful centaurs, while at the opposite end two men are competing in controlled, nonlethal combat, the two poles united by the central scenes of communal cultic activity in the form of dance.

—JMP

### BIBLIOGRAPHY

Hecht 1995, 9.

### NOTES

1 Reichel 1942; Cook 1951; Ohly 1953; Schweitzer 1971, 186–200; Coldstream 1977, 60–61, 123–25, 198; Sapouna-Sakellaraki 1997. The earliest Attic examples, with simple zigzag ornament, are from Middle Geometric I graves, ca. 850–830 (Coldstream 1977, 60–61). Contemporary diadems from Lefkandi (Euboia) and Knossos (Crete) are more Orientalizing in style (Coldstream 1977, 64, 100–101).

2 Ohly 1953, 69–70.

3 Coldstream 1977, 123. Ohly (1953, 14–15) believed the matrices were of stone. For some bronze matrices of later date, see Stuart Jones 1896; Williams 1984–85.

4 For a fragment of a gold sheet with multiple bands, from Eleusis, see Ohly 1953, pl. 3; Schweitzer 1971, pl. 229.

5 Ohly's Groups I–II (Ohly 1953, 15–33, pls. 1–8); see also Schweitzer 1971, 186–87, pls. 222–23; Coldstream 1977, 123, fig. 38a–c.

6 Ohly's Groups III–IV (Ohly 1953, 33–46, pls. 9–12); see also Schweitzer 1971, 187–88, pl. 224; Coldstream 1977, 123–24, fig. 38d.

7 Ohly 1953, 46–52, pls. 13–14; Coldstream 1977, 199, fig. 64.

8 This manner of holding two branches is common among centaurs in Attic Geometric vase-painting: e.g., Paris, Louvre CA 3256 (Boardman 1998, 45, fig. 70); Baghdad IM 52041 (Coldstream 1977, 118, fig. 36b). Cf. also the lead seal in Princeton (cat. no. 16).

9 For pyrrhic dances, see Poursat 1968.

10 Athens, Nat. Mus., formerly Stathatou Collection; Copenhagen, Nat. Mus. 741: see Cook 1951, pl. 10; ohly 1953, 35, figs. 19, 40–42, nos. A20, A20A, Beilage S.40, pls. 10.1, 12.4; Schweitzer 1971, 187, fig. 107; Schiffler 1976, 265, cat. A-S3, A-S4; Coldstream 1977, 123, fig. 38d. Dancers, horsemen, and centaurs are again combined in the two friezes of a gold band in Berlin (GI 310): Baur 1912, 5–6, no. 5, fig. 3; Ohly 1953, 35, fig. 20; Schiffler 1976, 265, cat. A-S2.

11 For fish and horses, see Langdon 1989.

12 Best known is a fragmentary bronze tripod handle from Olympia with two helmeted warriors, each holding one leg of a tripod: Olympia B 1730; Ohly 1953, pl. 28.2; Schweitzer 1971, pl. 213; Coldstream 1977, 336, fig. 108b; Ahlberg-Cornell 1992, 279, fig. 28. Ahlberg-Cornell (p. 26) is among those who prefer to interpret the scene as a boxing match, but the helmets make this unlikely.

13 See n. 10 above. Schweitzer (1971, 188) identifies two pairs of figures on the Copenhagen diadem as wrestlers or boxers, but the boxers contending for a tripod on this diadem are unparalleled. The subject appears on a handful of Geometric vases: e.g., a fragment in the Sarajevo Museum (Ahlberg-Cornell 1992, 279, fig. 29). On a Geometric kantharos in Copenhagen (Nat. Mus. 727: Ohly 1953, pl. 18), boxers are shown fighting next to a pair of warriors similar to those on the diadem; they, too, may be dancing a pyrrhic. The combination of boxers and tripod appears later on a seventh-century bronze matrix in Oxford (G 437: Stuart Jones 1896; Williams 1984–85, 26, figs. 8a, 9a), on archaic bronze shield-band reliefs from Olympia (Kunze 1950, pl. 14, IIIa; pl. 66, XLIIb), and on Attic black-figure vases, e.g., Rome, Vatican, Astarita 27: Poliakoff 1987, fig. 90.

14 Ohly 1953, 75–82.

# 18

# Pair of Plaques with Centaurs

Greek, Rhodian, from Kameiros, ca. 645–635 B.C.
Electrum
Plaque 99.386: height 6.3 cm., width 3.4 cm.
Plaque 99.388: height 5.8 cm., width 3.4 cm.
Museum of Fine Arts, Boston, Henry Lillie Pierce Fund
(99.386, 99.388)

CONDITION
Both plaques are substantially intact, with some
losses. On plaque 99.386, the upper left corner, much
of the tab and its attached rosette, and two of the
suspended spheres at the bottom are missing. On
plaque 99.388, the lower left corner, part of the tab
and its attached rosette, and all five suspended
spheres are missing.

One of two techniques was used in the fabrication of
these rectangular plaques, found at Kameiros, on Rhodes.
Each plaque is made of electrum, a natural alloy of
gold and silver, worked into a thin sheet and then either
pressed into a mold or carefully hammered onto a core
sculpted in relief.[1] Additional ornamentation, seen in the
multiple borders and raised bosses, was worked into the
metal sheet from the back, apparently with stamps.

The two plaques were made from the same mold or
core. Each features a centaur with a fully human body that
is modeled as if independent of the rest of the creature,
comprising the hindquarters of a horse. The human part
resembles a beardless kouros wearing a belt composed of
two rings, an attribute with heroic associations.[2] His torso
and head are shown frontally, while the rest of his body,
both human and horse, is in profile to the left.[3] His right
arm is raised to his chest, and in his left hand he clutches
a small animal, probably a fawn, by the neck.[4]

Both plaques are perforated along the bottom for the
attachment of small spheres suspended from single links:
three are preserved on plaque 99.386 and may represent
pomegranates. There are two additional perforations of
uncertain function at the left and right sides of each
plaque. A double beaded border surrounds each plaque,
while at the bottom, each has an additional register of

circular bosses, and at the top, a register of vertical
indentations. Two rosettes, the bottom one slightly larger,
occupy the area near the upper right corner. The plaques
possibly were affixed to a woman's garment by means
of the hooked tab at the top; the perforations in these
tabs may have accommodated rivets used to attach an
electrum rosette.[5]

Plaques of this type were made in Rhodes in the
period about 660–620 B.C. The frontal-facing human
heads are executed in the Daedalic style, with triangular
faces framed by wiglike tresses with stacked horizontal
lines. Examples may be dated according to the sequence
Early, Middle, and Late Daedalic;[6] this pair probably
dates about 645–635 B.C. and accordingly are Middle
Daedalic. There are fifteen known examples that feature
centaurs.[7] Other subjects include a winged Artemis as
"Mistress of Animals" (*Potnia Theron*), who commonly
holds lions at her sides; a winged bee-woman; a sphinx;
a griffin; as well as others.[8] Indeed, Rhodian electrum
plaques present a menagerie of composite creatures of
Near Eastern origin with human and animal features, many
of which became increasingly popular in Greek art. On
the Boston plaques, the centaur has subdued a fawn, a
demonstration of authority over the natural world that
may be thematically related to the image of the *Potnia
Theron*, but that probably was not as imbued with divinity.
—MB

BIBLIOGRAPHY
Chase and Vermeule 1963, 45, fig. 39 (99.386); Laffineur 1978, 3, 11,
13–14, 16, 22, 26, 29–30, 81, 166, 194–95, nos. 13 and 15, pl. IV;
Laffineur 1980, 18, 28, fig. 5; *LIMC* 8 (1997), 681, no. 120, s.v. "Kentauroi
et Kentaurides" (Leventopoulou et al.).

NOTES
1 See Laffineur 1980, 18–19.
2 See Bennett 1997. For belted figures in archaic Greek art, see Guralnick
1989, 173–74; Bennett 1999, 12–14.
3 For a list of plaques with this motif, see Laffineur 1978, 22.
4 Laffineur 1978, 22 n. 1.
5 Laffineur 1978, 14 n. 6. Compare with a plaque in the British Museum:
Marshall 1911, 88, no. 1115, pl. 11; see also Greifenhagen 1970, 29,
nos. 2–4, 6.
6 See Jenkins 1936, 89–91; Higgins 1980, 115–17.
7 Laffineur 1978, 22.
8 Laffineur 1978, 15–26.

## 19

## Statuette of a Centaur
## Holding a Quadruped

**Cypriote, ca. 600 b.c.**
**Hand-modeled terracotta**
**Height 15.2 cm., length 11.2 cm., width 7.0 cm.**
**Strahlendorff-Plechner Collection**

CONDITION
**The handmade, solid figure is well preserved, with only slight loss of the painted slip on its proper right side.**

The centaur is fully human in front, including the front legs and feet. He has a prominent black beard and ski-jump nose. The hair is modeled separately and resembles a cap, except it covers the back of the neck. The ears are small lumps of clay, also added. The centaur clasps in its proper right arm a small quadruped with long ears. The eye of the animal is indicated as a circle and central dot in black slip; there are traces of red on its ears and neck. On the centaur, black slip is used to outline the exterior surface of the legs with horizontal lines that connect the vertical lines in groups of three black and three red. In front, the verticals and horizontals end near the putative waist; at the back they pass over the rump in a continuous pattern from one side to the other. The interior surfaces of the front legs are covered with four horizontal black lines; the interior of the rear legs is unpainted. Black is used for the eye, eyebrow, and beard of the centaur, and alternating groups of black and red lines encircle the arms and suggest the fingers on both hands. The tail, curled back on the proper right haunch, was solid black but is now much worn. Patches of red cover the groin and the back of the torso.

The date of the centaur is difficult to determine with any precision, but the human front legs suggest influence from Greece in the seventh century b.c.[1] Bearded centaurs from Cyprus are not rare and occur in both the seventh and sixth centuries.[2] A centaur carrying a small animal in its arms is infrequent. The type may derive from Assyria. An example, preserved only in a drawing,[3] is known from Layard's excavations at Nineveh, where a monumental lion-centaur guarding a doorway holds a stag or goat in its right arm up against its chest. Three other Cypriote examples

are known to me: the earliest, possibly of the eighth century, from Kourion, is now in Paris;[4] another, from Ayia Irini, is in Stockholm;[5] and the third, the latest, probably of the late sixth century, is in London.[6] All three hold the animal they carry with the left instead of the right arm. On the basis of the painted decoration, the centaur under discussion here probably should be dated close to 600 b.c.

The general sense of the centaur as a creature of the wild and as a protective spirit may explain why he carries a small animal in his arms, but it is unclear whether there are other reasons. Certainly the function of the figure at Nineveh was to guard the passageway against the incursion of evil forces. The very protective gesture of the Cypriote centaur's proper left arm suggests a related interpretation, even though he seems to be stroking his beard. A comparison of this centaur with the Princeton

Cypriote centaur (cat. no. 20), a figure with upraised arms that is interpreted as a companion of the gods, suggests a possible connection with centaurs that gently carry animals in their arms. Both earlier Assyrian (cat. no. 12) and later Greek centaurs, however, often carry dead animals, sometimes hanging from a stick, which indicates that they are hunters. In such cases, the centaur holds up an animal as if it were prey. By contrast, Cypriote centaurs cradle the animal they carry, and this is very different from the gesture of a hunter. Thus, the meaning remains uncertain.
— WAPC

**BIBLIOGRAPHY**

Sotheby's, London, July 10, 1990, lot 307; Karageorghis 1996, 7, no. A17, pl. V.5.

**NOTES**

1   Centaurs with human front legs appear in the earliest Attic Geometric representations of the late eighth century and continue into the early sixth century: *LIMC* 8 (1997), 674, nos. 3 and 6, pl. 416; 682, no. 132, pl. 422; 683, pl. 423, no. 137, etc., s.v. "Kentauroi et Kentaurides" (Leventopoulou et al.). For Cypriote centaurs with human front legs, see Karageorghis 1996, nos. A9 and A10, both from Ayia Irini; a third from the same site is illustrated on p. 6, fig. 3. They are dated from the late seventh century into the first half of the sixth century B.C. (p. 5).

2   Karageorghis 1996, 16–22, nos. A9, A10,

3   Layard 1849–53, vol. 1, 5, pl. 42: Nimrud, Room B, entrance d on plan 3, pl. 100.

4   Paris, Louvre CA 2139: Caubet, Hermary, and Karageorghis 1992, 94–95, no. 105; Karageorghis 1996, 2, no. A1, pl. I.1 (dated early eighth century); Caubet, Fourrier, and Queyrel 1998, 151–52, no. 199 (dated late eighth to early seventh century, i.e., Cypro-Geometric III–Cypro-Archaic I).

5   Stockholm no. 2340, 2328, and 2373: Karageorghis 1996, 5, no. A7, pl. III.1.

6   London, Brit. Mus. A 227: Bailey and Hockey 2001, 126, no. 21, fig. 9.25 (dated to the late sixth century: p. 113); *LIMC* 8, 681, no. 117, pl. 421, s.v. "Kentauroi et Kentaurides." Cf. the hostile attitude of Greek centaurs to other animals: *LIMC* 8, 681, nos. 111–15, 120.

# 20

# Statuette of a Centaur

**Cypriote, seventh century B.C.**
**Terracotta**
**Height 9.51 cm., length 8.45 cm., maximum width (arms) 5.0 cm.**
**Princeton University Art Museum, Fowler McCormick, Class of 1921, Fund (2002–279)**

**CONDITION**
**The handmade, solid clay figure is unbroken and in an excellent state of preservation, with most of the original bichrome (red and black) slip preserved.**

The centaur stands with all four hooves on the ground and raises its two arms forward to about neck height. The figure has two small breasts, which might indicate that it is female, but the type is quite common on Cyprus, some examples of which have male genitalia.[1] One example, however, has long hair falling on its shoulders and is elaborately garbed and painted, as though the sculptor wished to portray a female centaur.[2] A famous female centaur on a Cycladic relief-pithos, now in Paris, was used to depict the Gorgon Medusa (see this volume,

Tsiafakis, "ΠΕΛΩΡΑ," fig. 13), but otherwise the type is unknown in Greece.[3]

Black is used to outline the eyes, which are small dots of clay, and perhaps to represent the mouth (the trace is faint). Black also delineates all four legs with horizontal lines joining the verticals. A box shape outlined in black and filled with red is best preserved on the left rear leg. Six black lines cross the animal's back and end on its sides. Red is used along the neck up to the head, across the shoulders and the tops of the arms, the front of the forelegs to mid-chest, and the back of the hind legs up to the point of the tail.

The animal component of this centaur is not certain. Cypriote centaurs have a strong affinity to a cow or bull;[4] this connection may be suggested by the broad legs of the present figure that have nothing horselike about them. A comparison with the Cypriote horse and rider statuette in Princeton (cat. no. 48) confirms this observation. The curious forward curve of the tail with a furrow in the middle of its rear plane is known from a terracotta figurine of a goat of a much later date.[5] Given the simple forms of the creature, it seems wise to refrain from identifying its quadruped element. The upraised arms suggest comparison with votive figurines of people in the same pose. Since centaurs appear quite regularly in Cypriote sanctuaries, it has been suggested that they

are attendants to the divinity worshiped, a relationship suggested by the upraised arms.[6] In this case, Cypriote centaurs would be closely related to the various Oriental composite creatures, many of whom were divine servants.[7]

This centaur has a distinctive, sharply sloping facial surface, which in frontal view is roughly triangular in form with broad curved ends.[8] These characteristics indicate a date no later than the seventh century. Comparison can be made with heads of the Cypro-Geometric period[9] and particularly the Cypro-Archaic I period as embodied in small figurines of men holding shields.[10]

— WAPC

**BIBLIOGRAPHY**

Unpublished.

**NOTES**

1 Karageorghis 1996, pls. II–IV. See also Padgett 1995, 401 n. 10.

2 Karageorghis 1996, 2, 8–9, A23, pl. VI.4.

3 Schefold 1966, 32, pl. 15b; Ahlberg-Cornell 1992, 113, no. 115, fig. 198.

4 Karageorghis 1966.

5 Karageorghis 1996, 37, cat. no. K11, pl. XXI.8 (Amathous tomb 204, dated Cypro-Archaic II–Cypro-Classical I).

6 Karageorghis 1966, 164–66.

7 See Childs, "The Human Animal," fig. 4 and accompanying text, in this volume.

8 The configuration is very old and tenacious on Cyprus. Cf. Karageorghis 1993a, 32, cat. no. L12, pl. XIX.4, dated to the Late Bronze Age.

9 Karageorghis 1993a, pl. XXVII.7. Cf., e.g., a figurine in New York (Met. Mus. 74.51.1609: Karageorghis, Mertens, and Rose 2000, 141, cat. no. 212 [Cypro-Geometric II/III]).

10 Karageorghis 1995, pls. XII–XIII.

## 21

### Statuette of a Centaur

**Greek, Boiotian, end of the seventh century B.C.**
**Said to be from Schimatari (Tanagra)**
**Terracotta**
**Height 11.9 cm., length 8.4 cm., width 6.9 cm.**
**Museum of Art and Archaeology, University of**
**Missouri-Columbia (58.20)**

#### CONDITION

The pinkish buff clay (Munsell 5YR 7/4) contains lime particles. The figurine is solid and handmade. The tail, beard, chin, and thumbs are broken away. There are chips in both hands and small chips in the chest and right side of the head. The slip is worn on both arms. There are traces of pale incrustation.[1]

This centaur has human forelegs and genitals. The handmade figure is very simply modeled. The limbs, both horse and human, are little more than tapering cylinders, but the human feet are clearly indicated. The centaur raises both arms in an emphatic gesture, the palms held vertically and facing the sides of the head. The thick, rounded nose melds into the oval head, which has an even simpler appearance than intended, since the beard and chin have been broken away. Traces of black slip on the head and neck suggest an attempt to differentiate the hair and beard from the rest of the centaur's human anatomy, which otherwise is painted with dark, orange-brown slip. The latter extends back to a darker, almost black stripe around the barrel of the "horse"; beyond this, the hindquarters are reserved in the lighter color of the clay. There are horizontal stripes down the backs of both hind legs, giving the rear view quite a different appearance from the front.

Excluding those from Cyprus (e.g., cat. nos. 19, 20) and the precocious Protogeometric centaur from Lefkandi, in Euboia (see this volume, Padgett, "Horse Men," fig. 3), fewer than a score of Geometric and Archaic Greek terracotta centaurs are known. Examples from the eighth and early seventh centuries are rare and come from Athens and the Peloponnese.[2] Centaurs like the one in Missouri are somewhat later in date and have been recognized as Boiotian, despite a paucity of excavated examples.

Miklós Szabó included the Missouri figurine in his "Centaur Workshop," which he dated to the second half of the seventh century on the basis of similarities of technique, form, and painted decoration with the class of Boiotian terracotta chariot teams and the fact that centaurs of this type are not found in the same sixth-century graves as the more numerous class of Boiotian terracotta horsemen (e.g., cat. no. 49).[3] Although he did include some earlier horsemen in his Centaur Workshop, Szabó called the Missouri centaur a "hybrid" because the stripes on its hind legs also occur on horses.[4] One centaur produced in that workshop is not a single figure but instead is shown in combat with a human hero,[5] like the famous bronze group from Olympia in the Metropolitan Museum of Art (cat. no. 13). Other centaurs from this group raise their arms in the same manner as the one in Missouri.[6] Beginning in Geometric times, most painted and bronze centaurs were represented carrying a branch or sapling, but such an accoutrement apparently was considered too fragile for terracotta. These early Boiotian figurines are empty-handed, but later examples with molded heads, from the late sixth and fifth centuries, may carry an object or even another figure.[7]

The ponderous sincerity of this centaur and others like it is as appealing to us as it apparently was to the ancient Boiotians. As a grave offering, anything beyond the simplest details was considered superfluous to the purpose at hand, which was to accompany the dead and convey some quality or essence to the afterlife that we, at this remove, can only guess at. The connotations of wealth and status implicit in the offering of a clay horse and rider, like those found in many Archaic Boiotian tombs, are at best subliminal in a horse-man like this, and it may be only coincidental that the two types have not been found together in the same grave.

—JMP

#### BIBLIOGRAPHY

Szabó 1973, 4–5, no. 1, 6–7, figs. 3–4; Szabó 1994, 29, 31–32, fig. 15.

#### NOTES

1  I am indebted to Jeffrey Wilcox for information about the figure's condition and fabric.

2 *Geometric*: Munich 5236 (from Athens?): Schiffler 1976, 265, cat. A-S 1, pl. 5. Athens, 3rd Ephoria 2333: Schiffler 1976, 265, cat. A-S 6; Stavropoulos 1964, 58, pl. 55α; *LIMC* 8 (1997), 675, no. 21, s.v. "Kentauroi et Kentaurides" (Leventopoulou et al.). Olympia 853: *LIMC* 8, 675, no. 23; Kardara 1988, 115–16, pl. 34ε–στ'. *Early seventh-century*: Corinth Museum: Shear 1931, 425, fig. 2; Schiffler 1976, 271, cat. K-S 2; *LIMC* 8, 675, no. 24.

3 Szabó 1973, 3–14, figs. 1–6; Szabó 1994, 29–32, figs. 11, 14–15. "Similar types and technical features no longer occur among the finds of the Rhitsona cemetery at the beginning of the 6th century" (Szabó 1994, 32). To the five centaurs that Szabó included in his Centaur Workshop should be added at least three more examples: (1) Athens, Goulandris Museum, ΣΠ 34 (*LIMC* 8, 675, no. 22, pl. 417, s.v. "Kentauroi et Kentaurides" [Leventopoulou dates it to the first half of the seventh century, but it belongs with those of the second half]); (2) Zürich, der Archäologischen Sammlung der Universität 4312 (Peege 1997, 29, no. 3, and cover); (3) once art market, Galerie Günter Puhze, Katalog 6, *Kunst der Antike* [Freiburg 1985], no. 136.

4 Szabó 1973, 13.

5 Athens, Nat. Mus. 12504: Kunze 1930, 44–45, pls. 38.2, 39; Szabó 1973, 5, 8, 10–11, figs. 5–6; Schiffler 1976, 277, cat. B-S 2; Szabó 1994, fig. 11; *LIMC* 8, 682, no. 133, pl. 422, s.v. "Kentauroi et Kentaurides."

6 Although centaurs in black-figure vase-painting may raise both hands when hurling stones (e.g., Würzburg L 405: *ABV* 190.18; *LIMC* 8, no. 114, pl. 421, s.v. "Kentauroi et Kentaurides"), or raise one hand and lower the other while running (e.g., Athens, Kerameikos 658: *ABV* 3; *Paralipomena* 1; *BAdd*[2] 1), the raising of empty hands is otherwise uncommon among centaurs; cf. those on a seventh-century seal in Munich (Münzsammlung A 1312: *LIMC* 8, no. 45, pl. 418,) and on an eighth-century Cypriote White Painted III oinochoe in Nicosia (Cyprus Museum 1985/X-19/1: Karageorghis 1986, 51–52, pl. X.5). The gesture is well known among handmade Archaic votive figurines from Greece and Cyprus and is customarily explained as an expression of worship or awe (for examples of the "goddess with uplifted arms" from the Princeton excavations at Marion [Polis], Cyprus, see Serwint 1991, pl. LVId–e). Since centaurs are not noted for their piety, it seems more likely that the action of the terracotta centaurs is self-referential: "Here I am!"

7 E.g., Athens, Nat. Mus. 1820 (Winter 1903, I 36, fig. 2; Schiffler 1976, 278, cat. B-S 12), which holds a child, suggesting an identification with Cheiron. For later Boiotian terracotta centaurs with molded faces, see Szabó 1973, 13 n. 26; Schiffler 1976, 277–78, cat. B-S 9–13, pl. 8; Szabó 1994, 80, figs. 82–83; Schmidt 1994, 42, no. 35, pl. 10.

## 22

# Statuette of a Centaur (Cheiron?)

**East Greek, late sixth century B.C.**
**Bronze**
**Height 6.02 cm., width 2.98 cm., length 7.12 cm.**
**Collection of Shelby White and Leon Levy**

**CONDITION**
**The statuette is complete and has a dark, shiny green patina.**

This charming centaur, with his right arm extended forward, his left arm bent and placed on the side of his equine body, seems to be in the act of greeting. Given the full body of a human with the hindquarters of a horse attached to his back, he stands facing straight ahead with his two human feet placed firmly on the ground, his right rear leg extended slightly forward. He is bearded and has lightly impressed circles for eyes and pupils and a short, irregular incision for a mouth. The modeling of the figure is broad with simple planes. His spade-shaped beard is not differentiated from his checks, and his large nose

appears to become part of his forehead. Both hands are simple masses without any attempt to render fingers. Long and tubular in shape, his equine body ends with a thick tail that extends almost to the ground. To make all four feet, human and equine, the wax of the model was simply pinched forward. A round lump at the lower part of his torso represents his penis.

The centaur belongs to a large group of Archaic bronze statuettes that were most likely manufactured in the East Greek world. The core of this group, most of which is now in the British Museum, was published by D. E. L. Haynes and includes mythological creatures such as mermen, sirens, sphinxes, and other centaurs, and figures such as ploughmen, fighting men and women, and various types of animals.[1] Some of the shared stylistic traits include the rough modeling of the surface, the spade-shaped beards and large noses of the male figures, and the pinched feet. Based upon a nineteenth-century catalogue containing descriptions of some of the bronzes, Haynes argued that the group was most likely found in Çesme, a city on Aegean coast of Turkey.[2] Their small size, subject matter, and freestanding nature suggest that they may have functioned as votive offerings.[3]

The centaur's lack of attributes makes an individual identification difficult to determine. What should not go unnoticed, however, is the gesture of the right hand. The same positioning of the arm can be seen in another statuette of a centaur from the Haynes group.[4] Both stand in quiet, static poses, as if waiting for or greeting someone. When compared with the New York Morgan centaur, another Archaic bronze (cat. no. 26), the amicable quality of the Haynes statuettes becomes even clearer.[5] The Morgan centaur, who once held a branch above his head, charges aggressively forward toward an unknown opponent. In sharp contrast, these East Greek centaurs are presented as friendly and welcoming creatures, not hostile aggressors.

From Greek mythology, we learn of two friendly centaurs: Pholos, the leader of a tribe of centaurs inhabiting Mount Pholoë in Arcadia (see cat. no. 29), and Cheiron, the tutor of the young Achilles. During this period, Pholos is normally represented with the torso of a human attached to the body of a horse, while Cheiron, at least until the Classical period, has the full body of a human with an equine body extending from his back, that is, in the same manner as the centaur in the exhibition.[6] As Madeleine Gisler-Huwiler has pointed out, Cheiron is also most frequently depicted draped in a chiton, a hima-tion, or a combination of the two, and sometimes carries a branch.[7] There are, however, several exceptions to the rule. On a black-figure Siana cup dated to 560 B.C., for example, a nude Cheiron welcomes the young Achilles.[8] Moving quickly to the right toward Peleus, who is cradling Achilles in his arms, the centaur extends his left arm in a manner similar to that of the small bronze, whose gesture clearly symbolizes welcoming. A comparable scene can be found on another black-figure Siana cup dated to 550 B.C., where a nude Cheiron stands with his left arm lifted toward Achilles and Peleus, which again is meant to express this centaur's welcoming of his new pupil.[9]

The ambiguous nature of the statuette in the exhibition means that an identification of it as Cheiron must remain tentative. If the statuette is simply a generic representation of a centaur, then it may have been made as a reminder of the ambivalent nature of these beings, defined not only by their brutality, but also by their closeness to man.

—JYC

### BIBLIOGRAPHY

Mitten and Doeringer 1967, 74, no. 68; Schiffler 1976, 289, cat. O-S5; Bothmer 1990, 105, no. 86.

### NOTES

1 Haynes 1952, 74−79.

2 Haynes 1952, 78.

3 Based upon their subject matter, Haynes also suggested that they could have functioned as votive offerings to Cybele, whose cult was popular in Lydia during the Archaic period. Without more informa-tion about their find spot, however, their precise function must remain open to question. See Haynes 1952, 79.

4 London 1875.3-13.12 (height 7 cm., length 7.7 cm.): Haynes 1952, 75−76, pl. IId.

5 See Bothmer 1967, 221−22.

6 For Pholos, see *LIMC* 8 (1997), 706−10, nos. 348−67, pls. 456−67, s.v. "Kentauroi et Kentaurides" (Leventopoulou et al.); for Cheiron, see *LIMC* 3 (1986), 243−48, s.v. "Cheiron" (Gisler-Huwiler).

7 *LIMC* 3, 247−48, s.v. "Cheiron."

8 Palermo 1856: *ABV* 65.45; Beazley 1986, 48, pl. 43.3; *LIMC* 1 (1981), 46, no. 30, s.v. "Achilleus" (Kossatz-Deissmann).

9 Würzburg 452: *ABV* 63.6; Beazley 1986, 47−48, pl. 43.1−2; *LIMC* 1, 46, no. 35, s.v. "Achilleus."

## 23

# Statuette of a Centaur

**Greek, Laconian, ca. 540–530 B.C.**
**Found on the Athenian Acropolis in 1835; formerly in the Oppermann Collection**
**Bronze**
**Height 10.0 cm., length 9.5 cm.**
**Paris, Bibliothèque Nationale de France, Cabinet des Médailles (514)**

### CONDITION

**The figure is well preserved except for the left human foot, the lower hind legs of the horse part, and the tail, all of which are missing. The patina ranges from black to green.**

In a strong movement, the centaur strides to the right, the equine part in full profile, the human part turned toward the viewer in three-quarter view; the sense of tor-sion is intensified by the raising of the broad, bearded head. In his raised left hand the centaur holds a branch or club over his left shoulder, while his right arm rests on his horse flank. This last gesture constitutes the only con-vincing link in an otherwise very loose composition of parts, the human having its full size, the equine only half of it. The equine hind legs are meant to be galloping, since they stay close together, "giving a most unnatural effect, as though the inert equine body were being dragged along."[1] The muscles of the human legs and arms are well developed, and a powerful breast and broad shoulders emerge from the narrow waist. Already these features sug-gest a date well advanced in the third quarter of the sixth century B.C.[2] This dating is confirmed by the formal details of the head, which also may assist in attributing the work to a particular regional school.

The face is dominated by rather big, almond-shaped eyes, plastically accentuated eyelids and eyebrows, thick lips, and a prominent nose.[3] The hair above the fore-head is angled in the center and divided into short, parallel courses, as are the moustache and the beard. On top of the head the scaling of the hair continues, ending at the back in a long, straight, vertical mass. All the features of the head point to a Laconian (Spartan) origin for this centaur.[4]

This centaur has always been compared with a second bronze centaur from the Athenian Acropolis that, however, is of an earlier date (see Padgett, "Horse Men," fig. 6, this volume). This second centaur, a masterpiece of the Laconian style, has not attracted the attention it deserves.[5] It exhibits the same iconography as the centaur in Paris but is smaller (height 6.7 cm., length 6.5 cm.). The hind legs with the base and the tail are preserved. The earlier dating, in the second quarter of the sixth century, is based on the simpler, plainer modeling of both the human and animal parts.[6]

Both centaurs may have served as decorations on the shoulders of cauldrons (dinoi), together with others of their kind. Such groups can be interpreted as representing the centaurs that, according to the myth, assaulted Herakles on Mount Pholoë and were driven off by the hero's arrows.[7] Herakles and Pholos, together with other centaurs, are depicted on a Laconian clay dinos of about 545–535 B.C.[8] that is roughly contemporary with the centaur in the Bibliothèque Nationale. Pholos has a fully human body, unlike the other centaurs, who have four horse legs.[9] Of the two types, the four-legged was more satisfying from an artistic point of view because the human part is less isolated from the equine part. This type was popular in Athens (cf. the bronze centaur in Princeton, cat. no. 24), whereas the other was preferred in Sparta and Corinth.[10]

The two bronze centaurs from the Acropolis would remain rather isolated[11] if we could not compare them with some bronze silens/satyrs closely related in style and iconography.[12] This can be illustrated by a bronze satyr from Spain, now in the Louvre (see Padgett, "Horse Men," fig. 23).[13] Apart from such typical satyr features as the shape of the ears and the fact that a satyr would not brandish a club or branch as the centaurs often do, its general iconographic posture is much the same. Its original height of about 10.0 centimeters comes very near to that of the centaur in Paris. The general structure and musculature of the satyr's body also is similar: note the narrow hips and voluminous breast. The characteristic Laconian features of the satyr's head and hair, like the heavy eyelids, the incised eyebrows, the scaled pattern of the hair and beard, and the long mass of braids on the back, cannot be overlooked.[14] The relationship between centaurs and satyrs becomes all the more apparent if one looks at the development of the types in Attica, where bronze satyrs are equipped with horse tails, ears, and hoofs.[15]

—CMS

**BIBLIOGRAPHY**

Babelon and Blanchet 1895, 219, no. 514; Baur 1912, 98, no. 237; Babelon 1929, no. 29, pl. 22; Lamb 1929, 101, pl. 39a; Niemeyer 1964, 11, pl. 32a; Rolley 1969, 132; Schiffler 1976, 154, 320, cat. V 16; Herfort-Koch 1986, 61, 69, 121, no. K154.

**NOTES**

1 This is a somewhat exaggerated observation by Baur (1912, 98), originating from the fact that the lower hind legs are missing.

2  The flesh on the hips is clearly accentuated, as becomes the rule after
   550 B.C. The chest makes an outward, convex curve, instead of inward as
   in earlier times. The pubic hair has a slightly angular upper contour
   and is more or less detached from the groin; the design of the stomach
   is already more natural and less geometric than it was in the second
   quarter of the sixth century.

3  For this feature of Laconian bronzes, see Stibbe 1996, 356.

4  Attributions hitherto have been made rather haphazardly. The piece
   has been called Attic by Lamb (1929, 101) and Niemeyer (1964, 11)
   because of the find spot. That, however, is not a good argument
   ("Perhaps no sufficient proof"), as Niemeyer (1964, 10) himself has
   stated. In fact, there is a whole series of Laconian bronzes from the
   Athenian Acropolis: a list is published for the first time in Stibbe-Vasić
   2002, chapter 8, n. 8. That the piece could not be Attic anyway is stated
   by Schiffler (1976, 155). The first to recognize the Laconian origin (with
   good arguments) was Herfort-Koch (1986, no. K154).

5  Athens, Nat. Mus. 6680: see the bibliography in Herfort-Koch 1986,
   121, no. K155. Because of the find spot, this centaur has been called
   Attic by Lamb (1929, 101), Niemeyer (1964, 11), and Rolley (1969, 132),
   but has been rightly attributed to Laconia on stylistic grounds by
   Herfort-Koch. Niemeyer (1964, 11) erroneously calls it "a humble small
   work" ("ein bescheidenes Werkchen") and dates it (p. 30) about 525 B.C.

6  Cf. the bodies of the handle-kouroi in Stibbe 2000b, 27–34, Group A,
   dated 575–555 B.C.

7  Rolley 1983, 108. For the myth see LIMC 8 (1997), 672, s.v. "Kentauroi
   et Kentaurides" (Leventopoulou et al.).

8  Louvre E 662.

9  Pipili (1987, 7   10) treats the case extensively.

10 Schiffler 1976, 59–66 (Corinth) and 67–70 (Laconia).

11 A third example, with a fully human body attached to the body and
   hind legs of a horse, is in an American private collection (see Padgett,
   "Horse Men," fig. 8, this volume). This piece, of excellent quality, is
   well preserved, except for the club in the centaur's right hand, most of
   its right hind leg, and its tail, which are missing. Judging only from
   photographs, the hair and the features of the face seem to be Laconian.

12 The relationship has been noted before by Herfort-Koch 1986, 61; see
   also LIMC 8 (1997), 1108, s.v. "Silenoi" (Simon).

13 Paris, Louvre Br 133, from Llano de la Consolación (near Montealegre
   del Castillo, prov. Albacete); height 9.0 cm.; black-brown patina. See
   the bibliography in Herfort-Koch 1986, 121, no. K153. The Spanish
   provenance is important in relation to another satyr from Spain, which
   is presented here as a local imitation (see cat. no. 25, n. 4).

14 Cf. also a satyr from Laconia (Amyklaion): Herfort-Koch 1986, 120, no.
   K152; Pipili 1987, 68, 117, no. 189; and another satyr, from the acropolis
   of Sparta: Herfort-Koch 1986, 120, no. K151, pl. 21.9; Pipili 1987, 68–
   69, 117, no. 187, fig. 100, with further references.

15 LIMC 8, 1108–10, s.v. "Silenoi." On the differences between Laconian
   and Attic satyrs, see Pipili 1987, 65–68.

## 24

# Statuette of a Centaur

**Greek, Attic, ca. 530 B.C.**
**Bronze**
**Height 11.1 cm., length 11.9 cm., depth 3.9 cm.**
**Princeton University Art Museum, gift of Damon**
**Mezzacappa (1997–36)**

CONDITION

**The solid-cast centaur is well preserved except for
the lower legs, which are missing. A single hoof
survives (inv. 2002–383), but its association with
this centaur is uncertain; it does not join the broken
legs but is of the same scale and identical patina.
Also missing is the branch that the centaur probably
held over his right shoulder.[1] The tail is bent forward,
almost touching the left hind leg (the very tip is
missing). The nose is flattened, but the features are
otherwise unmarred. An indentation in the back
of the head may have served to accommodate a
structural element, like the upper end of the arched
support of a tripod.[2] The slight curvature of the
body and the absence of incision in the hair on the
back of the head point in the same direction.[3] In
several places, especially on the back, the dull green
patina is overlaid with hard brown incrustation.
The breaks of the legs also are encrusted.**

The centaur is represented walking vivaciously to the
right. His raised left elbow and left foreleg underline his
energetic movement. Both of the centaur's right legs are
pulled back, like a pacing horse. In contrast to the animal
part, the human upper body shows a torsional motion
to the creature's right, turning toward but not quite facing
the viewer. In spite of these contrasting elements, the
artist succeeded in creating a convincing composition,
thanks to the harmonious and balanced transition
between the bodies of the two parts, horse and man.
In both parts, the rendering of the flesh and muscles is
convincingly naturalistic and shows a mature level of
craftsmanship. Details like the equine genitals, the anus
(represented by a short distinct protrusion), and the
hair at the top of the tail, which is indicated by stacked

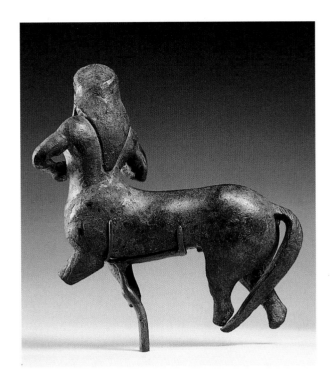

chevrons incised in the wax, are all finely worked. The nipples on the chest are not depicted, but the hair of the chest is represented by horizontal rows of short, chiseled strokes, cold-worked in the finished bronze: four rows on the right breast and five on the left, where they extend over the top of the shoulder. Since the chisel could not reach the chest beneath the beard, there is but a single row of strokes across the bottom. Clear traces of filing are visible on the forearms and the left elbow.

The centaur's human head offers a compendium of the characteristic features of this bronze worker's style. Large bulging eyes are framed by differently arched lids and eyebrows modeled in relief. The prominent nose, now flattened, has carefully detailed nostrils. The rather broad mouth has thick smiling lips that accentuate the high cheekbones and highlight the apparent absence of a moustache. The face as a whole seems almost egg-shaped, since it is framed by masses of hair carefully modeled in the round. The impressive beard runs from ear to ear in a half circle, as if it were artificial and unconnected with the flesh. This impression is strengthened by the gradated series of rather long, discrete strands, each scored in the wax with slanting parallel strokes. A row of parallel, hatched locks describes a semicircle above the forehead. In contrast, the hair over the shoulders, which falls behind the large flat ears, is divided into narrow horizontal bands of short

vertical strokes. The hair in the back is in the form of an elongated triangular mass, without incision or modeling.

Stylistically the centaur combines elements taken from different schools: the rendering of the eyes and eyebrows, for example, is characteristically Laconian,[4] while the broad, horizontally layered hair above the shoulders is a common Corinthian feature.[5] Other elements, however, like the powerful, accomplished modeling of the muscles and the harmonious composition of contrasting elements, point to a third production center: Athens.[6] In fact, the facial features of this centaur are encountered again on an earlier Attic monument, on the heads of a serpentine-bodied monster, the so-called Bluebeard, from a poros lime-stone pediment on the Athenian Acropolis, dated about 570 B.C.[7] A later head of Zeus from another pediment on the Acropolis has a face of the same shape combined with a beard featuring a similar series of long discrete strands.[8]

The attribution of the centaur to an Attic workshop is confirmed by its general iconography. In Attica, the harmonious, more organic solution of the problem of how to connect the two bodies of a horse and a man, as shown in this centaur, was adopted at an early date and maintained throughout the sixth century B.C.[9] In Corinth and Laconia, however, the more old-fashioned solution, which attaches the horse part at the back of a complete human figure, as in the bronze centaur in Paris (cat. no. 23) remained the preferred one.[10] Other iconographic elements, such as the extraordinarily long beard and the hair on the breast and shoulders, are more traditional features which indicate the wild nature of the centaurs. They are also found in other Greek production centers,[11] as is the tree or branch that should be imagined resting on the centaur's right shoulder.

Among the centaurs mentioned in ancient literature, only two, Cheiron and Pholos, are said to have a less wild, more friendly and human nature, the first being known as a player of music and the educator of heroes like Peleus and Achilles, and the second as the host of Herakles.[12] The Princeton centaur does not show any special identifying attribute, nor is there any reason to suppose that he would have been part of a group, as would likely be the case with Cheiron or Pholos. He therefore should be considered as an ordinary representative of his kind. In our

appreciation of this centaur as an artistic achievement, however, the small bronze occupies an exceptional place, for there is no other centaur of such high artistic quality known from the Archaic period.

The date of the centaur can be determined only through analysis of the stylistic elements of the two parts of its body.[13] As already stated above, they point to a mature stage of development within the Archaic period. The human part can be compared with, among others, the bronze statuette of a youth once in Berlin, dated about 520, which also has the same elongated triangular contour of the hair in the back.[14] The centaur's horse part has a predecessor in a well-known horse and rider from Dodona, now in the Louvre, in which the tail is bent forward in the same fashion.[15] A date between these two, about 530 B.C., should be appropriate for the Princeton centaur.

Finally, the centaur's smile. If this were an isolated phenomenon in the period to which we have assigned this masterpiece, it would throw an interesting light on the centaur's own character. Most centaurs are wild and ferocious creatures, and a friendly smile would suggest that he is instead one of the two "civilized" centaurs: Cheiron or Pholos. We have to consider, however, that a smile such as this is a common feature in Archaic Greek sculpture, found even on such horrifying monsters as Gorgons and gorgoneia. We therefore may explain the smile on the face

of this centaur as the expression of a general feeling or attitude that contrasts sharply with the nature of the average centaur. The conventional "Archaic smile" may thus be understood as the expression of a general feeling characteristic of the period: the feeling of being young and full of energy and beauty, which even today makes young people smile.

—CMS

**BIBLIOGRAPHY**

*Apollo* 146, no. 430 (Dec. 1997), 13 with illus.; *Record* 57.1–2 (1998) 194, 196 with illus.

**NOTES**

1 The right hand has a circular depression in the top. It probably held, according to the usual iconography of centaurs (see Schiffler 1976, 15), a branch or club, although it is not clear whether this was made separately or cast in one piece with the rest of the figure.

2 Cf. the positioning of the cows on the tripod from Metapontum, in Berlin, Fr. 768: Stibbe 2000b, 82, fig. 53.

3 Cf. the same treatment of the back hair on a bronze komast in Corfu: Dontas 1969, figs. 1–2.

4 E.g., see Herfort-Koch 1986, pl. 11, figs. 10–11, and pl. 13, figs. 1, 3.

5 E.g., see Wallenstein 1971, pls. 18.2, 19.4, 21.1, 22.2.

6 Niemeyer (1964, 11) defines the character of Attic art of the period with the following words: "that energetic, as it were challenging, active Attic manner" ("jene energische, gleichsam fordernde, tatbereite attische Art"), referring to Homann-Wedeking 1950, 89. Langlotz (1927, 73) had earlier characterized the "disengaged cheerfulness" ("freie Heiterkeit") and the "greater vivacity of life" ("grössere Regsamkeit des Lebens") as typically Attic.

7 Boardman 1967, 140–41, fig. 85; Knell 1990, 4–9, fig. 16; Ridgway 1993, 285–87, fig. 115.

8 Knell 1990, 4–9, fig. 15; Ridgway 1993, 288, 117.

9 Schiffler 1976, 15–58, 69.

10 Schiffler 1976, 59–66 (Corinth) and 67–70 (Laconia); Pipili 1987, 7–10.

11 Schiffler 1976, 15, 59, 61, 67, 70.

12 *LIMC* 8 (1997), 672, 706–10, s.v. "Pholos" (Leventopoulou); Schiffler 1976, 30–37 (Cheiron), 37–41 (Pholos).

13 The features of the face that point to an Attic origin, as shown above, do not contribute in the same way to the dating of the statuette.

14 Richter 1960, 128, 142–43, no. 175, figs. 515–17: early in the Ptoon 20 Group. Comparable also is the body of the bronze statuette of Zeus, ca. 530–520 B.C., in Munich (4339): Kopcke 1976, 7–28; Rolley 1983, 92; Mattusch 1988, 68–69; Thomas 1992, 69.

15 Wallenstein 1971, 145, no. 25, dated 570–560 B.C. or a little later.

# 25

# Statuette of a Centaur

Probably local Iberian, ca. 540–530 B.C.
From Rollos, near Caravaca, province of Murcia
Bronze
Height 11.2 cm., length 10.8 cm.
Madrid, Museo Arqueológico Nacional (18536)

CONDITION
The solid-cast figure is well preserved except for
the left arm, the tail, and the lower legs, which are
missing. The patina is dark green, almost black,
with brown patches.

This centaur walks quietly to the right, his left arm raised and extended and his left foreleg advanced. His complete human body is neatly separated from the equine part by the contour of the buttocks and by the rendering of the muscles, which are well developed. In contrast, the equine part is more meager, the muscles being indicated only by an almost abstract linear modeling. Moreover the equine body, which is disproportionately smaller than the human portion, is seen in profile while the human upper body is turned almost in full frontal view. The centaur's right arm touches his right flank; the missing left arm very likely was raised to hold a branch or small tree, the common weapon of these wild creatures.

As with the bronze centaur in Paris, from the Acropolis of Athens (cat. no. 23), the part of the figure that particularly lends itself to attribution to a specific regional school is the head. The features of this Spanish centaur are most peculiar. The big round head is framed by a sickle-shaped beard running from ear to ear and by a plain cap of hair offset above the forehead in an almost horizontal line. At the back, the hair is divided into two robust, coarsely scaled and tapering braids, one of which falls on the breast. The face is dominated by large eyes with heavy eyelids, a broad nose, and a mouth with thick lips. If one compares this centaur with the centaur in Paris, and with another Laconian example, also from the Acropolis (see Padgett, "Horse Men," fig. 6, this volume), it is evident that it follows the general iconography of these prototypes and, more particularly, that the musculature

of its human part resembles that of the centaur in Paris. Consequently the date of its production should not differ much from that of the Paris statuette: about 540–530 B.C. Much more problematic is the attribution, as is evident from the different opinions expressed by specialists so far.[1]

It has been thought an improvement over the centaur in Paris that this Spanish centaur shows "a correct attitude for a walking centaur."[2] This "improvement," however, is due to a difference in the iconography, since the Greek centaurs are galloping. We may speak instead, and more convincingly, of a remarkable difference in conception in this centaur, one that requires explanation.[3] In one sense, it is in line with the striking features of the head, which differ greatly from the Laconian prototypes. Some of these features recur on a bronze satyr, also from Spain, found at Capilla (Badajoz), which has the same artificial-looking beard and the same shape of the face, eyes, nose, and mouth.[4] In comparison with an imported Laconian satyr from Spain, now in the Louvre (Padgett, "Horse Men," fig. 26, this volume), which we have mentioned in relation to the centaur in Paris,[5] the satyr from Capilla has lost in spirit and vigor, and the dancing movement has been altered, possibly as an adaption to local requirements and habits. The underlying Greek model nonetheless can be recognized in details like the ear.

Because of the similarities of the satyr from Capilla and the centaur from Rollos, we may conclude that both are products of local Iberian workshops.[6] In this connection, it should be stressed that Iberian bronze workers were familiar with imported Greek prototypes, as shown by the Laconian satyr in the Louvre, which was found near Montealegre del Castillo, in the province of Albacete.[7]

Laconian and other Greek imports in southern Spain should be understood in the context of commercial contacts, not as the result of colonization; the only Greek colony in Spain, Ampurias (Emporion), on the northeast coast, was a sixth-century daughter foundation of the Greek colony Massalia (Marseille), in southern France. Greek pottery and other Greek products arrived in southern Spain from 700 B.C. onward, often through the mediation of Phoenician traders and trading posts such as Tartessos, in the bay of Cadiz.[8]
—CMS

**BIBLIOGRAPHY**

Hübner 1898, 121–22; Bauer 1912, 99, no. 239 (with older literature); Thouvenot 1927, no. 5, pl. 1; García y Bellido 1948, vol. 2, 87 no. 7, pl. 24; *Guiat de los Museos de Espana I, Museo Arqueológico Nacional* (Madrid 1954), fig. 11, pl. 109; Riis 1959, 44, no. 5B; Schiffler 1976, 154, 321, cat. V 17; Shefton 1982, 362; Olmos Romera 1983, 377–88; De Caro, Borriello, and Cassani 1993, 385–86 (illus. in color); Caratelli 1996, 756, no. 411; Rouillard 1996, 46–63, with color fig. on p. 51; Blech 2001, 614, pl. 210, with bibliog.

**NOTES**

1 The centaur has been interpreted as Ionic (Bauer 1912, 99); as Attic or Argive (García y Bellido 1948, 87); as possibly Campanian (Riis 1959, 44); and as Peloponnesian (Shefton 1982, 362).

2 Baur 1912, 99.

3 A bronze centaur in an American private collection (see Padgett, "Horse Men," fig. 8, this volume), apparently Greek, walks with the same quiet gait as the centaur from Spain. The latter, therefore, may well have followed a Greek, probably Laconian, prototype.

4 Madrid 71145/1: from Capilla, on the River Guadiana, province of Badajoz; height 11.0 cm. See Olmos Romera 1977; Olmos and Picazo 1979, 189, pl. 30a; Almagro-Gorbea 1977, 252–53; Shefton 1982, 363 n. 71.

5 See cat. no. 23, n. 13.

6 The existence of local Iberian bronze workshops in the sixth century B.C., operating in the southeast of the Iberian peninsula, is suggested by quite a few other statuettes, such as a bull with a human head from Balazote (Baur 1907, 187, fig. 6; Blech 2001, 619, pl. 216c). They often are attributed, erroneously in my opinion, to Greek, colonial Greek, and Etruscan workshops (see Rouillard 1991, 187–89; Blech 2001, 216, pl. 216c). Another interesting case is a well-preserved bronze oinochoe from Don Benito (prov. Badajoz), which shows two couchant lions, one on each side of a female protome, at the upper attachment of the handle (reproduced in color in De Caro, Borriello, and Cassani 1993, 505–6, no. 468). This is a most unusual composition for a Greek oinochoe (see Pelagatti and Stibbe 1999, passim), but it is conceivable in a local Iberian workshop (Blech 2001, 572, pl. 131, with bibliography).

7 See this volume, cat. no. 23, n. 13. Another instance of an import from Laconia into Spain is a bronze statuette of a girl in a peplos, dated about 540–530 B.C.: see Herfort-Koch 1986, 90, no. K38, with bibliography.

8 Boardman 1999, 213–18, 277. On the "Tartessian culture," see Blech 2001, 305–48.

# 26

# Statuette of a Centaur

Campanian, late sixth – early fifth centuries B.C.
Bronze
Height 11.3 cm., length 14.3 cm.
The Metropolitan Museum of Art, gift of J. Pierpont
Morgan, 1917 (17.190.2070)

CONDITION
The statuette is in good condition: only the tip of
the tail, the left ear, and most of the branch that the
centaur holds in his hands are missing. It is a solid
lost-wax casting with a dark green-black patina. An
original casting flaw is visible where bronze did not
fill the mold of the inner thigh of the left hind leg.

The centaur lunges forward with his arms raised over
his head; he holds a rounded object with both hands,
most likely a branch of a tree. His body inclines forward
slightly, with his forelegs planted as though he were
about to deal a blow. He has been described as galloping
but is more likely in the midst of lunging at an opponent,
as his muscular torso with its broad angular chest and
the large head are turned slightly to his right. Moreover,
the equine forelegs are on the "ground," not in the air
as is characteristic for the flying gallop in ancient Greek
art. The forelegs appear smaller than, and disproportion-
ate to, the hind legs, adding to the sense of forward
motion and placing a greater emphasis on the human
torso of the centaur, which appears even larger from the
front view. The tail is carefully rendered with four distinct pairs of thick stylized tresses of hair at the base that
flow into longer, carefully incised tail hair. Other features
of the centaur's hair are also stylistically distinct: the
spade-shaped beard (echoed in the line of the long hair
at the back of his head), a long pointed moustache, and
the artificial broad mass of hair that covers his forehead.[1]
The coiffure derives from a typical Archaic Greek hairstyle in which the hair is wrapped around a fillet; the
centaur's hair is gathered in the back at the nape of the
neck, but the fillet is not rendered. He has a small
mouth, broad nose, and almond-shaped eyes. Only the
right ear is carefully articulated. All four hooves are

firmly joined to the narrow base plate, which is flat but
has a slightly curved form.

It is most likely that the statuette was attached to a
vessel rim or lid because of the curved plinth. It could
have served as a handle or simply as a decorative element.
For many years this centaur was considered to be a Greek
work of the Ionian style.[2] However, it has been noted that
the practice of attaching figures in this way is not typical
of Greek manufacture but occurs on bronze vessels from
Campania, especially dinoi.[3] Stylistic considerations are
also suggestive of an Etruscan workshop in Campania,
where Greek, Etruscan, and Italic peoples were living in
close proximity to one another.[4] One imagines the centaur
as part of a group placed around the rim or lid of a large
vessel, perhaps at the front of a band of centaurs attacking
Herakles or another opponent.
—SAH

SELECTED BIBLIOGRAPHY
Sambon 1906a, pl. 1; Baur 1912, 71, fig. 12; Richter 1917, 64, 67,
fig. 35; Richter 1927, 76 ff., fig. 44; Richter 1937, no. 70; Richter 1953, 51
n. 20, pl. 36g; Bothmer 1967, 221–22; Schiffler 1976, 321, cat. V-18.

NOTES

1 This mass of hair was apparently affixed as a single strip of wax to the model.

2 Sambon 1906a, pl. 1; Baur 1912, 71.

3 Bothmer 1967, 221. On the technique of attaching the figures to the Campanian dinoi, see Formigli and Heilmeyer 1984, 405–7. The Campanian bronze dinoi, many of which been found at Capua, one of the most important Etruscan settlements in Campania during the Archaic period, were used as cinerary urns. In Archaic and Classical Greece, this type of vessel, also known as a lebes, was often used as an athletic prize together with the stand that supported it. For a discussion of the shape, see Richter 1935, 9–10.

4 For example, compare the similar treatment of hair on a Campanian bronze statuette in Mainz: Bossert-Radtke 1990, pl. 60. Bothmer (1967, 221) also saw Etruscan stylistic affinities with the Morgan centaur. On the Etruscans in Campania and their considerable bronze workshops, see Jovino 2000, 163–67.

# 27

# Black-Figure Siana Cup with the Death of Kaineus

Greek, Attic, ca. 560 B.C, attributed to the
Painter of Boston C.A.
Ceramic
Height 12.9 cm., diameter 26.2 cm.
J. Paul Getty Museum, Malibu, California (86.AE.154)

CONDITION
The cup has been reconstructed from numerous fragments with some modern fill. Added white slip is largely lost from the tripod device on Kaineus's shield (visible as a ghost), the baldrics of the warriors flanking him, the underbelly of the centaur on the left, the boulders held by the other centaur, the shield of the warrior on the right; and, on side B, the dog on the boar's back. Added red has partially flaked away from the boar's neck, hunter's tunic, and, on the interior, the horse's chest.

Siana cups (so called after a cemetery on Rhodes where two such cups were found in the late nineteenth century) were a popular form of kylix in early-sixth-century Athens.[1] Taller and wider than their Corinthian prototypes, their exteriors were painted either in "double-decker" fashion, with the lip and handle zone treated as two separate fields, or "overlapping," as here, with figures straddling both zones and a narrow horizontal line marking the division. Widely exported, they have come to light throughout Greece, in Italy, and in Egypt. Although many have been recovered from tombs, they also were employed at symposia, and their decoration reflects—indeed, projects and celebrates—the dominant cultural values of the men who drank from them.

The exterior of this cup is decorated with active, heroic scenes: a centauromachy (A) and a boar hunt (B); inside, an elaborate border surrounds a horseman. The focal point of the centauromachy is the Lapith hero Kaineus attacked by two shaggy-haired, fully equine centaurs. Kaineus is depicted from the thighs up, partially sunken into the earth. Wide-eyed, looking to the right, he drives his spear into the chest of a centaur wielding two

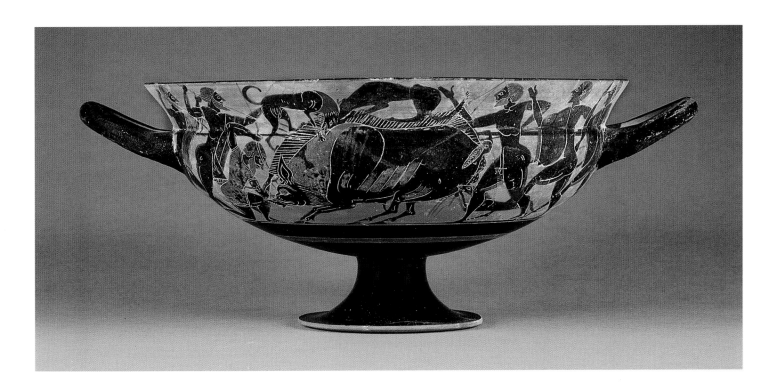

boulders, who bleeds profusely. In contrast to the brutish weapons of the centaurs, all of whom carry stones, Kaineus has full hoplite armor: high-crested Corinthian helmet, metallic breastplate with spirals, short tunic, shield (with tripod device), baldric, and sheathed sword. His long hair, typical of Archaic Greek heroes, falls forward over his right shoulder.

Lapith-centaur pairs flank the central three-figure group. On the left, a warrior carrying a Boiotian shield (seen from the interior) strides forward brandishing a spear as if to assist Kaineus. Behind him, a rearing centaur, whose body extends underneath the handle, holds a small rock in his lowered right hand and gestures emphatically with his left. On the right, a warrior armed with a spear and round shield (seen in profile) turns back to stab a rearing centaur, who prepares to hurl a rock. Overall, the violent composition is carefully balanced but nonetheless conveys the tumult of battle through emphatic gestures and vibrant color.

None of the figures is named, but Kaineus is readily identified by his half-sunken position, common not only on pots of various shapes — including the famous François Vase, where the combatants' names are inscribed — but also in metalwork, terracotta, and, later, on architectural sculpture. The earliest preserved example of the scene is on a seventh-century bronze plaque at Olympia, where the doomed hero wields two swords and no shield, as might be expected, for according to myth Kaineus was invulnerable. The centaurs could only defeat him by pounding him into the ground with stones and branches, burying him alive. Still, Kaineus is more often shown with a shield, as here, the earliest depiction of the myth on a black-figure cup. The heraldic composition with two flanking centaurs is also common, although Kaineus is sometimes depicted at an earlier stage of the conflict, standing, kneeling, or fallen, or later, further underneath the ground line, buried to his waist or chest.[2]

The myth of Kaineus is not fully told in surviving literature before Ovid's *Metamorphoses* (12.189–209). Homer and Hesiod both mention him as a companion of the Thessalian king Peirithoos, whose wedding was disrupted by drunken centaurs (*Il.* 1.264 and *Shield of Herakles* 179). According to a better-preserved fragment of the early-sixth-century B.C. *Catalogue of Women*, also traditionally ascribed to Hesiod (Fr. 87 MW), the hero was born as Kainis, daughter of the Lapith king Elatos. She caught the eye of Poseidon, who, after seducing her, offered to fulfill any wish. Apparently not wanting to repeat the experience, she asked to be a man. The god threw in invulnerability for good measure. Kaineus thus became a great warrior, joining the Argonauts and participating in the hunt of the Kalydonian boar. His/her story is also mentioned by Pindar, Apollonios, Virgil, and other authors, some of whom suggest that he later angered the gods by worshiping his spear.[3] There is, however, no overt reference to this in the visual tradition, nor to the hero's female origins before the early fourth century B.C. On this sixth-century Siana cup, Kaineus embodies the virtue of a steadfast warrior, to be emulated by viewers, although for those aware of his hubris, his demise might serve as a warning.

Nothing identifies any of the six men attacking the giant boar on the other side of the cup as Kaineus, though one stands out from the others: bearded, kneeling in a short tunic, with sheathed sword at his waist. He drives his trident into the boar's head, apparently stopping the forward movement of the menacing beast, to judge from the position of its legs. The boar is rendered with considerable detail: large tusks, pointed ears, bristling mane, and curly tail. Two dogs have jumped onto its back and tear at its neck, while a third draws blood from its rump. To the left, two bearded men, nude but for cloaks over their shoulders, also wield tridents. A fourth bearded man, nude and carrying a trident, stands behind the beast. Further to the right, two beardless youths with cloaks balance this conventional composition.

The hunt of the Kalydonian boar, sent by Artemis as a punishment for being omitted from a sacrifice by King Oineus of Kalydon, was frequently depicted in just this manner. It also occasionally was paired with the centauromachy, as on the François Vase and on other cups by the artist of this vessel, whom scholars call the "Painter of Boston C.A." (see cat. no. 93).[4] The usual protagonists, Meleager and Atalante (alone identifiable without an inscription by means of her gender), cannot be recognized here, however, and scholars have debated whether the painter has blended the mythical with the real, as is so often the case in Greek art.[5]

While the two exterior scenes may be linked by the heroic exploits of Kaineus, the interior depicts a scene from the life of Greek elites. Within a border of red and black tongues, dots, and circles, a beardless rider in a short tunic holds a spear in his left hand. Such figures are common in Athenian vase-painting, though they usually face left, hold their weapons in their right hand, and often are accompanied by a second, riderless horse. The forelegs of this lone stallion, overlapping the border, are sharply bent, while the straight-spined rider leans back. Depending on the orientation of the cup, the horse might be interpreted as rearing, galloping, or even kneeling,[6] but the artist seems to have intended to depict cantering — a moderate three-beat gait.

The precise identity of this youthful horseman remains unclear. Three blobs behind him take the place of letters. (Similar blobs are located beneath the centaur to the left of Kaineus.) The practice of writing such nonsense, sometimes with actual letters, was widespread, but writing, whether it said anything or not, could serve as more than identification or decoration. As literacy was far from universal, allusion to this relatively new technology had serious social implications — just as the cup's images of mythical warriors, brave hunters, and a horseman on a fine stallion all provided positive models for emulation.

—KDSL

### BIBLIOGRAPHY

Schauenburg 1962a; True and Frel 1983, 22–23, no. 11; Brijder 1983, 134; Laufer 1985, pl. 3, fig. 4; *LIMC* 5 (1990), 885, no. 10, pl. 565, s.v. "Kaineus" (Laufer); *CVA* J. Paul Getty Museum 2, USA 25, 39–41, pls. 82–84, 89.1; Barringer 2001, 150–51, fig. 83; *Getty Handbook* 2002, 59.

### NOTES

1 Brijder 1983; Cook 1997, 75.

2 For Kaineus imagery, see Cohen 1983; Laufer 1985; *LIMC* 5, 884–91, s.v. "Kaineus." The Olympia plaque is Arch. Mus. BE 11a: Laufer 1985, 3–5, 38 (M1), pl. 1; *LIMC* 5, 888, no. 61, pl. 573, s.v. "Kaineus."

3 For the literary tradition, see *LIMC* 5, 884, s.v. "Kaineus," and especially Gantz 1993, 280–81.

4 For the Painter of Boston C.A. (C.A. for "Circe-Acheloos"), see *ABV* [2] 69, 682; *Paralipomena* 28; Boardman 1974, 33; Brijder 1983, 134.

5 For hunting in general as well as the Kalydonian boar hunt, see Barringer 2001, with pp. 4–5 and 150–51 in particular for the ambiguity of this and other representations.

6 For kneeling horses, see Xen. *Eq.* 6.16, 7.3–4; Poll. *Onom.* 1.213; and for Alexander the Great's favorite, Bucephalus, see Curtius 6.5.18.

# 28

## Red-Figure Dinos Fragments with the Reclamation of Helen and the Death of Kaineus

Greek, Attic, ca. 470–460 B.C., the body attributed to the Copenhagen Painter (Syriskos) and the lid to the Syriskos Painter
Ceramic
Body and rim fragment: height 18.3 cm., width 39.4 cm., height of rim and neck 6.4 cm., width of rim 5.75 cm.
Lid fragment: diameter 42.5 cm., height 6.4 cm., thickness 0.95–1.23 cm.
Princeton University Art Museum, Fowler McCormick, Class of 1921, Fund
(y1986–34a–b)

CONDITION

These are two of sixteen non-joining fragments from the same vessel, one preserving roughly half of the lid, the other composed of contiguous sections of the rim, neck, shoulder, and upper body. The two fragments are themselves repaired from smaller pieces, with gaps restored in synthetic material tinted black (lid) or reddish orange (neck and shoulder). The breaks are sharp and irregular. The surfaces are in excellent condition, with glossy black slip and only minor chips and scratches. Of the fourteen fragments not illustrated here, eleven are from the rim, neck, and shoulder, the largest (length 37.5 cm.) repaired from several pieces. Of the remaining fragments, one is from the edge of the lid, another—painted with drapery folds—is from the body, and the last comprises nearly the entire foot of the vessel.

These fragments are apparently from a small dinos or lebes, a handleless cauldron with a wide mouth, overhanging rim, and depressed, spherical body. Instead of a foot, a dinos normally has a rounded base designed to sit on a separately made stand, an arrangement originating in the seventh century B.C. and lasting to the end of the fourth century.[1] Red-figure dinoi are smaller and less numerous than black-figure and often were equipped with a lid.[2] This example is unusual in having a large disk foot

(height 4.36 cm.; diameter 29.4 cm.).[3] On the reserved underside of the shallow conical lid there is a substantial flange that fitted within the mouth of the dinos, allowing an approximation of its original diameter (31.5 cm.). The wide, overhanging rim has an ovolo molding decorated with an egg pattern. Both sides of the neck are coated with black slip, as is the underside of the rim. The top of the rim is painted with a frieze of loosely addorsed red-figure palmettes that are enclosed in tendrils emerging from an uncommonly naturalistic stem. Circling the shoulder of the vessel, above the figure frieze, is a band of egg pattern above a wider band of alternating palmettes and flowering lotuses. All the elements of the ornament are contoured with relief lines.

The upper halves of four figures are preserved in the principal frieze on the body; at the far right are the helmet, hand, and raised spear of a fifth figure, a warrior attacking to the right. The subject is the so-called Reclamation of Helen, presumably part of a larger depiction of the sack of Troy that circled the entire vessel.[4] The composition is standard, with Menelaos charging toward Helen, who recoils in fright. The column at the far left places the setting within the house of Deiphobos, the Trojan to whom Helen was given after the death of Paris.[5] Menelaos intended to kill his wife for running off with Paris, but upon seeing her again he was so overwhelmed by her beauty that he forgave her. Menelaos wears a cuirass and an Attic helmet and carries a shield with a lion device. The scabbard at his hip is empty, proving that the vase-painter followed the standard formula of showing Menelaos either carrying his sword or dropping it when he sees his wife. Helen wears a sakkos, himation, and chiton, as well as a short mantle. She is identified by a retrograde inscription in red letters, as is Menelaos. Helen looks back at her wrathful husband as she runs to the left, extending both arms toward a second woman, as though seeking her help. This is surely Aphrodite, who often appears in depictions of the Reclamation as Helen's protector.[6] The goddess wears a long headband, a spotted peplos, and a himation draped over both shoulders.[7] She alone of all the figures in the scene stands unmoving and serene, confident in her power. A third draped female rushes up from the left while

looking back at some unseen menace. With her left hand
she pulls a short veil from her face, recalling scenes of
the Reclamation in which Aphrodite unveils Helen at the
critical moment to reveal her astounding beauty.[8] The
third female has been tentatively identified as Kassandra,
the sister of Paris;[9] this is possible but does not explain
the two letters — *MO* — next to her head.

Robert Guy attributed this scene to the Copenhagen
Painter, an artist whose real name is now known to have
been Syriskos, for his signature as painter appears on a
calyx-krater in Malibu that Guy also attributed to the
Copenhagen Painter.[10] His somewhat austere style stands
at the transition from Late Archaic to Early Classical.
He is known for the lush originality of his subsidiary
ornament, but the configuration of palmettes and florals
on this dinos is not exactly paralleled elsewhere in his
oeuvre.[11] The subject, too, is otherwise unknown among

his extant work. However, it is portrayed on a hydria in London by the Syriskos Painter, whom Beazley called the "brother" of the Copenhagen Painter.[12] The Syriskos Painter is named after a vase in Rome with the signature of Syriskos, this time signing not as painter but as potter.[13] Beazley occasionally found it hard to distinguish the works of the Copenhagen and Syriskos Painters, and the recent discovery that Syriskos was in fact the Copenhagen Painter has raised the question of whether the two painters were really one.[14] The Princeton vase conclusively demonstrates that they are not, for Guy recognized that the lid of the dinos was not painted by the Copenhagen Painter but rather by his "brother," the still anonymous Syriskos Painter.[15]

The lid of the dinos was painted with another grand mythological battle, the Thessalian centauromachy, with centaurs and armored Lapiths locked in combat. The action takes place on Mount Pelion rather than indoors at the wedding of Peirithoos, for the centaurs wield boulders and red-leaved trees instead of table legs and stools. The action occupies a frieze framed below by the egg pattern around the edge of the lid and above by the band of black palmettes circling the missing knob. Preserved are four complete figures and parts of two more. In the center, Kaineus is being pounded into the ground by a trio of centaurs, the only way in which they could overcome the otherwise invulnerable Lapith. The composition is canonical for the subject (cf. cat. no. 27).[16] Kaineus fends off one centaur with his shield and hacks at a second with his sword, all in vain.

The Syriskos Painter is somewhat freer in his draftsmanship than the Copenhagen Painter/Syriskos, but as in the Reclamation scene, all the figures on the lid are contoured with relief lines. He is distinguished from his "brother" by, among other things, his treatment of hair and beards. He took pains to distinguish the three centaurs by giving one a full head of hair, another a balding pate and a brown beard drawn with dilute slip, and the third—rendered in three-quarter view—a bald forehead and black beard. The elegant dilute tresses of the Copenhagen Painter are not in evidence. Faint lines of musculature are drawn with dilute glaze, and there are numerous sketch lines on the figures. At either end of the fragment are parts of two Lapiths who move to left and right, their faces lost. Both wear helmets and greaves; the one on the right carries a sword and is nude save for a billowing cloak; the left one wears a cuirass. They remind us that although these centaurs may have the upper hand against Kaineus, their brethren on the missing side of the lid probably were not faring as well.

The attribution of the lid to the Syriskos Painter is supported by comparison with the centauromachies on the shoulders of three splendid pointed amphorae by the Copenhagen Painter, one of which, in the collection of Shelby White and Leon Levy, also features the death of Kaineus.[17] The stylistic and compositional affinities between these scenes and that on the Princeton lid are unmistakable, but so are the distinctions in detail and spirit that support the attributions to two different painters. Theseus and Peirithoos are named on the White/Levy amphora and in the centauromachy on a pointed amphora in a German private collection.[18] The Lapith who is knocked to the ground, but not sunk into it, on the shoulder of the third amphora, in Zürich, also may represent Kaineus.[19] The principal scene on the body of the White/Levy amphora is the Wedding of Peleus and Thetis, with the couple greeted by the groom's surrogate parents, the centaur Cheiron and his mother Philyra. The connection with the centauromachy on the shoulder is evident, as it is on the amphora in Zürich, where the main subject is the rearming of Achilles by his mother Thetis.[20] The relationship between the subjects on the Princeton vase is more subtle. Both concern the attempted break-up of marriages, with the centaurs disrupting the wedding of Peirithoos and Hippodameia on the lid, and on the body Menelaos reclaiming the wife usurped by Paris and Deiphobos, acts of hubris that in both cases did not go unpunished.

—JMP

## BIBLIOGRAPHY

*Record* 46.1 (1987): 45, 46 (illus. of Reclamation scene only); *LIMC* 4 (1988), 544, pl. 342, no. 278, s.v. "Helene" (Kahil); Mangold 2000, 195, no. IV 38 (not illus.).

## NOTES

1 For black-figure dinoi, see discussion under cat. no. 53.

2 For a typical red-figure dinos and stand, slightly later in date than the Princeton fragments and attributed to Polygnotos, cf. Ferrara 9380: *ARV²* 1029.17, 1707; *Paralipomena* 442; *BAdd²* 317; Matheson 1995, 16, pl. 8, 350, no. P 18.

3 The underside of the hollow foot is concave and reserved. The top surface is black, and the side is reserved except for a single line around the middle. A smaller vase in Malibu (89.AE.7), attributed to the Syleus Painter, has been described as a handleless stamnos, but it could as easily be called a footed dinos: *GettyMusJ* 18 (1990), 167.

4 For the Reclamation of Helen, see Kahil 1955; Clement 1958; Simon 1964; *LIMC* 4, 537–52, pls. 329–57, s.v. "Helene"; Robertson 1995; *LIMC* 8 (1997), 839–40, pl. 565, s.v. "Menelaos" (Kahil); Dipla 1997. In sixth-century black-figure, Menelaos does not attack Helen but either stands before her or leads her away. The earliest depiction of Menelaos threatening Helen with a sword is on a red-figure amphora by Oltos of about 510 B.C. (Paris, Louvre G 3: *ARV²* 53.1; *BAdd²* 162–63).

5 Helen's marriage to Deiphobos was mentioned both in the *Little Iliad* of Lesches and the *Iliupersis* of Arktinos: see Evelyn-White 1982, 510–11, 520–21.

6 See *LIMC* 2 (1984), 140–41, pls. 143–45, s.v. "Aphrodite" (Delivorrias).

7 Cf. the same combination of garments on one of the Nereids on the pointed amphora Zürich University L 5, attributed by Cornelia Isler-Kerenyi to the Copenhagen Painter: *ARV²* 1656.2 bis (as the Oreithyia Painter); *BAdd²* 250; Isler-Kerenyi 1977, fig. 7a; Robertson 1995, 142, fig. 145.

8 E.g., the skyphos Boston 13.186, signed by Makron: *ARV²* 458.1, 1654; *Paralipomena* 377; *BAdd²* 243; *LIMC* 4, 540, no. 243, pl. 334, s.v. "Helene"; Robertson 1995, 432, fig. 26.1. Robertson (1995, 431–34) argues that the scene may depict not the Reclamation but rather an earlier Greek embassy to Troy. Ancient literature, however, does not mention such an earlier meeting between the estranged Menelaos and Helen. There could have been only one such dramatic encounter, and we know that it occurred at the sack because it was described in the *Little Iliad* (Schol. Ar. *Lys.* 155; Evelyn-White 1982, 518–19), in which context it is

mentioned also by Euripides (*Andr.* 627–31). In some vase-paintings, Eros also flies in to make certain that Menelaos is well and truly smitten: e.g., Princeton 2002-166 (*LIMC* 4, 544, no. 279 bis, pl. 342, s.v. "Helene").

9 Mangold 2000, 195, no. IV 38.

10 Malibu 92.AE.6: Shapiro 1993, 220, fig. 181, no. 145; *Getty Masterpieces* 1997, 46; Lubsen Admiraal 1998, pl. 22. For the Copenhagen Painter, see *ARV²* 256–59, 1640; *Paralipomena* 351; *BAdd²* 204; Isler-Kerenyi 1977; Robertson 1995, 135–42.

11 Cf. the related palmette-and-lotus chains on the necks of two pointed amphorae by the Copenhagen Painter, one in London (Brit. Mus. E 350: *ARV²* 256.2; *BAdd²* 204; Isler-Kerenyi 1977, fig. 5b) and the other in a German private collection (Cahn 1988; Tiverios 1991). Cf. also the florals on some amphorae and lekythoi of the Group of the Floral Nolans: *ARV²* 218–19, 1636; *Paralipomena* 346; *BAdd²* 197; Kurtz 1975, 24, pl. 66.2.

12 London, Brit. Mus. E 161: *ARV²* 262.41; *BAdd²* 205; *CVA* London 5, Great Britain 7, pl. 71.1. For the Syriskos Painter, see *ARV²* 259–67, 1640–41; *Paralipomena* 351–52; *BAdd²* 204–5; Robertson 1995, 135–42.

13 Rome, Villa Giulia 866: *ARV²* 264.67; *Paralipomena* 351; *BAdd²* 205; Boardman 1975a, fig. 204.

14 Boardman (1975a, 113–14) believed they were the same, along with the P.S. Painter, but Robertson (1995, 140), with what turns out to have been admirable prescience, preferred to keep them separate.

15 Robert Guy presented his arguments in an unpublished paper, "A Lidded Vessel in Princeton by the Syriskos and Copenhagen Painters," at the 3rd Symposium on Ancient Greek and Related Pottery, Copenhagen, August 31–September 4, 1987.

16 For Kaineus, see the discussion and references under cat. no. 27 and in Padgett, "Horse Men," both in this volume.

17 Bothmer 1990, 168–71, no. 121; Oakley and Sinos 1993, 36–37, 112–14, figs. 108–11; *LIMC* 7 (1994), 233, no. 5, pl. 172, s.v. "Peirithoos" (Manakidou); Reeder 1995, 347–49, no. 109.

18 See n. 11 above. For details of the centauromachy, see Cahn 1988, 113–14, figs. 8–9.

19 See n. 7 above. For details of the centauromachy, see Isler-Kerenyi 1977, 25, fig. 9a–d.

20 A fragmentary and unpublished bell-krater with the arming of Achilles, in a private collection, also can be attributed to the Cophenhagen Painter.

# 29

# Black-Figure Neck-Amphora with Herakles and Pholos

Greek, Attic, ca. 520–510 B.C., attributed to the
Group of Würzburg 199
Ceramic
Height 47 cm., diameter 25.5 cm.
Collection of Shelby White and Leon Levy

CONDITION
The vase has been reconstructed from many
fragments but is essentially complete. Some breaks
have been retouched, and there is minor chipping
along the edge of the rim. The vessel was bumped
before being fired, resulting in a small dent on the
lower right side of the Dionysiac scene. The surface of
the body of the satyr to the left of Dionysos is worn.

The scene depicted on the obverse side illustrates the
hospitable character of Pholos, the leader of a tribe of
centaurs who inhabited Mount Pholoë in Arcadia. During
his journey through this region, Herakles was invited to
dinner by the centaur. When Herakles asked for a drink
of wine from the centaurs' communal jar, Pholos warned
him in vain not to open it. Although Pholos was able to
control himself in front of the wine, the aroma from the
opened pithos ignited the other centaurs' insatiable thirst.
Maddened, the centaurs armed themselves with branches
and rocks and attacked their leader and his guest. In the
ensuing battle, the hero was able to drive off the savage
horde, first with hot brands from the fire, then using his
bow, but in the aftermath Pholos was accidentally killed
by one of Herakles' poisoned arrows.[1]

At the center of the scene is the large pithos, partially
sunken into the ground to keep it from tipping over.
Herakles, at left, bends over the vessel supporting himself
with his left hand, which rests on the rim. With his right
hand, he dips in his kantharos to draw his first taste of
wine. The hero is dressed in a short chiton and belted
lion's skin, and carries his bow, quiver, and club on his
back; his sword is visible at his left side. The inclusion
of his weapons in this otherwise friendly scene may have
been meant as an allusion to the battle that would soon

occur.[2] To the right stands Pholos, his gaze fixed on
Herakles. The bearded centaur has the torso of a human
and the body of a horse, as well as long, wavy hair, prominent horse ears, round eyes, and a thick nose. In addition,
he is shown clothed; three vertical lines run down his
left side indicating that he wears a short chiton, an appropriate garment for hunting. Resting on his left shoulder
is a large tree branch from which hangs a fox and a hare,
game surely hunted for the intended banquet. In his right
hand he holds his own kantharos, which will be filled
momentarily. Nonsense inscriptions echo the curve in
Herakles' back and frame the top of the scene.

Although the narrative is not continued onto the
other side, a related scene is depicted. The bearded and
heavily draped Dionysos stands at the center. In his left
hand he lifts his characteristic rhyton, while in his right he holds
a bunch of grape vines. The god turns his head over his
right shoulder toward two members of his *thiasos*, a dancing
satyr and a *krotala*-playing maenad; to his left is another
dancing satyr holding an oinochoe in his right hand. As

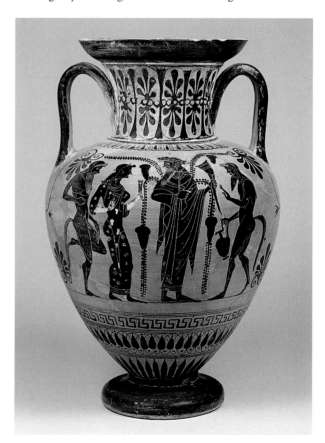

the god of wine, Dionysos is thematically linked to the event on the other side. Pholos was also the son of Silenos and a nymph, and it could be that the vase-painter was making indirect reference to the centaur's lineage with this scene.[3]

The fullest accounts of Herakles' encounter with Pholos are found in the much later sources of Diodoros and Apollodoros, who both treat the episode during the hero's third labor, the capture of the Erymanthian boar.[4] From a fragment of the *Geryoneis* of Stesichoros, which dates to the second half of the sixth century and was primarily concerned with Herakles' tenth labor (fetching the cattle of Geryon), we know that this Sicilian poet also narrated the story.[5] The preserved fragment records that Pholos served wine to Herakles but does not mention when the event occurred. Whether the encounter was originally attached to his tenth labor or simply mentioned by the poet as a reminiscence is, therefore, uncertain.[6]

In Archaic art, the episode becomes popular with Attic vase-painters in the last quarter of the sixth century B.C.[7] Pholos is most frequently represented welcoming Herakles, offering him wine or banqueting with him, that is, in friendly, tranquil scenes.[8] On these vases, the centaur is normally depicted with at least one of three attributes —holding a kantharos, wearing a short chiton, and carrying a branch with game suspended from it. On this vase, he is shown with all three. The latter two are significant in defining his character. By representing this centaur wearing a chiton, his more civilized nature is emphasized. Pholos is not only able to exercise self-control when drinking wine, but he also welcomes guests, providing Herakles with the hospitality expected in the civilized realm. In addition to suggesting his role as a hunter, the chiton also illustrates his humanlike cultivation, a characteristic not normally associated with centaurs. Further, while a tree branch is the centaur's weapon of choice, Pholos does not use it in this manner. Instead, he carries the game from his successful hunt, further indication that he intends to entertain his guest in a civilized manner.[9]

The amphora has been attributed to the Group of Würzburg 199 by J. Robert Guy. The painters of this group are considered part of the circle of the Antimenes Painter, whose preserved works date between 525–510 B.C.[10]

—JYC

**BIBLIOGRAPHY**

Uhlenbrock et al. 1986, 104–5, no. 8.

**NOTES**

1 Apollod. *Bibl.* 2.5.4. Lebessi (1996, 153 n. 57) overlooks this passage in arguing that Cheiron was the only centaur killed by Herakles' poison arrows.

2 Uhlenbrock et al. 1986, 105.

3 Apollod. *Bibl.* 2.5.4.

4 Diod. Sic. 4.12.3–8; Apollod. *Bibl.* 2.5.4–5.

5 Davies 1991, frag. 181, line 2 for this fragment of the *Geryoneis*; see also Brize 1980, 52–54, 146–49.

6 Gantz 1993, 390.

7 Gantz 1993, 709–10.

8 Verbanck-Piérard 1982, 147–48. For representations of Herakles banqueting with Pholos, see Schauenburg 1971; Wolf 1993, pls. 123–30.

9 During the Archaic period, there are some iconographic similarities between Pholos and Cheiron, the other centaur friendly to humans. Cheiron, too, is frequently represented wearing a chiton and holding a branch with game. In his case, these attributes refer to his role in teaching Achilles how to hunt. Cheiron, however, is usually depicted with the full body of a human and only the hindquarters of a horse. One could suggest that because of his participation in the education of a hero, Cheiron was considered even closer to man than Pholos and was, thus, given a more humanlike appearance. For Cheiron, see *LIMC* 3 (1986), 237–48, esp. 247–48, with additional bibliography, s.v. "Cheiron" (Gisler-Huwiler).

10 For the Group of Würzburg 199, see *ABV* 287–90; *Paralipomena* 126. For the Antimenes Painter, see *ABV* 266–75, 691; *Paralipomena* 117–21; Burow 1989.

## 30

## Kotyle with an Archer Attacking a Centaur

**Greek, Middle Protocorinthian IB/II, ca. 675–650 B.C.[1]**
**Ceramic**
**Height 8.6 cm., width including handles 14.3 cm.,**
**diameter of rim 9.70 cm., diameter of base 3.6 cm.**
**Virginia Museum of Fine Arts, Richmond, The Adolph**
**D. and Wilkins C. Williams Fund (80.27)**

CONDITION
**The vase, made of pale, creamy buff clay, was broken and has been repaired. Several lacunae, including most of one handle, are restored in plaster but not repainted. The slip has flaked in places, especially on the boar and rams.**

A kotyle is a variety of skyphos, a deep wine cup, with tapering body, thin walls, straight rim, simple base ring, and two horizontal handles. In Corinth, the shape took form in the Geometric period and continued in use until the Classical period. This cup is in the Protocorinthian style of the third quarter of the seventh century: the traditional Geometric elements — crosses, zigzags, swastikas, groups of vertical and horizontal lines — are joined by curvilinear motifs and abstract floral designs, such as the zone of black rays on the lower body and the pendant coils in the adjacent band, reflecting the influence of imported Near Eastern metalwork, textiles, and ivories. The pattern work on the cup's rim, with a wide band of vertical zigzags, is based on a formula found on Late Geometric and Early Protocorinthian kotylai, but the use of vivid red slip for alternate zigzags is a noticeable innovation.[2]

The main figural frieze, which circles the cup below the handles, is misfired, so that the bodies of the animals and the hair and garments of the human figures mostly appear red instead of the intended dark brown. The somewhat eccentric composition features another Orientalizing formula: the heraldic arrangement of a pair of animals — rams — on either side of an abstract floral motif, in this case a flowery whorl of particular inventiveness, with volute-like tendrils that terminate in ivy leaves.[3] Instead of occupying a central position between the

handles, as one might expect, the entire group is skewed to the left, with the left ram placed beneath a handle. The rams lower their heads as though about to butt horns. Their sturdy bodies are drawn in the black-figure technique, a Corinthian invention of this period, in which details of dress and anatomy are incised with a needle on a dark silhouette, revealing the lighter clay beneath. The horn of the right ram is tinted with added red slip, the matt texture and purplish hue of which distinguish it from the misfired slip of the animal's body. In contrast, the horn of the left ram is drawn in outline directly on the clay ground, a combination of techniques repeated elsewhere in the frieze.

Beyond the left ram, farther left, two beardless young hunters attack a boar, whose entire body, except for its curling tail, is misfired red. The limbs and faces of the hunters are drawn in outline, but their long hair and short-sleeved tunics are rendered in black-figure.[4] The boar lowers its head defensively between its forelegs, its bristling razorback stiffly erect as it prepares to rip its tusks into the approaching hunter. The latter leans forward over his extended right leg, ready to stab the pig with the spear in his left hand but instead unwisely reaches for its head with his bare right hand. His more cautious companion hangs back at the right, crouching to draw his bow. The close encounter with a wild beast, the ingenuous style, and the combination of black-figure and outline drawing recall the lion hunt on the so-called Chigi Vase, a masterpiece of the Late Protocorinthian style in which the figures are drawn with even greater detail and felicity.[5]

To the left of the boar, beneath the second handle, a centaur runs to the right, fleeing from another bowman, who stands back-to-back with one of the rams on the reverse. The centaur's fully human body is drawn in outline while the equine portion behind is misfired red.[6] The centaur's head is lost, but his black hair is clearly longer than that of the hunters. He lifts his left leg to flee while spreading his arms wide in a gesture of desperation and despair. His missing left hand probably held a branch; its tip is preserved, touching the rump of the adjacent boar. Like the other two hunters, the face and limbs of the archer are outlined while his hair and tunic are largely

misfired red. Unlike the first archer, he has a quiver on his back and is running rather than crouching.

It is possible to read this curious composition as a group of three hunters converging on both a centaur and a boar, but this is unlikely. Centaurs are not game, like boars, but the foes of heroes, and all centauromachies are by definition mythological.[7] This is not to say that the artist did not wish to draw an analogy between the two "hunts," and indeed, he has run them together in a way that makes it difficult to separate them. On one level, the thematic relationship is obvious: the human hunters fight the wild boar the way the hero battles the wild centaur. But while the centaur seems about to encroach on the hunters' space, it necessarily occupies a different conceptual

realm: despite its propinquity and formal affinity, the boar hunt is a separate reality.[8]

In this period, when Greek artists were still experimenting with narrative and the portrayals of particular characters and stories were not yet standardized, the criteria for identification are less secure. In myth and in later art, the opponents of the centaurs are Herakles and the Lapiths: if the archer pursuing the centaur is to be identified with a particular figure, he ought to be one of these. He cannot be a Lapith, for their battle with the centaurs is a melée, and even when a Lapith is shown fighting a centaur in single combat, he can be represented as an armored hoplite but not as an archer.[9] Instead, the bowman must be Herakles, in spite of the absence of the club and lion's skin by which in later vase-painting he would be readily recognizable. The question then arises whether the centaur is to be identified as Nessos or as one of the thirsty centaurs of Mount Pholoë, in Arcadia, who interrupted Herakles' visit with Pholos. Benson opted for Nessos, but Splitter is surely correct in seeing this scene as derived from the Pholos myth.[10] Even when Pholos is absent, the Arcadian fight usually can be distinguished from the encounter with Nessos both by the number of centaurs and by the absence of Deianeira. In art, Herakles normally uses his club or a sword against Nessos (e.g., cat. nos. 35, 37). On a Middle Protocorinthian oinochoe in Syracuse, Herakles — again lacking his later attributes — advances with drawn sword against a single centaur, whose identity as Nessos is suggested by his running toward Herakles rather than away from him.[11] Only rarely is Herakles shown attacking Nessos with a bow,[12] even though ancient authors agree that Nessos was killed by an arrow tipped with the poisonous venom of the Hydra, a necessary precondition for the centaur's tainted blood that would eventually be Herakles' undoing.[13]

Depictions of the kneeling Herakles peppering a group of fleeing centaurs with arrows appear on a few other Protocorinthian and Corinthian vases, and these have rightly been identified as representing events on Mount Pholoë.[14] Among the gilt ivory reliefs on the Chest of Kypselos, at Olympia, Pausanias mentions a man, "obviously Herakles," shooting at a group of centaurs, but he makes no mention of Pholos.[15] His elimination is a logical step, and there seems little doubt that instances of Herakles shooting at a single centaur, as on this cup, are simply reduced versions of the same subject.[16]

—JMP

**BIBLIOGRAPHY**

Siegal 1981, 18–20, figs. 3–6; Amyx 1988, 541, 630, 666, no. 1 (not illus.); Benson 1995b, 168–69, pl. 38.f–I; Splitter 2000, 67, no. 8 (not illus.).

**NOTES**

1 Amyx (1988, 541) assigns the cup to MPC II, which he dates ca. 675–650 B.C. (p. 399). Benson (1995b, 169 n. 23), prefers to call it MPC IB, which he dates ca. 675–660 B.C., explaining: "The precocity of the floral ornament in stark contrast with the geometric rim pattern signals a stylistic *cul de sac* calling for a total rethinking of style direction. That

came in MPC II." For Protocorinthian vase-painting, see Friis Johansen 1923; Payne 1931, 1–27, 94–98, 269–73; Payne 1933; Amyx 1988, 15–49.

2 Cf. the red filling ornaments, including crosses, on a pair of Protocorinthian kotylai from Rhodes, now in London and Florence (Friis Johansen 1923, pl. 25.1–2; Payne 1931, pl. 5.).

3 An exact Protocorinthian parallel is wanting, but the whorl shape is perhaps ancestral to the pinwheels that decorate the bases of later Corinthian aryballoi: e.g., cat. no. 47.

4 This combination of outline and black-figure techniques differs from the later "Polychrome Style" of the Chigi Vase and related works, in which the flesh of the figures is painted pale brown (Payne 1931, 95). For the Chigi Vase (Rome, Villa Giulia 22679), see Friis Johansen 1923, pls. 39–40; Payne 1931, 272, no. 39; Payne 1933, pls. 27–29; Amyx 1988, 32, no. A-3; Hurwit 2002.

5 Chigi Vase (see n. 4 above); for a detail of the lion hunt, see Hurwit 2002, 11, fig. 7. The posture of the spearman on this kotyle is particularly close to that of one of the lion hunters on a fragmentary Late Protocorinthian oinochoe from Erythrai in Asia Minor, likely from the Chigi Group: see M. Akurgal 1992; Hurwit 2002, 8, fig. 4. For boar hunts on Corinthian vases, see Payne 1931, 116, 133–34; Schnapp 1979, figs. 1–2, 4–7; Amyx 1988, 665–66; Langridge 1991; Schnapp 1997, 278–85.

6 On a MPC II oinochoe from Tavros, near Athens, with a fight between lions and centaurs, the human parts of the centaurs are intentionally painted a pale red and the equine parts black: Schilardi 1973, 57; *AR* 1977–78, 10, fig. 17. For the unusual subject, cf. the pair of branch-wielding centaurs charging a panther on a MPC dinos in Basel (Boardman 1970, pl. 44.2).

7 On some Little Master cups by the Centaur Painter, men with throwing-sticks (*lagobola*) pursue centaurs instead of their usual prey, but the centaurs fight back with stones; this is a battle, not a hunt: see Jongkees-Vos 1971; Schnapp 1997, 257–61; Barringer 2001, 16–17. The same "hunters" appear in a more conventional centauromachy on a cup in Toronto (285: *ABV* 190.3; Baur 1912, 25, no. 58, fig. 6).

8 On the oinochoe from Erythrai (see n. 5 above), the scene of Herakles kneeling to shoot at a centaur is separated from the nearby lion hunt by a sphinx, a fantastic creature who serves to demarcate the mythical and everyday realms.

9 Cf. *LIMC* 8 (1997), nos. 166–67, pl. 424, s.v. "Kentauroi et Kentaurides" (Leventopoulou et al.). Much later, in the metopes of the Parthenon, nude Lapiths are shown battling individual centaurs, but together they constitute a series of duels within a larger battle.

10 Benson 1995, 169; Splitter 2000, 67. Amyx (1988, 541) says the scene is not necessarily mythological: "possibly, but not surely, Herakles in the episode on Mt. Pholoë" (p. 630).

11 Syracuse 42648: Payne 1931, pl. 7. Disturbed that "Herakles is not clearly characterized," Amyx (1988, 631) suggested that the centaur's opponent is a Lapith, but this identification is less supportable.

12 E.g., on an Attic red-figure cup (New York, Met. 1989.382.2) attributed

to Euphronios, where Herakles is absent but Nessos, who carries Deianeira, is peppered with arrows: *Euphronios der Maler* 1991, 224, no. 52. For examples in black-figure, see *LIMC* 6 (1992), 842, nos. 81–82, pl. 548, s.v. "Nessos" (Díez de Velasco).

13 E.g., Soph. *Trach.* 566–67. A fragment (Fr. 147) of Archilochos suggests that the motif of the poisoned arrow was known much earlier than Sophokles (see Bérard 1981). If the "wound" on the leg of the Lefkandi Centaur identifies him as Cheiron, the motif may be as old as the tenth century.

14 Cf. the MPC aryballos Berlin 2686: Payne 1933, pl. 21; Amyx 1988, 37, no. 1; Ahlberg-Cornell 1992, 104, 355, fig. 178; *LIMC* 8, 691, pl. 441, no. 235. The same subject occurs on a Middle Corinthian column-krater, Corinth C-30-103: Weinberg 1943, 74–75, pl. 38, no. 312; Ahlberg-Cornell 1992, 357, fig. 182; Boardman 1998, fig. 397. When Pholos himself is present, as on the name-vase of the Pholoë Painter (Paris, Louvre MNC 677: Baur 1912, 93–94, fig. 12, no. 228; Payne 1931, pl. 31.9–10; *LIMC* 8, 693, no. 252, pl. 445), there is no question about the subject. For other examples, with and without Pholos, see Ahlberg-Cornell 1992, 102–5; Amyx 1988, 630–31; Splitter 2000, 66–68, 89–90.

15 Pausanias 5.19.9. The so-called Chest of Kypselos may have been dedicated by the Corinthian tyrant Periander, late in the first quarter of the sixth century, rather than by Kypselos himself, who ruled at Corinth ca. 657–625 B.C. (Payne 1931, 351 n. 4; Carter 1989). Splitter's new reconstruction of the chest (Splitter 2000, 49–50, and following p. 173) is said to be based on Corinthian vase-paintings, but in fact it differs from them in showing the centaurs charging toward Herakles instead of running away from his deadly arrows.

16 For another Protocorinthian example, cf. the alabastron Florence 79252: Ahlberg-Cornell 1992, 112, text fig. 7; *LIMC* 8, 691, no. 236, pl. 442. The same reduced depiction of the subject is found in Attic black-figure, e.g., Hannover 1972.1: *CVA* Hannover 2, Germany 72, pl. 25.1 and 5. Cf. also a bronze relief from Olympia (Athens, Nat. Mus. 6444: Brize 1985, pl. 23.2).

## 31

## Aryballos with Herakles (?) Battling a Centaur (?)

**Greek, Middle Protocorinthian I, ca. 680 B.C.,[1]
attributed to the Ajax Painter[2]
Ceramic
Height 7.3 cm., diameter of shoulder 4.4 cm.,
diameter of mouth 3 cm.
Museum of Fine Arts, Boston, Catharine Page Perkins
Fund (95.12)**

**CONDITION**
**The fabric is fine, pale brown clay. The lip and handle were broken off and reattached. Below and to the left of the lower handle attachment is a spall. There is a small loss on the edge of the foot and a rectangular patch of abrasion in the main figural frieze.**

This small perfume flask has a flat mouth-plate, columnar neck, strap handle, and an ovoid body that tapers sharply toward a narrow foot. It is decorated in the black-figure technique, with many details in added red slip. Much of its surface is adorned with pattern work, including concentric bands of tongues, curls, and short triangular rays around the mouth. The handle is decorated with a complex guilloche ornament, and a row of broken maeanders runs along the edge of the mouth and the sides of the handle. Three fine lines frame the main figural frieze, while long rays encircle the lower body. A variety of delicate and fanciful ornaments fill the field of the figural frieze, and the flask's underside displays a central dot placed within two circles.

On the shoulder of the aryballos is an early example of the type of animal frieze that became ubiquitous in later Greek vase-painting.[3] It includes a roaring lion, a walking ram, and a grazing goat. The larger figural frieze encircling the vessel's body is of particular interest, however, because it represents an early use of pictorial narrative.[4]

On the back, below the handle, a beardless nude male of robust proportions holds a sword in one hand and runs toward a vessel sitting on a stand. This object, perhaps a bronze cauldron, is represented as if seen from

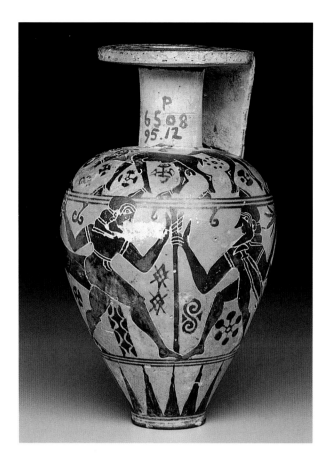
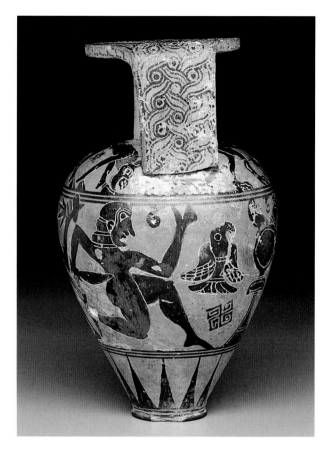

above; it is flanked by a pair of birds in flight, and another pair perches on its rim. On the front of the flask is a beardless centaur in the form of a human male with equine hindquarters projecting from his backside. He steps boldly forward to the right, his arms spread wide, a branch in one hand and an upright object, perhaps the shaft of a staff or scepter, in the other. He wears a belted tunic, and his long hair is tied in a queue. A bearded male advances on the centaur from the right, grasping the same spear or scepter shaft with his right hand and at the same time brandishing a four-pronged object in his raised left hand. His hair is also tied back, and he, too, wears a tight-fitting tunic. A sheathed sword hangs at his side.

While this is obviously a battle scene, scholars have debated over its exact meaning ever since the Museum of Fine Arts, Boston, acquired the vessel at the end of the nineteenth century.[5] Two theories identify the mysterious, four-pronged object as a thunderbolt.[6] The first contends that the bearded man is Zeus, who wields a thunderbolt against the monstrous Typhon in a struggle for world dominion.[7] The beardless, running

figure is ancillary, having no apparent connection with the cosmic battle. The second theory, which takes a more holistic approach, interprets the scene as a struggle for supremacy between Zeus and a centaur at Delphi, a site sacred to the god Apollo. The cauldron, the birds, and the running figure — identified as Apollo himself — suggest the setting.[8]

It has also been argued, however, that the four-pronged object is not a thunderbolt, but rather a burning brand, and that the scene depicts an episode from the legendary encounter of Herakles with the hospitable centaur Pholos.[9] In the story as related by Apollodoros (*Bibl.* 2.5.4), the hero uses just such a weapon to rout the pack of troublesome centaurs that attacked him on Mount Pholoë, emboldened by the aroma of wine wafting from a freshly opened jar. This interpretation is based in part on a scene on a much later Corinthian wine cup that depicts Herakles scattering the centaurs with a very similar object, apparently snatched from a blazing altar nearby.[10]

There is no way to conclusively prove or disprove these theories, and the debate continues.[11] The vase does,

however, offer irrefutable evidence that a boldly imaginative Corinthian vase-painter of the early seventh century B.C. used his work to tell a story, and in the process captured a moment in time when the now familiar iconography of Greek gods, heroes, and monsters was still in the process of being formed.

—KM

**BIBLIOGRAPHY**

Jacobsthal 1906, 15–16; Johansen 1923, 92–93, no. 8, pl. 22.2a–d; Fairbanks 1928, 150, no. 398, pl. 41; Buschor 1934, 128–32, fig. 1; Dunbabin and Robertson 1953, 176, no. 6; Schefold 1966, 29–30, fig. 4; Fittschen 1969, 113–14, no. SB 5, 119, 124–26, 217; Wallenstein 1971, 19, 170 n. 85; Simon 1980, 27–28, fig. 15; Hurwit 1985, 155–56, fig. 64 (center), fig. 65; Amyx 1988, 23–24, no. A-4, 301, 367, 631, 714; Benson 1989, 44, no. 4, pl. 15.2; Ahlberg-Cornell 1992, 102–4, cover illus., 111, fig. 6; Benson 1995a, 353–54, figs. 20.16a–e; Benson 1995b, 168, pl. 38d; Boardman 1998a, 86, fig. 174; Snodgrass 1998, 83–85, fig. 30; Splitter 2000, 66–67.

**NOTES**

1 Amyx 1988, 367 (MPC II, ca. 675–50 B.C.); Benson 1986, 99, 106 and 1989, 33–44 (MPC IA, ca. 690–75 B.C.).

2 Dunbabin and Robertson 1953, 176, no. 6. For more on the Ajax Painter, see Amyx 1988, 23–24, 367; Benson 1995a, 335–62.

3 Amyx 1988, 367.

4 Dunbabin and Robertson 1953, 172–73, 176; Amyx 1988, 23, 367; Benson 1995a, 351–53; Benson 1995b, 163–65, 175–76; Boardman 1998a, 86. On the origin of narrative in the Geometric period, Stansbury-O'Donnell 1999, 31–53.

5 Splitter 2000, 66–67.

6 Jacobsthal (1906, 15–16) was the first to identify this object as a thunderbolt.

7 First proposed by Buschor (1934, 128–29), followed by Schefold (1966, 29), Hurwit (1985, 155 n. 40), Fittschen (1969, 119–24), and Amyx (1988, 23–24, 367), all of whom agree that Zeus is battling Typhon in the guise of a horse-monster, before the latter's iconography was firmly established (cf. the Yale alabastron, cat. no. 98). Benson (1995a, 352) suggests that the scene may illustrate Zeus battling either Kronos or Typhon.

8 Simon 1980, 27–28.

9 Fittschen 1969, 113–14, 119–25; Ahlberg-Cornell 1992, 103–4. Ahlberg-Cornell's suggestion that the running figure might be Herakles at an earlier moment in the narrative is less persuasive. For the iconographic development of the centaur, see Padgett, "Horse Men," in this volume. For the Pholos adventure, see *LIMC* 8 (1997), 706–10, s.v. "Kentauroi et Kentaurides" (Leventopoulou et al.).

10 Paris, Louvre MNC 677 (L 173): Baur 1912, 93–94, no. 228, fig. 12; Payne 1931, pl. 31.9–10; Ahlberg-Cornell 1992, 104, 357, fig. 183.

11 Splitter 2000, 66–67.

# 32

# Relief-Decorated Lamina with Herakles Battling a Centaur

Greek, probably South Italian, ca. 625 – 575 B.C.
Silver gilt
Fragment with Herakles and centaur:
height 4.1 cm., width 6.8 cm.
Fragment with *Potnia Theron*:
height 5.4 cm., width 3.5 cm.
Fragment with Gorgon:
height 3.4 cm., width 3 cm.
Fragment with female figure:
height 3.2 cm., width 2.2 cm.
Fragment with tongue pattern:
height 1.2 cm., width 2.3 cm.
The Metropolitan Museum of Art, New York,
Fletcher Fund, 1927 (27.122.23)

CONDITION

The silver lamina, or thin sheet metal, is preserved in
five fragments of which two appear to join but have
not been reattached. The fragment with the *Potnia
Theron* consists of two reattached pieces, while that
with the tongue pattern consists of four pieces. The
fragment with the Gorgon consists of six reattached
pieces.[1] All the edges of the fragments are broken;
none appears to be finished. The relief work on the
fragment with the Gorgon is less well preserved than
on the other fragments.

The scenes on the lamina are composed within panels
in a metope-like arrangement framed above and below by
a tongue pattern between three horizontal grooves and by
vertical dividers decorated with two vertical series of circular impressions separated by a shallow groove. The
largest fragment depicts an archer battling a centaur. The
centaur, represented with the body of a man attached to
the hindquarters of a horse, brandishes a branch and
moves to the right in one panel. In the adjacent panel, the
archer, surely the hero Herakles, braced on one knee, his
quiver slung on his back, faces to the left and aims his bow
squarely at the centaur's chest. Behind Herakles, in the
next panel, a winged female figure faces to the left, in the
direction of the battle, and holds an animal in each hand,
symmetrically positioned. She is a *Potnia Theron* (Mistress
of Animals), an iconographic type with a long tradition
in the Near East who perhaps is best identified here in a
Greek context as the goddess Artemis (see Tsiafakis,
"ΠΕΛΩΡΑ," this volume).

The two remaining fragmentary panels appear to
depict distinct compositions, but their precise placement
cannot be determined. The fragment restored on the far
left features a female figure in left profile leading a second
figure to the left, possibly in a dance.[2] Her left arm is bent
at the chest and raised in front of her face while her right
arm, bent down and at her side, is grasped at the wrist by
the figure behind. She has long braided or curly hair, like
the winged goddess, and wears a full-length garment belted at the waist, the skirt of which is elaborately decorated
with a symmetrical pattern that indicates sumptuous and

ornate cloth. Only the hand, forearm, and tip of the nose of the second figure are preserved.

In the panel at the far right, a winged Gorgon fills the panel with her massive frontal head, snaky hair, open mouth, and protruding tongue as she runs to the right in the typical *Knielauf* position. Her preserved boot is winged, and she wears an elaborately decorated bib-like garment.

The centaur's body and the lower part of the dividing column behind are covered in a thin second sheet of gilt silver that is still adhering to a thicker first sheet. Both sheets appear to have been hammered into the same mold[3] and attached by means of rivets placed symmetrically at the top and bottom of the vertical dividing columns. Five rivets are preserved on the fragment with Herakles and the centaur; one rivet hole and most of a second are preserved on the fragment with the Gorgon.

The scene of Herakles battling a centaur is best identified as representing the myth of Herakles and the centaur Pholos.[4] During the hunt for the Erymanthian boar, which Herakles was to capture alive, Herakles was received by the centaur Pholos, who provided him with roasted meat. When Pholos hesitated to give Herakles wine, since the wine jar he had was the common property of the centaurs, Herakles insisted. As soon as the jar was opened, the rest

of the centaurs arrived, attracted by the smell, and a fierce battle began. Accounts of the myth mention Herakles using his bow and arrows, which are dipped in the poisonous venom of the Hydra from Lerna.[5] It is conceivable that the panel with the *Potnia Theron* relates to the narrative scene. Her static, primarily emblematic iconography has a long association with warriors in the Near East.[6] Here as Artemis, goddess of the hunt, she is clearly depicted on the side of Herakles, and perhaps also sets the scene in the context of the labor of the Erymanthian boar.

The lamina once may have decorated a box in the tradition of the famous chest dedicated at Olympia by Kypselos, the tyrant of Corinth.[7] While its provenance is unknown, the lamina was acquired in Italy and may have been found there.[8] Another panel with a nearly identical Gorgon has been identified as belonging to the same lamina or at least to the same workshop.[9] This second fragment was found together with an amber sculpture at Gissi di Chieti in the Abruzzo region of Italy.[10] Other examples of such metalwork are known from South Italy, notably Sybaris.[11] A secure attribution is not possible at present, but scholars have tentatively attributed the Metropolitan's lamina to a Corinthian,[12] Spartan, or Tarantine[13] workshop.
—SAH

**BIBLIOGRAPHY**

Alexander 1929, 201–2, fig. 2; Richter 1953, 32 n. 22, pl. 20b; Schiffler 1976, 271, cat. K-S4; Müller 1978, no. 192; Guzzo 1987, 163–69, pl. 100.1; Rocco 1995, 5–8, pl. 3; *LIMC* 8 (1997), 695, no. 279, s.v. "Kentauroi et Kentaurides" (Leventopoulou et al.).

**NOTES**

1 The upper piece illustrated separately in some of the earlier publications (Alexander 1929, fig. 2; Richter 1953, pl. 20b; Guzzo 1987, pl. 100b) is incorrectly attached to the fragment with a Gorgon. As now restored, it does not allow for three grooves, only two.

2 Compare, for example, the dancing figures on the top register of the later François Vase (Florence 4209: *ABV* 76.1).

3 An example of such a mold in stone, dated in the seventh century B.C., with relief- decorated panels, was found on Corfu and is now in Oxford (G 437): see Treister 1995, 97 n. 114, pls. 4–5.

4 *LIMC* 8, 695, s.v. "Kentauroi et Kentaurides." The encounter of Herakles with Pholos begins first on Corinthian vase-painting of the seventh century and was especially popular in Magna Graecia during the Archaic period. Of particular interest are the metopes from the Heraion at Foce del Sele, where Herakles also fights centaurs across separate metopes. A gold relief band of the Late Archaic period from Vergina (Theodossiev 2000, 194–95, fig. 10) attests to the widespread existence of the scene in fine metalwork of the Archaic period.

5 The earliest reference to the myth is a fragment by Stesichoros (Campbell 1991, 81, S 19), and a more complete version appears in Apollodoros (*Bibl.* 2.5.4); see Rose 1959, 216–17; Arnold 1972, 184–87.

6 For a detailed discussion, see Marinatos 2000, esp. 1–31, 67–109.

7 Pausanias 5.17.5–11. The so-called Chest of Kypselos had similar iconographic motifs including a winged Artemis, Herakles fighting centaurs, and Gorgons. For discussion and a reconstruction drawing, see Splitter 2000, 23–49, pls. 1–3; and Padgett's comments in cat. no. 30, n. 15, in this volume.

8 Richter 1953, 32.

9 See Rocco 1995, 5–8, pl. 2; Guzzo 1987, 164, pl. 100.2. Guzzo was uncertain of the whereabouts of this fragment; he knew only that at one time it belonged to an antiquities dealer in Rome, but Rocco details its modern history: it is now in the collection of the Vatican Museums. It is interesting to note that the Vatican's fragment and those in the Metropolitan were acquired in the same year, 1927, adding to the probability that they are related.

10 Rocco 1995, 5.

11 Compare also an Archaic Greek gilded silver lamina with mythological relief panels in Malibu (83.AM.343), attributed to a workshop in Magna Graecia (Brommer 1984a, 135–38, fig. 1).

12 *LIMC* 8, 695, s.v. "Kentauroi et Kentaurides."

13 Guzzo (1987, 169) suggests either Spartan or Tarantine manufacture. Rocco (1995, 6) leans toward Guzzo's attribution.

---

## 33

# Tyrrhenian Amphora with Herakles Battling the Centaurs

**Greek, Attic, ca. 560–550 B.C., attributed to the Fallow Deer Painter**
**Ceramic**
**Height 36.8 cm., width including handles 23.8 cm., diameter of rim 16.0 cm., diameter of foot 11.1 cm.**
**Private collection**

**CONDITION**
The vase is broken and repaired, with only a few small lacunae. There is in-painting of cracks and minor restoration of small gaps: for example, the rump of the right-hand sphinx beneath handle B/A. The surface is in good condition, but most details in added white slip are eroded, especially the faces and wings of the sphinxes and sirens. There are traces of wear on the handles. Slumping of the reverse shoulder gives the vase a slightly lopsided stance.

This is a classic example of a "Tyrrhenian" amphora, a distinctive type of Attic black-figure neck-amphora produced in the second quarter of the sixth century B.C. The great majority are found in Italy, and the name reflects the assumption that they were made specifically for export to the Etruscans, known to the Greeks as the *Tyrrhenoi*.[1] The shape and decorative scheme of this example are characteristic: tall, tapering body; concave neck with floral decoration; echinus mouth and foot; two cylindrical handles; extensive use of added color; multiple animal friezes on the lower body; a human figural frieze in a broader zone between the handles. The exterior of the otherwise black mouth is decorated with a band of upright lotus buds, alternately closed (red) and open (white). The handles and foot are black on the outside and reserved underneath; a red stripe circles the foot's lower edge. There is a "festoon" of interlaced palmettes on either side of the neck, and a red fillet marks the juncture of neck and shoulder, the latter circled by a band of black and red tongues. The usual zone of black rays above the foot is rendered in two tiers. Paired lines frame the two animal

friezes, which are separated from the main figural frieze by a band of dots.

The obverse is identified by the use of added red on the neck festoon and by the symmetrical compositions of the animal friezes. In the uppermost animal frieze, a pair of seated, confronted sphinxes are framed by a pair of cocks, themselves flanked by sirens with outstretched wings. Pairs of standing, confronted sphinxes are placed below either handle, while the center of the reverse is occupied by seated, confronted sphinxes framed by sirens. The incision is cursory in places, but the artist took pains to vary the depiction of the wings. In the lower frieze, a symmetrical group again fills the center of the obverse: two sirens with folded wings flank a third with wings outstretched. A pair of panthers stands to either side. In the center of the reverse, another pair of panthers approaches a stag, the left cat followed by a soaring eagle.

In the principal scene of the obverse, Herakles battles a group of four centaurs that wield their usual weapons:

boulders and uprooted trees. Three black stones lie on the ground. The centaurs have human torsos and equine forelegs. Herakles kneels to the right and draws his bow; the artist apparently had trouble deciding on which side of the adjacent centaur to place the weapon, resulting in a tangle of bow, tail, tree, and arms. There is a red quiver of white-feathered arrows on Herakles' back. The paws of his lion's skin dangle between his legs, the trophy of another wild creature that came to grief at his hands. The varied textures of the skin are rendered with incised dots and strokes. The face and beard of the hero are painted red, as are the breasts of the centaurs. The centaurs at the right have red hair and beards, while those of the left pair are incised with parallel lines. The equine legs of the centaurs are drawn with lean grace and in a variety of postures. The centaur behind Herakles kicks at him with a foreleg while raising a large white boulder. The wild barbarity of the horse men is emphasized by their bold features: shaggy hair, full lips, pointed ears, and long, upturned noses. The five rows of letters angling through the spaces around the protagonists recall the inscriptions identifying the centaurs on the François Vase, but these nonsensical "inscriptions" are not so informative: they are mere design elements that mimic more literate models.

On the reverse is a subject seemingly unrelated to that on the front, except in its theme of combat. Two naked warriors attack one another with raised spears, their round shields clashing. Both wear red greaves and Corinthian helmets with long white crests. The helmet of the left warrior is red, and there is red on the interior of his shield. The pinwheel device on the exterior of his opponent's shield is turned toward the viewer. The inscriptions that surround them are again nonsensical. Prancing up on either side of the warriors is a pair of horses. The right one, with a rippling mane of red and black, is ridden by a bearded man in a red cloak; the horse at the left has a bristling red mane and a younger, beardless rider, also cloaked in red. Both horsemen pull back sharply on the reins, restraining their mounts, who nevertheless kick out with their forelegs, as though eager to join the fray.

Many elements—the relatively small size, the dot band at mid-body, the decorated rim, the arrangement of the animals, the curl of the panthers' tails, the pinwheel device on the shield, details of the armor and lion's skin, the nonsense inscriptions—support the attribution to the Fallow Deer Painter.[2] He is particularly fond of horsemen and dueling warriors, although usually on different sides.[3] He represents Herakles killing a centaur on two other vases, in Munich and in a private collection, but in both cases the victim is Nessos, the centaur who tried to ravish Herakles' wife Deianeira.[4] On this vase, however, the subject instead is Herakles' encounter with the centaurs of Mount Pholoë, in Arcadia. When Herakles was the guest of the wise centaur Pholos, he used his bow to run off a pack of wilder centaurs that had been attracted by the smell of wine (see cat. no. 29). The subject is distinguished from the fight with Nessos both by the number of centaurs and by the absence of Deianeira, although neither feature alone would be sufficient to eliminate Nessos as a possibility. In art, Herakles normally uses a club or sword against Nessos (see cat. nos. 35, 37), but occasionally he does employ a bow.[5] Even when Deianeira is present and the subject is not in doubt, Nessos may be accompanied by other centaurs shown rushing to his aid, as they do on another amphora by the Fallow Deer Painter, in Munich.[6] In a melée like this one, however, with Herakles kneeling to shoot at two fleeing centaurs, neither of whom is distinguished in any significant way from his fellows, the subject is surely the violent denouement of the meeting with Pholos.

—JMP

## BIBLIOGRAPHY

New York, Royal-Athena Galleries, *Art of the Ancient World*, vol. 6, pt. 1 (November 1990), *One Thousand Years of Ancient Greek Vases from Greece, Etruria, and Southern Italy*, no. 27.

## NOTES

1 For Tyrrhenian amphorae, see *ABV* 94–106, 683–84; *Paralipomena* 34–43; *BAdd*[2] 25–28; Thiersch 1899; Bothmer 1944; Schauenburg 1962b; Meyer-Emmerling 1979; Carpenter 1983; Carpenter 1984; Ginge 1988; Kluiver 1992; Kluiver 1993. Attempts to down-date the Tyrrhenian Group to ca. 560–530 (Carpenter 1983) and to locate their production in Etruria (Ginge 1988) or closer to Euboia (Carpenter 1984) have not found wide acceptance (e.g., Boardman 2001b, 48, 236), although Tuna-Nörling (1997, 438) explicitly accepts Carpenter's lower dates. New finds in Turkey, Rhodes, and Egypt show that the workshop's products reached a wider audience than previously realized and make an Italian origin even more unlikely (see Tuna-Nörling 1997).

2 The author of the attribution is not known. If the single deer ever had the white spots that give the artist his name, they have worn away. The Fallow Deer Painter was named by D. von Bothmer (Bothmer 1944, 165), who initially identified eight works by the artist (*Paralipomena* 37–38, nos. 23, 32, 40, 76, 77, 84, 93, and p. 41), later adding another pair in the Swiss art market (Basel, *MuM*, Auktion 63, *Kunstwerke der Antike*, June 29, 1983, nos. 20–21, pl. 8), and an amphora formerly in the J. L. Theodor Collection (New York, Sotheby's, December 17, 1998, lot 66). To these, Kluiver (1992, 1993) has added at least four more: another amphora from the Theodor Collection (New York, Sotheby's, December 17, 1998, lot 65); an unpublished amphora in Paris (Louvre C 12070: Tuna-Nörling 1997, 445 n. 11); an amphora in Munich (1430: *ABV* 101.92; *CVA* Munich 7, Germany 32, pls. 321–22.1–2); and a fragmentary volute-krater from Phocaea (Izmir 9634: Tuna-Nörling 1997, 435–38, figs. 1–6). To these is added an amphora in the De Menil Collection, Houston, on loan to Rice University: Hoffmann 1970, 342–47, no. 165.

3 On an amphora in Paris (Louvre C 10504: *Paralipomena* 41), the duel between Achilles and Memnon takes place between both the combatants' mothers and a pair of horsemen. Kluiver is said to reject Bothmer's attribution of this vase (Tuna-Nörling 1997, 445 n. 11).

4 Munich 1428 (*ABV* 98.40; *CVA* Munich 7, Germany 32, pl. 322.3–4, and 323) and a vase formerly in the Theodor Collection (see n. 2 above): New York, Sotheby's, December 17, 1998, lot 65. In both cases, Herakles attacks the falling Nessos with a sword. On the Munich vase, Nessos is still carrying Deianeira, but on the Theodor vase she and another woman stand on either side proffering wreaths of victory. The Theodor vase also has a decorated rim, and the figures of Herakles and Nessos are in many details quite close to their counterparts on the amphora catalogued here.

5 See cat. no. 37 and n. 8 of that entry. It should be noted that there also are many vase-paintings of Herakles using a sword or club against a group of fleeing centaurs, instead of a bow: e.g., a Tyrrhenian amphora by the Kyllenios Painter (Hobart, University of Tasmania 59; *Paralipomena* 40; *BAdd*[2] 29); and an amphora by an artist close to the Tyrrhenian Group, in a private collection (Schauenburg 1973, 15, fig. 1). The number of centaurs, their headlong flight, and the absence of a female figure indicate that these scenes also represent the fight on Mount Pholoë. For criteria to differentiate such mythical centauromachies, see Ahlberg-Cornell 1992, 103.

6 For the Munich vase, see n. 4 above. On the reverse of the artist's other vase with Nessos, formerly in the Theodor Collection (see n. 4 above), an armored warrior is spearing a centaur about to exit the scene, as though running to the aid of Nessos on the obverse. For other examples of centaurs rushing to help Nessos, cf. four Tyrrhenian amphorae: Rome, Vatican 308 (*ABV* 98.39; Schauenburg 1973, 31, figs. 42–43); Kassel T 385 (*ABV* 105.2; Schauenburg 1962b, 65, fig. 6); Hamburg 1960.1 (*LIMC* 6 [1992], 839, pl. 535, no. 3. s.v. "Nessos" [Díez de Velasco]); and Munich 1433 (*ABV* 98.37; *Paralipomena* 37; Baur 1912, pl. 1, no. 36).

# 34

# Black-Figure Neck-Amphora with Herakles Battling the Centaurs

Greek, Attic, ca. 500–475 B.C., attributed to the
Diosphos Painter
Found in Sicily[1]
Ceramic
Height 17.0 cm., maximum diameter 14.3 cm.,
diameter of mouth 10.3 cm., diameter of foot 7.8 cm.
Private collection

CONDITION
The vessel is made of orange-red clay; it is well fired,
with lustrous black slip. A short section of the foot
is restored, but otherwise the vase is unbroken and in
excellent condition.

This vase belongs to a special class of small, "very fat" neck-amphorae, of which Sir John Beazley identified only four examples.[2] Two of these, including this vase, he attributed to the Diosphos Painter, a prolific painter of small black-figure vases, mostly lekythoi (e.g., cat. no. 39), who was active in the first quarter of the fifth century B.C.[3] Characteristic of this special shape are an almost spherical body, triple-reeded handles, an echinus mouth, and a broad disk foot. On either side of the concave neck are three black palmettes, lying to the right and linked by enclosing tendrils. The two figural scenes are in reserved panels framed by single lines, with a band of unframed tongues above. The lean, leggy figures are typical creations of the Diosphos Painter, with parallels elsewhere in his oeuvre.[4]

On the obverse, Herakles battles a pair of centaurs with human torsos and four equine legs. The hero charges to the right, his left leg raised, his white club clenched in his right hand. He has inflicted two bloody wounds on a centaur, who falls to one knee, his hind legs flailing wildly against the picture frame.[5] The centaur screams in pain as Herakles jerks him by the tail. The hero wears his lion's skin like a hood, its white-clawed paws knotted at his throat and dangling between his sinewy legs. He wears a short red chiton and a red belt; a white baldric supports a bow and scabbard. A second centaur, swinging a pine branch with both hands, attacks Herakles from behind. The centaurs are balding and have red beards, white bellies, and white dappling on the withers and croup.[6]

On the reverse is a fight between a warrior and a centaur with a red beard and white belly. The centaur attacks with a tree branch, but the warrior spears his human belly, causing a gush of red blood. The warrior wears a bell cuirass and a Corinthian helmet pushed up on his head. He holds his red-rimmed shield high on his left arm, concealing his face. Added white is used for the shield device (a chariot wheel, only half visible), the tail of the helmet crest, and dots on the crest and on the hem of the warrior's chitoniskos. The short inscription in the field beneath the centaur is nonsensical, like those on the Tyrrhenian vase with Herakles and the centaurs (cat. no. 33).

Paul Baur identified the subject of the obverse as Herakles battling the centaurs on Mount Pholoë, where he had gone to visit the centaur Pholos (cf. cat. no. 29).

This is likely correct, since the number of centaurs and the absence of Deianeira ought to rule out the encounter with Nessos (see the discussion under cat. no. 35). Again following Baur, the fight on the reverse between a centaur and a Greek warrior apparently derives from the Lapith centauromachy, at which Herakles was not present. It is questionable, however, whether the Diosphos Painter was punctilious in separating the two myths.[7]

—JMP

## BIBLIOGRAPHY

Paris, *Collection d'antiquités. Vente 18–20 mars 1901*, pl. 3, no. 20; Baur 1912, 37, no. 107; *ABV* 517.1; Paris, *Antiques, Vente Hôtel Drouot 11–12 juin 1959*, pl. 3, no. 55; *Paralipomena* 250, 255; Brommer 1973, 85, no. A14; Schiffler 1976, 250, pl. 2, cat. A-79; *BAdd²* 128; Basel, Jean-David Cahn, A.G., Auktion 2, *Kunstwerke der Antike*, June 26, 2000, pl. 14, no. 41; New York, Royal-Athena Galleries, *Art of the Ancient World*, vol. 12 (2001), no. 186.

## NOTES

1 Originally in the Bourguignon Collection, Naples; thereafter with the Comte Chandon de Briailles, Chaource, and in the art markets of Paris, Basel, and New York.

2 Three were black-figure (*ABV* 510.26; 517.1–2). The fourth was a red-figure work by the Berlin Painter (Oxford 1924.3: *ARV²* 200.45).

3 Beazley at first did not recognize this vase as the work of the Diosphos Painter (*ABV* 517.1), but later attributed it to him (*Paralipomena* 250, 255). Two other amphorae of this type, both formerly in the art market, also can be attributed to the artist: London, Sotheby's, December 12, 1988, lot 343; and New York, Sotheby's, June 12, 2001, lot 257. For the Diosphos Painter, see *ABL* 94–130, 232–41, pls. 37–39; *ABV* 508–511, 702–3, 716; *Paralipomena* 248–50, 255; *BAdd²* 127–28; Haspels 1972; Kurtz 1975, 97–99; Jubier 1999.

4 For the figure of Herakles charging to the right with raised left leg, cf. a neck-amphora in Richmond (60-11): *Paralipomena* 250; Shapiro 1981, no. 24. For the drawing of the centaurs, cf. the figure of Nessos on an amphora in Rome (Museo Barracco 223: *ABL* 240.149; Bothmer 1992, 24, figs. 14–15. For the warrior with raised shield concealing his face, cf. New York, Met. 56.171.25: *ABL* 239.137; Boardman 1974, fig. 271.

5 The flailing of limbs against the border recurs on another neck-amphora of this shape, which Beazley did not believe was by the Diosphos Painter (Rome, Antiquarium Forense: Pinza 1905, 263, fig. 105; *ABV* 517.2).

6 Dappling is uncommon on both horses and centaurs in black-figure; for another dappled centaur, cf. Rome, Vatican 308: *ABV* 98.39; Schauenburg 1973, 31. For a dappled horse, cf. a neck-amphora formerly in the art market, attributable to the Diosphos Painter: London, Sotheby's, January 29, 1968, lot 145.

7 Cf. New York, Met. 41.162.103, with Herakles and Nessos on one side and a Lapith fighting a centaur on the other: *LIMC* 8 (1997), 685, pl. 424, no. 166, s.v. "Kentauroi et Kentaurides" (Leventopoulou et al.). Only rarely are Herakles and a warrior represented together in the same centauromachy: e.g., a red-figure cup by the Nikosthenes Painter (Los Angeles A 5933.50.21: *ARV²* 125.11; *CVA* Los Angeles 1, USA 18, pl. 38.1) and a lekythos formerly in the art market (Basel, *MuM*, Auktion 51, *Kunstwerke der Antike*, March 14–15, 1975, pl. 29, no. 135).

## 35

# Hydria with Herakles and Nessos

Greek, Middle Corinthian, ca. 590–570 B.C.
Ceramic
Height 20 cm., maximum diameter 22 cm., diameter
of rim 9.4 cm.
The Metropolitan Museum of Art, New York,
Fletcher Fund, 1938 (38.11.8)

CONDITION
The vase is in very good condition. Only the side
handles have broken off and been reattached. There
are copious remains of matte red slip preserved as
broad bands on the outer rim, neck, and foot, and
beneath the reserved panel as well as on the tongue
pattern and the figures.

The vessel with its spheroid body, sharp contours, tall
neck, and heavy vertical rim sits on an inverted echinus
foot. A single combat scene in a reserved panel between
the low side handles decorates the front of the vase. At
the center of the scene, a bearded man, nude except for his
baldric and sword sheath, grabs the hair of a centaur as
he prepares to thrust his long sword into the beast. The
centaur, whose head and right knee are bent in submission, stretches out his arms in a gesture of supplication;
he may even be touching Herakles' beard with his right
hand.[1] Represented as a man attached to the hindquarters
of a horse, the centaur is bearded and without a weapon.
A tall sphinx is seated at the left of the scene. A bird flies
to the right above the centaur. A tongue pattern borders
the top of the panel and rosettes fill the field.

The scene almost certainly represents the hero Herakles
dealing the deathblow to the centaur Nessos, who had
attempted to abduct Herakles' wife, Deianeira. According
to the myth, best preserved in the fifth-century B.C. play
*Women of Trachis* by Sophokles,[2] Herakles, after killing his
first wife, Megara, and their children in a fit of madness,
married Deianeira, daughter of Oineus of Kalydon.
Herakles won her hand by defeating the river god Acheloos,
with whom he wrestled. On the journey home, Herakles
and his new bride came upon a flooded river, the Euenos,
which Deianeira could not cross. A centaur, Nessos, offered

to carry Deianeira across while Herakles waded for himself.
Herakles agreed, but then Nessos tried to abduct Deianeira
and Herakles slew him. While he lay dying, Nessos suggested to Deianeira that she save some of the blood from his
wound as a charm. Nessos told her that by getting Herakles
to wear a garment covered with his blood she could win
back Herakles if he should ever become unfaithful.[3] The
scene is a pivotal one in the life of Herakles because years
later when he is unfaithful to Deianeira with Iole, Deianeira
used the blood of Nessos, which was deadly poison, and
gave Herakles the garment to wear. When Herakles donned
the garment, it clung to his flesh and burnt so terribly that
he killed himself by consuming his body in a great pyre of
wood on the top of Mount Oita.[4]

The fundamental iconography of this popular myth
can be traced at least sixty years earlier to the Protoattic
New York Nessos amphora, where one sees a similar representation of Herakles and Nessos portrayed in even
greater detail.[5] The identification of the centaur as Nessos
here is supported by Herakles' use of a sword (although
literary sources say he used a bow),[6] since he nearly always
uses a sword or club in artistic representations of the
Nessos myth. Also, the centaur is but one, not a band, is
unarmed, and is not fleeing, all elements consistent with an
identification as Nessos. A contemporary example of the
scene that includes Deianeira appears on the bronze shield
band signed by Aristodamos of Argos (cat. no. 36), and
an even more complete rendering can be seen in the later
(ca. 530–520 B.C.) Attic panel amphora of Type B in the
J. Paul Getty Museum, attributed to the Medea Group
(cat. no. 37). It is unlikely that the bird and sphinx have
any specific connection to the mythological scene; rather,
they are decorative motifs, as is so often the case on
Archaic Corinthian pottery.[7] Their general placement,
however, does visually reinforce the victory of Herakles.

The three-handled water jar was a common pottery
shape throughout the ancient Greek world but was apparently not popular in Corinth as a fine ware shape.[8] This
small hydria is one of only a few examples datable to the
Middle Corinthian period.[9] The vase has been attributed
to or is placed near to the Painter of Athens 931, a close
follower of the Dodwell Painter.[10]

—SAH

BIBLIOGRAPHY

Alexander 1939, 98–99, fig. 1; Amyx 1971, 25, no. 8; Schiffler 1976, 270, cat. K-26; Amyx 1988, 213, 499, 631.

NOTES

1 Alexander 1939, 99.

2 Soph. *Trach.*, esp. lines 9–34, 555–81.

3 For a discussion of the myth, see Rose 1959, 209–10.

4 Rose 1959, 219. Scenes of the self-immolation of Herakles on top of the pyre appear in later Greek and Roman art, notably in Classical Athenian vase-painting. See *LIMC* 5.1 (1990), 128, esp. nos. 2909 and 2910, s.v. "Herakles at the Pyre" (Boardman).

5 New York, Met. 11.210.1. For a discussion of the vase, see Morris 1984, 65–70, pl. 15.

6 Sophokles (*Trach.* 572–77) explains that the blood of Nessos is poisoned by the arrow, characteristically tipped with the Lernaian Hydra's deadly poison blood, with which Herakles shot him. Since many of the early representations of the myth show Herakles using a sword, there must have been an alternate explanation that is now lost for why Nessos's blood is so fatal to Herakles.

7 For a discussion of Corinthian vases with scenes of Herakles and centaurs, see Amyx 1988, 630–31. On the use of animal symbolism in Greek vase-painting, see Edlund 1980a, 31–35.

8 For a discussion of hydriae and their use in Attica, see Richter 1935, 11–12.

9 See Amyx 1988, 498–99. It is an interesting predecessor to the Late Corinthian hydriae that imitate Attic pottery and also exhibit mythological scenes.

10 Amyx 1971, 25, no. 8; Amyx 1988, 213. On the Painter of Athens 931, see also Lawrence 1996, 136–37.

## 36

# Shield Band with Nessos and Deianeira

**Greek, Argive, ca. 575 B.C., signed by Aristodamos of Argos**
**Bronze**
**Height 16.2 cm., width 8.0 cm.**
**J. Paul Getty Museum, Malibu, California (84.AC.11)**

CONDITION

The original strap, of which this fragment of a shield band was a part, would have extended to almost the full diameter of a shield, approximately 80 to 90 centimeters. The fragment was cleaned and consolidated in 1983 with a backing of fiberglass applied so that the original rear surface is no longer visible. Two figural panels remain of the original decoration, and although parts of both scenes are missing, enough of the iconography survives for their identification and interpretation. There is also a corner of a third panel, possibly figural.[1] A light corrosion layer covers the bronze. In the upper of the two complete panels, there are two areas of fill, one on the right edge in the border, the other in the head of the male figure.

The centaur Nessos and Deianeira, bride of Herakles, are identified by inscriptions in the lower panel. Nessos is bearded, holds a pine branch in his left hand, and turns his head to face Deianeira, who sits sidesaddle on his back. Her demeanor is calm.[2] She wears a belted peplos decorated with a lattice pattern. In the background, a waterbird, probably a heron,[3] flies behind Deianeira's head. An omen,[4] here it sets the scene as that of the moment of Nessos's crossing the River Evenus.[5] Inscribed in retrograde at the top of the panel is Ἀριστόδαμος ἐποίϝεσε ηαργεῖος

(Aristodamos from Argos made me), the earliest recognized signature of a Greek metalworker.[6]

Nessos is formed from the combination of a fully human head and upper torso with the body and legs of a horse. The style of the human half of Nessos suggests features reflected in early kouroi. For example, his hair is long and wiglike, similar to the hair on a kouros from Delphi.[7] His triangular-shaped torso with squared shoulders, the pronounced epigastric arch, and arms with bulging biceps recall similar features on the statues of Kleobis and Biton.[8] This shield band is just one of three known that depict Nessos, and this the only one that includes both Nessos and Deianeira.[9]

The upper panel contains a scene of a woman being led by the wrist at sword point by a man wearing only a cuirass. Athena stands at the right, identified by the inscription beside her. The woman holds the edge of her mantle, which would have covered her head, out from her face with her left hand, a gesture of brides and married women.[10] The warrior grasps the woman's wrist in a manner associated with abduction and wedding iconography.[11] Thus, the relationship between the two is more than likely that of husband and wife. In the background between the couple is a lizard chasing an insect, another omen, perhaps here symbolic of a troubled relationship between the two.[12] A rooster, sign of virility, pugnacity, and a common love gift,[13] sits on the lower border of the panel between the legs of the warrior. Considering all the elements, the iconography of the scene is closest to that of King Menelaos of Sparta recovering his wife, Helen, from Troy after the Greeks' victory in the Trojan War.[14]

Many such shield bands have been recovered from the sanctuary of Zeus at Olympia, where worshipers left elaborate shields as dedications.[15] These hammered strips of bronze, typically decorated with a series of figural panels containing mythological or monstrous scenes, were used to attach the arm loop (*porpax*), the device by which a warrior held his shield, to the interior of the shield. The city of Argos was the major production site of this art form, as the Argive artist's signature on this fragment attests.[16]

—JBG

**SELECTED BIBLIOGRAPHY**

"Acquisitions/1984," *GettyMusJ* 13 (1985): 166–67, no. 12; *SEG* 35 (1985), 83, no. 266 bis; Bol 1985, 62–63; Bol 1989, 52, 54, 70, 76, 89, 100; Beck, Bol, and Bückling 1990, 508, no. 2; Jeffery 1990, 444 C, pl. 74.6; Rolley 1991, 286; *LIMC* 6 (1992), 843, no. 97, s.v. "Nessos" (Díez de Velasco); Frel 1994, 12; Bodel and Tracy 1997, 9; *Getty Masterpieces* 1997, 30; *Getty Handbook* 2002, 33.

**NOTES**

1 Two incised tapering arcs rest on the top of the horizontal guilloche band that separates this panel from one below containing the scene of Menelaos and Helen. The original notice of the shield band ("Acquisitions/1984," 166) identified the two forms as landscape elements, possibly rocks, but if that were the case it would be unique in the iconography of shield bands. It is more likely that the two forms belong to a decorative pattern of pointed tongues or feather tips. For example, see such patterns in Bol 1989, pls. 52.H21a, 78.H70α–β, 85.H94.

2 Deianeira perched calmly on the back of Nessos, in a seemingly cooperative attitude, is seen in only a few other visual representations (*LIMC* 6, 843, nos. 98–99, 100–102, s.v. "Nessos"). These nonviolent images give no hint of the imminent rape attempt.

3 The neck, folded in upon itself, is characteristic of herons in flight, as opposed to cranes, which fly with their necks stretched out (Voous 1960, 16–18).

4 Pipili 1987, 2–3; Pollard 1977, 68–69, 116–29. Herons are also commonly placed in women's scenes on Greek vases (Woysch-Méautis 1982, 50; Barringer 1995, 121–23).

5 Soph. *Trach.* 557–65.

6 This artist's signature is also preserved on a shield-band fragment from Olympia (Olympia B236: Kunze 1950, 43, no. 76, 212, no. 2a, Beil. 12.1).

7 Bronze kouros from Delphi, ca. 650–625 B.C. (Delphi 2527: Stewart 1990, 108, fig. 36).

8 Kleobis and Biton from Delphi, ca. 600–575 B.C. (Delphi 467 and 980: Stewart 1990, 109, fig. 56).

9 Bol 1989, 54 n. 231.

10 Oakley and Sinos 1993, 25–26, 30.

11 Oakley and Sinos 1993, 32.

12 The shape of the insect is that of several modern species of bees and flies found in Greece (Zahradník 1977, 238, no. 8; 298, nos. 2–3; 304, nos. 3–5). The shape of the lizard is close to two modern species found in Greece, Kotschy's Gecko and the Agama stellio (Arnold and Burton 1978, 110–11). On meaning, see *CVA* Braunschweig, Herzog-Anton-Ulrich-Museum 12, Deutschland 4, pls. 3–4; Kunze 1950, 106 n. 2; Edlund 1980b, 31–35. The lizard and insect motif is seen on other shield bands, e.g., placed between the figures of Ajax and Kassandra on a band in the Delphi Museum (B237: *LIMC* 7 [1994], 961, no. 49a, pl. 673, s.v. "Kassandra I" [Paoletti]). Faunal motifs on armor may have had a talismanic significance, especially those of a species hunting its prey, as here (Faraone 1992, 3–17, 58–59 [discussion of animal motifs on the baldric of Herakles]).

13 Pollard 1977, 88–89; Woysch-Méautis 1982, 47; Barringer 2001, 90–93 (in context of homosexual courtship scenes). The cock also has associations with Athena (Pollard 1977, 144, 147).

14 The visual evidence is extensive and much richer (Kahil 1955; *LIMC* 4 [1988], 498–563, s.v. "Helene" [Kahil]; *LIMC* 8 [1997], 834–41, s.v. "Menelaos" [Kahil]) than surviving literary accounts, which exist among the fragments known as The Epic Cycle (Evelyn-White 1982, 519 [*The Little Iliad* 13] and 521 [*The Sack of Ilium* 1]). Because of the presence of Athena, other mythological couples are worth considering: Ajax and Kassandra (Frel 1994, 12); Paris abducting Helen from Sparta (also noted by Frel); and Tydeus killing Ismene (Robertson 1995, 434–36). There are problems, however, with those identifications: Kassandra is typically shown distraught, at a reduced scale in a half-kneeling position, and placed between Ajax and Athena (*LIMC* 7, 961, nos. 48–55, s.v. "Kassandra I," as representative of the type); Helen is not led at sword point by Paris (*LIMC* 1 [1981], 511, no. 64, pl. 388, s.v. "Alexandros" [Hampe] as representative of the iconography); Ismene is usually depicted partially undressed, with Tydeus actively either killing or threatening her (*LIMC* 5 [1990], 797, nos. 3–4, 6, s.v. "Ismene I" [Krauskopf], as typical examples). So, even taking into account the unexpected presence of Athena in the scene, the couple is best identified as Helen and Menelaos (*LIMC* 4, 547–48, nos. 306–14, s.v. "Helene").

15 Kunze 1950.

16 Bol 1989.

## 37

## Black-Figure Amphora with Herakles and Nessos

**Greek, Athens, ca. 530–520 B.C., attributed to
the Medea Group**
**Ceramic**
**Height 34 cm., diameter of foot 13 cm., maximum
diameter of body 22.1 cm.**
**J. Paul Getty Museum, Malibu, California (88.AE.24)**

CONDITION
**The amphora has been broken and repaired from
several large fragments. A chip from the lip and a
small area adjacent to the left figure on side *B* have
been filled and in-painted. The vase is otherwise in
excellent condition. The surfaces of the vase are
clean and probably have been coated with wax or
another finishing material.**

Amphorae were used by the Greeks and Romans to store a wide variety of perishable materials, including grains, olives, and wine. The Type B amphora was popular during the latter part of the sixth century B.C. and is the most common shape for a black-figure amphora. The flaring mouth, round black handles, and echinus-shaped foot are its distinguishing features. The panel-amphora is a variety of Type B amphora and is called after the single reserved panel on each side of the vase, designed to provide the painters with a distinctive field for their figural compositions. Decoration outside the panel is always minimal. Here, forty rays extend from the base of the vase, and each panel is crowned with a row of pendant lotus buds.

Amphorae frequently display scenes from heroic mythology paired with so-called genre scenes. In the center of side *A*, Herakles attacks the centaur Nessos for assaulting his wife, Deianeira, who witnesses the event from the left. Deianeira unveils her himation in an action frequently used by female figures and specific to married women and young brides.[1] In the absence of inscriptions, this action helps to identify her as the hero's wife (cf. cat. no. 36, shield band, upper panel). She extends her right hand in rigid alarm.

Herakles wears a tunic covered by a breastplate. A sheathed sword, bow, and quiver with arrows hang on his back. Though fully armed with these weapons, he attacks Nessos with his most characteristic attribute, the club. Holding this upraised in his right hand, he grabs the centaur's upper right arm with his left hand as he prepares to strike him. Nessos fights back with a cry, brandishing white rocks in both hands.[2] Despite his ferocious stance and screaming mouth, the centaur's front legs buckle under the advance of Herakles. The elderly man standing to the right can only be Oineus, Deianeira's father. Compositions including onlookers who flank combat scenes are remarkably common in this period, especially on amphorae. Often these figures are anonymous, but this painter has made the figures part of the narrative by including hints that suggest their identity, in this case, the old man's receding white hair, and the clothing and action of a young but unhappy bride.

The most powerful description of the story comes from Deianeira herself in Sophokles' *Trachiniae* (553–76): trusting the centaur to ferry her across the River Evenos, she instead found herself fighting off his unwanted advances midstream.[3] Witnessing this conflict, Herakles quickly shot an arrow (tipped in poisonous blood from the Lernaian Hydra) sizzling into the lungs of the centaur. As Nessos lay dying on shore, he gave Deianeira some of his congealed blood, still potently poisonous, passing it off as a love charm. Deianeira would have reason to use it many years later, with deadly results for Herakles.

Side *B* shows Athenian youths engaged in three of the sports that comprised the pentathlon. A javelin-thrower sprints to the left, while another contestant kneels to choose a javelin from among several that are piled upon the ground. In the foreground, in front of the kneeling javelin-thrower, a discus-thrower readies himself, and to the right a jumper holds the weights he will use to extend his leap. This amphora was very likely used in the household as one of the functional wine storage vessels associated with the *symposion*, the drinking party, and the scenes upon it reflect the interests of the male elite who frequented such gatherings.

A graffito of three convergent triangles (Johnston type 40A) is incised in the center of the underside of the

amphora's base.[4] Trademarks consisting of designs (rather than letters) were favored by potters and tradesmen in the Athenian Kerameikos during the last quarter of the sixth century B.C. While some trademarks are acknowledged to indicate cost, either ownership or craftsmanship is more likely implied in this case.[5] White pigment largely remains for Deianeira's flesh, the hair and beard of Oineus, the rocks held by Nessos, and the ornament on the weapons of Herakles. Added red enlivens the himation of Deianeira, the cloak of Oineus, the beards and hair framing the faces of Herakles and Nessos, and the latter's tail.

The painter and potter of this vase remain unknown. They (or he) belonged to an important group of late-sixth-century artists known as the Medea Group.[6] Painters belonging to this group produced works characterized by use of straightforward narrative, compositional clarity, and stylistically clean lines. In their style and subject matter, they show influence from the slightly earlier and greater black-figure potter and painter Exekias (ca. 545–530 B.C.). The Medea Group's surviving pots exhibit subject matter that favors Herakles—not surprising for aristocratic art in late-sixth-century Athens, where Herakles was promoted as a civic hero.

This painting of the story of Herakles and Nessos is an interesting example of the iconographic flexibility artists typically display when they combine mythical and pictorial narratives. Sophokles wrote the *Trachiniae* about one hundred years after this vase was produced.[7] His use of the bow and arrow for Herakles' weapon varies from most of the earlier vase-paintings that prefer to show Herakles wielding either sword or club.[8] By using the bow and arrow to kill Nessos, Sophokles referenced Herakles' future rather than his past. In contrast, the anonymous vase-painter chose to emphasize the hero's youthful vigor by arming him with his club rather than with the instruments of his death.

—MLH

**BIBLIOGRAPHY**

"Acquisitions/1988," *GettyMusJ* 17 (1989): 112; "U.S. Museum Acquisitions," *Minerva* 1.6 (1990): 47; Grossman 2002, 30.

**NOTES**

1  Oakley and Sinos 1993, 25–26, 30.
2  Black-figure iconography often has Nessos defending himself with rocks. For comparative examples, see *LIMC* 6 (1992), figs. 40, 43–45, 48–49, s.v. "Nessos" (Díez de Velasco); figure 48, by the Painter of the Vatican Mourner, is especially close to the Getty amphora, as is the amphora in San Antonio (79.59.15), attributed to Group E (Shapiro, Picón, and Scott 1995, 89–90, no. 41).
3  For Deianeira crossing the river on the back of Nessos, cf. the lower panel on the shield band discussed in this volume as cat. no. 36.
4  A similar mark appears on an amphora in Naples (RC199), attributed to the Group of Würzburg 199 (*ABV* 288.18), a group of painters contemporary with the Medea Group. See Johnston 1979, 88.
5  For a summary of the uses and interpretation of trademarks on vases, see A. Johnston, in Rasmussen and Spivey 1991, 219–25.
6  The name "Medea Painter" was first coined in 1945 by H. R. W. Smith after an amphora in the British Museum (B 221), with a scene of Medea rejuvenating the ram (Smith 1945, 473). Smith collected three other pots together under this name, which was changed to the Medea Group by Beazley (*ABV* 321.1–4), who later added three more vases (*Paralipomena* 141.1–6; see also *BAdd*[2] 87).
7  Sophokles lived from about 496 to 406 B.C. and entered his first dramatic competition in 468 B.C. Although the date of the *Trachiniae* is unknown, H. Lloyd-Jones (1994, vol. 1, 9) conjectures that it may belong to the "fifties or the forties of the fifth century," along with *Antigone*.
8  See *LIMC* 6, 842, nos. 81–82, s.v. "Nessos." Very few surviving Attic vases show Herakles using the bow and arrow against Nessos.

# 38

## Red-Figure Bell-Krater with the Wedding of Cheiron

Greek, Attic, ca. 440–430 B.C., attributed to the
Eupolis Painter
Ceramic
Height 36.5 cm., diameter 38.8 cm., width including
handles 43.4 cm.
Private collection

CONDITION
The vase is intact except for a minor repair in the rim
on side B. There is moderate misfiring on side B and
some loss of black glaze in the handle zone. Details in
added red and white slip are largely worn away.

A centaur escorts his bride in their wedding procession
on this red-figure bell-krater by the Eupolis Painter.[1]
A woman follows the couple, bearing the torches that indicate the nocturnal procession from the bride's house to
that of the groom.[2] The centaur, with shaggy hair and
beard, wears a spotted animal skin (deer?) over one shoulder, tied in a knot across his chest. A large, leafless branch
serves as his walking stick. He looks intently at his bride.
His right hand rests on her shoulders and guides her forward. His mouth is slightly open, perhaps speaking words
of encouragement. The bride, adorned with a crown and
necklace, wears a pleated chiton under a himation bordered
with a dark-colored ball fringe. The himation covers her
hands and her head, which tilts downward slightly in a
modest and submissive gaze. A long curl from her unbound
hair shows on either side of her face. The woman bearing
torches also is dressed in a chiton and himation, but she
wears no crown and her uncovered hair is bound by three
white fillets (now lost) and tied loosely at the back.

Centaurs usually interact with women under circumstances of conflict, and their relations are more aptly
characterized as rape than as marriage. Often the centaurs'
naturally brutish natures are inflamed by wine. The centaurs carrying off the brides of the Lapiths at their
wedding feast is a version of this encounter that appears
frequently in art. As seen in the west pediment of the
temple of Zeus at Olympia and numerous Athenian

vase-paintings, the centaurs and their victims struggle
vigorously, even as the Lapith men fight to defend their
brides. Here, by contrast, the atmosphere could not be
more decorous and calm. The centaur walks slowly forward. He gently guides the woman with his hand, while
the branch, frequently a weapon in the hands of a centaur,
rests harmlessly on the ground. His gaze reveals intensity
but not aggression. His companion stands still, but her
body reveals no resistance to the idea of walking with
him. No violence is expressed in their interaction. Their
relationship appears to be one of trust, or at least consent.

The idea that this is a wedding is confirmed both
by the garb and crown of the centaur's companion and by
the torches carried by the woman who follows the pair.
The best-known centaur marriage in ancient literature is
that of Cheiron,[3] who married the nymph Chariklo,[4] and
it is undoubtedly that wedding that is represented here,
so far without parallel.

Cheiron was exceptional among centaurs and, in the
view of some writers, a god. He was the son of Kronos[5]
and Philyra,[6] a daughter of Okeanos. Intelligent, wise,
benign, skilled in music and medicine, Cheiron was the
companion and teacher of gods and heroes. Homer called
him the "most righteous of the centaurs."[7] He helped
Peleus capture Thetis (cf. cat. nos. 39, 96) and was present
at their wedding. When their son Achilles was born, the
parents brought the child to Cheiron to raise, in the cave
on Mount Pelion where he lived with his wife and mother,
and reared Jason and other heroes.[8] He taught hunting,
which he learned from Apollo and Artemis, to Achilles,
and healing to Asklepios.[9] He and Chariklo had children
of their own.[10]

The extraordinarily human personality of Cheiron is
vividly depicted in vase-painting, especially by Attic black-
figure artists. Unlike other centaurs, Cheiron is often shown
with a full human body, clad in a himation or chlamys, the
rear part of a horse's body protruding from the center of
the human back. Following sculptural prototypes, this form
disappears by the middle of the fifth century in favor of
centaurs who are human only to the waist, with artists rely-
ing on context to indicate that the centaur is Cheiron.[11]

Cheiron and Chariklo appear together on Greek vases
in scenes of the Wedding of Peleus and Thetis, and of

Peleus (and sometimes Thetis) bringing their son Achilles to Cheiron (cf. cat. no. 40).[12] Scenes including Chariklo are far less common than those with Cheiron alone. Sophilos, on his dinos in the British Museum, and Kleitias, on the François Vase, feature Cheiron and Chariklo in early representations of the wedding scene. Sophilos makes Chariklo one of the four goddesses who are the first guests to be welcomed by Peleus: Hestia and Demeter, Leto and Chariklo. They are followed by Dionysos, then Hebe, then Cheiron. Kleitias, in his glorious procession of the gods at the wedding, places Cheiron as the first guest to meet Peleus at his house, his prominence reflecting his role in arranging the marriage. Chariklo appears with the same three goddesses in the part of the procession that falls on the other side of the vase. In a later variant of this subject, Cheiron and his

women are alike in wearing chiton and himation, but only the one on the right has covered her hair. Lacking inscriptions naming the figures, the scene cannot be linked to the wedding scene on the obverse.

—SBM

**BIBLIOGRAPHY**

*LIMC* 7 (1994), 387, no. 3, pl. 327, s.v. "Philyra" (Kossatz-Deissmann).

**NOTES**

1 Attributed by Michael Padgett. The published attribution to the Methyse Painter (*LIMC* 7, 387, no. 3, s.v. "Philyra") erroneously ascribed to R. Guy. Cf. especially the drawing of the women on a kalpis by the Eupolis Painter in Rome (Vatican 17939: *ARV*² 1074.18).

2 Ghosts of added red flames are preserved. On weddings, see Oakley and Sinos 1993.

3 On Cheiron, including citations to ancient sources for Cheiron's character and skills as enumerated here, see *LIMC* 3 (1986), 237–48, pls. 185–97, s.v. "Cheiron" (Gisler-Huwiler). On centaurs, see Baur 1912; Schiffler 1976 (on Cheiron, 30–37, 257–61, pl. 4).

4 On Chariklo, see *LIMC* 3 (1986), 189–91, pls. 150–51, s.v. "Chariklo I" (Finster-Hotz).

5 Some sources say of Poseidon or Ixion; see *LIMC* 3, 237, s.v. "Cheiron."

6 On Philyra, see *LIMC* 7, 386–87, pls. 326–27, s.v. "Philyra"; this vase: 387, no. 3, pl. 327.

7 Hom. *Il.* 11.832, trans. R. Lattimore (Chicago 1951). For Philyra as the nymph of the linden/lime tree, see Colvin 1880, 134–36.

8 Jason: Hom. *Il.* 11.832; also Pind. *Pyth.* 4.103–6.

9 Pind. *Nem.* 3.43–58.

10 On these, see *LIMC* 3, 237, s.v. "Cheiron."

11 For examples of both, see ibid. passim.

12 On these scenes, see Shapiro 1994b, 99–105. For the Sophilos dinos, see Williams 1983.

13 Collection of Shelby White and Leon Levy: Shapiro 1994b, 102, figs. 68–69; Bothmer 1990, no. 121. All figures on the vase are named; this is the only known inscription naming Philyra. For Philyra as the leader of the procession, see Oakley and Sinos 1993, 6.

14 Paris, Cab. Méd. no number; Schiffler 1976, 269, cat. K-21; *LIMC* 3, 190, no. 4, s.v. "Chariklo I"; *LIMC* 3, 241, no. 56, pl. 192, s.v. "Cheiron." Another possible example, although lacking inscriptions, is on a Siana cup by the Heidelberg Painter (Würzburg L 452), where the women standing behind Cheiron may include both Chariklo and Philyra: *ABV* 63.6; *LIMC* 7, 387, no. 2, pl. 326, s.v. "Philyra."

mother Philyra serve as the parents of Peleus in a wedding scene by the Copenhagen Painter from about 470 B.C.: the centaur stands outside the door of the groom's house in the spot normally reserved for the father, while Philyra, bearing torches and named by inscription, leads the procession to the marriage bed.[13] Likewise, the woman with torches following Cheiron and Chariklo on this krater should also be identified as Philyra. Chariklo appears only rarely in scenes of the young Achilles being delivered to Cheiron. On a Corinthian plate of about 600 B.C., for example, Cheiron receives Achilles from his father, while Chariklo stands behind her husband; both figures are named in inscriptions.[14] Compared to the range and prominence of Cheiron, Chariklo's presence in vase-painting is extremely rare, and, other than on this krater, is restricted to Corinthian and Attic black-figure vases.

On the reverse of this vessel, a man with white hair and beard (now worn away) appears between two women. The old man, wearing a long himation over his shoulder, walks slowly to the right, aided by a staff, toward a woman who stands at right, facing him. He turns back toward the woman at left, his arm outstretched toward her while she stands, unresponsive, enveloped in her himation. The

## 39

# Black-Figure Lekythos with Cheiron Watching Peleus Wrestle Thetis

Greek, Attic, ca. 490 B.C., attributed to the
Diosphos Painter
Ceramic
Height 19.9 cm., diameter of body 7.4 cm., diameter
of mouth 4.0 cm., diameter of foot 5.5 cm.
Arthur M. Sackler Museum, Harvard University Art
Museums, bequest of Joseph C. Hoppin (1925.30.49)

CONDITION
The fine-grained red clay is hard-fired and slightly
pinkish. The foot, mouth, and handle have been
reattached, the handle repair disguised with black
slip. On the body there are three small scratches on
the figure of Thetis. The mottled appearance in
many areas of the vase may be due to imperfection
of the glaze at firing.

The shoulder, clearly distinct from the body, marks this
vase as a Type II lekythos. It is an early, black-figure version of the straight-bodied, cylinder type[1] and is similar
in shape to some of the lekythoi painted by the Leagros
Group and the Bowdoin Workshop.[2] The reserved white
shoulder neck, the lotus-bud chain on the shoulder, the
checkerboard pattern at the top of the body, and the foot
in two degrees also identify the vase as belonging to Type
DL, the Diosphos Painter's type.[3] C. H. E. Haspels attributed this vase to the Diosphos Painter and identified it as
one of seven, including three lekythoi, on which the artist
depicted Peleus and Thetis.[4] The subject of Peleus and
Thetis seems to have been particularly popular on black-
figure/white-ground lekythoi in this period.[5] As is common with the Diosphos Painter, the painted inscriptions
on the vase are meaningless.[6]

The main decoration consists of the tall black-figure
scene that encircles most of the body except for a small
gap at the back, beneath the handle. The black figures are
painted on a ground of creamy white slip. On the left side
is the centaur Cheiron. He has the full body of a robed

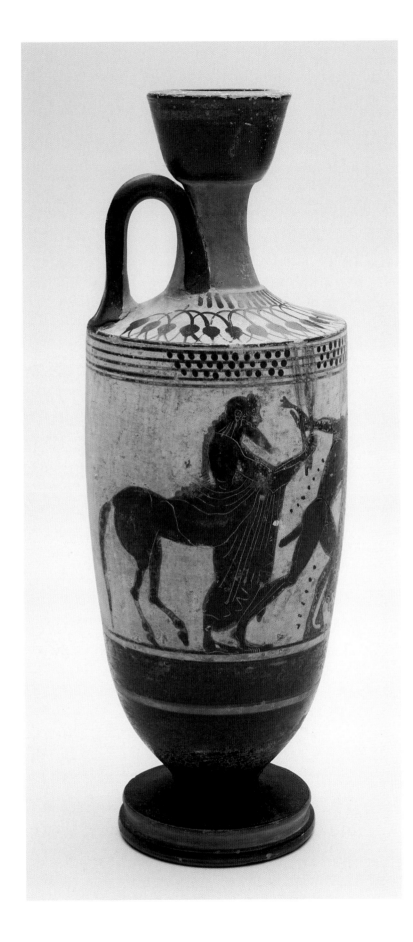

man attached to the body, hindquarters, and hind legs of a horse.[7] He has long, curly hair and a long, pointed beard. An himation is draped over his left arm. He steps forward slightly and extends his arms, grasping in each hand a blazing torch with flames rendered in brown diluted slip. In front of Cheiron is a naked male figure, Peleus, the son of Aiakos, who wrestles with the sea nymph Thetis. Peleus braces himself to exert the greatest force, his left leg forward and bent, his right leg stretched behind him. The straining of the muscles in his legs and torso are shown with incisions, and his face is in a grimace. His arms are wrapped around the waist of Thetis, and his head is hunched against her right shoulder. Like the centaur, Peleus has long, curly hair and wears a fillet. There is a sword at his waist but no baldric to hold it.

Thetis tries to pull away from her attacker, her left hand braced against his forehead in an attempt to push him away. Her body is turned frontally but her head is in profile to the left, facing the centaur: she seems to look straight at him, and her right arm stretches toward him. Her hair, in a *krobylos*, is long and curly, draping down her back; there are small curls at her forehead and temples. Flames, again drawn with diluted glaze, leap up from both shoulders. Her left elbow connects to a snake that lies atop an altar decorated with volutes. A palm tree stands behind the altar, which together with the altar, symbolizes a sanctuary, possibly connected to Artemis or Zeus Herkeios.[8] At the far right is another woman, a Nereid, who, looking back toward her sister Thetis, leaps forward with her left leg as she tries to escape from the scene. She brandishes a dolphin in her right hand, a sign of her watery nature.

Because the white body of the lekythos is a continuous panel with no obvious breaks or repetition of figures, we might be tempted to say that the representation shows a single moment of the story. If we take into account Apollodoros's version of the myth, however, we see that the Diosphos Painter is actually combining several episodes —he is conflating time. According to Apollodoros, Zeus and Poseidon had desired Thetis, but Themis had prophesied that any son that Thetis bore would be stronger than his father. The two gods naturally lost interest, but the centaur Cheiron, mentor to Peleus, encouraged the young man to seize and hold her no matter what shape she might take. Unhappy at the prospect of marriage to a mere mortal, Thetis turned herself into fire, water, and beasts in an effort to elude him. She was unsuccessful; the pair was married before all the gods, and the hero Achilles was born not long after.[9]

Cheiron's benevolent presence—his upturned lips seem to smile—echoes a previous moment in which he encouraged the abduction. The fire on Thetis's shoulders and the snake at her elbow represent separate chronological actions in the story, as she did not turn herself into all these different elements at once.

There are two elements painted on the vase that are not mentioned in the account of Apollodoros. The first is the Nereid, who, in a form of prolepsis, may be a symbolic reference to a future event—the upcoming marriage. Nereids are common in both funerary and conjugal contexts, and according to Judith Barringer, they "serve as escorts of an individual undergoing a critical life transformation," so that in this case they might represent the transformation of a "wild virgin to tamed matron."[10] But since it is also common in this period to find the sisters of the victim or other groups of young women in the iconography of abduction scenes, the Nereid's role here may be not only to evoke the future, but also to provide context for the moment just before the abduction.[11]

The other element not mentioned by Apollodoros, the combination of altar and palm tree, may also refer to the future marriage, but again, there is uncertainty. Christiane Sourvinou-Inwood has argued that this combination of images in the fifth century B.C. is a representation of the ritual involved in young women's preparation for marriage. Altars were used as dedications and shrines for wedding amphorae and hydriae on the south slope of the Acropolis,[12] and for animal sacrifice to the gods of matrimony (*theoi gameloi*) during the wedding ceremony. However, if the altar and palm tree were instead a reference to Zeus Herkeios, the altar might have been painted in order to locate the scene in a palace court, namely, that of Nereus.[13] The torches that Cheiron holds are almost certainly a reference to the marriage ceremony, in which torches were carried during the procession.[14] If this is the case, the torches not only proleptically allude to the wedding but also indicate Cheiron's active involvement in it.

Thus, the painting on the Sackler lekythos illustrates the conflation of different scenes from the mythological narrative, beginning with the presence and support of Cheiron, continuing with the multiple transformations of Thetis, simultaneously shown, and possibly also with the Nereid and the altar-palm tree configuration as a foreshadowing of marriage.

—ABS

## BIBLIOGRAPHY

*CVA* USA 1, 11–12, pl. 19.1 and 3; *ABL* 233, 20.

## NOTES

1 Kurtz 1975, 77–78. According to Kurtz, "the first cylinder lekythoi may have been red-figure—the new shape and new technique appearing together—but our earliest examples are black-figure."

2 For shape comparanda, see Kurtz 1975, pls. 3.1, 13.1–2; *ABL* 233, nos. 18 (pl. 36.4), 19, and 31. For the Diosphos Painter, see *ABL* 94–130, 232–41; *ABV* 508–11, 702–3; *Paralipomena* 248–50; *BAdd*² 127–28; Haspels 1972; Kurtz 1975, 96–102.

3 Kurtz 1975, 40.

4 Of these, two are on small neck-amphorae, one in Vienna (IV 3599: *ABL* 240, 148; Baur 1912, 108, no. 264) and one in Capua (7555: *ABL* 240, 152; *ABV* 703). Other versions are on an amphora in Munich (1582: *ABL* 241, 161); an alabastron in Amsterdam (318: *CVA* The Hague, Musée Scheurleer 1, Netherlands 1, pl. 1 [37], 1; *ABL* 237, 103); and three lekythoi: the Harvard vase; one in Berlin, which is particularly close to the Harvard version (Berlin F 2003: *ABL* 234, 39; Baur 1912, 106–7, no. 258; *LIMC* 7 [1994], 261, no. 167, pl. 198, s.v. "Peleus" [Vollkommer]); and another in Paris (Louvre CA 1887: *ABL* 233, 35). Beazley added an eighth example, a neck-amphora formerly in the New York market (*ABV* 510, 26). Schiffler added another alabastron with this subject (Athens, Kerameikos 1531; Schiffler 1976, 259, cat. A/Ch 25, pl. 4). The Diosphos Painter's close companion, the Sappho Painter, also painted this subject on a white-ground lekythos (Paris, Louvre CA 156: Baur 1912, 107, no. 259; *ABL* 226, 11, pl. 33, 2), with Cheiron emerging from a cave holding a pair of torches.

5 For examples, see *LIMC* 8 (1997), 260, nos. 121–22, 124–26, pl. 194, s.v. "Thetis" (Vollkommer).

6 Each figure has an inscription next to it consisting of dabs of paint that do not even have the shape of Greek letters. Moreover, the number of "letters" does not correspond to the number that would be in each name. The Diosphos Painter apparently was not fully illiterate; however, Haspels lists four vases with inscriptions that make sense (*ABL* 96–97).

7 This corresponds to Baur's so-called Type B centaur (Baur 1912, 100–110).

8 Sourvinou-Inwood (1985, 127) argues for the association between Artemis as protector of the *parthenoi* and the "altar with palm tree" in scenes of pursuit and abduction.

9 Apollod. *Bibl.* 3.13.4–6.

10 Barringer 1995, 69.

11 For examples, see Kaempf-Dimitriadou 1979, figs. 361, 363, 364, 389, and 393 (Oreithyia). Abduction scenes in which young women, such as Thetis, Oreithyia, Persephone, Europa, or Aigina, are accompanied by a sister or bands of young women are fairly common.

12 Webster 1973, 135.

13 Ferrari (2002, 36) has written: "[T]he altar of Zeus Herkeios is a standard feature of the representation of ancient palaces, where it is located in the court."

14 See Sourvinou-Inwood 1985, 129 and, for comparanda on wedding torches, Oakley and Sinos 1993, figs. 108–11. Beazley (1927, 148) believed that these are torches; Baur (1912, 107), however, did not think that they are specifically related to weddings (but provided no reasons). In this connection, it might be useful to study in greater detail Cheiron's role in the myth of Peleus and Thetis.

## 40

# Black-Figure Lekythos with Cheiron Receiving Achilles from Peleus

Greek, Attic, ca. 510–500 B.C., attributed to
the Edinburgh Painter
Ceramic
Height 33.3 cm., maximum diameter 11.8 cm.,
diameter of foot 7.3 cm.
Private collection

### CONDITION

A break in the shoulder has been repaired, and a
small hole in the lower body has been filled and
painted black. The figure of the woman is quite
worn, as are the handle and three of the shoulder
palmettes, but the surface is otherwise in good
condition except for minor chips and spalls.

At the end of the sixth century B.C., Athenian potters
developed a new lekythos shape with a tall, nearly
straight-sided cylindrical body that would become the
standard throughout the next century. Among the first to
popularize the shape was the Edinburgh Painter, a black-
figure artist who at the beginning of his career was associated with the Leagros Group and later established the
fashion for white-ground lekythoi.[1] His early lekythoi
usually have seven black palmettes on the shoulder below
a band of simple tongues, and a band of net-pattern
around the top of the cylinder. This lekythos is typical of
the painter's early style and probably dates no later than
500 B.C. In addition to the figure frieze, the neck, the side
of the disk foot, and the top of the mouth also are
reserved in the reddish orange color of the clay. The lower
body, the top of the foot, and the sides of the mouth
and handle are coated with black slip.

In the principal scene, Peleus brings the young
Achilles to be raised by Cheiron, the wise centaur who
also was said to have taught Jason, Asklepios, and several
other heroes and demigods, although it was his rearing
of Achilles that provided the model for these others.[2]
Although the majority of examples date to the last

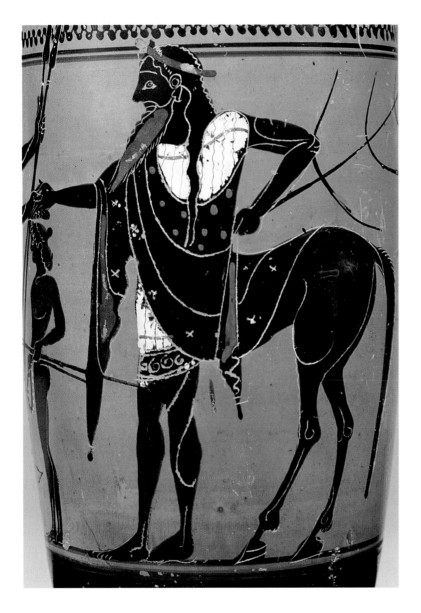

spangled with crosses and white dots. His beard and the broad-brimmed petasos on his head are painted red. He holds a pair of long spears in his left hand. As is customary in depictions of Cheiron, the centaur is shown with the barrel and hindquarters of a horse attached in front to a fully human body, the latter dressed in a short chiton of added white and a red-spotted himation that falls on his equine back like a horse blanket.[5] He wears a red fillet, and there are red stripes across the incised pleats of his chitoniskos. Cheiron's beard is larger than Peleus's, and his long hair hangs nearly to his waist. In his left hand he holds a small tree, a rude weapon commonly carried by centaurs that in this context is surely meant to recall the famous ash spear that he gave to Peleus and that Achilles carried to Troy.[6] He holds the tree at a curious angle — the root ought to pass in front of his body but does not — and, in general, his stance is more awkward than that of Peleus or Achilles, with most of his two bodies in profile to the left but his human torso turned to a frontal position.

Standing behind Peleus is a woman in a poor state of preservation. She wears a peplos and, over this, a himation, which she drapes over her head and shoulders.[7] Both garments are edged in red. She raises the himation with her covered left hand; her right arm is flexed. The added white on her face and right hand is lost, but traces remain on her feet. The pair of leafless vines that seem to emerge from her right shoulder is a common motif on small vases of this period. The woman has been identified as Philyra,[8] the mother of Cheiron, but this is unlikely. Philyra is only rarely represented in art (cf. cat. no. 38), and her many counterparts in other depictions of this subject, who usually stand behind Peleus, are customarily identified as Thetis, the daughter of Nereus, whose marriage to Peleus was Cheiron's doing: "He brought to pass the marriage / of Nereus's daughter of the shining breasts, and reared / her magnificent son, waxing his heart to all things becoming."[9]

The Edinburgh Painter returned to this subject on three other occasions: a fragment from a lekanis lid in Paris,[10] a lekythos in Syracuse,[11] and a white-ground lekythos in Athens.[12] In all four versions the core composition is basically the same, with Achilles represented as a young boy carrying a pair of javelins. On the examples

quarter of the sixth century B.C., the subject had a long history in Attic vase-painting, first appearing as early as the mid-seventh century on fragmentary Middle Protoattic vases by the Polyphemos Painter and the Ram Jug Painter.[3] In most cases, Achilles is represented as a babe in arms, but nearly as often he is shown as a young boy, as he is here.[4] The naked Achilles stands between Peleus and Cheiron, who shake hands above his head. The boy faces his father, a pair of short hunting javelins in one hand and the throwing-thong in the other. His long hair is tied up in a krobylos. Peleus is dressed for the hunt in a short chiton and a red-striped chlamys, both

in Paris and Syracuse, Achilles faces Cheiron, while on the
Athens lekythos—the closest parallel—he again faces
Peleus and holds both the javelins and the thong. Standing
next to him on the Athens vase is a fawn, an allusion to the
woodland setting and, perhaps, his future provender.[13]
—JMP

### BIBLIOGRAPHY

Basel, *MuM*, Auktion 40, *Kunstwerke der Antike*, December 13, 1969, no. 76,
pl. 27; Brommer 1973, 330, no. 17; *LIMC* 1 (1981), 46, no. 36, pl. 60, s.v.
"Achilleus" (Kossatz-Deissmann); *LIMC* 3 (1986), 241, no. 50, pl. 191,
s.v. "Cheiron" (Gisler-Huwiler); New York, Christie's, December 7,
2000, no. 440.

### NOTES

1 For the Edinburgh Painter, see *ABL* 86–89, 215–21; *ABV* 476–78,
700; *Paralipomena* 217–19; *BAdd²* 120–21; Boardman 1974, 147; Kurtz
1975, 13–14.

2 For Cheiron, see the discussion and notes in cat. no. 38 in this volume.
No literary account describes Herakles as the pupil of Cheiron, but on
a black-figure neck-amphora, of the same date as this lekythos, Hermes
is shown carrying the infant hero, his name inscribed, to the centaur
(Munich 1615A: *ABV* 484.6; *LIMC* 4 [1988], 832 [drawing], no. 1665, s.v.
"Herakles" [Boardman]).

3 Polyphemos Painter, Aigina Museum: Morris 1984, 39, pl. 4. Ram Jug
Painter, Berlin 31573 A9: *LIMC* 1, 45, pl. 58, no. 21, s.v. "Achilleus"; Morris
1984, 55–56, pl. 12; Beazley 1986, 9–10, pl. 9.3–4.

4 For vase-paintings of Peleus bringing Achilles to Cheiron, see Brommer
1973, 330–31; Friis Johansen 1939; Beck 1975, 9–12, pls. 1–3; *LIMC* 1,
45–47, pls. 58–61, s.v. "Achilleus"; *LIMC* 3, 24, pls. 191–92, s.v.
"Cheiron"; *LIMC* 7 (1994), 267–68, pl. 209, s.v. "Peleus" (Vollkommer).

5 In contrast, when drawing Nessos or the centaurs of Mount Pholoë,
the Edinburgh Painter represented them with human torsos and equine
forelegs: cf. Munich 1905 WAF (*ABL* 218.49; *Veder Greco* 1988, 107, no. 9);
and another lekythos formerly in the art market (Basel, *MuM*, Auktion
51, *Kunstwerke der Antike*, March 14–15, 1975, no. 135). The artist often
painted chitons and chitoniskoi in added white: e.g., that of Odysseus
on a lekythos in Athens (Nat. Mus. 1130: *ABL* 217.27, pl. 29.3;
*Paralipomena* 217; *BAdd²* 120).

6 Hom. *Il.* 16.139–44; Apollod. *Bibl.* 3.13.5. Stewart (1983, 64–65, 72 n.
50), while acknowledging that the literature mentions centaurs fighting
with fir and pine trees instead of ash, makes a good case for Cheiron's
tree being the ash that yielded the spear of Achilles.

7 The Edinburgh Painter often hooded the heads of women in this fashion: cf. Deianeira on the Nessos lekythos in Munich (see n. 5 above);
and the Artemis on a lekythos in the Borowski Collection, Jerusalem,
here attributed to the Edinburgh Painter (Bernheimer 2001, no. 75).

8 New York, Christie's, December 7, 2000, no. 440.

9 Pind. *Nem.* 3.56–58, trans. R. Lattimore.

10 Paris, Cab. Méd. [no number]: *ABL* 219.60; *CVA* Bibliothèque National
2, France 10, pl. 83, no. 22.

11 Syracuse 18418: *ABL* 217.38; Beck 1975, pl. 3, fig. 13.

12 Athens, Nat. Mus. 550: *ABL* 217.28, pl. 28; Friis Johansen 1939, 195,
fig. 6; Beck 1975, pl. 3, fig. 19; *LIMC* 1, 45, pl. 58, no. 19.

13 "[Cheiron] fed him honeycombs and the marrow of fawns" (Philostr.
*Her.* 45.4, trans. J. K. B. Maclean and E. B. Aitken [Atlanta 2001]).

# 41

# Fragment of a Kantharos with Centaur

**Italy, Faliscan, third quarter of the seventh century B.C.**
**Ceramic (impasto)**
**Height 14.8 cm., width 19.7 cm., diameter 7.8 cm.**
**Princeton University Art Museum, gift of Allan**
**Marquand, Class of 1874 (y1950–40)**

CONDITION
**The fragment is of dark gray clay with mineral inclusions; the core is browner. There are irregular breaks on all sides. A section of the flange has been reattached. The surface is in good condition except for patches of light brown incrustation. The exterior is burnished, but not the interior, which is scored with irregular wheel marks.**

The single large fragment preserves parts of both the upper and lower body, along with a section of the knobbed flange separating them at the vessel's widest circumference. The burnished gray fabric can be considered an improved form of impasto, not yet the fully developed Etruscan black bucchero of the sixth century B.C. The lower body has a spherical curve while the straight walls of the upper body slope inward. The lower walls are twice as thick (0.8 cm.) as the upper (0.4 cm.). The sturdy flange (max. depth 3.6 cm.) has two rather droopy triangular protrusions, which originally continued at intervals around the body.

A slight carination marks the transition from the flange to the upper wall, which is decorated with an incised centaur of peculiar type, walking to the right. The incised lines are relatively wide and shallow, with a few faint traces of red pigment, especially on the centaur's face and on the "tail" at the upper right. The centaur's fully human body is rendered in a lively, cartoonlike manner, with rubbery legs and a triangular torso. His head is oversized, with a long neck, full lips, a pointed beard, and a nose to match. Half of the right eye is preserved, but there is no trace of either hair or ears (one wonders if the latter were human). The centaur's wasp waist is cinched with a belt, from which a sort of loincloth extends along

the top of his raised left thigh. He is otherwise nude, as attested by the careful incision of the nipples and the pendulous but not ithyphallic genitals. The horse part of his anatomy is attached to his right shoulder like a trailer on a hitch, completely supplanting his right arm. The horse's barrel chest looms behind the adjacent human waist but does not touch it. The body of the horse is bordered with an inner line and crossed by four vertical lines near the flank and three zigzags across the ribs. The left hind leg, which also has an inner border, is fully preserved, while the right leg is lost. The hock and fetlock are sharply delineated. The creature's long tail curls around to cross the body of the horse, terminating in a bushy tip. He extends his left hand—crudely rendered, with a huge thumb—toward a slender object dangling from a rounded mass at the upper right. It may be a tail, for the tip resembles that of the centaur's own, though how another animal could be placed so much higher in the field is unclear.

This type of impasto kantharos, with a nearly biconical body surrounded by a spiked flange, was produced in the second half of the seventh century B.C. in the Faliscan territory north of Rome, where such vessels have been found in the cemeteries at Falerii Veteres (Città Castellana), Narce, and Capena.[1] Examples were traded into neighboring regions of Etruria—Chiusi and Orvieto—and into Latium, whose inhabitants were of related Indo-European stock. The name *kantharos*, a type of Greek wine cup with two tall, vertical handles, is frequently applied by scholars to vessels of similar shape, even when they are not Greek. We do not know the actual Faliscan name for cups like this, and even calling a vessel of such size a cup may not be entirely accurate, although its descendants in the bucchero repertory were, indeed, wine cups of classic kantharos form (e.g., cat. no. 42). The handles are frequently of complex shape: twisted, doubled with connecting latticework, topped by ram's heads, or in the form of human mourners.[2]

The distinctive decoration of the Faliscan kantharoi also had a strong influence on regional styles. The bodies have incised or scraped designs, often filled with red pigment, in the form of Orientalizing floral ornament and of highly stylized animals, most often horses, both "real"

and fantastic, with wings and Chimaera-like animal appendages. The outlining of the equine anatomy on this centaur is characteristic, but the creature itself is unique.[3] The artist may have seen a centaur on an imported Protocorinthinian cup or aryballos (e.g., cat. nos. 30, 31), which he imitated in his own inimitable way, grafting the body and hind legs of a horse stylized in the usual Faliscan manner onto a bearded human of earnest but simple aspect.

—JMP

**BIBLIOGRAPHY**

Unpublished.

**NOTES**

1  For the type, with bibliography, see Hayes 1985, 42.

2  For some examples exhibiting a diversity of handle shapes and incised decoration, see Hayes 1985, 43, B20; Jucker 1991, 167, no. 203; De Lucia Brolli 1991, 31, fig. 8; Chamay 1993, 194—99, nos. 97—100; *In Celebration* 1997, 11, no. 8; *CVA* Rome, Museo Prehistorico L. Pigorini 1, Italy 21, pls. 2.3, 3.3, 4.1, 6.1, 7.4—7, 8.6; *CVA* Copenhagen 5, Denmark 5, pl. 198.2—5.

3  A slightly later kantharos in Brussels (A 3352), more bucchero than impasto, has incised on one handle a crude centaur with forelegs but *no* arms: Weber-Lehmann 1988, 721, pl. 482, no. 3. The attachment between man and horse, however, is broader and less tenuous than on the Princeton centaur.

# 42

# Kantharos with Monsters and Animals

Etruscan, end of the seventh century B.C.
Ceramic (bucchero)
Height with handles 20.9 cm., height to rim 14.5 cm.,
width including handles 30.1 cm., diameter of
foot 9.6 cm.
Private collection, Princeton Class of 1973

CONDITION
The bucchero fabric is fired black throughout. The
smooth, reflective surface is thoroughly burnished
and is somewhat soapy in texture. The vase is
complete, with repaired breaks in the foot and on
the reverse. Two large reattached fragments on
the reverse are slightly worn.

A kantharos is a wine cup, usually footed, with a deep
body and two handles that rise high above the rim on
opposite sides. This kantharos is in bucchero, the quintessential Etruscan ceramic fabric distinguished by its black
color and burnished surface. Bucchero first appeared at
Cerveteri, in southern Etruria, in the second quarter of the
seventh century B.C.,[1] having developed from the impasto
fabric of the preceding two centuries (e.g., cat. no. 41).
The tall straight walls of this kantharos and the height
and shape of its hollow conical foot are characteristic of
Rasmussen's kantharos Type 3e, a numerous class that
begins in the last quarter of the seventh century and persists until the middle of the sixth.[2] The ribbon handles are
much wider at the base (7.2 cm.) than at the top (2.5 cm.),
where they are flanged. The bands of serrated notches
defining the juncture of the upper walls and lower body
are a common feature on kantharoi and some other early
bucchero shapes, particularly chalices and kyathoi.

Kantharoi of this type are normally not decorated,
but a small number, generally attributed to the region of
Cerveteri and Veii, are, like this cup, larger than usual and
have animal friezes incised directly into the burnished
surface.[3] The decoration on this example is particularly
fine. On each handle are four panels enclosing saltires and,
where the handle meets the rim, a row of dotted fans,

common ornament on early bucchero. On either side of
the body is a figural frieze (h. 4.6–5.0 cm.), above which
is a band of fans framed by paired lines terminating in
volutes. In the center of the obverse, a griffin and a sphinx
face one another in heraldic fashion over a stubby palmette. This is the height of the Orientalizing period in
Etruria, and the composition is certainly derived from
Near Eastern models in which sphinxes, griffins, and lions
face one another over a stylized Tree of Life. The Etruscan
artist may have based his design on an imported
Phoenician bowl, like those from the Bernardini tomb at
Praeneste,[4] but combined a griffin with a sphinx in a way
that no eastern artisan would have done. Other incised
bucchero vases of this period also feature heraldic sphinxes, griffins, lions, and even centaurs, always with a plant
of some kind between them.[5]

The leonine bodies of the sphinx and griffin are
incised with particular care, each raising a foreleg to cross
its counterpart's above the palmette. The sphinx has long
curly hair but is of indeterminate sex. A second palmette
grows beneath the griffin, whose beaked mouth is open,
its tongue protruding between incongruous rows of teeth.
At the far left, a third palmette hangs from the upper
border next to a seated leopard. It raises a paw to touch
the griffin's rump and turns its face toward the viewer.
The type is familiar from Corinthian and East Greek
vase-paintings of the period, as, indeed, are the griffin
and sphinx, which also appear in contemporary Etruscan
metalwork in association with the same kind of long-
stemmed palmettes.[6] The fourth figure, a seated lion at
the far right, has more native roots. Emerging from its
jaws are the torso and legs of a human male, a motif that
occurs on many Etruscan vases of the late seventh and
early sixth centuries.[7]

The frieze on the reverse begins with a pendant palmette and a horse and rider to right. The horse is low to
the ground, its hind legs bent, its forelegs fully extended;
it may be rising, or perhaps the rider has pulled in the
reins he holds in both hands and the horse is skidding to
a halt. An inscription in Etruscan fills the space beneath
the horse's legs (see below). Farther right, a toothless lion
is walking to the right in front of a tall tree or plant. The
beast raises a foreleg to touch the tail of a centaur, who

walks in the same direction. In front the centaur has a
fully human body. Like the horseman, he wears a tunic.
He carries a tree in one hand and a long-stemmed palmette in the other, which he raises like a weapon. Another
palmette grows from the ground behind him. There are
five *sigma*-shaped zigzags on the barrel of the centaur's
equine body and a curvilinear mark on his rump, possibly
a brand (the mounted horse has the same mark). The
centaur's hair is not curly like the sphinx's but is tied
behind the ears in the same way.

The combination of real and fantastic animals on
the reverse does not constitute a narrative; the horseman is
separated from the centaur, and in any case the latter's
mythical antagonists are never mounted. Centaurs seldom
join the processions of animals and monsters on incised
bucchero vases.[8] Horsemen are even less common in such
contexts, and the combination of the two in the same animal frieze is almost unprecedented.[9] Like the heraldic
group on the obverse, animal friezes of this type imitate
those on imported Greek pottery and Near Eastern metalwork, although only in the Corinthian repertory does
one find centaurs as part of the mix.[10]

—JMP

### THE INSCRIPTION

An inscription is engraved beneath the horse and rider
on the reverse. It is written from left-to-right, and there is
no punctuation or spacing separating the words. The
shapes of the letters, particularly the variation in the form

of *sigma*, and the left-to-right direction, point to a southern Etruscan origin—Caere (Cerveteri) is a likely candidate—and to a date near the end of the seventh century.

The inscription is the record of a gift given by or to
Licine Velchaina: *mi mulu licine`si velcaina`si.* Possible translations are: "I (was) given by Licine Velchaina," or "I (am)
a gift for Licine Velchaina."

A copy of the inscription is found on a bucchero
skyphos from Caere,[11] which raises the question of possible forgery. But since other Etruscan inscriptions engraved
on ceramic appear in duplicate or even triplicate, the mere
fact that this inscription is attested twice does not necessarily mean that either of the two is suspect.

—RW

BIBLIOGRAPHY

Unpublished.

NOTES

1 Rasmussen 1979, 106.

2 Rasmussen 1979, 104–6, pls. 31–32 (cf. esp. pl. 32, no. 172).

3 For bucchero kantharoi with incised figures scenes, see Bonamici 1974, nos. 8, 18, 24–26, 38–40, 46, 52, 76, 90; Hayes 1985, 75.

4 Neri 2000. The examples in the Bernardini tomb do not actually feature heraldic animals; cf. instead the griffins and sphinxes on a bowl from Kourion in Cyprus (New York, Met. 74.51.4554: Neri 2000, 36, fig. 13; Markoe 1985, 259, no. Cy8).

5 Bonamici 1974, no. 52, pl. 25 (griffins; sphinxes); no. 71, pl. 32 (lions); no. 90, pl. 44 (sphinxes); no. 103, pl. 53 (leopards); no. 99, pls. 48–49 (sphinxes; leopards); no. 100, pl. 51 (lions). Camporeale 1991, no. 101, pl. 86 (griffins); no. 102, pl. 87 (griffins; griffin and winged lion). *In Celebration* 1997, 11, no. 8 (lions). For a pair of heraldic centaurs on a bucchero kantharos in Toronto (959.17.75), see Hayes 1985, 75–76, no. C21; *LIMC* 8 (1997), 722, no. 22, pl. 484, s.v. "Kentauroi (in Etruria)" (Weber-Lehmann). There is no plant between the heraldic horses on a ring askos in the C.A. collection, but they do cross their raised forelegs in the same (unusual) manner as the griffin and sphinx on this vase: Camporeale 1991, no. 142, pl. 106.

6 For leopards with raised paws and frontal faces, see Childs 2001, 54. For the influence of Corinthian imports on bucchero artists and the possibility of immigrant Corinthian artisans in Etruria, see Rasmussen 1979, 157–58. For metalwork parallels to the griffin, sphinx, and palmettes, see Johansen 1979, 78, fig. 16 (griffin), and 86, fig. 25 (sphinx).

7 Szilágyi 1958, 274–75, figs. 5 and 7; Bonamici 1974, nos. 19, 25, 28, 45, 46, 55, 73, 76, 77, 89, 92, pls. 11, 12, 14, 22, 23, 26, 34, 37, 38, 42, 46; Martelli 1987, 98, no. 46, and 101, no. 48; Jucker 1991, 181, no. 227; Camporeale 1991, pl. 28.

8 Some examples: Baur 1912, 115–16, nos. 290–92; Bonamici 1974, nos. 38, 76, 97, pls. 19, 37, 47; Schiffler 1976, 311, cat. E-S11–216; Hayes 1985, 75–76, no. C 21; Jucker 1991, 179–81, nos. 226–27; Camporeale 1991, no. 81, pl. 68; *LIMC* 8, 723, nos. 24–35, pl. 486, s.v. "Kentauroi (in Etruria)." Centaurs also are rare in animal friezes on Attic vases: e.g., a band-cup formerly in the art market (London, Sotheby's, July 17–18, 1985, lot 571).

9 On a kyathos in a Rome private collection, a horseman rides behind a centaur holding a raised branch: Bonamici 1974, no. 107, pl. 55. For other examples of horsemen, see Poupé 1963, pl. 22, no. 3; Camporeale 1991, pl. 56; Bonamici 1974, pl. 31, no. 70, and pl. 38, no. 77.

10 E.g., Dunbabin 1962, no. 240, pl. 14; Boardman 1970, pl. 44.2.

11 Colonna 1964, 167, no. 2, pl. 33, 3–4; Rix 1991, Cr 3.13.

## 43

# Statuette of a Centaur

**Etruscan, mid-sixth century B.C.**
**Probably once in the Tyszkiewicz Collection[1]**
**Bronze and iron**
**Height 8.5 cm., length of base 6.7 cm., width of base 2.3 cm.**
**Museum of Fine Arts, Boston, gift of Harold W. Parsons (09.291)**

CONDITION

The statuette itself is intact, but most of the iron pin is lost. The dark green patina retains light incrustation in the crevices and between the lower legs.

This little solid-cast centaur has human forelegs and genitals. He stands stiffly at attention with his slender human legs held perfectly straight. He is nude, as evidenced by his genitals, but when viewed from the front, his slender hips, the rounded modeling of his torso, and the web of bronze between his lower legs give him somewhat the appearance of a peplos-clad kore, an effect heightened by the absence of a beard, the small chin, and the mass of long hair pushed behind the ears and covering the nape. His upper arms are close to the body, but the lower arms are bent perpendicular and extended with open hands, the latter crudely executed, with only the thumbs modeled. The slender, almost tubular barrel of the centaur's equine body forms an abrupt right angle with the human portion, following the line of the extended forearms. Like the forelegs, the hind legs are set close together, and the curve of the hocks is exaggerated to emphasize their equine character. The ropelike tail, which is scored with incised lines, falls straight down to connect with the flat, rectangular plinth.

Archaic Etruscan bronze centaurs are as scarce as their Greek counterparts but do not approach them in quality. Most are basically similar in type to the Boston centaur, with human forelegs, extended forearms, and a narrow, rectangular plinth.[2] They are usually beardless, but an earlier example in Hannover is bearded and differs also in wearing a loin cloth and in holding a small, unidentified object in one hand.[3] A centaur in Florence

wears a chiton, and—uniquely—has human feet on all four legs.[4] In Greek art, centaurs in human garb almost always represent either Cheiron or Pholos, but the centaur in Florence is beardless and consequently is insufficiently venerable to be identified with one of these wise counselors.

The Boston centaur was once attached to another object, as attested by the remains of an iron pin that extended vertically through the equine body and the plinth below. A few other Etruscan bronze centaurs have the same feature.[5] Why the pin should have extended all the way up through the body of the centaur is a mystery, since the connection with the plinth alone ought to have been sufficient to firmly secure it to an object, for instance, the lid of a cista. The answer could be that the pin once extended higher to connect with an object above, but this is conjecture. Like so many Etruscan bronzes, such figures may have served as handles or sculptural adjuncts on larger bronze vessels, but no complete ensembles that include centaurs are preserved.[6] These are generic monsters, independent of narrative, and were perhaps considered apotropaic.

—JMP

## BIBLIOGRAPHY

*RSGR* V, 401.1; Baur 1912, 117, fig. 30, no. 296; Comstock and Vermeule 1971, 159, no. 181.

## NOTES

1  Comstock and Vermeule 1971, 159.

2  Baur 1912, 117–18, nos. 294–300; *RSGR* II, 692.1–4, 6; Schiffler 1976, 315–16, cat. E-S45–S52, pls. 13–14.

3  Hannover 3097 (from Vulci, early sixth century); Baur 1912, 118, no. 297; *RSGR* II, 692.1; Giglioli 1935, pl. 85.2; Schiffler 1976, 312, cat. E-S22; Gercke 1996, no. 240.

4  Baur 1912, 118, no. 300; *RSGR* III, 285.4.

5  Baur 1912, 117–18, nos. 294, 297, 300; Schiffler 1976, 316, cat. E-S46–S47, pl. 13.

6  One exception is a pair of the earliest Etruscan bronze centaurs, from the seventh-century Bernardini tomb (Rome, Villa Giulia 61634); they stand not on plinths but directly on a complex figural handle, where they interact with human figures: Schiffler 1976, 310, cat. E-S2; *LIMC* 8 (1997), 724, no. 39, pl. 487, s.v. "Kentauroi (in Etruria)" (Weber-Lehmann).

# 44

# "Pontic" Amphora with Centaurs

Etruscan, ca. 530 B.C., attributed to the Paris Painter
Ceramic with slip decoration
Height 35.87 cm.
Jamieson Collection

## CONDITION
The vase has been restored from numerous fragments. A section of the neck and portions of the lower body are missing, as is the foot. The slip is chipped in places.

This exuberantly colorful neck-amphora features a row of three centaurs marching in single file to the left on each shoulder. The last centaur on each side is cut off at mid-body by the panel of the handle (as if it were emerging from behind a wall), which suggests that the procession is meant to be continuous. Each centaur carries an uprooted leafy sapling in his left hand and holds out his empty right hand with fingers extended. The centaurs have long red hair and beards, except for one that is unbearded and so perhaps younger.

Centaurs in Etruscan vase-painting are usually portrayed as wild, unruly creatures, often using trees as weapons.[1] They often appear in narrative episodes, either rushing around in combat or galloping for a taste of Pholos's wine, as on the Tityos Painter's oinochoe in Cleveland.[2] Here, however, they are tamed, calm, even stately. The Paris Painter had a decided preference for processions of centaurs, which he depicted in the shoulder zone of many of his neck-amphorae. The amphorae in Würzburg and in Rome with two and a half centaurs per side are the closest parallels.[3] The painter varies the details of his *Mischwesen*, giving them either human or equine front legs, and human or equine ears.

Characteristic of his style are the incised vertical lines on the front legs of his animals, the zigzag incision at the knee joint of the rear legs, the white belly, and the red strokes indicating the haunch muscles. Typical facial features include a long pointed nose and heavy beard. Also characteristic is the bifurcated root of the tree carried by the centaurs.[4]

The remainder of the vase is decorated with bands of floral decoration: black ivy vine on the neck, alternating red and black ivy vine at the greatest diameter, and alternating palmettes and lotus on the lower body. Below is a zone of diagonally stacked wavy lines in black and white. White is used for the dots on the vines, and the hearts of the palmettes and lotus. This vase also has the traditional black rays at the base, black round handles, and echinus lip.

The Paris Painter derives his name from the charming amphora in Munich that depicts the Judgment of Paris.[5] The term "Pontic" is a misnomer applied to this class of vases because the scholar who named the group thought they represented tribesmen from the Black Sea region. They were the earliest black-figure vases produced in Etruria, possibly by an immigrant from East Greece since the style of painting is North Ionian.[6]

—JN

## BIBLIOGRAPHY
London, Christie's, July 10, 1991, lot 145 (as Attic); New York, Christie's, June 12, 2000, lot 144.

## NOTES
1 For centaurs in Etruscan art, see Schiffler 1976, 125–50, 303–18; *LIMC* 8 (1997), 721–27, pls. 482–93, s.v. "Kentauroi (in Etruria)" (Weber-Lehmann).
2 Cleveland 1986.88: see Neils 1998.
3 Würzburg L 778: Hannestad 1974, 44 no. 2; Schiffler 1976, 304, cat. E-17; *CVA* Würzburg 3, Germany 51, pls. 27, 30; *Pferdemann* 1999, 71, no. 7.1. This amphora has more figural decoration with nude youths on the neck and a subsidiary zone of sphinxes and lions. It represents a hierarchical ordering of human, half-human/half-animal, and animal. Rome, Villa Giulia 48070, from Cerveteri: *MonAnt* 42 (1955), cols. 538–40, fig. 130; Hannestad 1974, 47, no. 22; Schiffler 1976, 305, cat. E-19. This amphora has a lotus and palmette band below the shoulder scene. Other closely related vases are: New York, Met. 55.11.1 (Bothmer 1956; Hannestad 1974, 45, no. 9.), with three entire centaurs per panel; and Berlin F 1675, from Tarquinia (Hannestad 1974, 47, no. 21; Schiffler 1976, 305, cat. E-18, pl. 11), with only two centaurs per panel.
4 For a thorough description of this painter, see Hannestad 1974.
5 Munich 837: Beazley 1947a, 1, pl. 1.3–4.
6 For "Pontic" vases, see Ducati 1932; Rizzo 1987.

# 45

## Geison Revetment with Charging Centaur

South Etruscan, ca. 525–490 B.C.
Terracotta, painted [1]
Height 25.2 cm., width 27.8 cm., depth 2 cm.
Private collection

### CONDITION

Reconstructed from nine fragments, the plaque preserves its original vertical edge on the left but is broken on the right, including the lip of the overhanging cavetto molding. The cracks through the design are repainted. A missing triangular fragment at the left, which took with it the top of the centaur's tail and part of the branch he carries, is restored in plain fashion, as is a smaller piece at the lower edge.

In small religious buildings like the one that this plaque originally decorated, the roof joists, the raking structural supports for the terracotta tiles, were tied into horizontal beams atop the building's sidewalls. Called the trabeation or the geison beams, these often were sheathed with terracotta plaques: those running along the exterior long sides are called geison revetments. Placed end-to-end, geison revetments provided a continuous surface for decoration at the top of the wall (see the architectural drawing in the Glossary). In Italy, those decorated with figural images seem to have achieved particular popularity in indigenous Italic contexts,[2] but there also are examples from Greek Sicily and South Italy (Magna Graecia).[3] The medium is normally painted relief, mold-made and repetitive, thereby ignoring the potential for narrative development inherent in its friezelike field. Geison revetments with figures executed in free painting, like this example, are less common, appearing only in southern Etruria at Caere (modern Cerveteri),[4] and in Sicily at Naxos, Gela, and Grammichele.[5] On these, there is even greater potential for narrative development, but there is little evidence that it was exploited.

Most Etrusco-Campanian geison revetments, whether decorated in relief or painted, have a mold-made cavetto decorated with concave leaves or "strigils" in alternating colors occupying the upper third of the face. On this example, the horizontal framing device separating the leaves from the figure field is a low, half-round molding.

The subject is a centaur, a relatively rare image in Etruscan architectural decoration. This creature, brandishing a tree limb in his withdrawn right hand, charges from left to right. He is beardless and has a long nose and jutting chin. He stretches his left arm forward, its missing hand perhaps grasping at another centaur whose tail is overlapped by this centaur's left front leg. Black is used for outlines, hair, and inner details, as well as the plastically rendered outlines around the leaves, the half round separating the leaves from the figure field, and alternating leaves. The centaur's equine body, the framing stripe at the bottom of the figure field, the red "strigilated" leaves, and the vertical face of the lip at the top of the cavetto are painted in red. The centaur's human upper body is light taupe in color, as is the tail of the otherwise missing centaur to the right, while a darker shade of taupe is used for the tree limb the centaur carries in his right hand.

In what is said to be an Italic technique, grainy grog-filled clay is used throughout, but an extra thick slip was applied to the figure field, producing a smooth surface for the fine linear detail of the painted figures. Use of a separate mold for the concave leaves in the cavetto allowed the artisan to vary the height of the figure field below according to the height of the beam to be covered.

Like the gorgoneion and the satyr, the centaur's meaning on a building is likely to have been apotropaic — averting evil and misfortune — a function enhanced by the creature's reputation for male libidinousness.[6] The closest comparanda are a pair of fragmentary revetments from Caere, now in the Ny Carlsberg Glyptotek, Copenhagen.[7] This plaque is probably Caeretan, too; indeed, it and the Copenhagen plaques are so similar in style that they may have been painted by the same hand.
—JFK

**BIBLIOGRAPHY**
Unpublished.

**NOTES**

1 Red clay fabric (Munsell 2.5YR, 6/4) with creamy white slip (7.5YR, 7/4). Paints are red (2.5YR, 5/4), black, and two shades of taupe (5YR, 6/4 and 5YR, 6/3).

2 Andrén 1940, CXVI–CLI, esp. CXXX–CLI and CLXXXVI–CXCI; Andrén 1971–74, 1–16, pls. 1–40.

3 Mertens-Horn 1992; Kenfield 1993, 21–28; Greco 1997, 83–94; Lentini 1997, 129–31, figs. 6–7.

4 Andrén 1940, 25–26, pls. 7.2 and 8.22–23.

5 Lentini 1997, 129–31, figs. 6–7.

6 Lulof 1997a, 135 and 142; Holloway 1988, 177–83, fig. 2.

7 Christiansen 1985–87, 140–45, figs. 7–8; Cristofani 1992, 47–49, pl. IV, nos. B36–37, with comparanda from the Ny Carlsberg Glyptotek at the bottom.

# 46

# Columen Plaque with a Centaur in Relief

Etruscan, southern Etruria or Latium, ca. 500–480 B.C.
Terracotta, painted[1]
Height 29.1 cm., width 20.6 cm., depth 13.8 cm.,
thickness of frame 4.4–4.6 cm.
Princeton University Art Museum, gift of Ali and
Hicham Aboutaam (1995–129)

CONDITION
The left half of the plaque is missing, including the
rear half of the centaur's body, right foreleg, right
arm, and the tip of the club or branch brandished in
his raised left hand. Large chips are missing from
the left foreleg, the left side of the centaur's beard,
and the outer edge of the raised frame, especially at
the lower right corner. The paint is well preserved
but worn on the head, face, and left elbow. On the
decorated surfaces there are numerous scratches,
chips, and small areas of abrasion. The irregular break
runs vertically along the fragment's left side before
turning horizontally at the level of the centaur's
pectoral muscles. There is light incrustation over
all surfaces.

The superstructures of the modest religious buildings
to which the architectural terracotta revetments in this
exhibition were applied contained three great beams
running the length of the building: the ridge pole, or
columen, at the peak of the roof and the geison beams on
top of the sidewalls (see the architectural drawing in the
Glossary). On buildings with a deep prostyle porch, there
was no need for a pediment wall filling the gabled end at
the front of the building; it therefore often was left open
except for the exposed ends of these three beams. Like the
other exposed wooden elements of the superstructure,
the beam ends needed protection from the elements and
so were reveted with terracotta: a columen plaque for the
ridge pole and two antepagmenta or mutuli plaques for
the geison beams. All three of these plaques offered additional areas for decoration. In Campania, Rome, Latium,
and southern Etruria, where prostyle porches and open

pediments were the norm in the late Archaic period,
examples decorated with multifigure scenes from Greek
mythology in painted relief are common.[2]

The clay fabric of this fragmentary relief is a
yellowish taupe with copious black grog (i.e., artificially
introduced inclusions). The decorated surface is covered
with a creamy, pale yellow slip that is painted over with
reddish brown color for the centaur's face, chest, and
surviving left arm. The background is black, as is the
raised mass representing the hair, the beard, the outlines
around the eyes, the pupils, the nipples, the hair on
the chest, and internal details on the equine front legs,
which otherwise are reserved in the color of the slip.
The semicircular black line visible on the centaur's equine
body, just inside the vertical break line on the left, may
indicate that other internal details were painted in black.
The eyeballs are painted white. The zigzag or *denti di
lupo* [wolf's teeth] motif on the frame is painted in red
and black, separated by the color of the slip.

The centaur is modeled by hand. As is the case
with the other indigenous Italic (as opposed to colonial
Greek) architectural terracottas in this exhibition, the

technique of using clay infused with large grains of grog produces a form lacking fine plastic detail. The break on the left reveals that the clay was pressed into the mold in three separate layers, probably to allow each layer to dry to the proper consistency before superimposing another.

The surviving edge at the upper right is cut at an angle of seventeen degrees, which provides the pitch of the roof under which it was placed. The centaur is grappling with an opponent, either Herakles or a Lapith,[3] whose arm is preserved at the very top, grabbing the centaur by the neck. It thus is likely that the surviving fragment is less than half the width of the original plaque, and that the complete revetment was used to cover the end of a columen at the apex of the open gable. The knee of the centaur's surviving left leg, as well as his raised left hand and the branch or club it holds, overlap the raised frame, creating a baroque effect.

—JFK

**BIBLIOGRAPHY**

*Record* 56.1 (1997): 61–62 (illus.); Lulof 1997a, 135–42 (136, fig. 1).

**NOTES**

1 Fabric color (Munsell): 10YR, 7/3; slip color: 10YR, 8/4; reddish brown paint: 2.5YR, 4/6.

2 Lulof 1997a, 135 n. 1; Lulof 1997b, 85–114; Lulof 1999, 241–44, figs. 93–94; N. A. Winter, "The Origin of the Recessed Gable in Etruscan Architecture," a talk delivered on November 7, 2002, in a conference at the American Academy in Rome entitled *Deliciae Fictiles* III. The proceedings of this conference are to be published under this same title as a forthcoming volume of *MAAR*.

3 Lulof (1997a, 142) suggests Herakles and Nessos. She reconstructs four other relief fragments in the Princeton University Art Museum (y1995-126/128) as the remnants of the accompanying mutuli plaques from the same temple, the entire ensemble presenting a centauromachy, presumably between Lapiths and centaurs. If this hypothesis is correct, then this columen plaque should not represent Herakles and Nessos, a one-on-one centauromachy having nothing to do with the marriage of Peirithoos. See her reconstruction, p. 140, fig. 6.

# 47

# Aryballos with Bellerophon and Pegasos

**Greek, Early Corinthian, ca. 625 – 600 B.C., attributed to the Heraldic Lions Painter**
**Ceramic**
**Height 6.7 cm., maximum diameter 6.85 cm., diameter of mouth 4.2 cm.**
**Princeton University Art Museum, museum purchase, Carl Otto von Kienbusch Jr. Memorial Collection Fund (y1994–9)**

**CONDITION**
**The vase, made of creamy buff, slightly yellowish clay, is unbroken and in excellent condition. There are chips in the lower edge of the rim and some flaking of the decoration, especially the added white. The surface is lightly spotted with brown incrustation.**

In shape, this is a typical Early Corinthian aryballos, a small oil bottle with a depressed spherical body and rounded base, a short, concave neck, small mouth, wide circular rim with a concave surface, and a wide, flat handle from shoulder to rim. Aryballoi of this type were produced in great numbers at Corinth in the late seventh and sixth centuries B.C. and were exported all over the Mediterranean, along with the perfumed oils they contained. The decoration is in the black-figure technique, with some details in red and white slip. The artist is the Heraldic Lions Painter, the leading artist of the Lion Group, Early Corinthian vase-painters whose aryballoi tend to have similar subsidiary ornament: two vertical black stripes on the handle; the mouth circled by four concentric lines and a band of slender tongues that fills the bowl of the rim; a row of dots around the outer edge of the rim; a band of simple, unframed tongues on the shoulder below the neck; and a large pinwheel design on the rounded base, its circular boundary serving as the ground line for the figures.[1]

Pegasos, the mythical winged horse, rises from the ground line as if from the sea or a cloud.[2] His forelegs, with their hairy fetlocks, rest upon the ground line, and his long tail stretches out behind, almost circling the vase

to meet its owner coming in the other direction. His hind legs are not represented, and his body rises only high enough to make it clear that he is a stallion. The mane is a cascade of rippling lines and stripes of added red. The wings overlap, so that only one is represented; it sweeps back from the shoulder to curl forward at the tip, the primary feathers alternately red and white, the secondaries solid red, and the coverts a mass of red and white scales. The added white is now quite worn, making the wings look redder than the artist intended.

Upon the back of Pegasos rides the hero Bellerophon, a beardless youth dressed in a short-sleeved tunic, his long hair bound with a fillet and gathered in a clump at the nape. He holds the white-spotted reins with both hands, his right hand also clutching a riding crop. His round eye is as vacant as that of his mount, but a slight smile animates his features.

In Book 6 of the *Iliad*, the Lycian warrior Glaukos confronts Diomedes and gives him a long, discursive account of his ancestry, which he traces back to Bellerophon and his grandfather, Sisyphos.[3] Bellerophon left his birthplace of Ephyre, near Corinth, to take refuge at Argos because of a blood feud. There he angered Anteia (Stheneboia in later accounts), wife of King Proitos, by refusing her advances; enraged, she told her husband that Bellerophon had tried to seduce her. Proitos dispatched Bellerophon to Lycia, in southern Turkey, with a letter to King Iobates (named in later sources) requesting that he kill the bearer. Iobates sent him to deal with the Chimaera, a ferocious beast that was part lion, part snake, and part goat. After killing the monster, Bellerophon subdued the Solymi and the Amazons and returned to thwart Iobates' treachery and marry his daughter.

Nowhere in Glaukos's account is there any mention of Pegasos, the winged horse sired by Poseidon and born from the neck of the decapitated Medusa.[4] Hesiod, however, says that Pegasos teamed with Bellerophon to kill the Chimaera,[5] a myth first given visual form in the mid-seventh century on two Late Protocorinthian vases: a fragmentary kotyle from Aigina and a pointed aryballos in Boston.[6] Pindar relates how Bellerophon, using the golden bit given to him by Athena, tamed the flying horse at the spring of Priene, in Corinth, and there is no doubt that the city claimed both hero and horse as its own, placing Pegasos on its classical coins.[7] Curiously, after the two Protocorinthian examples, Bellerophon and Pegasos appear together again only once more in Corinthian vase-painting, on this aryballos.[8]

Like the Sphinx, Pegasos was an individual in myth but was multiplied at the whim of the artists, both with and without riders.[9] Not a "human animal" but the descendant of many a Near Eastern winged horse, Pegasos is but one example of the diversity of half-horse creatures devised by the Greek imagination, from the centaurs and satyrs to the seagoing hippocamp, with its serpentine tail, and the fantastic hippalektryon, with the body of a rooster.[10]

—JMP

BIBLIOGRAPHY

*Record* 54.1 (1995): 68, 70 (illus.).

NOTES

1 Attributed by Jasper Gaunt. For the Lion Group, see Payne 1931, 289;
Amyx 1988, 118. For the Heraldic Lions Painter, see Amyx 1988, 119, 377.
This is the artist's only depiction of this subject, but he did paint four
aryballoi with the Chimaera alone (Amyx 1988, 119, nos. 2–5, pl. 50.1).

2 Cf. the portrayal of Europa and the bull on the Attic lip-cup in the
Steinhardt Collection (cat. no. 95), where the bull half rises from a
ground line surely meant to represent the surface of the sea. In contrast, the painter of this aryballos may simply have wished to save space
for a larger and more detailed rendering of the figures.

3 Hom. *Il.* 6.150–211.

4 Hes. *Theog.* 280–81. For Pegasos, see Yalouris 1987; *LIMC* 7 (1994),
214–30, pls. 142–71, s.v. "Pegasos" (Lochin).

5 Hes. *Theog.* 325.

6 Aigina 1376: Friis Johansen 1923, pl. 35.3a; Payne 1931, pl. 4.1–2; Payne
1933, pl. 17.1; Yalouris 1987, fig. 7; Amyx 1988, 28, no. 1, pl. 8; *LIMC* 7,
227, no. 212, pl. 167, s.v. "Pegasos." Boston 95.10: Friis Johansen 1923,
pl. 30.2a–d; Payne 1933, pl. 20.2–5; Yalouris 1987, fig. 6; Amyx 1988, 37,
no. 2; *LIMC* 7, 227, no. 213, pl. 167, s.v. "Pegasos."

7 Pind. *Ol.* 13.60–92; see also Paus. 2.4.1. For the coinage of Corinth, see
Ravel 1936 and Ravel 1948.

8 The vase was not known to Amyx, who found the absence of the subject in the Corinthian repertory puzzling and a "fact that begs for an
explanation" (Amyx 1988, 627). Bellerophon and Pegasos do appear a
generation later in early Attic black-figure, notably on the name-vase of
the Bellerophon Painter (Athens, Nat. Mus. 16389: *ABV* 2.1; Yalouris
1987, figs. 11–12; *LIMC* 3 [1986], 254, no. 80a, pl. 204, s.v. "Chimaira"
[Jacquemin]) and on later, mid-century Corinthian painted plaques
from Perachora (*LIMC* 7, 221, nos. 103–103a, pl. 152, s.v. "Pegasos").

9 E.g., the paired Pegasoi on a Late Corinthian aryballos by the Pegasos
Painter: *CVA* Göttingen 2, Germany 73, pl. 5.1–3. Poseidon and two
attendants ride winged horses on a Late Corinthian column-krater in
Bari: Payne 1931, 329, no. 1459; Amyx 1988, 266, no. 1.

10 *LIMC* 8 (1997), 634–37, pls. 391–95, s.v. "Hippokampos" (Icard-
Gianolio); *LIMC* 5 (1990), 427–32, pls. 301–308, s.v. "Hippalektryon"
(Williams).

## 48

# Statuette of a Horse and Rider

Cypriote, ca. 700 B.C.
Terracotta
Height 20.4 cm., length 20.9 cm., maximum
width 6.2 cm.
Princeton University Art Museum, gift of
Gillett G. Griffin (2002–360)

CONDITION
The handmade, solid figurine is in excellent
condition except that the painting is largely lost
on its left side.

The rider stands on the back of the horse in the so-called
"snowman" form: a plain tubular body with no articulation
of the legs. He raises both arms to grasp the horse's mane
well up the neck. The horse and the rider are decorated
with black lines and areas of red slip. Broad black lines follow the lateral edges of all four legs of the horse, in the
front extending all the way up to the tip of the mane.
These vertical lines are joined by a variety of narrow horizontal lines on the sides of the legs; on the upper front legs
these become diagonal. On the right rear leg, where the
decoration is well preserved, there is a crossed circle on the
upper leg. Groups of narrow horizontal black bands decorate the neck, upper mane, and chest of the horse. The
horse's eye is indicated in black, as is the face of the rider
(eye, mouth, beard), and there are parallel short strokes of
black on the rider's arm. Red is used up the front of the
horse and on the head and muzzle, the tail, and patches on
the upper legs. Red is also used on the back of the rider,
around his throat, and on the top of his cap.

The horse and rider belong to a particularly homogeneous group of such figurines found widely on Cyprus and
dating to the late Cypro-Geometric III and the Cypro-
Archaic I periods, that is, the late eighth century and the
whole span of the seventh century.[1] The Princeton piece
belongs in the earlier range of these dates, that is about
700 B.C. or slightly later, on the basis of the forms and
painted decoration.[2]

The identity of the rider remains uncertain: god,
hero, or mortal. Later Archaic riders sometimes carry

sword and/or shield.[3] Although commentators associate the figurines with a male cult,[4] some sanctuaries have votives of both sexes, although perhaps a preponderance of one over the other. Such is the case at Ayia Irini and also the sanctuary of the Classical period excavated by Princeton at Polis Chrysochous (ancient Marion).[5] In the latter case, the explanation may lie in the existence of multiple cults within a relatively confined area, though there is no proof of this yet. Horses, of course, represent an elite status of the rider. Actual representations of horse with rider are a relatively late phenomenon. They are not nearly as popular in the Late Bronze Age as in the Late Geometric/Archaic periods when figurines of the type here in consideration abound.[6]

—WAPC

**BIBLIOGRAPHY**
Unpublished.

**NOTES**
1 Karageorghis 1995, 61–64, pls. XXIX–XXXIII.
2 Cf. particularly a horse in the Louvre (MNB 370: Caubet, Hermary, and Karageorghis 1992, no. 196 [CG III]; Caubet, Fourrier, and Queyrel 1998, 118, no. 140), which compares well in size: height 20 cm., length 12.7 cm., width 6.2 cm.
3 Karageorghis 1995, pls. XXXVI–XXXVII.
4 Caubet 1979, 36.
5 Serwint 1991.
6 Karageorghis 1993a, 16–17, 65–67.

## 49

# Statuette of a Horse and Rider

**Greek, Boiotian, ca. 550 B.C.**
**Terracotta**
**Height 14.6 cm., length 13.6 cm., width 6.3 cm.**
**Princeton University Art Museum, museum**
**purchase (y1937 – 338)**

### CONDITION

The figurine is solid and handmade of beige tan clay with a red-buff core, fired hard. The decoration is in dark brown slip, misfired red on much of the right side. The tail is lost; the hole in the noticeably fat stub is from a previous restoration. Aside from minor paint flaking and a chip in the left hind leg, the piece is otherwise unbroken and in excellent condition.

The body of the horse is a simple cylinder; the legs taper almost to points, with no attempt at modeling. The crested mane projects slightly above the forelock, which is made from a separate piece of clay. The ears are short. Slight swellings define the eyes. The male rider has unnaturally stumpy legs, but they are distinctly modeled and do not simply merge into the horse's flank. The rider sits well forward, seeming to clutch the mane with both hands but actually grasping painted reins, the line of which passes up both arms and around his back. The modeling of his raised head is limited to a gash separating nose and jaw. This is supplemented with a few painted details: a tiny dot for the left eye; strands of long hair falling on the nape. A brown band circles his waist, and there are horizontal stripes on his legs. Parallel lines cover most of the horse except for the underbelly and the insides of the legs. There are horizontal stripes on each leg and rows of vertical stripes down the length of the body on both sides. A rectangular area on the horse's back, behind the rider, represents the saddlecloth, which is decorated with zigzag lines and the silhouette of a flying bird. Crossed lines once extended down the tail. On the horse's breast are three horizontal bands framing trios of brown dots.

Archaic terracotta horsemen of this type are well known from Boiotian graves at sites like Rhitsona and Tanagra, where they were found with pottery and other figurines, including riderless horses and flattened female "idols."[1] The horsemen have been studied by Jan Østergaard, who divided them into an earlier group of "Black" figurines from the first half of the sixth century, the more numerous striped ("Black on Brown") horsemen from the middle and third quarter of the century, of which this is an example, and the "Red on White" riders of the late sixth and early fifth centuries.[2] The Princeton rider is an excellent example of Østergaard's Group G, the largest subdivision of the Black on Brown variety, "comprising what to most people must be the typical Archaic Boiotian terracotta horseman."[3] The combination of horizontal and vertical stripes and the rows of dots on the chest are typical, but the horse's ears are normally not represented, and the provision of even truncated legs for the rider is a rare feature.[4] The bird on the blanket, although crude, has the soaring outline of an eagle, like those that give their name to the contemporary class of Boiotian "Bird Bowls."[5] Its presence on the horse blanket may allude to the swiftness of the steed.

A figure such as this differs fundamentally from the bronze horses and painted riders of the Geometric Period, being more simple than stylized, more abbreviated than condensed. But although the detail provided is only just enough to distinguish a horse and human rider from, say, a mule and satyr (cf. cat. no. 55), the conceptual threshold is clear, and in its modest way the figure brings with it all the heroic symbolism of the man on horseback. The horseman acted both as a container of particular societal values and as their conveyor into the afterlife. In this sense, at least, it is more understandable as a funerary offering than the clay centaurs from earlier Boiotian tombs (e.g., cat. no. 21), while at the same time it illuminates the possible significance of those more fantastic horse men.

—JMP

### BIBLIOGRAPHY

Østergaard 1991, 136, figs. 35, 37, no. G55, 180 n. 97.

### NOTES

1 For the Archaic cemeteries at Rhitsona, see Burrows and Ure 1907/8; Burrows and Ure 1909; Ure 1934, 4–15; Kurtz and Boardman 1971, 182–83. For Archaic burials at Tanagra, see Higgins 1986, 44–49. For female "idols," see Ure 1934, 54–61, pls. 13–14; Paul 1958/59; Higgins 1986, 71–83; Szabó 1994, 43–54, 60–70, 73–79. Most Boiotian terracotta centaurs, like the one in Missouri (cat. no. 21), are earlier in date.

2 Østergaard 1986; Østergaard 1991. See also Winter 1903, 7, nos. 1–3, 5; Ure 1934, 61–60, pl. 15; Szabó 1994, 33–35, 54–60, figs. 16–18, 29–32, 41, 44–46, 48–49, 51–53. There are examples in museums worldwide: e.g., Breitenstein 1941, nos. 151–52; Higgins 1954, pl. 105, nos. 782–86.

3 Østergaard 1991, 133.

4 Østergaard 1991, 138.

5 Østergaard 1991, 174, fig. 76d, 185 n.1. He cites a second example on a horseman of this type, in Copenhagen (Ny Carlsberg 3694), possibly the same as the one on the market in London (Sotheby's, July 9, 1990, no. 42). The eagles on Boiotian Bird Bowls are not in silhouette; see Schmaltz 1977/78; Higgins 1986, 46, figs. 32–33; Boardman 1998a, 109, fig. 233. There is an unpublished Bird Bowl in the Princeton University Art Museum (inv. y1951-15). Similar eagles appear on contemporary Boiotian female idols: see Winter 1903, 5, fig. 3; Szabó 1994, figs. 60–61.

## 50

# Statuette of a Horse and Rider

**Greek, mainland, early fifth century B.C.**
**Bronze**
**Height 8.3 cm., length 7.5 cm., width 2.5 cm.**
**Princeton University Art Museum, gift of Frank Jewett Mather Jr. (y1948–8)**

### CONDITION

**The statuette is in good condition, missing only the lower hind legs, the tip of the tail, the rider's lower left leg and foot, and most of the base plate. The right front hoof and a small section of the base plate are bent outward at a steep angle. There are modern metal pins in both hind legs and the right front hoof. The patina is almost black, with green spots.**

The horse walks to the right, its left leg raised. Its head is large in proportion to its stocky body and short legs. It holds itself proudly erect, the neck vertical, the head at a forty-five degree angle. The eyes are large and slightly bulging; the nostrils flare. The muscles of the breast and flanks are well modeled; the hooves, knees, and fetlocks are described but not emphasized. The curvaceous tail is attached to the hock of the left hind leg. The mane is neatly clipped and scored with horizontal lines; it arcs above the head where it terminates between the ears in a high forelock, from which pairs of scored tresses part to descend on either side of the face. The horse wears a bridle with a noseband. Its mouth remains closed in spite of the bit.

The rider may be a boy: he is beardless, and his feet barely extend past the horse's belly. His short hair bulges slightly above the forehead and may be rolled over a fillet, but this is not clear. He is nude, but unlike the horse, his genitals are not represented. He rides bareback, his posture erect but not stiff. The reins pass through the horse's mane on the right side to emerge on the left, where the rider holds them in his left hand, his right hand lowered to his thigh. The reins are taut, accounting for the erect posture of the horse. "Through the slight turn of the rider's head to one side, the group becomes more relaxed in its pose and signals the tendency of the period to break away from rigid postures."[1]

It has been suggested that the flat piece of metal beneath the horse's right front hoof is part of the cauldron or other vessel to which it once was attached.[5] This is unlikely, for no bronze vessel with sculptural adornment of this type has been found in Greece, and if one should be, the horse probably will be attached by rivets.[6] In this case, the surviving section of the base is cast in one piece with the hoof and is surely the remains of a narrow base plate, like that found on many of the few freestanding bronze horses that have retained their lower legs.[7] This does not mean that the horseman was not once attached to a vessel, but it would have been attached by a rivet through the plate. Another possibility is that the boy and his mount may have been votive offerings in a sanctuary, a dedication from a member of the horse-owning aristocracy, albeit a less expensive one than the marble horsemen of the Acropolis.

—JMP

### BIBLIOGRAPHY

*Record* 13.1 (1954): 3 (illus.); Kunze, Schleif, and Eilmann 1941, 147, fig. 108; Jones 1960, 38–39; Mitten and Doeringer 1967, 67, no. 58; Wangenheim 1988, no. 22, pl. 14.

### NOTES

1  Jones 1960, 39.
2  Comstock and Vermeule 1971, 34, no. 32; Wangenheim 1988, no. 23, pl. 14.
3  For details, see Gjødesen 1963, pl. 76, fig. 40; Wangenheim 1988, pls. 9, 11.
4  Mitten and Doeringer 1967, 67; Comstock and Vermeule 1971, 34. For the marble horsemen from the Acropolis, see Payne and Mackworth-Young 1950, 77, pls. 134–40; Eaverly 1996. For the bronze from the north slope, see Broneer 1938, 203–8, figs. 38–40; Wangenheim 1988, 7–8, no. 1, pl. 1.
5  Jones 1960, 39; Mitten and Doeringer 1967, 67.
6  The horses on the shoulder of the bronze hydria from Pesaro, for example, stand not on the vessel itself but on the snakes that, like them, are part of the cast handle, which is attached by rivets; see Caratelli 1996, 387.
7  E.g., the horse in New York (Met. 58.180.1: Mertens 1985, 29, no. 16; Wangenheim 1988, no. 34, pl. 18) and the famous horseman from Dodona (Athens, Nat. Mus. KAR 27 X 16547: Wangenheim 1988, no. 46, pl. 23; Tzachou-Alexandri 1989, no. 32). Cf. also the section of the base plate retained beneath the hind legs of a centaur from the Acropolis (Athens, Nat. Mus. 6680: Niemeyer 1964, pl. 27; see also this volume, cat. no. 23, n. 5 and Padgett, "Horse Men," fig. 6).

This statuette has been compared to a slightly earlier horse and rider in Boston, said to have been found at Mantineia, in Arcadia.[2] The Boston horse also is bridled and has a forelock and parted tresses like the Princeton horse; moreover, the young rider holds his hands in the same positions. Some of the appliqué chariot horses on the Laconian bronze volute-krater from Vix have similar forelocks, while others have the pendant tresses.[3] However, these Peloponnesian parallels need not indicate a similar origin for the Princeton bronze; indeed, both David Mitten and Cornelius Vermeule also note a general affinity with the Archaic marble horsemen from the Athenian Acropolis and with bronze statuettes from the Acropolis and its vicinity, in particular a horse and rider discovered in a well on the north slope.[4]

## 51

# Fragment of a Relief-Amphora with Horse and Rider

Greek, Cretan, ca. 660–630 B.C.
Ceramic
Height 19.07 cm., width 19.7 cm., maximum
thickness 2.45 cm.
Tampa Museum of Art, gift of Mr. and Mrs. William
Knight Zewadski in honor of J. Michael Padgett,
Curator of Classical Art, 1990–1992 (1991.023.001)

CONDITION

The medium red to light brown clay is coarse
and contains mica and darker red inclusions. The
fragment is broken on all sides. The surface is
worn, and there are chips in the horse's tail and
the raised band below.

A horse gallops to the right, its body, legs, and tail
stretched out and elongated in order to accentuate our
perception of its great speed. A male human figure wearing a belted tunic rides bareback, his head and upper body
turned frontally to face the viewer. While holding onto
the reins with his left hand, his right hand is swung back,
clutching a riding crop, now largely effaced. The details
of the rider's head are worn, but the inverted triangular
shape of the face and the wavy, wiglike tresses framing it
are characteristic of the Daedalic style of the middle and
third quarter of the seventh century B.C. The bridle of
the horse, its face, and the locks of hair on its mane are
better preserved and carefully rendered. The figural frieze
is bordered at top and bottom by triple ridged bands running horizontally. Below, in another frieze, a decoration
in the form of an undulating line is partly preserved.

The fragment comes from a decorative band on
the front of a Cretan relief-amphora, from just below the
shoulder of the vessel.[1] Complete examples of such
amphorae are rare: there is one in the Louvre[2] and another
in the Ashmolean Museum.[3] The applied figures and relief
decoration were produced by freehand modeling, in molds
(as in this example), or by stamping directly into the clay
walls. The horizontal ridged bands and wavy decoration
are standard motifs and, like the figures, were confined to
one side of the vase, the back of which was left undecorated. Varying in height from approximately .50 to 1.70
meters, the Cretan amphorae are similar in shape to painted Attic Geometric amphorae, although relief vessels were
not popular in Athens. Crete was one of the most prolific
centers of production for relief pottery, with workshops
based in Arkades, Phaistos, and Prinias.[4] In addition to
Crete, relief-amphorae and pithoi also were produced in
Boiotia, Tenos, Rhodes, and Laconia from the late eighth
through the mid-sixth century B.C. Imitating simple,
undecorated storage jars in basic form, these decorated
examples not only could have functioned as storage jars
but also as votive offerings, vessels for burial, or, taking
into account their monumental size, grave markers.

The Cretan relief-amphorae often are decorated
with animals and fabulous creatures from the East such as
sphinxes and griffins. A few examples have religious or
mythological scenes. Horsemen like this are uncommon.[5]
He probably was one of several in the same frieze, and

the crop in his hand and his mount's flying gallop suggest that they were contestants in a horse race, perhaps an allusion to funeral games in honor of the deceased. The context is not narrative. Centaurs and satyrs do not appear on the Cretan amphorae, only human "horsemen."

The technique of relief decoration and the subject matter of this class of vessel are closely related to metal vases; the horseman on this fragment, for example, finds a close parallel in a later, sixth-century bronze appliqué from the sanctuary of Zeus at Dodona.[6] The bronze relief, depicting a young horseman in a pose very similar to that of this rider, with the head turned toward the viewer, was made to be attached to a bronze krater, probably in a Corinthian workshop.

—AJP

### BIBLIOGRAPHY

Erlenmeyer 1960, 128; London, Sotheby's, December 13–14, 1990, lot 167; Borell and Rittig 1998, 119, 138, 215, pl. 61.3.

### NOTES

1 For Cretan relief-amphorae, see Eals 1971; Weinberg 1973; Anderson 1975, 41–61. For Greek relief-amphorae and pithoi in general, including Cretan, see Schäfer 1957; Anderson 1975.

2 Paris, Louvre CA 4523: *Greek Art of the Aegean Islands* 1979, 132–33, no. 79.

3 Oxford, Ashmolean: Eals 1971, 26, fig. 1. Another such amphora was recently in the art market: New York, Christie's, June 12, 2002, lot 9.

4 Anderson 1975, iii–iv, 99–100.

5 For fragments of other relief amphorae depicting a horse and rider, see Blome 1990, 51, nos. 81–82; Dörig 1975, no. 128.

6 Athens, Nat. Mus. KAR 36: Tzachou-Alexandri 1989, 302–4, no. 192. For another bronze appliqué in the form of a horse and rider, now in Malibu (96.AC.46), see True and Hamma 1994, 58–59, no. 18.

## 52

# Fragment of a Black-Figure Louterion

**Greek, Attic, ca. 590–570 B.C.**
**Ceramic**
**Height 9.8 cm., length 24.2 cm.**
**Private collection**

### CONDITION

The fine clay fabric is reddish pink. The fragment itself has been repaired from six large pieces, with no in-painting or plaster fills. The black slip has peeled in places and is misfired in others, particularly on the body of the horse on the right. Some of the decoration has been abraded, especially the face and body of the siren.

This large fragment derives from a louterion, a ceramic vessel in the shape of a wide, rounded bowl, similar to a dinos but more shallow, with a spout on one side and two upright loop handles, circular in section, attached to the shoulder. Surviving louteria are few in number and range in date from the Late Geometric period to the fourth century B.C., most examples dating before 550 B.C.[1] Early Attic black-figure louteria usually have an echinus foot. The long, narrow reserved panels on either side of black-figure louteria are often painted with various combinations of three elements: horsemen or pairs of confronted animals, such as boars and lions, with a floral ornament or a smaller animal, like a swan, placed between them. This fragment preserves the center and right half of the figural panel from the shoulder and body of the vessel, opposite the side with the spout.

Two horsemen face one another on either side of a centrally placed siren. The body of the siren faces right, but the head is turned around to face the horse and bearded rider at the left, of whom only the heads, necks, and upper chests are preserved. There is a central rosette above the siren's head and another rosette on the right, above the rump of the second horse, which is almost completely preserved, along with its beardless young rider. Both horsemen carry a spear while holding the reins. The youth at the right wears a sleeveless tunic in added

red, with borders at the neck and a lower hem indicated by double incised lines. Both horses are fitted out with simple halters, identified by a long cheek-strap ending at a noseband and throat lash, all three joined together by a large ring represented by two concentric circles.

Added red slip is used for the beard and hair of the older horseman and for the tunic of his young companion. The petals of the rosettes and the alternating locks of hair of the horses' manes also are painted red, as are the forelock and chests of both horses and the eye and rump of the horse at the right. There are traces of red on the hair and body of the siren. Two horizontal red bands preserved at the lower right accentuate the ground line of the figural panel. The figural scene is bordered above and at the right side of the panel by two dilute glaze lines; another dilute line forms the ground line. The interior surface of the fragment is covered uniformly with glossy black slip, care having been taken to evenly coat the underside of the curved shoulder. At the upper left part of the fragment, a small, vertical spur indicates the beginning of the vessel's rim, which is otherwise not preserved.

The halters on the horses are very similar to those depicted on Attic Horse-head amphorae, a distinctive class roughly contemporary in date with this fragment.[2] Indeed, the heraldic composition of the horse heads on the louterion resembles that of facing horses on some early Horse-head amphorae,[3] both possibly having their origin in the ritual arrangement of horses found in early burials, like those in the dromos of the Mycenaean tomb at Marathon.[4]

The louterion is an uncommon shape that may have cultic significance.[5] It is associated with Mycenaean burials at Menidhi[6] and with the complex at Vari that dates from the late seventh to the early sixth century.[7] Possibly the vessel held bath water for the deceased or was used for offerings of water to the dead.[8] A relatively complete louterion found in the area of the cemetery of the ancient city on Corfu is a close parallel to this louterion fragment in date, shape, and decorative scheme, as is an example by Sophilos in Athens.[9]

—AJP

235

**BIBLIOGRAPHY**
Unpublished.

**NOTES**

1 For louteria, see Callipolitis-Feytmans 1965; Moore and Philippides 1986, 32–33, pls. 56–57. For a Geometric example, ca. 710–700 B.C., cf. Toronto 919.5.18 (formerly C199): Hayes 1992, 31–32, no. 31. For an early black-figure example, ca. 625–600 B.C., cf. that by the Nettos Painter, Berlin 1682: *ABV* 5.4; *Paralipomena* 2–3.8; Callipolitis-Feytmans 1965, 18–19, no. 8. For a red-figure example, ca. 440 B.C., cf. Athens, Agora P 12641: Shefton 1962, 330–368; Callipolitis-Feytmans 1965, 35–36, no. 1; Moore 1997, 222–23, no. 584, pls. 59–60.

2 For halters and bits, see Anderson 1961, 40–43. For Horse-head amphorae, see Birchall 1972.

3 E.g., Boston 63.1611: Vermeule 1979, 60, fig. 15; *CVA* Boston 1, USA 14, pl. 1.1–2.

4 Vanderpool 1959, 280, pl. 74.6.

5 For the significance of louteria in cult, see Kenner 1935.

6 Whitley 1994a, 222–23.

7 Callipolitis-Feytmans 1965, 19, no. 11; 20, no. 13; 28, nos. 1–2; 33, no. 1.

8 Shefton 1962, 332.

9 For the louterion in the Corfu Museum (E61.09), see Daux 1962, 751, 753, 756, figs. 11–12; Callipolitis-Feytmans 1965, 19–20, no. 12, pls. Vb, VI–VIII; *Paralipomena* 19. On the side with the spout are two lions on either side of a lotus-palmette cross. The side opposite the spout depicts three horsemen at a gallop (see Callipolitis-Feytmans 1965, pls. 6–8). On a comparable louterion by Sophilos, from Vari (Athens, Nat. Mus. 16385: *ABV* 40.19, *Paralipomena* 18), the spout side is painted with a swan between two boars.

# 53

# Fragment of a Black-Figure Dinos with Satyrs

**Greek, Attic, ca. 580 B.C., attributed to Sophilos**
**Ceramic**
**Height 9.4 cm., width 11.7 cm., thickness 0.4–0.8 cm.**
**Collection of Arthur S. Richter**

**CONDITION**

The orange-red clay is burnished and well fired. There are chips and irregular breaks on three of four sides. There is minor surface wear, especially on the third satyr, and spots of brown incrustation. The inner surface is coated with black slip that is slightly iridescent, as are the black figures.

This Attic black-figure fragment is probably from a dinos, a large, handleless cauldron with a wide mouth and depressed, spherical body, the rounded base of which sat on a stand that was separately made.[1] The shape is based on hammered bronze cauldrons from the Near East and Cyprus that were exported to Greece in the late eighth and seventh centuries B.C. and copied in both metal and clay.[2] Painted dinoi and stands were among the showpieces of early Attic black-figure, serving as centerpieces at aristocratic drinking parties (symposia).

Parts of three hairy, ithyphallic satyrs (or silens: they are the same in this period) are preserved, all proceeding from left to right, the middle one running. Their heads and feet are missing, and of the first satyr much more. The second and third retain their long, flowing tails; their legs, too, are equine in form, with well-defined hocks. The torso of the third satyr is tinted with added red, but the bodies of the other two are completely covered with hair, represented by many short, incised lines. The pointed ends of the second satyr's shoulder-length locks are preserved, and part of the first satyr's stringy beard. The first holds a red wine cup, a *karchesion*, a type of footless kantharos with two vertical handles from base to rim. The hands of the other two satyrs are lost: the second raised his hands above his head, while the third one may have been holding something, possibly himself.[3]

Beside the second satyr's right arm is a fragmentary inscription in red letters: *[S]TRATOS*. This is probably his name, for it can be neither part of the artist's signature nor, at this date, a *kalos* inscription praising a young boy's beauty.[4] It is possible, even likely, to be the end of a longer name, such as Elasistratos, the name given to another satyr on a slightly later amphora.[5] The lively posture of this satyr could indicate that he is dancing, but his long stride is more suggestive of aggression, and the congruence of his preternaturally long phallus with the rump of the third satyr is surely meant to be interpreted in the simplest way, as an act of satyr buggery. This is not too surprising, considering the number of deer, goats, donkeys, and mules that receive the same treatment.[6] It is unlikely to have any significance as symbolizing fecundity or procreation, since no such outcome could result, and instead is more likely an intentional and presumably humorous commentary on the bestial, antisocial qualities of the satyrs, whom Hesiod called "good for nothing."[7]

The artist has been identified as Sophilos, an innovative and influential vase-painter of the first quarter of the sixth century who decorated a variety of shapes, including amphorae, kraters, spouted bowls (louteria), and dinoi.[8] His lively style and multifigured compositions, often featuring friezes of animals in the Corinthian manner, relate him to the Gorgon Painter, who may have been his teacher (see cat. no. 82). The spiky tresses and the linear incision of the tails are characteristic, as are such minor details as the distinctive way in which the fingernails of the first satyr are rendered by incising a line across the folded fingertips.[9] Two other dinos or krater fragments attributed to Sophilos also feature satyrs; on one of these, in Istanbul, the satyr grabbing the arm of a nymph has the same hairy body and prominent phallus.[10] These are among the earliest surviving depictions of satyrs in Greek art, if one discounts earlier "wild men," who display the hirsute tumescence of the satyrs but are without noticeably equine features.[11] These earliest satyrs are not shown in the company of Dionysos, and it is debated whether they have anything to do with the god until their appearance together a decade later on the François Vase, in the earliest portrayal of the Return of Hephaistos.[12]

—JMP

### BIBLIOGRAPHY

Atlantis Antiquities 1988, 55, fig. 48; Isler-Kerenyi 2001, 82 n. 11, 109, fig. 37.

### NOTES

1 For dinoi, see Milne and Richter 1935, 9–10, who point out that the name is a misnomer, a dinos instead probably being a type of drinking cup. The actual Greek name was *lebes*.

2 For Greek bronze cauldrons and their oriental models, see Jantzen 1955; Herrmann 1966; Herrmann 1979; Coldstream 1977, 362–65.

3 For masturbating satyrs, see Dover 1978, 97; *LIMC* 8 (1997), pls. 764–66, s.v. "Silenoi" (Simon).

4 The artist, Sophilos, did leave his signature on at least four vases, the first Attic vase-painter to do so. *Kalos* inscriptions did not come into vogue until the last quarter of the sixth century.

5 Cerveteri Museum: *LIMC* 3 (1986), 708, no. 1, s.v. "Elasistratos" (Kossatz-Deissmann). See also Kossatz-Deissmann 1991, 152.

6 See Lissarrague 1990c, 62; Dover 1978, 97; *LIMC* 8, pl. 755, nos. 52 and 55, s.v. "Silenoi"); Vierneisel and Kaeser 1991, 406–7. The Nymphs, too, are not exempt from penetration *a tergo*: cf. Würzburg 354: Langlotz 1932, pl. 26, no. 164.

7 Strabo 10.3.19; Merkelbach and West 1967, 60, fr. 123. This fragment is now known to be from the Hesiodic *Catalogue of Women*: see Carpenter 1986, 78–79; West 1985, 59. For an overview of satyrs in Classical art,

with extensive bibliography, see *LIMC* 8, 1108–33, pls. 746–83, s.v. "Silenoi."

8 For Sophilos, see *ABV* 37–43, 681, 714; *Paralipomena* 18–19; *BAdd*[2] 10–12; Bakir 1981. For dinoi by the artist, see Bakir 1981, 64–66, nos. A.1–7; and the discussions in Williams 1983 and Brownlee 1988.

9 There are many parallels: for the tresses, cf. those of the sphinxes on an amphora in Paris (Louvre E 819: *ABV* 38.5; Bakir 1981, pls. 13–14); for the incised tails, cf. the horses on the painter's London dinos with the Wedding of Peleus and Thetis (Brit. Mus. 1971.11-1.1: *Paralipomena* 19.16 bis; *BAdd*[2] 10–11; Williams 1983, 25–27, figs. 29–33); for the fingernails, cf. the left hand of Zeus on a krater fragment in Athens (Nat. Mus. Acrop. 587; *ABV* 39.15; Bakir 1981, pl. 4, fig. 6, no. A.2.)

10 Istanbul 4514: *ABV* 42.37; Bakir 1981, pl. 35, fig. 66, no. A.35; Carpenter 1986, pl. 18a. It is unknown whether this satyr had human or horse legs. The third satyr by Sophilos, on a fragment in New York (Met. 1977.193), is unpublished. In his only centauromachy, on a fragmentary krater in Athens (Nat. Mus. 2035: *ABV* 40.21 and 42.36; *Paralipomena* 18; Bakir 1981, pl. 9, fig. 17, no. A.20), Sophilos incised the hair of one centaur in the same manner as the satyrs, but not the other two centaurs in the same scene, which, like the third satyr on this fragment, he did not incise, a contrast suggesting a degree of individuality among the otherwise visually homogeneous creatures.

11 E.g., the hairy man on a Protattic krater in Berlin, which Beazley suggested might be a "proto-satyr" (Berlin A 33: Beazley 1986, 8; Metzger 1972, 32, fig. 1). That figure is not ithyphallic, but the "wild man" on a Late Corinthian aryballos in Brussels (A83) is both hairy and aroused (Payne 1931, 320, no. 1258; Amyx 1988, 620 n. 8). For the identity of such figures, see Metzger 1972; Carpenter 1986, 80–81 n. 19; Hedreen 1992, 128–29. See also Padgett, "Horse Men," n. 199, in this volume.

12 For the earliest satyrs and the question of whether or not they precede an association with Dionysos, see Brommer 1937, 26; Carpenter 1986, 80–82, 90–91; Hedreen 1992, 74–75, pl. 25. Hedreen (p. 74) thinks the karchesion/kantharos carried by the satyr on this fragment is a link with Dionysos. In this period, however, the kantharos is not yet associated with the god (Carpenter 1986, 117); on Sophilos's dinos in London, for instance, it is Peleus who carries a kantharos, not Dionysos (see n. 9 above); for details of Peleus and Dionysos, see Carpenter 1986, pl. 2; Williams 1983, 23–24, figs. 26–27). For the Return of Hephaistos on the François Vase (Florence 4209: *ABV* 76.1), see *Vaso François* 1980, pl. 92; Carpenter 1986, pl. 4a; Hedreen 1992, pl. 1; *LIMC* 8, 1113, no. 22, pl. 747, s.v. "Silenoi."

## 54

# Statuette of a Satyr

**Greek, Boiotian, ca. 500 B.C.**
**Terracotta**
**Height 12.9 cm., width 7.1 cm., depth 7.9 cm.**
**Princeton University Art Museum, gift of**
**Gillett G. Griffin (2002 – 35)**

CONDITION
**The figure is solid and handmade of brown clay with a smooth burnished surface. There are faint traces of white slip but no color. The left ear and both hands are missing, but it is otherwise complete. The head, tail, and left arm have been reattached.**

This little satyr is simply made but full of vitality. His head is raised and cocked slightly to his left, giving him a somewhat quizzical air. His rubbery limbs are unmodeled, but his feet are clearly humanoid. He leans back slightly, supported by a long tail, bent nearly perpendicular, which combines with his legs to form a stable tripod. He is ithyphallic, but his anatomy otherwise is without detail or definition. The torso is slender, the buttocks nonexistent. He holds both arms before him, the left above the right, but it is not clear whether the missing hands ever held anything. The head is nearly flat and only sketchily modeled, with a faint indication of hair in the back. The face is broad, with a flat jutting beard, a large nose, and short equine ears. The eyes are not modeled and may have been painted.

The satyr is related to a large class of early- to mid-fifth-century clay statuettes of satyrs, monkeys, and grotesque figures who are seated on their tails in this same fashion.[1] These "tripodic" figures have simple, handmade bodies, but their heads are normally molded and frequently oversized. A satyr riding a mule, from the Museum of Fine Arts, Boston (cat. no. 55), has a molded head typical of this type, albeit without the tripod tail. Most examples come from tombs in Boiotia and adjacent regions, but there has been disagreement as to whether they are of Boiotian or Corinthian manufacture.[2] This satyr is unusual in that its head is not molded but made by hand; its straight, unflexed legs are also a modest departure from

the norm, and he is taller than most tripodic figures. Taken together, these features suggest a slightly earlier date, at the very beginning of the fifth century.[3]

Although some tripodic satyrs have been found in sanctuaries, most come from graves, and we may postulate a similar origin for this figure. The reasons for burying figurines of satyrs with the dead are obscure. Did they play a magical role, perhaps connecting the deceased with the happy realm of Dionysos? We do not know, but they are unlikely to have been toys or dolls, and it is hard to imagine that they were household furnishings or objets d'art. The satyr figurines cannot be interpreted in isolation from the other types of Boiotian terracottas found in tombs, like the centaur in Missouri (cat. no. 21) or the Pan in Boston (cat. no. 100). Like many *Mischwesen*, their meaning probably changed depending on their circumstances, so that those from the Theban Kabirion sanctuary may have played a different role from that of their funerary counterparts.[4] Herbert Hoffmann believed they may have been inspired by lost satyr plays, like those of the tragic poet Pratinas, who was active at the beginning of the fifth century.[5] The molded heads, many of comically large dimensions, do resemble masks, and when the satyrs are preserved in a group, like the trio in Cleveland, they form a sort of chorus, like those of the rustic satyr mummers whose ecstatic dances and songs in honor of Dionysos were the basis of the first Greek theatrical performances. Without a mise-en-scène, however, or the presence of a mythological protagonist like Herakles, there is little justification for identifying individual figures with specific satyr plays.

—JMP

## BIBLIOGRAPHY
Unpublished.

## NOTES
1 For the type, see Winter 1903, 219, 1–11; Hoffmann 1964; Higgins 1954, 253–54, pl. 133, nos. 932–34. Examples are found in many museums: e.g., the Danish Nat. Mus., Copenhagen (Breitenstein 1941, pl. 38, no. 317); the Liebieghaus-Museum alter Plastik, Frankfurt (Bol 1981, 48, figs. 54–55); the Goulandris Museum, Athens (Marangou 1985, 131, no. 194). Three of the finest are the satyrs formerly in the Schimmel Collection and now in the Cleveland Museum of Art, said to have been found in a tomb near Megara (Cleveland 1992.352.1–3: Hoffmann 1964, 67, pl. 18.1–3, pl. 19.1; Muscarella 1974, no. 46). For some grotesque tripodic figures that are neither satyr nor monkey, see Breitenstein 1941, pl. 38, nos. 319–21; Higgins 1954, pl. 133, no. 937; New York, Christie's, May 30, 1997, no. 136.

2 Hoffmann believed that all the tripodic satyrs were Boiotian and noted that some had been found in the Theban Kabirion (Hoffmann 1964, 67; Winter 1903, 219, 1 b–g; Schmaltz 1974, pl. 30, no. 418). Spectrographic analysis of a related but anomalous satyr in Boston, who stands on one leg, supported a Boiotian origin (Hoffmann 1964, 70 n. 44, pl. 21.4). Higgins believed the clay of the three satyrs in London was Corinthian (Higgins 1954, 253); one was said to be from Tanagra and the other two from Athens, but the provenances are unreliable. The brown clay of the Princeton satyr looks more Boiotian than Corinthian, but it has not been tested. Hoffmann apparently agreed with Higgins that the closely related tripodic figurines of monkeys are Corinthian (Hoffmann 1964, 69, pl. 18.4–5; Higgins 1954, pl. 133, no. 936). Higgins dated the monkeys to the early fourth century, but a tripodic satyr of mid-fifth-century type, in the Goulandris Museum, Athens, has a similar monkey on his shoulder (Kanellopoulou 1980, pl. 130). Some tripodic figures have been found far from mainland Greece: e.g., a female (Aphrodite?) holding a dove from a mid-fifth-century tomb at Camarina, Sicily (Orsi 1990, pl. 17, 711.2).

3 Few tripodic figures can be dated much earlier than this. A Boiotian satyr with a molded face in the Kestner Museum, Hannover, has stripes on its legs like those on Boiotian terracotta horses of the mid-sixth century (e.g., cat. no. 49), suggesting it is of similar date (Liepmann 1975, 52, no. T28). The stripes make it clear that, in this instance, we are to interpret the figure's legs as those of a horse. A tripodic satyr in the art market may have a handmade head: Freiburg am Breisgau, Galerie Günter Puhze, Katalog 17, *Kunst der Antike* (Freiburg 2003), no. 107. Cf. also Boston 13.98.

4 See n. 2 above.

5 Hoffmann 1964, 68–69.

## 55

## Statuette of a Satyr Riding a Mule

**Greek, Boiotian, early fifth century B.C.**
**Terracotta**
**Height 15.8 cm., length 16.4 cm.**
**Museum of Fine Arts, Boston, gift of E. P. and**
**Fiske Warren (08.290)**

### CONDITION

**The statuette is made of fine brown, slighty micaceous clay. The end of the mule's tail and the satyr's lower left leg are missing. There are mended breaks in the mule's tail and right hind leg, and in the satyr's torso and neck. The satyr's left shoulder has been restored. The painted surface is worn.**

A satyr rides bareback on a mule, clutching the mane in his fingerless hands, his tail extending behind him along the animal's back. The mule is sexless, but the satyr is unostentatiously ithyphallic, the shaft attached to his belly along its entire length. The satyr's molded head is too large for his handmade body and has outsized features: a bald dome, rounded cheeks, flaring equine ears, drooping mustache, and full, spreading beard. Both satyr and mule are coated with white slip, over which the satyr's beard and upper body are painted red, his legs pink. A red stripe crosses the mule's lower neck, and there are traces of red on its eyes and mouth. The mule's head is bony and sharp-featured, with long, laid-back ears. Its head and body are molded, and the hollow body is vented through a hole in the anus.

The painting of details in red slip on a white ground relates this figurine to the latest of the Archaic Boiotian horsemen, Jan Østergaard's Group L.[1] But although a few of these late horsemen have molded heads, the earliest dating about 510 B.C.,[2] the horses are always solid and handmade. The satyr and mule in Boston are modeled with greater volume and plasticity and must instead have been made in the first half of the fifth century, a date confirmed by the close affinity between the satyr's molded head and those on "tripodic" satyrs from Boiotian graves of that period.[3] Indeed, the same mold could have been

used to provide the head for a tripodic satyr, but there is no parallel close in date and style for this pairing of satyr and mule. An earlier, sixth-century figurine in Boston, said to be from the Theban Kabirion, shows a fluting satyr mounted backwards on a solid, handmade mule with striped legs.[4] In addition, there are fifth-century Boiotian donkeys and mules ridden by monkeys, comic actors, and other characters,[5] as well as an abundance of mounted satyrs in Attic black-figure and red-figure vase-paintings.[6]

Although of independent origin, satyrs began their association with Dionysos early in the sixth century B.C. Donkeys and mules joined the god's retinue at the same time, their first connection occurring in the earliest and fullest depiction of the Return of Hephaistos, on the François Vase, after which both satyrs and donkeys become standard participants not only in the Return, but also in the canonical Dionysiac thiasos that evolved from this mythical procession.[7] Herbert Hoffmann took it for granted that this and other Boiotian terracotta satyrs were inspired by satyr plays, but there is little support for this assumption.[8] As the vase-paintings demonstrate, such imagery was widespread long before the first satyr plays were produced at the end of the sixth century. As with most such Archaic Boiotian terracottas, like the centaur in Missouri and the tripodic satyr in Princeton (cat. nos. 21 and 54), their principal "meaning" must be sought in the realm of funerary cult. A desire for an afterlife in the happy realm of Dionysos is certainly one possibility, but the means of expressing this desire—a satyr riding a mule—is curiously indirect, and one cannot forget that it follows a long line of human riders from Boiotian graves. Satyrs worm their way into many areas of public and private art where their significance is also poorly understood, and "explaining" a figurine such as this must necessarily be a subjective undertaking.[9]

—JMP

### BIBLIOGRAPHY

Hoffmann 1964, 69–70, pl. 21.2.

### NOTES

1 Østergaard 1991, 159–68, figs. 67–74. See also Higgins 1954, pl. 109, nos. 804–5.
2 Østergaard 1991, 183 n. 160. On a figurine in the Kurashiki Ninagawa

Museum, Tokyo (Simon 1982a, no. 129), the heads of both horse and rider are molded, but the solid bodies are handmade.

3   These are discussed, with references, under cat. no. 54. Østergaard (1991, 182 n. 130) dates the Boston satyr and mule to "ca. 500 B.C.?," but that is probably a little early.

4   Boston 01.8011: Hoffmann 1964, 70, pl. 21.1; Østergaard 1991, 153, fig. 61. A wheel-made horse in the Thera Museum, probably dating to late fifth century, is ridden by a satyr: Winter 1903, 215, no.1. A figurine in Bloomington, with a satyr reclining on a mule (Indiana University Art Museum 63.105.109), dates to the third century: Rudolph and Calinescu 1988, 166, no. 161.

5   Monkey (London, Brit. Mus. 75.3-9.16): Higgins 1954, pl. 136, no. 966. Comic actor (Copenhagen, Nat. Mus. 749): Breitenstein 1941, pl. 39. An unpublished fifth-century Boiotian figurine in the Princeton University Art Museum (y1964-116) represents a grotesque female with molded head riding sidesaddle on a donkey.

6   In one of their earliest (ca. 580 B.C.) pairings in Attic vase-painting, a black-figure lekythos in Buffalo (Albright-Knox Gallery G 600: *ABV* 12.22; Boardman 1974, fig. 15), a satyr already is shown riding a donkey, but most subsequent depictions of mounted satyrs date to the late sixth and fifth centuries: see Hoffmann 1983, 69 n. 25; Padgett 2000, 54 n. 37. With few exceptions, satyrs ride donkeys or mules rather than horses. They ride other animals as well, including goats (e.g., London, Brit. Mus. B 168: *ABV* 142.3; *CVA* London 3, Great Britain 4, pl. 31.2), bullocks (e.g., Oxford 1934.308: Lissarrague 1988, 341, fig. 4), dogs (e.g., Cologne, once Niessen Coll.: Brommer 1943, 131, fig. 8), and deer (e.g., Berlin 3242: *ARV²* 1608; Hoorn 1951, fig. 310).

7   François Vase (Florence 4209): *ABV* 76.1, 682; Paralipomena 29; *BAdd²* 21. For the Return of Hephaistos, see *LIMC* 4 (1988), 637–45, pls. 390–401, s.v. "Hephaistos" (Hermary and Jacquemin); Carpenter 1986, 13–29; Hedreen 1992, 13–30; Brommer 1978, 10–17, 199–205, pls. 1–11. For satyrs, donkeys, and mules in Dionysiac imagery, see Padgett 2000, 49–59.

8   See the comments under cat. no. 54 in this volume.

9   A different approach might be to consider possible foreign models for a connection between donkey riders and mortuary cult. For example, an Egyptian faïence statuette of a boy riding a donkey, ca. 750–525 B.C., has been interpreted as symbolizing the victory of the child Horus over the god Seth, represented by the donkey, in revenge for Seth's murder of Horus's father Osiris; see Noblecourt 1997.

## 56

# Statuette of a Satyr

**Greek, perhaps Peloponnesian, ca. 530–520 B.C.**
**Bronze**
**Height 9.56 cm., width across knees 5.59 cm.,**
**depth 2.9 cm.**
**Collection of Michael and Judy Steinhardt, New York**

**CONDITION**
The tail is broken off, but the figure is otherwise complete. There is a casting bubble in the satyr's left eye. The patina is dark green with brown mottling showing through, and spots of lighter green corrosion throughout.

His legs drawn up, his right hand clasping his slightly protruding belly, his left resting on his upper leg and knee, this satyr looks out eagerly at the world before him. Wide, round eyes are outlined with raised contour; the eyebrows are both modeled in relief and strengthened above with an incised line. A wide moustache with vertical incision is offset from a trim, luxuriant beard, patterned with dicing. A fillet arranges his long hair, which is pulled forward in long strands around the face and in back falls below his shoulders, where it terminates in a sharp, horizontal ridge. Lines incised in the wax give texture to the pubic hair, the hair around the hooves, and the hair inside the pointed equine ears. Punched circles define the nipples. A small stump at the base of his back marks the place where the tail has broken off. The soft, broad modeling of the body emphasizes the crisp precision of the face.

A small tang below each foot indicates attachment to something else. Scale, shape, and subject matter suggest that the most likely context would have been either a tripod or a stand. A number of tripods have been preserved with figural elements.[1] Although these generally seem to have been cast as a single object, some were assembled from more than one piece.[2] A second possible context is a stand (*hypokraterion*), such as the one in Belgrade from a tomb at Trebenishte.[3] In both cases, the satyr would, appropriately enough, have decorated a vessel intended to contain wine.

Typologically, this satyr goes with large groups of squatting figures: dwarves,[4] komasts,[5] negroes,[6] boys asleep out of doors,[7] and also satyrs.[8] These latter exist in representations from both Greece and the West: a series of terracottas from Lindos, on Rhodes,[9] and representations on Attic vases[10] may be compared with a group of Etruscan bronze handles that have been associated with a workshop in Vulci working in the purest Greek style.[11] The pose in some ways also recalls the rider on the Grimani oinochoe in Budapest.[12]

The question of this bronze's place of manufacture is necessarily uncertain. The proportions of the face and the treatment of the beard recall in particular the reclining bronze satyrs from Olympia.[13] Other bronzes that share something with this one are the Stathatos Kriophoros,[14] the Princeton centaur (cat. no. 24),[15] and the rather later Spencer-Churchill satyr,[16] all considered mainland Greek. The taut style and crisp modeling both strongly suggest a mainland Greek workshop, and one of the very best.

—JG

**BIBLIOGRAPHY**
Unpublished.

**NOTES**

1 For tripods with figural elements, see Stibbe 2000b, 127–42.

2 E.g., London, Brit. Mus. 1971.3-23.1: Stibbe 2000b, 80, fig. 52.

3 Belgrade 174/1; Stibbe 2000b, 88–98, figs. 56–62.

4 Dasen 1993.

5 Dasen 2000, 89–97.

6 E.g., Oxford 1884.585: Vafopoulou-Richardson 1981, 28–29, no. 27.

7 Bothmer 1979, 63–67.

8 Bulle 1893, 37.

9 Blinkenberg 1931, 562–64, nos. 2319–29, pl. 108, and 576–77, nos. 2381–82, 2384, pl. 112.

10 E.g., the satyr on the kyathos once in the Hirschmann Collection: Bloesch 1982, 56, no. 26; London, Sotheby's, December 9, 1993, lot 25.

11 Boston 99.464: Comstock and Vermeule 1971, 360–61, no. 507, with references. The handle cited there as being in a private collection in Haverford, Pennsylvania, is now at Harvard (1998.101).

12 Budapest 56.11.A: Bothmer 1979, 63–67; Szabó 1988, 229–32. The tangs below the feet, which would have pierced the vessel, make it unlikely that this bronze came from an oinochoe, although it is by no means impossible, as bronze oinochoe and hydria handles are regularly riveted.

13 Olympia B 4232, 4200, 4700: Herfort-Koch 1986, 119–20, nos. K 146–48. Contrast these with the Baker satyr, New York, Met. 1972.118.66: Bothmer 1950, 8, no. 19.

14 Kunze 1953, pls. 1–3. For others from the same series, see M. True, in Kozloff and Mitten 1988, 77–86.

15 Princeton 1997-36: *Record* 57 (1998): 194, 196.

16 London. Brit. Mus. 1966.3-28.2: Higgins 1967b, 49, 11b, 50, fig. 12.

# 57

# Neck-Amphora with Satyr Masks

Greek, Attic, ca. 530 B.C.
Ceramic
Height 38.5–39.6 cm., diameter of mouth
18.3 cm., diameter of body 27.7 cm., diameter of
foot 13.2 cm.
Art Institute of Chicago, Costa A. Pandaleon Fund
(1980.75)

CONDITION

The vase is in very good condition. A hole in the
body has been repaired and partially restored. There
are small chips on the inner edge of the lip and minor
abrasion overall. The foot has been reattached.
Remains of root marks occur on the neck of side B.

This neck-amphora, which once had a lid, was a storage
jar.[1] The artist has not been identified, but it is thought
that he was associated with the Antimenes Painter.[2] The
vase has an echinus mouth above an offset neck with
moldings above and below, a robust ovoid body, tripartite
handles, and a disk foot. The body is set unevenly on the
foot, causing the vase to cant slightly forward and to the

right when viewed from side A. Lustrous black slip covers
much of the vase, including the inner mouth and neck.
The lip and upper shoulder are reserved, but the outer
neck and a zone on the shoulder are coated with creamy
white slip.[3] Delicate palmettes with tightly coiled tendrils
are drawn in black slip on the shoulder. There are three
reserved pattern bands, including tongues on the upper
shoulder, right-facing keys framed by three fine bands on
the body below the lower handle attachments, and rays
above the foot. A fine band of red slip was applied to the
inner and outer edge of the lip and also to the moldings
at the place where the neck joins to the body and the body
attaches to the foot. There are two red bands above the
rays and a single, very fine band on the top of the foot.
A merchant's mark is scratched into the reserved underside of the foot.

On either side of the neck is a frontal face, or mask,
of a wreathed satyr, each rendered in a combination of
outline drawing and black-figure technique and framed
to the left and right by black vines.[4] The mask on side
A has a broad, rather genial face with slender, arching
eyebrows, while the mask on side B has a narrower, more
somber countenance, with thick eyebrows that meet
over the bridge of his nose. Both satyrs have long horse
ears with open tips. Four long locks of hair, each hastily
incised with a single irregularly etched line, hang from
the sides of their heads. A relief line occurs along the
edge and down the center of the unkempt beards of
both satyrs.

This amphora belongs to a group of vessels made
for use at drinking parties, mostly cups, neck-amphorae,
column-kraters, and hydriae, featuring frontal faces that
stare boldly at the viewer. Favorite subjects include the
gorgoneion, satyrs, and Dionysos, the latter two often
depicted between a pair of giant eyes. Their prevalence in
the last third of the sixth century B.C. has been tied to the
resurgence in the worship of Dionysos that occurred during the period of Peisistratid rule, which saw the estab-
lishment of the Greater Dionysia, an enormously popular
civic festival in the god's honor.[5]

Ideas abound about the origin, inspiration, and
meaning of these disembodied heads.[6] They have been
thought to possess defensive or protective powers[7] or

to have been inspired by the masks used in rituals or dramatic performances.[8] It also has been argued that they represent mask-idols of Dionysos and satyrs of the type shown on Lenaia vases, which were the focus of ritual worship.[9] Another theory, which draws heavily on the evidence of literature and vase imagery, proposes that the sole purpose of these wide-eyed faces on vases designed for convivial use was to amuse the ancient viewer.[10] A suggestion also has been put forward that in the context of the drinking party these frontal heads functioned as symbolic mirrors; when looking at a satyr mask, the ancient spectator would have seen a reflection of his own hedonistic desires held in check by the demands of civilized conduct, but yearning to be released through the liberating power of wine.[11]

In contrast to other composite creatures that figured prominently in Greek art, satyrs were relative latecomers to the scene.[12] They may have originally had an independent existence,[13] but as these shaggy hybrids became firmly established in Attic iconography during the course of the sixth century B.C., they also became inextricably linked to Dionysos. Their brutish appearance, base behavior, and insatiable appetites perfectly symbolized the irrational side of human nature that was the domain of the wine god.

—KM

## BIBLIOGRAPHY

Mertens 1977, iv; Art Institute of Chicago, *Annual Report 1979—1980* (Chicago 1980), 31 (illus.); Pedley 1994, 40—41, no. 22 (illus.).

## NOTES

1 The author is grateful to Joan Mertens for generously sharing her thoughts about the amphora. The vase had its original lid in modern times, but the two became separated before 1980, when the Art Institute of Chicago purchased the amphora.

2 Mertens 1977, iv; Pedley 1994, 40—41.

3 A difference in color and texture of the added white around the handle roots raised concern that these areas were restored in modern times. When the material proved resistant to acetone, the vase was microscopically examined by Suzanne R. Schnepp, associate conservator of objects at the Art Institute of Chicago. She concluded that both types of white slip were applied in antiquity.

4 Frontal heads usually appear on the body of an amphora, e.g., the famous neck-amphora in the Tarquinia Museum (RC 1804: *CVA* Tarquinia 2, Italy 26, pl. 32.4).

5 Shapiro 1989, 84—100.

6 Henrichs 1993, 36—39.

7 Korshak 1987, 2—5 (with references to earlier sources). See also Carpenter 1986, 97 and n. 95.

8 Bell 1977, 9—10.

9 Bell 1977, 10—11; Korshak 1987, 18—20; Hedreen 1992, 169—70 (following Ferrari 1986, 5—20); Carpenter 1997, 80—82. For Lenaia vases, see Peirce 1998, 59—95, with bibliography.

10 Carpenter 1986, 97.

11 Frontisi-Ducroux 1989, 150—65.

12 Boardman 1974, 232—33; Carpenter 1986, 80—81. For earlier representations, see *LIMC* 8 (1997), 1114, no. 29c, pl. 751, 1132, s.v. "Silenoi" (Simon).

13 Carpenter 1986, 76, 80—82. For a different opinion, see *LIMC* 8, 1108, s.v. "Silenoi."

## 58

# Janiform Kantharos with Satyr and African

Greek, Attic, ca. 470–460 B.C., assigned to the
Toronto Class
Ceramic with slip decoration
Height 19.6 cm., width at handles 17.2 cm., diameter
of rim 15.3 cm., diameter of base 8.5 cm.
Cleveland Museum of Art, purchase,
John L. Severance Fund (1979.69)

CONDITION
The vase is intact. The black glaze at the top of
the African's forehead and the white of his beard
are chipped.

Unique in its combination of the head of a black man with that of a satyr, this janiform kantharos belongs to a class of head vases that were popular as wine vessels in Athens during the fifth century B.C.[1] The heads were made in molds and then combined with a tall vertical lip that had been thrown on a wheel. The attachment of two hefty vertical handles at the sides makes the vessel a kantharos, a form of drinking cup that is often depicted as an attribute of the wine god Dionysos.

It is appropriate then that over one-half of this vase consists of the head of a satyr. Black-haired, black-bearded and with bushy black eyebrows, this satyr stares intently at the viewer. Over his balding forehead he wears a white relief band covered with rows of small clay pellets, suggesting wool. His long reserved moustache and red lips frame his bared white teeth. He is recognizable as a satyr by his prominent equine ears, which are separately molded and jut forward at the sides of his face. The artist has used fine, widely spaced, incised wavy lines to delineate the tufts of the splaying beard that encircles the satyr's lower face like a ruff.

On the opposite side is the head of a black African. The modeling of his face is similar to that of the satyr, but his skin is darkened with shiny black glaze. His tightly curled hair is indicated by rows of raised dots around his head as well as on his short tripartite beard. Oddly, his hair is painted red, but his beard and eyebrows are white,

perhaps to contrast with the black of his flesh. His moustache is short, his lips are thick, and his open mouth displays clenched white teeth. He is depicted as aged not only by his white beard and eyebrows but also by the wrinkles painted around his eyes.

While these two heads share a number of similarities — for example, each has a tonguelike area in relief (reserved) on the chin — they are also deliberately contrasted. The satyr with his woolen garland is depicted as a reveler and symposiast, while the black is probably to be understood as a careworn servant.[2] More common combinations used by Athenian potters include a woman and satyr, a woman and Herakles, and a woman and a black.[3] The white Greek male never appears on these vases, and it has been suggested that his absence is due to his sense of superiority over women, animal-human hybrids, and barbarians, i.e., non-Greeks.[4] Less-than-ideal types were

utilized for these utilitarian vessels that were featured at male drinking parties, thus reinforcing the Greek male's identity in contrast to his opposite, whether in gender, species, or ethnicity.[5]

Often the lip of these kantharoi is decorated with a figurative scene having to do with Dionysos or his retinue. Here, however, there is simply a red-figure ornament: a double addorsed palmette-lotus chain. A pair of anomalous lotus buds appears just off center above the right eye of the black.

—JN

**BIBLIOGRAPHY**

*BClevMus* 67.3 (March 1980): 95, no. 2, illus. p. 63; *BClevMus* 67.6 (June 1980): illus. p. 166; Kozloff 1980, 206–11, figs. 2–3 and color covers; Neils 1982, 18, no. 20; Kozloff 1989, 4, fig. 8; *CVA* Cleveland 2, USA 35, 40, pl. 78.

**NOTES**

1 For head vases in general, see Beazley 1929; Lissarrague 1995. For the Toronto Class, see *ARV*[2] 1537–38; *BAdd*[2] 386–87.

2 In spite of attempts by some scholars (e.g., Snowden 1970) to suggest that there was little or no color prejudice in ancient Greece, most blacks are depicted in subservient or otherwise demeaning roles. In contrasting Ethiopians and Thracians, Xenophanes (fr. 16) refers to the red hair of the Thracians, who also were household servants in ancient Athens.

3 This combination of the head of a Greek woman and that of a black man, with the latter made in the same mold as that in Cleveland, is found in a janiform kantharos at San Simeon (9997: see Kozloff 1980, 210–11, figs. 8–11).

4 See Lissarrague 1995.

5 Beazley (1929, 39) had a different explanation for the presence of the black on these head vases: "The black man gets in not because he has strong prophylactic properties, nor because he is more addicted to wine, or perfume, than the white man, nor because there were both perfumes and black men in Egypt, but because it seemed a crime not to make negroes when you had that magnificent black glaze."

## 59

## Antefix with Satyr Head

**Western (South Italian) Greek, probably Tarentine,
525 – 480 B.C.**
**Terracotta, painted[1]**
**Height 21.5 cm., width 22.2 cm., depth 1.7 – 2.4 cm.**
**Cleveland Museum of Art, the Charles W. Harkness
Endowment Fund (1926.552)**

CONDITION
**The antefix is repaired from two large pieces; the
lower left-hand corner is restored. Large chips are
missing from the upper lip. The face is incrusted
with accretions not present on the reverse, including
organic material in the depressions of the relief.
At high points in the relief some abrasion appears,
and the surface is worn and weathered.**

The openings of the cover tiles along the eaves of
ancient Greek and Italic roofs needed to be closed in
order to prevent both windblown water damage to the
structure below and nesting places for unwanted animals.
Two alternative solutions were devised, the use of a lateral sima or of antefixes (see the architectural drawing in
the Glossary). Antefixes are the norm for the temples of
mainland Greece but are confined to more modest buildings in East Greece and Magna Graecia. The figure fields
they provide are small and discontinuous, so the preference was for large single images that would be easily recognizable at a distance. The medium of decoration varies
from high relief to painting. When rendered plastically,
the image is almost always mold-made and repetitive,
though sometimes one set of antefixes alternated with a
second set bearing a different image. The molds were
itinerant, carried from site to site and even region to
region. This diffusion is probably due to traveling workshops, but it is also possible that molds were bought and
sold. Thus, the provenance of an antefix does not necessarily correlate with the origin of the mold or the workshop using it.

Among the options available for antefix decoration,
the staring face, sometimes divinely beautiful, at others
monstrous, is one of the most effective and widely used,

especially in northwestern Greece and Magna Graecia.
According to Pliny (*HN* 35.151 – 52), the face antefix was
the invention of a Sicyonian sculptor named Butades.
The earliest examples, however, come from sanctuaries in
northwestern Greece, such as that of Apollo at Thermon,
in Aitolia, and of Hera at Mons Repos, on Corfu.[2] Since
the material record at Thermon indicates cultural connections with Sicyon,[3] Butades' idea may have come to
Aitolia from Sicyon. Two Cretan sculptors, Dipoinos
and Skyllis, sons of the legendary Daidalos, may have
been the agents. They are said, again by Pliny (*HN* 36.9),
to have emigrated from Crete to Sicyon, from there to
Aitolia and eventually to Magna Graecia, a route of
artistic exchange increasingly confirmed by the archaeological evidence, especially in the realm of architectural
sculpture in terracotta.[4]

Two types of antefixes with faces in relief appear in
this exhibition: the satyr head, represented by this South
Italian Greek example, and the gorgoneion, Medusa's
severed head, represented by two examples, one South
Italian Greek (cat. no. 88), the other southern Etruscan or
Campanian (cat. no. 89). Both of the Western Greek antefixes were possibly made in the same center and belong
to a series best known through the many examples from
Taras (Tarentum; modern Taranto).[5]

Antefixes decorated with a satyr head appear to
be a more recent phenomenon than those decorated with
the gorgoneion and are found almost exclusively in Magna
Graecia, Sicily, and in the lands of the hellenized Italic
cultures.[6] The oldest surviving satyr heads used as architectural sculpture appear as water spouts on the later roof
of the temple of Apollo at Thermon.[7] As old or older
than the satyr-head antefixes in Italy and Sicily, the spouts
may have prompted use of satyr images on antefixes.
Although normally considered Dionysiac, satyr-head
antefixes often appeared on buildings not associated with
Dionysos. Antefixes depicting full-figured satyrs, both
in relief and painted, almost invariably show them
engaged in sexual acts. Though not as explicit, satyr heads
surely allude to the same unbridled male libido, and,
since images of sexual penetration and male genitalia were
regarded as apotropaic, their function must be similar
to that of the gorgoneion.[8]

This antefix is mold-made of fine-bodied sedimentary clay, fired beige and containing small rounded, naturally occurring inclusions rather than temper. Polychrome slip is visible on the front surface: a dark red for the hair and lighter red for the flesh of the face. The herringbone pattern of the beard and the beaded locks at the sides of the head (seven on the right, eight on the left) may have been made with a rolling stamp. The color of the incrusted eyes and beard are not discernable. On the reverse, a Laconian cover tile is attached flush with the antefix's semicircular contour. On the obverse, this upper contour is marked by a thin half-round molding, as is the case with the Tarentine gorgoneion antefix (cat. no. 88). The bottom edges of the cover tile end 9.5 centimeters above the bottom of the antefix, so it must have been positioned in front of its two adjoining pan tiles at the eaves, overlapping and covering the seam between them.

The similarity of the clay to that of the Tarentine Greek gorgoneion antefix should be noted. In low relief compared to contemporary Sicilian Greek and Etrusco-Campanian satyr-head antefixes, this antefix's plasticity is greater than that of its gorgoneion sister, as can be seen in the rendering of the nose and cheeks. While a furrowed brow is a common feature on satyr-head and gorgoneion antefixes, the similarity of this feature on the two Tarentine Greek examples in this exhibition, in addition to their shared fabric and the use of a torus molding to delineate the curving contour of the decorated surface, suggests that the molds for both antefixes were created by the same hand. Workshops that used these molds traveled widely, so although many antefixes made in the same or parallel molds have been found at Taras, the molds and indeed the workshop itself may not have been native to that city.[9] In spite of the low relief, the connection between outer appearance and inner anatomical structure, so visible in the cheekbones, is purely Greek.[10] It is a plastically sensitive rendering of a brutish face. Like its gorgoneion sister, the naturalism of the nose and the tear ducts at the inner corners of the eyes suggest a date in the late sixth or early fifth century B.C.

Another detail of this naturalism is the rendering of the eyelids, as well as the subtle vertical groove that bisects the full lower lip. Great care was taken to provide textural articulation to the moustache and beard, and to the rows of woolly curls that descend from the crown of the head to the hairline. Nevertheless, when painted and mounted on the eaves of a building, these subtle plastic details, so typical of Greek sculpture in terracotta, would not have been visible to even the most keen-eyed viewer. —JFK

## BIBLIOGRAPHY

Rossiter 1927, 21–22; H. Rossiter, *BClevMus* 15 (1928): 46.

## NOTES

1 Fabric color (Munsell 7.5YR, 8/2); red paints (10R, 4/4; 10R, 3/4; 10R, 6/4; 7.5R, 6/4).

2 The antefixes from the temple of Artemis Orthia at Sparta may be the earliest, in the third quarter of the seventh century (Winter 1993, 98–100, 106–7), followed closely by those from the early temple of Apollo at Thermon (Winter 1993, 112–15; Mertens-Horn 1978, 30–65) and the early temple of Hera at Mons Repos, on Corfu (Winter 1993, 63–65).

3 Jeffery 1990, 139, 225; Winter 1993, 112.

4 Torelli 1977, 310–11; Mertens-Horn 1992, 83–91.

5 Laviosa 1954, 229–35, pl. LXVIII.1–5.

6 The only example from the Aegean comes from the site of Xoburgo on the island of Tenos: see Winter 1993, 268.

7 Van Buren 1926, 142–43, figs. 127, 128, 136; Winter 1993, 114, 117, 131–32, pls. 55–56.

8 Holloway 1988, 177–83, fig. 2.

9 Van Buren 1973, 145, fig. 62; Edizione Alinari no. 21162. Another example was formerly in the Basel art market: *Monnaies et Medailles*, S.A., Auktion 14, June 19, 1954, lot 12, pl. 5.

10 Holloway 1975, 1–15.

# 60

# Black-Figure Lekythos with Satyrs Dancing a Pyrrhic

Greek, Attic, ca. 490 – 480 B.C., attributed to the
Athena Painter [1]
Ceramic
Height 25.3 cm., maximum diameter 8.8 cm.,
diameter of foot 7.0 cm.
Collection of Michael and Judy Steinhardt, New York

CONDITION
The mouth and upper neck are restored; otherwise,
the vase is in near perfect condition.

The lekythos is a tall, slender jug used to contain olive oil.
This example is decorated in the black-figure technique on
a white-ground.[2] It has a deep mouth and a long, narrow
neck. The shoulder is decorated with three black-glazed
palmettes, and most of the cylindrical body is coated with
white slip.[3] At the top of the body is a band of black net
pattern. Pairs of reddish dilute lines frame the figure zone.
The lower body is glazed black. A red band marks the join
of the body to the foot, which has an unusual profile,
sometimes described as "in two degrees." The top surface
is black, but the tapering side is reserved; a black band is
painted around the upper half of the torus below. The
underside of the foot is concave and reserved.

This lekythos has been attributed to the Athena
Painter,[4] a prolific artist active in the first decades of the
fifth century who displayed his special devotion to the
patron goddess of Athens by creating a number of lekythoi
that feature images of her head. The Athena Painter also
was fond of depicting satyrs,[5] such as the three on this vase,
who are identified by their distinctive equine ears, shaggy
beards, and long tails, as well as the erect phalloi sported by
two of them. The satyr in the middle plays the double
flutes, or auloi, for his two compatriots.[6] A pointed amphora, or wine jar, lies empty on its side behind the satyr at the
right. The vines that seem to emerge from the satyrs' shields
are a common motif on small black-figure vases of this
period and a reminder of the satyrs' association with the
wine god Dionysos. Incision is used throughout, and many
details are in added red slip.

The two flanking satyrs are armed, outfitted with Attic helmets, spears, and a type of curved shield called a pelta, in this case fitted with short leather aprons to protect the legs.[7] Spurred on by the tune of the flautist, who sets the rhythm, the satyrs dance with right legs bent at the knee and left legs extended before them. Their mouths are open in song, and they seem to be beating their spears on their peltae. They move in unison, which suggests that they are practicing the pyrrhic, a vigorous dance of war maneuvers performed in partial armor that constituted part of the physical training of young men.[8]

The artist's choice of a military theme may have been inspired by the ongoing conflict between Athens and the powerful Persian kingdom to the east. Satyrs, however, with their indiscriminate, unheroic behavior, are an odd choice for representing the highly disciplined Athenian armed forces, unless, of course, the scene is a gleeful

parody of soldiers preparing for war. Lusty and undisciplined, satyrs are associated above all with Dionysos. But Dionysos was also the god of drama, and, as such, also may be associated with the performance of the pyrrhic; it is this connection that may provide the basis for understanding this scene.

In his thorough study of the early character of Athenian drama, John J. Winkler drew on the evidence of ancient vase-painting, literature, and etymology to suggest that the chorus members who performed in the city's great Dionysiac theatrical productions were some of Athens's finest young soldiers or recruits-in-training. There they had the opportunity to display their disciplined mastery of close-order maneuvers learned during military training.[9] Divided into groups of twelve to fifteen, these young men proved their endurance by remaining on stage during the course of three tragedies

and a satyr play. Their performance consisted of taking up different positions or by repeatedly turning from the actors to face the audience and back again, all while singing their parts. Winkler speculated that these young men were called *tragōidoi*, which literally means "billy-goat singers," and that the prize given to the winning chorus was a male goat. Perhaps the Athena Painter conceived of the scene on this lekythos as a witty commentary on contemporary ritual, casting the "billy-goat singers" as the bestial, half-horse companions of Dionysos, who, like the god, are frequently represented in association with goats. The satyr, with his erect phallus, tendency toward errant behavior, and presumably foul smell, presents the ideal figure through which to poke good-natured fun at the elite corps of the chorus, who, despite their status and accomplishments, were caught in the awkward transition from youth to manhood.

—KM

**BIBLIOGRAPHY**
Unpublished.

**NOTES**

1 Michael Padgett attributed the vase and also provided information to this author about its condition. For the Athena Painter, see *ABL* 141–65, 254–60; *ABV* 522–33, 704–5; *Paralipomena* 260–62; *BAdd²* 130–32; Karouzou 1972, 240–41; Boardman 1974, 113–14, 147–48.

2 For other vases in the exhibition decorated in the same technique, see cat. nos. 57, 61, and 99.

3 For the palmette motif, see Kurtz 1975, 13.

4 See n. 1 above.

5 Among examples not known to Haspels or Beazley are a white-ground lekythos in a private collection with satyrs playing ball (Bothmer 1990, 151–52, no. 114); a lekythos in a Palermo private collection with satyrs dancing with goats (Isler and Sguaitamatti 1990, 124–25, pl. 28, no. 180); a white-ground lekythos in a New York private collection with three satyrs carrying a sword and two bows (unpublished); a white-ground lekythos formerly on the London market with Dionysos, maenad, and satyr (London, Bonhams, sale catalogue, July 4, 1996, lot 138); a white-ground lekythos formerly on the New York art market with Dionysos seated between two satyrs (unpublished); and in this exhibition, a white-ground oinochoe in a private collection with a satyr spanking an empty amphora (cat. no. 61).

6 For another white-ground lekythos by the Athena Painter with a very similar depiction of the same subject, cf. Athens, Nat. Mus. 18567: *ABL* 255.20; Karouzou 1972, 240–41, pls. 21.1–3, 22.1–2; Greifenhagen 1974,

239, figs. 3–4; Hedreen 1992, pl. 36. The subject appears also on an earlier red-figure amphora by Smikros (Berlin 1966.19: *Paralipomena* 323.3bis; Greifenhagen 1974, 239, figs. 1–2). The Athena Painter also decorated lekythoi with human pyrrhic dancers (*ABL* 258.90; *Paralipomena* 261). On dancing satyrs, see Buschor 1943.

7 For satyrs with peltae, see Lissarrague 1990b, 172–73. Satyrs also carry shields in representations of Dionysos battling the giants (e.g., Orvieto 1044: *ARV²* 657.1; Carpenter 1997, pl. 6).

8 For depictions of the pyrrhic in Attic vase-painting, see Poursat 1968; Hedreen 1992, 109–10. Several ancient authors mention the dance: Plato (*Leg.* 7.815), Dionysios of Halikarnassos (13.40), Pausanias (3.25.2), and Athenaeus (14.629b–c).

9 Winkler 1990, 20–62. The following synopsis is a gross oversimplification of a complex and well-argued theory that depends, in part, as the author notes, on evidence that is circumstantial rather than concrete.

## 61

# Black-Figure Oinochoe with Two Satyrs

Greek, Attic, ca. 490–480 B.C., attributed to the Athena Painter[1]
Ceramic
Height 20.2 cm., maximum diameter 13 cm., diameter of foot 7.3 cm.
Private collection

CONDITION

The vase has been reconstructed from fragments and partially restored.[2] The black glaze and white slip have suffered pitting and abrasion. The handle was broken off and reattached in antiquity, and some of the surface around the base of the handle has worn away. A misfired patch extends from behind the satyr on the left to the lower body of the vessel.

Decorated in the black-figure technique on a white ground, this vessel, an oinochoe, served as a pitcher for pouring libations or dispensing wine at drinking parties. It belongs to the Sèvres Class of oinochoai, which Sir John Beazley described as "shape II, but the vase not very broad; short black neck with spreading mouth; no collar; lowish round handle; torus foot, without base-fillet."[3] In this example, the three-lobed mouth, cylindrical handle, lower body, and spreading foot are black. The shoulder and much of the body are covered with a cream-colored slip. A band of crude tongue pattern—really just short, black lines—occupies the upper shoulder below the neck, and a black, leafy vine trails from the base of the handle to each side of the vase. Red was applied to the outer face of the rotelle, where the handle attaches to the rim, and along the rim between the rotelle. Three red bands encircle the vessel, one around its neck and two on the lower body. Above the main scene is a small drip of glaze. The underside of the foot is reserved.

The pitcher features a figural scene depicting three vessels associated with drinking parties and two ithyphallic satyrs. The details of the painted vessels and the contours of the creatures' muscles are meticulously incised, and hatching is employed to create the bristly edges of the

satyrs' hairy features, except for their tails. Red is applied to the beasts' unkempt beards and forelocks.

The creature on the left behaves in a most unusual fashion, straddling an empty wine jar, an amphora, grabbing it by one handle and vigorously spanking it with a sandal. His companion, playing the double flutes, or auloi, crouches before him. Drinking cups are scattered around: a kantharos resting behind the abuser and a rhyton before the flautist.

In Attic vase-painting, the earliest known depiction of these irrepressible and incorrigible hybrid beasts in combination with wine, music, and the pleasures of the flesh occurs on the François Vase, in Florence, which was

made about 570 B.C. In a fragmentary scene on this large vessel, a partially preserved image of Dionysos is followed by a mule bearing Hephaistos (see Padgett, "Horse Men," fig. 24, in this volume). Behind the lame god is a procession of satyrs, one carrying a wineskin on his back, a second playing the auloi, and a third, only partly extant, clutching a female in his arms.[4] Thereafter, hundreds of images on Athenian vases appear that show human and mythical celebrants of the wine god enjoying wine, music, and carnal pleasures. Typically, these devotees used alcohol to enter a state of trancelike rapture, in which they are known to have often participated in a wide variety of sexual acts. Flautists are often seen accompanying the revelers as they journey into communion with their god.[5]

On this vase, the satyr flautist plays for his companion, whose reason for beating the amphora is unclear. Is he punishing the jar for being empty? Is he trying to force more wine from it? Is he a drunken jug-band virtuoso who here uses the amphora as a drum to beat out a rhythm for the flautist? Or is he mocking a real-life practice? His actions recall images on vases that show men hitting nude women with sticks and sandals. These assailants are presumably drunken revelers, who may have assaulted prostitutes either for their own sexual gratification or in an effort to force them into compliance.[6]

Perhaps the Athena Painter intended the scene to serve as a commentary on the vice and folly of his contemporaries or to remind ancient viewers of the untamed parts of their own natures that are reflected in the behavior of satyrs.
—KM

**BIBLIOGRAPHY**
Unpublished.

**NOTES**
1 Attributed by Michael Padgett. For the Athena Painter, see cat. no. 60, n. 1.
2 In the figural scene, there is an area of loss before the standing satyr's chest, including the edge of his beard, and behind him, including the tip of his tail and a section of the amphora. There is also a small loss in the field between the two satyrs. Using the incision and what remained of the original drawing as a guide, much of the flaked black slip was repainted, most notably the three vessels and the face, arms, lower torso, and thighs of the right satyr; it is unclear whether the ancient artist or modern restorer is responsible for his left hand having five fingers but no thumb.
3 *ABV* 524. The group is named for a representative example in the Musée Céramique, Sèvres (*ABV* 525.6).
4 Carpenter 1986, 80–83.
5 Frontisi-Ducroux 1989, 150–65.
6 Keuls 1985, 180–86.

## 62

# Red-Figure Oinochoe with Running Satyr

**Attic, ca. 470 B.C., attributed to Douris**
**Ceramic**
**Height 13 cm., width including handle 11.5 cm.,**
**maximum diameter 9.6 cm.**
**Allen Memorial Art Museum, Oberlin College,**
**Oberlin, Ohio, R. T. Miller Jr. Fund, 1955 (55.11)**

CONDITION
**The vase is fashioned from orange-red clay, the
exterior coated with lustrous black slip. The vase is
complete and in good condition. A break in the
spout has been repaired, and there is a crack in the
left side of the body. The black slip on the handle
and rim is worn, suggesting considerable use before
burial.[1] There are stains and black spots on the
body of the satyr.**

An oinochoe is a wine jug, of which there are no fewer than ten standard shapes in the Attic repertory.[2] This oinochoe is shape VII, a rare type largely confined to the second and third quarters of the fifth century B.C.[3] Characteristic are the bulbous body tapering to a flat base and the broad-lipped, beaked spout that rises high in the front but remains low in the back, not rising above the juncture with the handle. The wide mouth is pinched slightly on either side but is not truly trefoil. Only about thirty Attic oinochoai of shape VII are known, none of which is said to have been found in Greece. The shape is common in Etruscan red-figure, however, and it has been suggested that the Attic examples were produced with the Italian market in mind.[4]

Sturdy and functional, a small jug like this was perfect for dipping diluted wine from a krater. This role is reflected in the decoration, where a satyr from the entourage of the wine god Dionysos runs rapidly to the left. With his right hand he thrusts forward a phiale, a shallow dish for pouring libations of wine. The lobed surface of the phiale indicates that it is metal, probably gold or silver. The satyr is balding but has enough hair on the nape to tie in a short queue. Relief lines add bristle

to his long beard and are used to contour his muscular body, enhancing the contrast of the reserved red clay against the glossy black slip of the background. This contrast is further emphasized by the absence of a ground line, so that the satyr seems to hurry through a black void. Indeed, the rest of the vase is entirely black except for a reserved band with a frieze of tongues that runs around the shoulder and terminates under the handle.

For all his speed, the satyr is careful to hold the phiale steady and not spill a drop. He may be taking it to his master, Dionysos, else he likely would drink it himself. Satyrs are mischievous, randy, self-centered, and eternally thirsty, and only the god's command or the promise of sex or wine could induce such quick service as this.

Beazley attributed the drawing of this satyr to Douris, a prolific Attic red-figure vase-painter active in the first three decades of the fifth century.[5] Douris mostly painted kylikes (wine cups), frequently signing his name as painter and, on at least two occasions, as potter.[6] This is his only known oinochoe, a late work of about 470. Diana Buitron-Oliver compared the style to that of a fragmentary cup-skyphos in Bologna, where a satyr carries a jug behind Dionysos.[7] However, the lively posture, bald pate, lean

physique, and short queue of the Oberlin satyr call to mind even more strongly the capering satyrs on the painter's psykter in London, one of his finest creations, an earlier work of the 480s.[8]

The semi-equine nature of these satyrs is revealed in long ears and bushy tails, but they are far more human in appearance than their hairy predecessors on the early black-figure fragment by Sophilos (cat. no. 53).

—JMP

**BIBLIOGRAPHY**

*ARV*[2] 446.265; *BAdd*[2] 241; Capps 1955; Schauenburg 1975, 101, pl. 32, figs. 3–4; Buitron-Oliver 1995, 86, pl. 113, no. 244.

**NOTES**

1 The excellent condition of the vase, which is said to have been in an Italian private collection, indicates it was probably preserved in a tomb.

2 Beazley's classification of the ten oinochoe shapes (*ARV*[2] xlix–l) superseded all previous typologies (e.g., Milne and Richter 1935, 19–20). For a thorough description of each shape and its variants, see Green 1972.

3 For oinochoai of shape VII, see Green 1972, 8, pl. IId; Schauenburg 1975; Lezzi-Hafter 1976, 12–13; Buitron-Oliver 1995, 66–67. A vase in Rome is the only known black-figure example (Villa Giulia 1204: *ABV* 441; Schauenburg 1975, pl. 27, figs. 1–2).

4 Buitron-Oliver 1995, 67. For the shape in Etruscan red-figure, see Beazley 1947, 268.

5 For Douris, see *ARV*[2] 425–51, 1652–54, 1701, 1706; *Paralipomena* 374–76, 512, 521, 523–24; *BAdd*[2] 235–42; Boardman 1975, 137–39, figs. 281–99; Robertson 1992, 84–93; Buitron-Oliver 1995.

6 Potter signatures: *ARV*[2] 445.256; 447, 274.

7 Bologna 470: *ARV*[2] 445.253: Buitron-Oliver 1995, 39, 86, pl. 113, no. 242.

8 London, Brit. Mus. E 768: *ARV*[2] 446.262; *Paralipomena* 375; *BAdd*[2] 241; Boardman 1975a, fig. 299; Robertson 1992, 93, fig. 86; Buitron-Oliver 1995, 78, pls. 54–55, no. 84.

## 63

# Red-Figure Lekythos with Oedipus and the Sphinx

**Greek, Attic, ca. 460 B.C.**
**Ceramic**
**Height 23.0 cm., diameter at shoulder 8.4 cm.**
**Princeton University Art Museum, gift of Professor Edward Sampson, Class of 1914 (y1964–107)**

**CONDITION**
**The vase has been recomposed from fragments, with modest restoration along the seams. Sections of the mouth and the top of the handle have been restored. There are small lacunae, including significant portions of the palmettes and lotus buds. The black slip misfired red on the front near the base and on the back near the handle.**

Lekythoi, designed as oil containers, were associated with burial practices and rites of death. The fragility of white lekythoi in particular made them impractical for daily use, but even a red-figure lekythos could be linked with death, especially when, like this one, it is decorated with funereal iconography. Furthermore, a small hole in the underside of the base indicates that this particular lekythos could not have been used to hold oil and therefore probably was placed in a grave.

In shape, this lekythos is of Type II: cylindrical, with the shoulder sharply set off from the body, rather straight sides, and the base tapering in a rounded curve.[1] There is a fillet between the base and foot. Although this type is not exclusively decorated in the red-figure technique, Donna Kurtz postulates that the new shape emerged at the same time as the new painting style, about 530 B.C.[2] Even among Type II lekythoi there are a variety of subtle differences in shape. The Princeton lekythos, for instance, has a wide, flat shoulder and a particularly thin tapering foot. These characteristics resemble some earlier works: the foot, a lekythos by the Bowdoin Workshop;[3] the wide shoulder and slightly curved sides, some works by the Edinburgh Painter.[4]

The neck is decorated with an ovolo and dot pattern, and the shoulder features a central vertical palmette, two lateral horizontal palmettes, and two horizontal lotus

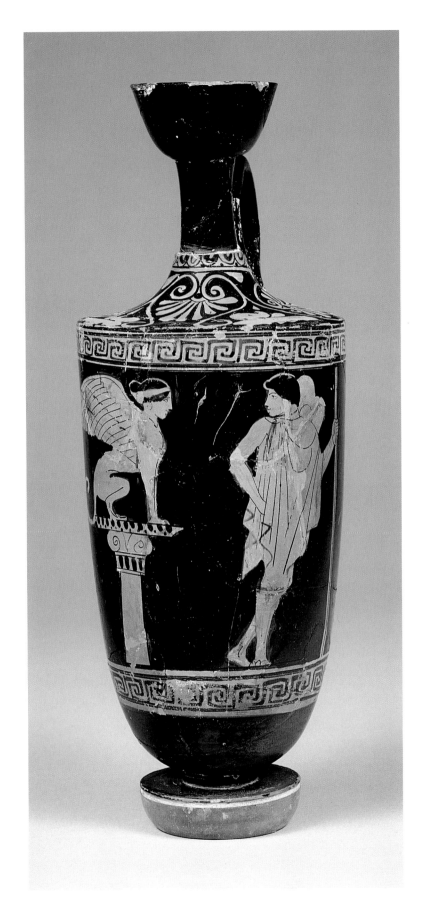

buds.[5] Tendrils spring from the heart of the central palmette and loop around the lateral palmettes. On the front
of the body, framed above and below by bands of broken
maeanders running to the right, a winged Sphinx with
raised haunches and upward- curling tail perches on an
Aeolic column and stares at the beardless youth before
her.[6] The youth wears a petasos tied around his neck and a
loosely hanging chlamys. This traveler must be Oedipus,
the riddle-solver, future king of Thebes, and tragic character par excellence.[7] He has journeyed to Thebes, where
each day the Sphinx kills a youth until someone can answer
her riddle: What has one voice and becomes first four-
footed, then two-footed, and finally three-footed? Kreon,
king of Thebes, has promised his sister, the widowed
queen Iocosta, to whomever answers the riddle. Oedipus
provides the correct response—"Man"—who first crawls
on hands and knees, then stands upright on two feet, and
finally uses a cane as a third support. He thus rids Thebes
of the Sphinx and marries, unknowingly, his own mother.[8]

The Princeton lekythos represents the moment the
Sphinx asks her riddle, indicated by meaningless words
painted in red and hovering before the monster's mouth.[9]
This moment is in a sense the height of Oedipus's life, for
he saves Thebes by the power of his intellect and becomes
the king, but it also marks the beginning of his downfall
—his incestuous marriage. The scene displays the full
tragedy of his fate, for while he perceives the answer to
the riddle, he is blind to the future that awaits him.

In earlier Attic vase-painting, the Sphinx attacks
young men (e.g., cat. no. 64) or poses the riddle to a
group of debating Thebans.[10] The encounter with
Oedipus begins about 490–480 B.C.,[11] and certain Attic
representations from the early fifth century could be
linked to the performance of Aischylos's satyr-play *Sphinx*,
in 467 B.C.[12] The tension on the Princeton lekythos is
unique, created through the eye contact of riddler and
answerer, the empty space between them, and Oedipus's
imbalance: he leans away from the Sphinx while turning
his head and arm toward her. Indeed, the Princeton
lekythos is one of the few instances where Oedipus is
not depicted from the back.[13]

When the Sphinx poses the riddle to the Thebans or
to Oedipus, she sits on a rock or on a column.[14] The latter

position closely resembles Attic grave monuments erected about 610–525 B.C. On these monuments, sphinxes first sit on a cavetto column capital, later they perch with raised haunches on a cavetto capital, and later still, perch on a double-volute column capital.[15] The Sphinx sitting on an Aeolic capital on this vase is unusual, although Aeolic capitals were used as supports for statues in other funerary contexts.[16] These instances of sphinxes on rocks or columns can be related to similar representations of sirens,[17] and show that sphinxes, too, were perceived as transporters of the dead and guardians of the grave (see Tsiafakis, "ΠΕΛΩΡΑ," in this volume).[18]

It has been noted that this piece resembles works related to the Providence Painter, the Oionokles Painter, and the Nikon Painter.[19] The painter of this Princeton lekythos shares the interest of the first two in the "language of the eyes" but lacks their attention to patterns and folds.[20] He is perhaps closer to the Nikon Painter, and some elements also bear resemblance to works by the Syriskos Painter.[21]

—NTA

**BIBLIOGRAPHY**

Ridgway and Pinney 1979, 92–93, no. 43; Moret 1984, 173, no. 70, pl. 40.1; *LIMC* 7 (1994), 3–4, no. 11, pl. 6, s.v. "Oidipous" (Krauskopf); Segal 2001, 34, fig. 2.

**NOTES**

1 Kurtz 1975, 77–78.
2 Kurtz 1975, 78.
3 Palermo 2792: *ABL* 262.2; *ABV* 524; Kurtz 1975, pl. 13.2.
4 E.g., Swiss private collection: *Paralipomena* 217; Kurtz 1975, pl. 7.2.
5 The three-palmette system is common on red-figure lekythoi of this period: see Kurtz 1975, 18 and fig. 9.
6 This lekythos represents one of the first instances of a beardless Oedipus: Moret 1984, 53.
7 The clothes indicate that he is a traveler, and the two spears perhaps allude to the third part of the riddle: the old man's staff that becomes his third "foot." On Oedipus as a traveler, see Zeitlin 1990, 132–33. Zeitlin (163–64) points to the heroic aspects of the end of Oedipus's life, which would make him a fitting figure for a funereal piece.
8 There is no ancient canonical literary version either of the Sphinx or of her encounter with Oedipus. The earliest reference to sphinxes is in Hesiod's *Theogony* (326–32), while Homer mentions Oedipus, but not the Sphinx, in Book 23 of the *Iliad* (679–80). Some of the fullest accounts of Oedipus and the Sphinx are in Apollodoros (*Bibl.* 3.5.8), Pausanias (9.26.2–4), and Euripides (*Phoen.* 49–50, 806–11, and 1019–42). For more complete listings of literary references, see *LIMC* 8 (1997), 1149–51, s.v. "Sphinx" (Kourou, Komvou, and Raftopoulou); and Edmunds 1981, 48–49. On the epics about Thebes composed between the seventh and fifth centuries, the *Oedipodeia* and the *Thebais*, which are known only from late summaries and fragments, see Segal 2001, 25.
9 Words also appear on the name-vase of the Oedipus Painter (Rome, Vatican 16541): *ARV*² 451.1; *LIMC* 7, 4, no. 19, pl. 7, s.v. "Oidipous."
10 Sphinx attacking youths: Moret 1984, pls. 3–15; *LIMC* 8, 1160, nos. 168–81, pls. 804–5, s.v. "Sphinx"; Sphinx posing riddle to group: Moret 1984, pls. 17–38, 41; *LIMC* 8, 1160–61, nos. 183–84, pl. 805, s.v. "Sphinx."
11 Moret 1984, 1. For representations of Oedipus and the Sphinx, see Moret 1984, pls. 42–46, 48; *LIMC* 7, 3–6, nos. 10–51, pls. 6–11, s.v. "Oidipous."
12 On the dating of Aischylos's satyr-play, see Segal 2001, 11 and 25.
13 Moret 1984, 54.
14 Sphinx on a rock: Moret 1984, pls. 46–47; *LIMC* 7, 4, nos. 22–23, pl. 7, s.v. "Oidipous." Sphinx on a column: Moret 1984, pls. 14–45; *LIMC* 7, 3–4, nos. 10–14, 19, pls. 6–7, s.v. "Oidipous."
15 Richter 1961, Types Ia–c. Richter's Type Ib (pp. 15–26), dated about 575–545 B.C., has raised haunches, which Hanfmann (1953, 229–30) described as creating a watchful alertness that contrasts with Egyptian reclining sphinxes.
16 Betancourt 1977, 100. See also the discussion in this volume under cat. no. 72.

17 E.g., a black-figure lekythos in Bloomington (Indiana Univ. 65.66: *LIMC* 8 [1997], 1098, no. 67, pl. 738, s.v. "Seirenes" [Hofstetter]).

18 On sphinxes as guardians of the grave, see Hanfmann 1953, 230; Richter 1961, 6; Vermeule 1979, 69 and 171. It should be noted that while the Sphinx's posture and setting resemble funerary monuments of the Archaic period, the depiction of the Sphinx herself, with gently curving wings and hair held in a bun by a *sphendone*, is Classical in style.

19 Ridgway and Pinney 1979, 92.

20 For these attributes of the Providence and Oionokles Painters, see Knauer 1986, 99–100. For similarities between these artists and the painter of the Princeton lekythos, cf. a lekythos attributed to the Providence Painter (Oxford 1925.68: *ARV²* 641.87; *CVA* Oxford 1, Great Britain 3, pl. 34.1); a Nolan amphora in the manner of the Providence Painter and close to our painter (Oxford 1914.732: *CVA* Oxford 1, pls. 17.5 and 18.6); a neck-amphora attributed to the Oionokles Painter (New York, Met. 09.221.41: *ARV²* 646.6; Knauer 1986, fig. 6); and a lekythos by the same artist (Cleveland 28.660: *ARV²* 648.37; Moon and Berge 1979, 164).

21 For similarities to the Nikon Painter, cf. a lekythos in Athens (Nat. Mus. 12779: *ARV²* 651.22; *CVA* Athens 1, Greece 1, pl. 32.4); another in Oxford (316: *ARV²* 651.23; *CVA* Oxford 1, pl. 34.3); and a third in Copenhagen (Nat. Mus. 13789: *ARV²* 652.33, *CVA* Copenhagen 1, Denmark 8, pl. 353.3a). For similarities to the Syriskos Painter, cf. a neck-amphora formerly in the Museum of Fine Arts, Boston (*ARV²* 261.22; New York, Sotheby's, December 17, 1997, lot 101), and a neck-amphora in Oxford (1920.105: *ARV²* 261.24; *CVA* Oxford 1, pl. 17.9).

## 64

# Black-Figure Siana Cup with Rampaging Sphinx

**Greek, Attic, ca. 560 B.C., attributed to the Heidelberg Painter**
**Ceramic**
**Height 14 cm., diameter 25 cm., diameter of foot 9.5 cm., diameter of tondo 14.1 cm.**
**Private collection**

### CONDITION

**The cup has been recomposed from fragments, the parts between the joins made good. Small losses between some of the figures on the reverse have been restored in plaster. There are traces of an ancient repair in the wreath to the left of the head of Dionysos. The interior is misfired red.**

The tondo in the interior shows Dionysos standing between two satyrs. He stands to right but looks back, holding up a drinking horn in his right hand while keeping his left hand across his waist. He wears a himation over a chiton and has a fillet in his hair. The two smaller, ithyphallic satyrs flank the god, facing inward, their arms gesturing. The tondo is framed by a myrtle wreath bordered by three lines on either side.

On one side of the exterior, the Sphinx is shown devouring a Theban youth.[1] The Sphinx had been sent to Thebes to punish Laios for his wrongful love for Chrysippos. She posed a riddle, asking what walked on four feet in the morning, two at midday and three in the evening: those who could answer were let free, but those who could not were killed. It was Oedipus who finally realized the answer to the riddle (mankind) and in turn killed the Sphinx. On this cup, the Sphinx is facing left in the center of the composition, her wings spread to either side. She has lifted the captured youth and drawn it under her chest. Three youths sprint away on each side, two of them looking back. All wear mantles hung loosely across their shoulders.

The other side shows six nude athletes in the palaestra, arranged in two groups of three. In the first group, a youth carries a discus to right and is met by

two companions whose hands are empty. In the second group, a youth bends forward to right. A companion, who faces him, carries high in his right hand a curved object, quite likely a jumping weight. The last athlete follows this one toward the center, his hands at his side. Bearded onlookers, possibly trainers, flank the two groups.

This representation of the Sphinx is one of the earliest of a group that has survived predominantly on Siana cups or cups derived from them:[2] the story must have had some special resonance for the painters and their patrons. Contemporary with these is a fragmentary bronze relief from the Acropolis.[3] The first representations all show the Sphinx crouching over the Theban's body. Sometimes, as here, the Sphinx actually lifts the victim from the ground, in the manner described by Aischylos,[4] and recalling, as Brijder has noted,[5] depictions of the escape of Odysseus under the ram.

The Heidelberg Painter[6] specialized in decorating Siana cups; this one dates from his late period, about 560 B.C. Siana cups, which take their name from a site on Rhodes where many were found, are characterized by a deep offset lip, wide bowl, and short flaring foot. On this example, the Heidelberg Painter has avoided pattern work on the lip, thereby enabling his figures to be larger, a device later favored by the potter Nikosthenes on his so-called overlap amphorae.[7]

Dionysos is a favorite subject for the Heidelberg Painter.[8] The tondo composition, with three figures rather than two, appears to be unique in the Heidelberg Painter's repertoire.[9] The synoptic representation of a variety of athletic events on this cup may have been inspired by the reorganization of the Panathenaic festival and its games in 566 B.C.[10] Depictions of several athletic events on a single vase become common only rather later in the sixth century. —JG

### BIBLIOGRAPHY

Atlantis Antiquities 1988, 43–44, 74, fig. 38; Brijder 1991, 359, 381, 392, 413–14, 437, 453–54, no. 385 bis, pl. 130 a–c.

### NOTES

1 For the Theban sphinx, see esp. Schauenburg 1982; Brijder 1983, 133; Edmunds 1981; Moret 1984; Brijder 1991, 381; Vollkommer 1991; *LIMC* 8 (1997), 1149–74, pls. 794–817, s.v. "Sphinx" (Kourou, Komvou, and Raftopoulou).

2 Brijder 1983, 133; Brijder 1991, 381.

3 Athens, Nat. Mus. Acropolis 6961a: *LIMC* 8, 1160, no. 176, s.v. "Sphinx."

4 Aesch. *Sept.* 543.

5 Brijder 1983, 133.

6 On the Heidelberg Painter, see *ABV* 65–67, 682, 716; *Paralipomena* 26–27, 90; Bothmer 1985, 39–40; Beazley 1989, 17–18; Brijder 1991.

7 *ABV* 216–17; *Paralipomena* 105.

8 For the Heidelberg Painter's contribution to Dionysian imagery, see Carpenter 1986, 30–54; Brijder 1991, 357–59.

9 Brijder 1991, 359.

10 Kyle 1992.

## 65

# Amathous-Style Amphoriskos with Sphinxes

**Cypriote, mid-sixth century B.C.**
**Ceramic**
**Height of upper part 16.8 cm., height of lower part 4.9 cm., diameter of mouth 7.9 cm., diameter of base 7.5 cm.**
**Private collection**

### CONDITION

**The vase is broken and now consists of two non-joining sections. The clay is whitish gray with black and dilute brown slip. There are touches of white in the eyes of the sphinxes; and incision articulates details on figures and ornaments.**

The vase is richly decorated with geometric and vegetal motifs above and below a broad central zone between the two vertical loop handles. Here two pairs of sphinxes face one another on either side of a central sacred tree, a common motif in almost all cultures of the ancient Near East. On one side (*A*), the sphinx on the left with very short legs strides to the right; her companion on the right sits. The figures are essentially painted in silhouette with internal details rendered in incision, with the exception of the faces, which are painted in outline. Both sphinxes wear the double crown of Egypt and a broad Egyptian collar. They both have large, curved wings; the wing of the sphinx on the left springs from the lower flank, while that of her counterpart on the right springs from the shoulder. The chest of each is decorated with a narrow incised band; on the left this is filled with cross-hatchings, on the right, tongues. What these bands are meant to represent is difficult to say, though the Phoenician character of the sphinxes suggests they depict in profile view the characteristic apron common to Phoenician sphinxes (cf. cat. no. 9).

The pair of sphinxes on side *B* closely resembles the two creatures on side *A*, except that the legs of the striding sphinx on the left are missing and the wing here is attached somewhat higher.

The sacred trees that the sphinxes flank are almost identical on the two sides of the vase. Each consists of two

horizontal volutes set on roughly triangular bases covered in scale pattern. Small volutes mark the juncture of the bases and the horizontal members. Tendrils with buds grow from the junctures and the tops of the bases: the lower buds are palmettes, the others look like papyrus plants. From the top horizontal member grow "paradise flowers."[1]

The lower fragment of the vase was decorated with an interlocking chain of flowers of which only the semicircular connecting lines are preserved. The bottom edge of the upper part of the vase preserves spreading leaves rendered in black slip with incision. On the shoulder and neck of the upper part of the vase are two series of decorative bands of which the rosettes in metope-type frames deserve particular mention—they are a common motif on Cypriote pottery.[2]

The sphinx had its origin in Egypt, where it was always male (even the sphinxes of Hatshepsut, the female pharaoh of the Eighteenth Dynasty, were male).[3] The female sphinx originated in the Levant; there the motif decorated all manner of objects and was particularly favored by Phoenician ivory carvers.[4] The Phoenicians borrowed many motifs from Egypt and were especially fond of the double crown, which is worn by all four sphinxes on this vase, although it is otherwise rare in

Cypriote iconography of sphinxes.[5] As already noted, the painted and incised bands along the chests of these four creatures probably were meant to represent the apron that the Phoenicians added to the iconography of the now universally female sphinx, as though to suggest a dress.[6]

The class of Amathous vases has been studied in detail. It comprises a series of some twenty-four small vases, usually amphoriskoi of the type being considered here and all probably from tombs, as well as approximately twenty to thirty fragments from the French excavations at Amathous itself.[7] The color of the clay, the dull black paint, and the use of incision are common to this class of vases which, more than any other group of Cypriote vessels, seem to imitate Greek prototypes. This type of vase first appeared around the middle of the sixth century and continued to be produced at least until the middle of the fifth century.[8] The decoration of this particular vase is especially rich, with extensive use of incision. The motif of sphinxes flanking a sacred tree occurs on two other vessels, an oinochoe in the museum at Newcastle upon Tyne[9] and an amphoriskos from tomb 251 at Amathous.[10] Sphinxes are represented at least twice on the fragments from the excavations of Amathous.[11] The date of this amphoriskos must fall early in the series, that is, near the middle of the sixth century.[12]

—WAPC

## BIBLIOGRAPHY

Karageorghis 1990.

## NOTES

1 Shefton 1989.

2 An amphoriskos in the British Museum (C 853) follows the decorative patterns of this vase rather closely: Karageorghis and Des Gagniers 1974, 507, no. 4.

3 Russmann 1989, 83–85, no. 37.

4 Barnett 1975, pls. CXXXIII, sup. 24, CXXXIV, sup. 23 and 33; Barnett 1982, pls. 49e, 51, 53 (from Salamis on Cyprus).

5 Karageorghis (1990, 123) notes that the double crown does not appear on other examples of sphinxes of Amthous-style vases, and occurs on only one of the pairs of sphinxes flanking a sacred tree of the earlier Bichrome classes of pottery: Karageorghis and Des Gagniers 1974, vol. 2, 124, vase no. XII.a.1. The crown is also lacking on sphinxes of Syrian-style ivories: Barnett 1975, pls. XIX (S13), XXI (S6), XXXIV (S50).

6 E.g., Barnett 1975, pls. CXXXIII, CXXXIV; Barnett 1982, pls. 51, 53.

7 Karageorghis and Des Gagniers 1974, vol. 1, 91–93; vol. 2, 504–17 (nos. 1–13); Hermary 1997, 158–59.

8 Karageorghis 1990, 124; Hermary 1997, 157, 159.

9 Karageorghis 1989, 84, pl. 16.1–3.

10 Karageorghis 1989, 84, pl. 15.6–7; Hermary 1997, 158, pl. LIIa (not the side with sphinxes).

11 Hermary 1986, 169–70, pls. XXXV.1a–c and 4; Hermary 1997, 159. As Karageorghis (1990, 122–23) points out, sphinxes appear on other classes of Cypriote vases and metalwork rather frequently, both individually and in pairs flanking a sacred tree: Karageorghis and Des Gagniers 1974, vol. 2, 124–35, nos. XII.a.1–9.

12 Karageorghis 1990, 124.

# 66

# Aryballos with Two Sphinxes

**Greek, Laconian, 570–560 B.C., attributed to the Rider Painter[1]**
**Ceramic**
**Height 6.3 cm., diameter of mouth 4.5 cm., diameter of body 6.5 cm., diameter of foot 4.5 cm.**
**Private collection**

CONDITION
The fine clay is light orange-brown. The vessel is intact. Small chips are missing from the rim and there are minor abrasions on the decorated surface. The proper right side of the handle is slightly misshapen.

This generously proportioned oil flask has a thick mouth-plate with a raised rim, an angled profile, and a molding around its lower edge. Below are a short neck, a squat, rounded body with a flat bottom, and a ring foot.[2] A broad, flat handle is attached to the back. A creamy slip covers much of the vase, except for the lip, part of the handle, the lower body, and the underside.

The upper part of the aryballos is decorated with pattern bands. Encircling the mouth, from the orifice to the rim, are black tongues framed by dilute glaze between two fine lines,[3] and alternating black and reserved rectangles between dots on a raised rim.[4] There are vertical lines on the edge of the mouth-plate and oblique lines on the molding. On the handle is an X with a small cross at its center.[5] Pattern bands continue on the shoulder, with black strokes radiating from the neck, followed by a zone of alternating black and reserved rectangles between dots.

This oil pot belongs to a small group of Laconian (i.e., Spartan) aryballoi that have flat bottoms and are decorated in the black-figure technique.[6] Here, on the body, two sphinxes face each other, separated by a broad, interlaced lotus-palmette complex with red hearts and thick volutes.[7] These beardless creatures have long hair and necks, attenuated leonine bodies, short forelegs, and large paws.[8] In his design, the artist buckled their back legs and lowered their hindquarters in order to fit them—raised sickle-shaped wings and all—neatly into the frieze.[9]

Long serpentine tails with tufted tips rise over their haunches and then curl back around a black dot. (The dot of the one on the viewer's left is considerably larger than the other one.) Red was applied to the upper edge of the sphinxes' wings and their bellies. The creature to the viewer's left also has a red stripe on the back of its head, two on its flank, one over its rump, and another on its haunch, all between incised lines. The other sphinx has a red stripe on its flank and two red stripes on its haunches, also between incised lines.

Below the thin ground line is a broad band overlaid with red. On the underside, in a black field, is a reserved cross; at the intersection of its arms is a small black circle within a larger one.[10] Surrounding this complex are a reserved circle, a narrow black circle, a reserved circle, a wide black circle with red overlay, and a reserved circle. Black was applied to the foot ring.

The sphinx appeared in Minoan and Mycenaean art and then apparently disappeared from Greece until after the middle of the eighth century B.C.[11] Although Sparta was connected to Egypt through the city of Naukratis on the Nile Delta, the Laconian sphinx is much more distantly related to its monumental stone ancestor at Giza than it is to the standing or crouching creature that is often found singly or in pairs on many Greek black-figure vases. Yet despite its regular appearance on Laconian pottery — most often in animal friezes, but occasionally as the principal subject for the tondo of a drinking cup[12] — this particular creature has yet to receive independent study as a regional icon.[13] The Spartan sphinx is not the monstrous *Mischwesen* that terrorized Thebes by devouring those who were unable to answer its riddle; rather it tended to be a benign and purely decorative creature of the type that enjoyed great popularity in the minor arts of Greece during the seventh and sixth centuries B.C.

—KM

**BIBLIOGRAPHY**
Unpublished.

**NOTES**

1 The vase was attributed by C. M. Stibbe, who (in correspondence, November 2002) stated that it is "a most welcome enrichment of our very limited knowledge of the early Rider Painter (Stibbe 1972, 162–65), for which we have hitherto only one specimen to compare: the aryballos in the Villa Giulia, inv. no. 45774 (Stibbe 1972, 165, 258–59, 285, no. 290, pls. 94.4 and 95.1–4)." I am grateful to Dr. Stibbe for his willingness to study photographs of the aryballos and offer his expert opinions about its shape, decoration, and attribution. The aryballos will be included in the addendum to his forthcoming supplement to Stibbe 1972.

2 Stibbe 2000a, 21–22, for the general shape, and 37–38, 120–21, Subgroup Ib, figs. 39–41, for the specific shape.

3 The use of the tongue pattern on the mouth-plates of Laconian black-figure aryballoi is uncommon, but it is found elsewhere among the

work of the Rider Painter. For two variants, see Stibbe 1972, 157, nos. 9 and 10.

4 For this pattern, see Stibbe 2000a, 190, no. 44.

5 For this pattern, see Stibbe 1997, 112–13, no. 93, fig. 30, and Stibbe 1972, 112, no. 16.

6 Stibbe 2000a, 36–38.

7 *LIMC* 8 (1997), 1156, nos. 87–100, pls. 799–800, s.v. "Sphinx" (Kourou, Komvou, and Raftopoulou).

8 Compare an aryballos in Richmond (80.170) with two sirens facing each other, flanking a floral ornament: *LIMC* 8 (1997), 1097, no. 44, s.v. "Seirenes" (Hofstetter) (attributed to the Naukratis Painter by G. Schaus); Stibbe 2000a, 37, 120, no. I7, pl. 4.5 (who identifies it as the work of the Rider Painter).

9 The closest parallels for these sphinxes, with the nearly circular treatment of their wing tips, are found among the works of the Rider Painter, including the aryballos in the Villa Giulia mentioned above (n. 1), with similar, if less carefully rendered pattern bands, and a kylix in New York (Met. 14.30.26: Stibbe 1972, 153–54, 168, 175, 285, no. 299, pl. 106.1–2).

10 Compare an aryballos in Tarquinia (R.C. 3502) without the central circle: Stibbe 2000a, 119, no. I1, fig. 36. A similar pattern appears on the underside of an East Greek round-mouthed oinochoe in Toledo (71.2; *CVA* Toledo 2, USA 20, pl. 68.1) and on an Italic cup in San Antonio (90.8.4; Shapiro et al. 1995, 258, no. 145).

11 *LIMC* 8, 1163, s.v. "Sphinx."

12 E.g., a kylix in Paris, attributed to the Naukratis Painter (Louvre E 664: Stibbe 1972, 49, 67, 270, no. 7, pl. 4.1); the kylix in New York mentioned above (n. 9); and another in Hamburg (1968.94), which has been identified as in the manner of the Rider Painter (Stibbe 1972, 174–75, 287, no. 324, pl. 116.1). The same painter also put heraldic sphinxes in the tondo of a cup in the Louvre (Cp10492: Stibbe 1972, 175, 287, no. 325 [where the inv. no. is given as 10.492], pl. 116.2).

13 Pipili 1987, introduction (n.p.).

# 67

## Fragmentary Pinax with Relief of Sphinx and Griffin

Greek, possibly Samian, ca. 600–570 B.C.
Said to be from Lokri
Terracotta
Height 8.1 cm., width 11.3 cm., thickness 1.4 cm.
Arthur M. Sackler Museum, Harvard University Art
Museums, David M. Robinson Fund
(1980.2)

### CONDITION

The right-hand portion of the plaque is missing except
for the head of the griffin. There is collateral damage
along the break to the neck of the griffin and two legs
of the sphinx. There are flecks of gray incrustation on
the sphinx's chin, wings, and right hind leg.

This pinax, or tablet, with relief decoration, features
two confronted mythological composite creatures: a
sphinx facing right and a griffin facing left, the latter
entirely lost except for its head. The mold from which the
relief figures were impressed was very fresh, rendering
such details as the hair, scales, and feathers of the sphinx
with meticulous precision. The clay is buff-colored and
hard-fired; the edges are finished by hand (distinct fingerprints). There is no trace of paint.

The sphinx has a muscular lion's body with S-curving-
tail, a forepart consisting of overlapping scales representing the covert feathers, and a sickle-shaped wing with
feathers curving outward and upward, each delineated by a
low ridge. A slender concave band with diagonal markings
forms the boundary from which the wing emerges from
the sphinx's scaly shoulders. She wears a dotted fillet and
has three wavy tresses hanging from the back of her head,

each with individual locks delineated. Three curling spiral locks adorn her forehead. A small palmette rises from the top of her head, from which, on either side, emerge two double curving tendrils terminating in volutes. The griffin has an open eagle's beak, a large eye, a vertical pointed ear rising above the head, and a circular knob on the forehead from which hangs a small spiral. A hole for attachment perforates the tablet between the sphinx's wing and the edge of its tail; another such hole presumably occupied the space opposite, above the griffin. Enough is preserved to show that the two creatures stood on a molded ground line consisting of two small raised ridges.

In a study of an intact pinax with a relief depicting the same pair of confronted sphinx and griffin, in the J. Paul Getty Museum, Angelika Dierichs identified numerous parallels to the composition in Archaic terracotta reliefs and scenes on relief-pithoi, as well as on hammered bronze reliefs.[1] Although there are close parallels from Magna Graecia and Crete, Dierichs makes a convincing argument that the Getty plaque was probably made at the temple of Hera on Samos. The Harvard pinax is clearly impressed from the same mold as the Getty pinax and therefore also may come from the Heraion. The question remains whether these plaques were produced at the Heraion or were imported from some other location in the Archaic Greek world. Their function within the sanctuary may have been votive, apotropaic, or decorative; or indeed, all three, since the perceived distinctions among these roles are artificial and would have been meaningless to the maker of the plaques and their owners.

—DGM

BIBLIOGRAPHY

*LIMC* 8 (1997), 1163, no. 232, pl. 808, s.v. "Sphinx" (Kourou et al.).

NOTE

1 Dierichs 1993. Cf. also the confronting sphinx and griffin on the Etruscan bucchero kantharos in this exhibition (cat. no. 42).

## 68

# Fikellura Oinochoe with Sirens and Sphinxes

East Greek, Milesian, ca. 550–540 B.C., attributed to the Altenburg Painter
Ceramic
Height 26.7 cm., diameter of foot 9.2 cm., width of mouth 12.9 cm.
Private collection

CONDITION
The reddish tan clay is micaceous. Most of the surface is coated with creamy white slip. The vase has been repaired from large fragments but is complete, with only minor inpainting of cracks. The black slip on the left side is misfired red while that on the right is quite worn in places: hare, deer, dog, adjacent ornament, and left side of the foot. The mouth also is worn, inside and out, with damage to the eyes.

Fikellura ware is a distinctive East Greek pottery produced from about 560 to 520 B.C. It is named after a site on Rhodes, the island where it was long assumed to have been made, but analysis of the clay now has established that Miletos, on the west coast of Asia Minor, was its principal producer.[1] The most favored shapes were the amphora and the oinochoe, of which this vase is a classic example: biconical body with steep shoulder; wide trefoil mouth; echinus foot; triple-reeded handle rising high above the rim, the juncture marked by circular disks (*rotelle*). Fikellura decorative schemes vary, but many elements on this vase are characteristic: animal friezes on the shoulder and lower body; broad bands of maeanders and concentric boxes on the neck and around the middle of the body, each running below a more slender band of short vertical lines; a band of lotus buds, alternately closed and open, on the lower body; a band of tongues above the foot and another below the neck, the latter with red tongues among the black. There are black crosses on the rotelle and diagonal slashes on the handles. The foot, the back of the neck, and the sides of the handles are black, as is the rim, which is decorated with white rosettes and red and white eyes, a standard feature on these jugs.

The decoration resembles the black-figure of Attic and Corinthian vases, and of some East Greek fabrics, but the technique is different, beginning with the white ground, which offers a better contrast for the black silhouetted figures than the duller clay of the pot. More importantly, there is no use of incision; instead, all internal details—wings, muscles, spots, eyes, ears—are left carefully "reserved," defined by the white ground beneath. Some silhouetted details, such as wings, bellies, and haunches, are highlighted with added red slip. Filling ornaments, mostly dot rosettes and Maltese crosses, are interspersed among the figures, and lotus buds hang from the upper borders. The shape, technique, subject matter, and subsidiary ornament are all rooted in the tradition of earlier, seventh-century Milesian pottery of the Wild Goat Style.[2] In the latter, the figures have reserved heads and painted internal details, while in Fikellura they are drawn as black silhouettes with reserved details, a more difficult and coloristic technique.

In the center of the upper frieze, a pair of rather elongated sphinxes stands on either side of a fallow deer, which has dropped to one knee. Behind each sphinx is a siren, who walks in the opposite direction, toward the base of the handle, which is flanked by a pair of goats. The female heads of the sirens resemble those of the sphinxes, with large eyes, pointed noses, and long hair pushed behind the ears (cf. the East Greek siren alabastron, cat. no. 78). The lower frieze of nine animals has no central group; instead, it repeats three times the sequence of hound, hare, and deer. The hounds and hares are shown with both of their forepaws in the air at the same time, a conventional means of representing rapid, quadrupedal motion, in this instance handled with notable grace.[3]

Despite the formulaic compositions and figure types, the monsters and animals in both friezes are rendered with the liveliest animation, their bodies drawn with a vivacious elegance that, paradoxically, achieves naturalism with an abundance of stylization. The hounds seem to grin as they chase their quarries, not caring if they catch them or not. Certain elements—the carefully reserved details in the animals, the types of filling ornament, the polychrome tongues on the shoulder, the drawing of the hounds and

hares—permit an attribution to Schaus's Altenburg Painter, "the pioneer of the Fikellura style."[4] More fluid than his earliest work of about 560 B.C. but with none
of the carelessness that marks his later production, this vase probably dates to about 550–540 B.C.

The sphinxes and sirens, while rendered in a distinctive East Greek style, are basically indistinguishable from their counterparts on the Greek mainland or, indeed, from anywhere in the Greek world of the sixth century. Their "function" is the same as on Corinthian or Attic pottery, to provide a pleasing design employing traditional motifs imbued with well-understood but seldom articulated apotropaic powers, all against a faintly resonant background of elitist privilege grounded in the hunt and the monopoly of Eastern luxury goods.

—JMP

### BIBLIOGRAPHY
Unpublished.

### NOTES
1 For Fikellura pottery, see Cook 1933–34; Schaus 1986; Cook 1992, 260–63; Cook and Dupont 1998, 77–91. For analysis of Fikellura clay, see Dupont 1983; Jones 1986; Schaus 1986, 283–84; Cook and Dupont 1998, 77.
2 For the Wild Goat Style, see Cook 1992; Cook and Dupont 1998, 32–70; Käufler 1999. See also Schiering 1957; Kardara 1963; Walter 1968; Walter-Karydi 1973.
3 Cf. the hounds and hares on contemporary East Greek bronze plaques in the Princeton University Art Museum (Childs 2001a, 46–47, nos. 21–27).
4 Cook and Dupont 1998, 78. For the Altenburg Painter, see Schaus 1986, 253–70, pls. 13–15; Cook and Dupont 1998, 78–81. For comparison of some individual figures and motifs, see CVA London 8, Great Britain 13, pl. 1 (hounds and hares, filling ornament, polychrome tongues, bands of vertical lines); pl. 8.9 (sphinx with raised paw next to deer); pl. 11.2 (sphinxes with raised paws flanking a goat); pl. 12.1–2 (maeander and squares on the neck).

## 69

# Fragment of a Fikellura Oinochoe

East Greek, Miletos, ca. 550–520 B.C.
Ceramic
Height 9.0 cm., width 7.5 cm., thickness 0.5 cm.
Collection of William R. Suddaby

### CONDITION
The clay fabric is light pinkish beige with mica inclusions. The fragment is itself repaired from four pieces. The exterior is covered with an off-white clay slip and is thoroughly burnished. The figure is painted in dark brown slip, with reserved lines to depict details.

The fragment is from an oinochoe, a wine jug, in the Fikellura style, like the vase in the preceding entry (cat. no. 68).[1] The curvature of the vessel shoulder is preserved at the top of the fragment. The city of Miletos, on the Aegean coast of Asia Minor, is now credited with the production of classic Fikellura ware,[2] with the possible exceptions of a few local imitations found at Histria and Olbia.[3]

A winged figure, identifiable as a male sphinx, is shown running to the left in a highly animated but semi-crouching position. The preserved part of the figure's human upper right arm extends straight out, while the left arm, missing the wrist and hand, extends forward and downward. The right leg, preserved to just below the calf, is bent in the so-called *Knielauf* position; the preserved upper thigh area of the left leg appears to extend back from the figure, perhaps bent in a position similar to that of the right leg. What is remarkable is that both legs appear to be human in form. The horizontal continuation of dark brown glaze from the left buttock may represent the beginning of a tail or the upper part of the extended left leg. Beneath the figure is a curved tendril terminating in a pendant lotus blossom. At the upper right, above the end of the figure's wing, a small bit of black glaze on the edge of the fragment may be part of a volute tendril, or possibly the end of a long curving tail. A large spot of black glaze, an obvious mistake on the part of the vase-painter, is located between the curving front part of the wing and the back of the figure's head, giving the false impression of a second wing.

The figure's face is drawn with great care and, at least for Fikellura, unusual sensitivity. A combination of outline technique, common in early Orientalizing vase-painting, and the rendering of figures in silhouette, typical of later, black-figure style, is used to depict the head of the figure, with no use of incision. The eye, nose, and mouth are carefully outlined in slip, while the remaining parts of the head make use of the reverse technique, with the chin, cheek, ear, and hair painted in silhouette and details delineated by reserved lines.[4]

The subject, a male sphinx, is unusual and possibly unique, at least in this form. Greek sphinxes are normally female, and although a few bearded sphinxes are known,[5] their sex is indicated by the beard, whereas the male genitals of this smooth-shaven monster make its gender explicit. One might be tempted to identify the figure simply as a winged male, such as Boreas or Eros, but the body is quite horizontal, like a normal Fikellura sphinx (cf. cat. no. 68). Moreover, the figure's hair is reminiscent of an Egyptian-style wig, lending a particularly foreign air to the figure and associating it with other East Greek sphinxes. We cannot know for certain why the artist created this hybrid in which the human part of the sphinx's nature is given an unprecedented precedence.

—AJP

**BIBLIOGRAPHY**

Paul 2001, no. 52.

**NOTES**

1  For Fikellura pottery, see Cook and Dupont 1998, 77–91; Cook 1933–34; Cook 1992, 260–63; Cook 1997, 123–27; *CVA* London 8, Great Britain 13, pls.1–14; Schaus 1986, 251–95; Greenewalt 1971; Kardara 1963; Walter 1968; Walter-Karydi 1973; Schiering 1957; Vallet 1978.

2  Cook and Dupont 1998, 77; Cook 1997, 123.

3  Cook and Dupont 1998, 88–91; Cook 1997, 127.

4  For the use of reserve and black-figure technique in the Wild Goat and Fikellura styles, see Cook and Dupont 1998, 78–79.

5  *LIMC* 8 (1997), 1158, nos. 129–34, pls. 801–2, s.v. "Sphinx" (Kourou, Komvou, and Raftopoulou).

# 70

# Appliqué in the Form of a Recumbent Sphinx

Greek, perhaps Peloponnesian (Laconian?), ca. 540 B.C.
Bronze
Height 4.39 cm., length 5.97 cm.
Collection of Michael and Judy Steinhardt, New York

CONDITION
There are small losses on the nose, proper right cheek, shoulder, and forepaw. The end of the tail is broken off. The patina is smooth and grayish green in color. A reddish incrustation remains in the incisions.

The sphinx reclines to left, forepaws extended. She looks outward and upward toward the viewer. On her head she wears a small, undecorated, concave polos. Her hair is arranged in eleven tresses of four beads over the forehead and falls to the neck behind in seven tresses of eight beads. Her forelegs are differentiated, the left with four claws, the right with two. The wing is divided at the front by a strip of rope pattern, and six pairs of incised lines, front and back, denote the feathers. The long tail would have doubled back on itself. She lies on a flat Ionic capital, hatched on the side with a zigzag above a rope pattern. The back, head, shoulder, upper wing, and body are fully modeled, but the lower side of the figure is cut away to fit snugly against the shoulder of the vessel.[1]

Among bronze appliqués from vessels, a distinction may be drawn between those with a flat base, which would have been placed on top of the rim, and those (much rarer) whose back or underside are curved and cut away, suggesting attachment at the shoulder or at the edge of a substantial convex lip.[2] Elaborate vertical handles of bronze hydriae and amphorae often have animals (notably lions or rams) to either side below (e.g., cat. no. 85); these, however, are generally cast integrally with the handle, and sphinxes occur only rarely.[3] More likely, therefore, this appliqué comes from the shoulder of a mixing bowl, a dinos or lebes, where it may have been one of three. An attachment to an item of furniture cannot, however, be ruled out.[4]

The Ionic capital that supports the sphinx is a common device on other small bronzes.[5] Together with the sphinx, it echoes the series of sculptural dedications of which the Naxian offering at Delphi is the most famous.[6]

Stylistically, the Steinhardt sphinx most closely approaches bronzes from Selinunte,[7] from Lokri,[8] and from Gela.[9] In terms of workmanship, it is by no means inferior to a splendid sphinx from Perachora,[10] which suggests, despite the South Italian and Sicilian parallels, that it instead originated in a mainland Greek atelier. The esteem in which such bronzes were held is demonstrated by provincial Etruscan imitations.[11]

To the ancients, wine could slowly reveal truth (*in vino veritas*), not always pleasantly.[12] The Theban Sphinx, in asking the riddle, sought a true answer. Perhaps this accounts for one aspect of the popularity of the sphinx in the Archaic period as a subject for decorating vessels for mixing wine with water.

—JG

## BIBLIOGRAPHY

*Hesperia Art Auction*, New York, November 27, 1990, lot 9.

## NOTES

1 For archaic bronze vessels and their attachments, see esp. Jantzen 1937; Rolley 1982; Herfort-Koch 1986; Gauer 1991; Stibbe 2000b. For a recent discussion of sphinxes, see *LIMC* 8 (1997), 1149–74, pls. 794–817, s.v. "Sphinx" (Kourou, Komvou, and Raftopoulou); for bronze ones, Stibbe 2001.

2 E.g., Boston 52.188 (Comstock and Vermeule 1971, 292 no. 417); New York, Met. 1976.11.2 and 1976.11.3 (Mertens 1985, 30–31 no. 17); private collection (small ram).

3 Diehl 1964; Bothmer 1965; Stibbe 2000b.

4 Descamps-Lequime 2002.

5 Besides sphinxes, cf. Louvre Br 4467 (Joffroy 1979, 69, fig. 52); St. Petersburg 1870 1/1 (Joffroy 1979, 69, fig 53); Athens, Nat. Mus. 6113 (Gauer 1991, 296, var. 72, pl. 110.1).

6 *LIMC* 8, 1153, no. 31, pl. 796, s.v. "Sphinx."

7 Palermo 8269: Di Stefano 1975, 96, no. 172, pl. 37.

8 Baltimore 54.770: Hill 1949, 121–22, no. 279, pl. 54.

9 One in Boston (98.656) and another in Weimar: Jantzen 1937, 70, nos. 27–28, pls. 32–33, nos. 132–39; Comstock and Vermeule 1971, 284, no. 409.

10 Payne 1940, 135–36, pl. 43.1–2.

11 Liebermann 1971, no. 140, pl. 19.

12 Rösler 1995, 106–12.

# 71

# Red-Figure Stemmed Dish with Iris and a Sphinx

**Greek, Attic, ca. 520 B.C., attributed to the Euergides Painter**
**Ceramic**
**Height 25.35 cm., width 17.18 cm., depth 17.18 cm., diameter of foot 11.9 cm.**
**The Metropolitan Museum of Art, New York, Rogers Fund (65.11.14)**

CONDITION

**The upper part of the vase has been restored from fragments, of which only a few are missing, including small fragments from the lower part of the sphinx and a large fragment from Iris's left side. The vase is otherwise in an excellent state of preservation.**

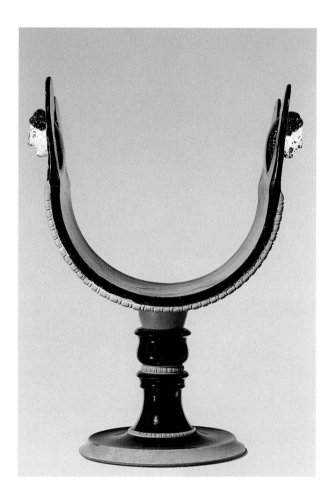

This vase and another very similar to it form a unique pair.[1] The shape is a half-cylinder lying on its side and resting on a tall, richly molded stem and low, broad, circular foot. The rims of the cylinder are decorated with a notched, beaded molding and a painted kymation pattern. Each side of the cylinder is decorated with a winged female figure whose wings and plastic head have been added separately. On one side a sphinx, a mythical creature part woman and part lion, with the wings of an eagle, wears a delicate necklace and crouches on her four paws, her tail curled at attention. She appears to be gazing down from a high perch, an effect that is heightened by the curve of the vessel and the tall stem. On the other side is a winged female figure, also wearing a necklace, and carrying a *kerykeion*, a herald's staff, in her left hand (no longer preserved). She wears a short chiton and runs in the characteristic *Knielauf* position. She may be Nike, the personification of victory, or, more likely, Iris, goddess of the rainbow and messenger of the gods.[2] In Archaic Greek vase-painting, Iris is sometimes represented as a lone traveler beset by centaurs or satyrs, and it is quite possible that a similar connotation of danger on the road is meant here by her juxtaposition with the sphinx.[3]

The vase is an outstanding example of Attic painted ceramics at a time when the red-figure technique was still coming into vogue. The applied white slip for female flesh and the wing coverts, incised on a black ground, follow black-figure conventions, while the sphinx's feline body and the drapery of Iris's short chiton are rendered in the new red-figure technique. The primary feathers are done in outline technique. The kymation frame of the rims is executed on a white ground. The firm attribution of such an unusual vase is difficult. It has been suggested that the potter may have been Sikanos, who produced some unusual stemmed plates,[4] while the Euergides Painter, whose seated sphinxes are similar to those on the dishes, has been proposed as the red-figure artist responsible for their decoration.[5]

The shape of the vase is otherwise unknown in Attic ceramics but has a long history in Etruscan bucchero ware.[6] It was almost certainly made for export to Etruria, where Attic vases were popular at this time, and is likely to have been a special commission, quite possibly ordered together with the very similar vase now also in New York.[7] The precise function of the vase is not known. The hypothesis

that it is an elegant container for solid items, such as asparagus, celery, or fennel, is more plausible than the suggestion that it was used as a headrest.[8]

—SAH

**BIBLIOGRAPHY**

Bothmer 1966, 184; Sparkes and Talcott 1970, 138 n. 1; Hoffmann 1971, pl. 13; Bothmer 1972, 83–92; Bothmer 1975, 124; Langlotz 1975, 189 n. 62; Brommer 1980, 337 n. 9; Moret 1984, 23 n. 2, 74 n. 9; Spivey 1991, 140–41; Sparkes 2000, 323–24, 329 n. 3, fig. 3; Descœudres 2001, 111–14.

**NOTES**

1   The vases appeared on the European art market together and were originally offered as a pair (Bothmer 1972, 83). The second vase, formerly belonging to Norbert Schimmel, is also in New York (Met. 1980.537: D. von Bothmer, in Muscarella 1974, no. 58; Bothmer 1981a, 35–36; Bothmer 1981b, 14; Milleker 1992, 43). It differs slightly in decorative details and represents a sphinx on both sides rather than Iris and the sphinx. A third vase of this type, published by J.-P. Descœudres (2001, 114), has been identified as a forgery.

2   The iconography of Iris and Nike is not always easy to distinguish in this early period (*LIMC* 6 [1992], 852, s.v. "Nike, Archaische Zeit" [Moustaka]). Nike is also sometimes represented with the kerykeion, Iris's most characteristic attribute.

3   For her encounter with centaurs, see, e.g., a fragmentary red-figure skyphos in Florence (4218) attributed to the Kleophrades Painter: *LIMC* 5 (1990), 756, no. 167, pl. 499, s.v. "Iris" (Kossatz-Deissman). Images of Iris with satyrs are listed in *LIMC* 5, 751–52, nos. 105–20.

4   Bothmer 1972, 92; Moret 1984, 23; Sparkes 2000, 323–24.

5   D. von Bothmer, in Muscarella 1974, under no. 58; Boardman 1975, 60, pl. 103; Spivey 1991, 140.

6   For a discussion of the Etruscan bucchero precedents, which are centered inland in northern Etruria, especially Chiusi, see Bothmer 1972, 86–91. For a discussion of other Attic vases that were exported to Etruria, see Rasmussen 1985, 33–39, esp. 39; Spivey 1991, 131–50.

7   See n. 1 above for publications and relevant discussion in many of the other references cited in the bibliography.

8   See Bothmer 1972, 89. Descœudres (2001, 113–14), looking to Egyptian parallels and the evident funerary context of most of the Etruscan bucchero examples, makes the suggestion that the type served as a headrest.

# 72

# Fragment of an Altar
# with a Seated Sphinx

Greek, probably Calabria, Early Classical period,
480–460 B.C.
Terracotta
Height 21.5 cm., width 11.7 cm., depth 9.5 cm.
Museum of Fine Arts, Boston, gift of Ariel Herrmann
in memory of Lucia Torossi (2001.851)

CONDITION
The piece is made from orange-brown clay with
many coarse white impurities. It is finished at the left
rear but broken on all the other edges.

The Greek tragic poets describe the sphinx as a winged
young woman with the body of a lion[1] or a dog.[2] In
this case, the lean body seems canine and the large paws
leonine. The swelling chest reflects the intermingling of
woman and animal. The female part is fashionably elegant; the sphinx wears globular earrings and a hair net
(*sakkos*), which covers the rear part of her head. The netting
of the *sakkos* is indicated with incised cross-hatching.

The sphinx sits on top of an engaged Aeolic column
with seven visible flutes. If continued as a full round column, it would have had nine flutes. The capital lacks the
logic seen in built architecture: the point or wedge separating the volutes is below rather than above them, and
both volutes are turned counterclockwise rather than in
contrasting orientations. Nonetheless, the basic elements
and the proportions are canonically Aeolic: large volutes
are set close together above a narrow column. In Attica
at least, the order tended to be used not in architecture
but for votive or funerary columns.[3]

Capital, column, and monster are all rendered in high
relief; they seem to have been largely modeled freehand and
retouched with a knife or stick. Only some elements, such
as the face, were apparently made with molds. The blank
eyes still preserve Archaic tradition, but the absence of a
smile and the relatively soft hair indicate a slightly post-
Archaic date. The head has something in common with the
sub-Archaic and Early Classical terracotta heads of Lokri[4]
and Medma,[5] but its dainty chin also links it to Sicilian

figures.[6] The coarse, dark clay, which is much like that of
Medma or Lokri, indicates an attribution to Calabria.

In spite of the feminine charm seen in sculptures
such as this, the Sphinx was a terrible creature in Greek
literature. Her primary association is with Thebes and the
Oedipus legend, where she is a brutal killer, descending
daily from her mountain home to devour the men of
Thebes.[7] She did, however, give her victims the possibility
of escape by asking them a riddle. A fearsome image also
emerges in an epigram from a monument in Thessaly, in
which a sphinx seated on top of the construction or tomb
is called "the dog of Hades."[8]

In funerary art throughout antiquity, the sphinx
acted as a watchdog over the tomb. Although the rationale
is not made explicit, her savagery could evidently be
thought of as turned against those who would disturb
the dead.[9] J.-M. Moret and Herbert Hoffmann offer a
different perspective.[10] Mixtures of human and animal,
such as the sphinx, are creatures of the boundaries
between two different realms, and as such, they preside
over rites of passage between different states of human
experience, whether from life to death or from ephebe to
warrior. Initiation into manhood can be seen as a symbolic death, justifying the participation of this murderous
creature. This metaphoric interpretation of visual imagery,
however, lacks textual support.

The sphinx has a role in the public realm that poses
the interpretive problem in different terms. Despite her
negative mythological baggage, the sphinx evidently had
positive connotations that permitted her display in sacred
spaces. The earliest surviving example may well be the
monumental marble sphinx on an Ionic column erected
by the Naxians about 580–560 B.C. at Delphi.[11] Sphinxes
were also set up in sanctuaries at Delos and Cyrene.[12] To
explain this killer's prominent presence, Émile Bourguet
has evoked the Sphinx's "prophetic character."[13] In other
words, her riddle becomes a metaphor for the obscure but
enlightening utterances of priests at these famous oracular
shrines. There is an admonitory implication as well; those
who cannot seriously consider or interpret such ambiguous pronouncements should advance no further.

Literary support for this sacred monitory role for the
sphinx emerges in a passage of Clement of Alexandria

(ca. A.D. 200): "Therefore also the Egyptians place Sphinxes in front of their temples to indicate that the discourse about god is enigmatic and obscure. Perhaps one should both love and fear the divine: to love it as gentle and kind to the pious, to fear it as implacably just to the impious. For the Sphinx shows enigmatically at the same time the image of a wild beast and of a human being."[14] Although Clement refers this role of the sphinx to Egyptian temples, it is equally relevant in a Greek setting.

This terracotta sphinx seated on a column may well have belonged to an object with sacred connotations. Sphinxes (though not on columns) are known from many small ceramic altars (*arulae*) from South Italy and Sicily,[15] whose find spots suggest a ritual (non-funerary) function: i.e., to receive various sorts of offerings.[16] An identification of this piece as an *arula* is, however, not entirely certain. While *arulae* are highly variable in their proportions,[17] this fragment is unusually shallow. (The original left rear edge is preserved.) Behind the engaged column, moreover, the support tapers, flaring upward both in front and side view, more like a table leg than an altar. The side panel expands from 5.8 centimeters below to 6.7 centimeters above. Altars whose form suggests tables are known,[18] and the maker of this piece may also have borrowed from furniture design. There seem to be no close parallels, however, for the specific form of this example.

—JJH

**BIBLIOGRAPHY**
Unpublished.

**NOTES**

1  Eur. *Phoen.* 806, 1019, 1042; *LIMC* 8 (1997), 1150, s.v. "Sphinx" (Kourou, Komvou, and Raftopoulou).

2  Aesch. *Sphinx, TrGF* III F 236; Soph. *OT* 391; cf. Palaiphatos 4 Festa; *LIMC* 8, 1149–50, s.v. "Sphinx."

3  Betancourt 1977, 100–104, pls. 55–59. See also the discussion under cat. no. 63 in this volume.

4  Higgins 1954, cat. no. 1202.

5  Holloway 1975, 6–8, figs. 31–58.

6  Higgins 1954, cat. nos. 1144, 1153; Holloway 1975, figs. 82, 93, 94.

7  *LIMC* 8, 1149–50, s.v. "Sphinx."

8  Ibid., 1150.

9  Vermeule 1979, 171; Woysch-Méautis 1982, 87.

10  Moret 1984. Hoffmann 1997, chapter 6.

11  Betancourt 1977, 106–9, fig. 51; École française d'Athènes 1991, 31–33

12  Betancourt 1977, 106–8, fig. 50; *LIMC* 8, 1131, no. 31, s.v. "Sphinx."

13  Bourguet 1914, 131.

14  Clement of Alexandria, *Stromateis* V.31.5; passage suggested by Annewies van den Hoek.

15  Van der Meijden 1993, 63–64, 282–89, pls. 49–50.

16  Van der Meijden 1993, 153–80.

17  Van der Meijden 1993, Beil. 1–5.

18  Van der Meijden 1993, form G, p. 7, 281, FA 3, 5, 11, 50, pl. 47.

## 73

# Statuette of a Siren

Greek, perhaps Peloponnesian, ca. 750 – 700 B.C.
Bronze
Height 4.0 cm., length 4.3 cm., preserved width 1.85
(wings)
Sol and Colleen Rabin Collection

CONDITION
The smooth dark green patina has areas of damage
on the underside and lower left side of the siren's
body, as well as on the breast, chin, and back of the
head. The end of the nose is missing. Most of the
left wing is broken off.

This cast bronze statuette is one of the earliest known
sculptural representations of a siren. The rounded underside and the jutting neck and head give it a high center
of gravity and prevent it from standing on its own. The
hole under the figure suggests that it was once attached to
another object and so held upright, a highly unusual
arrangement in a Geometric bronze. Possibly the figure
functioned as a finial or was part of a larger sculptural
assemblage.

The siren looks directly forward, its chin slightly
raised. Seen from the front, the breast and neck appear
flattened. Emphasis is placed on the head and tall neck,
which rises directly from the bird body. The triangular
head is not very deep, front to back, and features a strong
jawline ending in raised areas forming the ears, further
indicated by large drill holes. The ear formations are continuous with the planes of the face. Smaller drill holes
define the eyes, and a single slash, the mouth. Arched
brows, the left much more distinct than the right, appear
to have been executed in the wax before casting. These
features are similar in character to bronze human statuettes excavated at Delphi, dated from the middle to the
late eighth century B.C.[1] The short wings are placed
high on the body. The figure's back displays a concave
arc terminating in a raised, paddle-shaped tail. There are
no visible surface incisions indicating feathers or hair.

The closest comparison is an eighth-century B.C.
Greek bronze siren pendant, now in the J. Paul Getty

Museum, Los Angeles.[2] The Getty siren, however, differs in two important respects: it has a suspension loop on the back, and it lacks any discernable facial features.

In Homer's *Odyssey*, the sirens' beguiling but deadly songs attracted sailors to their island, but their appearance is not described.[3] Instead, Homer describes the sirens as endowed with omniscient memory, including complete knowledge of the Trojan War.[4] Sirens also have the power to quiet the winds.[5] In literature and art, their presence foreshadows, accompanies, or otherwise refers to death.[6] There may be some relationship between Greek sirens and the Egyptian *ba*-bird, in form and function (cf. cat. no. 8).[7] Sirens appear with increasing frequency in Greek art from the early seventh century on, both in sculpture and on painted vases. This little statuette is among the earliest known representations, before the canonical type was established. There is nothing about the features to suggest whether it is male or female, and it is only by association with what came after it that we identify it as a siren at all.

—MB

**BIBLIOGRAPHY**
Unpublished.

**NOTES**
1 See Rolley 1969, 22–56; cf. esp. 28–29, no. 8.
2 True and Hamma 1994, 47. For similar pendants, see Kilian-Dirlmeier 1979. The Greek bronze siren pendant will eventually be housed in the Getty Villa, Malibu.
3 Hom. *Od.* 12.39–54, 158–200.
4 *Od.* 12.189–91; Bennett 1997, 151–52.
5 *Od.* 12.168–70.
6 In art: Buitron and Cohen 1992, 108–11; Hofstetter 1990. In epic: Doherty 1995; Segal 1992, 3–29; Pucci 1979, 121–32.
7 Cooney 1968, 262–71, figs. 1–3.

## 74

# Siren from the Rim of a Lebes

**Greek, from Olympia, ca. 650 B.C.**
**Bronze**
**Height 5.2 cm., width 20.5 cm., length (head to tail) 13.5 cm.**
**Museum of Fine Arts, Boston, Henry Lillie Pierce Fund (99.458)**

CONDITION
**The siren attachment is intact. The crusty patina is a greenish blue, and the back is covered with a calcareous deposit.**

Designed for attachment to the rim of a cauldron (lebes), this cast bronze siren has its wings outspread, on the top of which its arms are outstretched. Another like it would have been positioned at the opposite side of the vessel; the two sirens would have stared at one another across the mouth of the cauldron, their heads and shoulders above the vessel's rim. The siren's hair emerges from a flattened cap in four thick strands, two falling in front of the shoulders and two down the back.[1] A central U-shaped element, cast in relief at the back of the figure, joins the wings and tail with the arms at the elbows, and is mirrored by the curved slope of the siren's shoulders. The flaring tail is balanced by the similar shape of the torso in a continuous profile forming the edges of the siren's sleeved garment. It is difficult to determine whether the figure is male or female. The lobes segmenting the wing and tail feathers are further differentiated with incisions. The lug at the middle of the back is not pierced. There are two rivets, one in each wing, positioned under the wrists. They are hammered flat at the top of the wings and protrude underneath, where, on the lower torso, there are two incised letters, a Λ above a K.

The Boston siren attachment is one of a matched pair; the other was excavated at Olympia, which would seem to establish the provenance of this piece.[2] Each cast attachment was once riveted to a cauldron made of hammered sheet bronze. These attachments, the products of Greek craftsmanship, ultimately derive from Near Eastern prototypes whose possible origins have been debated.[3] The Oriental attachments are commonly in the form of

composite creatures with bearded male heads and bird bodies. Proposed centers of production include Urartu, North Syria, and Assyria. The Greek siren cauldron attachments, now numbering perhaps twenty-six, provide valuable evidence of the Greek modification of Near Eastern motifs and art forms in the seventh century B.C., the Orientalizing period. It is reasonable to assume that Greeks interpreted the Oriental cauldron attachments as sirens, inspiring Greek bronze craftsmen to produce examples more in keeping with their conception of the mythical creature. Both imported and locally made siren attachments have been found at Olympia and Delphi. Delos, Ptoion, and Argos have yielded only imported Oriental examples, while at Athens and Samos only locally made siren attachments have been excavated.[4]

The siren continued to be used to ornament Greek bronze vessels and mirrors, becoming widely popular in the mid-fifth century B.C., especially on hydriae (cat. no. 80).[5] These images, more decorative than threatening, suggest that by this time their dangerous reputation, first found in Homeric poetry, had softened.[6]

—MB

### BIBLIOGRAPHY

Kunze 1930, 158 n. 2; Hampe 1936, 33, Abb.16; Hampe and Jantzen 1937, 73 n. 2; Chase 1950, 36–37, fig. 7; Jantzen 1958, 36 n. 8; Ducat 1964, 601; Herrmann 1966, 92, no. A23; Kaulen 1967, 199, B8; Comstock and Vermeule 1971, 279–80; Weber 1974, 37, 39, 41, 45; Sturgeon 1987, 34; Comstock and Vermeule 1988, no. 402 (with bibliography); M. True, in Kozloff and Mitten 1988, 57; Muscarella 1992, 20.

### NOTES

1 For similarly modeled locks of hair on early Greek bronzes, see M. True, in Kozloff and Mitten 1988, 52–57, and note on p. 57.
2 Herrmann 1966, pls. 32–33; see also Bothmer et al. 1979, 174, no. 132; Muscarella 1992, 20.
3 Muscarella 1992, 16–24.
4 Muscarella 1992, 21.
5 Cf. the kalpis handle from the Fleischman Collection, now in the J. Paul Getty Museum (True and Hamma 1994, 69–70, with related bibliography); also the mirror from Locri Epizephirii (Reggio Calabria 4496: Bennett, Paul, and Iozzo 2002, 214–15); and the mirror handle in Cleveland (67.204: Cooney 1968, 262–71).
6 For sirens in Greek literature and art, see Vermeule 1979, 201–6; *LIMC* 8 (1997), 1093–1104, pls. 734–44, s.v. "Seirenes" (Hofstetter and Krauskopf).

## 75

# Round-Bodied Pyxis

**Greek, Corinthian, ca. 570 B.C., attributed to the Chimaera Painter**
**Ceramic**
**Height 21.8 cm., diameter of body 22.2 cm.**
**J. Paul Getty Museum, Malibu, California (88.AE.105)**

CONDITION
The vessel is complete, having been reconstructed from fragments. The surface is well preserved, and the added color remains intense and bright. The added red is lost from the base and the band at the front of the vessel, as well as on the garment of the female bust on side B/A. Black has been lost on the backside of the goat and the facing panther's head as well as on the hair of the female bust on side B/A.

Pyxides generally functioned as containers for cosmetics such as rouge, or for perfumed oils and powders, although the large size of this pyxis may indicate a function as a container of a different sort. Pyxides came in various shapes and sizes, both with convex and concave sides. Those with convex sides, or "round-bodied," are not found in the Protocorinthian or Transitional periods; they made their first appearance in Early Corinthian, in the last quarter of the seventh century B.C., became common in the sixth century, and remained widely used by various schools of vase-painting until the fifth century.[1]

This round-bodied pyxis is decorated from rim to foot with a series of friezes in the black-figure technique. A chain of lotus and palmettes, alternately reversed, rings the shoulder, and around the neck and foot are solid bands of red. Concentric bands circle the inside of the mouth and under the foot. The exterior of the rim displays a lively zigzag pattern. Attached at the rim and shoulder, the handles have been fashioned as busts of dark-haired females, each wearing a red garment and a beaded necklace. The plastic heads have inverted triangular faces and hair arranged in waves. The large primary frieze around the belly consists of creatures both real and fantastic.[2] On the front of the vessel stands a bearded siren at the center of a heraldic composition. He moves to the viewer's right with

head turned back and is flanked by two standing panthers with ruffed heads facing front.[3] Next to the panther on the right is a standing bull, facing right, with head down. Another panther with frontal head stands next to the bull, its body moving to the left. In the center of the back of the vessel is a wild goat (mouflon) grazing. And finally, to the right of the goat, a panther faces out with tail curving up, mirroring the tail of the ruffed panther on the front of the pyxis. The stylized and clearly outlined figures of the animals are evenly spaced around the vessel. The symmetry of the composition is reflected in the carefully rendered space-filling rosettes. Incised drawing and substantial amounts of added red pigment enliven and highlight details on the figural and floral decoration.

The bearded siren occupies a prominent position in the decoration of this pyxis.[4] Placed in the center, he stands in profile, with upraised wings. The history of

the bearded siren in Greek art is relatively short-lived. Human-headed birds first appeared in Greece in the eighth century B.C. on imported bronze cauldrons dedicated at sanctuaries in Olympia, Delphi, and Athens. The cauldrons often had protomes in the shape of birds with human heads and arms (e.g., cat. no. 74). These heads were made both bearded and unbearded and were likely a direct influence on the Greek siren.[5] Initially imported from the Near East, these cauldrons were subsequently copied by Greek metalworkers for domestic manufacture.[6] In painted form, bearded sirens first appear on Early Protocorinthian vases; these creatures can also be found on painted vases of Rhodes, Boiotia, and Attica.[7] Yet, the popularity of the bearded siren is most notable in Corinthian art, where it became firmly established as a decorative and non-narrative motif lasting throughout the sixth century B.C.

is in St. Petersburg and the other in Bonn.[14] On the Getty pyxis, the delicately incised details on the figures, the composition of the friezes, the variety of animals, the abundance of small rosettes, and the Archaic style of the modeled heads support the attribution to the Chimaera Painter.

—CET

### BIBLIOGRAPHY

Neeft 1991, 50; Amyx and Lawrence 1996, 96 n. 175; *Getty Masterpieces* 1997, 32; Katz 1997, 15.

### NOTES

1  Amyx 1988, 451–52; Payne 1931, 293.

2  The artistic vocabulary of the "animal style" included animals (real and imaginary) in a continuous file, heraldic pairing, and often animals attacking one another. This style extended beyond the decoration of pottery; it can be seen in religious architectural sculpture and in the decorative arts, such as metalwork. For information on Corinthian decorative metalwork and sculpture, see Payne 1931, 222–47.

3  The presence of a ruff may indicate a male panther. See n. 14 below for the pyxis at the Hermitage with a similar depiction of a panther with ruff.

4  It is unknown whether the human-headed bird that first appeared in Greek art was referred to, or even thought of, as a siren. This attribution came in the sixth century B.C. with the first depiction of Homer's sirens in Corinthian vase-painting. For this reason, images of human-headed, bird-bodied creatures, from all periods, are conventionally referred to as "sirens."

5  See Hermann 1966, 27–113, pls. 1–2, 4–41; Neils 1995, 177.

6  Herrmann 1966, 90.

7  Hofstetter-Dolega 1990: for bearded sirens on Protocorinthian vases, 35–40; on Attic vases, 69–71; on Boiotian vases, 187–92; on Rhodian vases, 226–27.

8  Herrmann 1966, 51–52.

9  Buschor 1944, 13–14. For references to the influence of the *ba*-bird on the protomes of bronze cauldrons, see Herrmann 1966, 51.

10  Quirke 1992, 106.

11  Neeft 1991, 50. The original attribution was made by Darryl Amyx. In Amyx and Lawrence 1996, 96 n. 175, Lawrence writes that she does not believe the Getty pyxis is by the Chimaera Painter, but she provides no reason for this opinion.

12  Amyx 1988, 167.

13  Amyx and Lawrence 1996, 55–56.

14  For St. Petersburg 5551, see Lawrence 1959, 354, no. 12, pl. 90, figs. 18–23. For Bonn 666, see Lawrence 1959, 354, no. 13, pl. 92, figs. 24–25.

Human-headed birds have a long history in the art of the ancient Near East and were likely models for the creature that came to be known as the "siren" in Greek art. The Assyrian god Assur was depicted with the head and arms of a bearded man and the body of a bird. He was sometimes shown with a winged sun disk, the symbol of divinity.[8] Near Eastern human-headed birds were themselves probably inspired by the Egyptian *ba*-bird (e.g., cat. no. 8).[9] The *ba*-bird, representing the freedom and mobility of the spirit of the deceased,[10] was depicted both with a beard and as beardless.

The Getty pyxis has been attributed to the Chimaera Painter, the dominant artist of the Chimaera Group.[11] His work is first seen at the beginning of the Middle Corinthian period (590–570 B.C.). The Chimaera Painter's work is recognizable by strong, bold lines and expressive and abundant use of polychromy.[12] This artist worked on bowls, plates, clay plaques, and aryballoi, and alone within the Chimaera Group also decorated pyxides.[13] Two head-pyxides by the same artist are the closest parallels; one

76

## Aryballos with a Siren

Greek, Early Corinthian, ca. 600 B.C.
Ceramic
Height 18.2 cm., diameter 15.4 cm., diameter of
rim 8.35 cm.
Collection of Mr. and Mrs. Nicholas M. Evans

CONDITION
The vase is unbroken and in good condition. The
lower body is misfired a reddish brown, and there is
flaking of the painted decoration, particularly on
the handle, the rosette on the rim, and the lower
body, including the lower feathers and feet of both
the siren and the bird.

The shape is that of a classic Corinthian spherical oil
bottle, an aryballos, with a rounded base, cylindrical neck,
strap handle, and a small mouth surrounded by a wide
rim with an overhanging lip. The clay fabric is the light
creamy beige characteristic of Archaic Corinthian pottery.
The decoration is in black slip, with many details in
added red and white. The central decoration, opposite the
handle, consists of a siren facing right, its outstretched
wings reaching almost entirely around the spherical body.
The top of the siren's head, extending slightly above the
figural field, is decorated with a small, stylized lotus bud
between two long-stemmed, volute tendrils, which radiate
from a narrow base in the shape of a low cap, or polos.
The demon's female face is imbued with exceptional character, having a large nose, strong chin, and carefully drawn
eye. Her long hair, secured by a white-dotted fillet, falls
in a rippling mass across her right wing. On the opposite
side of the vase, near the handle, is a waterbird, a swan or
goose, which faces left with folded wings.

The top of the rim is concave and is decorated with
a rosette, the petals alternately red and black. The rosette
on the base is misfired red. There is a row of black dots
around the edge of the lip and a zigzag line painted
between two vertical lines on the handle. Two black lines
run around the shoulder of the vessel below a band of
alternating red and black tongues. Added red is used for
the bird's breast and wing, and for the siren's face, breast,

and polos-shaped cap, and in bands on the wings and
tail. Black, white, and red bands indicate wing and tails
feathers on both the siren and the bird, with bands of
white dots differentiating the principal parts of the wings.
There are white, *sigma*-shaped zigzags on the black bands
running along the upper edges of the siren's wings. The
background is filled with black rosettes and lotus buds,
the spaces between them are filled with abstract shapes.

The sirens mentioned by Homer in the *Odyssey* lured
human beings with their song,[1] leading them to perish
nearby on the island inhabited by these creatures. The
poet omitted any description of these malevolent mythological beings, but by the early sixth century B.C. they
appear on a Corinthian aryballos in Boston as human-
headed birds associated with the Homeric tale, with
Odysseus tied to the mast of a ship while two sirens stand
on a large rock nearby (see Tsiafakis, "ΠΕΛΩΡΑ," fig. 3,

in this volume).[2] Sirens, a favorite motif of Corinthian artists, were more commonly represented than other fabulous winged creatures such as sphinxes, winged lions, panthers, horses, griffin-birds, lion-birds, panther-birds, goat-birds, and phallus-birds.[3]

The aryballos is attributed to the Luxus Group, a small group of Early Corinthian aryballoi characterized by fine drawing, rich polychromy, and plenteous use of white-dot bands.[4]

—AJP

**BIBLIOGRAPHY**
Unpublished.

**NOTES**
1  Hom. *Od*.12.39−54, 158−200.
2  Boston 01.8100: Vermeule 1979, 202, fig. 25. For sirens, see Vermeule 1979, 201−3; Buitron and Cohen 1995, 108−11; *LIMC* 8 (1997), 1093−1104, s.v. "Seirenes" (Hofstetter). See also Tsiafakis, "ΠΕΛΩΡΑ," in this volume.
3  Payne 1931, 90−91.
4  For the Luxus Group: Amyx 1988, 87, 397; Lawrence 1998. Lawrence (1998, 317 n. 74) notes that she and C. W. Neeft have independently identified several vases by the same hand as the Evans aryballos, whom she calls the Painter of Louvre E 516 but whom Neeft refers to as the Royal Athena Painter.

## 77

# Aryballos in the Shape of a Siren

Greek, Middle Corinthian, ca. 575 B.C.
Ceramic
Height 8 cm., length 7.4 cm., width of body 4.35 cm.
Museum of Fine Arts, Boston, Seth K. Sweetser Fund
(65.566)

CONDITION
The color of the fabric is buff. The vessel is intact,
except for the loss of a section of hair to the left of the
siren's face. Some of the glaze, which is dark brown
and matte, has worn away. Residual dirt remains in
crevices alongside the face, below the left jaw,
between the legs, and on the underside of the tail.

Modeled in the shape of a siren, with the head of a
woman and the body of a bird, this aryballos was once a
flask for special oil.[1] It was filled and emptied through the
simple hole on the top of the head. A cord was strung
through the perforations alongside the neck for carrying
the vase or to hold a stopper. The nearly round body
was made on the wheel and the head was fashioned in a
mold,[2] while the tail and legs were formed by hand.

The siren's head, which is large in relation to her
body, faces forward atop a slightly craned neck. Her eyes
are delineated by light and dark glaze, and her shoulder-
length hair, which was first painted black and then overlaid with bright red, now has a mottled appearance. The
figure has no wings; instead, the sides and back of her
body are stippled with dots of glaze, and a zigzag is
painted on her belly. A dark band encircles the base of
her short, flaring tail. The siren's dark brown legs are
tucked under her body; because they are unequal in
thickness, she tilts slightly to her left.[3]

Although the origin and development of siren iconography in early Greek art is the subject of an essay in this
catalogue,[4] it bears mentioning here that a creature combining a human head and an avian body had been adopted
from the Near East by the beginning of the seventh century
B.C.[5] In its earliest manifestations, a Greek siren might have
the head of a man[6] or a woman, but in the sixth century,
female representations became predominant.[7]

During the last half-century, Corinthian siren
aryballoi have been studied by a handful of scholars, who
categorize these works differently but generally agree
about their chronology and development.[8] Siren aryballoi
are typically understood as belonging to one of two
groups. Those of the first, smaller type, were made in the
Early Corinthian period, about 620–590 B.C., and are
characterized by winged, ovoid bodies. The Boston siren
belongs to the later, larger group of vases, which have
round, wingless bodies that are decorated with dots or
various ornaments.[9] They were manufactured during the
Middle Corinthian and Late Corinthian I periods, about
595–550 B.C.[10] By all accounts, this example was made
about 575 B.C.

We can only surmise whether or not aryballoi of
this shape had a particular symbolic value.[11] Given the
bewitching nature of the Homeric sirens, however, it

is tempting to think that such vases might have contained perfumed substances that granted their wearers the same mesmerizing power of seduction. Although it may be hard to see the subject of this innocent little aryballos as a rapacious temptress, the source of the siren's dread power was, in fact, her ability to deceive by means of charm.

Despite the siren's traditional significance as a portent of death, aryballoi of this shape have been discovered in graves only rarely. In this setting their function is unclear: perhaps the vases contained aromatic substances used in funerary rites, or were themselves placed alongside the dead either as prized possessions from life or farewell gifts from loved ones.[12] Indeed, it may have been thought that the sirens' beguiling song was a fitting lament to accompany grieving souls as they journeyed from their short life on earth to eternity in the underworld.[13]

Many siren aryballoi have been found while excavating the sanctuaries of female deities with whom these creatures had a special association. These goddesses included Hera and Artemis,[14] whose domains encompassed marriage and birth, which brought forth life but also took it away. These very special votives were most certainly placed in shrines by imploring and grateful devotees. Regardless of its original purpose, this delightful little vessel, like the mythical sirens of the past, possesses the magical power to enchant us even today.

—KM

### BIBLIOGRAPHY

M. B. Comstock, in *MFAB* 63 (1965): 213 (left); 1965: *The Museum Year, The Ninetieth Annual Report of the Museum of Fine Arts, Boston* (Boston, 1966), 67; Wallenstein 1971, 60, 131, no. V/A 7d; *LIMC* 8 (1997), 1095, no. 17c (where the inventory number is cited as 65.566.67), s.v. "Seirenes" (Hofstetter); Biers 1999, 140, 141, fig. 4 (left), 145, no. 12.

### NOTES

1 On the identification of the contents, see Biers, Gerhardt, and Braniff 1994, which is briefly summarized in Biers 1999, 136.

2 The head of this siren shares a certain likeness to molded handle attachments on Corinthian round-bodied head-pyxides, such as Malibu 88.AE.105 (cat. no. 75).

3 On the basis of shape and decoration, this vessel belongs to a group Biers (1999, 144–45) categorizes as having a "more globular body, without wings." Another aryballos of this type was recently in the London art market (London, Charles Ede, Ltd., *Corinthian and East Greek Pottery XII* [2002], no. 12). Among its closest comparisons is the aryballos Bonn 901, after which the "Groupe de la Sirène de Bonn" got its name (Ducat 1963, 450, no. V.1, fig. 22).

4 See Tsiafakis, "ΠΕΛΩΡΑ," in this volume.

5 Buitron and Cohen 1992, 109.

6 A bearded siren appears in the animal frieze on the Corinthian round-bodied head-pyxis mentioned in n. 2 above.

7 Buitron and Cohen 1992, 109; *LIMC* 8, 1103, s.v. "Seirenes."

8 Biers 1999, 140–41, where there is a summary of the scholarship.

9 Amyx 1988, 528–29 nn. 352, 353; Biers 1999, 141, 144–45, nos. 9–37. For a variant of this type, with the siren's head turned to the left and an ovoid body with stippled decoration, in the collection of Mr. and Mrs. Jonathan P. Rosen, see Buitron and Cohen 1992, 112, no. 34. For a hybrid combining a Gorgon's head and a round body like this siren, in the Museum of Art and Archaeology, University of Missouri, Columbia (87.106), see Biers, Gerhardt, and Braniff 1994, 11, no. 11, 12, fig. 4.

10 Amyx 1988, 528.

11 Biers, Gerhardt, and Braniff 1994, 5; Bevan 1986, 300–301, 309–11, 312–18.

12 Biers 1999, 137.

13 Vermeule 1979, 200–206.

14 Biers 1999, 138–39.

## 78

# Oil Bottle in the Form of a Siren

East Greek, sixth century B.C., Aphrodite Group
Ceramic
Height 13.1 cm., length 19.7 cm., diameter 9.2 cm.
Princeton University Art Museum, museum
purchase, gift of John B. Elliott, Class of 1951
(y1989–31)

CONDITION
The pale brown clay is micaceous, with a slight
orange tint. It is unbroken but has surface damage
along the front of the body and the top of the tail.
Many areas are coated with a thin, hard incrustation,
especially noticeable on the face, which is also
covered with root marks. A more fugitive brown
incrustation is evident in spots, particularly on
the breast and the underside of the tail.

The body of this vase is in the form of a bird with folded
wings, probably a dove. The legs, tucked close to the body,
are fully modeled but the feet are indistinct. The head,
turned to the right, is that of a woman, with an oval face,
high cheekbones, rounded chin, slanted almond eyes, long
pointed nose, and full lips arranged in a subdued smile.
Her long hair is tucked behind her ears and falls in ropelike tresses, three on her right shoulder, two on her left.
The hair in back is a single, ridged mass with the tips of
the tresses fringing the bottom.

The vessel was made in a double mold, front and
back; the long spreading tail was added last. The mouth
of the vessel is on top of the woman's head; the rim
is a flat, wheel-made disk, like that of an aryballos or
an alabastron. The flat, pierced lug behind the neck has
a hole for a cord of string or leather, the other end of
which could have been tied around the mouth or attached
to a stopper.

The surface damage and incrustation make it difficult
to reconstruct the figure's original color scheme. There

are many traces of white slip and, over this, areas of deep red slip, matt in texture, which is best preserved on the mouth and handle, the sides of the tail feathers, and the folded wing on the left side.

The bird with the head of a woman is a siren, one of the monsters who, in Homer's *Odyssey*, lured sailors to their death and whose seductive song Odysseus resisted only by having himself tied to the mast of his ship.[1] Homer does not describe their appearance, but from the seventh-century B.C. on, Greek artists always represented them as birds with female heads, perhaps influenced by the example of the Egyptian *ba*-bird (e.g., cat. no. 8). Along with the Sphinx, the winged lion with a female head, sirens became commonplace in Greek art of the Orientalizing and Archaic periods, normally in contexts remote from Homer's narrative or any other.[2]

Mold-made ceramic vessels in the form of sirens were produced in a number of places, but by far the most numerous are the little oil bottles manufactured in Corinth in the early sixth century (e.g., cat. no. 47) and the larger East Greek sirens of the Aphrodite Group,

of which this vase is a classic example.[3] The exact location of the Group's manufacture is uncertain, with Samos and Rhodes the principal candidates. The vessels developed out of and alongside the plastic vases of the early-sixth-century Gorgoneion Group (e.g., cat. no. 83); the canonical Aphrodite types were established by mid-century, and many of them persisted for another fifty years. The Group's name comes from a series of hollow clay figurines and plastic vessels in the form of a woman, probably Aphrodite, who stands rigidly frontal, like a stone kore, draped in a chiton and Ionic himation and holding a dove to her chest with one hand and clutching her chiton with the other. The goddess frequently wears a diadem, as do some of the sirens, and indeed the heads of both are essentially the same type. Other types associated with the Aphrodite Group include seated women, seated and standing men, reclining male banqueters, crouching dwarfs, and a few others.[4] Widely exported, they probably were purchased as much for the scented oil they contained as for themselves, although we can presume they were retained, to be refilled when necessary.[5] In addition to

those from Rhodes and other eastern sites,[6] many have been found in graves in South Italy and Sicily, some imported and others made locally from imported molds.[7] Indeed, Herbert Hoffmann published this vase as "Western Greek, perhaps made from an imported Rhodian mold."[8] It does lack the smooth, "soapy" surface that characterizes many works of the Aphrodite Group, but this may be masked by the surface damage and incrustation; the color of the clay and the presence of mica point to an East Greek origin.

By the third quarter of the sixth century, when this vase was made, the siren had been a fixture of Greek art for well over a century. We lack hard evidence of the motivations of the consumers who wanted oil bottles in this shape, or in the shape of one of the Gorgons or a helmeted warrior. We are not even sure what kind of oils or unguents they contained, or if the iconography varied with the contents.[9] In Homer, the sirens are enchanters who lure men to their doom, the beach before their meadow "piled with the bones of men now rotted away."[10] This siren does not seem that threatening, but apparently neither did Homer's. Her "Archaic smile" is an artistic convention of the period and not an attempt to evoke what the sirens themselves described as "the honey sweet voice that issues from our lips."[11]

—JMP

### BIBLIOGRAPHY

Basel, *MuM*, A.G., Auktion 34, May 6, 1967, *Kunstwerke der Antike*, 53, pl. 28, no. 113; Hoffmann 1971, 158, fig. 133a–b; Buitron and Cohen 1992, 113, 125–26, no. 35.

### NOTES

1  Hom. *Od.* 12.39–54; 165–200.

2  For sirens in Greek art, see, in this volume, Tsiafakis, "ΠΕΛΩΡΑ," figs. 1–4 and 6, with accompanying text. See also Hofstetter 1990; Neils 1995; Tsiafakis 2001; *LIMC* 8 (1997), 1093–1104, pls. 734–44, s.v. "Seirenes" (Hofstetter).

3  Aphrodite Group: Winter 1903, I 226, no. 4; Higgins 1954, 53, pl. 16, nos. 75–77; Higgins 1967a, 32–37, pl. 14A. For other examples, see Hill 1953, 60–62, pl. 18a; Ducat 1966, pl. 10.1, 11.7; Bell 1981, 130, no. 51, pl. 12; Johansen 1994, 120, no. 63; *CVA* Hannover 2, Germany 72, pl. 16, 1–3; *Pferdemann & Löwenfrau* 1999, 76, no. 8.14; London, Sotheby's, July 10, 1972, no. 134; London, Sotheby's, July 14, 1975, no. 148; New York, Christie's, December 9, 1999, no. 291; Galerie Günter Puhze, Katalog 8, *Kunst der Antike* (Freiburg 1989), no. 170 and Katalog 13 (1999), no. 123; Basel, Jean-David Cahn, A.G., *Tier und Mischwesen II* (December 2001), no. 39. An example in Copenhagen (Nat. Mus. 7657: *LIMC* 8, pl. 734, no. 9, s.v. "Seirenes") is unusual in having the head of a bearded man wearing a tall hat. For a different approach to making a siren vase, cf. an ebullient Sicilian vessel of ca. 500 B.C., formerly in the art market, with a molded face and plump, wheel-made body: Basel, *MuM*, Auktion 56, *Kunstwerke der Antike*, February 19, 1980, pl. 17, no. 56.

4  For descriptions of the principal Aphrodite Group types, see Higgins 1967a, 34–37, pls. 12–14.

5  Higgins 1967a, 30.

6  For some siren vases excavated in tombs on Rhodes, see Maiuri 1923–24, 299, fig. 194; Jacopi 1929, 36, no. 14, fig. 20, and 112, fig. 106.

7  For an example from a grave at Morgantina, in Sicily, see Bell 1981, 130, no. 51, pl. 12. Others come from cemeteries at Gela (Orlandini 1978, pl. 58, fig. 41) and Taranto (Lo Porto 1978, pl. 65, fig. 9). Some South Italian sirens have the same form as the vases but are actually handmade figurines, e.g., one in New York (Met. 2000.276: *BMMA* [Fall 2001], 9). Imported molds for siren vases have been found at Olbia, in the Crimea (Hoffmann 1970, 258).

8  Hoffmann 1971, 158, figs. 133a–b.

9  For attempts to determine the original contents of Corinthian and East Greek plastic vessels through analysis of trace elements, see Biers, Gerhardt, and Braniff 1994.

10  Hom. *Od.* 12.45–46.

11  Hom. *Od.* 12.87–88.

# 79

# Amphora with a Siren

Etruscan, ca. 530 B.C., attributed to the Ivy-Leaf Group
Ceramic
Height 35.5 cm., diameter of body 20.6 cm., diameter
of mouth 15.7 cm., diameter of foot 12.7 cm.
Virginia Museum of Fine Arts, Richmond, the
Adolph D. and Wilkins C. Williams Fund (60.3)

CONDITION

The vessel, made from orange clay, is intact. Much
of the upper portion of side B, including most of the
siren, is misfired. A crack extends from near the
upper left-hand corner of the picture field through
the siren's head and wing to the base of handle B/A.
Some of the white is worn away and the dull black
glaze is cracked and abraded in places.

This belly-amphora was once used to store provisions. The
shape, which was borrowed from Attic imports, has a flaring
mouth, an unbroken contour along the length of its body,
cylindrical handles, and an echinus foot. The vase is entirely
black except for the reserved panels on front and back,
which are topped by a zone of interlaced pendant lotus
buds with dots above, and a zone of rays above the foot.

On side B, facing left, an elegant siren of ample
proportions fills the framed picture field. Resplendent in
her feathered finery, this matronly creature sniffs a small
blossom she holds in the delicate fingers of her right
hand. She has a placid expression, a dark eye, a pointed
nose, and a small mouth. Her ear is drawn with great care,
and from its lobe hangs an earring. She also wears two
necklaces, one with tiny pendants, and a fillet around her
head. Long locks of wavy hair fall over her raised left
wing, which is divided into three sections and terminates
in short flight feathers that curl upward at the tips. From

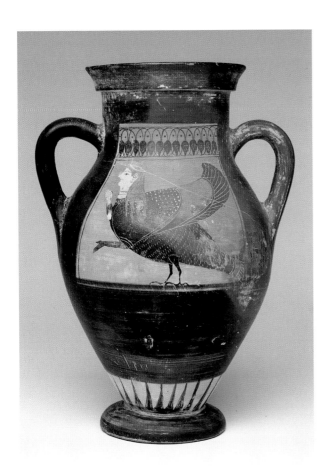

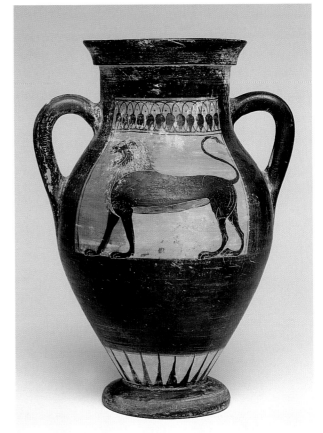

the figure's generous bosom emerge her arms, the left one set quite low and extended before her. The siren's long body, which is balanced on slender legs with large claws, tapers to a short, stubby tail.

This vase was painted by an artist adept in the black-figure technique, who used bold, diagonal lines to fill most of the trapezoidal picture field. Although the painter was a bit hasty with the engraver in some places, he used more or less parallel rows of short hatches to indicate the hair above the siren's forehead and the finer feathers on her body and at the tops of her legs. White dots contour her neckline and are aligned neatly across the shoulder of her wing. Her face, arms, and hair band are also white. Red slip was applied to the blossom, her hair, the broad midsection of her wing, and the band around her tail.

Originally it was believed that one artist decorated more than thirty vases that were linked by style; he was called the Ivy Painter, after his penchant for depicting dancers with oversized leaves of this plant on their backs.[1] Since there was eventually good reason to think that these

vessels were the product of a workshop rather than by a single artist, they were later assigned instead to the Ivy-Leaf Group.[2] During the half-century following the initial assembly, some vases have been removed and others added, with the total now exceeding fifty. The debate continues, however, about whether they came from one hand or were the product of a group.[3]

Unlike the ivy-bearers, the siren did not figure prominently among the painter's (or painters') favorite subjects. But one amphora, the current whereabouts of which is unknown, reportedly had a siren on both sides.[4] A third siren drawn on the back of an amphora formerly in the Ascona art market is strikingly similar in type, if not in detail, to the one on this vase; she, too, faces left and has small arms and a raised wing divided into three sections.[5] The Ascona amphora displays notable differences, however, in the shape and length of the siren's body, and the arrangement of her wing feathers, as well as the inclusion of a simplified lotus band above the picture field. Another amphora formerly in the art market also has a siren painted on its reverse.[6] Although she faces right, below a frieze of interlaced pendant pomegranates, and has outspread wings and no arms, there is little doubt that she belongs to the immediate family of the Richmond and Ascona sirens.

In the course of the swift westward flow of Near Eastern iconography during the Orientalizing period, the siren motif arrived in Italy by the seventh century B.C.,[7] either by way of Greece, which had adopted it from the East, or through Syrian or Phoenician imports.[8] In Etruria, some of these creatures were given arms, not unlike the Egyptian *ba*-bird, with whom this human-headed avian has been linked[9] (cf. cat. no. 8). But rather than serving as conveyors of souls or as portents of death, the bird-ladies on these vases seem to have been selected for their decorative appeal. While it is possible that their apparent sweetness in fact belies the suffering and death carried in their song, even a cursory glance at other monsters painted by the Ivy-Leaf Group suggests quite a different reading. In this work, like those, the artist reveals a greater interest in depicting a creature's unique physical presence than anything of the lethal threat she embodies. The Richmond siren appears no more menacing than a pet bird.

—KM

### BIBLIOGRAPHY

*Ancient Art in the Virginia Museum* 1973, 114, no. 130; Drukker 1986, 42, no. 31.

### NOTES

1 Dohrn 1937, 7–23 and 143–44; Scheffer 1977, 56; and Drukker 1986, 40. Shapes include cups, dippers, pitchers, and storage jars.

2 Beazley 1947a, 11.

3 Drukker 1986, 47–48.

4 Drukker 1986, 42, no. 32, which appeared on Dohrn's original list (no. 28).

5 Drukker 1986, 48 (addendum) and fig. 14. It is not clear in the illustration whether she, too, sniffs a blossom and wears jewelry.

6 *Kunstwerke archaischer Zeit*, H.A.C., Katalog 9 (Basel, January 1998), no. 37.

7 *LIMC* 8 (1997), 1104, s.v. "Anhang: Etruskische Sirenen" (Krauskopf); and Strøm, 1971, 131–34.

8 Strøm 1971, 209.

9 Strøm 1971, 209; Scheffer 1979, 49 n. 48; and Hummel 1984, 24–25.

# 80

# Hydria with Siren Handle

**Greek, perhaps Attic, ca. 440–430 B.C.**
**Bronze with inlaid silver**
**Height 37.8 cm., maximum circumference 87 cm.,**
**diameter of rim 12.5 cm., diameter of foot 12.5 cm.,**
**height of siren 7.73 cm.**
**Private collection**

CONDITION

**The vessel is complete except for three circular areas of restoration (diam. 2–3 cm.) on the upper walls and a narrow band of restoration around the lower body that reunites the upper and lower sections of the walls. The patina of the body and mouth is a golden brown, but the three handles are green, while the foot is a mottled combination of brown and green. There are irregular marks of mild corrosion on the body and a small area of heavy corrosion on the foot. Four evenly spaced drilled holes in the upper surface of the mouth may have held a lid in place, suggesting use as a cinerary urn. A dent and a small crack appear inside the mouth above the vertical handle, and signs of wear are evident under the handle itself, suggesting frequent use before burial.**

This vessel is a splendid example of the large class of Greek fifth-century "siren hydriae," first grouped by Erika Diehl.[1] Siren hydriae are always of the *kalpis* type, with a rounded, continuous profile and a vertical handle from shoulder to neck. Diehl's initial list has been considerably augmented, most recently with the publication of excavated material from ancient Thrace and Macedonia.[2] Precise dating of these *kalpides* is complicated by the fact that in antiquity bronze vessels were frequently buried long after they were produced.[3] Diehl's relative chronology has been convincingly raised by Vokotopoulou.[4]

The body of the hydria is moderately voluminous, somewhere between spherical and broadly ovoid, and the neck is well proportioned to it. The shoulders are high and not severely oblique. The Lesbian kymation on the handle roots and foot, together with its overall shape, make it comparable to two siren kalpides in Athens[5]

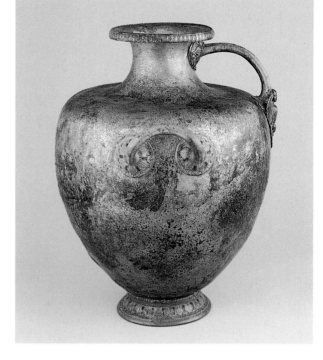

and a third in Thessaloniki with a winged Nike at the base of its vertical handle,[6] all dateable to about 440–430 B.C.

The body was raised by hammering. The mouth appears to have been cast with its egg-and-dart motif below a zone of beading on the lip. In the absence of any visible join, only X-radiology can reveal whether the body was hammered in a single piece to the middle of the neck or the two pieces were joined at the shoulder. Some hammer marks are visible inside the neck.[7]

The vertical handle with the siren at its base and the two horizontal handles, all apparently originally soldered in place, as well as the ring foot, are cast. The siren head is inlaid in silver, and there are raised silver volute eyes in the handle plaque as well as inlaid silver calyxes in the Lesbian kymation on all five handle roots and the foot. The single ovule directly over the vertical handle, of a width considerably more narrow than the others, suggests the handle's deliberate placement there. The dimensions of the two horizontal handles differ slightly, but variations in the stylized Lesbian kymatia on the four handle roots are minor. In three, the inlay channel of the calyx was omitted in the flower partially concealed behind the handle; in the fourth, the hidden flower was cast with a channel, apparently by oversight, and the silver appears.

On the high double-curve foot, the same Lesbian kymation is framed by beading at the top and bottom.

Below, a plain rounded molding spreads out to form the base of the foot. As the curve of the ornamented area is steeper than that of the horizontal handle roots and the floral forms more compressed (and narrow), the silver inlay that survives extends almost the full length of the flower.

The Lesbian kymation on the domed and oval root of the vertical handle follows the same pattern, with the same number of leaves (six) as on the roots of the horizontal handles and all the flower calyxes inlaid with silver. Under the arch of the handle, which has three flutes on its outer face, the spines of the leaves in the Lesbian kymation are worn down to a smooth surface. It is here that the fingers would have been placed to hold the handle for pouring, the thumb securing the grasp just inside the mouth, where there are also signs of wear.

Dominating the vessel by the intensity of its serious expression is the small, delicately modeled human face of the siren. She has a long, sturdy neck, large, wide-open eyes with irises and pupils indicated, a fine, thin-ridged nose, and a pursed, unsmiling mouth with bow-shaped upper lip. Her fully extended wings are sickle-shaped, formed of single long feathers that are modeled very simply, with rounded ends and a complete absence of texture. Their symmetrical, inward curving tips frame the inlaid head of the siren, which is already emphasized by the contrast of its silvery surface to the color of the bronze, and the attention of the viewer is thereby focused on her singular human characteristic. Fine incision defines the strands of her hair, which, parted in the middle, is pulled across her smooth brow in gentle curves on both sides. There are traces of gilding on these front tresses. The join of the inlay to the cast socket is cleverly disguised by engraved strands of hair flowing back from her face, cold worked to blend silver to bronze.

The siren's body of cast bronze swells slightly in front with a hint of human breasts. The join of inlaid neck to body, which is covered with a herringbone pattern of small feathers, is bordered with a molded V-neckline that echoes the shape of her body, the extension of her wings, and the outline of the handle plaque itself. Her bird's feet, which are not detailed, rest on an amorphous bronze shape suggesting the siren's traditional rocky habitat but also forming the heart of the palmette below. On each side, a series of four connected openwork volutes reaches up to a small palmette, the topmost petal of which joins the outer edge of a wing in a semicircle. The pierced, *à jour* volutes are modeled with low channels, and the eye of each is inlaid with a small, buttonlike form in silver.

The clear signs of wear on the hydria, both on the mouth above the vertical handle and on the kymation inside the handle's arch, suggest extensive use. It is probably not an accident that the principal restoration on the body is exactly where the other hand would have held the heavy bronze vessel when pouring—low on the wall opposite the vertical handle.

The hydria is a vessel found in Greek tombs throughout the Aegean and in South Russia,[8] both with and without cremation remains. It was used in funerary rites for pouring libations.[9] The siren was a particularly suitable decoration for a hydria intended for funerary use and is found in burials on other pouring vessels.[10] According to Ovid, sirens were the daughters of Acheloos, the river god, and skilled in song. They were companions of Persephone; when seeking in vain for her, they prayed to "float on beating wings above the waves." Getting their wish, they found themselves covered with golden plumage, but their soothing human voices and maidenly features remained (Ov. *Met.* 5.550–64). While their song was deadly to human sailors,[11] in Greek funeral rites the effective

aspect of their role may derive from their filial relationship to Acheloos, a god associated with the underworld, and their companionship with Persephone, the daughter of Demeter who was abducted by Hades into the underworld.
—BB-S

**BIBLIOGRAPHY**
Unpublished.

**NOTES**

1 Diehl 1964, 34–39 and 219–20, B 137–72 with pls. 14–21.

2 D. von Bothmer added to Diehl's original list in his review (Bothmer 1965, 603–5).

3 A phenomenon found in both Thrace (Archibald 1998, 173–74) and Macedonia (Vokotopoulou 1987), and probably elsewhere. Vokotopoulou discusses a hydria that she dates to 430 B.C., which was found in a cist grave dated by other material to 350 B.C

4 Vokotopoulou 1987, 158–69.

5 Both in Athens (Nat. Mus. 7914, from Thebes, and 13789, from the Kerameikos); see Vokotopoulou 1987, 167, pl. 23.2 and pl. 25.2 (Kerameikos), where both kalpides are dated to the third quarter of the fifth century. See also Diehl 1964, 35–36 and 219, nos. B 148 and B 149; pl. 15.4 (Thebes). The Lesbian kymation in the handle roots of the Kerameikos hydria has silver inlay in the spines of the leaves.

6 See Vokotopoulou 1987, pl. 21; she dates it ca. 430 b.c and considers it Attic. The ovules of the mouth are inlaid with silver.

7 X-rays of some fourth-century bronze hydriae have revealed a diffused, thickened area in the middle of the neck where the hammered body and the cast element with the mouth and upper neck were joined by hammering. A related process joined the cast mouths and hammered bodies of fifth-century bronze volute-kraters as early as the second quarter of the fifth century B.C. The area of overlap in those vessels is narrowly contained and influenced the profile of the vessel: see Barr-Sharrar 2000, 159–78. Other bronze hydriae are apparently produced in two pieces welded at the shoulder (see Bothmer 1965, 605–6). The body of a fifth- century bronze siren kalpis formerly in Athens was hammered in two parts with a horizontal join a few centimeters below the placement of the handles; the mouth and neck component was presumably added as a third element: see Andrioménou 1975, 535–36, fig 1.

8 Diehl 1964, 219, B 139, from Kul Oba, and B 144, from Kertsch.

9 On the subject, see Diehl 1964, ch. 2.

10 E.g., a bronze oinochoe, dated ca. 450 B.C., in Boston (99.48.1), from Spongano, near Vaste, in South Italy (Comstock and Vermeule 1971, 296–97, no. 423). It was said to have been found with a second bronze oinochoe and a monumental bronze volute-krater, also in Boston.

11 Living amid the bones of their victims, they sang seductively but in vain to both Odysseus and Jason on their respective voyages (Hom. *Od.* 12.170–200; Ap. Rhod. *Argon.* 4. 891–920).

# Black-Figure Neck-Amphora with Perseus and the Gorgons

*Greek, Attic, ca. 570–560 B.C., attributed to the Painter of London B 76*
*Ceramic*
*Height 46.1 cm., diameter of rim 19.3 cm.*
*Private collection*

### CONDITION

The vase has been repaired from fragments; half the foot is restored, but the vase is otherwise complete. There is repainting of cracks and adjacent areas of spalling, including the right thigh of Perseus, the right foot of the second Gorgon, and half of her face. The added colors are worn, particularly the white areas, such as the beard of Priam and the limbs and faces of the Gorgons.

The ovoid body of this neck-amphora proclaims its early date. Glossy black slip coats the echinus foot, cylindrical handles, and flat, overhanging rim. The body, too, is black, except for a zone of rays above the foot and two reserved panels for the pictures, each with a larger scene above a narrower frieze. Lines of added red slip circle the rim and foot and run above the rays and below the panels. Red fillets separate the body from the foot and neck, and another circles the lower edge of the foot. There are palmette-and-lotus festoons on either side of the neck. Above each panel is a band of red and black tongues.

This handsome vase features one of the earliest and finest depictions of the Ransom of Hektor, the subject of the concluding book of the *Iliad*. The composition is one repeated well into the fifth century, with the aged king Priam, garbed in himation and white chiton, approaching Achilles to request the return of the body of his son, Hektor, which lies on the floor.[1] Achilles reclines on a couch in his tent: "He had just now got through with his dinner, / with eating and drinking, and the table still stood by. / Tall Priam came in unseen by the other men and stood close beside him / and caught the knees of Achilles in his arms."[2] Dripping cuts of meat hang from the table above the corpse, which lies stiff and naked.[3]

Achilles stares in wonder at the old king, his left hand paused over a mound of viands, a metal phiale in his right hand. The artist agrees with Homer in having Priam grasp Achilles' knees, which are draped in a colorful, spotted cloak (by mistake, the incised end of the couch is visible through Priam's cloak). The two companions of Achilles mentioned by Homer are not depicted, however, and Hektor's corpse ought not to be present, for Achilles was careful that Priam not see it until his maids had washed and anointed it.[4]

Surrounding the figures, arrayed on tables, shelves, and pegs, are the arms of Achilles—shield, sword, cuirass, helmet, and greaves—all painted in red and white. This could be the armor lent by Achilles to Patroklos and subsequently taken from his corpse by Hektor, who in turn had it stripped from his own body by Achilles.[5] The fate of that battle-scarred panoply, the gift of the gods

to Achilles' father Peleus,[6] is not recorded, and this instead is more likely to be Achilles' second set of armor, fashioned by Hephaistos at the behest of Thetis, the hero's mother, and described by Homer in loving detail.[7] Its looming presence leads the viewer's mind to the eventual death of Achilles and the quarrel between Ajax and Odysseus over this very armor, resulting in Ajax's suicide. As much as Hektor's corpse, the armor represents death: when it first was delivered by Thetis, "Trembling took hold of the Myrmidons. None had the courage to look straight at it. They were afraid of it."[8]

The attribution of this and the other scene on the vase to the Painter of London B 76 is simplified by the existence of a similar version of the Ransom of Hektor on a hydria in Zürich, the composition of which, however, differs significantly.[9] The artist's interest in Homeric subjects is further attested by his name-vase in the British

Museum, with the chariot of Hektor, and by multiple versions of the Judgment of Paris, the Ambush of Troilos, and Achilles receiving his armor from Thetis.[10]

In the frieze beneath the Ransom are three galloping horsemen, the forelegs of their red-maned steeds all raised in unison.[11] Their rightward movement leads the eye toward the pictures on the reverse, where the subject of the upper panel is a chariot in profile to the left. A warrior and a white-gowned charioteer stand in the box. The warrior wears an Illyrian helmet and carries a colorful shield with a red rim and a black-and-white pinwheel device.[12] He is not identified, but we are free to assume that the setting is still the plain of Troy. The chariot may allude to the dragging of Hektor's corpse or to the chariot race at the funeral games for Patroklos.

In the frieze below is a scene of violence and pursuit, with the hero Perseus fleeing from the sisters of the

Gorgon Medusa. The decapitated Medusa, blood gushing from her neck, is shown falling to her knees at the far left. As is usual in such scenes, the two pursuing Gorgons turn their gruesome faces toward the viewer as they run, grinning horribly and baring their fangs, their hair alive with snakes. Their feminine, albeit monstrous, nature is signified by the added white of their flesh. Perseus sprints away at the far right, assisted by the winged boots and the cap of invisibility lent to him by Hermes. He wears a sword, but the bag, the famous *kibisis*, containing the Gorgon's head, is not depicted, an omission repeated by the artist in another version of this subject, on a hydria at Harvard.[13]

The adventures of Perseus, "the most pre-eminent of men,"[14] are mentioned briefly by Hesiod[15] and described in detail by Apollodoros.[16] Born of Zeus and Danaë, he and his mother were set adrift in a chest by King Akrisios but were rescued by the fisherman Diktys and brought to Seriphos. King Polydektes sent him to fetch the head of the Gorgon Medusa, whose glance turned her victims to stone. Aided by Athena and Hermes, Perseus cut off Medusa's head and eluded the pursuing Gorgons. After rescuing the princess Andromeda from a sea monster, he returned to Seriphos and turned Polydektes to stone for persecuting Danaë, later returning to Tiryns and killing Akrisios.

The escape of Perseus from the Gorgons was a favorite theme of Archaic artists. The composition on this vase descends from such forerunners as the painted metopes of the temple of Apollo at Thermon[17] and the ivory Chest of Kypselos at Olympia;[18] and from such notable earlier Athenian vase-paintings as the great Protoattic amphora from Eleusis,[19] and the name-vases of the Nettos Painter[20] and the Gorgon Painter.[21] Its placement on this vase in opposition to the Ransom of Hektor presented the ancient viewer with two depictions of a triumphant hero with the bloody corpse of his enemy, perhaps subtly evoking the victory of the soul over death.

—JMP

**BIBLIOGRAPHY**

Unpublished.

**NOTES**

1 For the subject, see Danale-Giole 1981; *LIMC* 1 (1981), 147−61, pls. 121−29, s.v. "Achilleus" (Kossatz-Deissmann).

2 Hom. *Il.* 24.475−78, trans. R. Lattimore.

3 The crown of Hektor's head is painted red and set off from the black curls on the brow and nape by an incised line, as though it had been scalped. Achilles dragged the corpse behind his chariot: "and all that head that was once so handsome was tumbled in the dust" (Hom. *Il.* 22.401−404).

4 Hom. *Il.* 24.581−85.

5 Hom. *Il.* 22.368−69.

6 Hom. *Il.* 17.195−97; 18.83−84.

7 Hom. *Il.* 18.477−612.

8 Hom. *Il.* 19.14−15.

9 Zürich, University, 4001: *Paralipomena* 32.1 bis; Isler 1986; Shapiro 1994a, 26, 31, 41, figs. 4−5; Miller 1995, 451, figs. 28.2−3. In the Zürich version, Priam does not actually clutch at Achilles' knees, Hektor's body is moved to one side, and there are other figures present, notably Hermes. Shapiro (1994a, 26, 31) identifies the armor in the Zürich scene as Hektor's, i.e., Achilles' first set, but there are actually parts of two panoplies present. A closer comparative study of the two versions is needed.

10 For the Painter of London B 76, see *ABV* 85−88, 683, 714; *Paralipomena* 32−33, 524; *BAdd²* 23−24. See also Bothmer 1948, 42. For the name-vase, London, Brit. Mus. B 76: *ABV* 85.1; Boardman 1974, fig. 54. For the Judgment of Paris (six): *ABV* 86.12−13; 87.15−16, 21, 23; *Paralipomena* 33.16 bis. For the Ambush of Troilos (two): *ABV* 85.2; 86. 8. For Achilles receiving his armor (four): *ABV* 86.9−11; 87.17; there is a fifth example, a column-krater in Madrid, with a Theban shield

identical to that on this amphora: London, Sotheby's, December 10, 1996, lot 162.

11 Cf. the horsemen on the painter's dinos in Boston, 34.212: *ABV* 87.18; Bothmer 1948, 44−45. figs. 2−3.

12 The Painter of London B 76 normally prefers to represent chariots in frontal view, as on his name-vase (see n. 10 above); this is his only profile chariot.

13 Harvard 1960.318; *ABV* 86.4; *CVA* Robinson Collection 1, USA 4, pl. 18. Medusa is absent on the Harvard vase, and on a third version, a neck-amphora formerly in the art market, here attributed to the same artist, only the two pursuing Gorgons are represented: Galerie Günter Puhze, Katalog 13, *Kunst der Antike* (Freiburg 1999), no. 114; New York, Sotheby's, June 13, 2002, lot 53.

14 Hom. *Il.* 14.320.

15 Hes. *Theog.* 280−83.

16 Apollod. *Bibl.* 2.4.1−4. For Perseus in art, see *LIMC* 7 (1994), 332−48, pls. 272−308, s.v. "Perseus" (Roccos).

17 Athens, Nat. Mus. 13401: *LIMC* 7, 340, no. 137, pl. 295, s.v. "Perseus."

18 Paus. 5.18.5; Splitter 2000, 37.

19 Eleusis Museum: Morris 1984, pl. 6; *LIMC* 4 (1988), 313, no. 312, pl. 184, s.v. "Gorgo, Gorgones" (Krauskopf and Dahlinger).

20 Athens, Nat. Mus. 1002: *ABV* 4.1: Beazley 1986, pl. 10.2−4; *LIMC* 4, 313, no. 313, pl. 184, s.v. "Gorgo, Gorgones."

21 Paris, Louvre E 874: *ABV* 8.1; Beazley 1986, pl. 14.1−3. For an example contemporary with this amphora, cf. a krater fragment by Kleitias, in Moscow (Pushkin Museum 2986: *ABV* 77.22). Other examples occur on Siana cups and vases of the Tyrrhenian Group, e.g., *LIMC* 4, 314, no. 315, pl. 18, s.v. "Gorgo, Gorgones"; *LIMC* 7, 340−42, no. 100, pl. 288, no. 154, pl. 298, and no. 165, pl. 301, s.v. "Perseus"; Schauenburg 1962b, 60, fig. 1; Brijder 2000, pl. 191a−b.

# 82

# Black-Figure Plate with Gorgoneion, Sphinx, and Sirens

Greek, Attic, ca. 590–580 B.C., attributed to the
Gorgon Painter
Ceramic
Height 4.2 cm., diameter 32.5 cm.
Walters Art Museum, Baltimore, Maryland (48.215)[1]

CONDITION
**The plate has been recomposed from fragments, with several losses. Missing fragments would have given the left cheek of the Gorgon; the wing and tail feathers of a siren above; and on the rim, most of a goat and of a lion, and much of a siren. A rim fragment with the hind legs of the lion below the Gorgon has been misplaced as the hind legs of the goat at left. The plate is misfired red in places.**

The magnificent gorgoneion in the tondo gives structural orientation to the decoration of this plate. Wide-eyed, and with a long tongue protruding from a slightly open, toothy mouth, the hair of the Gorgon is neatly arranged in snail-shell coils on top and in three corkscrew curls to either side. Her nostrils are rendered as Ionic volutes. From the top of her head emerge six long-bearded snakes, with forked tongues projecting from open mouths. The painted edge of a garment, with an incised zigzag border, appears below her neck.

Around this central tondo are two figural friezes, the inner one on the floor of the plate, the outer occupying the rim. In the former, the animals are arranged in two groups and a singleton. At the top are two confronting sirens with fillets in their hair. Below, heraldic lions flank a sphinx whose wings are extended; she, too, wears a fillet. At right, a youthful rider gallops to right; he wears a chitoniskos, carries a sword at his side, and has a fillet in his hair. Behind the horse is a rosette.

The rim has a procession of animals. The sequence begins with the two panthers at top that confront one another over an owl. From them, moving clockwise, we find a goat facing right; confronting sirens; a panther moving right, a lion facing right, with a rosette in front of him; and a goat facing left. The thickened edge of the rim has a row of small triangles; the underside is concave, with a glazed ring foot.

Much added red enlivens the figures, notably the Gorgon's tongue and the hair that fringes her forehead; the faces, forewings, and some tail feathers of the sirens; the manes and underbellies of lions; the panthers' shoulders; the horse's shoulder; and the rider's chitoniskos.

Both the subject matter and the scheme of decoration, with the animals arranged in concentric circles around a tondo, owe much to Near Eastern prototypes such as Phoenician bowls in bronze and precious metals (e.g., cat. no. 9).[2] Similar arrangements were also applied to decorated shields,[3] of which the literary one made by Hephaistos for Achilles was the most famous.[4]

The Baltimore plate is the most complete of the series of plates by the Gorgon Painter.[5] All seem to have been composed with a central tondo surrounded by one or two bands of figural decoration. (The plate of which fragments are divided among London, Oxford, and Toronto must have been particularly close.[6]) At least three are by the same potter.[7] They anticipate the Tyrrhenian plate in Würzburg, assigned by Denise Callipolitis-Feytmans to her Eridanos Workshop.[8] Similar in disposition of figure work and choice of subsidiary ornament are the Painter's dinoi and those of his pupil or follower Sophilos, whom Dietrich von Bothmer has proposed may have started his career as the potter for the Gorgon Painter.[9] The animal friezes by the Gorgon Painter are in turn much indebted to those on *lekanides* by the Nettos Painter.[10]

The animals on the Baltimore plate fall into three categories: the purely mythical, such as the Gorgon, the sphinx, and the sirens; those not indigenous to Greece, such as the felines; and the owl and goats that would have been more familiar. Almost buried among them is the most important figure in the composition, the youthful rider. The rosette behind him emphasizes his significance. He recalls the man between the lions on the Gorgon Painter's dinos in the Louvre.[11] Without an attribute to identify him as a particular mythological hero, we may perhaps think of him as an aristocratic youth, setting out boldly among heroic monsters to prove his *areté*. In some ways, he stands in the same relationship to them as do the Homeric heroes to

the animals in Homer's similes. Yet, unlike the hieratic images of gods among animals, such as Artemis *Potnia Theron*, Mistress of Animals, the relative place of humanity in the grander scheme is one of utter insignificance. Something of the same foreboding occurs on some early lekythoi of Deianeira type, some of which were decorated by the Gorgon Painter.[12] The same contrast is emphasized on the contemporary pediment of the temple of Artemis at Corfu.[13]

—JG

### BIBLIOGRAPHY

*Walters Handbook* 1936, 28; Papaspyridi-Karusu 1937, 123–24, pl. 65; Beazley 1944, 40, no. 12; Richter 1949, 6, fig. 6; Hill 1950, 96; *ABV* 9.18, 697; Scheibler 1961, 19, fig. 20 and 28, fig. 29; Karagiorga 1970, 36 n. 10, 154, no. VI 5; *Paralipomena* 7; Callipolitis-Feytmans 1974, 63–67, 309 no. 1, pl. 14.1; Floren 1977, 42–43, pl. 3.2; Markoe and Serwint 1985, 23, no. 16; *LIMC* 4 (1988), 291, no. 36, pl. 165, s.v. "Gorgo, Gorgones" (Krauskopf and Dahlinger); Beazley 1989, 3; Hofstetter 1990, 80 no. A 50.

### NOTES

1 Acquired by Henry Walters from Joseph Brummer in 1927.

2 Markoe 1985.

3 Kunze 1931; Bol 1989.

4 Hom. *Il.* 18.478–607. Cf. also the shield of Herakles in the Hes. *Scut.* 139–317.

5 *ABV* 9–10.18–21. On the Gorgon Painter, see *ABV* 8–13, 679; *Paralipomena* 7–9; Beazley 1989, 2–4; Rolley 1961; Scheibler 1961; Bakir 1978; Kilinski 1978; Grazia Marzi 1981; Hamilton-Margos 1985, 77-85; Williams 1986; Clark 1992.

6 *ABV* 9.19; Callipolitis-Feytmans 1974, pl. 15.4.

7 *ABV* 9–10.18, 19, and 21. For a different view, see Callipolitis-Feytmans 1974, 309–10.

8 Würzburg 167: *ABV* 105.135; Callipolitis-Feytmans 1974, 311, no. 14, pl. 18, fig. 20.

9 Dinos by the Gorgon Painter, Louvre E 874: *ABV* 8.1; Simon and Hirmer 1976, pls. 47–48. Dinoi by Sophilos: *ABV* 39–40.12–16; *Paralipomena* 19; Bakir 1981, passim; Williams 1983. To these, now add Harvard 1995.18.23 (Paul 1997, 23, no. 1, 46). For Sophilos as a "follower" of the Gorgon Painter, see *ABV* 37–38; as a "pupil," Williams 1985, 28. Papaspyridi-Karusu (1937) has not been followed in suggesting that the Gorgon Painter was an early phase of Sophilos. D. von Bothmer's proposal was first mentioned in a lecture at Oxford, February 15, 1999.

10 *ABV* 5.6–9.

11 Louvre E 874: *ABV* 8.1; detail, Scheibler 1961, 12, fig. 14. Cf. also a fragment, Hildesheim 1805: *ABV* 10.29.

12 Mertens 1993.

13 Rodenwaldt 1938.

# 83

# Aryballos in the Shape of a Gorgon

**Greek, Rhodian, ca. 580–570 B.C.**
**Ceramic**
**Height 7 cm., width of base 5.8 cm., diameter of mouth 2.05 cm.**
**Museum of Fine Arts, Boston, Henry Lillie Pierce Fund (99.510)**

### CONDITION

**The fabric is pale reddish brown. The vase is unbroken, but the rim is chipped. It is misfired on the proper left side, and the surface is covered with a fine web of root marks.**

Modeled in the shape of a Gorgon bust, this flask has a raised spout with a disk mouth-plate encircled on its upper surface by glazed dots. At the back is a small, flat handle, which once may have been threaded with a cord for hanging or affixing a stopper. The underside of the vase is undecorated.

The Gorgon's dark, reddish brown hair hangs before her bare shoulders in modeled locks, three on each side, and cascades down her back in a thick mass with gently waving ends. Her round face is framed by a teeming mass of ten serpents rendered in relief; some of these preserve red, white, and black painted dots along the length of their bodies. Writhing snakes emerge from the sides of her face and rise over her forehead, while others slither across her cheeks and chin to form a beard. Mouths open, they are ready to sink their venomous fangs into anyone foolhardy enough to approach the odious creature.

The Gorgon's widely arching eyebrows nearly meet on the bridge of her broad, flat nose. Her slightly projecting, almond-shaped eyes are outlined with glaze, and between the brows and eyes, a line of dilute glaze contours the eye socket. On the eyes themselves, the dark pupils are overlaid with red and the sclerae are painted white. Her lips are drawn back in a menacing leer that causes deep wrinkles to form across her cheeks and above her upper lip. Framed by long, sinister tusks, a red tongue lolls from her mouth.

Like the other, relatively small number of surviving Gorgon aryballoi, this vessel was made on Rhodes.[1] It exhibits features that distinguish the so-called East Greek plastic vases from their Corinthian counterparts, including the method of manufacture in a two-part mold, the addition of a wheel-made spout and disk mouthplate, and the use of incision and color in its decoration.[2] It would seem that the Gorgon was a popular subject in Rhodes, but it did not find favor among Corinthian potters of plastic vessels.[3]

The most frequently represented demon in antiquity,[4] the deadly Gorgon is a decidedly odd subject for a conventional cosmetic container. Although her iconographic ancestry can be traced back to the Near East, like so many supernatural creatures adopted by the Greeks during the Orientalizing period, she was fundamentally altered and Hellenized in the process.[5] According to Greek tradition, Gorgo, or Medusa, was one of three sisters born to the sea deities Phorkys and Keto, or, alternatively, was the daughter of Earth, Gaia. In time Medusa became quite lovely, but in her earliest manifestations she was, as shown here, a hideous monster whose frightening countenance could turn all who looked upon her into stone. She was hunted down and slain by the clever Perseus, who used the reflective surface of a shield as a mirror to avert her deadly gaze while severing her head. The blood that spurted from the left vein in her neck was said to be capable of harming mortals, while the blood that gushed from the other side could heal the sick and resurrect the dead.[6]

It is unclear whether the subjects of such plastic vases were related to their contents or use.[7] If they were, then perhaps the choice of the Gorgon's image for this precious little aryballos, like the later popularity of her mask on the interior of drinking cups where it warned about the ill effects of over-imbibing, symbolized the gradual taming of evil Medusa and the transformation of her formidable powers from the ominous to the protective, to aid rather than injure mankind. This vase may have held a special potion for warding off illness, harm, or evil, or contained oil used to anoint the bodies of the dead.

—KM

**BIBLIOGRAPHY**

Forman Sale Catalogue 1899, no. 273; Fairbanks 1928, 175, no. 498, pl. XLIX; *CVA* Oxford 2, Great Britain 9, 85; Lane 1971, 29, pl. 21c; Ducat 1966, 52, D.1, pl. VIII.1; *LIMC* 4 (1988), 292, no. 53, 319, pl. 167, s.v. "Gorgo, Gorgones" (Krauskopf).

**NOTES**

1 Ducat 1966, 51–54, pls. VII.4–6, VIII.1–2. This vase belongs to his Gorgoneia Type D, which is typologically distinctive for its inclusion of the shoulders, the way in which the details are accentuated, the almost straight fangs, the shape of its eyes, the presence of hair rather than serpents hanging before the Gorgon's shoulders, and the vertical groove down the middle of its relatively short tongue. Ducat gave it a date of 590–580 B.C. There is a similar Gorgon aryballos in Cophenagen (Ny Carlsberg 3300: Walter-Karydi 1985, 10, fig. 11). In addition to Types A–D, which were decorated in "vase technique," with dark glaze,

added color, and incision, Ducat also noted the existence of two other kinds of gorgoneion vessels. The first of these was based on an example once in the collection of Eric de Kolb (Basel, MuM, Auktion 26, October 5, 1963, *Kunstwerke der Antike*, no. 76, pl. 23; Basel, MuM, Auktion 60, September 21, 1982, *Kunstwerke der Antike*, no. 15, pl. 5), which was decorated in "terra-cotta technique," with slip and sometimes matte paint (see also *CVA* Oxford 2, Great Britain 9, 85). This Gorgon has protruding eyes and ears, and incised locks of hair at the back, and most of the upper torso is represented. A very similar vessel, although lacking the disk mouth that is characteristic of Rhodian plastic vases, was formerly in the Swiss art market: Basel, *Werke Antike Kleinkunst*, H.A.C., *Kunst der Antike*, Katalog 2 (December 1990), no. 1.

2   For a summary of East Greek plastic vases, see Biers, Gerhardt, and Braniff 1994, 3.

3   Amyx 1988, 516, 529–30.

4   *LIMC* 4, 288, s.v. "Gorgo, Gorgones."

5   Burkert 1984, 81.

6   Apollod. *Bibl.* 3.10.3.

7   For the significance and use of plastic vases, see Biers, Gerhardt, and Braniff 1994, 5. For the subject matter of plastic vases in general, see ibid. 10, and for East Greek pottery in particular, Walter-Karydi 1985, 7–16.

## 84

# Running Gorgon

**Greek, ca. 540 B.C.**
**Bronze**
**Height 8.85 cm., width 7.8 cm., depth 1.5 cm.**
**Yale University Art Gallery, gift of**
**Cornelius C. Vermeule III, in memory of**
**Emily Townsend Vermeule (2002.95.2)**

CONDITION
**The piece originally was an attachment for a large bronze vessel, which is not preserved. The figure is complete except for a small loss in the left snake; it is otherwise unbroken but for the rejoined tang extending from the proper left foot. A green and black patina covers the figure, with traces of a black copper oxide incrustation remaining in unexposed areas.**

This bronze figure of a running Gorgon apparently decorated the base of a handle of a large bronze volute-krater. Solid cast as a single piece with minimal modeling of the back, the figure was attached to a small platform, possibly in the form of an ionic capital, at the base of the handle. The Gorgon runs to the right, her legs and lower body in profile, her winged boots speeding her along. She wears a short chiton, with a deep central pleat in the skirt and short cap sleeves that stretch as she extends her arms outward. Two snakes form the belt, which she ties in a knot as the snakes coil up her arms. Her two sickle-shaped wings, formed as a single span across her back, extend from her shoulders, spreading wide and curling upward at their ends. Long corkscrew locks on each side of her face pass behind her prominent ears and fall nearly to her waist, while a triple row of curls frames her forehead. Her face is characteristically wide and mask-like, featuring long fearsome fangs, strong teeth, and an ugly distended tongue.

Gorgons are best known from the story of Perseus and Medusa, but their mythology extends beyond that single episode.[1] Born as the three daughters of the sea god Phorkys and the sea monster Keto, the Gorgons were, according to some ancient sources, turned into horrible

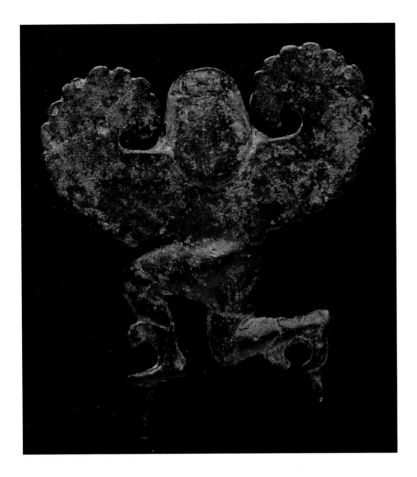

monsters by Athena, as punishment for Medusa's having lain with Poseidon in a grove sacred to the goddess. Medusa, at least, had the power to turn to stone anyone who gazed upon her hideous face. Perseus, sent by King Polydektes to fetch Medusa's head, succeeded with the help of Athena and Hermes in beheading the monster. Vase-paintings of the subject show Perseus looking away from Medusa to avoid being turned to stone as he grasps her hair and beheads her with his sickle-shaped sword. With the head in a bag and wearing Hermes' winged boots, the hero flies to Athena and delivers the head. Though separated from Medusa's body, the head retains the power to petrify, and even a goddess is not immune: a bell-krater by the Tarpoley Painter in the Museum of Fine Arts, Boston, shows Athena holding Medusa's head aloft while she and Perseus look at its reflection, properly upside down, in Athena's polished shield resting on the ground.[2] Athena later wore Medusa's head on her aegis as an apotropaic device. Other vases

show Perseus's flight, in some cases pursued by Medusa's sisters (cat. no. 81). They, too, have wings and winged boots, as does this bronze Gorgon, but Perseus has the added advantage of Hermes' winged hat, and he escapes.

The running Gorgon of the Perseus myth becomes the archetypical Gorgon figure of Archaic Greek art, second in popularity only to the separate image of the Gorgon's mask-like face. Like all Archaic Greek representations of Gorgons, the face of this bronze is frontal, emphasizing its horrible mask-like quality and its evil powers. Such frontality is otherwise rare in Archaic Greek art.[3] The petrifying power retained by the disembodied head of Medusa evolved into a power to ward off evil that was shared by all images of Gorgon's heads (gorgoneia), whether worn by Athena on her aegis or painted on a drinking cup to ward off the evils of over-consumption. It was used by warriors as a shield device, often and at least as early as the *Iliad*, where on Agamemnon's shield "circled in the midst of all was the blank-eyed face of the Gorgon with her stare of horror, and Fear was inscribed on it, and Terror."[4] Gorgons appear in monumental sculpture both in the Perseus myth and as central pedimental figures and acroteria on temples, where they served an apotropaic function. Gorgon heads as antefixes (cat. nos. 88, 89) must have served a similar purpose.

The running Gorgon in the round is among the least common of the types of bronze Gorgons that function as attachments for bronze vessels. Most popular is the mask-like gorgoneion, i.e., the head alone. These occur frequently at the base of the handle on hydriae and amphorae.[5] Second—and far more rare than the head type—is the bust type (cat. no. 86), in which the Gorgon is shown to the waist, arms and wings intact, with snakes emanating from the lower corners in place of the Gorgon's lower body and legs. This type occurs as part of the handles of large volute-kraters, nestled between the flanges at the base, the snakes often extending backward onto the body of the vessel.[6] Outstanding examples of these were found in the so-called tombs of the chieftains in Trebenishte, Macedonia, dated to the mid-sixth century B.C.[7] Rarest is the frontal kneeling Gorgon that appears above each of the clawed feet on the early-sixth-century Laconian stand (*hypokraterion*) for a volute-krater from Trebenishte tomb VIII.[8]

Bronze running Gorgons similar to this one have been found still attached to volute-krater handles, and others have been found separate from the vessels.[9] Details of these Gorgons vary: some have four wings instead of two; some do not show the long curls in front; some do not show the central pleat in the skirt of the chiton; some are barefoot; some do not show fangs; few show the snaky belt and even fewer show the Gorgon tying it. Some are more finished on the back. Some were attached to their vessels with rivets. Find spots indicate that the type was known in the Black Sea area, Greece (Attica, Corinth, Isthmia, Laconia, Olympia), and Magna Graecia.[10] Stylistic similarities to these examples, as well as parallels in Greek vase-painting, suggest an origin for the Yale Gorgon in Greece, most likely in Laconia, Corinth, Attica, or northern Greece, and a date of about 540 B.C.[11]

—SBM

**BIBLIOGRAPHY**
Unpublished.

**NOTES**

1  On Gorgons, see *LIMC* 4 (1988), s.v. "Gorgo, Gorgones" (Krauskopf and Dahlinger).

2  Boston 1970.237: Trendall and Cambitoglou 1978, 48, no. 3; Padgett et al. 1993, 66–67, no. 10.

3  See Korshak 1987.

4  Hom. *Il.* 11.36–37, trans. R. Lattimore.

5  E.g., Stibbe 2000b, 73, fig. 45, 75, fig.

6  Stibbe 2000b, 67, fig. 40.

7  Stibbe 2000b, 62, figs. 37–38, tomb I. Another, from Campania, is Munich 4262: Maass 1979, 50–53, no. 29.

8  Stibbe 2000b, 89, figs. 56–57, 94–95, figs. 60, 62.

9  On volute-kraters and these handle attachments, see Gaunt 2002. Examples, as collected by Gaunt (2002, 641–42), Jantzen (1937, 70), and Stibbe (2001), include: Athens, Nat. Mus. 6113 (from Olympia); Athens, Nat. Mus. 10703 (from near Phoiniki in Laconia); Boston 98.656; Paris, Louvre Br 4467 (from Cilicia); St. Petersburg DN 1870, 1/1 (from Martonoša); Weimar, Goethe Nationalmuseum; Isthmia Museum; and examples from Olympia and Perachora.

10  See, most recently, especially for the Greek finds, Stibbe 2001, 20–24, figs. 27–32.

11  I am grateful to a number of colleagues for these suggestions, expressed in personal communications, about the origins and date of the bronze. Parallels in terracotta and stone from South Italy and Sicily also support this date.

## 85

# Handle with Gorgoneion

Greek, Laconian, ca. 600–590 B.C.
Bronze
Height 23.5 cm., width 16.5 cm. (lions),
approximate original diameter of rim 11.4 cm.
Princeton University Art Museum, museum purchase, Carl Otto von Kienbusch Jr. Memorial Collection Fund (y1988–1)

CONDITION
The two lions are reattached, with minor restorations at the joins; the handle otherwise is unbroken and well preserved. It has a dark patina, almost black, tending to green in places.[1]

This robust handle consists of a twisted, hollow-cast grip, an upper attachment with two couchant rams, each lying on a base in the shape of a snake, and a lower attachment with a monstrous human head in relief, a gorgoneion, flanked by two couchant lions. The grip and the animals are filled with a clay core. Underneath the rams are two circular flanges with bronze rivets that attached to the neck of the vessel, while at the lower point of attachment, the bodies of the lions are pierced with an additional two rivets. Inside the handle there is a rusted iron pin that may have served as a fitting for the core material.[2] On the reverse side of the gorgoneion, a capital letter *A* was scratched in antiquity.

Bronze handles of this kind, cluttered with snakes, rams, lions and with a central device in the form of a gorgoneion, palmette, or another motif, are quite common within a well-defined group of early-sixth-century Laconian bronze vessels.[3] Within the range of possibilities of that group, this handle makes even a modest appearance, the only exceptional features being the twisted grip, the placement of the lions and rams, and the narrow diameter of the neck, which can be derived from the curve made by the rams at the upper attachment to the missing rim. Both features return with a group of narrow-necked amphorae of later date (ca. 560–545 B.C.), which still range within the orbit of the Laconian production of bronze vessels, suggesting that this handle also was

designed for an amphora.[4] The Princeton handle, therefore, may be a prototype for this later development. An example of comparably rich decoration, this time being the prototype for a later group of bronze narrow-necked hydriae, is in the Archaeological Museum of Sofia.[5] It has a vertical handle equipped with a similar gorgoneion, flanked by snakes, whereas the upper attachment shows couchant lions. This comparison only stresses the extraordinary nature of the Princeton handle.

There are a few more arguments in favor of the supposition that this handle belonged to an amphora, beginning with the letter *A* scratched at the back of the gorgoneion: such letters were used by ancient bronze workers to secure the handle in the right position on the vessel, in case of transport in separate units to distant destinations, or for other reasons.[6] In this case, the letter *A* would be of no use if there would not have been a second handle bearing the letter *B*, as may be expected with an amphora; it would be pointless to scratch such a letter on the back of the sole vertical handle of a hydria. Second, the possible counterpart of the handle under discussion actually turned up in the art market and was acquired by the Princeton University Art Museum in 1990.[7] It is only a fragment (fig. 1), but there can be no doubt that it came from the same mold as the complete handle.[8] This does not prove, of course, that we are dealing with two handles belonging to the same amphora, but at least the word "probably" should be appropriate here.

In 1989, in a grave at the necropolis of the ancient harbor town of Pydna, on the east coast of the Greek mainland, a bronze hydria was found, decorated at the lower attachment of its vertical handle with a gorgoneion that shows exactly the same features as the two on the Princeton handles.[9] This hydria is also otherwise equipped with rich figural decoration, placing it in the same group of Laconian bronze vessels to which we have assigned the Princeton handles. Because of the Pydna connection and because of its narrow-necked shape, the Princeton amphora, as we may call it now, can be associated with the northern trade route that extended from Laconia through the Aegean Sea to the Illyrian princes of the Balkans.[10]

One may wonder where the bronze worker responsible for the two handles at Princeton got the idea of

transforming the usual flattish shape of the grip into a twisted one. Such handles are found on clay amphorae as early as the eighth century B.C. in other production centers,[11] from whence the idea may have spread to Laconia, where it would have appealed to the experimental spirit characteristic of Laconian bronze workers at the end of the seventh century B.C.[12] This spirit betrays itself also in the positioning of the rams and the lions: their canonical places in the later sixth century, on hydriae and oinochoai, would be the other way around, with the lions at the upper attachment and the rams at the lower.[13]

An early date for the Princeton handles is also suggested by the shapes of the bodies of the animals: they are compactly modeled instead of lengthened, as in the middle of the century; the rams, moreover, have plain coats, whereas the canonic rams of the second quarter of the century show cross-hatching or even a plastically detailed rendering of the fleece.[14]

FIGURE I

Whatever their place, the animals were likely added to the central motif of the gorgoneion as protective, evil-averting devices. Rams were noted for "their sturdy belligerence and steadfast resistance," lions for their being "emblems of bravery, ferocity and majesty."[15] On the Princeton handles they all look toward the viewer, as if they would warn us against stealing or any other evildoing. In this respect, the Gorgon head or gorgoneion also had a long tradition in ancient art. In the seventh and sixth centuries it seems to have had a connotation as the quintessence of ugliness, the contrast and reversal of the beloved features of beauty. But by the end of the sixth century a process of humanizing starts, which ends up, from about 450 onward, in a beautiful female face framed by snakes and wings.[16]

The Princeton gorgoneion, with its horns, its flat, wrinkled nose, its broad mouth with tusks and pointed beard, is still the early Archaic Laconian type. Its fierceness seems to be mitigated only by one detail: the corners of its horrible mouth are pulled up so as to suggest a smile. But is this a smile at all? If so, it would be a sarcastic one, jeering at the viewer with a dangling tongue!

—CMS

**BIBLIOGRAPHY**

*Record* 48.1 (1989): 53—54 (illus.); Stibbe 1994b, 93—99, fig. 13; Stibbe 1996, 362; Stibbe 2000b, 74, 107, fig. 47, 165, no. 1.

**NOTES**

1 The handle was examined and conserved by the conservation laboratory of the Harvard University Art Museums in 1989. It originally was in three pieces, both lions having broken off. An analysis of the corrosion layers (black cassiterite and green malachite) found them to be consistent with an ancient date and long burial. This conclusion was supported by the thermoluminescence analysis of the clay core, conducted by the Research Laboratory for Archaeology at Oxford, which yielded an age of between 1900 and 2900 years. The metal itself is leaded bronze with the percentage of lead varying locally from 0.5 percent to 3.0 percent.

2 Similar iron pins were found in the cores of the side handles of an early Laconian bronze hydria, now in New York (Met. 1995.92); see Sommer 1994, 104, fig. 7.

3 The Grächwil-Treia-group of hydriae: see Stibbe 1992, 20—30, figs. 32—39; Stibbe 2000b, 111—15, figs. 68—72.

4 Stibbe 2000b, 166, nos. 3—6.

5 From Trebenishte, tomb III: see Stibbe 2000b, 61—62, 72—74, figs. 45—46, 163, no. l.

6 They are found, for example, on the backs of the appliqués on the neck of the bronze volute-kraters from Vix and Trebenishte: Stibbe 2000b, 59 n. 16.

7 Princeton University Art Museum, museum purchase, gift of Joyce von Bothmer (y1990-83); height 9.8 cm.; Hesperia Arts Auction Ltd., New York, November 21, 1990, no. 7; Stibbe 1994b, 93, 97–99, fig. 14; Stibbe 2000b, 74–75, no. 1, fig. 48.

8 The fragment is so incrusted and oxidized as to make it impossible to detect the letter B, which we would expect to be scratched on the reverse of the gorgoneion.

9 Vokotopoulou 1997, 117–19, pls. 105–8, with comments on pp. 246–47; Stibbe, 2000, 102–11, figs 63–66.

10 On this trade route, see Stibbe 2003, chapters 8–9.

11 See, e.g., the Italo-Corinthian Geometric amphora from Carthage in Gehrig and Niemeyer 1990, 200, no. 169. For later examples, one may mention the handles cited in n. 3 above, and a series of Corinthian late-sixth-century beaked jugs: Vokotopoulou 1975, 167 and passim.

12 See, e.g., Stibbe 1996, 361–64 and passim.

13 I know of only one other instance, a hydria handle in Paris (Louvre Br 2624), dated ca. 600 B.C., on which the rams are placed above, the lions below: Stibbe 1994b, 91 with fig. 18; Stibbe 1996, 360–64, pl. 27.1. For the canonical positioning, see Stibbe 1996, 362 nn. 35, 36.

14 On the development of the ram type, see Stibbe 1994a, 95; for the lions, Stibbe 1996, 362. For a more precise dating of the gorgoneia, cf. the other Laconian bronze gorgoneia of the same generation: one at Harvard (Mitten and Doeringer 1967, no. 71; Stibbe 1992, 29, 56, no. G6; Stibbe 1994b, 95–96, fig. 15); one from a narrow-necked hydria in Sofia, already mentioned above (see n. 5); and a series of superb Laconian terracotta Gorgons (Floren and Herfort 1983, 23–26). As a result, the Princeton gorgoneia are put on the same chronological level as the terra-cotta Gorgons, that is ca. 600–590, followed by the Sofia handle ca. 590–580, and the Harvard handle 580–570 (Stibbe 1994b, 93–95).

15 Mitten 1981, 80–81.

16 On the subject in general, see Krauskopf 1988, 322–23. On the Laconian output, see Pipili 1987, 14–17, with further literature; Rocco 1995, 5–8; Stibbe 2001, 20–24.

## 86

# Volute-Krater Handle with Gorgon

**Greek, possibly northern, ca. 550–525 B.C.**
**Bronze**
**Height 22.8 cm., width 10.7 cm., depth 12.2 cm., height of Gorgon 12.6 cm., width of Gorgon 16.1 cm., width of handle flange at sides 4.4 cm.**
**Collection of James E. and Elizabeth J. Ferrell**

CONDITION
**The Gorgon's right wing is bent; the left wing is broken away. The patina is a uniform dark gray, with patches of green and dispersed areas of red cuprite. There are additional areas of chalky white surface deposits. In several areas, the corrosion layers have worn through to reveal the bronze below.**

This elaborate handle, a tour de force of lost-wax casting, is one of a pair originally attached to a massive bronze volute-krater. The base is decorated in relief with the head and bust of a frontally posed winged Gorgon. The Gorgon uses both of her hands to support her breasts from the sides and below. The fingers are extended and held together, with thumbs raised. Her bent elbows protrude symmetrically on either side of her torso. She wears a cloak over a sleeved garment covered by an incised scale pattern,[1] terminated at the bottom by a raised ledge. There are running zigzags above the single incised line at the edge of the cloak and below the incised double neckline. A similar zigzag appears on the raised ledge at the bottom of the bust. The Gorgon's head is surrounded by a flatly rendered, wiglike hairstyle, parted near the middle of the forehead, from whence a series of deep diagonal furrows run left and right, ending behind the ears.

Framing the face and emerging from behind the ears are two flat masses of hair, which fall in front of the shoulders and end in straight lines above the breasts. These masses are embellished with parallel rows of vertical incisions marked by horizontal striations.[2] The Gorgon's round face is creased at the center of the forehead. Above the lidded, almond-shaped eyes, the arched eyebrows are decorated with hatching. The characteristic grimace is without fangs, revealing the tongue hanging down onto the cleft chin.

The preserved right wing curves up under a hanging palmette and is divided into a series of sickle-shaped sections suggestive of feathers. The snakes once present at the lower sides of the figure, which supported the handle against the shoulder of the vessel, have been broken off.[3] The edges of the handle flanges are ornamented with a beaded molding, and on the sloping inner and straight

outer sides there are tongues with double outlines. The handle's strap has a central raised band flanked by two recessed panels with incised zigzags along their edges. The strut at the bottom of the handle's left flange still retains the rivet used to attach the handle to the rim.

The handle was once part of a large bronze volute-krater of a type first produced in Laconia, the Spartan homeland, in the period 600–575 B.C.[4] The closest comparisons are the two volute-kraters from Trebenishte, Macedonia: one in Belgrade, the other in Sofia.[5] Unlike the earlier Vix krater, the Gorgons on the handles of the Trebenishte kraters seem to have lost their function as supports and have become purely decorative.[6] The Trebenishte kraters have been variously attributed by scholars to Laconian, Corinthian, and South Italian workshops.[7] The krater in Sofia is of much higher quality than the otherwise similar krater in Belgrade. The

Gorgon handle under discussion is larger than those from Trebenishte and appears to be a provincial variation of a Laconian prototype, perhaps of a slightly later date than the Trebenishte examples.[8] The different treatment of the Gorgon's facial features and hairstyle, as well as the unique gesture of the figure holding her breasts, clearly distinguish it from the Trebenishte Gorgon handles. Details of subsidiary decoration and incision confirm the impression that this handle was produced in a workshop informed by the influences seen in the Trebenishte kraters, with some variations.

According to Hesiod, the Gorgons were three sisters — Stheno, Euryale, and Medusa[9] — who lived in the extreme west, near the Hesperides and beyond Okeanos. Their sisters were the Graiai, who shared a single eye and tooth among them.[10] Perseus was directed by Polydektes to bring back the head of Medusa, a dangerous task made possible by several divine gifts from Hermes and Athena: a sickle, a cap of invisibility, winged shoes, and a bag to hold the severed head. After Perseus decapitated Medusa, she gave birth to the children conceived from her union with the god Poseidon: Chrysaor and the winged horse Pegasos.[11]

Gorgons begin to appear in Greek art in the early seventh century B.C. and were popular on painted vases, architectural sculpture in terracotta and stone, and on bronze vessels and armor. Their often-cited ability to ward off evil, possibly related to their ability to turn men into stone, made them a welcome decorative addition with many applications.

—MB

### BIBLIOGRAPHY

Gaunt 2002, 645, XI no. 17.

### NOTES

1 The scale pattern is seen on bronze caryatid figures, sphinxes as well as Gorgons. See Raubitschek 1998, 32–33 n. 69.

2 Cf. the hairstyle of the terracotta antefix with a satyr face in the exhibition (cat. no. 59), said to be from Taras (modern Taranto), a Laconian settlement in South Italy.

3 These snakes may comprise the belt of the Gorgon Medusa, rather than her legs (Hes. *Scut.* 229–37).

4 Stibbe 2000b, 59. For bronze volute-kraters, see Joffroy 1979; Hitzl 1982; Stibbe 2000b; Gaunt 2002.

5 Belgrade krater: Br 174/I; height 76.0 cm., ca. 520 B.C.; found in grave VIII at Trebenishte. See Vulić 1930, 296–99; Rolley 1981, 325, fig. 8; Hitzl 1982, 266–70, pls. 24–26, no. 17; Gaunt 2002, 635–36, XI no. 6; Stibbe 2003, 85, figs. 48–49. Sofia krater: no accession no., height 68 cm., ca. 530 B.C.; found in 1918 in Grave I at Trebenishte. See Hitzl 1982, 262–65, pls. 21–23a, no. 16; Gaunt 2002, 644–45, XI no. 15; Stibbe 2003, 75–79, figs. 33–38. For a notice of its discovery, see *AJA* 36 (1932): 250–52, fig. 6. For an overview of the Trebenishte finds, see Stibbe 2000b, 57–101; Stibbe 2003.

6 A point made by Stibbe 2000b, 63.

7 For a recent discussion see Stibbe 2000b, 63–68, 88–98.1

8 Suggested by J. Gaunt in a letter dated July 9, 2001.

9 Hes. *Theog.* 274–83.

10 Aesch. *Prometheus Desmotes* 792–97.

11 For the myth of Perseus and the Gorgon Medusa, see Apollod. *Bibl.* 2.4.1–5.

# 87

# Fragmentary Relief with Gorgon

**Greek, ca. 550–500 B.C.**
**Bronze**
**Height 24.7 cm., preserved width 17.2 cm.**
**Museum of Fine Arts, Boston, Henry Lillie Pierce Fund (98.652)1**

### CONDITION
**Much of the relief is missing; most of the proper right half of the Gorgon's face is preserved, minus the nose, but only the upper left quadrant of the surrounding plaque. There are small tears along the edges, and the surface is cracked and abraded. The patina is dark green with patches of incrustation.**

The fragmentary hammered and incised bronze relief was originally rectangular in form. Two nail holes are preserved: one near the upper edge and the other by the left edge. The original left edge is preserved, bent back in a uniform, curved arc, presumably in order to fit the plate onto another surface that terminated along this side. The relief depicts a gorgoneion, the frontally facing head of the Gorgon Medusa. Much of the proper right side of the head is preserved, with Medusa's well-known features worked into the sheet bronze with precision and fine detail. Her expression, more grimace than smile, is made more horrifying by the opposing curved fangs protruding past the border of her lips. The expected lolling tongue was in the missing section at the right. The hammered relief gives greater volume to her head and right ear than the five snakes that grow from her scalp like strands of hair. She probably also had a beard of flame-like locks, as suggested by other sixth-century Greek hammered sheet bronze reliefs from Olympia and South Italy.[2]

The fragment preserves five snakes in profile with open mouths exposing rows of teeth and extended tongues. Their bodies are covered with incised scale pattern up to their bellies, which are distinguished by rows of paired hatchings. They rise from the top of Medusa's head in S-shaped curves, and one appears to curl around her ear, its head facing left. A smaller snake is delicately incised under her ear, facing right. Two rows of incised

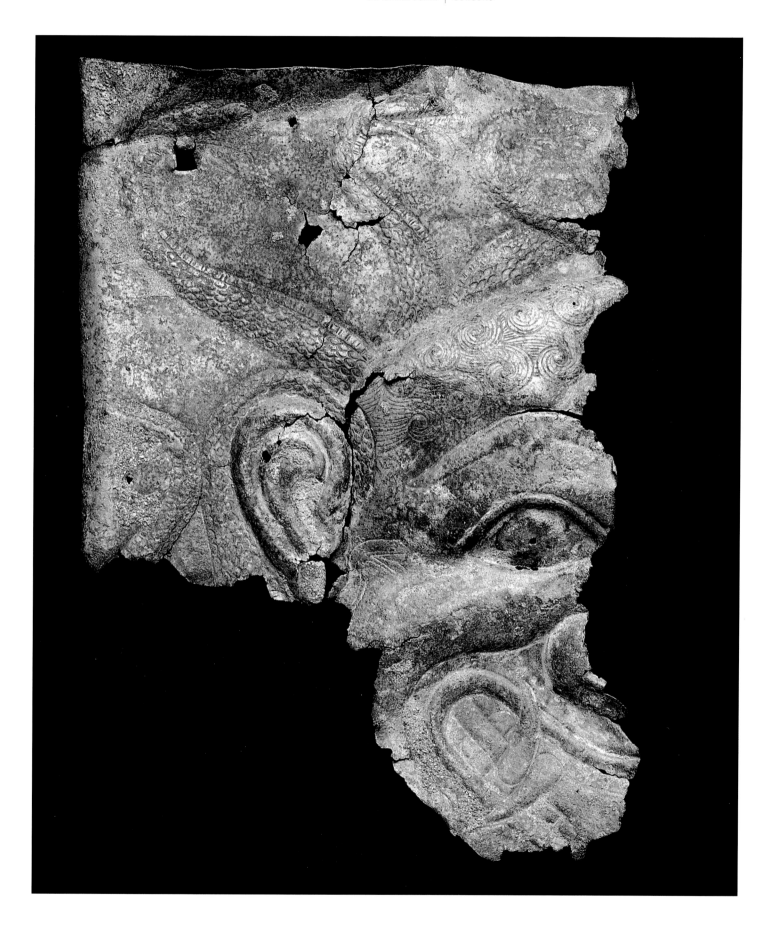

spiral curls with punched central bosses cover most of her short forehead. The thick eyebrow mirrors the sweeping line of the upper eyelid over the almond-shaped eye. Only the right nostril of the nose remains.

The function of the relief is unclear. Its shape and rolled-back left edge do not suggest a shield appliqué. Decorated seventh-century bronze sheets of similar dimensions from the Athenian Acropolis were used as facings for massive tripod legs.[3] Also from the Acropolis is a very different bronze cutout figure of a Gorgon, perhaps used to adorn a temple.[4] Most other early Greek bronze plaques are smaller, like those from the sanctuary of Aphrodite at Miletos,[5] and a related group in the Princeton University Art Museum, which have been interpreted as revetments and independent votives.[6]

—MB

BIBLIOGRAPHY

Comstock and Vermeule 1971, 450–51, no. 660.

NOTES

1 From the E. P. Warren Collection, purchased at Xylokastro in the Peloponnese, near Sicyon.

2 For example, on a shield band from Olympia (Kunze 1950, 28, 71–72, XXVIz) and a horse pectoral in Naples (5715: De Caro, Borriello, and Cassani 1996, 243).

3 Touloupa 1991, 242–54.

4 Touloupa 1969, pl. XX.

5 Brize 2002; cf. esp. the crude Gorgon on a votive shield, p. 566, fig. 11.

6 Childs 2001a. The gorgoneion does not appear among the Boston plaques.

# 88

# Antefix with Gorgoneion

**Western (South Italian) Greek, probably Tarentine, ca. 500–480 B.C.**
**Terracotta[1]**
**Height 17.5 cm., width 26 cm., depth at base 1.7 cm., depth at top with remnant of cover tile 4 cm.**
**Princeton University Art Museum, museum purchase (y1931–13)**

CONDITION

If the antefix once had painted decoration, it has worn off. The lower left corner and the curving periphery at the upper right side are damaged. Missing to the right are the snake's head, the outside of the Gorgon's ear, the upper surfaces of the two lowest locks of hair, and a portion of the narrow half-round molding that marks the antefix's curving edge. The cover tile formerly attached to the back is lost.

Although a monstrous appearance is emphasized, naturalistic anatomical features such as the nose, the ears (though placed too high), and the tear ducts at the inner corners of the eyes suggest a date in the late sixth to the early fifth century B.C. for this gorgoneion antefix. Unlike its Etrusco-Campanian counterpart (cat. no. 89), the stump of the neck is not represented at the bottom. The tusk-like locks below the cheeks and chin belong to the Gorgon's beard, as is made clear by a comparison with the flame-shaped locks of the gorgoneion antefix of catalogue number 89. The snakes that emerge from the jowls and curl down and away before recurving up and out again, just below the lobe of each ear, are an enduring convention, since they continue to flank heads of Medusa long after Classical humanism had metamorphosed her from the Archaic monster seen in this example into the face of a beautiful woman with disheveled hair.[2]

Remnants of a cover tile of Laconian type appear at the reverse, flush with the curving edge of the antefix. Since the cover tile's bottom edge ends 4.5 centimeters from the bottom of the antefix, the antefix must have overhung to that depth the edges of the adjoining eaves

tiles against which it rested, simultaneously concealing and covering the seam between them. Also on the reverse are horizontal striations, the marks of tooling used to smooth out the clay and feather it into the wall of the accompanying cover tile (see the architectural drawing in the Glossary).

The lack of large grit inclusions in the clay imparts a crisp, linear clarity to the low relief. Usually identified as Greek, this technique contrasts with the lack of plastic precision produced by the large-grained grog that permeates the clay of the accompanying Etrusco-Campanian example.[3] Numerous antefixes produced in different molds of the same series have been found at Taranto.[4]

—JFK

**BIBLIOGRAPHY**

Ridgway and Pinney 1979, 240–41, no. 117.

**NOTES**

1  The antefix is made from light red clay (Munsell 2.5YR, 6/4) with small, rounded, naturally occurring inclusions, shading to buff at the surface. Covered with a light creamy slip (7.5YR, 8/2), its many small pits were occasioned by bubbles that burst.

2  Laviosa 1954, 228, 235–43, pls. LXXII–LXXIII; Floren 1977, 116–217.

3  Lulof 1996, 175–82, nos. 278, 290; Kenfield 1997, 107–11.

4  Koch 1912, 11–14, fig. 64; Wuilleumier 1939, 425–26, pl. 38.2; Richter 1953, 30, pl. 19d–e; Higgins 1954, 336, 341, pl. 171, no. 1251; Laviosa 1954, 229–35, pl. LXVIII.1–5; Mollard-Besques 1954, 59, 74, pl. 47; van Buren 1973, 142–43, no. 28, fig. 58; Herdejürgen 1978, 87, no. C2; *LIMC* 4 (1988), 293, no. 67, pl. 169, s.v. "Gorgo, Gorgones" (Krauskopf and Dahlinger).

# 89

## Antefix with Gorgoneion

Etruscan, southern Etruria, Latium, or Campania,
ca. 525 – 480 B.C.
Terracotta[1]
Height 24 cm., width 17 cm., depth 8 cm.
Private collection

CONDITION
The piece is broken on all sides, with only the face
of the gorgoneion preserved. Abrasion is apparent
on raised surfaces such as the nose, cheeks, eyebrows, eyes, tongue, fangs, and the curly locks at
the top of the head.

Among the face or head antefix types that appeared first
on the temples in the northwestern Greek system, the
gorgoneion, Medusa's severed head, was the only one that
became ubiquitous in the contiguous Greek and Italic
worlds.[2] Its meaning, both in an architectural context and
elsewhere, seems to have been twofold: apotropaic, i.e.,
warding evil away from the structure it decorates and
physically protects (see the architectural drawing in the
Glossary); and inducing the fecundity of nature through
Medusa's association with Artemis.[3]

The clay of this antefix is full of large inclusions
added to promote the evaporation of water vapor during
the drying and firing processes. In a technique said to
be Italic (Etrusco-Campanian), these inclusions are
allowed to permeate the entire fabric, producing grainy,
less plastically precise forms, even when covered with a
cream-colored slip.

Comparison with other extant antefixes produced in
the same or a parallel mold reveals that major portions
of this antefix are broken away at the top, the sides, and
the bottom. At the sides and top, these features would have
included a surrounding shell of mold-made concave leaves,
as well as "Hathor" locks and a half-round molding ending in volutes at the shoulders and separating the hair and
ears from the surrounding leaves. On the antefix's left
side, a vertical break has taken away the ends of the flame-
shaped locks of the beard as well as the two rows of beaded locks that descend from behind and beneath the ears.

Beneath the neckline of the monster's tunic, a raised
molding and a recessed fascia, again visible on more complete examples, are broken away except for a small surviving fragment slightly left of center. Traces of red, black,
and white paint remain. The locks of the beard alternate
in red and black, as do the dots arranged in a pendent arc
on the neckline of the tunic. The pupils are black, as are
the hair and eyebrows. Red is used for the tongue and lips;
white for the teeth and fangs, and for the eyes surrounding
the black pupils. The anatomical details of the ears are
rendered in red, each lobe bearing an earring in relief, outlined and dotted at the center in red. All other features
of the face are reserved in the color of the slip.

Remnants of an attached cover tile of Laconian type,
its back or saddle painted black, appear on the reverse nine
centimeters below the preserved top of the antefix and
four centimeters above its bottom edge, thus revealing the
depth to which it overhung the edges of its adjoining eaves
tiles, concealing and protecting the seam between them.

The same or a parallel mold was used to produce gorgoneia for a variety of revetments at Capua, so a Capuan origin for the workshop seems plausible, a supposition enhanced by the grainy appearance of the modeled surface. Another example in Rome is of uncertain provenance but must be from that city or some site nearby.[4] At Caere (Cerveteri), many gorgoneion antefixes of the same series — made in a mold that is related but not the same — were found. Interestingly, this mold or a parallel example was also used to produce antefixes at Capua and Satricum.[5] Although trade in molds is a possible explanation for this diffusion, it is more likely that all were produced by an itinerant workshop.[6] The relief is higher than that of the Tarentine-type gorgoneion antefix (cat. no. 88) and it is much thicker, requiring clay well fortified with grog (crushed terracotta). Though less aesthetically pleasing at close range than the Tarentine antefix, the aesthetic deficiencies of the Etrusco-Campanian technique would scarcely have been noticed when the terrifying faces were painted and mounted on a roof at some distance from the viewer.

—JFK

**BIBLIOGRAPHY**
Unpublished.

**NOTES**
1  The thick fabric was fired to a brick red (Munsell 2.5YR, 5/4) at the surface, shading to a charcoal gray (5YR, 4/1) in the interior; covered with a cream-colored slip (10YR, 8/2). Red paint (10R, 4/6) was used.

2  Belson 1981.

3  Frothingham 1911; Howe 1954; Croon 1955; Kunze 1963; Feldman 1965; Rizza and Scrinari 1968, 260–63; Belson 1981, 183–95; Carter 1987.

4  Capua: Koch 1912, 37–38, pls. VI.3, XXVI.3b, XXVIII.5; Van Buren 1921, 7, Type IV, pl. 3.3. Rome (provenance unknown): Koch 1912, 37, n. 1, and 80, fig. 93, pl. VI, no. 3; Andrén 1940, 499, pl. 156, no. 523. For a splendid color photograph of an example from S. Maria Vetere made in the same or a parallel mold, see Torelli 2001, 156.

5  Koch 1912, pls. V.5–7, VI.1–2, VI.4, XXXIII.2; Andrén 1940, 34–35, pl. 10, no. 33, and 467, pl. 144, no. 502. Caere: Van Buren 1921, 6–8, Type IV, pl. II.2. Examples with no provenance can be found in the Danish National Museum, Copenhagen, and in the J. Paul Getty Museum, Malibu: see Breitenstein 1941, 79–80, no. 766, pl. 92. The definitive study of the series is Kästner 1989 (115–28); he presents an example in Berlin (TC 7019: 116, fig. 8), made in the same or a parallel mold.

## 90

# Bucchero Aryballos with Gorgoneion

**Etruscan, early sixth century B.C.**
**Ceramic**
**Height 6.8 cm., diameter of rim 2.4 cm., diameter of foot 1.6 cm.**
**Private collection**

**CONDITION**
**The vase has been repaired from large fragments, with no losses. There is minor incrustation around the handles and in the incised inscription.**

This vase is a minor masterpiece of Etruscan art. It is an aryballos, a small oil bottle, with a tapering pyriform body, a tiny foot, and a flat, disk rim. The shoulder is unusually broad, perhaps to accommodate the short inscription that fills over half of it (see below), although this was incised after the vase was fired. The shape is based on that of imported Protocorinthian aryballoi, like the one in Boston with a painted centaur (cat. no. 31). The shape is not common in bucchero, with most examples coming from the area of Caere (Cerveteri).[1] Their relative scarcity may be due to the lesser role played by olive oil in Etruscan culture, at least in this early period. At Corinth, the pyriform shape died out in the last quarter of the seventh century and was replaced by the spherical aryballos. In Italy, however, where the spherical type was only rarely imitated in bucchero,[2] the earlier type persisted into the sixth century.

What is remarkable — and, indeed, unique — about this aryballos is its handle, which is molded in the form of a gorgoneion, the disembodied head of the Gorgon Medusa. As is customary, the wide face is shown in a frontal scowl. The broad nose, prominent cheekbones, large eyes, and snake-like tresses are characteristic features, as is the long tongue lolling between fearsome fangs. The hair is pulled up and tied with a fillet, then continues upward, where it splits in two, each half coiling into a volute as it touches the rim. This remarkable treatment of the hair is almost certainly derived from the feather headdress routinely worn by the Egyptian god Bes.[3] Although it is uncertain to what extent the Greek

conception of the Gorgon is based on Bes (cat. no. 6), the Near Eastern demon Pazuzu (cat. no. 7), or some other combination of foreign monsters, in the case of this Etruscan vase, the Greek model apparently has been hybridized with the Egyptian god.

As it is in Greek art, the function of the gorgoneion is presumably apotropaic, averting evil; or perhaps it just looked good dangling from the wrist of a devil-may-care Etruscan youth. The Etruscans had their own demons, and the Greek Gorgon never achieved quite the same widespread popularity in Archaic Etruria as it had in Magna Graecia and on the Greek mainland. Although frequently encountered in Etruscan architectural terracottas (e.g., cat. no. 89), gorgoneia are rare on both painted vases and incised bucchero.[4]

—JMP

## THE INSCRIPTION

An inscription is engraved from right-to-left on the shoulder of the aryballos. The words are not separated by spacing or punctuation. The final letter of the inscription, the letter *san* >M<, represents the sound *s*, a pronunciation characteristic of inscriptions originating from northern Etruria. The style of the lettering points to an early date, probably in the sixth century B.C.

The inscription reads: *larqia ninie```s*. The text records the name of the owner of the aryballos and may be translated as "(The property) of Larth Ninie."

It is interesting to note that a Larth Ninie is known also from another Etruscan inscription: a sandstone grave marker (*cippus*) from the northern Etruscan city of Faesulae bears a funerary inscription with the name Larth Ninie: *larqia ninie`s* : "(The tomb) of Larth Ninie."[5] We may speculate that this handsome aryballos, whose provenance is otherwise unknown, was among the funeral objects placed in the tomb of Larth Ninie at Faesulae by members of the deceased's family.

—RW

**BIBLIOGRAPHY**
Unpublished.

**NOTES**

1 For bucchero aryballoi of this shape, the principal study is Poupé 1963; see also Bonamici 1974, pl. 2, no. 5, and pl. 12, no. 45; Camporeale 1991, pls. 108–9, nos. 146–49; Freeden 1992, 20, 22, no. 13. None has quite the same shape as this vase, which also has an unusually thick rim. For other inscribed aryballoi, see Poupé 1963, 242–54, nos. 30–36, pls. 25–26; Torelli 2001, 579, no. 126. Two other inscribed pyriform aryballoi were owned by an individual named Larth: one formerly in a private collection (Poupé 1963, 243–44, no. 30, pl. 24.1) and another, from Caere, in Cambridge (Fitz. GR.4.1929: Hutchinson 1930, pl. VIIIa).

2 For some bucchero aryballoi of spherical shape, see Bonamici 1974, pl. 35, no. 75; Camporeale 1991, pls. 110–11, nos. 151–53.

3 For Bes's feather headdress, see the numerous examples in *LIMC* 3 (1986), 98–112, pls. 74–86, s.v. "Bes" (Hermary).

4 For some other bucchero gorgoneia, see Bonamici 1974, pl. 39, no. 77 (same as *LIMC* 4 [1988], 331, no. 2, pl. 188, s.v. "Gorgones [in Etruria]" [Krauskopf]), and pl. 57, no. 109. For the Gorgon in Etruscan art, see *LIMC* 4, 322–45, pls. 188–95, s.v. "Gorgones (in Etruria)."

5 Rix 1991, Fs 1.1.

# Black-Figure Amphora with Theseus and the Minotaur

Attic, ca. 545 – 535 B.C., attributed to the
Princeton Painter
Said to have been found at Nola, in Campania
Ceramic
Height 42.8 cm., maximum diameter 28.4 cm.,
diameter of rim 17.6 cm., diameter of foot 15.3 cm.
Princeton University Art Museum, Trumbull-Prime
Collection (y168)

CONDITION
The vase has been repaired from several fragments,
with only small gaps: for example, in the chests of
Theseus and the youth to his left. The surface is worn
in places, especially the handles and the figures on
the obverse. On the reverse, most of the added white
slip is lost on the winged female at the right.

The decoration of this vase was attributed by Beazley to the Princeton Painter, named by him not for this amphora but for another at Princeton that was included in his initial list of the artist's works.[1] Active in the third quarter of the sixth century, the Princeton Painter decorated mostly amphorae and neck-amphorae, favoring heroic and mythological subjects, as well as scenes with warriors, chariots, and horsemen. These figures, with their pointed noses and chins, long red hair, and stiff postures, are entirely characteristic. Although not without talent, the Princeton Painter is known less for his skills as a draftsman or for the originality of his compositions than for the diversity of his amphora shapes and their sometimes elaborate subsidiary ornament.[2] This amphora, however, is unexceptional on both counts, being generally indistinguishable in shape and ornament from many contemporary works by the Swing Painter or the Painter of Berlin 1686. In shape, it is a classic belly amphora of Type B, with two cylindrical handles, a flaring rim, rounded shoulders, and a stout body tapering to an echinus foot. The decorative scheme is no less standardized, with the figures in reserved panels on either side and the rest of the vase coated with black slip, saving only the top of the rim, the

underside of the foot, and the zone of rays on the lower body. Lines of added red slip run above and below the panels, around the middle of the foot and neck, at the top of the inner and outer rim, and above the rays. The obverse panel is bordered above by a standard palmette-and-lotus festoon, while the reverse panel is topped by a chain of pendant lotus buds linked by tendrils.

On the obverse Theseus kills the Minotaur, seizing the bull-headed monster by the arm as he readies his sword for the fatal blow. The Minotaur has fallen to one knee, his right hand clutching at his attacker's arm while with his left he flails at him with a white rock. The monster is nude, as always, while Theseus wears an animal pelt over a short red chiton. The Minotaur's thick bull neck is tinted red, making a vivid contrast with the white of his muzzle. Watching the struggle from either side are two pairs of nude youths. Like Theseus, they have long red hair, but the hero's locks are tied together in the back and fringed with incision over the brow. On the ground, between Theseus's legs, is a folded himation draped over a stone, the garment identified by its colored stripes and dot-rosettes.[3]

The offspring of the unnatural union between the Cretan Bull and Pasiphaë, the wife of King Minos of Crete, the Minotaur was housed in the Labyrinth, a maze devised by the artisan Daidalos, from which neither the monster nor his victims could escape.[4] Aigeus, the king of Athens, was forced to send an annual tribute to Minos in the form of seven youths and seven maidens, to be killed by the Minotaur. Volunteering to go as one of them, Aigeus's son Theseus won the love of Minos's daughter Ariadne, who told him to mark his path through the Labyrinth with a ball of thread. With this assistance he slew the Minotaur and escaped, taking Ariadne with him. Archetypal in its symbolism of death, the maze of the underworld, and ultimate resurrection, the story is one of great antiquity, although efforts to associate it with the bull cult of the Greek Bronze Age and the labyrinthine sub-basements of the Minoan palace at Knossos remain speculative.

The slaying of the Minotaur was depicted in a variety of media as early as the mid-seventh century but only began to occur regularly on Athenian pottery in the second quarter of the sixth, appearing also on a metope

version of the subject by the Princeton Painter, in Madrid, there are six male and female onlookers.[7]

On the reverse of the amphora, a bearded king, identified as such by his scepter, sits to the right on a folding stool. He wears a long himation with colored stripes and dot-rosettes and has a fringed red beard, a red fillet, and long hair tied in a queue. Standing to either side, dressed in short red-and-black chitons, are a pair of winged, white-skinned goddesses, who raise their hands near the head of the seated king. Behind each goddess is a nude, red-haired youth, like those flanking the action on the obverse. The same group, without the youthful onlookers, appears on an amphora in Rome by the Swing Painter, and on a few other vases.[8] These scenes, including the one in Princeton, have been interpreted by Dietrich von Bothmer as the moment before the Birth of Athena, with Zeus attended by Eileithyia, the goddess of childbirth, here shown in double form, as frequently happens.[9] The Eileithyiai gesture at Zeus's head because it is from there that Athena is about to spring fully armored, a subject depicted by the Princeton Painter on at least two other amphorae.[10] In the latter, Zeus is attended by a mixture of gods and gesturing goddesses, none of whom are winged. Indeed, the Eileithyiai normally are not winged, whether in depictions of the actual Birth or of the moment before, as on another amphora by the Princeton Painter, in New York.[11] There is disagreement whether the winged goddesses are, in fact, the Eileithyiai, and consequently whether the subject is the incipient Birth of Athena. However, the suggestion by Ricardo Olmos that these figures are instead "messenger deities" is not convincing:[12] messengers do not come in pairs, and the actions and postures of the winged women are identical to those of the wingless Eileithyiai.[13]

Unlike most portrayals of the Birth of Athena, vase-paintings focusing on the pregnant moment before the actual delivery seem almost intentionally ambiguous, leaving the identity of Zeus in some doubt by placing him on a stool rather than a throne and giving him a scepter but not the more defining attribute of a thunderbolt.[14] The resulting uncertainty contributes to an air of tense expectancy suitable to the subject.

—JMP

of the Athenian Treasury at Delphi soon after 500 B.C.[5] The scene on this vase is canonical in composition, with the hero seizing the struggling monster with one hand and stabbing him with the other. The rock wielded by the Minotaur is a mark of his rude nature, as it is with centaurs, although in some earlier depictions Theseus, too, fights with stones.[6] The four youths could be interpreted as some of Theseus's Athenian companions, but identical onlookers were part of the Princeton Painter's stock repertory—two of them turn up in the scene on the reverse—and we cannot be certain whether they are real protagonists or space-filling afterthoughts. On another

**BIBLIOGRAPHY**

*ABV* 299.19; *BAdd*[2] 78; Prime 1879, 69, fig. 41; Bothmer 1953, 56; Boardman 1974, fig. 138; Padgett 1996, 108, fig. 1.

**NOTES**

1  Princeton y169: *ABV* 298.6; Beazley 1931–32, pl. 9.2. For Beazley's initial list of attributions to the Princeton Painter, see Beazley 1931–32, 17–18. For the Princeton Painter, see also *ABV* 297–99, 692; *Paralipomena* 129–30; *BAdd*[2] 78; Chamay and Bothmer 1987.

2  Bothmer (in Chamay and Bothmer 1987, 66) notes that "no two of his vases look as if they had been made by the same potter."

3  The same cloak and stone frequently recur in other black-figure versions of this subject: e.g., a panel amphora by the Taleides Painter (New York, Met. 47.11.5: *ABV* 174.1; *CVA* New York 3, USA 12, pl. 11). The garment may have more significance than we know, for it ought to belong to neither the Minotaur nor the chiton-clad Theseus.

4  For the entire story, see Apollod. *Bibl.* 3.1.34; 3.157–16.9. See also Tsiafakis, "ΠΕΛΩΡΑ," in this volume.

5  See Young 1972; Brommer 1973, 226–43; *LIMC* 6 (1992), 574–81, pls. 316–25, s.v. "Minotauros" (Woodford); *LIMC* 7 (1994), 940–41, pls. 661–62, s.v. "Theseus" (Woodford). For the Delphi metope, see Boardman 1978, fig. 213.9; Schefold 1992, 166, fig. 204.

6  See Schefold 1992, fig. 201.

7  Madrid 10925: *ABV* 298.11; *BAdd*[2] 78; *CVA* Madrid 1, Spain 1, pl.2.1. Beazley also attributed an amphora with this subject in the Krefeld Museum (32/1911) to the manner of the Princeton Painter: *ABV* 300.7; *BAdd*[2] 79; *CVA* Krefeld (Nordrhein-Westfalen) 1, Germany 49, pls. 34.3–4, 35.1–2.

8  Rome, Vatican G. 37 (*ABV* 305.13; *BAdd*[2] 80; Böhr 1982, pl. 22); see Brommer 1961, pls. 33–35; for other examples, see *LIMC* 3 (1986), 691, nos. 52–54, s.v. "Eileithyia" (Olmos).

9  Bothmer 1953, 56. For Eileithyia, see *LIMC* 3, 685–99, pls. 534–40, s.v. "Eleithyia." The goddess is referred to in double form by Homer (*Il.* 11.271). For the Birth of Athena, see Brommer 1961; *LIMC* 2 (1984), 986, pls. 742–43, s.v. "Athena" (Demargne).

10  Geneva MF 154 (*ABV* 299.18; *Paralipomena* 130; *BAdd*[2] 78; *CVA* Geneva 2, Switzerland 3, pl. 48; *LIMC* 3, 688, pl. 535, no. 20, s.v. "Eileithyia"); and a vase formerly in the art market (London, Sotheby's, December 10, 1996, lot 170).

11  New York, Met. 53.11.1: *ABV* 298.5; *BAdd*[2] 78; Bothmer 1953, 52; Böhr 1982, pl. 169.

12  *LIMC* 3, 691, s.v. "Eileithyia."

13  In the earliest known depiction of the Birth of Athena, on a seventh-century relief-amphora in the Tenos Museum (*LIMC* 2, 988, pl. 745, no. 360, s.v. "Athena"), the Eileithyiai are winged, as is Zeus.

14  In the scene of a departing warrior on an amphora in Dunedin (Otago Museum E 53.62), which Beazley related to works in the manner of the Princeton Painter, a very similar draped man holding a scepter, also seated on a folding stool, is clearly not Zeus, but rather a mortal king: *ABV* 301.2; *Paralipomena* 131; *BAdd*[2] 79; *CVA* New Zealand 1, pl. 9.1–3.

## 92

# Statuette of Acheloos

**Greek, probably from South Italy, early fifth century B.C.**
**Bronze**
**Height 7.45 cm., length 9.77 cm., width 2.63 cm.**
**Private collection**

**CONDITION**
**The figure is intact. The patina is dark green, with lighter green patches on the right flank and the right hind leg.**

This statuette represents Acheloos, the longest river in Greece, personified as a bull with the head of a bearded man. The stocky and somewhat angular bovine body stands on flat hooves with no base plate; the left front and both hind legs are stepping forward.[1] The weight of the figure inclines slightly to the right side, but it stands steadily. The legs are thick, with heavy fetlocks. After rising at the base, the tail drops almost perpendicular to the ground. The prominent dewlap falls from beneath the chin and is gently rounded at the bottom. The scrotum is close to the body and the penis sheath dangles down. The human face of the river god features well-defined lips, a "Roman" nose, large eyes, and very prominent brow ridges, above which the short forehead slopes back at a sharp angle. Accentuating the profile of the face, the spade-shaped beard juts strongly forward while the bovine ears are angled back in line with the beard and do not rise above the head. The god's long tresses are rendered with horizontal ridges held close to the cranium before fanning out over the shoulders, reaching a point near the middle of the back.[2] Above the ears, the short horns curve up neatly over the head.[3]

Acheloos is not a common subject among Greek bronze statuettes. The closest parallel for this figure is a smaller statuette formerly in the British art market,[4] which lacks the long hair and hanging dewlap and has a longer tail, nearly reaching the ground. A statuette in the British Museum dated to the first half of the fifth century B.C. shows the river god lying down with his forelegs folded beneath his body.[5]

The personification of rivers as man-headed bulls is an Archaic tradition for which Near Eastern prototypes

have been suggested.[6] Acheloos is commonly represented in this way in Greek art, becoming the quintessential Greek river god.[7] Man-headed bulls also appear on the coins of South Italy and Sicily, notably those of Gela and Katane, representing not Acheloos but the river gods Gelas and Amenanos respectively.[8]

The River Acheloos flows southward from Mount Pindus in Epirus for a distance of about 130 miles. It separates Akarnania and Aitolia before emptying into

the Ionian Sea near the entrance to the Gulf of Corinth. In Hesiod, Acheloos is one of nineteen rivers, the sons of Okeanos and Tethys;[9] he also is mentioned in Homer.[10] Herakles fought with Acheloos for Deianeira, and in the process broke off his horn (see cat. no. 93), which later came to be associated with the cornucopia.[11] This myth was known in South Italy and is illustrated on a terracotta altar from Locri dated about 470–450 B.C., now in the Museo Archeologico Nazionale, Reggio Calabria.[12] Acheloos is represented with a human body and bull's horns on a coin from Metapontum, dated about 440–430 B.C., with the legend ΑΕΘΛΟΝ ΑΧΕΛΟΙΟ, a reference suggesting that this stater was given as a prize in athletic games held in the river god's honor.[13] The residents of Metapontum evidently considered themselves to be related to the Aitolians of the Greek mainland, the source of the Acheloos cult.[14] These associations suggest that this statuette of Acheloos would not have been out of place in South Italy and may well have been made there.

—MB

**BIBLIOGRAPHY**
Unpublished.

**NOTES**

1 The lack of any noticeable curvature in the body and the absence of a base plate argue against the statuette having been a vessel attachment.

2 As seen also on the name-vase of the Acheloos Painter, an Attic black-figure vase-painter of the last quarter of the sixth century (Berlin 1851; *ABV* 383.3; *BAdd*² 101). On the Berlin neck-amphora, however, Acheloos has arms and a human torso, like a centaur.

3 These short curving horns are reminiscent of Near Eastern human-headed bulls (e.g., cat. no. 1).

4 London, Sotheby's, December 13–14, 1982, lot 241.

5 Walters 1899, 20, no. 211; *LIMC* I (1981), 17, no. 66, pl. 23, s.v. "Acheloos" (Isler).

6 Gais 1978, 356 n. 3.

7 See Isler 1970, 123–91; *LIMC* I, 12–36, pls. 19–54, s.v. "Acheloos."

8 See Jenkins 1970, 165–70; *LIMC* I, 15–16, pl. 22, s.v. "Acheloos."

9 Hes. *Theog.* 337–45.

10 Hom. *Il.* 21.193–95.

11 Ov. *Met.* 9.87.

12 Reggio Calabria 94062; Bennett, Paul, and Iozzo 2002, 208–9, no. 40.

13 Kraay 1976, 179. Kraay shows the legend with a variant form of **X**. See Noe 1984, 55–56, 70.

14 Kray 1976, 179 n. 2.

## Black-Figure Siana Cup with Herakles and Acheloos

Attic, ca. 560–545 B.C., attributed to the
Painter of Boston C.A.
Said to have been found at Thebes
Ceramic
Diameter 26.9 cm.
Museum of Fine Arts, Boston, Henry Lillie Pierce
Fund (99.519)

CONDITION
The cup is repaired from fragments, with only
minimal in-painting. There are several lacunae on
side A, notably the head of Circe and parts of the
two crewmen on either side of her. Much of the
sphinx in the tondo is lost. The handles and foot are
lost. The foot is restored incorrectly as that of a
Little Master cup; the original foot would have
resembled that of catalogue number 27, attributed
to the same painter.[1]

Beazley designated this fragmentary cup the name-piece
of his Painter of Boston C.A. (Circe-Acheloos), who was
active in the late second and early third quarters of the
sixth century and apparently decorated only Siana cups.[2]
The latter are of both the "overlap" variety, with the
figures overlapping the offset of the lip, and "double-
deckers," like this example, with the figures confined to
the lower body. This cup is a somewhat experimental variation on the double-decker scheme, with a short dark
lip. The base is decorated with a band of red and black
tongues above a zone of rays. In the reserved handle zone,
the painter has given us two scenes of transformation, a
theme which he seems to have favored, often depicting
composite human and animal creatures such as bull-men,
satyrs, sphinxes, and centaurs (cf. the centaurs on cat. no.
27). On side A, the sorceress Circe transforms Odysseus's
men into animals, while on side B, Herakles struggles with
the river god Acheloos, who has transformed himself into
a bearded, human-headed bull. In the interior, a seated
sphinx faces to the right and looks back over her shoulder,

one paw raised to touch the tondo border of black and red tongues. There is a red fillet in her hair, which hangs over her left ear; her flesh was painted in added white.

On side *B*, Herakles struggles with Acheloos, who falls to his knees in submission.[3] Herakles holds the god by the horn and threatens him with his sword. The hero wears his usual attire, a short unpleated chiton under the belted skin of the Nemean lion, which is pulled up over his head, the lion's paws knotted at his chest. Watching the battle are six bearded onlookers, four on the left and two on the right, who wear long himations decorated with red rosettes with seven white dots. There is extensive use of added red and white slip; even the face of Herakles is red.

In this early depiction of the subject, Acheloos has only a human head, a type that persists well into the Classical period, although by the second half of the sixth century the more common way of representing the god was with not just a human head but also a torso and arms.[4] In that form Acheloos resembles a centaur, but he is

distinguished by his bovine body and genitalia, and above all by his horn. Ovid describes how Herakles broke off the horn of Acheloos and then used it as a horn of plenty that the Naiads filled with fruits and flowers (*Met.* 9.87).

On side *A*, Circe offers the transforming magic potion to Odysseus's men in a high-stemmed lip cup resembling a Little Master cup, the favored cup type at symposia in the middle and third quarter of the sixth century.[5] A hunting dog sits frontally between Circe and the companion to her right, recalling sympotic scenes where the dog usually sits under the symposiasts' couch.[6] This man's head is lost, but the other crewmen of Odysseus have been transformed, their heads turned into those of animals: lion, cock, bridled horse, wolf, panther, and goat. These are the same animals that frequent Little Master cups, but it is normally only in depictions of this subject and of Theseus's defeat of the bull-headed Minotaur (e.g., cat. no. 91) that one finds this particular kind of composite creature, with an animal's head on a

high-stemmed cup may retain its potency as part of the imagery of transformation. For example, on a late Archaic scaraboid in Bonn, a centaur (Pholos?) reclines as a symposiast with a drinking horn and plays kottabos with a high-stemmed cup.[8]

—JTH

### BIBLIOGRAPHY

*ABV* 69.1, 682; *Paralipomena* 28; *BAdd*² 18; Luce 1923, 426, fig. 1 and 428, fig. 3; Himmelmann-Wildschütz 1967, pl. 5; Touchefeu-Meynier 1968, no. 170, pl. 14.1; Isler 1970, 135, pl. 4, no. 68; Blatter 1975, 76, pl. 29,1; *CVA* Boston 2, USA 19, pl. 87; Bérard 1981, 10, fig. 2; *LIMC* 1 (1981), 25, no. 215, pl. 45, s.v. "Acheloos" (Isler); Brommer 1984b, pl. 25; *LIMC* 6 (1992), 960, no. 139, pl. 631, s.v. "Odysseus" (Touchefeu-Meynier); B. Andreae, in *Ulisse* 1996, 52, fig. 11.

### NOTES

1 On cups by the Painter of Boston C.A., "[t]he wall of the usually low foot is concave and flaring" (*CVA* Amsterdam 2, Netherlands 8, p. 35 [Brijder]).

2 For the Painter of Boston C.A., see *ABV* 69, 682; *Paralipomena* 28; *BAdd*² 18; Haldenstein 1982, 10–14; *CVA* Amsterdam 2, Netherlands 8, 35–38 (Brijder). For the relations among Siana, Gordion, and Little Master cups, see Brijder 2000, 549–65.

3 For Acheloos, see Isler 1970; *LIMC* 1, 12–36, pls. 19–54, s.v. "Acheloos"; Gantz 1993, 431–34. See also Hes. *Theog.* 337–45; Archil. 287W.

4 Isler 1970, pls. V–VII; *LIMC* 1, 27–28, pls. 50–53, s.v. "Acheloos."

5 For Little Master cups, see Beazley 1932; *ABV* 159–97; *Paralipomena* 67–80; Haldenstein 1982. For Circe, see Touchefeu-Meynier 1968, 81–131; Blatter 1975; Buitron and Cohen 1992, 77–80; *LIMC* 6 (1992), 48–59, pls. 24–30, s.v. "Kirke" (Canciani).

6 A similar dog occupies the same position between Circe and a crewman on the Merrythought cup (Boston 99.518: *ABV* 198; *LIMC* 6, 52, no. 14, pl. 25, s.v. "Kirke"), where Circe again holds a Little Master cup.

7 See Heesen 1996, 127–29, no. 29, fig. 81, for a cup related to the Painter of the Boston C.A. with a painted inscription—*SOTER* (savior or guardian)—on the shield of a stone-wielding warrior in the tondo. On the exterior, centaurs wield boulders.

8 Zwierlein-Diehl 2000, 398, figs. 1–3.

fully human body, a type more at home in Egypt and the Near East than in Greece.

Odysseus, nude, enters on the left with sword drawn; a short cloak, a chlamys, dotted with rosettes, hangs over his left arm. Behind him, between the roots of the missing handle, is a bystander in a himation, like those on side *B*. Homer relates that when Odysseus went up to Circe's great house, he was met by Hermes "in the likeness of a young man with the first down on his lip," who told him, "When Circe shall smite thee with her long wand, then do thy draw thy sharp sword from beside thy thigh, and rush upon Circe, as though thou wouldst slay her. And she will be seized with fear, and will bid thee lie with her" (*Od.* 10.277–79, 293–96). Thereafter Odysseus recalled, "she prepared me a potion in a golden cup, that I might drink" (*Od.* 10.316–17); but Hermes had given him a preventive antidote, and he drew his sword and forced the sorceress to restore his men to human form.

It could be said that Odysseus and the nude youths, his animal-headed companions, are like initiates in a process of transformation, a ritual rite of passage. Initiates, *mystes*, are an integral part of the use and iconography of Little Master cups. Using a familiar narrative, the cup painters developed a catalogue of images to express ritual status.[7] Even when black-figure gives way to the red-figure style, there is reason to believe that the

## 94

# Handle in the Form of Triton

**Etruscan, late sixth century B.C.**
**Bronze**
**Height with pin 4.6 cm., length 8.3 cm., width 2.3 cm.**
**Museum of Fine Arts, Boston, gift by contribution**
**(01.7508)**

CONDITION
**The right arm is broken off at the elbow, the left hand at the wrist. One tail fin is missing. The face is somewhat worn. The surface is pitted in places and has a dark green patina. There are traces of an attachment pin below the front body.**

This elegant sea monster was certainly a handle, the curve of its body providing the perfect grip. The shape of the vessel it adorned is uncertain: perhaps the lid of a large pyxis. It may be compared with another Etruscan bronze in Boston, the statuette of a centaur (cat. no. 43), which also may have functioned as a handle.

The creature's human torso, like that of a centaur, rises vertically at the front. The serpentine part extends behind, originally terminating in a horizontal tail fin like that of a whale or dolphin. A single ventral fin rises from the top of the central undulation. He is bearded, and his long hair extends down his back and in discrete tresses over his chest. His features are refined and somewhat somber.

The figure is a borrowing from the Greek repertory, where Herakles wrestles with the mermen Triton and Nereus (e.g., cat. no. 96). Depictions of this contest are rare in Archaic Etruscan art, but Tritons and other fishtailed creatures abound, alone or in multiples, on metalwork, sculpted tomb monuments, and black-figure vases.[1] Demons, including a variety of fishtailed monsters, were a notable feature of the Etruscan afterlife. The association with funerary iconography is strong, and not simply because Tritons were conveniently suited to fill the narrow ends of painted gables in rock-cut tombs.[2] Most bronze examples are handles or handle ornaments, where their functional and decorative qualities were undoubtedly combined with an apotropaic role.[3] Not all such vessels can have been made for funerary use.

—JMP

**BIBLIOGRAPHY**

Shepard 1940, 31, pl. VI, fig. 42; Comstock and Vermeule 1971, no. 214; *LIMC* 8 (1997), 87, no. 32, s.v. "Tritones (in Etruria)" (Camporeale).

**NOTES**

1 For Tritons in Etruscan art, see Shepard 1940, 31–35, pls. VI–VII; *LIMC* 8, 85–90, pls. 60–68, s.v. "Tritones (in Etruria)."

2 Shepard 1940, pl. VII, fig. 48a.

3 Walters 1899, 67, no. 485; Shepard 1940, pl. VI, fig. 49; *LIMC* 8, 87, nos. 28–41, pls. 62–63, s.v. "Tritones (in Etruria)."

# Lip-Cup with Europa and Triton

Greek, Attic, ca. 540 B.C., signed by Tleson as potter
and attributed here to the Tleson Painter
Ceramic
Height 14.7 cm., depth of lip 23.2 cm., width
with handles 30.5 cm., depth of foot 9.55 cm., height
of lip 3.2 cm.
Collection of Michael and Judy Steinhardt, New York

CONDITION
The cup has been recomposed from fragments. On
the reverse, five letters of the inscription are missing.
There are five holes, 2 millimeters wide, from ancient
repairs at the top of the stem and on the cup wall
beneath Europa, where a small fragment is lost,
taking with it part of the inscription.

Europa, daughter of Phoinix, king of Tyre, was picking
flowers in a meadow with her friends when she caught
Zeus's eye. He transformed himself into a saffron-
breathing bull, attracted her attention, and carried her
off across the sea to Crete, where she bore him Minos,
Radamanthys, and, in some versions, Sarpedon.[1]

Here, it is the voyage from Tyre to Crete that is
depicted. The architecture of the cup has allowed the
painter to treat the ridge at the base of the offset lip as the
sea, indicated by a glazed line. On one side, Europa sits
sidesaddle on the bull, whose upper body only is shown
(the legs would be under water). With her right hand she
steadies herself on the bull's back and places her left on its
neck. She wears disk earrings, bracelets, and a belted peplos with incised pattern work. Her flesh is in added white.
The bull's neck is in added red, as are stripes on its
haunches, while its dappled hide is indicated by four large,
white triangular markings. On the other side, Triton (or
perhaps Nereus) skims the waves. His upper part is portrayed as an old man, with trim beard and white hair tied
neatly behind. His extended arms (his left with palm up)
convey both a sense of speed and a gesture of welcome
rather than alarm. He wears a short-sleeved red tunic: the
borders of its sleeves, neck, and waist, and a central vertical panel are decorated with incised zigzags between rows

of white dots. His lower body continues as a fish, with a forked tail and a dorsal fin. Incision is used for the backbone, a row of scales along the lower body, and zigzag lines between red dots along the body.

The signature of the potter Tleson runs in bold, lapidary letters below each figure: ΤΛΕΣΟΝ ΗΟ ΝΕΑΡΧΟ ΕΠΟΙΕΣΕΝ (Tleson, the son of Nearchos, made [this]). The cup is otherwise minimally decorated. An eleven-frond palmette extends from each handle root, a red line intersecting the stem on three of them. The body (except for a reserved band), stem, and foot are black. Under the foot are five diluted black lines, a set of three between singletons at the inner and outer edges. Inside, a reserved tondo (diam. 7.29 cm.) may have had a black central dot and band.

This cup may have the very earliest representation of Europa and the bull in Attic art yet known to us. It joins three other more or less contemporary cups, in Rhodes,[2] Florence,[3] and Cambridge, Massachusetts.[4] This cluster

of Attic representations coincides with a rekindled and widespread interest in the story of Europa throughout the Greek world in the middle of the sixth century.[5] The reasons underlying this cannot now be reconstructed with any confidence, but they may have included the treatment of the story by the poet Stesichoros.[6]

Common to most of these early artistic representations is the voyage over the sea. Europa does not cling to the bull by the horn as in later versions and the accounts in Moschos and Lucian.[7] She seems relaxed enough: indeed, on the Boston cup, Europa adjusts her veil in a bridal gesture.

The sea monster, perhaps Triton, on the other side, represents the marine thiasos that accompanies Europa on the bull. As in Homer, when Poseidon rides in a chariot across the waves, " the sea beasts came up from their deep places and played in his path, and acknowledged their master."[8] He is especially close to the Triton on a lip-cup fragment from the Athenian Acropolis, which is by the same

ivory or woodwork (whence it is transferred also to stone and metal). A possible connection with Samos,[19] where small vessels and cups were often decorated with similarly delicate lines (including some under the foot), becomes the more intriguing in the light of the Samian Little Master cup in Riehen whose subject in the tondo (a swan preening itself) is a favorite of the Tleson Painter.[20]

The many cups signed by Tleson as potter raise the question of the identity of their painter, whom we know by convention as the Tleson Painter,[21] and of whom Sir John Beazley speaks as the most "typical" of the Little Masters.[22] John Boardman has suggested that potter and painter are one and the same,[23] but Henry Immerwahr has cautioned that we may do better to consider them as separate individuals.[24] Mythological representations, such as Pegasos[25] or Theseus and the Minotaur,[26] are quite rare in his work. Much commoner are his beloved animals— swans preening, grazing deer, cockerels, hens. In style, the Steinhardt cup most closely approaches the fragmentary siren from the Acropolis.[27]

The choice of subject for the shape may have been prompted by the Greek nexus of ideas and rituals that interwove the sea and wine.[28] In Homer, the sea is "wine-dark." When the cup was filled with wine, the symposiast would have enjoyed the associations whereby the wine inside would have become, as it were, the sea over which Europa sped.

—JG

**BIBLIOGRAPHY**
Unpublished.

**NOTES**
1 For the story, see *Enciclopedia dell'arte antica* 3 (1960), 542–45, s.v. "Europa" (Pincelli), 542–45; [changed from Pincelli 1960] Zahn 1983; Dombrowski 1984; *LIMC* 4 (1988), 76–92, pls. 32–48, s.v. "Europa 1" [write as? 76–92, no. 1, pls. 32–48, s.v. "Europa" or stet?] (C. M. Robertson); Arafat 1990, 135–39; I. Morris 1992, 175–76 (on Near Eastern prototypes). For South Italian versions, see Jentoft-Nilsen 1983, 139–48. For girls being seduced while picking flowers, see Richardson 1974, 140–42. For the saffron-breathing bull, see Schol. AB Hom. *Il.* 12.292, conveniently in Merkelbach and West 1970, 154, no. 140. 1. For the story, see *Enciclopedia dell'arte antica* 3 (1960), 542–45, s.v. "Europa" (Pincelli), 542–45; Zahn 1983; Dombrowski 1984; *LIMC* 4 (1988), 76–92, pls. 32–48, s.v. "Europe 1" (Robertson); Arafat 1990,

hand;[9] and may be compared with one on a lip-cup in Rhodes[10] and on a South Italian clay altar in the Louvre.[11]

The delicate lines under the foot[12] first occur on cups signed by the potter Nearchos, the father of the potter of the Steinhardt cup.[13] Shortly after come two others, one signed by the potter Eucheiros and another close in style.[14] Later are cups signed by Hermogenes as potter in Toulouse,[15] a fragmentary cup signed by "… kles" in Florence,[16] a lip-cup foot in the Louvre that is joined to the wrong body,[17] and finally an eye-cup of Type A in Boston.[18] The motif may have been inspired by turned

135–39; Morris 1992, 175–76 (on Near Eastern prototypes). For South Italian versions, see Jentoft-Nilsen 1983, 139–48. For girls being seduced while picking flowers, see Richardson 1974, 140–42. For the saffron-breathing bull, see Schol. AB Hom. *Il.* 12.292, conveniently in Merkelbach and West 1983, 154, no. 140.

2  *LIMC* 4, 78, no. 26, s.v. "Europa" (Robertson).

3  Florence, private coll., Ceccanti: Lepora 1998, 271–80; Brijder 2000, 669, 724, Malibu Painter Addenda no. 17, pl. 247a.

4  Goldfarb, Wolsky, and Vermeule 1993, 9–11, perhaps by the Xenokles Painter.

5  See *LIMC* 4, 76–92, pls. 32–48, s.v. "Europe 1" (Robertson).

6  Brize 1980, 103. The influence of Stesichoros on artists in the Athenian Kerameikos was first argued by C. M. Robertson (1969, 207–21).

7  Mosch. *Ep. Bion.* 2.115–30; Lucian, *Enalioi dialogoi* no. 15.

8  Hom. *Il.* 13.27–28, trans. R. Lattimore. On Triton, see *LIMC* 8 (1997), 68–73, s.v. "Triton" (Icard-Gianolio).

9  Graef and Langlotz I, pl. 82, no. 1575.

10  Rhodes Museum 10527: *ABV* 162.1; *LIMC* 8 (1997), 74, no. 8, pl. 47, s.v. "Triton" (Icard-Gianolio).

11  Paris, Louvre CA 5956: Van der Meijden 1993, 302–3, no. MY 24; *LIMC* 8, 70, no. 20, pl. 44, s.v. "Triton."

12  On these, see Beazley 1932, 168 n. 8; Bothmer 1962, 255–56.

13  Cups signed by Tleson as the son of Nearchos: Civitavecchia Museum and Rome, Guglielmi Collection (*ABV* 83, middle); New York, Met. 61.11.2 (*Paralipomena* 74.3 bis; Bothmer 1962, 255–56, pl. 65, figs. 1–3).

14  London, Brit. Mus. B 417: *ABV* 162.2; *CVA* 2, pl. 11.1. Madrid, Museo Arqueologico Nacional: Korres 1972, 208–33, pl. 84.

15  Toulouse 26.177: *ABV* 165.

16  *ABV* 187, top.

17  Louvre F 97: *CVA* Louvre 12, pl. 87.12. D. von Bothmer (1962, 256) suggests that this should be the foot either of the lip-cup signed by Neandros in the Louvre (F 82: *ABV* 167.1; *CVA* Louvre 12, pl.78.9 and 79.2), or F 66 (unattributed: *CVA* Louvre 12, pl. 77.8 and 12).

18  Boston 03.784: *CVA* 2, pl. 100.

19  Robertson 1954.

20  Riehen: Schefold 1960, 163 III 151; Walter-Karydi 1973, 128–29, no. 427, pl. 48.

21  On Tleson the potter and the Tleson Painter, see Beazley 1947b, 1–6 (Beazley 1989a, 1–5); *ABV* 178–83, 688; *Paralipomena* 74.6, 523; Beazley 1989, 50–51; Boardman 1974, 60; Heesen 1996, 140–42.

22  Beazley 1951, 55; Beazley 1986, 50–51.

23  Boardman 1974, 60.

24  Immerwahr 1990, 53.

25  New York, Met. 55.11.13: *Paralipomena* 74.3 bis.

26  Toledo 1958.70: *Paralipomena* 75.1 bis.

27  Acropolis 613: *ABV* 180.36.

28  On these interrelated ideas, see Davies 1978, 72–95.

## 96

# Band-Cup with Cheiron, Peleus, and Thetis; and Herakles and Nereus

**Greek, Attic, ca. 540–530 B.C., attributed to the Oakeshott Painter**
**Ceramic**
**Height 14.18–14.30 cm., depth with handles 30 cm., depth of lip 22.7 cm., depth of foot 9.75 cm., height of figural band 2.6 cm.**
**Michael C. Carlos Museum of Emory University, Carlos Collection of Ancient Greek Art (2000.1.2)**

### CONDITION

**The cup, recomposed from fragments, is essentially complete, with minor repainting at the joins. The fragments on the reverse are smaller, with the result that more is lost. The surface on the obverse is somewhat worn at the left.**

The two sides of this cup are intimately connected by both theme and composition. The less ambiguous side, the reverse, gives Peleus wrestling Thetis (see detail in Padgett, "Horse Men," fig. 16, in this volume).[1] Daughter of Nereus and Doris, Thetis had attracted the attention of Zeus until he discovered that it had been decreed by fate that the offspring would be greater than the father. Here the mortal hero Peleus, wearing a chitoniskos and carrying a sword at his side, has caught up with Thetis. He grasps her with his left arm behind her back and his right hand on her left shoulder. Even as Thetis flees, she looks back at her pursuer. She wears a belted, diamond-patterned peplos, incised necklace and earrings, and bracelets. Beside this group a small garment hangs in the field, perhaps Peleus's mantle. Behind them is a small altar, its patterned wall suggesting stone masonry, with offerings placed on top. The two large birds that perch on the upturned volutes at the edges of the altar convey the momentous significance of the events that unfold nearby. Similar altars, indicating that the story takes place in a sanctuary, often occur in representations on Greek vases;[2] from literature we know only that some authors

set the scene by the seashore.[3] Cheiron,[4] the centaur who would be entrusted with the education of Achilles, son of Peleus and Thetis, approaches from the left. He carries a branch over his right shoulder and extends his left arm, palm up, in a gesture either of welcome or demonstration. His forepart is fully human and is draped in a chitoniskos.

This central composition is framed to left and right by three women who look back as they flee the scene. Their widely spaced legs and extended arms give an impression of speed. Each wears a belted peplos, incised necklace and earrings, and painted bracelets. Their flesh, as with Thetis, is in added white. In pose, they are indistinguishable. No two peploi are identical, but the patterning of the fabric panels, with rosettes in red dots surrounded by white, is very similar.

Turning to the front of the cup, we encounter six more women, three flanking either side of the central scene, who are interchangeable with those on the back. They witness Herakles wrestling with a sea monster, while Poseidon hastens up behind, accompanied by a dolphin.[5] The long red mantle that Poseidon wears over his shoulders covers a black peplos with rosettes. The god carries

a trident in his right hand and gestures with his left in much the same manner as Cheiron. Herakles, who is nude, sits astride the sea monster, whose neck he grasps with his left hand, while brandishing his club in his right. A quiver, its open lid revealing several arrows, is suspended on his back. The monster is conceived with the forepart of an old man, his hair shoulder-length, his full beard trim. He carries a dolphin by the tail in his left hand, while his right appears beside Herakles. He wears a chitoniskos patterned with rosettes. Below the garment, his body emerges as a scaly fish, with one dorsal and two ventral fins and a forked tail. The outline and center of each scale along the back is incised, while the softer flesh along the belly is indicated in added red. The central section of each tripartite fin is in added white.

The identity of the sea monster with whom Herakles wrestles has been much discussed recently. Inscribed vases offer two mutually exclusive possibilities: that he is Nereus (son of Pontos)[6] or Triton (son of Poseidon and Amphitrite).[7] The literary accounts reveal that Herakles wrestled Nereus to discover where the Garden of the Hesperides lay; but they do not record a struggle between Herakles and Triton. The Nereus story seems suddenly to

have been supplanted by Triton, prompting some scholars to seek an explanation in political and historical terms.[8]

Ruth Glynn proposed that the diagnostic element in the iconography of Nereus is that he mutates, whereas Triton does not.[9] She suggested therefore that the sea monster on this cup is Triton. In the case of Thetis, however, both mutating and non-mutating depictions are known. While Glynn is right that a mutating sea monster cannot be Triton, it does not follow that a non-mutating sea monster cannot be Nereus.

Indeed, on this band-cup, it seems much more likely that the sea monster is Nereus. Just as he is caught up in wrestling with Herakles, so his most famous daughter, Thetis, wrestles with Peleus on the other side. This in turn brings up the identities of the fleeing women on either side of both scenes. Similar women are often present at the wrestling of Peleus for Thetis. But they also appear intermittently in other scenes involving Herakles, for example, when he wrestles the Marathonian bull or the Libyan giant Antaios.[10] In all these cases, they must be local dwellers. Judith Barringer has recently suggested that in the case of Herakles and Nereus, the women might be nymphs, who were instrumental in leading Herakles to Nereus.[11] She believes that the women are unlikely to be Nereids because daughters would not wish to betray their father. There are, however, no literary sources indicating nymphs in the story of Peleus wrestling with Thetis, and furthermore, the similarities between the women on the two sides of the cup are so great that they must be considered together. It would seem likely, therefore, that since Nereus was famous for his daughters, it is the Nereids who are present on this cup.

The subjects of the two sides—heroes wrestling with marine deities—are complementary. The victory of Herakles over the sea monster perhaps reflects at some level a desire to master the ocean in the search for trade. The danger of seafaring and its misery is a topos in ancient literature that begins with Hesiod.[12] If the obverse can be taken to symbolize professional work that carries one far away into unknown dangers of the deep, the reverse—showing a man winning his wife—returns us safely to a domestic context, albeit a contentious one.

The attribution to the Oakeshott Painter suggested here is based on comparison of the women on this cup with the maenads on a cup in New York;[13] the Thetis on the Atlanta cup is especially close, and the spacing of the figures is also similar. The meaningless inscriptions recall those on the painter's name-piece in Oxford, which are also nonsensical although some of the letters appear real.[14]

The interior of the Atlanta cup is glazed except for a reserved tondo (diam. 6.61 cm.), with central dot, circle, and band. The exterior of the body and foot are also glazed, except for a reserved stripe below the figural zone, on the inside of the handles, and the edge and underside of the foot.

—JG

## BIBLIOGRAPHY

Brommer 1960, 116, no. 101.1 (Herakles) and 243, no. 49 (Peleus); Brommer 1973, 323, no. 72 (Peleus); *Antika Vaser, Samling Henning Throne-Holst* (private publication, Stockholm 1975), no. 10; Glynn 1981, 128, no. 24; Ahlberg-Cornell 1984, 31, nos. 12, 34, 37, 120, fig. IV.12; London, Christie's, June 8, 1988, lot 36; Barringer 1995, 185, no. 59.

## NOTES

1  For Peleus and Thetis, see Krieger 1973; *LIMC* 7 (1994), 251–69, pls. 182–209, s.v. "Peleus" (Vollkommer); Barringer 1995, 69–77; *LIMC* 8 (1997), 7–14, s.v. "Thetis" (Volkommer).

2  *LIMC* 7, 251–69, pls. 182–209, s.v. "Peleus"; Barringer 1995, 72–73.

3  Ov. *Met.* 11.238.

4  For Cheiron, see Schiffler 1976; Vogel 1978; *LIMC* 3 (1986), 237–48, pls. 185–97, s.v. "Cheiron" (Gisler-Huwiler).

5  For Herakles and the sea monster, see esp. Luce 1922; Shepard 1940; Brize 1980, 103; Glynn 1981; Ahlberg-Cornell 1984; *LIMC* 4 (1988), 409–10, s.v. "Halios Geron" (Glynn); Brommer 1983a; Brommer 1984b, 111–13; *LIMC* 6 (1992), 824–37, s.v. "Nereus" (Pipili); *LIMC* 6 (1994), 470, s.v. "Poseidon" (Simon); Barringer 1995, 155–62; *LIMC* 8 (1997), 68–73, s.v. "Triton" (Icard-Gianolio); Mommsen 2002.

6  E.g., Basel, Cahn Collection 1173: Glynn 1981, pl. 21, fig. 1.

7  E.g., Berlin F 1906: *ABV* 675; *LIMC* 8, 69, no. 7, pl. 42, s.v. "Triton."

8  Boardman (1972, 59 and 1975b, 10) suggests that the Herakles-Triton motif reflects the Athenian domination of the island of Salamis and the removal of Megarian residents. Glynn (1981, 130–32) speculates instead that the Athenian seizure of Sigeion may have been the driving force.

9  Glynn 1981, 126–28.

10  E.g., Taranto 20335 (*ABV* 195.4; *LIMC* 5 [1990], pl. 78, no. 2331) and Paris, Louvre G 103 (*ARV*² 14.2; Pasquier and Denoyelle 1990, 67–76, no. 3).

11  Barringer 1995, 155–56.

12  Hes. *Op.* 618; West 1978, 313–14.

13  New York, Met. 17.230.5: *Paralipomena* 78.1; Beazley 1951, pls. 24–25.

14  Oxford 1972.162: *Paralipomena* 78.2; Vickers 1975, figs. 73–76.

# Red-Figure Neck-Amphora with Nereus

Greek, Attic, ca. 490 B.C., attributed to the
Berlin Painter
Ceramic
Height 30.8 cm., diameter 18.0 cm.
Arthur M. Sackler Museum, Harvard University Art
Museums, gift of Edward P. Warren, Esq. (1927.150)

## CONDITION

The amphora is intact and in excellent condition, with lustrous black glaze. There is a crack in the rim, which is slightly chipped at that point. The dent in the tail of the triton was caused when the clay was not yet dry. The tiny graffito in the form of the letter *psi* on the inside of the foot may be modern.

This type of small neck-amphora, redesigned by red-figure potters and painters from the black-figure neck-amphorae of the second half of the sixth century B.C., was one of a great variety of shapes decorated by the Berlin Painter, one of the leading draftsmen of Athenian red-figure vase-painting during the first quarter of the fifth century B.C. Called a "doubleen," it derives its name from its double handles, consisting of pairs of conjoined cylinders. This example has a tall neck, a flaring rim, and a disk foot. A small fillet marks the juncture of the neck and shoulder, and a thicker fillet divides the foot from the tapering lower body. The doubleen is related to the so-called Nolan amphora, named after the site of Nola, in Campania, east of Mount Vesuvius, where these imported Attic vases were first found.[1] Nolan amphorae are customarily painted in a distinctive decorative scheme characterized by a minimum of subsidiary ornament and the highlighting of the red figures against an unframed expanse of black slip. This doubleen, while not a true Nolan amphora, is decorated in the "Nolan" style.

The august, fish-tailed creature on the main side of the vase, the obverse, is most likely Nereus, the wise "Old Man of the Sea," who was forced by Herakles to reveal the way to the Garden of the Hesperides. His spotted tail is tinted with brown dilute glaze and has two pairs of fins.

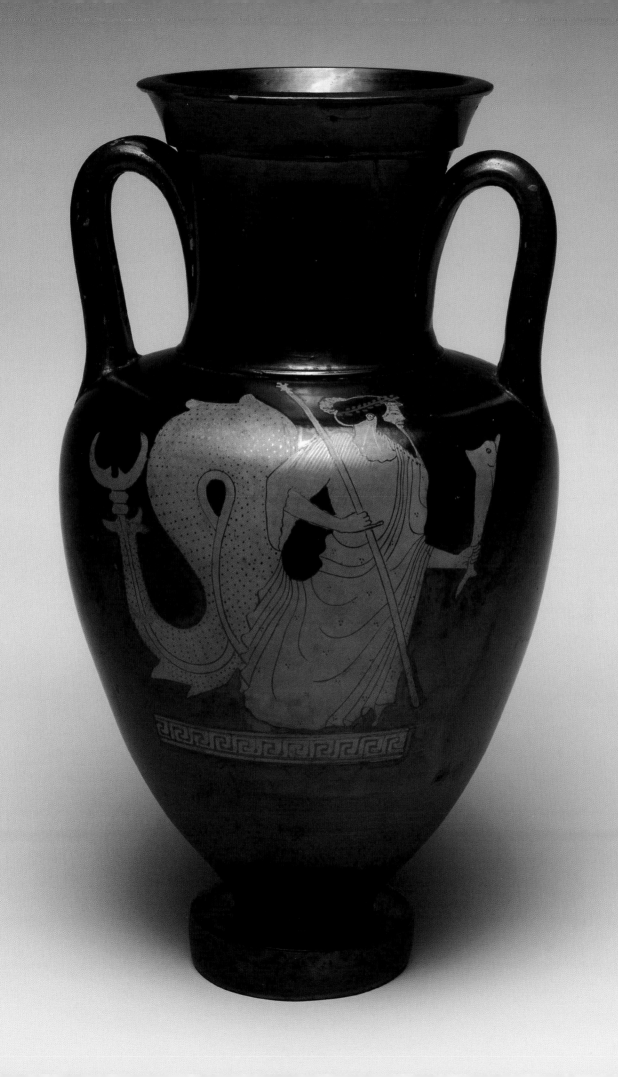

He carries a long, palmette-tipped scepter in his right hand and grasps a dolphin by its tail in his left. His human torso is clothed in a himation worn over a chiton; the relief-line folds of the himation are in bold contrast to the golden, diluted slip used for the chiton's pleats. He wears a wreath of leaves drawn in purple slip around his head, securing his long hair in a bun, a *krobylos*. His costume, which conceals the junction between his human and fish sections, is analogous to the garments worn by Cheiron, the wise senior centaur and tutor of heroes (e.g., cat. nos. 39, 40), whom the Berlin Painter elsewhere also portrayed with the civilized attributes of clothing, albeit on a body with human legs.[2] The portrayal of the fish-tailed Nereus with a draped human torso, however, was not directly borrowed from the iconography of Cheiron but developed in tandem with it: in the earliest Attic vase-paintings of Herakles wrestling with Nereus, of about 590 B.C., the sea god already has a draped human torso.[3] His civilized attire distinguishes Nereus from depictions of Triton, another fish-tailed merman with whom Herakles is often represented in combat, especially on black-figure vases of the preceding century, during which time the iconography of the two characters became conflated in ways still not completely understood.[4] The scepter is another identifying attribute, and on a hydria in London, the Berlin Painter actually depicted Nereus as a normal old man, dressed in a chiton and himation and clutching his scepter and fish.[5]

Nereus and his wife Doris had many sea-nymph daughters, the Nereids, the best known of whom is Thetis, the mother of Achilles. On the reverse, the draped female figure who runs to the left with arms outstretched is almost certainly a Nereid. Although she is not specifically identified by an inscription, her posture is identical to that of the Nereid on a stamnos by the Berlin Painter in Munich, who runs to her fish-tailed father with the news of Peleus's rape of Thetis.[6] On the Munich vase, Nereus again wears human garb, as does Cheiron, who on the opposite side of the vase receives the same news from another of Thetis's sisters.

Both Nereus and the Nereid are situated above ground lines consisting of a short segment of maeander, or key, pattern. The design of the painting on the obverse —where the curving coil of Nereus's fishlike form lends an added tension to the swelling body of the amphora— is masterful. Beazley considered this vase to be an early work by the Berlin Painter, which would date it somewhere around 490 B.C. The Berlin stamnos with the rape of Thetis was painted more than a decade later, about 480– 470 B.C., and thus was not the model for the imagery of the Harvard vase but rather an expanded recollection of it.
—DGM

**BIBLIOGRAPHY**

*CVA* Fogg-Gallatin, USA 8, 33, pl. 16.3; *ARV*[2] 200.49; *BAdd*[2] 191; Kurtz 1983, pls. 10.17, 43 c–d; *LIMC* 8 (1997), 73, no. 1, pl. 42, s.v. "Triton" (Icard-Gianolio); Paul 1997, 8 nn. 6–8.

**NOTES**

1  For Nolan amphorae, see Euwe 1986.

2  Paris, Louvre G 186: *ARV*[2] 207.140; *BAdd*[2] 194; Schnapp 1997, 447, fig. 542.

3  In particular, cf. Boston 1888.827 (*ABV* 13.45; *Paralipomena* 8; *BAdd*[2] 4) and a fragment in the Samos Museum (*ABV* 25.18; *Paralipomena* 15; *BAdd*[2] 7; *LIMC* 6 [1992], 826, pl. 519, s.v. "Nereus" [Pipili]).

4  For the iconography of Nereus and Triton, see Glynn 1981; Brommer 1983a; *LIMC* 4 (1988), 409–410, s.v. "Halios Geron" (Glynn); *LIMC* 6, 824–37, pls. 516–34, s.v. "Nereus"; *LIMC* 8, 68–73, pls. 42–46, s.v. "Triton."

5  London, Brit. Mus. E 162: *ARV*[2] 209.165; *BAdd*[2] 195; Glynn 1981, pl. 22, fig. 5; *LIMC* 6, 828, no. 42, pl. 521, s.v. "Nereus."

6  Munich 8738: *ARV*[2] 209.161; *Paralipomena* 343; *BAdd*[2] 195; *CVA* Berlin 5, Germany 20, pls. 259–62; *LIMC* 6, 830, no. 74, pl. 525, s.v. "Nereus"; Barringer 1995, pls. 80–83.

## 98

## Alabastron with Typhon

**Greek, Early Corinthian, ca. 610–600 B.C.**
**Ceramic**
**Height 25.9 cm., width 11.9 cm., depth 11.9 cm.**
**Yale University Art Gallery, Harold A. Strickland Jr.**
**Collection (1998.23.2)**

CONDITION

**The vessel is intact. There is slight wear on the
mouth and minor pitting on the body. Any added
white has worn away.**

Half human, half snake, the composite monster Typhon
virtually encircles this large Early Corinthian alabastron.
Propelled by his powerful tail and his red-and-black
striped sickle-shaped wings, Typhon is in motion, his
arms held in a pose characteristic of running figures in
Archaic Greek art. His upper body, which is frontal, is
human to the waist and garbed in a short-sleeved red chiton with plain and patterned black bands down the front
and across the neck and shoulders. His face and arms
are red. His head in profile, he wears a full beard and long
wavy hair that is held in place by a broad fillet and tied
in a snood at its end. The lower, serpentine part of his
body, a central band of solid red bordered by bands of
alternating red and black segments, swirls around the
vase. A large black dolphin, with red spots lining the base
of its beak and the folds in front of its pectoral flippers,
swims under the vessel's handle, suggesting a watery setting.
Black rosettes, some with red centers, fill the background.

Typhon, the most powerful and malevolent of
the serpentine monsters in Greek myth, embodied the
destructive forces of wind and fire.[1] Known at least as
early as Homer (*Il.* 2.783–84), Typhon appears frequently
in ancient literature. Son of Gaia and Tartaros, he is
varyingly described but invariably monstrous in size.
Apollodoros says that he was bigger than the mountains
and that his head touched the stars.[2] The same author,
who calls him Typhon, describes him as human to the
waist, but with legs that became huge hissing vipers that
reached up to his head; his arms reached out to the east
and west, and from each hand a hundred dragon heads

projected; his body bore wings; his wild hair and beard
streamed out on the wind; fire flashed from his eyes.
Hesiod calls him Typhoeus, and refers to the "scorch and
breath of his storm winds" and "the wonderful heads set
about on the dreaded monster," that is, the hundred
snakes' heads that grew from his shoulders, "that licked
with dark tongues" and "from [which] fire flared from his
eyes' glancing."[3] Hesiod, unlike most writers, apparently
gives Typhon human legs and feet ("the feet of the powerful god were tireless"). Both writers add noise—hissing,
horrible voices, "every sort of horrible sound." Mated to
the grisly, ageless nymph Echidna, Typhon fathered other
monsters, including, according to Apollodoros, the
Chimaera, the Nemean lion, and the Sphinx.[4]

Although not a giant, Typhon is associated with the
battle of the gods and giants as the last adversary of Zeus.
As told by Apollodoros, Typhon, the child of Earth, was
born after the gods had defeated the giants, inspired by
Earth's anger at the gods' victory. Grown to his full monstrous size and fury and driven to control the world,
Typhon challenged heaven itself with burning rocks and
hissing jets of fire, chasing the gods to Egypt. Only Zeus
stood and fought back, hurling thunderbolts and striking
the monster down with a sickle. But when Zeus leapt on
Typhon, the monster grasped the god with his snaky legs,
and, stealing the sickle, severed the tendons in the god's
hands and feet. Helpless, Zeus was carried off to a cave in
Cilicia, but Hermes rescued him and restored his tendons.
Renewed, Zeus charged out of heaven in a chariot after
Typhon, pelting him with thunderbolts. Typhon fought
back, hurling mountains at the god, but the thunderbolts
were more powerful, and Typhon went down. As he fled
through the Sicilian sea, Zeus buried him with Mount
Etna, which still breathes fire.

Typhon first appears in art in Corinth, where he
was a favorite subject on Corinthian terracotta alabastra
of the seventh century B.C.[5] This early Corinthian example is among the largest and boldest of the representations, but it is consistent with the more modest images on
smaller vessels. Typically, as here, Typhon's upper body is
upright on the vase, shown frontally with the arms held
out—"to the east and to the west"—and wings outstretched behind them. His bearded head faces right, his

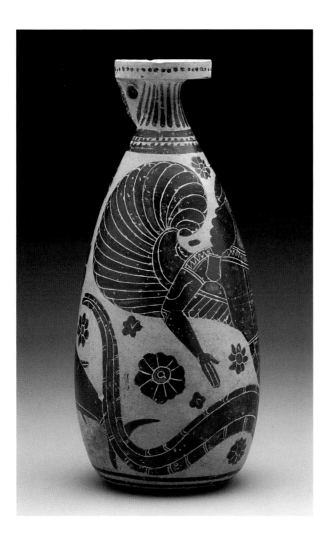

long hair hanging loosely or tied at the end. Below the waist, his body is that of a snake, which curves back on itself and circles around to the back of the vase. Generally there is an animal—here a dolphin, elsewhere a lion, eagle, swan, or other bird—in the space between the hands and wingtips on the back of the vase. There is little on these Corinthian alabastra that reproduces the literary description of Typhon: no hundred snakes emerging from hands or shoulders, no fire flaming from eyes. Variants include a double Typhon—one image superimposed on another—and possibly a centaurlike Typhon on a small aryballos attributed to the Ajax Painter (cat. no. 31), although this identification is now questioned.[6]

At least one vase shows Typhon with a double serpentine tail,[7] a detail that links it to images of Typhon on

early Argive-Corinthian bronze shield bands from Olympia decorated with reliefs of mythological scenes.[8] Some of the reliefs show Typhon as a single figure, like the Corinthian vases, while others show him as the last adversary of Zeus. These small vignettes typically show Zeus grasping Typhon around the neck with his left hand while holding a raised thunderbolt in his right. Typhon faces Zeus, "standing" on his tail(s), his wings spread or behind him, and, in one case, snakes emerging from his waist.

Outside of Corinth, a Typhon with a double tail appears on a Laconian cup in Cerveteri.[9] His tail is more fishy than serpentine, and he lacks wings, but the seventeen snakes that emerge from his waist, ends and both sides of his tails, and his wild beard and hair, are actually closer to the literary descriptions of Typhon than the

Corinthian vases. A Laconian fragment shows Typhon, apparently from a scene as the adversary of Zeus.[10] Typhon does not appear in Attic art, which suggests that the subject in art may be a Peloponnesian invention.[11] Perhaps the best known surviving example of the Typhon-Zeus confrontation is on a Chalcidian hydria in Munich of about 540–530 B.C.[12] Again, Typhon has a double tail, and he faces Zeus, who is named, in a composition like that of the shield bands.

The double-tailed Typhon is echoed by a figure on the Chest of Kypselos, one of the famous lost works of the Archaic period. Described by Pausanias, it was dedicated at Olympia by the Corinthian tyrant Kypselos in the seventh century B.C. and probably was of Corinthian manufacture.[13] In one of the carved ivory relief panels on the upper register of the chest, Boreas, the god of the north wind, is seen carrying off the maiden Oreithyeia. According to Pausanias, Boreas is shown with "serpent tails instead of feet."[14] This is one of the earliest representations of Boreas, who later appears in purely human form, and the artist appears to have appropriated the contemporary Typhon iconography to express the malevolent and chthonic aspects of the wind god.[15]

Typhon also appeared on a famous monumental work of art known to us only through literary sources and scant archaeological remains: the throne of Apollo at Amyklai, near Sparta, by Bathykles of Magnesia, erected around the middle of the sixth century B.C. As described by Pausanias,[16] Typhon "stands" with Echidna as two among a group of figures supporting the throne.

—SBM

## BIBLIOGRAPHY

*Yale University Art Gallery Bulletin* 1999 (September 2000): listed p. 197, ill. p. 199.

## NOTES

1 On Typhon, see *LIMC* 8 (1997), 147–51, pls. 112–13, s.v. "Typhoeus-Typhon" (Touchefeu-Meynier).

2 Apollod. *Bibl.* 1.6.3, trans. Loeb ed.

3 Hes. *Theog.* 820–81, trans. R. Lattimore; for references to discussion of authenticity of this passage, see *LIMC* 8, 147, s.v. "Typhoeus-Typhon."

4 Echidna: Hes. *Theog.* 304–5, 309–27. Monsters: Apollod. *Bibl.*1.6.3.

5 For these alabastra, see *LIMC* 8, 148, nos. 1–10, pl. 112, s.v. "Typhoeus-Typhon." For the Typhon Painter, see Amyx 1988, 56–57, pl. 18.

6 For the double Typhon, see Hamburg 1966.12: *LIMC* 8, 148–49, no. 10, pl. 112, s.v. "Typhoeus-Typhon." For the centaurlike Typhon by the Ajax Painter, see Boston 1895.12: Amyx 1988, 23, cat. no. 4, and p. 367; but see K. Manchester, in this volume (cat. no. 31), following Fittschen, for an alternative identification.

7 Paris, Cab. Méd. 135: *LIMC* 8, 148, no. A9, pl. 112, s.v. "Typhoeus-Typhon."

8 On the shield bands, see J. B. Grossman in this catalogue (cat. no. 36); see also Kunze 1950, and for a selection, *LIMC* 8, 149, nos. 16–19, s.v. "Typhoeus-Typhon."

9 Cerveteri 67658: Pipili 1987, 69, fig. 102.

10 London, Brit. Mus. B 7.6, from Naukratis: Pipili 1987, 69, fig. 101.

11 Pipili 1987, 69.

12 Munich 596: *LIMC* 8, 149, no. 14, pl. 112, s.v. "Typhoeus-Typhon."

13 Chest of Kypselos: Pausanias 5.17.5–19.10, trans. Pollitt 1990, 210–15; Splitter 2000.

14 Pausanias 5.19.1, trans. Pollitt 1990, 214.

15 Simon 1967, 111.

16 Throne of Apollo: Pausanias 3.18.9–19.5, trans. Pollitt 1990, 23–26.

# 99

## Black-Figure Oinochoe with Hermes and Pan

**Greek, Attic, ca. 490–480 B.C., attributed to the Theseus Painter**
**Ceramic**
**Height 22.6 cm., maximum diameter 14.3 cm., diameter of foot 7.7 cm.**
**Private collection**

### CONDITION

The vase is unbroken and in excellent condition. The black slip is misfired a smoky gray on much of the front, including the lower body, the spout and foot, and the figure of Pan. There is minor flaking of the black slip on the rim and handle.

Like the oinochoe with satyrs by the Athena Painter (cat. no. 61), this wine jug is of the Sèvres Class, an Attic black-figure shape with a plump, tapering body, a short neck, trefoil mouth, low cylindrical handle, and torus foot.[1] Most Sèvres Class oinochoai are white-ground; that is, their black-figure decoration is executed on a ground of creamy white slip, which coats two-thirds of the body, the rest of the vase being black. A pair of slender rotelle flanks the juncture of the rim and handle, each with a red face. Two lines of cherry red slip run beneath the white zone, and there are single red stripes circling the edge of the foot and the juncture of body and neck, below which is a band of simple black tongues.

The subject is a pair of deities, father and son. Hermes is seated to the right on a block; he is playing the auloi, the double flutes, which he holds in both hands. He is bearded and wears his usual winged boots, tunic, short cloak (chlamys), and petasos, a hat for sun and rain much favored by travelers and hunters and particularly associated with Hermes. This petasos is of the "Robin Hood" variety, with a tall peak and a single brim in front. The tunic and chlamys are decorated with red dots. Facing Hermes at the right is his son Pan, the Arcadian god of flocks who is always represented either as a goat, as he is here, or with a human torso and arms and only the head and legs of a goat.[2] The artist distinguishes the

god from a mere goat by having him stand erect like a man and dressing him in a spotted chlamys. As a final touch, he is shown leaning on a knotty walking stick, the essential accessory of the Greek male. Pan has impressively long horns and a full beard striated with incised lines. Behind him, four black dots fall in suspicious propinquity to his posterior;[3] there is a another dot in front, however, below his elbow, and it seems likely that all five have dripped accidentally from the painter's brush. On the back of the vase, a pair of vines issues from the root of the handle, branching to either side to touch the cap of Hermes and fill the space between the two gods. Two large birds, possibly ravens, stand behind the figures at left and right. Ravens are sacred to Apollo, the god of music. They are listening to Pan, whose mouth is open as he sings: "Not even that bird can surpass him in song / Who in blossoming springtime pours forth her lament / From her leafy bower, grieving in honeysweet tones."[4]

Most Sèvres Class oinochoai are painted by the Athena Painter or members of his workshop, but this jug has been attributed to the Theseus Painter.[5] The artist's hand is recognizable in such things as the wiry limbs of Hermes, his slender beard, the drawing and incision of his hands on the auloi, and above all the birds, which have direct correspondents on more than one of his vases.[6] The grapevines in the background are found on most Sèvres Class oinochoai but also on other shapes; indeed, they are a common motif in the work of many black-figure vase-painters of the late sixth and early fifth centuries, not excepting the Theseus Painter. The vines have no narrative function, nor are they purely decorative; the vast majority are on vessels associated with the serving and drinking of wine, and their ubiquity is a constant reminder of the pervasive power of Dionysos.

Pan was not one of the Twelve Olympians, but an Arcadian deity whose earliest depictions in Greek art date from just this period, immediately after the Battle of Marathon in 490 B.C., before which he was said to have assured the Athenians of his special favor (Hdt. 6.105). This charming portrayal of the god listening to the fluting Hermes is unique, but there are other musical goats. On a pelike by the Eucharides Painter in Samothrace, the seated Hermes is again playing the auloi, but this time

his audience consists of a satyr and a dancing goat that rears up on its hind legs.[7] The goats standing erect on either side of Dionysos on a lekythos by the Athena Painter at Dartmouth College are not in apparent motion, but on a black-figure hydria in Capetown and a red-figure cup in Rome, whole flocks rise up to dance to the tune of fluting satyrs.[8] A culmination of sorts is reached on a lekythos by the Athena Painter in the Collisani Collection, Palermo, where a satyr aulist is joined by two mixed pairs of goats and satyrs, who join hands (and hooves) in a kind of Dionysiac waltz.[9] It is unclear whether these caprine choruses are associated with the new popularity of Pan after 490 or are evidence for a pre-established receptiveness to his introduction into the Athenian pantheon at this time.

—JMP

## BIBLIOGRAPHY

Unpublished.

## NOTES

1 *ABL* 260.129–32, 261.30–35; *ABV* 524–25; *Paralipomena* 263; *BAdd²* 131; Mertens 1977, 71–77.

2 For Pan, see *RE* Suppl. 8 (1956), 949–1008, s.v. "Pan" (Brommer); Bourgeaud 1988; *LIMC* 8 (1997), 923–41, pls. 612–35, s.v. "Pan" (Boardman); Boardman 1998b. This vase joins the few depictions of Pan as completely caprine in form, all dating to the early fifth century (*LIMC* 8, 924, nos. 3–6, pl. 612). This conception of the god quickly gave way to his being thought of as half goat and half human, as he is described by Herodotus (2.46) and Plato (*Cra.* 408d).

3 Attic vase-painters were not above the graphic depiction of defecation, e.g., Athens, Nat. Mus. 1045: *ABV* 186.

4 *Hymn. Hom. Pan.* 16–19, trans. T. Sargent (1973).

5 Attributed by Walter Gilbert. This is the only oinochoe of this shape that the Theseus Painter is known to have painted and is added testament to his close relationship with the Athena Painter. For the Theseus Painter, see *ABL* 141–65, 249–54; *ABV* 518–21, 703–4, 716; *Paralipomena* 255–60; *BAdd²* 129–30; Boardman 1974, 147; Borgers 1999.

6 Cf. the fluting Hermes and goat (not Pan) on a skyphos by the Theseus Painter in South Hadley, Mass. (Mt. Holyoke College 1925 BS II.3: *ABV* 519, with no. 18; Buitron 1972, 54–55, no. 22). Goats turn up in many scenes by the Theseus Painter, as do aulists: e.g., a pelike in San Antonio (86.134.157: *Paralipomena* 257; Shapiro, Picón, and Scott 1995, 114–15, no. 56). On another pelike by the artist, in a private collection, two goats accompany a pair of fluting satyrs (London, Sotheby's, June 12, 1967, lot 139; *Paralipomena* 257). For the painter's distinctive birds, cf. Naples 2458 (*ABL* 250.33; *Paralipomena* 255; *BAdd²* 129); Lecce 560 (*ABL* 250.34; *Paralipomena* 255; Bernardini 1981, 34–35); Athens, Nat. Mus. 13916 (*Paralipomena* 259 ["near the Theseus Painter"]; *CVA* Athens 4, Greece 4, 50–51, pl. 42 [M. Pipili gives it to the artist himself]).

7 Samothrace Museum 57.565: *ARV²* 232.1; *Paralipomena* 174.23 bis; Price 1971, pl. 94, fig. 6. Price identified the goat as Pan, but it lacks any attributes, and there are other dancing goats of this type (see n. 8 below).

8 Dartmouth College, Hanover, Hood Museum of Art: *Paralipomena* 261; Terrace 1957, 6–7, fig. 15. Capetown, South Africa, Museum H 4827: *Paralipomena* 268.46; Boardman and Pope 1961, pl. III, no. 4. Rome, Villa Giulia 64224: Lissarrague 1988, 343, fig. 7.

9 Isler and Sguaitamatti 1990, pl. 28, no. 180.

# Statuette of Pan

**Greek, Boiotian, mid-fifth century B.C.**

**Terracotta**

**Height 12.9 cm., length of base 10.5 cm.**

**Museum of Fine Arts, Boston, gift by contribution (01.7777)**

## CONDITION

The fine-grained clay is light brown. The statuette has been repaired but is largely complete. The right arm, left hand, and the tip of the phallus are reattached. Missing are the right foot, the right horn, and the tips of the rhyton, left thumb, and right ear. There is some slight incrustation.

The goat god Pan is half reclining on a rock, representing the slope of a mountain. He raises both hands, probably to play the syrinx, the "Pan pipes," now lost.[1] A rhyton, a horn-shaped drinking cup, lies by his leg. The god's humanoid torso is lean and well muscled, but the limbs are more simply modeled, with hands like flattened mittens. The flaccid genitals are naturalistic, not idealized (i.e., small). The left leg is fully preserved and terminates in a cloven hoof. The solid body is handmade, but the face is molded, a combination frequently encountered in contemporary Boiotian terracotta satyrs (e.g., cat. no. 54). The corners of the mouth and the inside of the eyes are deepened with a pointed tool. The face is clearly that of a goat but with an almost human beard, though not as full and rounded as those of the clay satyrs. Two horns (the right one is missing) rise in a crescent from the top of the head, mirrored by the large caprine ears. There are traces of red and greenish yellow beneath the incrustation on the rock, and of pale blue on the horns. The underside of the rock is hollow.

E. P. Warren bought this statuette in Athens, but its fabric, technique, and style leave no doubt that it is a product of Boiotia, perhaps from one of the tombs at Tanagra or from the Kabirion sanctuary at Thebes. Paul Baur identified it as Tityros, a shepherd deity of goatish form, believing that it and another figurine from Thebes could not represent Pan because they have human legs

down to the hoofs, while "the legs of Pan are those of a goat from the trunk of the body down."[2] Most depictions of Pan are as he describes, including the numerous Boiotian class of standing, molded terracotta Pans that began toward the end of the fifth century and continued through most of the fourth.[3] There are, however, more than a few Pans with human legs, and even human feet,[4] and considering the popularity of the god in this period and the obscurity of Tityros, whose iconography is otherwise nonexistent, this figure's identity is not in doubt. The casual posture and the relationship to the handmade satyrs with molded faces suggest a date before the standardization of the series of terracotta Pans mentioned above. Among the latter are a few seated and reclining examples,[5] but none as free in their handling as this creature, created for a time and place in which it was still possible to believe in the wild spirits of the mountains.
—JMP

## BIBLIOGRAPHY

Baur 1905, 161–62, pl. V; Hoffmann 1964, 70–71, pl. 21.4.

## NOTES

1 Baur (1905, 161) thought he was playing the auloi, the double pipes, but Hoffmann (1964, 71) pointed out that the hands then ought to be open; he mentions a suggestion by Ines Jucker that he is instead playing a syrinx, and this is surely correct. For Pan, see the references in cat. no. 99.

2 Baur 1905, 157.

3 Winter 1903, pt. I, 220–21; Sieveking 1916, pl. 26; Higgins 1954, pl. 129, no. 891; Mollard-Besques 1954, pl. 63 (C44); Jurriaans-Helle 1997, pl. V; *LIMC* 8 (1997), 925, no. 30, pl. 614, s.v. "Pan" (Boardman).

4 For example, cf. the Pan (his name is inscribed) with human legs and feet on an Attic red-figure volute-krater in the Stanford University Art Museum (70.12: Raubitschek and Raubitschek 1982, pl. 15b; *LIMC* 8, 936, no. 243, pl. 631, s.v. "Pan").

5 Seated: Winter 1903, pt. I, 221.3; Higgins 1954, pl. 49, no. 297 (playing the syrinx); *LIMC* 8, 929, no. 122, pl. 622, s.v. "Pan." Reclining: *LIMC* 8, 929, no. 124, pl. 622.

# Glossary

**Acheloos**
River in northwest Greece; river deity with the body of a bull and the head of a man, the son of Okeanos and Tethys or Gaia.

**addorsed**
Arranged back-to-back.

**Aeolic capital**
Column capital in the form of two palm-like volutes emerging from the top of the shaft and spreading to either side.

**Akkadian**
Southern Mesopotamian culture of ca. 2500–2250 B.C.; the Semitic language of the Akkadians and its dialects.

**akroterion (pl. akroteria)**
Three-dimensional ornament or sculpture placed at the peaks and corners on the roof of a gabled building. See the architectural drawing.

**alabastron**
Flask for scented oil, slender or bag-shaped, with a rounded base, small mouth, and wide rim.

**amphora (pl. amphorae)**
Jar with two vertical handles, used for oil, water, and wine.

**amphoriskos (amphoriskoi)**
Miniature amphora.

**anta (pl. antae)**
Pilaster or corner post of slight projection at the end of the lateral walls of a cella.

**antefix**
Vertical, decorative plaque at the lower end of a cover tile, arranged in a row along the eaves of a roof. See the architectural drawing.

**apkallu (pl. apkallē)**
One of the Near Eastern "Seven Sages," often represented in the form of a fish-man or bird-man, who guarded the home and passageways from evil demons and disease.

**apotropaic**
Able to ward off evil.

**Archaic**
Period and style of Greek art, ca. 600–480 B.C.

*areté*
The Greek ideal of manly virtue.

**aryballos (pl. aryballoi).**
Small oil bottle, usually spherical or with a sharply tapering lower body.

**askos (pl. askoi)**
Small vessel with a spout and a single, curved handle on top.

**Assyrians**
A people of northern Mesopotamia, second to first millennia B.C.; see Neo-Assyrian

**Attic**
Refers to Attica, the region around Athens.

**auloi (sing. aulos)**
Double pipes, played simultaneously, one in each hand.

*ba*-bird
Egyptian human-headed bird representing the mobile aspect of the soul.

**band-cup**
Type of Little Master cup with a distinctive shape and decorative scheme, being mostly black except for a decorated reserved band in the handle zone.

**bell-krater**
Krater with a deep, rounded profile, an offset rim, and two handles at mid-body or higher.

**black-figure**
Technique of vase decoration in which the figures are silhouetted in black slip on a reddish clay ground, linear details are incised with a needle, and additional details are painted with white and cherry-red slip.

**Boreas**
Personification of the north wind.

**bucchero**
Etruscan pottery, seventh–sixth centuries B.C., fired black throughout, whose burnished surface was either plain or decorated by modeling, stamping, or incision.

**calyx-krater**
Krater with tall straight walls, a wide mouth, and two handles on the bulbous lower body.

**cavetto**
Concave, quarter-round molding.

**cella**
The enclosed inner sanctuary of a temple; in Greek, *naos*.

**centaur**
Mythical creature, half horse and half man, sometimes with four equine legs and a human torso, other times with equine hindquarters attached to a fully human body.

**centauromachy**
Battle with centaurs.

**Chalcidian**
Type of Archaic black-figure pottery, probably made at the Chalcidian colony of Rhegion, in Calabria.

**chasing**
Metal ornament consisting of indentations made with a hammer and a tool.

**Cheiron**
Immortal and civilized centaur, the son of Kronos and Philyra, who reared and trained several Greek heroes.

**Chimaera**
Monstrous daughter of Echidna and Typhon, killed by Bellerophon; normally represented as having the body of a lion with a goat's head on its back and a snake-headed tail.

**chiton**
Long gown, often of linen, sometimes buttoned along the arms to form sleeves; may be worn under a himation.

**chlamys**
Short cloak, pinned at one shoulder; often worn by hunters, travelers, and Hermes.

**Classical**
Period and style of Greek art, ca. 480–323 B.C.

**columen plaque**
Decorative plaque at the apex of a temple gable, affixed to the end of the wooden beam that supports the peak of the roof. See the architectural drawing.

**Corinthian**
Style of black-figure vase decoration in Corinth, ca. 640–550 B.C., characterized by animal friezes and copious filling ornament; divided into Transitional (640–625 B.C.), Early (ca. 625–600 B.C.), Middle (ca. 600–575 B.C.), and Late (ca. 575–550 B.C.).

**cuneiform**
The principal form of ancient Near Eastern writing, based on wedge-shaped impressions in clay, adapted to write many languages.

**cylinder seal**
Near Eastern stone seal of cylindrical shape, carved with an intaglio design and rolled onto clay to create an impression.

**Cypro-Archaic**
Period and style of Cypriote art, ca. 725–475 B.C.

**Cypro-Geometric**
Period and style of Cypriote art, ca. 1050–725 B.C.

**Daedalic**
A style of Greek art in the second half of the seventh century B.C.; figures have triangular faces and wig-like hair.

**Dark Ages**
Obscure period of Greek history, ca. 1100–950 B.C., between the decline of the Mycenaean civilization and the revival of Greek culture in the Early Iron Age.

**Deianeira**
Second wife of Herakles; daughter of Oineus.

**dinos (pl. dinoi)**
Large, handleless cauldron, with a wide mouth and depressed, spherical body, used for mixing wine and water (cf. lebes).

**Dorians**
Legendary northern invaders of Greece at the end of the second millennium B.C.; historical Greek speakers of Dorian dialects, including the Spartans and the Corinthians.

**dromos**
Race or race-course.

**echinus**
"Pillow"-shaped element of a Doric column capital; similarly shaped foot or mouth of a vessel.

**egg-and-dart**
Pattern applied to the Ionic ovolo molding, consisting of eggs alternating with slender darts.

**Enkidu**
The wild-man companion of Gilgamesh.

**Etruscans**
The people who dominated north-central Italy from the seventh to the fourth century B.C.

**Eros**
Greek god of sudden, passionate love; son of Aphrodite.

**Faliscans**
An Italic people centered on Falerii Veteres, under Etruscan cultural and political influence.

**Fikellura**
A type of East Greek pottery, ca. 560–520 B.C., named after a site on Rhodes but apparently made at Miletos.

**geison**
In small wooden temples, the beams running along the tops of the lateral cella walls and along the eaves above the lower ends of the roof joists.

**geison revetments**
Clay plaques decorating the geison beams. See the architectural drawing.

**Geometric**
Period and style of Greek art, ca. 900–700 B.C., divided into Early (900–850 B.C.), Middle (850–750 B.C.), and Late (750–700 B.C.).

**gigantomachy**
Mythical battle between the gods and the giants.

**Gilgamesh**
Mythical first king of the Sumerians, famed for heroic exploits.

**gorgoneion**
The disembodied head of the Gorgon Medusa.

**Gorgons**
Daughters of Phorkys and Keto (or Gaia), three monstrous sisters with hideous faces, fangs, beards, and snaky hair; the gaze of Medusa, who was beheaded by Perseus, turned people into stone.

**graffiti**
Incised linear writing, such as that incised directly onto the surface of clay pots.

**griffin**
Mythical animal with the body of a lion and the wings and head of a beaked bird.

**Harpies**
Winged beings who snatch and carry off people and things; they tormented Phineus and were driven off by the sons of Boreas.

**Hellenistic**
Period and style of Greek art between the death of Alexander the Great and the end of the Roman Republic, ca. 323–31 B.C.

**Herakles**
Widely popular Greek hero, son of Zeus and Alkmene; he completed twelve Labors and earned immortality.

**himation**
Large rectangular cloth garment draped over the shoulder and wrapped around the body; worn by both men and women.

**hoplite**
Greek infantryman who went to battle clad in bronze armor and carrying a spear and a heavy shield.

**Humbaba**
A monster killed by Gilgamesh and Enkidu.

**hydria (pl. hydriae)**
Water jar with two horizontal handles and a vertical handle in the back.

**impasto**
Type of Villanovan and early Etruscan pottery, ninth—early seventh centuries B.C.., with a burnished surface and incised or relief decoration.

**Ionians**
Greeks speaking the Ionic dialect, including the Athenians; the Greeks of Ionia on the central Aegean coast of Turkey and adjacent islands.

**janiform kantharos**
Wine cup with two vertical handles and a mold-made body in the form of addorsed heads.

**Kaineus**
Lapith warrior, originally female, who was changed by Poseidon into an invulnerable man but was killed when the centaurs drove him into the ground.

**kantharos (pl. kantharoi)**
Wine cup with a deep body and two vertical handles, often rising high above the rim; associated with Dionysos.

**Kassites**
A Near Eastern people who controlled central and southern Mesopotamia in the second half of the second millennium B.C.

**Ker**
Homeric goddess of violent death; daughter of Nyx and Erebos.

**Kerameikos**
The potters' quarter in Athens; a cemetery in the same district.

**kerykeion**
A herald's staff, carried by Hermes; in Latin, *caduceus*.

**Keto**
Daughter of Gaia and Okeanos; wife of Phorkys; mother of the Gorgons, Skylla, and other monsters.

**kibisis**
A pouch or wallet, used by Perseus to carry the head of Medusa.

**kithara**
Large concert lyre with a wooden sound-board and seven strings.

*Knielauf*
German term referring to a stylized posture adopted by running figures in Archaic Greek art, with the legs and arms flexed in pin-wheel fashion.

**komasts**
Drunken revelers.

**kore**
Archaic Greek statue of a young female.

**kottabos**
Game in which the object is to fling at a target the wine dregs in one's cup.

**kotyle**
A variety of skyphos, a deep wine cup, with tapering body, thin walls, straight rim, simple base ring, and two horizontal handles.

**kouros**
Archaic Greek statue of a young man.

**kourotrophos**
Refers to the rearing of children; a nursing mother.

**krater**
Large, wide-mouthed bowl used for mixing wine and water; basic varieties are bell, calyx, column, and volute.

**krateriskos**
Miniature krater.

**krobylos**
Long hair tied in a queue and pulled up under a headband to fall back over the top.

**Kronos**
Youngest son of Heaven (Ouranos) and Earth (Gaia) and the leader of his siblings against the Titans; father of Zeus and Cheiron.

**kudurru**
Type of decorated Mesopotamian—particularly Kassite—boundary stone.

**kylix (pl. kylikes)**
Wine cup with a wide, shallow bowl and two horizontal handles.

**kymation**
Curved, S-shaped molding, with the protruding upper portion either concave (cyma recta) or convex (cyma reversa).

**Laconian**
Refers to Laconia, the area around Sparta.

**laḫmu**
Powerful hero in Near Eastern mythology.

**Lamaštu**
Near Eastern goddess/demon who was part-lion; an enemy of pregnant women, women in childbirth, and babies.

**Lapiths**
Mythical tribe of Thessalian Greeks who battled the centaurs at the wedding of Peirithoos.

**Late Bronze Age**
In the eastern Mediterranean and the Near East, the period roughly encompassing the second half of the second millennium B.C.

**lebes**
Handleless cauldron with a wide mouth, overhanging rim, and depressed, spherical body; in pottery also called a dinos.

**lekanis (pl. lekanides)**
Wide, shallow, lidded dish with two horizontal handles.

**lekythos**
Tall oil vessel with a tapering or cylindrical body, slender neck, and single vertical handle.

**limu**
Eponymous yearly magistrate during the Middle Assyrian period.

**lip-cup**
Type of Little Master cup with figural decoration confined to the reserved lip and to the circular tondo in the bowl.

**Little Master cup**
Greek wine cup, ca. 560–530 B.C., with slightly offset lip, moderately deep bowl, tall, stemmed foot, and miniaturist decoration.

**lost-wax**
Bronze-casting process in which a wax model, sometimes built around a clay core, is covered with clay and then fired; bronze is poured in to replace the melted wax, after which the outer clay shell is removed.

**louterion**
Wide, rounded bowl with a spout on one side and two upright loop handles on the shoulder.

**maenads**
Frenzied female worshipers of Dionysos; also called bacchantes.

**maeander**
Ornamental pattern consisting of lines making consecutive right-angle turns into a center.

**metopes**
Panels in a Doric frieze that alternate with triglyphs and frequently have sculpted decoration.

**Middle Assyrian**
Assyrian art and culture, ca. 1521–1021 B.C.

**Minoan**
Bronze Age civilization of Crete, ca. 3000–1100 B.C.

**Minotaur**
Mythical monster, son of Queen Pasiphaë and the Cretan Bull, with a human body and the head of a bull; lived in the Labyrinth; killed by Theseus.

**Mischwesen**
German term meaning "mixed beings," i.e., composite creatures.

**Mitanni**
People who dominated North Syria and northern Meopotamia in the mid-second millennium B.C.

**modius**
A corn measure.

**mutulus plaque (pl. mutuli)**
In a small wooden temple, a decorative plaque affixed to the end of the lateral geison beam. See the architectural drawing.

**Mycenaean**
Late Bronze Age civilization of Greece, ca. 1580–1100 B.C., centered on the Greek mainland but also subsuming the older Minoan civilization of Crete.

**neck-amphora**
Amphora with an offset neck.

**Neo-Assyrian**
Assyrian art and culture, ca. 911–612 B.C., when the Assyrian empire dominated much of the Near East.

**Neo-Babylonian**
Resurgent Babylonian culture, ca. 626–539 B.C., from the fall of Assyria to the capture of Babylon by the Persians.

**Nereus**
Wise sea-god, father of Thetis, who mutated while Herakles wrestled him, eventually revealing the way to the Garden of the Hesperides; often confused with Triton.

**Nessos**
Centaur killed by Herakles for attempting to molest Deianeira while carrying her across a river.

**Nolan amphora**
Type of fifth-century Attic red-figure amphora distinguished by its slender shape and elegant decoration.

**nymphs**
Female nature spirits representing the divine powers of mountains, water, woods, and trees.

**Oedipus**
Mythical king of Thebes who solved the riddle of the Sphinx; he unwittingly killed his father and married his mother.

**oinochoe (pl. oinochoai)**
One-handled jug for pouring liquids.

**Orientalizing period**
The seventh century B.C., a period of strong Near Eastern influence on Greek art.

**orthostat**
Upright stone slabs arranged at the base of a wall.

**ovolo**
Rounded, convex molding.

**palmette-lotus chain**
Decorative pattern consisting of an interlocking chain of addorsed palmettes alternating with addorsed lotus buds.

**Pan**
Olympian god of flocks; the son of Hermes, represented in the form of a goat or a hybrid of goat and man.

**Panathenaic Games**
Athletic games in honor of Athena, held every four years in Athens at the Greater Panathenaia.

**parthenoi**
Maidens, virgins.

**patina**
Corrosion product formed on bronze or copper.

**Pazuzu**
Malignant Near Eastern demon of the underworld and guardian against Lamaštu; usually portrayed with a leonine or dog-like head.

**Pegasos**
Winged horse born from the slain Medusa; tamed by Bellerophon.

**Peleus**
Mythical Greek hero who was raised by Cheiron; wrestled with Atalanta at the funeral games of Pelias; forced Thetis to be his wife; and brought his son Achilles to Cheiron.

**Peloponnesian War**
Fought intermittently from 431 until 404 B.C. between Athens and Sparta, and their allies.

**pelora**
Malevolent monsters of Greek myth.

**pelta**
Small, light shield of crescent shape.

**peplos**
Sleeveless woolen garment, secured by a pin at each shoulder; worn by women.

**Perseus**
Mythological hero who killed the Gorgon Medusa; son of Zeus and Danaë.

**petasos**
Wide-brimmed hat worn by travelers, hunters, and Hermes.

**Phoenicians**
The people of ancient Lebanon, renowned as sea traders.

**Pholos**
Mythical centaur, of a mild and hospitable nature; he entertained Herakles on Mount Pholoë in Arcadia.

**Phorkys**
Son of Nereus and Gaia; father of the Gorgons.

**pinax**
Flat clay plaque decorated with painting or relief.

**pithos**
Very large ceramic storage jar.

**polos**
Cylindrical female headdress.

**Pontic**
The earliest black-figure vases in Etruria, ca. 560–500 B.C., possibly produced by immigrant East Greek artisans.

**Pontos**
Okeanós, son Gaia, father of Nereus, Phorkys, and Acheloos; region of northern Asia Minor bordering the Black Sea.

**Potnia Theron**
Divine "Mistress of Animals," often associated with Artemis.

**prostyle**
Temple with a portico of columns in the front.

**prothesis**
The laying out of a deceased person for mourning.

**Protoattic**
Attic pottery style, ca. 700–630 B.C.

**Protocorinthian**
Corinthian pottery style, ca. 720–640 B.C.

**Protogeometric**
Period and style of Greek art, ca. 1050–900 B.C

**protome**
Forepart of an animal.

**pyrrhic**
Ritual war dance performed in partial armor.

**pyxis (pl. pyxides)**
Small, lidded box.

**raking sima**
The sima that runs along the edge of a pediment. See the architectural drawing.

**red-figure**
Technique of vase decoration in which the background is painted with black slip and the figures are left reserved in the reddish orange color of the clay.

**repoussé**
Relief ornament produced by hammering the opposite side of a metal sheet.

**reserved**
Section of a vase that is not coated with slip, e.g., the reddish orange clay of Attic black-figure and red-figure vases.

**rhyton (pl. rhyta)**
One-handled drinking cup, often molded in the form of an animal's head.

**sakkos**
Cloth snood.

**saltire**
X-shaped cross.

**satyr**
Mythical creature, part man and part horse, with equine tail and ears, and sometimes hooves; associated with Dionysos; also called a silenos.

**Siana cup**
Type of Attic black-figure kylix, ca. 570–550 B.C., with an offset lip and short flaring foot.

**silenos**
Generically, a satyr; also a specific mythical satyr (Silenos), known for his wisdom, who was captured by King Midas.

**sima**
The clay or stone gutter of a building, often decorated and frequently pierced by lion's head spouts.

**siren**
Mythical monster with the body of a bird and the head of a woman, who lured sailors to their death.

**situla**
Bucket-shaped vase with a bail handle.

**skyphos**
Deep wine cup with two handles near the rim; see kotyle.

**slip**
Blend of refined clay and water mixed to creamy consistency; the black gloss ("glaze") on Greek vases is a slip.

**sphendone**
Headband resembling a sling and worn by women.

**Sphinx**
Mythical monster with the body of a winged lion and the head of a woman; its deadly riddle was solved by Oedipus.

**stamnos**
Wide-mouthed jar with an offset neck and two horizontal handles.

**Theseus**
Mythical Athenian hero, son of Aigeus or Poseidon; slayer of the Minotaur.

**Thessaly**
Region in northeast Greece, south of Macedonia.

**Thetis**
Sea nymph, daughter of Nereus; wife of Peleus; mother of Achilles.

**thiasos**
The riotous retinue of Dionysos, including satyrs, nymphs, and/or maenads.

**thymiaterion**
Vessel for burning incense.

**thyrsos**
Fennel wand tipped with ivy, associated with Dionysos and carried by maenads.

**Titans**
Older gods predating the Olympians; the children of Heaven (Ouranos) and Earth (Gaia); defeated by Zeus.

**tondo**
Decorated circular field in the interior of a kylix or plate.

**Triton**
Mythical sea monster with the upper body of a man and the lower body and tail of a fish; in art, he is shown wrestling with Herakles.

**Typhon**
Mythical monster, son of Gaia and
Tartaros; husband of Echidna; father of
the Chimaera, the Nemean lion, and
the Sphinx; commonly represented with
a serpentine lower body; defeated by
Zeus and buried under Mount Etna.

**Tyrrhenian amphora**
Type of Attic black-figure amphora,
ca. 570–550 B.C., with a distinctive ovoid
shape, multiple animal friezes, and a
figural frieze on the shoulder; apparently
made primarily for export to Etruria.

**volute-krater**
Krater with two high handles in the form
of Ionic volutes.

**white-ground**
White clay slip applied to the surface of
a vase before decoration.

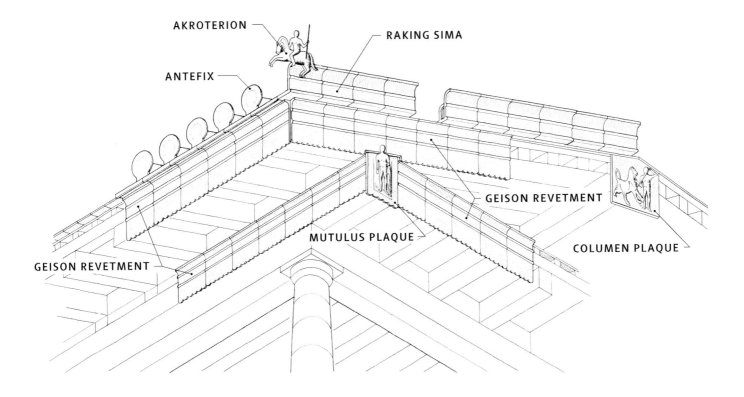

# Bibliography of Works Cited

**AHLBERG-CORNELL 1884**
Ahlberg-Cornell, G. *Herakles and the Sea-Monster in Attic Black-Figure Vase-Painting.* Stockholm 1984.

**AHLBERG-CORNELL 1992**
Ahlberg-Cornell, G. *Myth and Epos in Early Greek Art: Representation and Interpretation.* Studies in Mediterranean Archaeology 100. Jonsered 1992.

**ÅKERSTROM 1966**
Åkerstrom, Å. *Architektonischen Terrakotten Kleinasiens.* Lund 1966.

**ÅKERSTROM 1978**
Åkerstrom, Å. "Ionia and Anatolia, Ionia and the West. The Figured Architectural Terracotta Frieze: Its Penetration and Transformation in the East and the West in the Archaic Period." In *Proceedings of the Tenth International Congress of Classical Archaeology, Ankara-Izmir 1973,* 319–27. Ankara 1978.

**AKURGAL 1949**
Akurgal, E. *Späthethitische Bildkunst, Ankara Üniversitesi, Dil ve Tarih-Cografya Fakültesi yayimlari* no. 60. *Arkeoloji Enstitüsü* [yayimlari] no. 4. Ankara 1949.

**AKURGAL 1961**
Akurgal, E. *Die Kunst Anatoliens von Homer bis Alexander.* Berlin 1961.

**AKURGAL 1968**
Akurgal, E. *The Art of Greece: Its Origins in the Mediterranean and Near East.* Trans. W. Dynes. New York 1968.

**AKURGAL 1992**
Akurgal, E. "Zur Enstehung des griechischen Greifenbildes." In *Kotinos: Festschrift für Erika Simon,* ed. H. Froning, T. Hölscher, and H. Mielsch, 34–52. Mainz 1992.

**AKURGAL 1992**
Akurgal, M. "Eine protokorinthische Oinochoe aus Erythrai." *IstMitt* 42 (1992): 83–96.

**AKURGAL AND HIRMER 1961**
Akurgal, E., and M. Hirmer. *Die Kunst der Hethiter.* Munich 1961.

**ALEXANDER 1929**
Alexander, C. "Miscellaneous Accessions in the Classical Department." *BMMA* 24.8 (1929): 201–4.

**ALEXANDER 1939**
Alexander, C. "Greek Vases, Recent Accessions." *BMMA* 34.9 (1939): 98–100.

**ALMAGRO-GORBEA 1977**
Almagro-Gorbea, M. *El bronce final y el periodo orientalizante en extremadura.* Madrid 1977.

**AMANDRY 1958**
Amandry, P. "Objets orientaux en Grèce et en Italie aux VIIIe et VIIe siècles av. J.-C." *Syria* 35 (1958): 73–109.

**AMIET 1956**
Amiet, P. "Le Symbolisme cosmique du répertoire animalier en Mésopotamie." *RAssyr* 50 (1956): 113–26.

**AMIET 1976A**
Amiet, P. *Les Antiquités du Luristan.* Paris 1976.

**AMIET 1976B**
Amiet, P. "Introduction à l'étude du panthéon systématique et des panthéons locaux dans l'Ancien Orient." *Orientalia* 45 (1976): 15–32.

**AMIET 1980**
Amiet, P. *La Glyptique mésopotamienne archaïque.* 2d ed. Paris 1980.

**AMYX 1971**
Amyx, D. A. "Dodwelliana." *CSCA* 4 (1971): 1–48.

**AMYX 1988**
Amyx, D. A. *Corinthian Vase-Painting of the Archaic Period.* 3 vols. Berkeley and Los Angeles 1988.

**AMYX AND LAWRENCE 1996**
Amyx, D. A., and P. Lawrence. *Studies in Archaic Corinthian Vase-Painting.* Princeton 1996.

**ANCIENT ART IN THE VIRGINIA MUSEUM 1973**
*Ancient Art in the Virginia Museum.* Richmond 1973.

**ANDERSON 1961**
Anderson, J. K. *Ancient Greek Horsemanship.* Berkeley and Los Angeles 1961.

**ANDERSON 1975**
Anderson, L. H. *Relief Pithoi from the Archaic Period of Greek Art.* Ph.D. diss., University of Colorado 1975.

**ANDRÉN 1940**
Andrén, A. *Architectural Terracottas from Etrusco-Italic Temples.* Lund 1940.

**ANDRÉN 1971–74**
Andrén, A. "Osservazioni sulle terrecotte architettoniche etrusco-italiche." *OpRom* 8 (1971–74): 1–16.

**ANDRIOMENOU 1975**
Andrioménou, A. "Vases et lampes de bronze dans des collections privées d'Athènes." *BCH* 99 (1975): 535–80.

**ARAFAT 1990**
Arafat, K. W. *Classical Zeus: A Study in Art and Literature.* Oxford 1990.

**ARCHIBALD 1998**
Archibald, Z. H. *The Odrysian Kingdom of Thrace.* Oxford 1998.

**ARNOLD 1972**
Arnold, R. *The Horse-Demon in Early Greek Art and His Eastern Neighbors.* Ph.D. diss., Columbia University 1972.

**ARNOLD AND BURTON 1978**
Arnold, E., and J. Burton. *A Field Guide to the Reptiles and Amphibians of Britain and Europe.* London 1978.

**ASHMEAD 1999**
Ashmead, A. H. *Haverford College Collection of Classical Antiquities: The Bequest of Ernest Allen.* Philadelphia 1999.

**ASHMOLE AND YALOURIS 1967**
Ashmole, B., and N. Yalouris. *Olympia: The Sculptures of the Temple of Zeus.* London 1967.

**ATLANTIS ANTIQUITIES 1988**
Atlantis Antiquities. *Greek and Etruscan Art of the Archaic Period.* New York 1988.

**BABELON 1929**
Babelon, J. *Choix de bronzes et de terres cuites des collections Oppermann et de Janzé.* Paris 1929.

**BABELON 1930**
Babelon, E. *Bibliothèque Nationale, Cabinet des Médailles et Antiques. Les Pierres gravées. Guide du visiteur.* Paris 1930.

**BABELON AND BLANCHET 1895**
Babelon, E., and J. A. Blanchet. *Catalogue des bronzes antiques de la Bibliothèque Nationale.* Paris 1895.

**BAILEY AND HOCKEY 2001**
Bailey, D. M., and M. Hockey. "'New' Objects from British Museum Tomb 73 at Curium." In *Cyprus in the Nineteenth Century A.D.: Fact, Fancy and Fiction,* ed. V. Tatton-Brown, 109–33. Oxford 2001.

**BAKIR 1978**
Bakir, G. "Der Maler von Istanbul 7314." *AA* 1978, 26–43.

**BAKIR 1981**
Bakir, G. *Sophilos: Ein Beitrag zu seinem Stil.* Mainz 1981.

**BARNETT 1967**
Barnett, R. D. "Layard's Nimrud Bronzes and Their Inscriptions." *Eretz-Israel* 8 (1967): 1–7.

**BARNETT 1975**
Barnett, R. D. *A Catalogue of the Nimrud Ivories.* 2d ed. London 1975.

**BARNETT 1976**
Barnett, R. D. *Sculptures from the North Palace of Ashurbanipal at Nineveh (668–627 B.C.).* London 1976.

**BARNETT 1982**
Barnett, R. D. *Ancient Ivories in the Middle East, Qedem.* Monographs of the Institute of Archaeology, The Hebrew University of Jerusalem 14. Jerusalem 1982.

**BARNETT AND FORMAN N.D.**
Barnett, R. D., and W. Forman. *Assyrian Palace Reliefs and Their Influence on the Sculptures of Babylonia and Persia.* London n.d.

**BARRINGER 1995**
Barringer, J. *Divine Escorts: Nereids in Archaic and Classical Greek Art.* Ann Arbor 1995.

**BARRINGER 2001**
Barringer, J. M. *The Hunt in Ancient Greece.* Baltimore 2001.

**BARRON 1972**
Barron, J. P. "New Light on Old Walls: The Murals of the Theseion." *JHS* 92 (1972): 20–45.

**BARR-SHARRAR 2000**
Barr-Sharrar, B. "Observations on the Derveni Tomb: A Bronze Volute-Krater." In ΜΥΡΤΟΣ: μνημή Ιουλία Βοκοτοπούλου, ed. D. Pantermales, 159–78. Thessaloniki 2000.

**BASISTA 1979**
Basista, W. "Hektors Lösing." *Boreas* 2 (1979): 5–36.

**BAUR 1905**
Baur, P. "Tityros." *AJA* 9 (1905): 157–65.

**BAUR 1907**
Baur, P. "Pre-Roman Antiquities in Spain." *AJA* 11 (1907): 51.

**BAUR 1912**
Baur, P. V. C. *Centaurs in Ancient Art.* Berlin 1912.

**BEAZLEY 1927**
Beazley, J. D. "Review of CVA Hoppin and Gallatin, *USA* 1." JHS 47 (1927): 148–49.

**BEAZLEY 1929**
Beazley, J. D. "Charinos." *JHS* 49 (1929): 38–78.

**BEAZLEY 1931–32**
Beazley, J. D. "Groups of Mid-Sixth-Century Black-Figure." *BSA* 32 (1931–32): 1–22.

**BEAZLEY 1932**
Beazley, J. D. "Little-Master Cups." *JHS* 52 (1932): 167–204.

**BEAZLEY 1939**
Beazley, J. D. "Two Swords, Two Shields." *BABesch* 14.1 (1939): 4–14.

**BEAZLEY 1944**
Beazley, J. D. "Groups of Early Attic Black-Figure." *Hesperia* 13 (1944): 38–57.

**BEAZLEY 1947a**
Beazley, J. D. *Etruscan Vase-Painting.* Oxford 1947.

**BEAZLEY 1947b**
Beazley, J. D. "Some Attic Vases in the Cyprus Museum." *Proceedings of the British Academy* 33 (1947): 195–244.

**BEAZLEY 1951**
Beazley, J. D. *The Development of Attic Black-Figure.* Berkeley 1951.

**BEAZLEY 1954**
Beazley, J. D. "Some Inscriptions on Greek Vases: VI." *AJA* 58 (1954): 187–90.

**BEAZLEY 1986**
Beazley, J. D. *The Development of Attic Black-Figure.* 2d ed. Rev. by D. von Bothmer and M. Moore. Berkeley 1986.

**BEAZLEY 1989**
Beazley, J. D. *Some Attic Vases in the Cyprus Museum.* Ed. D. C. Kurtz. Oxford 1989.

**BECK 1975**
Beck, A. G. *Album of Greek Education: The Greeks at School and at Play.* Sydney 1975.

**BECK, BOL, AND BÜCKLING 1990**
Beck, H., P. Bol, and M. Bückling, eds. *Polyklet: Der Bildhauer der griechischen Klassik.* Frankfurt am Main 1990.

**BELL 1977**
Bell, E. E. "Two Krokotos Mask Cups at San Simeon." *CSCA* 10 (1977): 1–15.

**BELL 1981**
Bell, M., III. *Morgantina Studies.* Vol 1, *The Terracottas.* Princeton 1981.

**BELSON 1981**
Belson, J. D. *The Gorgoneion in Greek Architecture.* Ph.D. diss., Bryn Mawr College 1981.

**BENNETT 1997**
Bennett, M. J. *Belted Heroes and Bound Women: The Myth of the Homeric Warrior-King.* Lanham 1997.

366

**BENNETT 1999**
Bennett, M. "The Belted Hero Figurine: New Evidence." In Docter and Moormann 1999, 12–14.

**BENNETT, PAUL, AND IOZZO 2002**
Bennett, M., A. J. Paul, and M. Iozzo. *Magna Graecia: Greek Art from South Italy and Sicily*. Exhib. cat. Cleveland Museum of Art. Cleveland 2002.

**BENSON 1967**
Benson, J. L. "The Central Group of the Corfu Pediment." In *Gestalt und Geschichte: Festschrift Karl Schefold*, ed. M. Rohde-Liegle, H. A. Cahn, and H. C. Ackermann, 48–60. *AntK* Beiheft 4. Bern 1967.

**BENSON 1970**
Benson, J. L. *Horse, Bird, and Man: The Origins of Greek Painting*. Amherst 1970.

**BENSON 1986**
Benson, J. L. "Middle Protocorinthian Periodization." In *Corinthiaca: Studies in Honor of Darrell A. Amyx*, ed. M. Del Chiaro, 97–106. Columbia (Missouri) 1986.

**BENSON 1989**
Benson, J. L. *Earlier Corinthian Workshops*. Amsterdam 1989.

**BENSON 1995a**
Benson, J. L. "Human Figures, the Ajax Painter, and Narrative Scenes in Earlier Corinthian Vase Painting." In Carter and Morris 1995, 335–62.

**BENSON 1995b**
Benson, J. L. "Human Figures and Narrative in Later Protocorinthian Vase Painting." *Hesperia* 64 (1995): 163–77.

**BENTZ 1998**
Bentz, M. *Panathenäische Preisamphoren*. *AntK* Beiheft 18. Basel 1998.

**BERAN 1957**
Beran, T. "Assyrische Glyptik des 14. Jahrhunderts." *ZA* 18 (1957): 141–215.

**BÉRARD 1981**
Bérard, C. "Achéloos ou Nessos? (Archiloque 273–277 LB)." *Études de lettres*, ser. 4, vol. 4.2 (1981): 3–14.

**BERNARDINI 1981**
Bernardini, M. *I vasi attici del Museo Provinciale di Lecce*. 2d ed. Galatina 1981.

**BERNHARD-WALCHER 1991**
Bernhard-Walcher, A. *Alltag, Feste, Religion: Antikes Leben auf griechischen Vasen*. Vienna 1991.

**BERNHEIMER 2001**
Bernheimer, G. M. *Glories of Ancient Greece: Vases and Jewelry from the Borowski Collection*. Exhib. cat. Bible Lands Museum. Jerusalem 2001.

**BERTI 1991**
Berti, F. *Dionysos: Mito e mistero*. Ferrara 1991.

**BESIG 1937**
Besig, H. *Gorgo und Gorgoneion in der archaischen Kunst*. Berlin 1937.

**BETANCOURT 1977**
Betancourt, P. *The Aeolic Style in Architecture*. Princeton 1977.

**BEVAN 1986**
Bevan, E. *Representations of Animals in Sanctuaries of Artemis and Other Olympian Deities*. Oxford 1986.

**BIERS 1999**
Biers, W. R. "'Plastic' Sirens from Corinth: An Addendum to Amyx." *Hesperia* 68 (1999): 135–146.

**BIERS, GERHARDT, AND BRANIFF 1994**
Biers, W. R., K. O. Gerhardt, and R. A. Braniff. *Lost Scents: Investigations of Corinthian "Plastic" Vases by Gas Chromatography-Mass Spectrometry*. MASCAP 11. Philadelphia 1994.

**BIRCHALL 1972**
Birchall, A. "Attic Horse-Head Amphorae." *JHS* 92 (1972): 46–63.

**BLACK 1988**
Black, J. A. "The Slain Heroes: Some Monsters of Ancient Mesopotamia." *Bulletin of the Society for Mesopotamian Studies* 15 (1988): 19–25.

**BLACK AND GREEN 1992**
Black, J., and A. Green. *Gods, Demons, and Symbols of Ancient Mesopotamia*. Austin 1992.

**BLATTER 1975**
Blatter, R. "Frühe Kirkebilder." *AntK* 18 (1975): 76–78.

**BLECH 2001**
Blech, M., M. Koch, and M. Kunst, eds. *Hispania antiqua: Denkmäler der Frühzeit*. Mainz 2001.

**BLEGEN 1937**
Blegen, C. *Prosymna: The Helladic Settlement preceding the Argive Heraeum*. Cambridge 1937.

**BLINKENBERG 1931**
Blinkenberg, C. *Lindos: Fouilles de l'acropole, 1902–1914*. Berlin 1931.

**BLOESCH 1982**
Bloesch H., ed. *Greek Vases from the Hirschmann Collection*. Zürich 1982.

**BLOME 1990**
Blome, P. ed. *Orient und frühes Griechenland: Kunstwerke der Sammlung H. und T. Bosshard*. Basel 1990.

**BOARDMAN 1963**
Boardman, J. *Island Gems: A Study of Greek Seals in the Geometric and Early Archaic Periods*. London 1963.

**BOARDMAN 1967**
Boardman, J. *Pre-Classical: From Crete to Archaic Greece*. London 1967.

**BOARDMAN 1968**
Boardman, J. *Archaic Greek Gems: Schools and Artists in the Sixth and Early Fifth Centuries B.C.* London 1968.

**BOARDMAN 1970**
Boardman, J. "A Protocorinthian Dinos and Stand." *AntK* 13 (1970): 92–94.

**BOARDMAN 1972**
Boardman, J. "Herakles, Peisistratos, and Sons." *RA* 1972, 57–72.

**BOARDMAN 1974**
Boardman, J. *Athenian Black-Figure Vases*. Oxford 1974.

**BOARDMAN 1975a**
Boardman, J. *Athenian Red-Figure Vases: The Archaic Period*. London 1975.

**BOARDMAN 1975b**
Boardman, J. "Herakles, Peisistratos, and Eleusis." *JHS* 95 (1975): 1–12.

**BOARDMAN 1978**
Boardman, J. *Greek Sculpture: The Archaic Period. A Handbook*. Norwich 1978.

**BOARDMAN 1980**
Boardman, J. *The Greeks Overseas: Their Early Colonies and Trade*. 2d ed. London 1980.

**BOARDMAN 1984**
Boardman, J. "Centaurs and Flying Rocks." *OJA* 3 (1984): 123–26.

**BOARDMAN 1985**
Boardman, J. *Greek Sculpture: The Classical Period*. London 1985.

**BOARDMAN 1987**
Boardman, J., "'Very Like a Whale'—Classical Sea Monsters." In Farkas, Harper, and Harrison 1987, 73–84.

**BOARDMAN 1995**
Boardman, J. *Greek Sculpture: The Late Classical Period*. London 1995.

**BOARDMAN 1998a**
Boardman, J. *Early Greek Vase Painting, 11th–6th Centuries B.C.: A Handbook*. London 1998.

**BOARDMAN 1998b**
Boardman, J. *The Great God Pan: The Survival of an Image*. New York 1998.

**BOARDMAN 1998c**
Boardman, J. "Herakles' Monsters: Indigenous or Oriental?" In *Le Bestiaire d'Héraclès. Troisième rencontre héracléenne: Actes du colloque organisé à l'Université de Liège et aux Facultés universitaires Notre-Dame de la Paix de Namur, du 14 au 16 novembre 1996*, ed. C. Bonnet, C. Jourdain-Annequin, and V. Pirennée-Delforge, 27–35. *Kernos Supplément*. Liège 1998.

**BOARDMAN 1999**
Boardman, J. *The Greeks Overseas: Their Early Colonies and Trade*. 4th ed. London 1999.

**BOARDMAN 2001a**
Boardman, J. *Greek Gems and Finger Rings*. London 2001.

**BOARDMAN 2001b**
Boardman, J. *The History of Greek Vases: Potters, Painters, and Pictures*. London 2001.

**BOARDMAN AND POPE 1961**
Boardman, J., and M. Pope. *Greek Vases in Capetown*. Capetown 1961.

**BODEL AND TRACY 1997**
Bodel, J., and S. Tracy. *Greek and Latin Inscriptions in the USA: A Checklist*. Rome 1997.

**BÖHR 1982**
Böhr, E. *Der Schaukelmaler*. Kerameus 4. Mainz 1982.

**BOEHMER 1965**
Boehmer, R. M. *Die Entwicklung der Glyptik während der Akkad-Zeit*. Untersuchungen zur Assyriologie und Vorderasiatischen Archäologie 4. Berlin 1965.

**BOL 1981**
Bol, P. *Liebieghaus: Museum alter Plastik. Guide to the Collection: Ancient Art*. Frankfurt am Main 1981.

**BOL 1985**
Bol, P. *Antike Bronzetechnik*. Munich 1985.

**BOL 1989**
Bol, P. *Argivische Schilde*. OlForsch 17. Berlin 1989.

**BONAMICI 1974**
Bonamici, M. *I buccheri con decorazioni graffite*. Florence 1974.

**BORELL AND RITTIG 1998**
Borell, B., and D. Rittig. *Orientalische und griechische Bronzereliefs aus Olympia: Der Fundkomplex aus Brunnen 17*. OlForsch 26. Berlin 1998.

**BORGEAUD 1988**
Borgeaud, P. *The Cult of Pan in Ancient Greece*. Chicago 1988.

**BORGEAUD AND CHRISTE 1985**
Borgeaud, P., and Y. Christe, eds. *L'Animal, l'homme, le dieu dans le Proche-Orient ancien. Actes du Colloque de Cartigny 1981*, 95–103. Les Cahiers du Centre d'Étude du Proche-Orient Ancien (CEPOA), Université de Genève. Louvain 1985.

**BORGER 1964**
Borger, R. "Austrahlungen des Zweistromlandes." *JEOL* 18 (1964): 317–30.

**BORGERS 1999**
Borgers, O. "Some Subjects and Shapes by the Theseus Painter." In Docter and Moormann 1999, 87–89.

**BOSANA-KOUROU 1979**
Bosana-Kourou, P. *The Sphinx in Early Archaic Greek Art*. Ph.D. diss., University of Oxford 1979.

**BOSSERT 1951**
Bossert, H. T. *Altsyrien*. Tübingen 1951.

**BOSSERT-RADTKE 1990**
Bossert-Radtke, C. "Eine campanische Bronzestatuette in Mainz." *Archäologisches Korrespondenzblatt* 20 (1990): 409–14.

**BOTHMER 1944**
Bothmer, D. von. "The Painters of Tyrrhenian Vases." *AJA* 48 (1944): 161–70.

**BOTHMER 1948**
Bothmer, D. von. "An Attic Black-Figured Dinos." *BMFA* 46 (1948): 42–48.

**BOTHMER 1950**
Bothmer, D. von. *Greek, Etruscan, and Roman Antiquities*. New York 1950.

**BOTHMER 1953**
Bothmer, D. von. "A Panathenaic Amphora." *BMMA* 12.2 (1953): 52–56.

**BOTHMER 1956**
Bothmer, D. von. "Two Etruscan Vases by the Paris Painter." *BMMA* 14.5 (June 1956): 127–32.

**BOTHMER 1962**
Bothmer, D. von. "Five Attic Black-Figured Lip-Cups." *AJA* 66 (1962): 255–58.

**BOTHMER 1965**
Bothmer, D. von. "Review of E. Diehl, *Die Hydria: Formgeschichte und Verwendung im Kult des Altertums* (Mainz 1964)." *Gnomon* 37 (1965): 599–608.

**BOTHMER 1966**
Bothmer, D. von. "Two Red-Figured Stands: An Attic Footnote on the Chalcidian Question." *AJA* 70 (1966): 184.

**BOTHMER 1967**
Bothmer, D. von. "The Case of the Morgan Centaur." *Archaeology* 20 (1967): 221–22.

**BOTHMER 1972**
Bothmer, D. von. "A Unique Pair of Attic Vases." *RA* 1972, 83–92.

**BOTHMER 1975**
Bothmer, D. von. "Greek and Roman Art." In *The Metropolitan Museum of Art Notable Acquisitions, 1965–1975*, 114–31. New York 1975.

**BOTHMER 1979**
Bothmer, D. von. "A Bronze Oinochoe in New York." In Kopcke and Moore 1979, 63–67.

**BOTHMER 1981a**
Bothmer, D. von. "Greek and Roman Art." In *The Metropolitan Museum of Art Annual Report for the Year 1980–1981*, 35–37. New York 1981.

**BOTHMER 1981b**
Bothmer, D. von. "Red-Figured Support. Notable Acquisitions, 1980–1981." *BMMA* 38.4 (1981): 14.

**BOTHMER 1981c**
Bothmer, D. von. "Amasis, Amasidos." *GettyMusJ* 9 (1981): 1–4.

**BOTHMER 1985**
Bothmer, D. von. *The Amasis Painter and His World: Vase-Painting in Sixth-Century B.C. Athens*. Malibu 1985.

**BOTHMER 1990**
Bothmer, D. von, ed. *Glories of the Past: Ancient Art from the Shelby White and Leon Levy Collection*. Exhib. cat. Metropolitan Museum of Art. New York 1990.

**BOTHMER 1992**
Bothmer, D. von. "The Subject Matter of Euphronios." In Denoyelle 1992, 13–32.

**BOTHMER ET AL. 1979**
Bothmer, D. von, et al. *Greek Art of the Aegean Islands*. Exhib. cat. Metropolitan Museum of Art. New York 1979.

**BOTHMER ET AL. 1983**
Bothmer, D. von, et al. *Wealth of the Ancient World: The Nelson Bunker Hunt and William Herbert Hunt Collections*. Exhib. cat. Kimbell Art Museum. Fort Worth 1983.

**BOTTINI AND GUZZO 1993**
Bottini, A., and P. G. Guzzo. "Orfeo e le sirene al Getty Museum." *Rivista di antichità* 2.1 (1993): 43–52.

**BOURGUET 1914**
Bourguet, E. *Les Ruines de Delphes*. Paris 1914.

**BRANDT 1968**
Brandt, E. *Antike Gemmen in deutschen Sammlungen*. Vol. 1.1, *Staatliche Münzsammlung München*. Munich 1968.

**BREITENSTEIN 1941**
Breitenstein, N. *Danish National Museum, Department of Oriental and Classical Antiquities. Catalogue of Terracottas: Cypriote, Greek, Etrusco-Italian, and Roman*. Copenhagen 1941.

**BRENDEL 1978**
Brendel, O. *Etruscan Art*. New York 1978.

**BRENTJES 1971**
Brentjes, B. "Equidengerät. Equiden in der Religion des Alten Orients." *Klio* 53 (1971): 77–96.

**BRIJDER 1983**
Brijder, H. A. G. *Siana Cups I and Komast Cups*. Amsterdam 1983.

**BRIJDER 1984**
Brijder, H. A. G. "Two Etruscan Centaurs." *BABesch* 59 (1984): 113–16.

**BRIJDER 1991**
Brijder, H. A. G. *Siana Cups II: The Heidelberg Painter*. Amsterdam 1991.

**BRIJDER 2000**
Brijder, H. A. G. *Siana Cups III: The Red-Black Painter, Griffin-Bird Painter, and Siana Cups Resembling Lip-Cups*. Amsterdam 2000.

**BRIJDER, DRUKKER, AND NEEFT 1986**
Brijder, H. A. G., A. A. Drukker, and C. W. Neeft, eds. *Enthousiasmos: Essays on Greek and Related Pottery Presented to J. M. Hemelrijk*. Amsterdam 1986.

**BRIZE 1980**
Brize, P. *Die Geryoneis des Stesichoros und die frühe griechische Kunst*. Würzburg 1980.

**BRIZE 1985**
Brize, P. "Samos und Stesichoros zu einem früharchaischen Bronzeblech." *AM* 100 (1985): 53–90.

**BRIZE 2002**
Brize, P. "Funde aus Milet X, Treibverzierte Bronzebleche." *AA* 2001, 559–73.

**BROKAW 1963**
Brokaw, C. "Concurrent Styles in Late Geometric and Early Protoattic Vase Painting." *AM* 78 (1963): 63–73.

**BROMMER 1937**
Brommer, F. *Satyroi*. Würzburg 1937.

**BROMMER 1941**
Brommer, F. "Bilder der Midassage." *AA* 1941, 36–52.

**BROMMER 1943**
Brommer. F. "Satyrspielterrakotten." *AA* 1943, 124–32.

**BROMMER 1959**
Brommer, F. *Satyrspiele: Bilder griechischer Vasen*. 2d ed. Berlin 1959.

**BROMMER 1960**
Brommer, F. *Vasenlisten zur griechischen Heldensage*. 2d ed. Marburg 1960.

**BROMMER 1961**
Brommer, F. "Die Geburt der Athena." *JbMusMainz* 8 (1961): 66–83.

**BROMMER 1973**
Brommer, F. *Vasenlisten zur griechischen Heldensagen*. 3d ed. Marburg 1973.

**BROMMER 1978**
Brommer, F. *Hephaistos: Der Schmeidegott in der antiken Kunst*. Mainz 1978.

**BROMMER 1978–79**
Brommer, F. "Huckepack." *GettyMusJ* 6–7 (1978–79): 139–46.

**BROMMER 1979**
Brommer, F. *The Sculptures of the Parthenon: Metopes, Frieze, Pediments, Cult-Statue*. London 1979.

**BROMMER 1980**
Brommer, F. "Krater Tyrrhenikos." *RM* 87 (1980): 335–39.

**BROMMER 1983a**
Brommer, F. "Herakles und Nereus." In *Image et céramique grecque. Actes du Colloque de Rouen, 25–26 novembre 1982*, ed. F. Lissarrague and F. Thelamon, 103–9. Rouen 1983.

**BROMMER 1983b**
Brommer, F. *Herakles: The Twelve Labors of the Hero in Ancient Art and Literature*. New Rochelle 1983.

**BROMMER 1983c**
Brommer, F. "Satyrspielvasen in Malibu." *Greek Vases in the J. Paul Getty Museum* 1 (1983): 115–20.

**BROMMER 1984a**
Brommer, F. "Ein Silberstreifen." *GettyMusJ* 12 (1984): 135–38.

**BROMMER 1984b**
Brommer, F. *Herakles II: Die Unkanonischer Taten des Helden*. Darmstadt 1984.

**BRONEER 1938**
Broneer, O. "Excavations on the North Slope of the Acropolis, 1937." *Hesperia* 7 (1938): 161–263.

**BROVARSKI, DOLL, AND FREED 1982**
Brovarski, E. J., S. K. Doll, and R. E. Freed, eds. *Egypt's Golden Age: The Art of Living in the New Kingdom*. Exhib. cat. Museum of Fine Arts, Boston. Boston 1982.

**BROWNLEE 1988**
Brownlee, A. B. "Sophilos and Early Attic Black-Figured Dinoi." In Christiansen and Melander 1988, 80–87.

**BUGH 1988**
Bugh, G. R. *The Horsemen of Athens*. Princeton 1988.

**BUITRON 1972**
Buitron, D. *Attic Vase-Painting in New England Collections*. Exhib. cat. Fogg Art Museum. Cambridge (Mass.) 1972.

**BUITRON-OLIVER 1995**
Buitron-Oliver, D. *Douris: A Master-Painter of Athenian Red-Figure Vases*. Kerameus 9. Mainz 1995.

**BUITRON AND COHEN 1992**
Buitron, D., and B. Cohen. *The Odyssey and Ancient Art: An Epic in Word and Image*. Exhib. cat. Bard College. Annandale-on-Hudson 1992.

**BUITRON AND COHEN 1995**
Buitron, D., and B. Cohen. "Between Skylla and Penelope: Female Characters of the Odyssey in Archaic and Classical Greek Art." In Cohen 1995, 29–58.

**BULLE 1893**
Bulle, H. *Die Silene in den archaischen Kunst der Griechen*. Munich 1893.

**BURKERT 1982**
Burkert, W. *Structure and History in Greek Mythology and Ritual*. Berkeley 1982.

**BURKERT 1984**
Burkert, W. *Die orientalisierende Epoche in der griechischen Religion und Literatur*. Heidelberg 1984.

**BURKERT 1985**
Burkert, W. *Greek Religion: Archaic and Classical*. Trans. J. Raffan. Cambridge (Mass.) 1985.

**BURKERT 1987**
Burkert, W. "Oriental and Greek Mythology: The Meeting of Parallels." In *Interpretations of Greek Mythology*, ed. J. Bremmer, 10–40. London 1987.

**BURKERT 1992**
Burkert, W. *The Orientalizing Revolution: Near Eastern Influence on Greek Culture in the Early Archaic Age*. Trans. E. Pinder. Cambridge (Mass.) 1992.

**BURN 1987**
Burn, L. *The Meidias Painter*. Oxford 1987.

**BUROW 1989**
Burow, J. *Der Antimenesmaler*. 1989. Kerameus 7. Mainz 1989.

**BURROWS AND URE 1907/8**
Burrows, R., and P. N. Ure. "Excavations at Rhitsona in Boeotia." *BSA* 14 (1907/8): 226–318.

**BURROWS AND URE 1909**
Burrows, R., and P. N. Ure. "Excavations at Rhitsona in Boeotia." *JHS* 29 (1909): 308–53.

**BUSCHOR 1934**
Buschor, E. "Kentauren." *AJA* 38 (1934): 128–32.

**BUSCHOR 1943**
Buschor, E. *Satyrtänze und frühes Drama*. Sitzungsberichte der Bayerischen Akademie der Wissenschaften, Philosophisch-historische Abteilung 1943, Heft 5. Munich 1943.

**BUSCHOR 1944**
Buschor, E. *Die Musen des Jenseits*. Munich 1944.

**CAHN 1988**
Cahn, H. "Okeanos, Strymon, und Atlas auf einer rotfigurigen Spitzamphora." In Christiansen and Melander 1988, 107–15.

**CALLIPOLITIS-FEYTMANS 1965**
Callipolitis-Feytmans, D. *Les "Louteria" attiques*. *ArchDelt* Suppl. 6. Athens 1965.

**CALLIPOLITIS-FEYTMANS 1972**
Callipolitis-Feytmans, D. "Deux Coupes à figures noires du Musée National d'Athènes." *RA* 1972, 73–82.

**CALLIPOLITIS-FEYTMANS 1974**
Callipolitis-Feytmans, D. *Les Plats attiques à figures noires*. Paris 1974.

**CAMPBELL 1991**
Campbell, D., ed. *Greek Lyric III. Stesichorus, Ibycus, Simonides, and Others*. Cambridge (Mass.) 1991.

**CAMPOREALE 1991**
Camporeale, G. *La Collezione C.A.: Impasti e buccheri*. Rome 1991.

**CANDIDA 1971**
Candida, B. "Ulisse e le sirene: Contributo al definizione di quattro oficine volterrane." *Rendiconti dell'Accademia Nazionale dei Lincei*, serie 8.26 (1971): 199–235.

**CAPECCHI ET AL. 1998**
Capecchi, G., et al., eds. *In memoria di Enrico Paribeni*. Archaeologica 125. Rome 1998.

**CAPEL AND MARKOE 1996**
Capel, A. K., and G. E. Markoe, eds. *Mistress of the House, Mistress of Heaven: Women in Ancient Egypt*. Exhib. cat. Cincinnati Art Museum. New York 1996.

**CAPPS 1955**
Capps, E., Jr. "A Red-Figured Pitcher by Dourus." *Allen Memorial Art Museum Bulletin* 13.1 (1955): 4–10.

**CARAPANOS 1878**
Carapanos, C. *Dodone et ses ruines*. Paris 1878.

**CARATELLI 1996**
Caratelli, G. P., ed. *The Western Greeks: Classical Civilization in the Western Mediterranean*. Exhib. cat. Palazzo Grassi. Venice 1996.

**CARPENTER 1983**
Carpenter, T. H. "On the Dating of the Tyrrhenian Group." *OJA* 2 (1983): 279–93.

**CARPENTER 1984**
Carpenter, T. H. "The Tyrrhenian Group: Problems of Provenance." *OJA* 3 (1984): 45–56.

**CARPENTER 1986**
Carpenter, T. H. *Dionysian Imagery in Archaic Greek Art: Its Development in Black-Figure Vase-Painting*. Oxford 1986.

**CARPENTER 1991**
Carpenter, T. H. *Art and Myth in Ancient Greece*. London 1991.

**CARPENTER 1997**
Carpenter, T. H. *Dionysian Imagery in Fifth-Century Athens*. Oxford 1997.

**CARPENTER AND FARAONE 1993**
Carpenter, T. H., and C. A. Faraone, eds. *Masks of Dionysos*. Ithaca (New York) and London 1993.

**CARTER 1972**
Carter, J. "The Beginning of Narrative Art in the Greek Geometric Period." *BSA* 67 (1972): 25–58.

**CARTER 1987**
Carter, J. B. "The Masks of Ortheia." *AJA* 91 (1987): 355–83.

**CARTER 1989**
Carter, J. B. "The Chests of Periander." *AJA* 93 (1989): 355–78.

**CARTER AND MORRIS 1995**
Carter, J. B., and S. P. Morris, eds. *The Ages of Homer: A Tribute to Emily Townsend Vermeule.* Austin 1995.

**CARUSO 1987**
Caruso, C. "Travestissements dionysiaques." In *Images et société en Grèce ancienne,* ed. C. Bérard, 103–10. Lausanne 1987.

**CASKEY AND BEAZLEY 1963**
Caskey, L. D., and J. D. Beazley. *Attic Vase-Paintings in the Museum of Fine Arts, Boston.* Vol. 3. Boston 1963.

**CASSON 1922**
Casson, S. "Bronze Work of the Geometric Period and Its Relation to Later Art." *JHS* 42 (1922): 207–19.

**CASSON 1927**
Casson, S. "Some Greek Seals of the 'Geometric' Period." *AntJ* 7 (1927): 38–43.

**CASSON 1933**
Casson, S. *The Technique of Early Greek Sculpture.* Oxford 1933.

**CAUBET 1979**
Caubet, A. *La Religion à Chypre dans l'antiquité.* Collection de la Maison de l'Orient, hors série 3. Lyon 1979.

**CAUBET, FOURRIER, AND QUEYREL 1998**
Caubet, A., S. Fourrier, and A. Queyrel. *L'Art des modeleurs d'argile: Antiquités de Chypre coroplastique, Musée du Louvre, Département des antiquités orientales.* Paris 1998.

**CAUBET, HERMARY, AND KARAGEORGHIS 1992**
Caubet, A., A. Hermary, and V. Karageorghis. *Art antique de Chypre au Musée du Louvre du chalcolithique à l'époque romaine.* Paris 1992.

**CHAMAY 1993**
Chamay, J. *The Art of the Italic Peoples from 3000 to 300 B.C.* Exhib. cat. Musée d'Art et d'Histoire, Génève. Geneva and Naples 1993.

**CHAMAY AND BOTHMER 1987**
Chamay, J., and D. von Bothmer. "Ajax et Cassandre par le Peintre de Princeton." *AntK* 30 (1987): 58–68.

**CHARBONNEAUX 1962**
Charbonneaux, J. *Greek Bronzes.* New York 1962.

**CHASE 1902**
Chase, G. H. *The Shield Devices of the Greeks.* Cambridge (Mass.) 1902.

**CHASE 1950**
Chase, G. H. "Three Griffins' Heads." *BMFA* 48 (1950): 33–37.

**CHASE AND VERMEULE 1963**
Chase, G. H., and C. C. Vermeule. *Greek, Etruscan, and Roman Art: The Classical Collections of the Museum of Fine Arts, Boston.* Boston 1963.

**CHILDS 1978**
Childs, W. A. P., ed. *Athens Comes of Age: From Solon to Salamis.* Princeton 1978.

**CHILDS 2001a**
Childs, W. A. P. "Early Greek Bronze Plaques in Princeton." *Record* 60 (2001): 30–63.

**CHILDS 2001b**
Childs, W. A. P. "Le Rôle de Chypre dans la naissance de la plastique monumentale en Grèce." *CECy* 31 (2001): 115–28.

**CHORMOUZIADES 1974**
Chormouziades, N. Σατυρικά. Athens 1974.

**CHRISTIANSEN 1985–87**
Christiansen, J. "Etruskike stumper." *MeddelGlypt* 41 (1985–87): 133–51.

**CHRISTIANSEN 1992**
Christiansen, J. *Greece in the Geometric Period: Catalogue, Ny Carlsberg Glyptotek.* Copenhagen 1992.

**CHRISTIANSEN AND MELANDER 1988**
Christiansen, J., and T. Melander, eds. *Proceedings of the Third Symposium on Ancient Greek and Related Pottery, Copenhagen, August 31–September 4, 1987.* Copenhagen 1988.

**CLARK 1992**
Clark, A. J. *Attic Black-Figured Olpai and Oinochoai.* Ph.D. diss., New York University 1992.

**CLARK AND GAUNT 2002**
Clark, A. J., and J. Gaunt, eds. *Essays in Honor of Dietrich von Bothmer.* Amsterdam 2002.

**CLEMENT 1958**
Clement, P. A. "The Recovery of Helen." *Hesperia* 27 (1958): 47–73.

**COHEN 1983**
Cohen, B. "Paragone: Sculpture versus Painting: Kaineus and the Kleophrades Painter." In Moon 1983, 171–92.

**COHEN 1995**
Cohen, B., ed. *The Distaff Side: Representing the Female in Homer's Odyssey.* New York 1995.

**COHEN 1997**
Cohen, B. "Red-Figure Vases Take Wing." In Oakley, Coulson, and Palagia 1997, 141–55.

**COHEN 2000a**
Cohen, B. "Man-Killers and Their Victims: Inversions of the Heroic Ideal in Classical Art." In Cohen 2000b, 98–131.

**COHEN 2000b**
Cohen, B., ed. *Not the Classical Ideal: Athens and the Construction of the Other in Greek Art.* Boston 2000.

**COLDSTREAM 1977**
Coldstream, J. N. *Geometric Greece.* London 1977.

**COLLON 1986**
Collon, D. *Catalogue of the Western Asiatic Seals in the British Museum: Cylinder Seals.* Vol. 3, *Isin-Larsa and Old Babylonian Periods.* London 1986.

**COLLON 1987**
Collon, D., *First Impressions: Cylinder Seals in the Ancient Near East.* London 1987.

**COLLON 1995**
Collon, D. *Ancient Near Eastern Art.* Berkeley 1995.

**COLLON 2001**
Collon, D. *Catalogue of the Western Asiatic Seals in the British Museum, Cylinder Seals.* Vol. 5, *Neo-Assyrian and Neo-Babylonian Periods.* London 2001.

**COLONNA 1964**
Colonna, G. "Rivista di epigraphia etrusca." *StEtr* 32 (1964): 161–63 and 165–67.

**COLONNA 1985**
Colonna, G. *Santuari d'Etruria.* Milan 1985.

**COLVIN 1880**
Colvin, S. "On Representations of Centaurs in Greek Vase-Painting." *JHS* 1 (1880): 107–67.

**COMSTOCK AND VERMEULE 1971**
Comstock, M., and C. C. Vermeule. *Greek, Etruscan, and Roman Bronzes in the Museum of Fine Arts, Boston.* Greenwich 1971.

**COMSTOCK AND VERMEULE 1976**
Comstock, M., and C. C. Vermeule. *Sculpture in Stone: The Greek, Etruscan, and Roman Collections of the Museum of Fine Arts, Boston.* Boston 1976.

**COMSTOCK AND VERMEULE 1988**
Comstock, M., and C. C. Vermeule. *Sculpture in Stone and Bronze: Additions to the Collections of Greek, Etruscan, and Roman Art, in the Museum of Fine Arts, Boston.* Boston 1988.

**CONNOR 1983**
Connor, P. J. "'Spotted Snakes with Double Tongue': An Unusual Gorgoneion Tondo." *AA* 1983, 23–31.

**COOK 1933–34**
Cook, R. M. "Fikellura Pottery." *BSA* 34 (1933–34): 1–98.

**COOK 1934–35**
Cook, J. M. "Protoattic Pottery." *BSA* 35 (1934–35): 165–211.

**COOK 1951**
Cook, J. "A Geometric Amphora and Gold Band." *BSA* 46 (1951): 45–49.

**COOK 1960**
Cook, R. M. *Greek Painted Pottery.* London 1960.

**COOK 1981**
Cook, R. M. *Clazomenian Sarcophagi.* Kerameus 3. Mainz 1981.

**COOK 1992**
Cook, R. M. "The Wild Goat and Fikellura Styles: Some Speculations." *OJA* 11 (1992): 255–66.

**COOK 1997**
Cook, R. M. *Greek Painted Pottery.* 3d ed. London and New York 1997.

**COOK AND DUPONT 1998**
Cook, R. M., and P. Dupont. *East Greek Pottery.* London 1998.

**COONEY 1968**
Cooney, J. D. "Siren and Ba, Birds of a Feather." *BClevMus* 55 (1968): 262–71.

**COOPER 1978**
Cooper, J. S. *The Return of Ninurta to Nippur.* Analecta Orientalia 52. Rome 1978.

**CRIELAARD 1992**
Crielaard, J. P. "How the West Was Won: Euboeans vs. Phoenicians." *HBA* 19/20 (1992): 235–60.

**CRISTOFANI 1992**
Cristofani, M. "Terrecotte decorative." In *Caere* 3, vol.1, *Lo scarico arcaico della Vigna Parrocchiale,* 29–57. Rome 1992.

**CRISTOFANI, MARZI, AND PERISSINOTTO 1981**
Cristofani, M., M. G. Marzi, and A. Perissinotto. *Materiali per servire alla storia del vaso François.* Bolletino d'Arte serie speciale 1. Rome 1981.

**CROON 1955**
Croon, J. H. "The Mask of the Underworld Daemon: Some Remarks on the Perseus-Gorgon Story." *JHS* 75 (1955): 9–16.

**CURTIS AND READE 1995**
Curtis, J. E., and J. E. Reade, eds. *Art and Empire: Treasures from Assyria in the British Museum.* Exhib. cat. Metropolitan Museum of Art. New York 1995.

**DALLEY 1989**
Dalley, S. *Myths from Mesopotamia.* Oxford 1989.

**DANALE-GIOLE 1981**
Danale-Giole, A. Τα Λύτρα του Έκτορος. Athens 1981.

**DANNER 1989**
Danner, P. *Griechischen Akrotere der archaischen und klassischen Zeit.* Rome 1989.

**DASEN 1993**
Dasen, V. *Dwarves in Ancient Egypt and Greece.* Oxford 1993.

**DASEN 2000**
Dasen, V. "Squatting Comasts and Scarab-Beetles." In Tsetskhladze, Prag, and Snodgrass 2000, 89–97.

**D'AURIA, LACOVARA, AND ROEHRIG 1988**
D'Auria, S., P. Lacovara, and C. H. Roehrig, eds. *Mummies and Magic: The Funerary Arts of Ancient Egypt.* Exhib. cat. Museum of Fine Arts, Boston. Boston 1988.

**DAUX 1962**
Daux, G. "Chronique des fouilles et découvertes archéologiques en Grèce en 1961." *BCH* 86 (1962): 629–974.

**DAVIES 1978**
Davies, M. I. "Sailing, Rowing, and Sporting in One's Cups on the Wine-dark Sea." In Childs 1978, 72–95.

**DAVIES 1991**
Davies, M., ed. *Poetarum melicorum Graecorum fragmenta.* Vol. 1. New York 1991.

**DE CARO, BORRIELLO, AND CASSANI 1993**
De Caro, S., M. R. Borriello, and S. Cassani. *De gabinete a museo: Tres siglos de historia.* Exhib. cat. Museo Arqueológico Nacional. Madrid 1993.

**DE CARO, BORRIELLO, AND CASSANI 1996**
De Caro, S., M. R. Borriello, and S. Cassani. *La Magna Grecia nelle collezioni del Museo archeologico di Napoli.* Exhib. cat. Naples 1996.

**DEIMEL 1950**
Deimel, P. A. *Šumerisches Lexikon.* Vol. 4.1, *Pantheon Babylonicum.* Rome 1950.

**DELAPORTE 1920–23**
Delaporte, L., *Catalogue des cylindres, cachets, et pierres gravées de style oriental. Musée du Louvre, Département des antiquités orientales et de la céramique antique.* Paris, 1920–23.

**DE LUCIA BROLLI 1991**
De Lucia Brolli, M. A. *Cività Castellana: Il Museo archeologico dell'Agro Falisco.* Rome 1991.

**DEMARGNE 1902**
Demargne, P. "Antiquités de Praesos et de l'antre Dictéen. 1. Plaquettes en terre cuite à reliefs de Praesos." *BCH* 26 (1902): 570–83.

**DEMARGNE 1929**
Demargne, P. "À propos d'une représentation de centaure." *BCH* 53 (1929): 117–28.

**DEMISCH 1977**
Demisch, H. *Die Sphinx.* Stuttgart 1977.

**DENOYELLE 1992**
Denoyelle, M., ed. *Euphronios peintre. Actes de la journée d'étude oganisée par l'École du Louvre et le Département des antiquités grecques, étrusques, et romaines du Musée du Louvre, 10 octobre 1990.* Paris 1992.

**DENOYELLE AND PASQUIER 1994**
Denoyelle, M., and A. Pasquier. *Chefs-d'œuvre de la céramique greque des collections du Louvre.* Paris 1994.

**DESBOROUGH, NICHOLLS, AND POPHAM 1970**
Desborough, V., R. V. Nicholls, and M. Popham. "A Euboean Centaur." *BSA* 65 (1970): 21–30.

**DESCAMPS-LEQUIME 2002**
Descamps-Lequime, S. "Une Sphinx en bronze: Élément de décor d'un trône archaïque?" In Clark and Gaunt 2002, 113–20.

**DESCŒUDRES 2001**
Descœudres, J.-P. "Head-rest or Celery Holder?" In *Zona Archaeologica: Festschrift für Hans Peter Isler zum 60. Geburtstag*, ed. S. Buzzi, 111–14. Bonn 2001.

**DESSENNE 1957**
Dessenne, A. *Le Sphinx: Étude iconographique.* Paris 1957.

**DIEHL 1964**
Diehl, E. *Die Hydria. Formgeschichte und Verwendung im Kult des Altertums.* Mainz 1964.

**DIERICHS 1993**
Dierichs, A. "Ein Terrakottenrelief mit Sphinx und Greif." *Studia Varia from the J. Paul Getty Museum* 1 (Malibu 1993): 33–54.

**DIJK 1983**
Dijk, J. van, *Lugal ud me-lám-bi Nir-gál. Le récit épique et didactique des Travaux de Ninurta, du Déluge et de la Nouvelle Création.* 2 vols. Leiden 1983.

**DIPLA 1997**
Dipla, A. "Helen, the Seductress." In Palagia 1997, 119–30.

**DI STEFANO 1975**
Di Stefano, C. A. *Bronzetti figurati del Museo Nazionale di Palermo.* Rome 1975.

**DOCTER AND MOORMANN 1999**
Docter, R. F., and E. M. Moormann, eds. *Proceedings of the Fifteenth International Congress of Classical Archaeology, Amsterdam, July 12–17, 1998.* Amsterdam 1999.

**DÖRIG 1975**
Dörig, J. *Art antique: Collections privées de Suisse romande.* Mainz 1975.

**DÖRIG 1985**
Dörig, J. *La Frise est de l'Hephaisteion.* Mainz 1985.

**DÖRIG AND GIGON 1961**
Dörig, J., and O. Gigon. *Der Kampf der Götter und Titanen.* Lausanne 1961.

**DOHERTY 1995**
Doherty, L. E. *Siren Songs: Gender, Audiences, and Narrators in the Odyssey.* Ann Arbor 1995.

**DOHRN 1937**
Dohrn, T. *Die schwarzfigurigen etruskischen Vasen aus der zweiten Hälfte des sechsten Jahrhunderts.* Berlin 1937.

**DOMBROWSKI 1984**
Dombrowski, B. *Der Name Europa auf seinem griechischen und altsyrischen Hintergrund.* Amsterdam 1984.

**DOMÍNQUEZ 1996**
Domínquez, A. J. *Los Griegos en la Peninsula Ibérica.* Madrid 1996.

**DONTAS 1969**
Dontas, G. "ΛΑΚΩΝ ΚΩΜΑΣΤΗΣ." *BCH* 93 (1969): 39–55.

**DOVER 1978**
Dover, K. J. *Greek Homosexuality.* Cambridge (Mass.) 1978.

**DRUKKER 1986**
Drukker, A. "The Ivy Painter in Friesland." In Brijder, Drukker, and Neeft 1986, 39–48.

**DUCAT 1963**
Ducat, J. "Les Vases plastiques corinthiens." *BCH* 87 (1963): 431–58.

**DUCAT 1964**
Ducat, J. "Périrrhantèria." *BCH* 88 (1964): 577–606.

**DUCAT 1966**
Ducat, J. *Les Vases plastiques rhodiens archaïques en terre cuite.* Paris 1966.

**DUCATI 1932**
Ducati, P. *Pontische Vasen.* Berlin 1932.

**DUCREY 1985**
Ducrey, P. *Guerre et guerriers dans la Grèce antique.* Paris 1985.

**DUGAS 1943**
Dugas, C. "La Mort du centaure Nessos." *REA* 45 (1943): 18–26.

**DUNBABIN 1962**
Dunbabin, T. J., ed. *Perachora: The Sanctuaries of Hera Akraia and Limenia.* Vol. 2, *Pottery, Ivories, Scarabs, and Other Objects from the Votive Deposit of Hera Limenia.* Oxford 1962.

**DUNBABIN AND ROBERTSON 1953**
Dunbabin, T. J., and M. Robertson. "Some Protocorinthian Vase-Painters." *BSA* 48 (1953): 172–81.

**DUPONT 1983**
Dupont, P. "Classification et détermination de provenance des céramiques grecques orientales archaïques d'Istros." *Dacia* 27 (1983): 19–43.

**EALS 1971**
Eals, N. R. "Relief Amphoras of Archaic Crete." *Muse* 5 (1971): 26–31.

**EAVERLY 1996**
Eaverly, M. A. *Archaic Greek Equestrian Sculpture.* Ann Arbor 1996.

**ÉCOLE FRANÇAISE D'ATHÈNES 1991**
École française d'Athènes. *Guide de Delphes. Le Musée.* Paris 1991.

**EDLUND 1980a**
Edlund, I. E. M. *The Iron Age and Etruscan Vases in the Olcott Collection at Columbia University.* TAPS 70.1. Philadelphia 1980.

**EDLUND 1980b**
Edlund, I. E. M. "Meaningful or Meaningless? Animal Symbolism in Greek Vase-Painting." *Meded* 42 (1980): 31–35.

**EDMUNDS 1981**
Edmunds, L. *The Sphinx in the Oedipus Legend.* Königstein 1981.

**EDMUNDS 1988**
Edmunds, L. "La Sphinx thébaine et Pauk Tyaing, l'Oedipe Birman." In *Metamorphoses du mythe en Grèce antique*, ed. C. Calame, 213–27. Geneva 1988.

**EDZARD 1997**
Edzard, D. O. *The Royal Inscriptions of Mesopotamia.* Vol. 3.1, *Gudea and His Dynasty.* Toronto 1997.

**EICHLER 1950**
Eichler, F. *Die Reliefs des Heroon von Gjölbaschi-Trysa.* Vienna 1950.

**EICHLER 1984**
Eichler, S. *Götter, Genien, und Mischwesen in der Urartäischen Kunst.* Berlin 1984.

**ELLIS 1977**
Ellis, R. S. "'Lion-men' in Assyria." In
*Essays on the Ancient Near East in Memory of Jacob
Joel Finkelstein*, ed. M. de J. Ellis, 67–78.
Memoirs of the Connecticut Academy of
Arts and Sciences. Hamden 1977.

**ENGEL 1987**
Engel, B. J. *Darstellungen von Dämonen und
Tieren in assyrischen Palästen und Tempeln nach den
schriftlichen Quellen.* Mönchengladbach 1987.

**ERLENMEYER 1960**
Erlenmeyer, M. L., and H. Erlenmeyer.
"Über Philister und Kreter. I." *Orientalia* 29
(1960): 121–50.

**ESPOSITO AND DE TOMMASO 1993**
Esposito, A. M., and G. de Tommaso.
*Museo Archeologico Nazionale di Firenze,
Antiquarium: Vasi attici.* Florence 1993.

**EUPHRONIOS DER MALER 1991**
*Euphronios der Maler.* Exhib. cat. Staatliche
Museen zu Berlin – Preussischer
Kulturbesitz. Berlin 1991.

**EUWE 1986**
Euwe, H. "The Shape of a Nolan Amphora
in Otterlo." In Brijder, Drukker, and Neeft
1986, 141–45.

**EVANS 1909**
Evans, A. J. *Scripta Minoa: The Written Documents
of Minoan Crete, with Special Reference to the
Archives of Knossos.* Vol. 1, *The Hieroglyphic and
Primitive Linear Classes, with an Account of the
Discovery of the Pre-Phoenician Scripts, Their Place
in Minoan History, and Their Mediterranean
Relations.* Oxford 1909.

**EVELYN-WHITE 1982**
Evelyn-White, H. G., trans. *Hesiod: The
Homeric Hymns and Homerica.* Cambridge 1982.
Reprint of Loeb ed. 1914.

**FAGLES 1998**
*Bacchylides. Complete Poems.* Trans., with a note
to the new ed., by R. Fagles. New Haven
1998.

**FAIRBANKS 1928**
Fairbanks, A. *Museum of Fine Arts, Boston.
Catalogue of Greek and Etruscan Vases.* Vol. 1,
*Early Vases, preceding Athenian Black-Figure Ware.*
Cambridge (Mass.) 1928.

**FALSONE 1985**
Falsone, G. "A Syro-Phoenician Bull-Bowl
in Geneva and Its Analogue in the British
Museum." *AnatSt* 35 (1985): 131–42.

**FARAONE 1992**
Faraone, C. *Talismans and Trojan Horses:
Guardian Statues in Ancient Greek Myth and Ritual.*
New York and Oxford 1992.

**FARKAS, HARPER, AND HARRISON 1987**
Farkas, A. E., P. O. Harper, and
E. B. Harrison, eds. *Monsters and Demons in
the Ancient and Medieval Worlds: Papers Presented
in Honor of Edith Porada.* Mainz 1987.

**FELDMAN 1965**
Feldman, T. "Gorgon and the Origins of
Fear." *Arion* 4 (1965): 484–94.

**FERRARI 1986**
Ferrari, G. "Eye Cup." *RA* 1986, 5–20.

**FERRARI 2002**
Ferrari, Gloria. *Figures of Speech: Men and
Maidens in Ancient Greece.* Chicago 2002.

**FILIPPAKIS ET AL. 1983**
Filippakis, S., et al. "Bronzes grecs et
orientaux: Influences et apprentissages."
*BCH* 107 (1983): 111–32.

**FINSTER-HOTZ 1984**
Finster-Hotz, U. *Der Bauschmuck des
Athenatempels von Assos. Studien zur Ikonographie.*
Rome 1984.

**FISCHER 1999**
Fischer, C. "Elitezugehörigkeit
und Harmonieverständis: Zu den mittelassyrischen Siegelabrollungen aus
Kār-Tukultī-Ninurta." *Mitteilungen der
Deutschen Orient-Gesellschaft zu Berlin* 131
(1999): 115–54.

**FITTSCHEN 1969**
Fittschen, K. *Untersuchungen zum Beginn der
Sagendarstellungen bei den Griechen.* Berlin 1969.

**FITTSCHEN 1970**
Fittschen, K. "Zur Herakles-Nessos-Sage."
*Gymnasium* 77 (1970): 160–71.

**FLOREN 1977**
Floren, J. *Studien zur Typologie des Gorgoneion.*
Münster 1977.

**FLOREN AND HERFORT 1983**
Floren, J., and M. Herfort. "Bemerkungen
zur lakonischen Plastik." *Boreas* 6 (1983):
23–30.

**FORMIGLI AND HEILMEYER 1984**
Formigli, E., and W.-D. Heilmeyer.
"Capuaner Aschenurne in Berlin." *AA*
1984, 395–407.

**FORMAN SALE CATALOGUE 1899**
*The Forman Collection: Catalogue of the Egyptian,
Greek, and Roman Antiquities, First Portion.*
Sotheby, Wilkinson, & Hodge (sales
catalogue), June 19, 1899. London 1899.

**FOSTER 1996**
Foster, B. R. *Before the Muses: An Anthology
of Akkadian Literature.* 2d ed. 2 vols. Bethesda
1996.

**FOWLER 1983**
Fowler, B. H. "The Centaur's Smile:
Pindar and the Archaic Aesthetic." In
Moon 1983, 159–70.

**FRANCIS 1972**
Francis, E. D. "'Chiron's Laughter'
(*Pyth.* 9,38)." *CP* 67 (1972): 288–91.

**FRANK 1908**
Frank, C. *Babylonische Beschwörungsreliefs:
Ein Beitrag zur Erklärung der sog. Hadesreliefs.*
Leipziger semitistische Studien. Leipzig
1908.

**FRANKFORT 1939**
Frankfort, H. *Cylinder Seals: A Documentary
Essay on the Art and Religion of the Ancient Near
East.* London 1939.

**FRANKFORT 1943**
Frankfort, H. *More Sculpture from the Diyala
Region.* Chicago 1943.

**FRANKFORT 1970**
Frankfort, H. *The Art and Architecture of the
Ancient Orient.* 4th ed. New Haven 1970.

**FREEDEN 1992**
Freeden, J. von. *Museum für Vor- und
Frühgeschichte. Archäologische Reihe Antikensammlung
5: Ausgewählte Werke.* Frankfurt am Main
1993.

**FREL 1994**
Frel, J. *Studia Varia.* Rome 1994.

**FREYDANK 1974**
Freydank, H., "Zu den Siegeln des
Bābu-aḫa-iddina." *FuB* 16 (1974): 7–8.

**FREYDANK 1991**
Freydank, H., *Beiträge zur mittelassyrischen
Chronologie und Geschichte. Schriften zur Geschichte
und Kultur des alten Orients* 21. Berlin 1991.

374

**FREYDANK 2001**
Freydank, H. "lēʾāni '(Holz)tafeln',
eine Grundlage der mittelassyrischen
Verwaltung." In *Kulturgeschichten:
Altorientalistische Studien für Volkert Haas zum
65. Geburtstag*, ed. T. Richter, D. Prechel,
and J. Klinger, 103–11. Saarbrücken 2001.

**FRIEDMAN 1998**
Friedman, F. D., ed. *Gifts of the Nile: Ancient
Egyptian Faience*. Exhib. cat. Rhode Island
School of Design. Providence 1998.

**FRIIS JOHANSEN 1923**
Friis Johansen, K. *Les Vases sicyoniens: Étude
archéologique*. Paris 1923.

**FRIIS JOHANSEN 1939**
Friis Johansen, K. "Achill bei Cheiron."
In ΔΡΑΓΜΑ: *MARTINO P. NILSSON A.D.
IV id. iul. anno MCMXXXIX dedicatum*,
181–205. Lund 1939.

**FRONTISI-DUCROUX 1989**
Frontisi-Ducroux, F. "In the Mirror of
the Mask." In *A City of Images: Iconography and
Society in Ancient Greece*, ed. C. Bérard et. al.
and trans. D. Lyons, 150–65. Princeton 1989.

**FROTHINGHAM 1911**
Frothingham, A. L. "Medusa, Apollo, and
the Great Mother." *AJA* 15 (1911): 349–77.

**FURTWÄNGLER 1890**
Furtwängler, A. *Olympia*. Ed. E. Curtius
and F. Adler. Vol. 4, *Die Bronzen und die übrigen
kleineren Funde von Olympia*. Berlin 1890.

**FURTWÄNGLER 1900**
Furtwängler, A. *Die antiken Gemmen*. Berlin
1900.

**GABBARD 1979**
Gabbard, K. E. *From Hubris to Virtu: Centaurs
in the Art and Literature of Fifth-Century Greece
and Renaissance Florence*. Ph.D. diss., Indiana
University 1979.

**GAIS 1978**
Gais, R. M. "Some Problems of River-God
Iconography." *AJA* 82 (1978): 355–70.

**GANTZ 1993**
Gantz, T. *Early Greek Myth: A Guide to Literary
and Artistic Sources*. Baltimore 1993.

**GARCÍA Y BELLIDO 1948**
García y Bellido, A. *Hispania graeca*. 2 vols.
Madrid 1948.

**GARDNER 1897**
Gardner, E. A. "Caineus and the Centaurs:
A Vase at Harrow." *JHS* 17 (1897): 294–305.

**GAUER 1991**
Gauer, W. *Die Bronzegefässe von Olympia*.
*OlForsch* 20. Berlin 1991.

**GAUNT 2002**
Gaunt, J. *The Attic Volute Krater*. Ph.D. diss.,
New York University 2002.

**GEHRIG AND NIEMEYER 1990**
Gehrig, U., and H. G. Niemeyer. *Die
Phönizier im Zeitalter Homers*. Hannover 1990.

**GERCKE 1996**
Gercke, W. B. *Etruskische Kunst im Kestner-
Museum Hannover*. Hannover 1996.

**GEROJANNIS 1927/28**
Gerojannis, K. "Γοργώ ή Μέδουσα." *ArchEph*
1927/28, 128–76.

**GETTY ANTIQUITIES 2002**
*The J. Paul Getty Museum: Handbook of the
Antiquities Collection*. Malibu 2002.

**GETTY HANDBOOK 2002**
*The J. Paul Getty Museum. Handbook of the
Collections*. Malibu 1986, 1988, 1991, 2002.

**GETTY MASTERPIECES 1997**
*Masterpieces of the J. Paul Getty Museum:
Antiquities*. London 1997.

**GIGLIOLI 1935**
Giglioli, G. Q. *L'arte etrusca*. Milan 1935.

**GINGE 1988**
Ginge, B. "A New Evaluation of the
Origins of Tyrrhenian Pottery: Etruscan
Precursors of Pontic Ceramics." In
Christiansen and Melander, 201–10.
Copenhagen 1988.

**GJØDESEN 1963**
Gjødesen, M. "Greek Bronzes: A Review
Article." *AJA* 67 (1963): 333–51.

**GLYNN 1981**
Glynn, R. "Herakles, Nereus, and Triton:
A Study of Iconography in Sixth-Century
Athens." *AJA* 85 (1981): 121–32.

**GOLDFARB, WOLSKY, AND VERMEULE 1993**
Goldfarb, H. T., F. Z. Wolsky, and
C. C. Vermeule III. *Passionate Acts in Greek
Myth*. Boston 1993.

**GOLDSTEIN 2001**
Goldstein, S. M. *Ancient Glass: Egypt to China*.
Exhib. cat. Miho Museum. Kyoto 2001.

**GOMBRICH 1960**
Gombrich, E. *Art and Illusion: A Study in the
Psychology of Pictorial Representation*. Princeton
1960.

**GRAEF AND LANGLOTZ 1925–33**
Graef, B., and E. Langlotz. *Die antiken
Vasen von der Akropolis zu Athen*. 2 vols. Berlin
1925–33.

**GRAY 1969**
Gray, J. *Near Eastern Mythology*. London 1969.

**GRAZIA MARZI 1981**
Grazia Marzi, M. "Un amfora della scuola
del Pittore del Gorgone." *Prospettiva* 26 (1981):
47–50.

**GRECO 1997**
Greco, G. "Frammenti di un fregio fittile
da Poseidonia." In Lulof and Moormann
1997, 83–94.

**GRECO 2001**
Greco, G. *Il Santuario di Hera alla Foce del Sele*.
Salerno 2001.

**GREEK ART OF THE AEGEAN ISLANDS 1979**
*Greek Art of the Aegean Islands*. Exhib. cat.
Metropolitan Museum of Art. New York
1979.

**GREEN 1972**
Green, J. R. "Oinochoe." *BICS* 19 (1972):
1–16.

**GREEN 1983**
Green, A. "Neo-Assyrian Apotropaic
Figures: Figurines, Rituals, and
Monumental Art, with Special Reference
to the Figurines from the Excavations
of the British School of Archaeology in
Iraq at Nimrud." *Iraq* 45 (1983): 87–96.

**GREEN 1985**
Green, J. R. "A Representation of *The Birds*
of Aristophanes." *Greek Vases in the J. Paul Getty
Museum* 2 (1985): 95–118.

**GREEN 1997**
Green, A. "Myths in Mesopotamian Art."
In *Sumerian Gods and Their Representations*,
ed. I. L. Finkel and M. J. Geller, 135–58.
Groningen 1997.

**GREEN AND HANDLEY 1995**
Green, J. R., and E. Handley. *Images of the
Greek Theater*. Austin 1995.

**GREENEWALT 1971**
Greenewalt, C. H., Jr. "Fikellura and 'Early Fikellura' Pottery from Sardis." *CSCA* 4 (1971): 153–80.

**GREIFENHAGEN 1970**
Greifenhagen, A. *Schmuckarbeiten in Edelmetall.* Vol. 1. Berlin 1970.

**GREIFENHAGEN 1974**
Greifenhagen, A. "Die Silene der Smikros-Amphora Berlin 1966.19." *AA* 1974.2, 238–40.

**GROPENGIESSER 1977**
Gropengiesser, H. "Sänger und Sirenen." *AA* 1977, 582–610.

**GROSSMAN 2002**
Grossman, J. B. *Athletes in Antiquity: Works in the Collection of the J. Paul Getty Museum.* Exhib. cat. Utah Museum of Fine Arts. Salt Lake City 2002.

**GSCHWANTLER AND BERNHARD-WALCHER 1988**
Gschwantler, K., and A. Bernhard-Walcher, eds. *Griechische und römische Statuetten und Grossbronzen.* Vienna 1988.

**GUGGISBERG 1947**
Guggisberg, P. *Das Satyrspiel.* Zürich 1947.

**GUGGISBERG 1996**
Guggisberg, M. A. *Frühgriechische Tierkeramik.* Mainz 1996.

**GURALNICK 1989**
Guralnick, E. "Greece and the Near East: Art and Archaeology." In *Daidalikon: Studies in Memory of Raymond V. Schoder, S.J.,* ed. R. F. Sutton Jr., 151–76. Wauconda 1989.

**GURNEY 1935**
Gurney, O. R. "Babylonian Prophylactic Figures and Their Rituals." *AnnLiv* 22 (1935): 31–96.

**GUY 1983**
Guy, J. R. *The Late Manner and Early Classical Followers of Douris.* Ph.D diss., University of Oxford, 1983.

**GUZZO 1987**
Guzzo, P.G. "Gioie clandestine." *RM* 94 (1987): 163–81.

**HAERINCK AND OVERLAET 1984**
Haerinck, E., and B. J. Overlaet. "Zur Funktion einiger Urartäischer Bronzegegenstände." *IrAnt* 19 (1984): 55–70.

**HALDENSTEIN 1982**
Haldenstein, J. T. *Little Master Cups: Studies in Sixth-Century Attic Black-Figure Vase-Painting.* Ph.D. diss., University of Cincinnati 1982; Ann Arbor 1983.

**HALLO 1997**
Hallo, W. W., ed. *The Context of Scripture.* Vol. 1, *Canonical Compositions from the Biblical World.* Leiden, New York, and Cologne 1997.

**HAMILTON 1991**
Hamilton, R. *Choes and Anthesteria: Athenian Iconography and Ritual.* Ann Arbor 1991.

**HAMILTON-MARGOS 1985**
Hamilton-Margos, R. "Une Amphore à figures noires proche du Peintre de la Gorgone." *Bulletin des Musées Royaux d'Art et d'Histoire* 56.1 (1985): 77–85.

**HAMPE 1935/36**
Hampe, R. "Korfugiebel und frühe Perseusbilder." AM 60/61 (1935/36): 269–99.

**HAMPE 1936**
Hampe, R. *Frühe griechische Sagenbilder in Böotien.* Athens 1936.

**HAMPE AND JANTZEN 1937**
Hampe, R., and U. Jantzen. *Bericht über die Ausgrabungen in Olympia.* JdI 52 (1937): 1–97.

**HANFMANN 1953**
Hanfmann, G. M. A. "On Sphinxes." *Archaeology* 6 (1953): 229–31.

**HANNESTAD 1974**
Hannestad, L. *The Paris Painter: An Etruscan Vase-Painter.* Copenhagen 1974.

**HANSEN 1963**
Hansen, D. "New Votive Plaques from Nippur." *JNES* 22 (1963): 145–66.

**HANSEN 1987**
Hansen, D. P. "The Fantastic World of Sumerian Art: Seal Impressions from Ancient Lagash." In Farkas, Harper, and Harrison 1987, 53–63.

**HANSON 1991**
Hanson, V. D., ed. *Hoplites: The Classical Greek Battle Experience.* London 1991.

**HARPER ET AL. 1995**
Harper, P. O., E. Klengel-Brant, J. Aruz, and K. Benzel. *Discoveries at Ashur on the Tigris: Assyrian Origins.* Exhib. cat. Metropolitan Museum of Art. New York 1995.

**HARTNER 1973–74**
Hartner, W. "The Vaso Vescovali in the British Museum. A Study on Islamic Astrological Iconography." *Kunst des Orients* 9 (1973–74): 99–130.

**HASPELS 1972**
Haspels, C. H. E. "Le Peintre de Diosphos." *RA* 1972, 103–9.

**HAUSMANN 1972**
Hausmann, U. "Oidipus und die Sphinx." *Jahrbuch der Staatlichen Kunstsammlungen in Baden-Württemberg* 9 (1972): 7–36.

**HAUSSIG 1965**
Haussig, H. W., ed. *Wörterbuch der Mythologie.* Vol. 1.1, *Götter und Mythen im vorderen Orient: Die alten Kulturwörter.* Stuttgart 1965.

**HAYES 1985**
Hayes, J. W. *Etruscan and Italic Pottery in the Royal Ontario Museum.* Leiden 1985.

**HAYES 1992**
Hayes, J. W. *Greek and Greek-Style Painted and Plain Pottery in the Royal Ontario Museum: Excluding Black-Figure and Red-Figure Vases.* Toronto 1992.

**HAYNES 1952**
Haynes, D. E. L. "A Group of East Greek Bronzes." *JHS* 72 (1952): 74–80.

**HAYNES 2000**
Haynes, S. *Etruscan Civilization.* Los Angeles 2000.

**HECHT 1995**
Hecht, R. E., Jr. *From a North American Collection of Ancient Art.* New York 1995.

**HEDREEN 1992**
Hedreen, G. M. *Silens in Attic Black-Figure Vase-Painting: Myth and Performance.* Ann Arbor 1992.

**HEDREEN 1994**
Hedreen, G. "Silens, Nymphs, and Maenads." *JHS* 114 (1994): 47–69.

**HEESEN 1996**
Heesen, P. *The J. L. Theodor Collection of Attic Black-Figure Vases.* Amsterdam 1996.

**HEEßEL 2002**

Heeßel, N. P. *Pazuzu: Archäologische und philologische Studien zu einem alt-orientalischen Dämon.* Ancient Magic and Divination 4. Leiden 2002.

**HEMINGWAY 1996**

Hemingway, S. "How Bronzes Were Made in Classical Antiquity." *Harvard University Art Museums Gallery Series* 19 (1996): 1–8.

**HENRICHS 1987**

Henrichs, A. "Myth Visualized: Dionysos and His Circle in Sixth-Century Attic Vase-Painting." In *Papers on the Amasis Painter and His World*, 92–124. Malibu 1987.

**HENRICHS 1993**

Henrichs, A. "'He has a god in him': Human and Divine in the Modern Perception of Dionysos." In Carpenter and Faraone 1993, 13–43.

**HERDEJÜRGEN 1978**

Herdejürgen, H. *Götter, Menschen, und Dämonen: Terrakotten aus Unteritalien.* Basel 1978.

**HERFORT-KOCH 1986**

Herfort-Koch, N. *Archaische Bronzeplastik Lakoniens.* Münster 1986.

**HERMARY 1986**

Hermary, A. "Divinités chypriotes II." *RDAC* (1986): 164–72.

**HERMARY 1997**

Hermary, A. "Le 'style d'Amathonte.'" In *Four Thousand Years of Images on Cypriote Pottery. Proceedings of the Third International Conference of Cypriote Studies, Nicosia, 3–4 May, 1996*, eds. V. Karageorghis, R. Laffineur, and F. Vandenabeele, 157–61. Brussels, Liège, and Nicosia 1997.

**HERRMANN 1964**

Herrmann, H.-V. "Werkstätten geometrischer Bronzeplastik." *JdI* 79 (1964): 17–71.

**HERRMANN 1966**

Herrmann, H.-V. "Die Kessel orientalisierender Zeit I: Kesselattaschen und Reliefuntersätze." *OlForsch* 6. Berlin 1966.

**HERRMANN 1972**

Herrmann, H.-V. *Olympia: Heiligtum und Wettkampfstätte.* Munich 1972.

**HERRMANN 1979**

Herrmann, H.-V. "Die Kessel der orientalisierender Zeit II: Kessel Protomen und Stabdreifüsse." *OlForsch* 11. Berlin 1979.

**HERRMANN 1987**

Herrmann, H.-V., ed. *Die Olympia-Skulpturen.* Darmstadt 1989.

**HEUZEY 1906**

Heuzey, L. "Les deux dragons sacrés de Babylone et leur prototype chaldéen." *RAssyr* 6.3 (1906): 95–105.

**HIGGINS 1954**

Higgins, R. A. *Catalogue of the Terracottas in the Department of Greek and Roman Antiquities, British Museum.* Vol. 1, *Greek: 730–330 B.C.* London 1954.

**HIGGINS 1959**

Higgins, R. A. *Catalogue of the Terracottas in the Department of Greek and Roman Antiquities, British Museum.* Vol. 2, *Plastic Vases of the Seventh and Sixth Centuries B.C., Plastic Lekythoi of the Fourth Century B.C.* London 1959.

**HIGGINS 1967a**

Higgins, R. A. *Greek Terracottas.* London 1967.

**HIGGINS 1967b**

Higgins, R. A. "Recent Acquisitions by the British Museum." *AR* 1966–67, 49–52.

**HIGGINS 1980**

Higgins, R. A. *Greek and Roman Jewellery.* 2d ed. London 1980.

**HIGGINS 1986**

Higgins, R. A. *Tanagra and the Figurines.* Princeton 1986.

**HILL 1949**

Hill, D. K. *Catalogue of Classical Bronze Sculpture in the Walters Art Gallery.* Baltimore 1949.

**HILL 1950**

Hill, D. K. "Animals in Your Museum." *Archaeology* 3.2 (1950): 96–97.

**HILL 1953**

Hill, D. K. "Two Plastic Vases." In *Studies Presented to David Moore Robinson on His Seventieth Birthday*, ed. G. Mylonas and D. Raymond, vol. 2, 60–64. St. Louis 1953.

**HIMMELMANN-WILDSCHÜTZ 1964**

Himmelmann-Wildschütz, N. *Bemerkungen zur geometrischen Plastik.* Berlin 1964.

**HIMMELMANN-WILDSCHÜTZ 1967**

Himmelmann-Wildschütz, N. *Erzählung und Figur in der archaischen Kunst.* Mainz 1967.

**HITZL 1982**

Hitzl, K. *Die Entstehung und Entwicklung des Volutenkraters von den frühesten Anfängen bis zur Ausprägung des kanonischen Stils in der attisch schwarzfigurigen Vasenmalerei.* Frankfurt am Main 1982.

**HOFFMANN 1964**

Hoffmann, H. "Some Unpublished Boeotian Satyr Terracottas." *AntK* 7 (1964): 67–71.

**HOFFMANN 1970**

Hoffmann, H. *Ten Centuries That Shaped the West: Greek and Roman Art in Texas Collections.* Exhib. cat. Institute for the Arts, Rice University. Houston 1970.

**HOFFMANN 1971**

Hoffmann, H. *Collecting Greek Antiquities.* New York 1971.

**HOFFMANN 1994**

Hoffmann, H. "The Riddle of the Sphinx: A Case Study in Athenian Immortality Symbolism." In *Classical Greece: Ancient Histories and Modern Archaeologies*, ed. I. Morris, 71–80. Cambridge 1994.

**HOFFMANN 1997**

Hoffmann, H. *Sotades. Symbols of Immortality on Greek Vases.* Oxford 1997.

**HOFFNER 1998**

Hoffner, H. A., Jr. *Hittite Myths.* 2d ed. Atlanta 1998.

**HOFSTETTER-DOLEGA 1990**

Hofstetter-Dolega, E. *Sirenen in Archaischen und Klassischen Griechenland.* Archäeologie 19. Würzburg 1990.

**HOGARTH 1914**

Hogarth, D. G. *Carchemish: Report on the Excavations at Djerabis on Behalf of the British Museum Conducted by C. L. Woolley and T. E. Lawrence.* Vol. 1. London 1914.

**HOLLOWAY 1975**
Holloway, R. R. *Influences and Styles in the Late Archaic and Early Classical Greek Sculpture of Sicily and Magna Graecia.* Louvain 1975.

**HOLLOWAY 1988**
Holloway, R. R. "Early Greek Architectural Decoration as Functional Art." *AJA* 92 (1988): 177–83.

**HOLLOWAY 2000**
Holloway, R. R. *The Archaeology of Ancient Sicily.* London 2000.

**HOMANN-WEDEKING 1950**
Homann-Wedeking, E. *Die Anfänge der griechischen Grossplastik.* Berlin 1950.

**HOMOLLE 1909**
Homolle, T. *Fouilles de Delphes.* Vol. 4.1, *Monuments figurés, sculpture: Art primitif, art archaïque du Péloponnèse et des iles.* Paris 1909.

**HOORN 1951**
Hoorn, G. van. *Choes and Anthesteria.* Leiden 1951.

**HOPKINS 1934**
Hopkins, C. "Assyrian Elements in the Perseus-Gorgon Story." *AJA* 34 (1934): 341–58.

**HOWE 1954**
Howe, T .P. "The Origin and Function of the Gorgon Head." *AJA* 58 (1954): 209–21.

**HOWES SMITH 1986**
Howes Smith, P. H. G. "A Study of 9th–7th Century Metal Bowls from Western Asia." *IrAnt* 21 (1986): 1–84.

**HUBER 2001**
Huber, I. *Die Ikonographie der Trauer in der griechischen Kunst.* Mannheim 2001.

**HÜBNER 1898**
Hübner, E. "Die Büste von Ilici." *JdI* 13 (1898): 114–34.

**HUMAN FIGURE 1987**
*The Human Figure in Early Greek Art.* Exhib. cat. National Gallery of Art, Washington, D.C., 1987.

**HUMMEL 1984**
Hummel, S. "Die etruskische Sirene und der ägyptische Ba-Vogel." *ÖJh* 55 (1984): 24–25.

**HURWIT 1985**
Hurwit, J. M. *The Art and Culture of Early Greece: 1100–480 B.C.* Ithaca (New York) and London 1985.

**HURWIT 1995**
Hurwit, J. "The Doryphoros: Looking Backward." In *Polykleitos, the Doryphoros, and Tradition,* ed. W. G. Moon, 3–18. Madison 1995.

**HURWIT 2002**
Hurwit, J. M. "Reading the Chigi Vase." *Hesperia* 71 (2002): 1–22.

**HUS 1961**
Hus, A. *Recherches sur la statuaire en pierre étrusque archaïque.* Paris 1961.

**HUTCHINSON 1930**
Hutchinson, R. W. "Two Etruscan Vases." *AnnalLiv* 17 (1930): 27–30.

**IMAI 1977**
Imai, A. *Some Aspects of the "Phoenician Bowls" with Special Reference to the Proto-Cypriote Class and the Cypro-Phoenician Class.* Ph.D. diss., Columbia University 1977.

**IMMERWAHR 1990**
Immerwahr, H. *Attic Script: A Survey.* Oxford 1990.

**IN CELEBRATION 1997**
*In Celebration: Works of Art from the Collections of Princeton Alumni and Friends of The Art Museum, Princeton University.* Exhib. cat. Princeton 1997.

**ISARD 1939**
Isard, A. *Le Centaure dans la légende et dans l'art.* Lyon 1939.

**ISLER 1970**
Isler, H. P. *Acheloos: Eine Monographie.* Bern 1970.

**ISLER 1978**
Isler, H. P. *Samos.* Vol. 4, *Das archaische Nordtor und seine Umgebung im Heraion von Samos.* Bonn 1978.

**ISLER 1986**
Isler, H. P. "Una idria del Pittore di Londra B76, con il riscatto di Ettore." *NumAntCl* 15 (1986): 95–123.

**ISLER AND SGUAITAMATTI 1990**
Isler, H. P., and M. Sguaitamatti, eds. *Die Sammlung Collisani/La Collezione Collisani.* Zürich 1990.

**ISLER-KERENYI 1977**
Isler-Kerenyi, C. *Lieblinge der Meermädchen: Achilles und Theseus auf einer Spitzamphora aus der Zeit der Perserkriege.* Zürcher Archäologische 3. Zürich 1977.

**ISLER-KERENYI 2001**
Isler-Kerenyi, C. *Dionysos nella Grecia arcaica: Il contributo delle immagini.* Pisa and Rome 2001.

**ISMAIL 1974**
Ismail, B. K. "Ein Pazuzu-Kopf aus Ninive." *Sumer* 30 (1974): 121–28.

**JACOBSTHAL 1906**
Jacobsthal, P. *Der Blitz in der orientalischen und griechischen Kunst.* Berlin 1906.

**JACOPI 1929**
Jacopi, P. *Clara Rhodos.* Vol. 3, *Scavi nella necropoli di Jalisso, 1924–1928.* Rhodes 1929.

**JACOPI 1953**
Jacopi, G. "Un askos di bronzo configurato da Crotone." *ArchCl* 5 (1953): 10–22.

**JANTZEN 1937**
Jantzen, U. *Bronzewerkstätten in Grossgriechenland und Sizilien.* JdI Erg. 13. Berlin 1937.

**JANTZEN 1955**
Jantzen, U. *Griechische Greifenkessel.* Berlin 1955.

**JANTZEN 1958**
Jantzen, U. "Greifenprotomen von Samos." *AM* 73 (1958): 26–49.

**JANTZEN 1972**
Jantzen, U. *Samos.* Vol. 8, *Ägyptische und orientalische Bronzen aus dem Heraion von Samos.* Bonn 1972.

**JEFFERY 1990**
Jeffery, L. H. *The Local Scripts of Archaic Greece: A Study of the Origins of the Greek Alphabet and Its Development from the Eighth to Fifth Centuries B.C.* Rev. ed. by A. W. Johnston. Oxford 1990.

**JENKINS 1936**
Jenkins, R. J. H. *Dedalica: A Study of Dorian Plastic Art in the Seventh Century B.C.* Cambridge 1936.

**JENKINS 1970**
Jenkins, G. M. *The Coinage of Gela.* Berlin 1970.

**JENTOFT-NILSEN 1983**
Jentoft-Nilsen, M. "A Krater by Asteas." *Greek Vases in the J. Paul Getty Museum* 1 (1983): 139–48.

**JOFFROY 1954**
Joffroy, R. "La Tombe de Vix (Côte-d' Or): Les Fouilles et les découvertes." *MonPiot* 48 (1954).

**JOFFROY 1962**
Joffroy, R. *Le Trésor de Vix: Histoire et portée d'une grande découverte.* Paris 1962.

**JOFFROY 1979**
Joffroy, R. *Vix et ses trésors.* Paris 1979.

**JOHANSEN 1979**
Johansen, F. "Etruskiske Bronzerelieffer I Glyptoteket." *MeddelGlypt* 36 (1979): 67–89.

**JOHANSEN 1994**
Johansen, F. *Greece in the Archaic Period.* Exhib. cat. Ny Carlsberg Glyptotek. Copenhagen 1994.

**JOHNS 1982**
Johns, C. *Sex or Symbol: Erotic Images of Greece and Rome.* London 1982.

**JOHNSTON 1979**
Johnston, A. W. *Trademarks on Greek Vases.* Warminster 1979.

**JONES 1960**
Jones, F. F. *Ancient Art in The Art Museum, Princeton University.* Princeton 1960.

**JONES 1986**
Jones, R. E. *Greek and Cypriote Pottery: A Review of Scientific Studies.* Athens 1986.

**JONGKEES-VOS 1971**
Jongkees-Vos, M. F. "The Centaur Painter." In J. H. Jongkees and M. F. Jongkees-Vos, *Varia Archaeologica*, 13–21. Alkmaar 1971.

**JORDAN 1988**
Jordan, J. *Attic Black-Figured Eye-Cups.* Ph.D. diss., New York University 1988.

**JOVINO 2000**
Jovino, M. B. "The Etruscan Expansion into Campania." In *The Etruscans*, ed. M. Torelli, 157–67. Milan 2000.

**JUBIER 1999**
Jubier, C. "Les Peintres de Sappho et de Diosphos, structures d'atelier." In Villanueva Puig et al. 1999, 181–85.

**JUCKER 1991**
Jucker, I. *Italy of the Etruscans.* Exhib. cat. Israel Museum, Jerusalem. Mainz 1991.

**JURRIAANS-HELLE 1997**
Jurriaans-Helle, G. "Fabelachtig! Wonderlijke wezens tussen mensen en goden." *Meded* 68 (1997): 6–25.

**KAEMPF-DIMITRIADOU 1979**
Kaempf-Dimitriadou, S. *Die Liebe der Götter in der attischen Kunst des 5. Jahrhunderts v. Chr. AntK* Beiheft 11. Bern 1979.

**KÄSTNER 1989**
Kästner, V. "Gorgoneionantefixe aus Süditalien." *FuB* 27 (1989): 115–28.

**KÄUFLER 1999**
Käufler, S. "Funde aus Milet II. Die Frühstufe des Middle Wild Goat I-Stils." *AA* 1999, 203–12.

**KAHIL 1955**
Kahil, L. *Les enlèvements et le retour d'Hélène dans les textes et les documents figurés.* Paris 1955.

**KANELLOPOULOU 1980**
Kanellopoulou, C. "Πήλινο ειδώλιο της συλλογής Καρόλου Πολίτη." In Στήλη: τόμος εις μνήμην Νικολάου Κοντολέοντος, 295–99. Athens 1980.

**KARAGEORGHIS 1966**
Karageorghis, V. "Notes on Some Centaurs from Cyprus." In Χαριστήριον εις Αναστάσιον Κ. Ορλάνδον, vol. 2, 160–69. Athens 1966.

**KARAGEORGHIS 1973**
Karageorghis, V. *Salamis.* Vol. 5.1–3, *Excavations in the Necropolis of Salamis, III.* Nicosia 1973.

**KARAGEORGHIS 1986**
Karageorghis, V. "Kypriaka IX." *RDAC* (1986): 45–54.

**KARAGEORGHIS 1989**
Karageorghis, V. "Some Remarks on the 'Amathus Style' in Cypriote Vase-Painting." In *Beiträge zur Ikonographie und Hermeneutik: Festschrift für Nikolaus Himmelmann*, ed. H.-U. Cain, H. Gabelmann, and D. Salzmann, 83–86. Bonn 1989.

**KARAGEORGHIS 1990**
Karageorghis, V. "The Princeton Amphoriskos of the Amathus Style." *RDAC* (1990): 121–25.

**KARAGEORGHIS 1991a**
Karageorghis, V., ed. *The Civilizations of the Aegean and Their Diffusion in Cyprus and the Eastern Mediterranean, 2000–600 B.C.* Larnaca 1991.

**KARAGEORGHIS 1991b**
Karageorghis, V. "A Cypriot Centaur Rediscovered." *CECy* 15 (1991): 25–28.

**KARAGEORGHIS 1993a**
Karageorghis, V. *The Coroplastic Art of Ancient Cyprus.* Vol. 2, *Late Cypriote II–Cypro-Geometric III.* Nicosia 1993.

**KARAGEORGHIS 1993b**
Karageorghis, V. *The Coroplastic Art of Ancient Cyprus.* Vol. 3, *The Cypro-Archaic Period: Large and Medium-Size Sculpture.* Nicosia 1993.

**KARAGEORGHIS 1995**
Karageorghis, V. *The Coroplastic Art of Ancient Cyprus.* Vol. 4, *The Cypro-Archaic Period: Small Male Figurines.* Nicosia 1995.

**KARAGEORGHIS 1996**
Karageorghis, V. *The Coroplastic Art of Ancient Cyprus.* Vol. 6, *The Cypro-Archaic Period: Monsters, Animals, and Miscellanea.* Nicosia 1996.

**KARAGEORGHIS 1998**
Karageorghis, V. *Greek Gods and Heroes in Ancient Cyprus.* Athens 1998.

**KARAGEORGHIS AND DES GAGNIERS 1974**
Karageorghis, V., and J. Des Gagniers. *La Céramique chypriote de style figuré: Age de fer (1050–500 av. J.-C.).* Istituto per gli Studi Micenai ed Egeo-Analotici: Biblioteca di antichità 2. Rome 1974.

**KARAGEORGHIS, MERTENS, AND ROSE 2000**
Karageorghis, V., J. R. Mertens, and M. E. Rose. *Ancient Art from Cyprus: The Cesnola Collection in the Metropolitan Museum of Art.* New York 2000.

**KARAGIORGA 1964**
Karagiorga, G. T. "Λακωνικά γοργόνεια." *ArchDelt* 19 (1964): 116–22.

**KARAGIORGA 1970**
Karagiorga, G. T. Γοργείη κεφαλή: καταγωγή και νόημα της γοργονικής μορφής στη λατρεία και την τέχνη των αρχαϊκών χρόνων. Athens 1970.

**KARDARA 1963**
Kardara, C. Ροδιακή Αγγειογραφία. Athens 1963.

379

**KARDARA 1988**
Kardara, C. Ἀφροδίτη Ἐρυκίνη: ἱερόν καὶ μαντεῖον εἰς τὴν Β. Δ. Ἀρκαδίαν. Athens 1988.

**KAROUZOU 1972**
Karouzou, S. "Satyroi pyrrhichistes sur un lécythe du Musée National d'Athènes." In Κέρνος: τιμητικὴ προσφορά, ed. G. Bakalakes, 58–71. Thessaloniki 1972.

**KATZ 1997**
Katz, P. "Hill-Stead 46.1.95, A 'Lost' Work of the Painter of Athens 931." *BABesch* 72 (1997): 1–20.

**KAULEN 1967**
Kaulen, G. *Daidalika: Werkstätten griechischer Kleinplastik des V. Jahrhunderts v. Chr.* Munich 1967.

**KAWAMI 1972**
Kawami, T. "A Possible Source for the Sculptures of the Audience Hall, Pasargadae." *Iran* 10 (1972): 146–48.

**KAWAMI 1974**
Kawami, T. "The Date of the Fish-Garbed Man from Assur." *FuB* 16 (1974): 9–13.

**KENDALL 1977**
Kendall, T. "Urartian Art in Boston: Two Bronze Belts and a Mirror." *BMFA* 75 (1977): 27–55.

**KENFIELD 1993**
Kenfield, J. F. "A Modelled Terracotta Frieze from Archaic Morgantina: Its East Greek and Central Italian Affinities." In *Deliciae Fictile*, ed. E. Rystedt, C. Wikander, and O. Wikander, 21–28. Stockholm 1993.

**KENFIELD 1997**
Kenfield, J. F. "Technical Variety in the Archaic Architectural Terracottas of Morgantina." In Lulof and Moormann 1997, 107–12.

**KENNER 1935**
Kenner, H. "Das Louterion in Kult." *ÖJh* 29 (1935): 109–54.

**KENNER 1939**
Kenner, H. "Flügelfrau und Flügeldämon." *ÖJh* 31 (1939): 83–95.

**KENNER 1946**
Kenner, H. *Der Fries des Tempels von Bassae-Phigaleia.* Vienna 1946.

**KEULS 1985**
Keuls, E. C. *The Reign of the Phallus: Sexual Politics in Ancient Athens.* New York 1985.

**KILIAN-DIRLMEIER 1979**
Kilian-Dirlmeier, I. *Anhänger in Griechenland von der mykenischen bis zur spätgeometrischen Zeit. Prähistorische Bronzefunde 11.* Vol. 2. Munich 1979.

**KILINSKI 1978**
Kilinski, K. "The Istanbul Painter." *AntK* 21 (1978): 12–16.

**KING 1912**
King, L. W. ed. *Babylonian Boundary-Stones.* London 1912.

**KIRK 1970**
Kirk, G. S. *Myth: Its Meaning and Functions in Ancient and Other Cultures.* Cambridge 1970.

**KLENGEL 1960**
Klengel, H. "Neue Lamaštu-Amulette aus dem Vorderasiatischen Museum zu Berlin und dem British Museum." *MIO* 7 (1960): 334–55.

**KLENGEL 1963**
Klengel, H. "Weitere Amulette gegen Lamaštu." *MIO* 8 (1963): 24–29.

**KLENGEL-BRANDT 1968**
Klengel-Brandt, E. "Apotropaische Tonfiguren aus Assur." *FuB* 10 (1968): 19–37.

**KLINGENDER 1971**
Klingender, F. *Animals in Art and Thought to the End of the Middle Ages.* London 1971.

**KLUIVER 1992**
Kluiver, J. "The 'Tyrrhenian' Group: Its Origins and the Neck-Amphorae in the Netherlands and Belgium." *BABesch* 67 (1992): 73–91.

**KLUIVER 1993**
Kluiver, J. "The Potter-Painters of 'Tyrrhenian' Neck-Amphorae: A Close Look at the Shape." *BABesch* 68 (1993): 179–94.

**KNAUER 1986**
Knauer, E. R. "ου γαρ ην αμις: A Chous by the Oionokles Painter." *Greek Vases in the J. Paul Getty Museum* 3 (1986): 91–100.

**KNELL 1990**
Knell, H. *Mythos und Polis. Bildprogramme griechischer Bauskulptur.* Darmstadt 1990.

**KNOLL 1998**
Knoll, K. *Alltag und Mythos. Griechische Gefässe der Skulpturensammlung.* Staatliche Kunstsammlungen. Dresden 1998.

**KOCH 1912**
Koch, H. *Dachterrakotten aus Campanien.* Berlin 1912.

**KOCH-HARNACK 1983**
Koch-Harnack, G. *Knabenliebe und Tiergeschenke. Ihre Bedeutung im päderastischen Erziehungssystem Athens.* Berlin 1983.

**KOCH-WESTENHOLZ 1995**
Koch-Westenholz, U., *Mesopotamian Astrology: An Introduction to Babylonian and Assyrian Celestial Divination.* Copenhagen 1995

**KÖCHER 1953**
Köcher, F. "Der babylonische Göttertypentext." *MIO* 1 (1953): 57–107.

**KOLBE 1981**
Kolbe, D. *Die Reliefprogramme religiös-mythologischen Charakters in neuassyrischen Palästen: Die Figurentypen, ihre Benennung und Bedeutung.* Europäische Hochschulschriften 38, Archäologie. Frankfurt am Main 1981.

**KOLDEWEY 1925**
Koldewey, R. *Das wieder erstehende Babylon: Die bisherigen Ergebnisse der deutschen Ausgrabungen.* Leipzig 1925.

**KOLDEWEY 1990**
Koldewey, R. *Das wieder erstehende Babylon.* Ed. B. Hrouda et al. Munich 1990.

**KOPCKE 1976**
Kopcke, G. "Eine Bronzestatuette in der Münchener Glyptothek." *MüJb* 27 (1976): 7–28.

**KOPCKE AND MOORE 1979**
Kopcke, G., and M. B. Moore, eds. *Studies in Classical Art and Archaeology: A Tribute to Peter Heinrich von Blanckenhagen.* New York 1979.

**KORRES 1972**
Korres, G. S. "Δίπαλτος καὶ Ὅρκιος Ζεὺς." *ArchEph* 1972, 208–33.

**KORSHAK 1987**
Korshak, Y. *Frontal Faces in Attic Vase Painting of the Archaic Period.* Chicago 1987.

**KOSSATZ-DEISSMANN 1982**
Kossatz-Deissmann, A. "Zur Herkunft des Perizoma im Satyrspiel." *JdI* 97 (1982): 65–90.

**KOSSATZ-DEISSMANN 1991**
Kossatz-Deissmann, A. "Satyr- und Mänadennamen auf Vasenbildern des Getty-Museums und der Sammlung Cahn (Basel), mit Addenda zu Charlotte Fränkel, *Satyr- und Bakchennamen auf Vasenbildern* (Hallee, 1912)." *Greek Vases in the J. Paul Getty Museum* 5 (1991): 131–99.

**KOUROU 1991**
Kourou, N. "Aegean Orientalizing versus Oriental Art: The Evidence of Monsters." In Karageorghis 1991a, 111–23.

**KOZLOFF 1980**
Kozloff, A. P. "Companions of Dionysos." *BClevMus* 67.7 (September 1980): 206–19.

**KOZLOFF 1989**
Kozloff, A. P. *Classical Art: A Brief Guide to the Collection.* Cleveland 1989.

**KOZLOFF AND MITTEN 1988**
Kozloff, A. P., and D. G. Mitten, eds. *The Gods Delight: The Human Figure in Classical Bronze.* Exhib. cat. Cleveland Museum of Art. Cleveland 1988.

**KRAAY 1976**
Kraay, C. M. *Archaic and Classical Greek Coins.* London 1976.

**KRIEGER 1973**
Krieger, X. *Der Kampf zwischen Peleus und Thetis in der griechischen Vasenmalerei.* Münster 1973.

**KÜBLER 1954**
Kübler, K. *Kerameikos.* Vol. 6.1, *Die Nekropole des 10 bis 8. Jahrhunderts.* Berlin 1954.

**KÜBLER 1970**
Kübler, K. *Kerameikos.* Vol. 6.2, *Die Nekropole des späten 8. bis frühen 6. Jahrhunderts.* Berlin 1970.

**KÜHNE 1980**
Kühne, H. *Das Rollsiegel in Syrien: Zur Steinschneidekunst in Syrien zwischen 3300 und 330 vor Christus.* Tübingen 1980.

**KÜHNE 1984**
Kühne, H. "Tell She Hamad/Dūr Katlimmu: The Assyrian Provincial Capital in the Mohafazat Deir Az-Zor." *AAS* 34 (1984): 160–81.

**KUNZE 1930**
Kunze, E. "Zu den Anfängen der griechischen Plastik." *AM* 55 (1930): 141–62.

**KUNZE 1931**
Kunze, E. *Kretische Bronzereliefs.* Stuttgart 1931.

**KUNZE 1932**
Kunze, E. "Sirenen." *AM* 57 (1932): 124–41.

**KUNZE 1950**
Kunze, E. *Archaische Schildbänder.* OlForsch 2. Berlin 1950.

**KUNZE 1953**
Kunze, E. *Drei Bronzen der Sammlung Hélène Stathatos.* Winckelmannsprogramm der archäologischen Gesellschaft zu Berlin 109. Berlin 1953.

**KUNZE 1963**
Kunze, E. "Zum Giebel des Artemistempels in Korfu." *AM* 78 (1963): 74–89.

**KUNZE, SCHLEIF, AND EILMANN 1941**
Kunze, E., H. Schleif, and E. Eilmann. *Olympische Bericht* 3 in *JdI* 56 (1941).

**KURTZ 1975**
Kurtz, D. *Athenian White Lekythoi: Patterns and Painters.* Oxford 1975.

**KURTZ 1983**
Kurtz, D. C. *The Berlin Painter.* Oxford 1983.

**KURTZ AND BOARDMAN 1971**
Kurtz, D., and J. Boardman. *Greek Burial Customs.* Ithaca (New York) 1971.

**KYLE 1992**
Kyle, D. G. "The Panathenaic Games: Sacred and Civic Athletics." In Neils 1992, 77–102.

**KYRKOU 1997**
Kyrkou, M. "Η πρωτοαττική πρόκληση. Νέες κεραμικές μαρτυρίες." In Oakley, Coulson, and Palagia 1997, 423–34.

**LAFFINEUR 1978**
Laffineur, R. *L'Orfèvrerie rhodienne orientalisante.* Paris 1978.

**LAFFINEUR 1980**
Laffineur, R. "L'Orfèvrerie rhodienne orientalisante." In *Études sur l'orfèvrerie antique,* ed. T. Hackens, 13–29. Louvain-La-Neuve 1980.

**LAMB 1929**
Lamb, W. *Greek and Roman Bronzes.* Chicago 1929.

**LAMBERT 1985**
Lambert, W. G. "The History of the *muš-ḫus* in Ancient Mesopotamia." In Borgeaud and Christe 1985, 87–94.

**LAMBERT 1987**
Lambert, W. G. "Gilgamesh in Literature and Art: The Second and First Millennia." In Farkas, Harper, and Harrison 1987, 37–52.

**LANE 1947**
Lane, A. *Greek Pottery.* New York 1947.

**LANE 1971**
Lane, A. *Greek Pottery.* 3d ed. London 1971.

**LANGDON 1923**
Langdon, S. *The Babylonian Epic of Creation Restored from the Recently Recovered Tablets of Assur: Transcription, Translation, and Commentary.* Oxford 1923.

**LANGDON 1989**
Langdon, S. "The Return of the Horse Leader." *AJA* 93 (1989): 185–201.

**LANGLOTZ 1927**
Langlotz, E. *Frühgriechische Bildhauerschulen.* Nuremberg 1927.

**LANGLOTZ 1932**
Langlotz, E. *Griechische Vasen in Würzburg.* Munich 1932.

**LANGLOTZ 1967**
Langlotz, E. "Der Sinn attischer Vasenbilder." *Wissenschaftliche Zeitschrift der Universität Rostock* 16.7–8 (1967): 473–80.

**LANGLOTZ 1975**
Langlotz, E. *Studien zur nordostgriechischen Kunst.* Mainz 1975.

**LANGRIDGE 1991**
Langridge, E. "The Boar Hunt in Corinthian Pottery." *AJA* 95 (1991): 323.

**LANGRIDGE 1993**
Langridge, E. M. *The Eucharides Painter and His Place in the Athenian Potters' Quarter.* Ph.D. diss., Princeton University 1993.

**LAPATIN 2001**
Lapatin, K. *Chryselephantine Statuary in the Ancient Mediterranean World.* Oxford 2001.

**LATTIMORE 1976**
Lattimore, R., trans. *The Odes of Pindar.* 2d ed. Chicago 1976.

**LAUFER 1985**
Laufer, E. *Kaineus: Studien zur Ikonographie.* RdA Suppl. 1. Rome 1985.

**LAUMONIER 1921**
Laumonier, A. *Catalogue de terres cuites du Musée Archéologique de Madrid.* Bordeaux and Paris 1921.

**LAVIOSA 1954**
Laviosa, C. "Le antefisse fittili di Taranto." *ArchCl* 6 (1954): 217–50.

**LAWRENCE 1929**
Lawrence, A. W. *Classical Sculpture.* London 1929.

**LAWRENCE 1959**
Lawrence, P. "The Corinthian Chimaera Painter." *AJA* 63 (1959): 349–63.

**LAWRENCE 1996**
Lawrence, P. "Dodwellians in the Potters' Quarter." In Amyx and Lawrence 1996, 131–47.

**LAWRENCE 1998**
Lawrence, P. "The Luxus Phenomenon I. The Taucheira Painter and Closely Related Hands." *Hesperia* 67 (1998): 303–22.

**LAYARD 1849**
Layard, A. H. *Nineveh and Its Remains.* Vol. 2. London 1849.

**LAYARD 1849–53**
Layard, A. H. *Monuments of Nineveh from Drawings Made on the Spot.* 2 vols. London 1849–53.

**LEBESSI 1973**
Lebessi, A. "Sanctuary of Hermes and Aphrodite near Kato Syme Viannou." *AAA* 6.1 (1973): 104–14 .

**LEBESSI 1996**
Lebessi, A. "The Relations of Crete and Euboea in the Tenth and Ninth Centuries B.C.: The Lefkandi Centaur and His Predecessors." In *Minotaur and Centaur: Studies in the Archaeology of Crete and Euboea Presented to Mervyn Popham*, ed. D. Evely, I. S. Lemos, and S. Sherratt, 146–54. Oxford 1996.

**LEBRUN 1985**
Lebrun, R. "Le zoomorphisme dans la religion Hittite." In Borgeaud and Christe 1985, 95–103.

**LEMOS 1997**
Lemos, A. "Athenian Black-Figure: Rhodes Revisited." In Oakley, Coulson, and Palagia 1997, 457–68.

**LEMOS 2000**
Lemos, A. "Songs for Heroes: The Lack of Images in Early Greece." In *Word and Image in Ancient Greece*, ed. N. K. Rutter and B. A. Sparkes, 11–21. Edinburgh 2000.

**LENTINI 1997**
Lentini, M. C. "Nuovi rivestiment architettonici di età arcaica a Naxos dal Santuario ad ovest del Santa Venera." In Lulof and Moormann 1997, 123–34.

**LEPORA 1998**
Lepora, L. "Di quattro kylikes attiche a figure nere della collezione Ceccanti." In Capecchi et al. 1998, 271–80.

**LEZZI-HAFTER 1976**
Lezzi-Hafter, A. *Der Schuwalow-Maler: Eine Kannenwerkstatt der Parthenonzeit.* Kerameus 2. Mainz 1976.

**LIEBERMANN 1971**
Liebermann, H. *Bronzen aus dem vorchristlichen Mittelmeerraum.* Kassel 1971.

**LIEPMANN 1975**
Liepmann, U. *Griechische Terrakotten, Bronzen, Skulpturen, Kestner Museum Hannover.* Hannover 1975.

**LISSARRAGUE 1988**
Lissarrague, F. "Les Satyres et le monde animal." In Christiansen and Melander 1988, 335–51.

**LISSARRAGUE 1990a**
Lissarrague, F. *The Aesthetics of the Greek Banquet.* Princeton 1990.

**LISSARRAGUE 1990b**
Lissarrague, F. *L'Autre Guerrier. Archers, peltastes, cavaliers dans l'imagerie attique.* Paris and Rome 1990.

**LISSARRAGUE 1990c**
Lissarrague, F. "The Sexual Life of Satyrs." In *Before Sexuality: The Construction of Erotic Experience in the Ancient Greek World*, ed. D. M. Halperin, J. J. Winkler, and F. I. Zeitlin, 53–81. Princeton 1990.

**LISSARRAGUE 1990d**
Lissarrague, F. "Why Satyrs Are Good to Represent." In Winkler and Zeitlin 1990, 228–36.

**LISSARRAGUE 1993**
Lissarrague, F. "On the Wildness of Satyrs." In Carpenter and Faraone 1993, 207–20.

**LISSARRAGUE 1995**
Lissarrague, F. "Identity and Otherness: The Case of Attic Head Vases and Plastic Vases." *Source* 15.1 (1995): 4–9.

**LLOYD-JONES 1994**
Lloyd-Jones, H. *Sophokles.* Cambridge (Mass.) 1994.

**LO PORTO 1978**
Lo Porto, F. G. "Le importazioni della Grecia dell'Est in Puglia." In Vallet 1978, 131–36.

**LUBSEN ADMIRAAL 1999**
Lubsen Admiraal, S. M. "The Getty Krater by Syriskos." In Docter and Moormann 1999, 239–41.

**LUCE 1922**
Luce, S. B. "Herakles and the Old Man of the Sea." *AJA* 26 (1922): 174–92.

**LUCE 1923**
Luce, S. B. "Heracles and Achelous on a Cylix in Boston." *AJA* 27 (1923): 425–37.

**LUCE 1924**
Luce, S. B. "Studies of the Exploits of Herakles on Vases, I. Herakles and the Erymanthian Boar." *AJA* 28 (1924): 296–325.

**LULLIES 1964**
Lullies, R. *Griechische Plastik, Vasen, und Kleinkunst. Leihgaben aus Privatbesitz.* Exhib. cat. Staatliche Kunstsammlungen Kassel. Kassel 1964.

**LULOF 1996**
Lulof, P. S. *The Ridge-Pole Statues from the Late Archaic Temple at Satricum.* Amsterdam 1996.

**LULOF 1997a**
Lulof, P. S. "An Etrusco-Italic Centauromachy in Princeton." In Lulof and Moormann 1997, 135–42.

**LULOF 1997b**
Lulof, P. S. "Myths from Greece: The Representation of Power on the Roofs of Satricum." *Meded* 56 (1997): 85–114.

**LULOF 1999**
Lulof, P. S. "The Image of Perseus in Archaic Roof Decoration in Central Italy." In Docter and Moormann 1999, 241–44.

**LULOF AND MOORMANN 1997**
Lulof, P. S., and E. M. Moormann, eds. *Deliciae Fictiles II. Proceedings of the Second International Conference on Archaic Architectural Terracottas from Italy, Held at the Netherlands Institute in Rome, 12–13 June 1996.* Amsterdam 1997.

**MAASS 1979**
Maass, M. *Greichische und römische Bronzewerke der Antikensammlungen.* Munich 1979.

**MAASS AND KILIAN-DIRLMEIER 1998**
Maass, M., and I. Kilian-Dirlmeier. "Aegina, Aphaia Tempel XVIII. Bronzefunde ausser Waffen." *AA* 1998, 57–104.

**MADHLOOM 1970**
Madhloom, T. A. *The Chronology of Neo-Assyrian Art.* London 1970.

**MADIGAN 1996**
Madigan, B. C. *The Temple of Apollo Bassitas.* Vol. 2, *The Sculpture*, ed. F. A. Cooper. Princeton 1996.

**MAIURI 1923–24**
Maiuri, A. "La necropoli arcaica di Jalisos." *ASAtene* 6–7 (1923–24): 257–341.

**MALLOWAN 1954**
Mallowan, M. E. L. "The Excavations at Nimrud (KALḪU), 1953." *Iraq* 16 (1954): 59–114.

**MALLOWAN 1966**
Mallowan, M. E. L. *Nimrud and Its Remains.* 3 vols. London 1966.

**MALLOWAN 1978**
Mallowan, M. E. L. *The Nimrud Ivories.* London 1978.

**MANGOLD 2000**
Mangold, M. *Kassandra in Athen. Die Eroberung Trojas auf attischen Vasenbildern.* Berlin 2000.

**MANNACK 2001**
Mannack, T. *The Late Mannerists in Athenian Vase-Painting.* Oxford 2001.

**MARANGOU 1985**
Marangou, L. I. *Ancient Greek Art: The N. P. Goulandris Collection.* Athens 1985.

**MARINATOS 1927/28**
Marinatos, S. "Γοργόνες και γοργόνεια." *ArchEph* 1927/28, 7–41.

**MARINATOS 2000**
Marinatos, N. *The Goddess and the Warrior: The Naked Goddess and Mistress of Animals in Early Greek Religion.* London and New York 2000.

**MARINATOS 2001**
Marinatos, N. "Medusa on the Temple of Artemis at Corfu." In *Archaische griechische Tempel und Altägypten. Internationales Kolloquium am 28. November 1997 am Institut für Ägyptologie der Universität Wien*, ed. M. Bietak, 83–88. Vienna 2001.

**MARKOE 1985**
Markoe, G. *Phoenician Bronze and Silver Bowls from Cyprus and the Mediterranean.* Berkeley 1985.

**MARKOE AND SERWINT 1985**
Markoe, G. E., and N. J. Serwint. *Animal Style on Greek and Etruscan Vases.* Exhib. cat. University of Vermont. Burlington 1985.

**MARSHALL 1911**
Marshall, F. H. *Catalogue of the Jewellery, Greek, Etruscan, and Roman, in the Department of Antiquities, British Museum.* London 1911.

**MARTELLI 1987**
Martelli, M., ed. *La ceramica degli Etruschi: La pittura vascolare.* Novara 1987.

**MATHESON 1995**
Matheson, S. B. *Polygnotos and Vase-Painting in Classical Athens.* Madison 1995.

**MATTHEWS 1990**
Matthews, D. M. *Principles of Composition in Near Eastern Glyptic of the Later Second Millennium B.C.* Orbis Biblicus et Orientalis, Series Archaeologica 8. Freiburg (Switzerland) and Göttingen 1990.

**MATTHEWS 1992**
Matthews, D. M. *The Kassite Glyptic of Nippur.* Orbis Biblicus et Orientalis 116. Freiburg (Switzerland) and Göttingen 1992.

**MATTUSCH 1988**
Mattusch, C. C. *Greek Bronze Statuary, from the Beginnings through the Fifth Century B.C.* Ithaca (New York) 1988.

**MAYER-OPIFICIUS 1986**
Mayer-Opificius, R. "Bemerkungen zur mittelassyrischen Glyptik des 13. und 12. Jhdts. v. Chr." In *Insight through Images: Studies in Honor of Edith Porada*, ed. M. Kelly-Buccellati, 161–69. Bibliotheca Mesopotamica 21. Malibu 1986.

**MAYO 1998**
Mayo, M. E. *Ancient Art: Virginia Museum of Fine Arts.* Richmond 1998.

**MAYOR 1994**
Mayor, A. "Guardians of the Gold." *Archaeology* 47.6 (1994): 53–59.

**MAYOR 2000**
Mayor, A. *The First Fossil Hunters: Paleontology in Greek and Roman Times.* Princeton 2000.

**MCNALLY 1978**
McNally, S. "The Maenad in Early Greek Art." *Arethusa* 11 (1978): 101–35.

**MCNIVEN 1995**
McNiven, T. J. "The Unheroic Penis: Otherness Exposed." *Source* 15.1 (1995): 10–16.

**MERCKLIN 1937**
Mercklin, E. von. "Kentaur auf Freierfüsse." *AA* 1937, 59–67.

**MERHAV ET AL. 1991**
Merhav, R., et al., eds. *Urartu: A Metalworking Center in the First Millenium B.C.E.* Exhib. cat. Israel Museum. Tel Aviv 1991.

**MERKELBACH AND WEST 1967**
Merkelbach, R., and M. L. West, eds. *Fragmenta Hesiodea.* Oxford 1967.

**MERKELBACH AND WEST 1983**
Merkelbach, R., and M. L. West. *Hesiodi Opera.* 2d ed. Oxford 1983.

**MERTENS 1977**
Mertens, J. *Attic White-Ground: Its Development on Shapes other than Lekythoi.* New York 1977.

**MERTENS 1985**
Mertens, J. R. *Greek Bronzes in the Metropolitan Museum of Art.* BMMA 43.2 (1985).

**MERTENS 1993**
Mertens, J. R. "Reflections of an Italian Journey on an Early Attic Lekythos?" *MMAJ* 28 (1993): 5–11.

**MERTENS-HORN 1978**
Mertens-Horn, M. "Beobachtungen an dädalischen Tondächern." *JdI* 93 (1978): 30–65.

**MERTENS-HORN 1990**
Mertens-Horn, M. "Archaische Tondächer west-griechischer Typologie in Delphi und Olympia." *Hesperia* 59 (1990): 235–48.

**MERTENS-HORN 1992**
Mertens-Horn, M. "Die archaischen Baufriese aus Metapont." *RM* 99 (1992): 1–122.

**METZGER 1972**
Metzger, H. "Satyres lanceurs de pierres." *RA* 1972, 31–34.

**MEYER-EMMERLING 1979**
Meyer-Emmerling, S. *Darstellungen auf tyrrhenischen Amphoren.* Ph.D. diss., University of Frankfurt 1979.

**MILLEKER 1992**
Milleker, E. "Red-Figure Stand with a Sphinx on Each Side." In *Ancient Art: Gifts from the Norbert Schimmel Collection*, 43–44. *BMMA* 49.4 (1992).

**MILLER 1995**
Miller, M. C. "Priam, King of Troy." In Carter and Morris 1995, 449–65.

**MILNE 1947**
Milne, M. "Peleus and Akastos." *BMMA* 5.10 (June 1947): 255–60.

**MILNE AND RICHTER 1935**
Milne, M. J., and G. M. A. Richter. *Shapes and Names of Athenian Vases.* New York 1935.

**MINTO 1955**
Minto, A. "La Centauromachia del Vaso François." In *Anthemon. Scritti di archeologia e di antichità classiche in onore di Carlo Anti*, introd. G. Fiocco, 21–40. Florence 1955.

**MINTO 1960**
Minto, A. *Il Vaso François.* Florence 1960.

**MITTEN 1975**
Mitten, D. G. *Classical Bronzes: Rhode Island School of Design, Providence. Museum of Art.* Providence 1975.

**MITTEN 1981**
Mitten, D. G. "Animals in the Classical World." In *Animals in Ancient Art from the Leo Mildenberg Collection*, 79–82. Exhib. cat. Cleveland Museum of Art. Cleveland 1981.

**MITTEN AND DOERINGER 1967**
Mitten, D. G., and S. F. Doeringer. *Master Bronzes from the Classical World.* Exhib. cat. Fogg Art Museum, Harvard University. Mainz 1967.

**MOLLARD-BESQUES 1954**
Mollard-Besques, S. *Catalogue raisonné des figurines et reliefs en terre cuite grecs, étrusques et romains, Louvre I: Époques préhellénique, géométrique, archaïque, et classique.* Paris 1954.

**MOMMSEN 2002**
Mommsen, H. "Das Tritonabenteuer bei Exekias." In Clark and Gaunt 2002, 225–32.

**MOON 1983**
Moon, W., ed. *Ancient Greek Art and Iconography.* Madison 1983.

**MOON AND BERGE 1979**
Moon, W. G., and C. Berge, eds. *Greek Vase-Painting in Midwestern Collections.* Chicago 1979.

**MOORE 1997**
Moore, M. B. *The Athenian Agora.* Vol. 30, *Attic Red-Figured and White-Ground Pottery.* Princeton 1997.

**MOORE AND PHILIPPIDES 1986**
Moore, M., and M. P. Philippides. *The Athenian Agora.* Vol. 23, *Attic Black-Figured Pottery.* Princeton 1986.

**MOOREY 1971**
Moorey, P. R. S. *Catalogue of the Ancient Persian Bronzes in the Ashmolean Museum.* Oxford 1971.

**MOOREY ET AL. 1981**
Moorey, P. R. S., E. C. Bunker, E. Porada, and G. Markoe. *Ancient Bronzes, Ceramics, and Seals: The Nasli M. Heeramaneck Collection.* Los Angeles 1981.

**MOORTGAT 1940**
Moortgat, A. *Vorderasiatische Rollsiegel: Ein Beitrag zur Geschichte der Steinschneidekunst, Staatliche Museen zu Berlin.* Berlin 1940.

**MOORTGAT 1941–42**
Moortgat, A. "Assyrische Glyptik des 13. Jahrhunderts." *ZA* 13 (1941–42): 50–88.

**MOORTGAT 1944**
Moortgat, A. "Assyrische Glyptik des 12. Jahrhunderts." *ZA* 14 (1944): 23–44.

**MOORTGAT 1967**
Moortgat, A. *Die Kunst des alten Mesopotamiens.* Cologne 1967.

**MOORTGAT-CORRENS 1964**
Moortgat-Correns, U. "Beiträge zue mittelassyrischen Glyptik." In *Vorderasiatische Archäologie: Studien und Aufsätze: Anton Moortgat zum 65. Geburtstag gewidmet von Kollegen, Freunden, und Schülern*, ed. K. Bittel, 165–77. Berlin 1964.

**MOORTGAT-CORRENS 1988**
Moortgat-Correns, U. "Ein Kultbild Ninurtas aus neuassyrischer Zeit." *AfO* 35 (1988): 117–33.

**MORAW 1998**
Moraw, S. *Die Mänade in der attischen Vasenmalerei des 6. und 5. Jahrhunderts v. Chr.* Mainz 1998.

**MORAWIETZ 1998**
Morawietz, G. *Die gezähmte Kentaur.* Ph.D. diss., University of Munich 1998.

**MORET 1984**
Moret, J.-M. *Oedipe, la Sphinx, et les Thébains. Essai de mythologie iconographique.* Rome 1984.

**MORRIS 1984**
Morris, S. P. *The Black and White Style. Athens and Aigina in the Orientalizing Period.* New Haven 1984.

**MORRIS 1988**
Morris, I. *Burial and Ancient Society: The Rise of the Greek City State.* Cambridge 1988.

**MORRIS 1992**
Morris, S. P. *Daidalos and the Origin of Greek Art.* Princeton 1992.

**MORRIS 1992/93**
Morris, I. "Law, Culture, and Funerary Art in Athens, 600–300 B.C." *Hephaistos* 11/12 (1992/93): 35–50.

**MÜLLER 1978**
Müller, P. *Löwen und Mischwesen in der archaischen griechischen Kunst: Eine Untersuchungen über ihre Bedeutung.* Ph.D. diss., University of Zürich 1978.

**MUNRO 1973**
Munro, P. *Die spätägyptischen Totenstela.* Gluckstadt 1973.

**MURRAY AND TECUSAN 1995**
Murray, O., and M. Tecusan, eds. *In Vino Veritas*. Oxford 1995.

**MUSCARELLA 1974**
Muscarella, O. W., ed. *Ancient Art: The Norbert Schimmel Collection*. Mainz 1974.

**MUSCARELLA 1988**
Muscarella, O. W. *Bronze and Iron: Ancient Near Eastern Artifacts in the Metropolitan Museum of Art*. New York 1988.

**MUSCARELLA 1992**
Muscarella, O. W. "Greek and Oriental Cauldron Attachments: A Review." In *Greece between East and West: 10th—8th Centuries B.C.*, ed. G. Kopcke and I. Tokumaru, 16—45. Mainz 1992.

**MYLONAS 1957**
Mylonas, G. Ο πρωτοαττικός αμφορεύς της Ελευσίνος. Athens 1957.

**MYLONAS 1980**
Mylonas, G. "Κρητο–Μυκηναϊκή Σφιγξ." In Πεπραγμένα του Δ΄ Διεθνούς Κρητολογικού Συνεδρίου, *Herakleion, August 29—September 3, 1976*, vol. 1, 352—62. Athens 1980.

**NACHBAUR 1999**
Nachbaur, G. "'Wenn aus der Stadt die geflügelte Jungfrau einen der Männer entführte?' Ein Vasenfragment des Eucharides-Malers." *ÖJh* 68 (1999): 21—32.

**NAPIER 1986**
Napier, A. D. *Masks, Transformation, and Paradox*. Berkeley 1986.

**NEEFT 1991**
Neeft, C. W. *Addenda and Corrigenda to D. A. Amyx, Corinthian Vase-Painting in the Archaic Period*. Amsterdam 1991.

**NEILS 1982**
Neils, J., ed. *The World of Ceramics: Masterpieces from the Cleveland Museum of Art*. Cleveland 1982.

**NEILS 1987**
Neils, J. *The Youthful Deeds of Theseus*. Rome 1987.

**NEILS 1992**
Neils, J. *Goddess and Polis. The Panathenaic Festival in Ancient Athens*. Hanover 1992.

**NEILS 1995**
Neils, J. "Les Femmes Fatales: Skylla and the Sirens in Greek Art." In Cohen 1995, 175—84.

**NEILS 1996**
Neils, J. "The Cleveland Painter." *Cleveland Studies in the History of Art* 1 (1996): 12—29.

**NEILS 1998**
Neils, J. "Hercle in Cleveland." *Cleveland Studies in the History of Art* 3 (1998): 6—21.

**NERI 2000**
Neri, D. *Le coppe fenicie della tomba Bernardini nel Museo di Villa Giulia*. La Spezia 2000.

**NICHOLLS 1952**
Nicholls, R. V. "Type, Group, and Series: A Reconsideration of Some Coroplastic Fundamentals." *BSA* 47 (1952): 217—6.

**NIEMEYER 1964**
Niemeyer, H. G. "Attische Bronzestatuetten der spätarchaischen und frühklassischen Zeit." *Antike Plastik* 3.1 (Berlin 1964): 7—76.

**NILSSON 1932**
Nilsson, M. P. *The Mycenaean Origins of Greek Mythology*. Cambridge 1932.

**NOBLECOURT 1997**
Noblecourt, C. D. "La Monture de l'enfant divin." In *Ancient Egypt, the Aegean, and the Near East: Studies in Honor of Martha Rhoads Bell*, vol. 1, 169—74. San Antonio 1997.

**NOE 1984**
Noe, S. P. *The Coinage of Metapontum*. Parts 1 and 2. New York 1984.

**OAKLEY 1990**
Oakley, J. H. *The Phiale Painter*. Kerameus 8. Mainz 1990.

**OAKLEY AND LANGRIDGE 1994**
Oakley, J. H., and E. M. Langridge, et al. *Athenian Potters and Painters: Catalogue of the Exhibit*. Gennadius Library, American School of Classical Studies. Athens 1994.

**OAKLEY AND SINOS 1993**
Oakley, J. H., and R. H. Sinos. *The Wedding in Ancient Athens*. Madison 1993.

**OAKLEY, COULSON, AND PALAGIA 1997**
Oakley, J. H., W. D. E. Coulson, and O. Palagia, eds. *Athenian Potters and Painters: The Conference Proceedings*. Oxford 1997.

**OBERLEITNER 1994**
Oberleitner, W. *Das Heroon von Trysa. Ein lykisches Fürstengrab des 4. Jahrhunderts v. Chr.* Mainz 1994.

**OHLY 1953**
Ohly, D. *Griechische Goldbleche des 8. Jahrhunderts v. Chr.* Berlin 1953.

**OHLY-DUMM AND HAMDORF 1981**
Ohly-Dumm, M., and F. W. Hamdorf. *Attische Vasenbilder der Antikensammlung in München nach Zeichnungen von Karl Reichhold*. Vol. 1, *Bilder auf Krugen und Schalen*. Munich 1981.

**OLMOS AND PICAZO 1979**
Olmos, R., and M. Picazo. "Zum Handel mit griechischen Vasen und Bronzen auf der Iberischen Halbinsel." *MM* 20 (1979): 184—201.

**OLMOS ROMERA 1977**
Olmos Romera, R. "El Sileno Simposiasta de Capilla (Badajoz)." *Trabajos de Prehistoria* 34 (1977): 371—82.

**OLMOS ROMERA 1983**
Olmos Romera, R. "El centauro de Royos e el centauro en el mundo iberico." In *Homenaje al Prof. Martin Almagro Bach*, vol. 2, 377—88. Madrid 1983.

**ORLANDINI 1954**
Orlandini, P. "Le nuove antefisse sileniche di Gela e il loro contributo alla conoscenza coroplastica siceliota." *ArchCl* 6 (1954): 251—56.

**ORLANDINI 1956**
Orlandini, P. "Altre antefisse sileniche di Gela." *ArchCl* 8 (1956): 47.

**ORLANDINI 1978**
Orlandini, F. "Ceramiche della Grecia dell'Est a Gela." In Vallet 1978, 93—98.

**ORSI 1990**
Orsi, Paolo. *La necropoli di Passo Marinaro a Camarina. Campagne di Scavo 1904—1909*. Rome 1990.

**ORTHMANN 1971**
Orthmann, W. *Untersuchungen zur spätethitischen Kunst*. Bonn 1971.

**ORTHMANN 1975**
Orthmann, W. *Der alte Orient.* Propyläen Kunstgeschichte 14. Berlin 1975.

**ØSTERGAARD 1986**
Østergaard, J. S. "Heste fra den boiotiske stald." *MeddelGlypt* 42 (1986): 81–108.

**ØSTERGAARD 1991**
Østergaard, J. S. "Terracotta Horses and Horsemen of Archaic Boeotia." *Acta Hyperborea* 3 (1991): 111–89.

**PADGETT 1995**
Padgett, M. "A Geometric Bard." In Carter and Morris 1995, 389–405.

**PADGETT 1995–96**
Padgett, J. M. "Attic Vase Paintings: Drawings in Clay." *Drawing* 17.4–6 (November 1995–March 1996): 80–84.

**PADGETT 1996**
Padgett, J. M. "The Collections of Ancient Art: The Early Years." *Record* 55 (1996): 107–24.

**PADGETT 2000**
Padgett, J. M. "The Stable Hands of Dionysos: Satyrs and Donkeys as Symbols of Social Marginalization in Attic Vase Painting." In Cohen 2000b, 43–70.

**PADGETT 2002**
Padgett, J. M. "A Unique Vase in the Metropolitan Museum of Art." In *Essays in Honor of Dietrich von Bothmer,* ed. J. Clark and J. Gaunt, 249–6. Amsterdam 2002.

**PALAGIA 1997**
Palagia, O., ed. *Greek Offerings: Essays on Greek Art in Honour of John Boardman.* Oxford 1997.

**PAPACHATZIS 1987**
Papachatzis, N. Η Θρησκεία στην αρχαία Ελλάδα. Athens 1987.

**PAPADOPOULOU-KANELLOPOULOU 1989**
Papadopoulou-Kanellopoulou, C. Συλλογή Κάρολου Πολίτη. Athens 1989.

**PAPASPYRIDI-KARUSU 1937**
Papaspyridi-Karusu, S. "Sophilos." *AM* 62 (1937): 111–35.

**PASQUIER AND DENOYELLE 1990**
Pasquier, A., and M. Denoyelle. *Euphronios, peintre à Athènes au VIe siècle avant J.-C.* Paris 1990.

**PAUL 1958/59**
Paul, E. "Die böotischen Brettidole." *Wissenschaftliche Zeitschrift der Karl-Marx-Universität Leipzig* 8 (1958/59): 165–206.

**PAUL 1997**
Paul, A. J. *Fragments of Antiquity. Drawing upon Greek Vases. Harvard University Art Museums Bulletin* 5.2 (1997).

**PAUL 2001**
Paul, A. J. *A View into Antiquity: Pottery from the Collection of William Suddaby and David Meier.* Exhib. cat. Tampa Museum of Art. Tampa 2001.

**PAYNE 1931**
Payne, H. G. G. *Necrocorinthia: A Study of Corinthian Art in the Archaic Period.* Oxford 1931.

**PAYNE 1933**
Payne, H. G. G. *Protokorinthische Vasenmalerei.* Bilder griechischer Vasen 7. Berlin 1933.

**PAYNE 1940**
Payne, H. G. G. *Perachora: The Sanctuary of Hera Akraia and Limenia.* Vol. 1, Architecture, Bronzes, Terracottas. Oxford 1940.

**PAYNE AND MACKWORTH-YOUNG 1950**
Payne, H. G. G., and G. Mackworth-Young. *Archaic Marble Sculpture from the Acropolis.* 2d ed. London 1950.

**PEDLEY 1994**
Pedley, J. G. "Greek Art." In *Ancient Art at the Art Institute of Chicago,* 32–53. *The Art Institute of Chicago Museum Studies* 20.1. Chicago 1994.

**PEEGE 1997**
Peege, C. *Die Terrakotten aus Böotien. Der Archäologischen Sammlung der Universität Zürich.* Zürich 1997.

**PEIRCE 1993**
Peirce, S. "Death, Revelry, and 'Thysia'." *ClAnt* 12.2 (1993): 219–66.

**PEIRCE 1998**
Peirce, S. "Visual Language and Concepts of Cult on the 'Lenaia Vases'." *ClAnt* 17 (1998): 59–95.

**PELAGATTI AND STIBBE 1999**
Pelagatti, P., and C. M. Stibbe. "Laconian Clay and Bronze Oinochoae with Plastic Decorations." *BABesch* 74 (1999): 21–62.

**PELTENBURG 1991**
Peltenburg, E. *The Burrell Collection: Western Asiatic Antiquities.* Edinburgh 1991.

**PENGLASE 1994**
Penglase, C. *Greek Myths and Mesopotamia.* London and New York 1994.

**PERROT AND CHIPIEZ 1911**
Perrot, G., and C. Chipiez. *Histoire de l'art dans l'antiquité.* Vol. 9. Paris 1911.

**PETROPOULOS 2001**
Petropoulos, J. C. B. "Myth and Art in Early Greece." *NumAntCl* 30 (2001): 11–24.

**PFERDEMANN & LÖWENFRAU 1999**
*Pferdemann & Löwenfrau: Mischwesen der Antike.* Exhib. cat. Martin von Wagner Museum der Universität Würzburg. Würzburg 1999.

**PICARD 1991**
Picard, O., ed. *Guide de Delphes. Le Musée.* École française d'Athènes, Sites et monuments 6. Paris 1991.

**PICOZZI 1971**
Picozzi, M. G. *Anfore attiche a protome equina.* Studi Miscellanei 18. Rome 1971.

**PINZA 1905**
Pinza, G. "Monumenti primitivi di Roma e del Lazio antico." *MonAnt* 15 (1905): 8–798.

**PIPILI 1987**
Pipili, M. *Laconian Iconography of the Sixth Century B.C.* Oxford 1987.

**POHLENZ 1965**
Pohlenz, M. Das Satyrspiele und Pratina von Phleius. Hildesheim 1965.

**POLIAKOFF 1987**
Poliakoff, M. B. *Combat Sports in the Ancient World.* London 1987.

**POLLARD 1977**
Pollard, J. *Birds in Greek Life and Myth.* London 1977.

**POLLITT 1990**
Pollitt, J. J. *The Art of Greece: Sources and Documents.* 2d ed. Cambridge 1990.

**POPE 1938**
Pope, A. U. *A Survey of Persian Art from Prehistoric Times to the Present.* Vol. 4, *Plates.* London 1938.

**POPHAM 1995**
Popham, M. "An Engraved Near Eastern Bronze Bowl from Lefkandi." *OJA* 14 (1995): 103–7.

**POPHAM AND LEMOS 1996**
Popham, M., and I. S. Lemos. *Lefkandi.* Vol. 3, *The Early Iron Age Cemetery at Toumba: The Excavations of 1981 to 1994.* London 1996.

**POPHAM, SACKETT, AND THEMELIS 1980**
Popham, M., L. H. Sackett, and P. G. Themelis. *Lefkandi.* Vol. 1, *The Iron Age Settlement: The Cemeteries.* London 1980.

**PORADA 1947**
Porada, E. *Mesopotamian Art in Cylinder Seals of the Pierpont Morgan Library.* New York 1947.

**PORADA 1948**
Porada, E. *The Collections of the Pierpont Morgan Library.* Corpus of Ancient Near Eastern Seals in North American Collections. Washington, D.C., 1948.

**PORADA 1952**
Porada, E. "On the Problem of Kassite Art." In *Archaeologica Orientalia in Memoriam Ernst Herzfeld,* ed. G. C. Miles, 179–87. Locust Valley (New York) 1952.

**PORADA 1995**
Porada, E. *Man and Images in the Ancient Near East.* Wakefield (Rhode Island) and London 1995.

**POTRATZ 1966**
Potratz, J. A. H. *Die Pferdetrensen des alten Orient.* Rome 1966.

**POUPÉ 1963**
Poupé, J. "Les Aryballes de bucchero imitant des modèles protocorinthiens." In *Études Étrusco-Italiques: Mélanges pour le 25ᵉ anniversaire de la chaire d'Étruscologie à l'Université de Louvain.* Louvain 1963.

**POURSAT 1968**
Poursat, J.-C. "Les Représentations de danse armée dans la céramique attique." *BCH* 92 (1968): 550–615.

**POURSAT 1973**
Poursat, J. C. "Le Sphinx minoen: Un nouveau document." In *Antichità cretesi: Studi in onore di Doro Levi,* ed. R. Giovanni, vol. 1, 111–14. Catania 1973.

**POWELL 1997**
Powell, B. B. "From Picture to Myth, from Myth to Picture. Prolegomena to the Invention of Mythic Representation of Greek Art." In *New Light on a Dark Age: Exploring the Culture of Geometric Greece,* ed. S. Langdon, 154–93. Columbia (Missouri) 1997.

**PRICE 1971**
Price, T. H. "'To Be or Not to Be' on an Attic Black-Figure Pelike." *AJA* 75 (1971): 431–34.

**PRICE AND WAGGONER 1975**
Price, M., and N. Waggoner. *Archaic Greek Coinage: The Asyut Hoard.* London 1975.

**PRIME 1879**
Prime, H. C. *Pottery and Porcelain of All Times and All Nations.* New York 1879.

**PRITCHETT 1993**
Pritchett, W. K. *The Liar School of Herodotos.* Amsterdam 1993.

**PUCCI 1979**
Pucci, P. "The Song of the Sirens." *Arethusa* 12 (1979): 121–32.

**QUIRKE 1992**
Quirke, S. *Ancient Egyptian Religion.* London 1992.

**RASMUSSEN 1979**
Rasmussen, T. *Bucchero Pottery from Southern Etruria.* Cambridge 1979.

**RASMUSSEN 1985**
Rasmussen, T. "Etruscan Shapes in Attic Pottery." *AntK* 28 (1985): 33–39.

**RASMUSSEN AND SPIVEY 1991**
Rasmussen, T., and N. Spivey. *Looking at Greek Vases.* Cambridge 1991.

**RAUBITSCHEK 1998**
Raubitschek, I. K. *Isthmia: Excavations by the University of Chicago under the Auspices of the American School of Classical Studies at Athens.* Vol. 7, *The Metal Objects.* Princeton 1998.

**RAUBITSCHEK AND RAUBITSCHEK 1982**
Raubitschek, I. K., and A. E. Raubitschek. "The Mission of Triptolemos." In *Studies in Athenian Architecture, Sculpture, and Topography Presented to Homer A. Thompson,* 109–17. Hesperia Supplement 20. Princeton 1982.

**RAVEL 1936**
Ravel, O. *Les "Poulains" de Corinthe: Monographie des statères corinthiens.* Vol. 1. Basel 1936.

**RAVEL 1948**
Ravel, O. *Les "Poulains" de Corinthe.* Vol. 2. London 1948.

**READE 1979**
Reade, J. E. "Assyrian Architectural Decoration: Techniques and Subject-Matter." *BaM* 10 (1979): 17–49.

**REEDER 1995**
Reeder, E. D. *Pandora: Women in Classical Greece.* Exhib. cat. Walters Art Gallery. Princeton 1995.

**REICHEL 1942**
Reichel, W. *Griechisches Goldrelief.* Berlin 1942.

**RHYNE 1982**
Rhyne, N. A. *The Aegean Animal Style: A Study of the Lion, Griffin, and Sphinx.* Ann Arbor 1982.

**RICCIONI 1960**
Riccioni, G. "Origine e sviluppo del gorgoneion e del mito della Gorgone-Medusa nell'arte Greca." *RivIstArch* 9 (1960): 127–206.

**RICHARDSON 1974**
Richardson, N. J. *The Homeric Hymn to Demeter.* Oxford 1974.

**RICHTER 1912**
Richter, G. M. A. "A New Early Attic Vase." *JHS* 32 (1912): 371–84.

**RICHTER 1917**
Richter, G. M. A. *The Metropolitan Museum of Art: Handbook of the Classical Collection.* New York 1917.

**RICHTER 1927**
Richter, G. M. A. *The Metropolitan Museum of Art: Handbook of the Classical Collection.* New York 1927.

**RICHTER 1929**
Richter, G. M. A. *Sculpture and Sculptors of the Greeks.* New Haven 1929.

**RICHTER 1930a**
Richter, G. M. A. *The Metropolitan Museum of Art: Handbook of the Classical Collection.* New York 1930.

**RICHTER 1930b**
Richter, G. M. A. *Sculpture and Sculptors of the Greeks.* 2d ed. New Haven 1930.

**RICHTER 1935**
Richter, G. M. A. *Shapes and Names of Athenian Vases.* New York 1935.

**RICHTER 1937**
Richter, G. M. A. "An Introduction to Greek, Etruscan, and Roman Bronzes." In *Master Bronzes Selected from Museums and Collections in America.* Buffalo (New York) 1937.

**RICHTER 1949**
Richter, G. M. A. *Archaic Greek Art against Its Historical Background: A Survey.* New York 1949.

**RICHTER 1953**
Richter, G. M. A. *Handbook of the Greek Collection of the Metropolitan Museum of Art, New York.* Cambridge (Mass.) 1953.

**RICHTER 1960**
Richter, G. M. A. *Kouroi: Archaic Greek Youths.* London 1960.

**RICHTER 1961**
Richter, G. *The Archaic Gravestones of Attica.* London 1961.

**RICHTER 1968**
Richter, G. M. A. *Engraved Gems of the Greeks, Etruscans, and Romans,* part 1, *Engraved Gems of the Greeks and the Etruscans.* London 1968.

**DE RIDDER 1896**
de Ridder, A. *Catalogue des bronzes trouvés sur l'Acropole d'Athènes.* Paris 1896.

**RIDGWAY 1993**
Ridgway, B. S. *The Archaic Style in Greek Sculpture.* 2d ed. Chicago 1993.

**RIDGWAY AND PINNEY 1979**
Ridgway, B. S., and G. F. Pinney. *Aspects of Ancient Greece.* Exhib. cat. Allentown Art Museum. Allentown (Penn.) 1979.

**RIIS 1959**
Riis, P. J. "The Danish Bronze Vessels of Greek, Early Campanian, and Etruscan Manufactures." *ActaArch* 30 (1959): 1–50.

**RITTIG 1977**
Rittig, D. *Assyrisch-babylonische Kleinplastik magischer Bedeutung vom 13.–6. Jh. v. Chr.* Münchener vorderasiatische Studien. Munich 1977.

**RIX 1991**
Rix, H. *Etruskische Texte.* 2 vols. Tübingen 1991.

**RIZZA 1960**
Rizza, G. "Stipe votiva di un santuario di Demetra a Catania." *BdA* 4 (1960): 247–62.

**RIZZA 1996**
Rizza, G. "Una kylix laconica del Pittore della Caccia a Catania." In *I Vasi attici ed altre ceramiche coeve in Sicilia. Atti del convegno internazionale, Catania, Camarina, Gela, Vittoria, 28 marzo–1 aprile 1990,* vol. 1, 135–43. *Cronache di archeologia* 29. Catania 1996.

**RIZZA AND SCRINARI 1968**
Rizza, G., and V. S. M. Scrinari. *Il santuario sull'acropoli di Gortina.* Rome 1968.

**RIZZO 1987**
Rizzo, M. A. "La ceramica a figure nere." In Martelli 1987, 31–42.

**RIZZO 1992–93**
Rizzo, M. A. "Gorgoneion bronzeo di importazione greca da Cerveteri." *ASAtene* 1992–93, 233–57.

**ROBERTSON 1954**
Robertson, C. M. "Attic or East Greek?" *ArchEph* 1953–54, 145–48.

**ROBERTSON 1969**
Robertson, C. M. "Geryoneis: Stesichoros and Vase-Painters." *CQ* 19 (1969): 207–21.

**ROBERTSON 1992**
Robertson, M. *The Art of Vase-Painting in Classical Athens.* Cambridge 1992.

**ROBERTSON 1995**
Robertson, M. "Menelaos and Helen in Troy." In Carter and Morris 1995, 431–36.

**ROBINSON 1942**
Robinson, D. M. "New Greek Bronze Vases: A Commentary on Pindar." *AJA* 46 (1942): 172–97.

**ROCCO 1995**
Rocco, G. "Una laminatta di argento nei Musei Vaticani." *Xenia Antiqua* 4 (1995): 5–8.

**ROCHBERG 1998**
Rochberg, F. *Babylonian Horoscopes.* TAPS 88.1. Philadelphia 1998.

**RODENWALDT 1938**
Rodenwaldt, G. *Altdorische Bildwerke in Korfu.* Berlin 1938.

**RODENWALDT 1939**
Rodenwaldt, G. *Die Bildwerke des Artemistempels von Korkyra.* Berlin 1939.

**ROES 1934**
Roes, A. "The Representation of the Chimaera." *JHS* 54 (1934): 21–25.

**RÖSLER 1995**
Rösler, W. "Wine and Truth in the Greek Symposium." In Murray and Tecusan 1995, 106–12.

**ROLLEY 1961**
Rolley, C. "Une Amphore inédite du peintre de la Gorgone." *BCH* 85 (1961): 539–43.

**ROLLEY 1969**
Rolley, C. *Fouilles de Delphes.* Vol. 5, *Monuments figurés,* part 2, *Les statuettes de bronze.* Paris 1969.

**ROLLEY 1982**
Rolley, C. *Les Vases de bronze de l'archaïsme récent en Grande Grèce.* Naples 1982.

**ROLLEY 1983**
Rolley, C. *Les Bronzes grecs.* Fribourg 1983.

**ROLLEY 1986**
Rolley, C. *Greek Bronzes.* Trans. R. Howell. London 1986.

**ROLLEY 1991**
Rolley, C. "Les Bronzes grecs et romains: Recherches récentes." *RA* 2 (1991): 281–96.

**ROLLEY 1994**
Rolley, C. *La Sculpture grecque.* Vol. 1, *Des Origines au milieu du Ve siècle.* Paris 1994.

**ROMBOS 1988**
Rombos, T. *The Iconography of the Attic Late Geometric II Pottery.* SIMA-PB 68. Jonsered 1988.

**ROSE 1959**
Rose, H. J. *A Handbook of Greek Mythology.* New York 1959.

**ROSSITER 1927**
Rossiter, H. "Greek Sculptures in Terracotta." *BClevMus* 1 (1927): 21–22.

**ROUILLARD 1991**
Ruillard, P., ed. *Les Grecs et la péninsule ibérique du VIIIe au IVe siècle avant Jésus-Christ.* Paris 1991.

**ROUILLARD 1996**
Rouillard, P. "Gli Iberi." *Archeo* 11(1996): 46–63.

**ROUSSOS 1986**
Roussos, E. "Τρίτωνας." In Ελληνική Μυθολογία, vol. 2, Οι Θεοί, ed. I. T. Kakridis, 246–48. Athens 1986.

**ROWLAND 1973**
Rowland, B. *Animals with Human Faces: A Guide to Animal Symbolism.* Knoxville (Tenn.) 1973.

**RUCKERT 1976**
Ruckert, A. *Frühe Keramik böotiens: Form und Dekoration der Vasen späten 8. und frühen 7. Jahrhunderts v. Chr. AntK Beiheft 10.* Bern 1976.

**RUDOLPH AND CALINESCU 1988**
Rudolph, W., and A. Calinescu. *Ancient Art in the V. G. Simkhovitch Collection.* Bloomington 1988.

**RUSSMANN 1989**
Russmann, E. R. *Egyptian Sculpture: Cairo and Luxor.* Austin (Texas) 1989.

**SAGGS 1959–60**
Saggs, H. W. F. "Pazuzu." *AfO* 19 (1959–60): 123–27.

**SAINT LOUIS ART MUSEUM 1975**
*The Saint Louis Art Museum: Handbook of the Collections.* St. Louis 1975.

**SAMBON 1906a**
Sambon, A. "Le Centaure." *Le Musée* 3 (1906): 4–13.

**SAMBON 1906b**
Sambon, A. "Bronzes et Terres Cuites." *Le Musée* 3 (1906): 428–32.

**SÁNCHEZ 2000**
Sánchez, C. *Los Griegos en España: Tras las Huellas de Heracles.* Exhib. cat. Museo Arqueológico Nacional. Madrid 2000.

**SAPOUNA-SAKELLARAKI 1995**
Sapouna-Sakellaraki, E. *Eretria: Site and Museum.* Athens 1995.

**SAPOUNA-SAKELLARAKI 1997**
Sapouna-Sakellaraki, E. "A Geometric Electrum Band from a Tomb on Skyros." In Palagia 1997, 35–42.

**SCHÄFER 1957**
Schäfer, J. *Studien zu den griechischen Reliefpithoi des 8.–6. Jahrhunderts v. Chr. aus Kreta, Rhodos, Tenos, und Boiotien.* Kallmünz uber Regensburg 1957.

**SCHAUENBURG 1960**
Schauenburg, K. *Perseus in der Kunst des Altertums.* Bonn 1960.

**SCHAUENBURG 1962a**
Schauenburg, K. "Eine neue Sianaschale." *AA* 1962, 746–76.

**SCHAUENBURG 1962b**
Schauenburg, K. "Zwei neue tyrrhenische Amphoren." *AA* 1962, 58–70.

**SCHAUENBURG 1970**
Schauenburg, K. "Zu griechischen Mythen in der etruskischen Kunst." *JdI* 85 (1970): 28–81.

**SCHAUENBURG 1971**
Schauenburg, K. "Herakles bei Pholos zu zwei frührotfigurigen Schale." *AM* 86 (1971): 51–78.

**SCHAUENBURG 1973**
Schauenburg, K. "Parisurteil und Nessosabenteuer auf attischen Vasen hocharchaischer Zeit." *Aachener Kunstblätter* 44 (1973): 15–42.

**SCHAUENBURG 1975**
Schauenburg, K. "ΕΥΡΥΜΕΔΩΝ ΕΙΜΙ." *AM* 90 (1975): 97–121.

**SCHAUENBURG 1976–77**
Schauenburg, K. "Unteritalische Kentaurenbilder." *ÖJh* 51 (1976–77): 17–44.

**SCHAUENBURG 1982**
Schauenburg, K. "Zur Thebanischen Sphinx." In *Praestant Interna. Festschrift für Ulrich Hausmann,* ed. B. von Freytag gen. Löringhoff et al., 230–35. Tübingen 1982.

**SCHAUS 1986**
Schaus, G. P. "Two Fikellura Vase-Painters." *BSA* 81 (1986): 251–95.

**SCHEFFER 1977**
Scheffer, C. "An Etruscan Black-Figured Amphora of the Ivy-Leaf Group." *MedMusB* 12 (1977): 53–61.

**SCHEFFER 1979**
Scheffer, C. "Sirens and Sphinxes from the Micali Painter's Workshop." *MedMusB* 14 (1979): 35–49.

**SCHEFFER 1994**
Scheffer, C. "Female Deities, Horses, and Death(?) in Archaic Greek Religion." In *Opus Mixtum: Essays in Ancient Art and Society,* ed. B. Alroth, 111–33. Stockholm 1994.

**SCHEFOLD 1960**
Schefold, K. *Meisterwerke griechische Kunst.* Basel 1960.

**SCHEFOLD 1964**
Schefold, K. *Frühgriechische Sagenbilder.* Munich 1964.

**SCHEFOLD 1966**
Schefold, K. *Myth and Legend in Early Greek Art.* Trans. A. Hicks. New York 1966.

**SCHEFOLD 1978**
Schefold, K. *Götter und Heldensagen der Griechen in der Spätarchaischen Kunst.* Munich 1978.

**SCHEFOLD 1988**
Schefold, K. *Die Urkönige, Perseus, Bellerophon, Herakles, und Theseus in der klassischen und hellenistischen Kunst.* Munich 1988.

**SCHEFOLD 1992**
Schefold, K. *Gods and Heroes in Late Archaic Greek Art.* Cambridge 1992.

**SCHEIBLER 1960**
Scheibler, I. *Die symmetrische Bildform in der frühgriechischen Flächenkunst.* Kallmünz and Regensburg 1960.

**SCHEIBLER 1961**
Scheibler, I. "Olpen und Amphoren des Gorgomalers." *JdI* 76 (1961): 1–47.

**SCHIERING 1957**
Schiering, W. *Werkstätten orientalisierender Keramik auf Rhodes.* Berlin 1957.

**SCHIFFLER 1976**
Schiffler, B. *Die Typologie des Kentauren in der antiken Kunst vom 10. bis zum Ende des 4. Jhs. v. Chr.* Frankfurt am Main 1976.

**SCHILARDI 1973**
Schilardi, D. U. "An Athenian Cemetery." *Archaeology* (1973): 54–57.

**SCHMALTZ 1974**
Schmaltz, B. *Das Kabirenheiligtum bei Theben.* Vol. 6, *Terrakotten aus dem Kabirenheiligtum bei Theben: Menschenähnliche Figuren, menschliche Figuren und Gerät.* Berlin 1974.

**SCHMALTZ 1977/78**
Schmaltz, B. "Zur Chronologie der böotischen Vogelschalen." *MarbWPr* (1977/78): 21–60.

**SCHMIDT 1994**
Schmidt, E., ed. *Martin von Wagner Museum der Universität Würzburg. Katalog der antiken Terrakotten.* Vol. 1, *Die figürlichen Terrakotten.* Mainz 1994.

**SCHMIDT-DOUNAS 1985**
Schmidt-Dounas, B. "Bemerkungen zu Kaineus." *IstMitt* 35 (1985): 5–12.

**SCHNAPP 1979**
Schnapp, A. "Images et programme: Les Figurations archaïques de la chasse au sanglier." *RA* 1979, 195–218.

**SCHNAPP 1988**
Schnapp, A. "Why did the Greeks Need Images?" In Christiansen and Melander 1988, 568–74.

**SCHNAPP 1997**
Schnapp, A. *Le Chasseur et la cite: Chasse et érotique dans la Grèce ancienne.* Paris 1997.

**SCHUMACHER 1890**
Schumacher, K. *Beschreibung der Sammlung antiker Bronzen. Grossherzogliche Vereinigte Sammlungen zu Karlsruhe.* Karlsruhe 1890.

**SCHWEITZER 1969**
Schweitzer, B. *Die geometrische Kunst Griechenlands.* Cologne 1969.

**SCHWEITZER 1971**
Schweitzer, B. *Greek Geometric Art.* London 1971.

**SEAFORD 1976**
Seaford, R. "On the Origins of Satyric Drama." *Maia* 28 (1976): 209–21.

**SEEBERG 1971**
Seeberg, A. *Corinthian Komos Vases.* London 1971.

**SEGAL 1992**
Segal, C. "Bard and Audience in Homer." In *Homer's Ancient Readers: The Hermeneutics of Greek Epic's Earliest Exegetes,* ed. R. Lamberton and J. J. Keaney, 3–29. Princeton 1992.

**SEGAL 2001**
Segal, C. *Oedipus Tyrannus: Tragic Heroism and the Limits of Knowledge.* New York 2001.

**SEIDL 1968**
Seidl, U. "Die babylonischen Kudurru-Reliefs." *BaM* 4 (1968): 7–220.

**SEIDL 1989**
Seidl, U. *Die babylonischen Kudurru-Reliefs: Symbole mesopotamischer Gottheiten.* Orbis Biblicus et Orientalis 87. Freiburg (Switzerland) and Göttingen 1989.

**SEIPPEL 1939**
Seippel, G. *Der Typhonmythos.* Greifswald 1939.

**SERWINT 1991**
Serwint, N. "The Terracotta Sculpture from Marion." In *Cypriote Terracottas. Proceedings of the First International Conference of Cypriote Studies, Brussels-Liège-Amsterdam, 29 May–1 June 1989,* ed. F. Vandenabeele, F. Laffineur, and R. Laffineur, 213–19. Brussels and Liège 1991.

**SETTIS 1985**
Settis, S., ed. *The Land of the Etruscans from Prehistory to the Middle Ages.* Florence 1985.

**SHAPIRO 1981**
Shapiro, H. A. *Art, Myth and Culture: Greek Vases from Southern Collections.* New Orleans 1981.

**SHAPIRO 1989**
Shapiro, H. A. *Art and Cult under the Tyrants in Athens.* Mainz 1989.

**SHAPIRO 1991**
Shapiro, H. A. "The Iconography of Mourning in Athenian Art." *AJA* 95 (1991): 629–56.

**SHAPIRO 1993**
Shapiro, H. A. *Personifications in Greek Art: The Representation of Abstract Concepts, 600–400 B.C.* Kilchberg 1993.

**SHAPIRO 1994a**
Shapiro, H. A. "Poet and Painter: *Iliad* 24 and the Greek Art of Narrative." *NumAntCl* 23 (1994): 23–48.

**SHAPIRO 1994b**
Shapiro, H. A. *Myth into Art.* London 1994.

**SHAPIRO, PICÓN, AND SCOTT 1995**
Shapiro, H. A., C. A. Picón, and G. D. Scott III, eds. *Greek Vases in the San Antonio Museum of Art.* San Antonio 1995.

**SHEAR 1931**
Shear, T. L. "The Excavation of Roman Chamber Tombs at Corinth in 1931." *AJA* 35 (1931): 424–41.

**SHEAR 2002**
Shear, I. M., "Mycenaean Centaurs at Ugarit." *JHS* 122 (2002): 147–53.

**SHEFTON 1962**
Shefton, B. "Herakles and Theseus on a Red-Figured Louterion." *Hesperia* 31 (1962): 330–68.

**SHEFTON 1982**
Shefton, B. B. "Greeks and Greek Imports in the South of the Iberian Peninsula." In *Die Phönizier im Westen,* ed. H. G. Niemeyer, 337–68. *Madrider Beiträge* 8. Mainz 1982

**SHEFTON 1989**
Shefton, B. B. "The Paradise Flower, a 'Court Style' Phoenician Ornament: Its History in Cyprus and the Central and Western Mediterranean." In *Cyprus and the East Mediterranean in the Iron Age,* ed. V. Tatton-Brown, 97–117. London 1989.

**SHEPARD 1940**
Shepard, K. *The Fish-Tailed Monster in Greek and Roman Art.* New York 1940.

**SIEGAL 1981**
Siegal, L. J. "Eastern Echoes in the Art of Ancient Greece." *Arts in Virginia* 21.2 (1981): 16–23.

**SIEVEKING 1916**
Sieveking, J. *Die Terrakotten der Sammlung Loeb.* Munich 1916.

**SIMON 1963**
Simon, E. "Ein Anthesteria-Skyphos des Polygnotos." *AntK* 6 (1963): 6–22.

**SIMON 1964**
Simon, E. "Die Wiedergewinnung der Helena." *AntK* 7 (1964): 91–95.

**SIMON 1967**

Simon, E. "Boreas und Oreithyia auf dem silbernen Rhyton in Triest." *AuA* 13 (1967): 101–26.

**SIMON 1980**

Simon, E. *Die Götter der Greichen.* 2d ed. Munich 1980.

**SIMON 1982a**

Simon, E. *The Kurashiki Ninagawa Museum: Greek, Etruscan, and Roman Antiquities.* Mainz 1982.

**SIMON 1982b**

Simon, E. "Satyr-Plays on Vases in the Time of Aeschylus." In *The Eye of Greece. Studies in the Art of Athens,* ed. D. Kurtz and B. Sparkes, 123–48. Cambridge and New York 1982.

**SIMON 1985**

Simon, E. *Die Götter der Greichen.* Darmstadt 1985.

**SIMON AND HIRMER 1976**

Simon, E., and M. Hirmer. *Die griechischen Vasen.* Munich 1976.

**SIMPSON 1972**

Simpson, W. K., ed. *The Literature of Ancient Egypt.* New Haven 1972.

**SLANSKI 2000**

Slanski, K. E. "Classification, Historiography and Monumental Authority: The Babylonian Entitlement Narûs (Kudurrus)." *JCS* 52 (2000): 95–114.

**SMITH 1892–93**

Smith, C. "Harpies in Greek Art." *JHS* 13 (1892–93): 103–14.

**SMITH 1945**

Smith, H. R. W. "From Farthest West." *AJA* 49 (1945): 473.

**SMITH 1965**

Smith, W. S. *Interconnections in the Ancient Near East.* New Haven 1965.

**SNODGRASS 1964**

Snodgrass, A. *Early Greek Armour and Weapons from the End of the Bronze Age to 600 B.C.* Edinburgh 1964.

**SNODGRASS 1993**

Snodgrass, A. "Hoplite Reform Revisted." *Dialogues d'histoire ancienne* 19.1 (1993): 47–61.

**SNODGRASS 1998**

Snodgrass, A. *Homer and the Artists: Text and Picture in Early Greek Art.* Cambridge 1998.

**SNOWDEN 1970**

Snowden, F. M. *Blacks in Antiquity: Ethiopians in the Greco-Roman Experience.* Cambridge 1970.

**SOMMER 1994**

Sommer, K. "Bemerkungen zur Herstellung, Restaurierung, und Rekonstruktion der 'Rosenbaum-Hydria'." *BABesch* 69 (1994): 103–13.

**SOURVINOU-INWOOD 1985**

Sourvinou-Inwood, C. "Altars with Palm-trees, Palm-trees, and Parthenoi." *BICS* 32. London 1985.

**SPARKES 2000**

Sparkes, B. "Sikanos and the Stemmed Plate." In Tsetskhladze, Prag, and Snodgrass 2000, 320–29.

**SPARKES AND TALCOTT 1970**

Sparkes, B., and L. Talcott. *The Athenian Agora.* Vol. 12.1, *Black and Plain Pottery of the Sixth, Fifth, and Fourth Centuries B.C.* Princeton 1970.

**SPIVEY 1991**

Spivey, N. "Greek Vases in Etruria." In *Looking at Greek Vases,* ed. T. Rasmussen and N. Spivey, 131–50. Cambridge 1991.

**SPLITTER 2000**

Splitter, R. *Die "Kypseloslade" in Olympia. Form, Funktion, und Bildschmuck: Eine Archäologische Rekonstruktion mit einem Katalog der Sagenbilder in der korinthischen Vasenmalerei und einem Anhang zur Forschungsgeschichte.* Mainz 2000.

**SPYCKET 1981**

Spycket, A. *La Statuaire du Proche-Orient ancien.* Leiden 1981.

**STANSBURY-O'DONNELL 1999**

Stansbury-O'Donnell, M. D. *Pictorial Narrative in Ancient Greek Art.* Cambridge Studies in Classical Archaeology. Cambridge 1999.

**STAVROPOULOS 1964**

Stavropoulos, P. "Άνασκαφαὶ καί τυχαῖα εὑρήματα ἐντός τῆς περιμετρικῆς ζώνης τῆς πόλεως τῶν Ἀθηνῶν." *ArchDelt* 19 (1964): Chronika, 46–64.

**STEARNS 1961**

Stearns, J. B. *Reliefs from the Palace of Ashurnasirpal II. AfO* Beiheft 15. Graz 1961.

**STEWART 1983**

Stewart, A. "Stesichoros and the François Vase." In Moon 1983, 53–74.

**STEWART 1990**

Stewart, A. *Greek Sculpture.* New Haven 1990.

**STIBBE 1972**

Stibbe, C. M. *Lakonische Vasenmaler der sechsten Jahrhunderts v. Chr.* Amsterdam and London 1972.

**STIBBE 1992**

Stibbe, C. M. "Archaic Bronze Hydriae." *BABesch* 67 (1992): 1–62.

**STIBBE 1994a**

Stibbe, C. M. "Eine archaische Bronzekanne in Basel." *AntK* 37 (1994): 108–20.

**STIBBE 1994b**

Stibbe, C. M. "Between Babyka and Knakion: Three Addenda." *BABesch* 69 (1994): 63–102.

**STIBBE 1996**

Stibbe, C. M. "Frauen und Löwen." *JbMusMainz* 43 (1996): 355–81.

**STIBBE 1997**

Stibbe, C. M. "Lakonische Keramik aus dem Heraion von Samos." *AM* 112 (1997): 25–142.

**STIBBE 2000a**

Stibbe, C. M. *Laconian Oil Flasks and Other Closed Shapes. Laconian Black-glazed Pottery, Part 3.* Allard Pierson Series Scripta Minora 5. Amsterdam 2000.

**STIBBE 2000b**

Stibbe, C. M. *The Sons of Hephaistos: Aspects of the Archaic Greek Bronze Industry.* Rome 2000.

**STIBBE 2001**

Stibbe, C. M. "La Sfinge, la gorgone, e la sirena. Tre bronzetti da Capo Colonna e i centri di produzione in età arcaica tra Sparta, Corinto, e Magna Grecia." *BdA* 116 (2001): 1–38.

**STIBBE 2003**

Stibbe, C. M. Trebenishte: The Fortunes of an Unusual Excavation. Rome 2003.

**STOESSL 1975**

Stoessl, F. "Silenos–Satyros." *Der Kleine Pauly* 5 (1975): 191–93.

**STRØM 1971**
Strøm, I. *Problems Concerning the Origin and Early Development of the Etruscan Orientalizing Style.* Odense 1971.

**STROMMENGER 1962**
Strommenger, E. *Fünf Jahrtausende Mesopotamien.* Munich 1962.

**STUART JONES 1896**
Stuart Jones, H. "A Greek Goldsmith's Mould in the Ashmolean Museum." *JHS* 16 (1896): 323–34.

**STUBBINGS 1962**
Stubbings, J. M. "Part II: Ivories." In Dunbabin 1962, 403–51. Oxford 1962.

**STUCCHI 1981**
Stucchi, S. "Delle figure del grande frontone di Corfu." *Divagazioni archeologiche* 1 (1981): 7–86.

**STURGEON 1987**
Sturgeon, M. C. *Isthmia: Excavations by the University of Chicago under the Auspices of the American School of Classical Studies at Athens.* Vol. 4, *Sculpture.* Princeton 1987.

**SZABÓ 1973**
Szabó, M. "Contribution à la question de la coroplathie béotienne du VIIe siècle av. N.E." *Bulletin du Musée Hongrois des Beaux Arts* 41 (1973): 3–19.

**SZABÓ 1988**
Szabó, M. "Remarques sur le décor plastique de l'oenochoé Grimani." In Gschwantler and Bernhard-Walcher 1988, 229–32.

**SZABÓ 1994**
Szabó, M. *Archaic Terracottas of Boeotia.* Rome 1994.

**SZILÁGYI 1958**
Szilágyi, J. G. "Italo-Corinthiaca." *StEtr* 26 (1958): 273–87.

**TAGALADOU 1993**
Tagaladou, E. *Weihreliefs an Herakles aus klassischer Zeit.* SIMA-PB 99. Jonsered 1993.

**TERRACE 1957**
Terrace, E. L. B. *Greek Vases at Dartmouth College.* Hanover 1957.

**TERRACE ET AL. 1966**
Terrace, E. L. B., et al. *The Pomerance Collection of Ancient Art: Catalogue of an Exhibition Held at the Brooklyn Museum, June 14 to October 2, 1966.* New York 1966.

**THEODOSSIEV 2000**
Theodossiev, N. "The Dead with Golden Faces: Other Evidence and Connections." *OJA* 19 (2000): 175–208.

**THIERSCH 1899**
Thiersch, H. *Tyrrhenische Amphoren.* Leipzig 1899.

**THIMME 1960**
Thimme, J. "Neuerwerbungen des Badischen Landesmuseums Karlsruhe." *AA* 1960, 36–69.

**THOMAS 1992**
Thomas, R. *Griechische Bronzestatuetten.* Darmstadt 1992.

**THOMPSON 1903–4**
Thompson, R. C. *The Devils and Spirits of Babylonia.* Luzac's Semitic Text and Translations Series. London 1903–4.

**THOUVENOT 1927**
Thouvenot, R. *Catalogue des figurines et objets de bronze du Musée Archéologique de Madrid.* Vol. 1. Madrid 1927.

**THOUVERIN 1990**
Thouverin, A. "Le Cratère de Vix: Technique de fabrication de la cuve." *Revue Archéologique de l'Est et du Centre-Est* 41 (1990): 301–4.

**THUREAU-DANGIN 1921**
Thureau-Dangin, F. "Rituel et amulettes contre Labartu." *RAssyr* 18 (1921): 161–98.

**THUREAU-DANGIN AND DUNAND 1931**
Thureau-Dangin, F., and M. Dunand. *Til-Barsib. Haut-commissariat de la République française en Syrie et au Liban. Service des antiquités.* Bibliothèque archéologique et historique. Paris 1931.

**TIVERIOS 1991**
Tiverios, M. "Ikonographie und Geschichte. Überlegungen anlässlich einer Abbildung des Strymon im Garten der Hesperiden." *AM* 106 (1991): 129–45.

**TÖLLE 1963**
Tölle, R. "Figurlich bemalte Fragmente der geometrischen Zeit vom Kerameikos." *AA* 1963, 642–64.

**TORELLI 1977**
Torelli, M. "Terrecotte architettoniche arcaiche da Gravisca e una nota a Plinio, NH XXXV, 151–52." In *Studi in onore di Filippo Magi,* ed. M. Bergamini and F. Magi, 305–12. Perugia 1977.

**TORELLI 2001**
Torelli, M., ed. *The Etruscans.* New York 2001.

**TOUCHEFEU-MEYNIER 1968**
Touchefeu-Meynier, O. *Thèmes Odysséens dans l'art antique.* Paris 1968.

**TOUCHEFEU-MEYNIER 1990**
Touchefeu-Meynier, O. "L'Humiliation d'Hector." *Metis* 5.1–2 (1990): 157–65.

**TOULOUPA 1969**
Touloupa, E. "Une Gorgone en bronze de l'Acropole." *BCH* 93 (1969): 862–84.

**TOULOUPA 1991**
Touloupa, E. "Early Bronze Sheets with Figured Scenes from the Acropolis." In *New Perspectives in Early Greek Art,* ed. D. Buitron-Oliver, 242–54. Hanover 1991.

**TREISTER 1995**
Treister, M. "A Bronze Matrix from Corfu in the Ashmolean Museum." *AM* 110 (1995): 83–102.

**TRENDALL AND CAMBITOGLOU 1978**
Trendall, A. D., and A. Cambitoglou. *The Red-Figured Vases of Apulia.* Vol. 1, *Early and Middle Apulian.* Oxford 1978.

**TRUE AND FREL 1983**
True, M., and J. Frel. *Greek Vases: Molly and Walter Bareiss Collection.* Malibu 1983.

**TRUE AND HAMMA 1994**
True, M., and K. Hamma. *A Passion for Antiquities: Ancient Art from the Collection of Barbara and Lawrence Fleischman.* Malibu 1994.

**TSETSKHLADZE, PRAG, AND SNODGRASS 2000**
Tsetskhladze, G. R., A. J. N. W. Prag, and A. M. Snodgrass, eds. *Periplous: Papers on Classical Art and Archaeology Presented to Sir John Boardman.* London 2000.

**TSIAFAKIS 1998**
Tsiafakis, D. Η Θράκη στην Αττική εικονογραφία του 5ου αιώνα π. Χρ. Komotini 1998.

**TSIAFAKIS 2000**

Tsiafakis, D. "The Allure and Repulsion of Thracians in the Art of Classical Athens." In Cohen 2000b, 364–89.

**TSIAFAKIS 2001**

Tsiafakis, D. "Life and Death at the Hands of a Siren." *Studia Varia from the J. Paul Getty Museum* 2 (Malibu 2001): 7–24.

**TUNA-NÖRLING 1997**

Tuna-Nörling, Y. "Attic Black-Figure Export to the East: The 'Tyrrhenian Group' in the East." In Oakley, Coulson, and Palagia 1997, 435–46.

**TZACHOU-ALEXANDRI 1989**

Tzachou-Alexandri, O., ed. *Mind and Body: Athletic Contests in Ancient Greece.* Exhib. cat. Athens National Museum. Athens 1989.

**UHLENBROCK ET AL. 1986**

Uhlenbrock, J. P., et al. *Herakles: Passage of the Hero through 1000 Years of Classical Art.* Exhib. cat. Bard College. Annandale-on-Hudson 1986.

**ULISSE 1996**

Andreae, B., and C. Parisi Presicce, eds. *Ulisse: Il mito e la memoria.* Exhib. cat. Palazzo delle Esposizioni. Rome 1996.

**URE 1927**

Ure, P. N. *Sixth- and Fifth-Century Pottery from Rhitsona.* London 1927.

**URE 1934**

Ure, P. N. *Aryballoi and Figurines from Rhitsona in Boeotia.* Cambridge 1934.

**VAERST 1980**

Vaerst, A. *Griechische Schildzeichen vom 8. bis zum ausgehenden 6. Jh.* Ph.D. diss., University of Salzburg 1980.

**VAFOPOULOU-RICHARDSON 1981**

Vafopoulou-Richardson, C. E. *Greek Terracottas.* Oxford 1981.

**VALLET 1978**

Vallet, G. *Les Céramiques de la Grèce de l'Est et leur diffusion en Occident. Actes du colloque, 6–9 juillet 1976.* Paris 1978.

**VAN BUREN 1921**

Van Buren, E. *Figurative Revetments in Etruria and Latium.* London 1921.

**VAN BUREN 1926**

Van Buren, E. *Archaic Fictile Revetments in the Archaic Period.* London 1926.

**VAN BUREN 1930**

Van Buren, E. D. *Clay Figurines of Babylonia and Assyria.* Yale Oriental Series, Researches 16. New Haven 1930.

**VAN BUREN 1946**

Van Buren, E. D. "The Dragon in Ancient Mesopotamia." *Orientalia* 15 (1946): 1–45.

**VAN BUREN 1973**

Van Buren, E. *Archaic Fictile Revetments in Sicily and Magna Graecia.* Washington, D.C. 1973. Reprint of 1923 ed.

**VAN DER MEIJDEN 1993**

Van der Meijden, H. *Terrakotta-arulae aus Sizilien und Unteritalien.* Amsterdam 1993.

**VANDERPOOL 1959**

Vanderpool, E. "News Letter from Greece." *AJA* 63 (1959): 279–83.

**VAN GELDER 1994**

Van Gelder, K. "A Protoattic Krater in a Swiss Private Collection." In *Studies in South Attica II. Miscellanea Graeca,* ed. H. Mussche, fasc. 9, 97–113. Ghent 1994.

**VAN KEUREN 1989**

Van Keuren, F. D. *The Frieze from the Hera I Temple at Foce del Sele.* Rome 1989.

**VAN LOON 1966**

Van Loon, M. N. *Urartian Art: Its Distinctive Traits in the Light of New Excavations.* Istanbul 1966.

**VEDDER 1985**

Vedder, U. *Untersuchungen zur plastischen Ausstatung attischer Grabanlagen des 4. Jhs. v. Chr.* Frankfurt am Main, Bern, and New York 1985.

**VEDER GRECO 1988**

*Veder Greco: Le necropoli di Agrigento.* Exhib. cat. Agrigento Museum. Rome 1988.

**VERBANCK-PIÉRARD 1982**

Verbanck-Piérard, A. "La Rencontre d'Héraklès et de Pholos: Varientes iconographiques du peintre d'Antiménès." In *Rayonnement grec: Hommages à Charles Delvoye,* 143–54. Brussels 1982.

**VERDÉLIS 1951**

Verdélis, N. M. "L'Apparition du Sphinx dans l'art grec aux VIIIe et VIIe siècles avant J.-C." *BCH* 75 (1951): 1–37.

**VERMEULE 1968**

Vermeule, C. C. "Archaic Terracotta Rider." *Antike Plastik* 8.1 (1968): 7–11.

**VERMEULE 1979**

Vermeule, E. *Aspects of Death in Early Greek Art and Poetry.* Berkeley 1979.

**VERMEULE AND KARAGEORGHIS 1982**

Vermeule, E., and V. Karageorghis. *Mycenaean Pictorial Vase Painting.* Cambridge (Mass.) 1982.

**VERNANT 1985**

Vernant, J.-P. *La Mort dans les yeux: Figures de l'autre en Grèce ancienne.* Paris 1985.

**VERNANT 1992**

Vernant, J.-P. Το Βλέμμα του θανάτου. Μορφής ετερότητας στην αρχαία Ελλάδα. Trans. from French by J. Pappas. Athens 1992.

**VICKERS 1975**

Vickers, M. "Recent Museum Acquisitions: Greek Antiquities in Oxford." *Burlington Magazine* 97 (June 1975): 381–86.

**VIERNEISEL AND KAESER 1991**

Vierneisel, K., and B. Kaeser, eds. *Kunst der Schale—Kultur des Trinkens.* Exhib. cat. Staatliche Anikensammlungen München. Munich 1991.

**VILLANUEVA PUIG ET AL. 1999**

Villanueva Puig, M.-C., et al., eds. *Céramique et peinture grecques: Modes d'emploi. Actes du colloque international, École du Louvre, 26–28 avril 1995.* Paris 1999.

**VOGEL 1978**

Vogel, M. *Chiron der Kentaur mit der Kithara.* Bonn 1978.

**VOKOTOPOULOU 1975**

Kouleimani-Vokotopoulou, I. Χαλκαί Κορινθιουργεῖς πρόχοι: συμβολή εἰς τὴν μελέτην τῆς ἀρχαίας ἑλληνικῆς χαλκουργίας. Athens 1975.

**VOKOTOPOULOU 1987**

Kouleimani-Vokotopoulou, I. "Η υδρία της Αίνειας." In ΑΜΗΤΟΣ. Τιμητικός τόμος για τον καθηγητή Μανόλη Ανδρόνικο, 157–78 and pls. 21–27. Thessaloniki 1987.

**VOKOTOPOULOU 1997**

Kouleimani-Vokotopoulou, I. Ελληνική τέχνη: αργυρά και χάλκινα έργα τέχνης στην αρχαιότητα. Athens 1997.

**VOLLKOMMER 1988**
Vollkommer, R. *Herakles in the Art of Classical Greece.* Oxford 1988.

**VOLLKOMMER 1991**
Vollkommer, R. "Zur Deutung der Löwenfrau in der frühgriechischen Kunst." *AM* 106 (1991): 47–64.

**VOOUS 1960**
Voous, K. *Atlas of European Birds.* London 1960.

**VULIĆ 1930**
Vulić, N. "Das neue Grab von Trebenischte." *AA* 1930, 296–99.

**WALDBAUM 1973**
Waldbaum, J. C. "Luristan Bronzes." *Record* 32.2 (1973): 8–15.

**WALDE AND LEY 1999**
Walde, C., and A. Ley. "Kentauren." *Neue Paulys* 6 (1999): 413–14.

**WALLENSTEIN 1971**
Wallenstein, K. *Korinthische Plastik des 7. und 6. Jahrhunderts vor Christus.* Bonn 1971.

**WALTER 1959**
Walter, H. "Korinthische Keramik." *AM* 74 (1959): 57–68.

**WALTER 1960**
Walter, H. "Sphingen." *AuA* 9 (1960): 63–72.

**WALTER 1968**
Walter, H. *Samos.* Vol. 5, *Frühe samische Gefässe: Chronologie und Landschaftsstile östgriechischer Gefässe.* Bonn 1968.

**WALTER-KARYDI 1973**
Walter-Karydi, E. *Samos.* Vol. 6.1, *Samische Gefässe des 6. Jahrhunderts vor Christus: Landschaftstile östgriechischer Gefässe.* Bonn 1973.

**WALTER-KARYDI 1985**
Walter-Karydi, E. "Die Themen der ostionischen figürlichen Salbgefäße." *MüJb* 36 (1985): 7–16.

**WALTER-KARYDI 2002**
Walter-Karydi, E. "Ταύτηση μια Αττικής επιτύμβιας σφίγγας και προσπάθεια ερμηνείας της." In Αφιέρωμα στη μνήμη του γλύπτη Στέλιου Τριάντη, Museum Benaki, Suppl. 1, 63–72. Athens 2002.

**WALTERS 1899**
Walters, H. B. *Catalogue of the Bronzes, Greek, Roman and Etruscan, in the Department of Greek and Roman Antiquities in the British Museum.* London 1899.

**WALTERS HANDBOOK 1936**
*Handbook of the Collection: The Walters Art Gallery.* Baltimore 1936.

**WANGENHEIM 1988**
Wangenheim, C. F. von. *Archaische Bronzepferde in Rundplastik und Relief.* Bonn 1988.

**WARREN 1995**
Warren, P. "Minoan Crete and Pharaonic Egypt." In *Egypt, the Aegean, and the Levant: Interconnections in the Second Millenium B.C.,* ed. W. V. Davies and L. Schofield, 1–18. London 1995.

**WEBER 1974**
Weber, M. "Zu frühen attischen Gerätfiguren." *AM* 89 (1974): 27–46.

**WEBSTER 1955**
Webster, T. B. L. "Homer and Attic Geometric Vases." *BSA* 50 (1955): 38–50.

**WEBSTER 1971**
Webster, T. B. L. *Illustrations of Greek Drama.* London 1971.

**WEBSTER 1973**
Webster, T. B. L. *Athenian Culture and Society.* Berkeley 1973.

**WEICKER 1902**
Weicker, G. *Der Seelenvogel in der alten mythologisch-archäologische Untersuchung.* Leipzig 1902.

**WEIDNER 1967**
Weidner, E. F. *Gestirn-Darstellungen auf babylonischen Tontafeln.* Vienna 1967.

**WEINBERG 1943**
Weinberg, S. S. *Corinth.* Vol. 7.1, *The Geometric and Orientalizing Pottery.* Cambridge (Mass.) 1943.

**WEINBERG 1973**
Weinberg, S. S. "Cretan Relief Amphora in Basel." *AntK* 16 (1973): 98–101.

**WESCOAT 1995**
Wescoat, B. "Wining and Dining on the Temple of Athena at Assos." In *The Art of Interpreting: Papers in Art History from the Pennsylvania State University,* vol. 9, 293–320. University Park 1995.

**WEST 1978**
West, M. L., ed. *Hesiod Works and Days.* Oxford 1978.

**WEST 1985**
West, M .L. *The Hesiodic Catalogue of Women.* Oxford 1985.

**WEST 1988**
West, M. L., ed. *Hesiod, Theogony.* Oxford 1988.

**WEST 1997**
West, M. L. *The East Face of the Helikon: West Asiatic Elements in Greek Poetry and Myth.* Oxford 1997.

**WHITLEY 1994a**
Whitley, J. "The Monuments That Stood before Marathon: Tomb Cult and Hero Cult in Archaic Attica." *AJA* 98 (1994): 213–30.

**WHITLEY 1994b**
Whitley, J. "Protoattic Pottery: A Contextual Approach." In *Classical Greece: Ancient Histories and Modern Archaeologies,* ed. I. Morris, 51–70. Cambridge 1994.

**WIGGERMANN 1981–82**
Wiggermann, F. A. M. "Exit talim. Studies in Babylonian Demonology, I." *JEOL* 27 (1981–82): 90–105.

**WIGGERMANN 1989**
Wiggermann, F. A. M. "Tišpak, His Seal, and the Dragon mušḫuššu." In *To the Euphrates and Beyond: Archaeological Studies in Honour of Maurits N. Van Loon,* ed. O. M. C. Haex, 117–33. Rotterdam and Brookfield (Vermont) 1989.

**WIGGERMANN 1992**
Wiggermann, F. A. M. *Mesopotamian Protective Spirits: The Ritual Texts.* Groningen 1992.

**WIKANDER 1986**
Wikander, C. *Sicilian Architectural Terracottas: A Reappraisal.* Stockholm 1986.

**WILLIAMS 1983**
Williams, D. "Sophilos in the British Museum." *Greek Vases in the J. Paul Getty Museum* 1 (1983): 9–34.

**WILLIAMS 1984–85**
Williams, E. R. "A Bronze Matrix in the Walters Art Gallery." *JWalt* 42–43 (1984–85): 24–31.

**WILLIAMS 1985**
Williams, D. *Greek Vases*. London 1985.

**WILLIAMS 1986**
Williams, D. "In the Manner of the Gorgon Painter: The Deianeira Painter and Others." In Brijder, Drukker, and Neeft 1986, 61–68.

**WILLIAMS 1992**
Williams, D. "The Brygos Tomb Reassembled and Nineteenth-Century Commerce in Capuan Antiquities." *AJA* 96 (1992): 617–36.

**WILLIAMS 1997**
Williams, D. "From Pelion to Troy: Two Skyphoi by the Kleophrades Painter." In Oakley, Coulson, and Palagia 1997, 195–201.

**WINKLER 1990**
Winkler, J. J. "The Ephebes' Song: *Tragōidia* and *Polis*." In Winkler and Zeitlin 1990, 20–62.

**WINKLER AND ZEITLIN 1990**
Winkler, J. J., and F. I. Zeitlin. *Nothing to Do with Dionysos? Athenian Drama in Its Social Context*. Princeton 1990.

**WINTER 1903**
Winter, F. *Die Typen der figurlichen Terrakotten*. 2 vols. Berlin and Stuttgart 1903.

**WINTER 1973**
Winter, I. J. *North Syria in the Early First Millenium B.C. with Special Reference to Ivory Carving*. Ph.D. diss., Columbia University 1973.

**WINTER 1993**
Winter, N. A. *Greek Architectural Terracottas from the Prehistoric to the End of the Archaic Period*. Oxford 1993.

**WOLF 1993**
Wolf, S. *Herakles beim Gelage*. Cologne 1993.

**WOLTERS AND BRUNS 1940**
Wolters, P., and G. Bruns. *Das Kabirenheiligtum bei Theben*. Vol. 1. Berlin 1940.

**WOODBURY 1972**
Woodbury, L. "Apollo's First Love: Pindar, Pyth. 9.26ff." *TAPA* 103 (1972): 561–73.

**WOODFORD 1974**
Woodford, S. "More Light on Old Walls: The Theseus of the Centauromachy in the Theseion." *JHS* 94 (1974): 158–65.

**WOOLLEY 1926**
Woolley, C. L. "Babylonian Prophylactic Figures." *JRAS* (1926): 698–713.

**WOOLLEY 1934**
Woolley, C. L. *Ur Excavations*. Vol. 2, *The Royal Cemetery*. London and Philadelphia 1934.

**WOYSCH-MÉAUTIS 1982**
Woysch-Méautis, D. *La Représentation des animaux et des êtres fabuleux sur les monuments funéraires grecs*. Lausanne 1982.

**WREDE 1928**
Wrede, W. "Der Maskengott." *AM* 53 (1928): 66–95.

**WUILLEUMIER 1939**
Wuilleumier, P. *Tarente*. Paris 1939.

**YALOURIS 1987**
Yalouris, N. *Pegasus, ein Mythos in der Kunst*. Rev. ed. Mainz 1987.

**YOUNG 1972**
Young, E. *The Slaying of the Minotaur: Evidence in Art and Literature for the Development of the Myth*. Ph.D. diss., Bryn Mawr College 1972.

**ZACHAROU-LOUTRARI 1998**
Zacharou-Loutrari, A. K. Χιακή Σφίγγα. Η διαχρονική πορεία ενός τοπικού συμβόλου. Chios 1998.

**ZAHN 1983**
Zahn, E. *Europa und der Stier*. Würzburg 1983.

**ZAHRADNÍK 1977**
Zahradník, J. *A Field Guide in Color to Insects*. Prague 1977.

**ZANCANI AND ZANOTTI 1954**
Zancani Montuoro, P., and U. Zanotti Bianco. *Heraion alla Foce del Sele*. Vol. 2, *Il primo thesauros*. Rome 1954.

**ZAPHEIROPOULOU 1985**
Zapheiropoulou, P. Προβλήματα της Μηλιακής αγγειογραφίας. Athens 1985.

**ZAZOFF 1969**
Zazoff, P. "Zur geometrischen Glyptik." In *Opus Nobile: Festschrift zum 60. Geburtstag von Ulf Janzten*, ed. W. Jantzen and P. Zazoff, 181–87. Wiesbaden 1969).

**ZEITLIN 1990**
Zeitlin, F. I. "Thebes: Theater of Self and Society in Athenian Drama." In Winkler and Zeitlin, 1990, 130–67.

**ZETTLER ET AL. 1998**
Zettler, R. L., et al. *Treasures from the Royal Tombs of Ur*. Exhib. cat. University of Pennsylvania Museum. Philadelphia 1998.

**ZIMMERMANN 1989**
Zimmermann, J.-L. *Les Chevaux de bronze dans l'art géométrique grec*. Mayence 1989.

**ZWIERLEIN-DIEHL 2000**
Zwierlein-Diehl, E. "A Centaur Playing Kottabos: A Late Archaic Scaraboid in the Akademisches Kunstmuseum, Antikensammlung der Universität Bonn." In Tsetskhladze, Prag, and Snodgrass 2000, 397–402.

# Photography and Drawing Credits

National Archaeological Museum, Athens
Childs (13), Padgett (6, 20)

Courtesy of the Michael C. Carlos Museum
of Emory University, Atlanta
96, Padgett (16, 30)

Walters Art Museum, Baltimore
82

Antikensammlung, Staatliche Museen zu Berlin—
Preussischer Kulturbesitz
Childs (3, 7), Padgett (25)

Museum of Fine Arts, Boston
8, 18, 31, 43, 55, 72, 74, 77, 83, 87, 93,
94, 100, Padgett (18, 27, 29), Tsiafakis (3)
(drawing: Suzanne Chapman; photos
©2003 Museum of Fine Arts, Boston)

Art Institute of Chicago
57 (photo ©The Art Institute of Chicago)

Cleveland Museum of Art
58, 59, 86 (photos ©The Cleveland Museum
of Art, 2002)

Nationalmuseet, Copenhagen
Childs (15)

Corfu Archaeological Museum
Tsiafakis (15)

Staatliche Kunstsammlungen Dresden
Tsiafakis (1)

Eleusis Archaeological Museum
Tsiafakis (14)

Eretria Archaeological Museum
Padgett (3)

Museo Archeologico Nazionale, Florence
Padgett (10, 17, 24)

Courtesy of the Arthur M. Sackler Museum,
Harvard University Art Museums
39, 67, 97 (photos © President and Fellows
of Harvard College)

Peter Harholdt
Padgett (30)

Archaeological Museum, Istanbul
Childs (14)

Justin Kerr
Padgett (28)

Leigh Photo & Imaging, LLC
Childs (2, 6, 12, 16, 17), Padgett (5, 11, 13),
Tsiafakis (5)

Hervé Lewandowski
Padgett (4), Tsiafakis (6, 11)

British Museum, London
Childs (1, 4, 5, 8), Padgett (12, 15),
Tsiafakis (4, 9, 17, 18, 19) (photos
©The British Museum)

Michael McKelvey
Padgett (16), 96

Archivo Fotográfico. Museo Arqueológico
Nacional, Madrid
25

The J. Paul Getty Museum, Malibu, California
27, 36, 37, 75, Tsiafakis (2, 7, 16) (photos
©The J. Paul Getty Museum)

Museum of Art and Archaeology, University
of Missouri-Columbia
21

Jill Moraca
Map, pp. xvii—xix (data: U. S. National
Imagery and Mapping Agency);
architectural drawing, p. 364, after Colonne
1985, 63, fig.3.1

Staatliche Antikensammlungen und Glyptothek, Munich
Tsiafakis (8, 10, 20)

Museo Archeologico Nazionale, Naples
Tsiafakis (21)

The Metropolitan Museum of Art, New York
13 (View 1 © 1996 The Metropolitan Museum
of Art, View 4 © 2002 The Metropolitan
Museum of Art), 26 (photo © 1994 The
Metropolitan Museum of Art), 32 (photo
© 1996 The Metropolitan Museum of Art),

35 (photo © 2002 The Metropolitan
Museum of Art), 71 (photo © 2002 The
Metropolitan Museum of Art), Padgett (19)
(photo © 1993 The Metropolitan Museum
of Art)

Courtesy of Christie's, Inc., New York
44

Courtesy of Sotheby's, New York
Padgett (14)

Cliché Bibliothèque Nationale de France, Paris
14, 23

Musée du Louvre, Paris
Childs (9, 10, 11), Padgett (4, 23), Padgett (23),
Tsiafakis (6, 11), Tsiafakis (12, 13) (photos
© Réunion des Musées Nationaux / Art
Resource, NY)

Professional Graphics, Inc.
61

Museo Nazionale di Villa Giulia, Rome
Padgett (7, 22)

John Seyfried
62 (photo © Allen Memorial Art Museum,
Oberlin College, Ohio)

Katherine Wetzel
6, 30, 79 (photos ©Virginia Museum of
Fine Arts)

Bruce M. White
Cover, frontispiece, 1-5, 7, 9—12, 15—17,
19, 20, 22, 24, 28, 29, 33, 34, 38, 40—42, 45—54,
56, 60, 63—66, 68—70, 73, 76, 78, 80, 81, 85,
88—92, 95, 99, Childs (frontispiece), Padgett
(frontispiece, 1, 2, 8, 9, 21), Tsiafakis
(frontispiece), frontispiece to catalogue

Martin von Wagner Museum der Universität
Würzburg, Würzburg
Padgett (26)

Yale University Art Gallery
84, 98

# Index

Thessalian, 14–17, 21, 23, 25, 39n.71, 40n.83, 44n.177, 135, 142, 168–69, 170–73, 191, 200, 224n.3; works: Aryballos with Herakles(?) Battling a Centaur(?), cat. no. 31, 11, 22, 42n.133, 97, 181–83, 327, 351; Kotyle with an Archer Attacking a Centaur, cat. no. 30, 11, 22, 177–81; Man Fighting a Centaur, cat. no. 13, 9, 23–24, 97, 133–36, 150; metopes from the Parthenon, London, **16**, 17, 25; pediment, temple of Zeus, Olympia, 14, 200; pointed amphora, 43n.163, 172, 202; west frieze of the Hephaisteion, 17. *See also works under* Herakles

Chariklo, 18–19, 200–202; works: alabastron, Cheiron and Chariklo, Rhodes, **17,** 18; Red-Figure Bell-Krater with the Wedding of Cheiron, cat. no. 38, 18, 25, 41n.109, 200–202; volute-krater, François Vase, Florence, 19, 201

Cheiron, 3, 9, 14, 17–18, 21–22, 25, 38n.26, 39n.71, 154–55, 161, 181n.13; and Chariklo, 18–19, 200–202; clothed, 18–19, 176n.9, 200, 203–4, 208, 347; death of, 20–21; and Herakles, 7, 209n.2; with human legs, 11, 18–19, 29, 41n.104, 43n.163, 154, 176n.9, 200, 203–4, 208, 344; as hunter, 19–20, 176n.9, 200; and Kronos, 18, 40n.93, 200; and Peleus, 19–20, 160; —and capture of Thetis, 20, 200, 204–6, 206n.4, 345; —rescue of, 19–20, 40n.102, 41n.107; —wedding of, 19, 172, 200–202; as teacher, 20, 154, 160, 176n.9, 200, 207, 344; works: alabastron, Cheiron and Chariklo, Rhodes, **17,** 18; Band-Cup with Cheiron, Peleus, and Thetis, cat. no. 96, **19,** 20, 45n.196, 65, 339, 343–46; Black-Figure Lekythos with Cheiron Receiving Achilles from Peleus, cat. no. 40, 18, 20, 207–9; Black-Figure Lekythos with Cheiron Watching Peleus Wrestle Thetis, cat. no. 39, 18, 41n.109, 190, 203–6; dinos, Cheiron at the wedding of Peleus, London, **18,** 19, 201, 238n.12; Red-Figure Bell-Krater with the Wedding of Cheiron, cat. no. 38, 18, 25, 41n.109, 200–202; stamnos, Munich, 348; vase, Paris, Louvre, 347; Statuette of a Centaur (Cheiron?), cat. no. 22, 12, 153–55; on volute-krater, François Vase, Florence, 19, 201

Chicago, Art Institute, Neck-Amphora with Satyr Masks, cat. no. 57, 246–48, 256n.2

Chimaera, 63, 65, 78, 83, 85, 226, 349;

Chimaera-sphinx, 97; works: aryballos, with human head, Boston, 63; orthostat blocks, Carchemish, **54,** 63; skyphos, Aigina, 63

Chimaera Painter, 290; cat. no. 75, 64, 74, 287–90, 294n.2

Chrysaor, 85, 89, 102n.117, 322; works: pediment, temple of Artemis, Corfu, 65, **89**

Chrysippos, 79, 264

Circe, 338; works: on Black-Figure Siana Cup, cat. no. 93, 169, 335, 336–38

Clement of Alexandria, 282–83

Cleveland, Museum of Art: Antefix with Satyr Head, cat. no. 59, 251–53, 322n.2; cosmetic vessel, Bes, 118; Janiform Kantharos with Satyr and African, cat. no. 58, 249–50; oinochoe, centaurs, 218; statuettes of satyrs, 240, 240n.1

Columbia, Museum of Art and Archaeology, University of Missouri–Columbia, Statuette of a Centaur, cat. no. 21, 150–52, 230, 240–41

constellations, 6, 54, 66, 130

Copenhagen, National Museum, kantharos, man devoured by lions, **61;** diadem, centaurs and dancers, 142, 143n.13

Copenhagen Painter (Syriskos), 171–72; cat. no. 28, 16, 142, 170–73; pointed amphora, Germany, 172; pointed amphora, White and Levy collection, 43n.163, 172, 202; pointed amphora, Zürich, 172, 173n.7

Corfu, Archaeological Museum: louterion, horsemen and lions, 235; pediment of the temple of Artemis, Corfu, 65, **89**

Corinthian, Early: cat. nos. 47, 76, 98

Corinthian, Middle: cat. nos. 35, 75, 77

Cretan: cat. no. 51

Cypriote: cat. nos. 19–20, 48, 65

**D**

Daidalos, 91, 251, 330

Danaë, 83, 306

Deianeira, 18, 25; and Herakles, 18, 23–25, 92, 192, 335; and Nessos, 18, 23–25, 40n.98, 43n.145, 137, 180, 180–81n.12, 189, 191–92, 196n.2, 197; works: Amyklai Throne, 42–43n.143; ivory relief, Athens, Nat. Mus., 25; Shield Band with Nessos and Deianeira, cat. no. 36, 18, 25, 192, 194–96; stamnos, London, 25; stamnos, Naples, 25; stand from the Argive Heraion, Athens, Nat. Mus., 24

Deidameia, 14

Deiphobos, 170, 173, 173n.5

Demeter, 19, 78, 201, 303

Dexamenos, 25; works: stamnos, Naples, 25

Diktys, 83, 306

Diodorus Siculus, 20–21, 39n.71, 176

Diogenes Laertius, 82

Dionysos, 27–29, 32, 34, 36, 176, 201, 238n.12, 241, 246, 249, 267, 353; and funerary cults, 45n.204, 240; with Herakles, 22; and maenads, 32, 174; mask-idols of, 248; and satyrs, 30, 32, 34, 36, 174, 238–39, 241, 248, 254–56, 256n.5, 258–59

Diosphos Painter: cat. no. 39, 18, 41n.109, 190, 203–6; cat. no. 34, 16–17, 22, 190–91

Dipoinos, 251

Doris, 343, 348

Douris: cat. no. 62, 27, 259–61; psykter, London, 261; kylix, **33,** 34, 45n.210

Dresden, Staatliche Kunstammlungen, hydria with siren, **75**

Dryas, 15–16

Dunnu, Theogony of, 66

**E**

East Greek: cat. nos. 18, 22, 68–69, 78, 83

Echidna, 65, 78, 83, 349, 352

Edinburgh Painter, 207–9, 209nn. 5 & 7, 261; cat. no. 40, 18, 20, 207–9; lekanis lid, Paris, Cab. Méd., 208–9; lekythoi, Athens, 77, 208–9; lekythos, Syracuse, 208–9

Egyptian: cat. nos. 6, 8

Eileithyia, 332

Eleusis Archaeological Museum, amphora, Gorgons pursuing Perseus, 62, **88,** 306

Endeis, 18, 40n.96

Enkidu, 108–10; works: cylinder seal impression, Munich, **52,** 53

Ergotimos, 15; François Vase, **15,** 16, 19, **29,** 30–32, 89, 102n.124, 168–69, 186n.2, 188, 201, 238, 241, 257–58; vase, Berlin, 35

Eretria, Archaeological Museum, Lefkandi Centaur, 7, **8,** 9–10, 37n.15, 64–65, 150, 181n.13

Eros, 82, 173n.8, 277

Etruscan: cat. nos. 42–46, 79, 89–90, 94

Euboian: cat. no. 17

Euergides Painter, 280; cat. no. 71, 280–81

Eupolis Painter, cat. no. 38, 18, 25, 41n.109, 200–202

Euripides, 20, 27, 29, 78, 90, 173n.8, 263n.8

Europa, 206n.11, 340–42; Lip-Cup with Europa and Triton, cat. no. 95, 340–43

Euryale, 83, 321

Eurystheus, 23

Eurytion, 14, 25, 39n.75